Accounting and Finance

for Managers

Updated Second Edition

Claud Pitts III, George K. Sharghi, Larry Gonzales

U N I V E R S I T Y   O F   P H O E N I X

School of Undergraduate Business and Management

Pearson
Custom
Publishing

Cover Design: Caldera Designs

Excerpts taken from:
Financial Accounting, Revised 3rd Edition, by Walter T. Harrison
and Charles T. Horngren
Copyright © 1998 by Prentice-Hall, Inc.
A Pearson Education Company
Upper Saddle River, New Jersey 07458

Introduction to Management Accounting, Tenth Edition,
by Charles T. Horngren, Gary L. Sundem, and William O. Stratton
Copyright © 1996, 1993, 1990, 1987, 1984, 1981, 1978, 1974, 1970, 1965 by Prentice-Hall, Inc.

Foundations of Finance, by Arthur J. Keown, David F. Scott, Jr.,
John D. Martin, and J. William Petty
Copyright © 1994 by Prentice-Hall, Inc.

Introduction to Financial Accounting, Sixth Edition
by Charles T. Horngren, Gary L. Sundem, and John A. Elliot
Copyright © 1996, 1993, 1990, 1988, 1987, 1984, 1981 by Prentice-Hall, Inc.

Essentials of Finance: An Integrated Approach,
by George W. Gallinger and Jerry B. Poe
Copyright © 1995 by Prentice-Hall, Inc.

Fundamentals of Financial Management, Ninth Edition,
by James C. Van Horne and John M. Wachowicz, Jr.
Copyright © 1995 by Prentice-Hall, Inc.

Basic Financial Management, Seventh Edition, by Arthur Keown,
David F. Scott, Jr., John D. Martin, and J. William Petty
Copyright © 1996 by Prentice-Hall, Inc.

Financial Management and Policy, Eleventh Edition,
by James C. Van Horne
Copyright © 1998 by Prentice-Hall, Inc.

This special edition published in cooperation with
Pearson Custom Publishing.

Printed in the United States of America

10 9 8 7 6 5 4

Please visit our website at www.pearsoncustom.com

ISBN 0–536–02117–1

BA 990900

PEARSON CUSTOM PUBLISHING
75 Arlington Street, Boston, MA 02116
A Pearson Education Company

CONTENTS

SECTION III   COST MANAGEMENT SYSTEMS

Chapter 5   Introduction to Cost Management Systems   91

Chapter 6   Analyzing Cost Behavior   121

SECTION IV   FINANCIAL PLANNING

Chapter 7   The Formal Budgeting Process   149

SECTION VII TIME VALUE OF MONEY AND THE PRINCIPLES OF CAPITAL BUDGETING

SECTION VIII WORKING-CAPITAL MANAGEMENT

SECTION IX   COST OF CAPITAL AND VALUATION OF LONG-TERM DEBT AND EQUITY

SECTION I
THE ACCOUNTING ENVIRONMENT

CHAPTER 1: Introduction to Accounting

CHAPTER 2: Accounting Concepts, Techniques, and Conventions

INTRODUCTION TO ACCOUNTING

WHAT IS ACCOUNTING?

Accounting is the system that measures business activities, processes that information into reports, and communicates the results to decision makers. The key products of any accounting system are the **financial statements,** which are the documents that report on a company's or organization's business activities in monetary amounts. This is why accounting is called "the language of business."

The Development of Accounting

The need for accounting has existed since the rise of business activity. Accounting records dating back to the ancient civilizations of China, Babylonia, Greece, and Egypt have been found. The rulers of Egyptian civilization used accounting systems to keep track of the costs of labor and materials used in building structures, such as the great pyramids. Business managers created accounting systems to report to the owners and others how their business was performing. To ensure that the business information produced was reliable and accurate, governing bodies were established to regulate the profession.

In the United States, the Securities and Exchange Commission (SEC) has legislative authority to set generally accepted accounting principles (GAAP). The SEC relies on the Financial Accounting Standards Board (FASB) to determine how accounting is practiced. The FASB works with the Securities and Exchange Commission and the American Institute of Certified Public Accountants (AICPA), the largest professional organization of accountants. Certified public accountants (CPAs) are licensed accountants who serve the general public rather than one particular company. The relationships among the SEC, the FASB, and the AICPA and the rules that govern them (GAAP) are diagramed in Exhibit 1-1.

Exhibit 1-1   Key Accounting Organizations

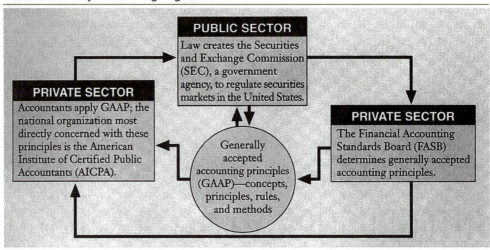

USERS OF ACCOUNTING INFORMATION: DECISION-MAKERS

The users of accounting information fall into the following categories.

Individuals use accounting information to manage their day-to-day affairs, evaluate job prospects, and make investment decisions.

Businesses. Business managers use accounting information to make decisions about their organizations, to evaluate the result of their operation, and to take corrective action.

Investors and Creditors analyze the financial statements of a business to determine what income they can expect on their investment. Banks and suppliers analyze the financial statements to determine if the company can meet their scheduled payments.

Government Regulatory Agencies. Many federal agencies require businesses to disclose certain financial information to the investing public. They also use the accounting information received from firms to develop controls and regulations.

Taxing Authorities. Local, state, and federal governments use accounting information to levy taxes on individuals and businesses. Businesses and individuals use their accounting records to determine the amount of taxes they must pay.

Nonprofit Organizations such as churches, hospitals, government agencies, and schools and colleges use accounting information the same way that profit-oriented businesses do. Both profit organizations and nonprofit organizations deal with such items as budgets, payrolls, and rent payments.

Other Users. Employees and labor unions make wage demands based on their employers' accounting information. Consumer groups and the general public are also interested in the amount of income businesses earn.

FINANCIAL ACCOUNTING AND MANAGEMENT ACCOUNTING

Even though the users of accounting information seem to be a diverse group, they still can be categorized as two user groups, external users or internal users. This distinction allows us to classify accounting into two fields: financial accounting and management accounting.

Financial accounting develops account information that is used by external parties such as stockholders, suppliers, banks, and government regulatory agencies in their decision making. **Management accounting** develops confidential accounting information that is used by managers within an organization. Management accounting is the process of identifying, measuring, accumulating, analyzing, preparing, interpreting, and communicating information that helps managers fulfill organizational objectives. The major distinctions between financial accounting and management accounting are listed in Exhibit 1-2.

Exhibit 1-2   Distinctions Between Financial Accounting and Management Accounting

	Financial Accounting	*Management Accounting*
Primary users	Outside parties such as investors and government agencies but also organization managers.	Organization managers at various levels.
Freedom of choice	Constrained by generally accepted accounting principles (GAAP).	No constraints other than costs in relation to benefits of improved management decisions.
Behavioral implications	Concern about how to measure and communicate economic phenomena. Behavioral considerations are secondary, although executive compensation based on reported results may have behavioral impacts.	Concern about how measurements and reports will influence managers' daily behavior.
Time focus	Past orientation: historical evaluation. Example: 19X6 actual performance versus 19X5 actual performance.	Future orientation: formal use of budgets as well as historical records. Example: 19X6 budget versus 19X6 actual performance.
Time span	Less flexible, usually 1 year or 1 quarter.	Flexible, varying from hourly to 10 to 15 years.
Reports	Summary reports: concern primarily with entity as a whole.	Detailed reports: concern about details of parts of the entity, products. departments, territories, etc.
Delineation of activities	Field is more sharply defined. Lighter use of related disciplines.	Field is less sharply defined. Heavier use of economics, decision sciences, and behavioral sciences.

ACCOUNTING'S POSITION IN THE ORGANIZATION

Line and Staff Authority

The organization chart in Exhibit 1-3 shows how a typical manufacturing company divides responsibilities. Notice the distinction between line and staff authority. Line authority is authority exerted downward over subordinates. Staff authority is authority to advise but not command. It may be exerted downward, laterally, or upward.

The Controller and Treasurer

The controller is the senior accounting position in an organization. In a government this position is called a **comptroller**. The controller is the key executive who is responsible for the managerial planning and control of the company. The treasurer is a senior financial person in an organization. The treasurer is primarily responsible for the acquisition of the company's capital needs, investor relations, and the administration of insurance.

Exhibit 1-3 Partial Organization Chart of a Manufacturing Company

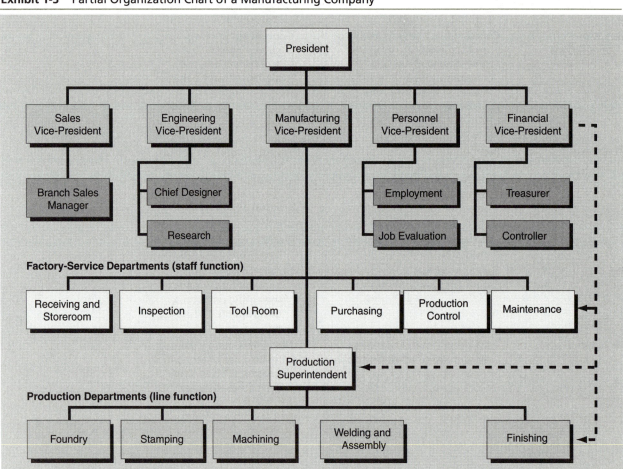

Dashed line represents staff authority of the finance staff to advise those in manufacturing operations.

Distinctions Between Controller and Treasurer

Many people confuse the offices of controller and treasurer. The Financial Executives Institute, an association of corporate treasurers and controllers, distinguishes their functions as follows:

Controllership	Treasurership
1. Planning for control	1. Provision of capital
2. Reporting and interpreting	2. Investor relations
3. Evaluating and consulting	3. Short-term financing
4. Tax administration	4. Banking and custody
5. Government reporting	5. Credits and collections
6. Protection of assets	6. Investments
7. Economic appraisal	7. Risk management (insurance)

As the table shows, the controller is concerned with operating matters while the treasurer is concerned mainly with the company's financial matters. The exact division of accounting and financial duties varies from company to company. In many cases the same person may function as controller and treasurer, especially in a small organization.

Legal Forms of Business Organizations

For legal, organizational, and accounting reasons, a business can take one of three forms. These three forms are a proprietorship, a partnership, and a corporation.

Proprietorships. A proprietorship has a single owner, called the proprietor, who is typically also the manager. Proprietorships tend to be small retail establishments or individual professional businesses, such as those of physicians, attorneys, and accountants. From the accounting viewpoint, each proprietorship is distinct from its proprietor. Thus, the accounting records of the proprietorship do not include the proprietor's personal financial records.

Partnerships. A partnership joins two or more individuals together as co-owners. Each owner is a partner. Many retail establishments, as well as some professional organizations of physicians, attorneys, and accountants, are partnerships. Most partnerships are small or medium-sized, but some are gigantic, exceeding 2,000 partners, Accounting treats the partnership as a separate organization, distinct from the personal affairs of each partner.

Corporations. A corporation is a business owned by stockholders, or shareholders, people who own stock, or shares of ownership, in the business. The corporation is the dominant form of business organization in the United States. Although proprietorships and partnerships are more numerous, corporations transact more business and are larger in terms of total assets, income, and number of employees. Most well-known companies, such as CBS, General Motors, and American Airlines, are corporations. Their full names include Corporation or Incorporated (abbreviated Corp. and Inc.) to indicate that they are corporations (for example, CBS, Inc., and General Motors Corporation). Some corporations bear the name "Company," such as Ford Motor Company. This title does not clearly identify the organization as a corporation because a proprietorship and a partnership can also bear the name "Company." Corporations need not be large. A corporation is a business entity formed under state law. From a legal perspective, a corporation is a distinct entity. The corporation operates as an artificial person that exists apart from its owners. The corporation has many of the rights that a person has; it can buy, own, and sell property. Assets and liabilities in the business belong to the corporation. The corporation may enter into contracts, sue, and be sued. Unlike proprietors and partners, a stockholder has no personal obligation for corporation liabilities. The most that a stockholder can lose on an investment in corporation stock is the cost of the investment. But proprietors and partners are personally liable for the debts of their businesses. The ownership interest of a corporation is divided into shares of stock. A person becomes a stockholder by purchasing the stock of the corporation. The Coca-Cola Company, for example, has 1.3 billion shares of stock owned by some 559,000 different shareholders. An investor with no personal relationship either to the Coca-Cola Company or to any other stockholder can become a co-owner by buying 30, 100, 5,000, or any number of shares of its stock.

The ultimate control of the corporation rests with the stockholders, who receive one vote for each share of stock they own. The stockholders elect the members of the board of directors, which sets policy for the corporation and appoints the officers. The board elects a chairperson, who usually is the most powerful person in the corporation. The board also designates the president, who is the chief operating officer in charge of managing day-to-day operations. Most corporations also have vice-presidents in charge of sales, manufacturing, accounting and finance, and other key areas.

Accounting Guidelines, Concepts and Principles

Accounting practices follow certain guidelines. The rules governing how accountants measure, process, and communicate financial information fall under the heading of Generally Accepted Accounting Principles (GAAP). Generally accepted accounting principles include not only principles but also concepts and methods that identify the proper way to produce accounting information. GAAP comprises all conventions, rules, and procedures that constitute accepted accounting practice at any given time. Generally accepted accounting principles are like the law—rules for conducting behavior in a way acceptable to the majority of people.

GAAP rests on a conceptual framework written by the Financial Accounting Standards Board (FASB). The primary objective of financial reporting is to provide information useful for making investment and lending decisions. To be useful, information must be relevant, reliable, and comparable. Accountants strive to meet these goals in the information they produce. To accomplish these goals the accountants adhere to the following basic concepts.

The Entity Concept

The basic concept in accounting is that of the entity. An accounting entity is an organization or a section of an organization that stands apart from other organizations and individuals as a separate economic unit. From an accounting perspective, sharp boundaries are drawn around each entity so as not to confuse its affairs with those of other entities.

Consider Julie DeFilippo, the owner of the catering firm, An Extra Hand. Suppose that her bank account shows a $2,000 balance at the end of the year. Only $1,200 of that amount grew from the business's operations. The other $800 was a gift from her grandparents. If DeFilippo follows the entity concept, she will account for the money generated by the business—one economic unit—separately from the money she received from her family, a second economic unit. This separation makes it possible to view An Extra Hand's financial position clearly.

Suppose DeFilippo disregards the entity concept and treats the full $2,000 as a product of An Extra Hand's operations. She will be misled into believing that the business has produced more cash than it has. Any steps needed to make the business more successful may not be taken.

Consider Toyota, a huge organization made up of several divisions. Toyota management evaluates each division as a separate accounting entity. If sales in the Lexus division were dropping drastically, Toyota would do well to identify the reason. But if sales figures from all divisions of the company were analyzed as a single amount, then management would not even know that the company was not selling enough Lexus automobiles. Thus, the entity concept also applies to the parts of a large organization, in fact, to any entity that needs to be evaluated separately.

In summary, the transactions of different entities should not be accounted for together. Each entity should be evaluated separately.

The Reliability (or Objectivity) Principle

Accounting records and statements are based on the most reliable data available so that they will be as accurate and useful as possible. This guideline is the **reliability principle,** also called the **objectivity principle.** Reliable data are verifiable. They may be confirmed by any independent observer. For example, Julie DeFilippo's $18 purchase of aprons is supported by a paid invoice. This is objective evidence of her cost of the aprons. Ideally, accounting records are based on information that flows from activities documented by objective evidence. Without the reliability principle, accounting records would be based on whims and opinions and subject to dispute.

Suppose that you want to open a stereo shop. To have a place for operations, you transfer a small building to the business. You believe the building is worth $155,000. To confirm its cost to the business, you hire two real estate professionals, who appraise the building at $147,000. Is $155,000 or $147,000 the more reliable estimate of the building's value? The real estate appraisal of $147,000 is because it is supported by external, independent, objective observation. The business should record the building at a cost of $147,000, the cost of acquiring the building.

The Cost Principle

The **cost principle** states that acquired assets and services should be recorded at their **actual cost** (also called **historical cost**). Even though the purchaser may believe the price paid is a bargain, the item is recorded at the price paid in the transaction and not at the "expected" cost. Suppose your stereo shop purchases stereo equipment from a supplier who is going out of business. Assume that you get a good deal on this purchase and pay only $2,000 for merchandise that would have cost you $3,000 elsewhere. The cost principle requires you to record this merchandise at its actual cost of $2,000, not the $3,000 that you believe the equipment to be worth. The cost principle also holds that the accounting records should maintain the historical cost of an asset for as long as the business holds the asset. Why? Because cost is a reliable measure. Suppose your store holds the stereo equipment for six months. During that time, stereo prices increase, and the equipment can be sold for $3,500. Should its accounting value—the figure "on the books"—be the actual cost of $2,000 or the current market value of $3,500? According to the cost principle, the accounting value of the equipment remains at actual cost, $2,000.

The Going-Concern Concept

Another reason for measuring assets at historical cost is the **going-concern concept,** which holds that the entity will remain in operation in the foreseeable future. Most assets—that is, the firm's resources, such as supplies, land, buildings, and equipment— are acquired to use rather than to sell. Under the going-concern concept, accountants assume that the business will remain in operation long enough to use existing assets for their intended purpose. The market value of an asset—the price for which the asset can be sold—may change during the asset's life. Therefore, an asset's current market value may not be relevant for decision making. Moreover, historical cost is a more reliable accounting measure for assets than is market value.

To understand the going-concern concept better, consider the alternative, which is to go out of business. A store that is holding a going-out-of-business sale is trying to sell all its assets. In that case, the relevant measure of the assets is their current market value. Going out of business, however, is the exception rather than the rule, and for this reason accounting records list assets at their historical cost.

The Stable-Monetary-Unit Concept

We think of a loaf of bread and a month's rent in terms of their dollar value. In the United States accountants record transactions in dollars because the dollar is the medium of exchange. British accountants record transactions in pounds sterling, and in Japan transactions are recorded in yen.

Unlike the value of a liter, a mile, or an acre, the value of a dollar or of a Mexican peso changes over time. A rise in prices is called inflation. During inflation a dollar will purchase less milk, less toothpaste, and less of other goods. When prices are stable—when there is little inflation—a dollar's purchasing power is also stable.

Accountants assume that the dollar's purchasing power is relatively stable. The **stable-monetary-unit concept** is the basis for ignoring the effect of inflation in the accounting records. It allows accountants to add and subtract dollar amounts as though each dollar has the same purchasing power as any other dollar at any other time. In South America, where inflation rates are high, accountants make adjustments to report monetary amounts in units of current buying power—a very different concept.

Accrual-Basis Accounting Versus Cash-Basis Accounting

There are two widely used bases of accounting: the accrual basis and the cash basis. In **accrual-basis accounting,** an accountant recognizes the impact of a business event as it occurs. When the business performs a service, makes a sale, or incurs an expense, the accountant enters the transaction into the books, whether or not cash has been received or paid. In **cash-basis accounting,** the accountant does not record a transaction until cash is received or paid. Cash receipts are treated as revenues, and cash payments are handled as expenses.

Generally Accepted Accounting Principles (GAAP) require that businesses use the accrual basis. This means that the business records revenues as they are earned and expenses as they are incurred, not when they receive cash. The reason GAAP requires

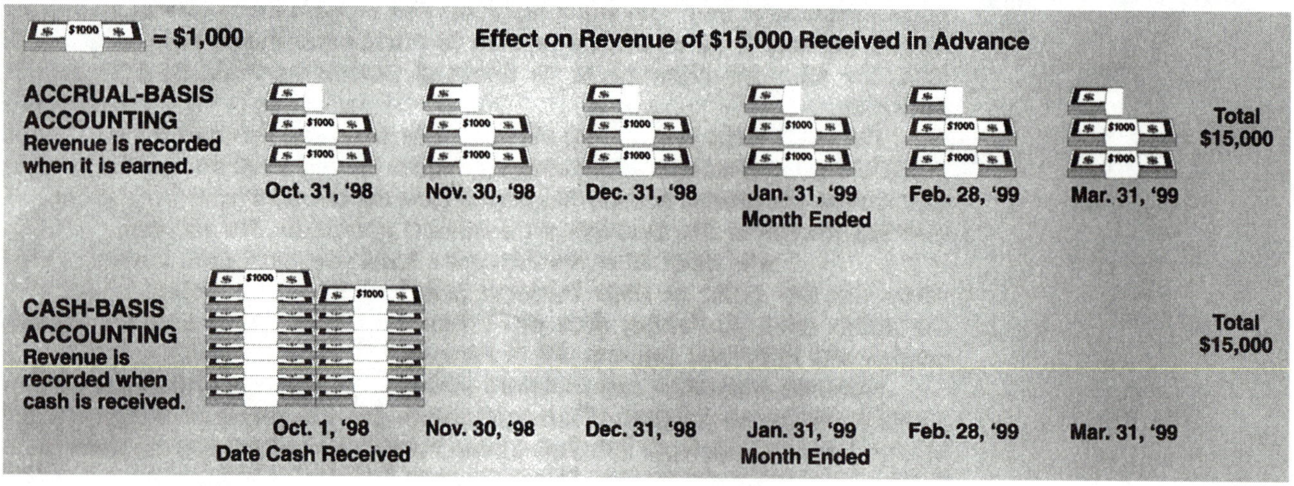

Exhibit 1-4 Accrual-Basis Accounting Versus Cash-Basis Accounting

that businesses use the accrual basis is shown in Exhibit 1-4; it provides more complete information about the businesses activities than cash-basis accounting does. This difference is important because the more complete the data, the better equipped decision makers are to reach conclusions about the firm's financial health and future prospects.

The following are three key concepts used in accrual-basis accounting:

The Time-Period Concept

The **time-period concept** ensures that accounting information is reported accurately in the proper period at regular intervals. The basic accounting period for most firms is one year. Under this concept the year is divided into monthly reporting periods to meet a business's need for periodic reports on its progress. These series of monthly statements can be combined to produce quarterly and semiannual reports.

The Revenue Principle

The **revenue principle** tells accountants (1) when to record revenue by making a journal entry and (2) the amount of revenue to record. The general principle guiding revenue recording says to record revenue when it has been earned—but not before. In most cases, revenue is earned when the business has delivered a completed good or service to the customer. The business has done everything required by the agreement and has transferred the good or service to the customer.

The Matching Principle

The **matching principle** is the basis for recording expenses. Recall that expenses, such as rent, utilities, and advertising, are the costs of operating a business. Expenses are the costs of assets that are used up in the earning of revenue. The matching principle directs accountants (1) to identify all expenses incurred during the accounting period, (2) to measure the expenses, and (3) to match the expenses against the revenues earned during that same period. To match expenses against revenues means to subtract the expenses from the revenues in order to compute net income or net loss for the period. Exhibit 1-5 illustrates the matching principle.

Professional Ethics

Members of the American Institute of Certified Public Accountants (AICPA) must abide by a code of professional conduct. Surveys of public attitudes toward CPAs have consistently ranked the accounting profession as having high ethical standards.

The code of professional conduct is especially concerned with integrity and independence. For example, independent auditors are forbidden to own shares of their client corporations. Moreover, the auditors must satisfy themselves that their clients' financial statements are prepared in accordance with GAAP.

Exhibit 1-5 Matching Principle

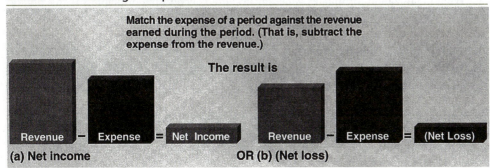

Match the expense of a period against the revenue earned during the period. (That is, subtract the expense from the revenue.)

The result is

Revenue − Expense = Net Income Revenue − Expense = (Net Loss)

(a) Net income OR (b) (Net loss)

The emphasis on ethics extends beyond public accounting. For example, members of the Institute of Management Accountants are expected to abide by that organization's code of ethics for management accountants. Auditors and management accountants have professional responsibilities regarding competence, confidentiality, integrity, and objectivity. Professional accounting organizations and state regulatory bodies have procedures for reviewing behavior alleged to violate codes of professional conduct.

SUMMARY

Accounting is an information system for measuring, processing, and communicating financial information. As the "language of business," accounting helps a wide range of decision makers. Accountants are expected to perform their jobs in an ethical manner consistent with generally accepted accounting principles (GAAP).

The three forms of business organization are the proprietorship, the partnership, and the corporation. In some cases, accounting procedures depend on which form of organization the business adopts.

Accountants are staff employees who provide information and advice for line managers. The head of accounting is often called the controller. Unlike the treasurer, who is concerned primarily with financial matters, the controller measures and reports on operating performance.

Accountants use the entity concept to keep the business' records separate from the personal records of the people who run it and to separate corporate divisions from one another. Other important concepts that guide accountants are the reliability principle, the cost principle, the going-concern concept, and the stable-monetary-unit concept.

In accrual-basis accounting, an accountant recognizes the impact of a business event as it occurs, whether or not cash is received or paid. In cash-basis accounting, the accountant does not record a transaction unless cash changes hands. The cash basis omits important events such as purchases and sales on account and distorts the financial statements. For this reason, generally accepted accounting principles require the use of accrual-basis accounting.

The revenue principle tells accountants (1) to record revenue when it has been earned, but not before and (2) to record revenue equal to the cash value of the goods or services transferred to the customer. The matching principle directs accountants to identify all the expenses incurred during the accounting period, to measure those expenses, and to match the expenses against the revenues earned during that period.

QUESTIONS

1. What is the difference between financial accounting and management accounting?
2. Identify five users of accounting information, and explain how they use it.
3. What organization formulates generally accepted accounting principles? Is this organization a government agency?
4. What is the role of the controller and treasurer?
5. Why do ethical standards exist in accounting?
6. Why is the entity concept so important to accounting?
7. Give four examples of accounting entities.
8. Briefly describe the reliability principle.
9. What role does the cost principle play in accounting?
10. Distinguish accrual-basis accounting from cash-basis accounting.

11. What two questions does the revenue principle help answer?

12. For each of the following activities, indicate whether it is most likely to be performed by the controller (C) or treasurer (T):

    a. Prepare credit checks on customers.

    b. Help managers prepare budgets.

    c. Advise which alternative action is least costly.

    d. Prepare divisional financial statements.

    e. Arrange short-term financing.

    f. Prepare tax returns.

    g. Arrange insurance coverage.

    h. Meet with financial analysts from Wall Street.

INTERNET EXERCISE

Go to the home page of the United States Securities and Exchange Commission (SEC) located at: **www.sec.gov/**

Required

    a. Briefly describe the role of the SEC. Which laws does it enforce?

    b. How many commissioners sit on the board of the SEC? Who is the current chairperson of the SEC? Who has the authority to appoint the chairperson?

    c. List three cities where regional or district offices of the SEC are located. (Hint: Washington, D.C. is not a regional or district office.)

    d. Name the principal divisions of the SEC.

CHAPTER 2

ACCOUNTING CONCEPTS, TECHNIQUES, AND CONVENTIONS

THE ACCOUNTING EQUATION

The most basic concept in accounting is the accounting equation. This accounting equation presents the resources of the business and the claims to those resources. Assets are the economic resources of a business that are expected to be of benefit in the future. Examples of a firm's assets are cash, office supplies, merchandise, furniture, land, and buildings. Any claims against these assets will fall into one of two categories, liabilities or owners' equity.

Liabilities are "outsider claims," which are economic obligations—debts—payable to outsiders. These outside parties are called creditors. For example, a creditor who has loaned money to a business has a claim—a legal right—to a part of the assets until the business pays the debt.

Owners' equity, or capital, are insider claims. These are the claims held by the owners of the business. An owner has a claim to the entity's assets because he or she has invested in the business. The $50 that Julie DeFilippo invested in An Extra Hand in the prior chapter is an example. Owners' equity is measured by subtracting liabilities from assets. The accounting equation in Exhibit 2-1 shows the relationship among assets, liabilities, and owners' equity. Assets appear on the left-hand side of the equation. The legal and economic claims against the assets—the liabilities and owners' equity—appear on the right-hand side of the equation. The two sides must be equal:

Exhibit 2-1

Economic Resources		Claims to Economic Resources
Assets	=	Liabilities + Owners' Equity

Let's take a closer look at the elements that make up the accounting equation. Suppose you run a business that supplies meat to McDonald's and other restaurants. Some customers pay you in cash when you deliver the meat. Cash is an asset. Other customers buy on credit and promise to pay you within a certain time after delivery. This promise is also an asset because it is an economic resource that will benefit you in the future when you receive cash from the customer. To you (the meat supplier), this promise is an account receivable. If the promise that entitles you to receive cash in the future is formally written out, it is called a note receivable. All receivables are assets. McDonald's promise to pay for its credit purchases creates a debt for the restaurant. This liability is an account payable of McDonald's. The debt is not written out; it is backed up by McDonald's reputation and credit standing. A written promise of future payment is a note payable. All payables are liabilities. Owners' equity is the amount of assets that remains after the liabilities are subtracted. For this reason, owners' equity is often referred to as net assets. We often write the accounting equation to show that the owners' claim to business assets is residual:

$$\text{Assets} - \text{Liabilities} = \text{Owners' Equity}$$

Owners' Equity in a Corporation

The owners' equity of a corporation—called stockholders' equity—is divided into two main categories: **paid-in capital** and **retained earnings.** For a corporation the accounting equation can be written as

$$\text{Assets} = \text{Liabilities} + \quad\quad\quad \text{Stockholders' Equity}$$
$$\wedge$$
$$\text{Assets} = \text{Liabilities} + \quad \text{Paid-In Capital} + \text{Retained Earnings}$$

Paid-in, or contributed, capital is the amount invested in the corporation by its owners. The basic component of paid-in capital is common stock, which the corporation issues to its stockholders as evidence of their ownership. Retained earnings is the amount earned by income-producing activities and kept for use in the business. Two types of transactions that affect retained earnings are revenues and expenses. Revenues are increases in retained earnings from delivering goods or services to customers. For example, a laundry's receipt of cash from a customer for cleaning a coat brings in revenue and increases the laundry's retained earnings. Expenses are the decreases in retained earnings that result from operations. For example, the wages that the laundry pays its employees is an expense and decreases retained earnings. Expenses are the cost of doing business and are the opposite of revenues. Expenses include office rent, salaries of employees, newspaper advertisements, and utility payments for light, electricity, gas, and so forth.

Businesses strive for profitability. When total revenues exceed total expenses, the result of operations is called net income, net earnings, or net profit. When expenses exceed revenues, the result is a net loss.

If the business is successful in earning a net income, it may pay dividends, which is the third type of transaction that affects retained earnings. Dividends are distributions to stockholders of assets (usually cash) generated by net income. Dividends are not expenses because the decision of whether or not to distribute them is made after expenses and revenues are recorded. First, the business measures its net income or net loss. Then, a corporation may (or may not) pay dividends. Exhibit 2-2 shows the relationships among retained earnings, revenues, expenses, net income or net loss, and dividends.

The owners' equity of proprietorships and partnerships is different. These types of business make no distinction between paid-in capital and retained earnings. Instead, the equity of each owner is accounted for under the single heading of capital—for example, Julie DeFilippo, Capital for a proprietorship. The partnership of Pratt and Muesli has a separate record for the capital of each partner: Pratt, Capital and Muesli, Capital.

Exhibit 2-2 Components of Retained Earnings

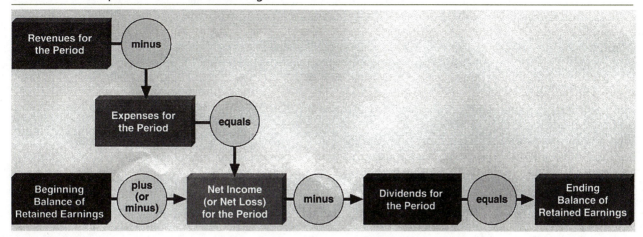

Double-Entry Accounting

Accountants use a double-entry accounting system to record the dual effects of a firm's financial transactions. As the term implies, the **double-entry system** requires at least two accounting entries for each transaction the firm has. This practice ensures that the accounting equation is always in balance. For example if your business purchases inventory with cash, you must make two accounting entries: (1) decrease your cash and (2) increase your inventory. Similarly, if you purchase supplies on credit, you would (1) increase your supplies and (2) increase your accounts payable. If you invest more money in your business, you would (1) increase your cash and (2) increase your owners' equity. In other words, every transaction affects two accounts.

Debits and Credits: The T-Account

Another universal method for keeping accounting records are debits and credits. To understand debits and credits, we first need to understand the **T-account.** The format for recording transactions takes the shape of a T, whose vertical line divides the account into two sides. As pictured below, for example, a firm's general accounting journal has the following T format:

Cash	
Left side	Right side
Debit	Credit

In accounting, debit and credit refer to the side on which account information is to be entered: The left column of any T-account is called the debit side, and the right column is the credit side:

$$\text{debit} = \text{left side}$$
$$\text{credit} = \text{right side}$$

When an asset increases, it is entered as a debit. When it decreases, it is entered as a credit. Exhibit 2-3 shows how the rules of the T-account are consistent with the terms of the accounting equation. Debits and credits provide a system of checks and balances.

Exhibit 2-3   The T-Account and the Accounting Equation

Assets		=	Liabilities		+	Owner's Equity	
Debit for Increase	Credit for Decrease		Debit for Decrease	Credit for Increase		Debit for Decrease	Credit for Increase

The double-entry system and T-accounts, therefore, provide an important method of accounting control: at the end of the accounting cycle, debits and credits must balance. In other words, total debits must equal total credits in the account balances recorded in the general ledger. An imbalance indicates improper accounting that must be corrected. "Balancing the books" is a control procedure to ensure that proper accounting methods have been used.

THE ACCOUNTING CYCLE

All accountants rely on record keeping to enter and track business transactions. Underlying all record-keeping procedures are the three key concepts of accounting: the accounting equation, double-entry accounting, and T-accounts for debits and credits. Exhibit 2-4 shows how the accounting cycle begins with the initial records of a firm's financial transactions.

Exhibit 2-4   Accounting Cycle

The accounting cycle is a comprehensive system for

Collecting			Analyzing	Communicating
Initial Records →	*Intermediate Records* →	*Final Records* =		*Financial Statements*
Examples:	General Accounting	Ledger, divided into		Balance sheet
Sales invoices	Journal or specialized	accounts such as		Income statement
Cash receipts	journals such as	cash		Statement of
Equipment purchases	cash	Accounts payable		cash flow
Materials purchases	Accounts payable	Accounts receivable		
Credit sales	Accounts receivable	Materials inventory		
		Merchandise		
		Inventory		

Journal Transactions

As initial transactions, records are received, sorted, and entered in chronological order in a journal with a brief description of the transactions. This process is called journalizing the transactions. These journal entries now become the firm's intermediate records.

The conventional form of the general journal includes the following:

1. The date and identification number of the entry make up the first two columns.
2. The accounts affected are shown in the next column, Accounts and Explanation. The title of the account or accounts to be debited is placed flush left. The title of the account or accounts to be credited is indented in a consistent way. The journal entry is followed by the narrative explanation, which can be brief or extensive. The length of the explanation depends on the complexity of the transaction and whether management wants the journal itself to contain all relevant information. Most often, explanations are brief and details are available in the file of supporting documents.
3. The Post Ref. (posting reference) column contains the number that is assigned to each account and is used for cross-referencing to the ledger accounts.

4. The money columns are for recording the amounts in the debit (left) or credit (right) columns for each account. No dollar signs are used.

The following is an example of how a transaction would be journalized. This entry records the acquisition of merchandise inventory for cash.

General Journal

Date	Entry No.	Accounts and Explanation	Post Ref.	Debit	Credit
1998					
Jan. 2	1	Merchandise inventory	130	150,000	
		Cash (acquired for cash)	100		150,000

These journal entries are examples of the accounting shorthand employees use to record the explanations for each business transaction. Its brevity would hamper any outsider's understanding of the transaction, but the entry's meaning would be clear to anyone within the organization.

Chart of Accounts

A key component in the accounting shorthand is the **chart of accounts.** Organizations have a chart of accounts, which is normally a numbered or coded list of all account titles. These numbers are used as references in the Post Ref. column of the journal. The following is the chart of accounts:

Account Number	Account Title	Account Number	Account Title
100	Cash	202	Note payable
120	Accounts receivable	203	Accounts payable
130	Merchandise inventory	300	Paid-in capital
140	Prepaid rent	400	Retained income
170	Store equipment	500	Sales revenues
170A	Accumulated depreciation	600	Cost of goods sold
	depreciation	601	Rent expense
	store equipment	602	Depreciation expense

Although an outsider may not know what the code means, accounting employees become so familiar with the code that they think, talk, and write in terms of account numbers instead of account names.

Posting to the Ledger

Posting to the ledger is the transferring of journal transactions to the appropriate accounts in the ledger. Posting to the ledger is usually done on a monthly basis. Like specialized journals, the ledger is divided into categories called accounts, such as cash, inventories, and receivables. The cash account, for example, is a detailed record of all the firm's changes in cash. Other accounts record changes in each type of asset and liability. Ledgers also feature an important column labeled "Balance," which shows the current total dollar amount in each account. If a balance in a given account is unexpectedly high or low, tracking backward to the corresponding journal entry should reveal the cause of the unexpected figure.

General Ledger

Cash						**Account No. 100**	
Date	**Explanation**	**Journ. Ref.**	**Debit**	**Date**	**Explanation**	**Journ. Ref.**	**Credit**
	(often blank because the explanation is already in the journal)			1998 1/2		1	150,000

Merchandise Inventory						**Account No. 130**	
Date	**Explanation**	**Journ. Ref.**	**Debit**	**Date Explanation**		**Journ. Ref.**	**Credit**
1998 1/2	.	1	150,000				

ACCOUNTING FOR BUSINESS TRANSACTIONS

A business transaction is any event that both affects the financial position of the business entity and can be reliably recorded. To illustrate the accounting for business transactions, let's assume that Gary and Monica Lyon open a travel agency that they incorporate as Air & Sea Travel, Inc. Let's now consider eleven events and analyze each in terms of its effect on the accounting equation of Air & Sea Travel, Inc.

Transaction 1. The Lyons invest $50,000 of their money to begin the business. Specifically, they deposit $50,000 in a bank account titled, Air & Sea Travel, Inc. As evidence of the corporation, Air & Sea Travel issues common stock to Gary and Monica Lyon. The stock is printed on certificates and issued by the corporation. It provides tangible evidence that the Lyons have an ownership interest in the corporation. The journal and ledger account entries are:

Journal entry:	Cash... 50,000	
	Common Stock	50,000
	Issued common stock to owners.	

Ledger accounts:	**Cash**	**Common Stock**
	(1) 50,000 |	|(1) 50,000

The effect of transaction #1 on the accounting equation of the business entity is shown in the following exhibit:

Assets / Cash	=	Liabilities	+	Stockholders' Equity Common Stock	Type of Stockholders' Equity Transaction
(1) +50,000				+50,000	Owner investment

For every transaction, the amount on the left side of the equation must equal the amount on the right side. The first transaction increases both the assets (in this case, Cash) and the owners' equity of the business (Common Stock). The transaction involves no liabilities because it creates no obligation for Air & Sea Travel to pay an outside party. To the right of the transaction we write "Issued stock to owners" to keep track of the reason for the effect on stockholders' equity.

Transaction 2. Air & Sea Travel purchases land for a future office location, paying cash of $40,000. The journal and ledger account entries are:

Journal   Land 40,000
entry: Cash 40,000
          Paid cash for land.

Ledger   **Cash**   **Land**
accounts: (1) 50,000 | (2) $40,000   (2) 40,000 |

The effect of transaction #2 on the accounting equation of the business entity is shown in the following exhibit:

Assets				Liabilities +	Stockholders' Equity	Type of Stockholders' Equity Transaction
Cash	+	Land			Common Stock	
(1) 50,000					50,000	Owner investment
(2) −40,000 +	40,000		=			
Bal. 10,000	40,000				50,000	
50,000					50,000	

The cash purchase of land increases one asset (Land) and decreases another asset (Cash) by the same amount. After the transaction is completed, Air & Sea Travel has cash of $10,000, land of $40,000, no liabilities, and stockholders' equity of $50,000. Note that the sums of the balances (abreviated as "Bal.") on both sides of the equation are equal. This equality must always exist.

Transaction 3. The business buys stationery and other office supplies, agreeing to pay $500 to the office-supply store within 30 days. This transaction increases both the assets and the liabilities of the business. The journal and ledger account entries are:

Journal   Office Supplies 500
entry: Accounts Payable 500
          Purchased office supplies on account.

Ledger   **Office Supplies**   **Accounts Payable**
accounts: (3) 500 | | (3) 500

The effect of transaction #3 on the accounting equation of the business entity is shown in the following exhibit:

	Assets					Liabilities +	Stockholders' Equity
	Cash	+	Office Supplies	+	Land	Accounts Payable +	Common Stock
Bal.	10,000				40,000		50,000
(3)			+500			+500	
Bal.	10,000		500		40,000	500	50,000
			50,500				50,500

The asset affected is Office Supplies, and the liability is an Account Payable. Because Air & Sea Travel is obligated to pay $500 in the future but signs no formal promissory note, we record the liability as an account payable, not as a note payable. We say that purchases supported by the buyer's general credit standing are made on open account.

Transaction 4. Air & Sea Travel earns service revenue by providing travel arrangement services for customers. Assume the business earns $5,500 and collects this amount in cash. The journal and ledger account entries are:

Journal   Cash.. 5,500
entry: Service Revenue....................   5,500
      Performed services for cash.

Ledger   **Cash**   **Service Revenue**
accounts: (1) 50,000 | (2) $40,000 | (4) 5,500
      (4) 5,500 |

The effect of transaction #4 on the accounting equation of the business entity is shown in the following exhibit:

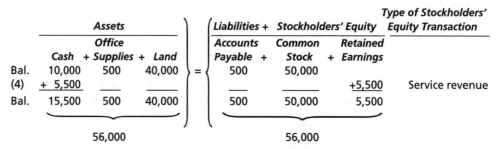

	Assets			Liabilities +	Stockholders' Equity		Type of Stockholders' Equity Transaction
	Cash	Office + Supplies	+ Land	Accounts Payable +	Common Stock +	Retained Earnings	
Bal.	10,000	500	40,000	500	50,000		
(4)	+ 5,500	____	_____	___	_____	+5,500	Service revenue
Bal.	15,500	500	40,000	500	50,000	5,500	
	56,000				56,000		

This revenue transaction caused the business to grow, as shown by the increase in total assets and in total liabilities plus stockholders' equity. Air & Sea Travel performs services for clients, so its revenue is called **service revenue**.

Transaction 5. Air & Sea Travel performs services for customers who do not pay immediately. In return for these services, Air & Sea Travel receives the customers' promise to pay $3,000 within one month. This promise is an asset to Air & Sea Travel, an account receivable because the business expects to collect the cash in the future. (In accounting, we say that Air & Sea Travel performed this service on account.) When the business performs a service for a client or a customer, the business earns revenue regardless of whether it receives cash immediately or expects to collect cash later. This $3,000 of service revenue is as real to the business as the $5,500 of revenue that it collected immediately in Transaction 4. Air & Sea Travel records an increase in the asset Accounts Receivable and an increase in Retained Earnings. The journal and ledger account entries are:

Journal   Accounts Receivable................ 3,000
entry: Service Revenue....................   3,000
      Performed services on account.

Ledger   **Accounts Receivable**   **Service Revenue**
accounts: (5) 3,000 | | (4) 5,500
               | (5) 3,000

The effect of transaction #5 on the accounting equation of the business entity is shown in the following exhibit:

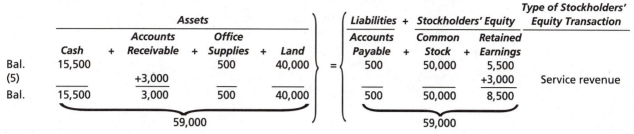

			Assets						Liabilities +	Stockholders' Equity		Type of Stockholders' Equity Transaction
	Cash	+	Accounts Receivable	+	Office Supplies	+	Land	=	Accounts Payable	+	Common Stock	+	Retained Earnings	
Bal.	15,500				500		40,000		500		50,000		5,500	
(5)			+3,000										+3,000	Service revenue
Bal.	15,500		3,000		500		40,000		500		50,000		8,500	
				59,000								59,000		

Like Transaction 4, this revenue transaction caused the business to grow.

Transaction 6. During the month, Air & Sea Travel pays $2,700 in cash expenses: office rent, $1,100; employee salary, $1,200 (for a part-time assistant); and total utilities, $400. The journal and ledger account entries are:

Journal entry:

Rent Expense............................	1,100	
Salary Expense..........................	1,200	
Utilities Expense	400	
Cash		2,700
Paid expenses.		

Ledger accounts:

Cash				Rent Expense		
(1)	50,000	(2) $40,000		(6) 1,100		
(4)	5,500	(6) 2,700				

Salary Expenses			Utilities Expense	
(6) 1,200			(6) 400	

The effect of transaction #6 on the accounting equation of the business entity is shown in the following exhibit:

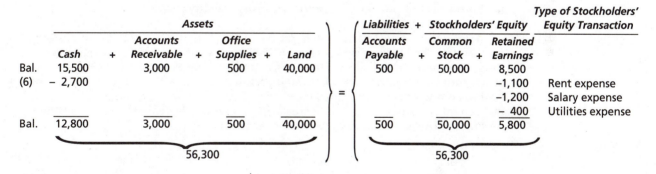

			Assets						Liabilities +	Stockholders' Equity		Type of Stockholders' Equity Transaction
	Cash	+	Accounts Receivable	+	Office Supplies	+	Land	=	Accounts Payable	+	Common Stock	+	Retained Earnings	
Bal.	15,500		3,000		500		40,000		500		50,000		8,500	
(6)	− 2,700												−1,100	Rent expense
													−1,200	Salary expense
													− 400	Utilities expense
Bal.	12,800		3,000		500		40,000		500		50,000		5,800	
				56,300								56,300		

Since expenses have the opposite effect of revenues, they cause the business to shrink, as shown by the smaller amounts of total assets and total liabilities and stockholders' equity. Each expense should be recorded in a separate transaction. Here, for simplicity, they are recorded together. As a result, the "balance" of the equation holds.

Transaction 7. Air & Sea Travel pays $400 to the store from which it purchased $500 worth of office supplies in Transaction 3. (In accounting, we say that Air & Sea Travel pays $400 on account. The journal and ledger account entries are:

Journal   Accounts Payable 400
entry: Cash   400
      Paid cash on account.

Ledger
accounts:

Cash		Accounts Payable	
(1) 50,000	(2) $40,000	(7) 400	(3) 500
(4) 5,500	(6) 2,700		
	(7) 400		

The effect of transaction #7 on the accounting equation of the business entity is shown in the following exhibit:

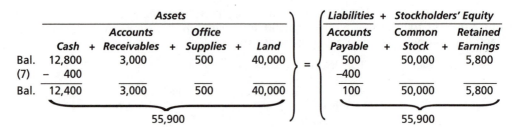

			Assets						Liabilities +		Stockholders' Equity	
			Accounts		Office				Accounts		Common	Retained
	Cash	+	Receivables	+	Supplies	+	Land		Payable	+	Stock +	Earnings
Bal.	12,800		3,000		500		40,000	=	500		50,000	5,800
(7)	– 400								–400			
Bal.	12,400		3,000		500		40,000		100		50,000	5,800
			55,900								55,900	

The payment of cash on account has no effect on the asset Office Supplies because the payment does not increase or decrease the supplies available to the business. The payment is not an expense; instead the business is paying off a liability.

Transaction 8. The Lyons remodel their home at a cost of $30,000, paying from personal funds. This event is not a transaction of Air & Sea Travel, Inc. It has no effect on Air & Sea Travel's business affairs and, therefore, is not recorded by the business. It is a transaction of the personal entity, the Lyon family, not the business entity Air & Sea Travel. We are focusing now solely on the business entity and this event does not affect it. This transaction illustrates the application of the entity concept.

Transaction 9. In Transaction 5, Air & Sea Travel performed service for customers on account. The business now collects $1,000 from a customer. (We say that it collects the cash on account.) Air & Sea Travel will record an increase in the asset Cash. Should it also record an increase in service revenue? No, because Air & Sea Travel already recorded the revenue when it performed the service in Transaction 5. The phrase "collect cash on account" means to record an increase in Cash and a decrease in the asset Accounts Receivable. The journal and ledger account entries are:

Journal   Cash 1,000
entry: Accounts Receivable   1,000
      Collected cash on account.

Ledger
accounts:

Cash		Accounts Payable	
(1) 50,000	(2) $40,000	(5) 3,000	(9) 1,000
(4) 5,500	(6) 2,700		
(9) 1,000	(7) 400		

The effect of transaction #9 on the accounting equation of the business entity is shown in the following exhibit:

		Assets					Liabilities +	Stockholders' Equity	
		Accounts		Office			Accounts	Common	Retained
	Cash +	Receivable +		Supplies +	Land		Payable +	Stock +	Earnings
Bal.	12,400	3,000		500	40,000		100	50,000	5,800
(9)	+ 1,000	−1,000				=			
Bal.	13,400	2,000		500	40,000		100	50,000	5,800
		55,900						55,900	

Total assets are unchanged from the preceding transaction's total. Why? Because Air & Sea Travel merely exchanged one asset for another. Also, liabilities and stockholders' equity are unchanged.

Transaction 10. An individual approaches the Lyons about selling a piece of the land owned by Air & Sea Travel. They and the other person agree to a sale price of $22,000, which is equal to the business's cost of the land. Air & Sea Travel sells the land and receives $22,000 cash. The journal and ledger account entries are:

Journal entry:
Cash.. 22,000
    Land 22,000
Sold land

Ledger accounts:

	Cash					Land	
(1)	50,000	(2)	40,000	(2)	40,000	(10)	22,000
(4)	5,500	(6)	2,700				
(9)	1,000	(7)	400				
(10)	22,000						

The effect of transaction #10 on the accounting equation of the business entity is shown in the following exhibit:

		Assets					Liabilities +	Stockholders' Equity	
		Accounts		Office			Accounts	Common	Retained
	Cash +	Receivables +		Supplies +	Land		Payable +	Stock +	Earnings
Bal.	13,400	2,000		500	40,000		500	50,000	5,800
(10)	+22,000				−22,000	=			
Bal.	35,400	2,000		500	18,000		100	50,000	5,800
		55,900						55,900	

Note that the company did not sell all its land; it still owns $18,000 worth of land.

Transaction 11. The corporation declares a dividend and pays Gary and Monica Lyon $2,100 cash for their personal use. The journal and ledger account entries are:

Journal entry:
Dividends 2,100
    Cash 2,100
Declared and paid dividends.

Ledger accounts:

	Cash				Dividends	
(1)	50,000	(2)	40,000	(11) 2,100	
(4)	5,500	(6)	2,700		
(9)	1,000	(7)	400		
(10)	22,000	(11)	2,100		

Each journal entry posted to the ledger is keyed by date or by transaction number. In this way, any transaction can be traced from the journal to the ledger and, if need be, back to the journal. This linking allows you to locate efficiently any information needed.

The effect of transaction #11 on the accounting equation of the business entity is shown in the following exhibit:

	Assets					Liabilities +	Stockholders' Equity		Type of Stockholders' Equity Transaction
	Cash	+ Accounts Receivable	+ Office Supplies	+ Land	=	Accounts Payable	+ Common Stock	+ Retained Earnings	
Bal.	35,400	2,000	500	18,000		100	50,000	5,800	
(11)	– 2,100							–2,100	Dividends
Bal.	33,300	2,000	500	18,000		100	50,000	3,700	
			53,800					53,800	

The dividend decreases the asset Cash and also the Retained Earnings of the business. Does the dividend decrease the business entity's holdings? The answer is "yes," because the cash paid to the stockholders is no longer available for Air & Sea Travel's business use. The dividend does not represent a business expense, however, because the cash is paid to the owners for their personal use. Therefore, we record this decrease in stockholders' equity as Dividends, not as an expense.

Accounts after Posting

Exhibit 2-5 shows how the ledger accounts look when the amounts of the preceding transactions have been posted. The exhibit groups the accounts under the accounting equation's headings. Each account has a balance, denoted as "Bal." This amount is the difference between the account's total debits and its total credits. For example, the balance in the Cash account is the difference between the debits, $78,500 ($50,000 + $5,500 + $1,000 + $22,000) and the credits, $45,200 ($40,000 + $2,700 + $400 + $2,100). Thus, the cash balance is $33,300. The balance amounts are not journal entries posted to the

Exhibit 2-5   Air & Sea Travel's Ledger Accounts After Posting

ASSETS	=	LIABILITIES	+	STOCKHOLDERS' EQUITY

Cash

(1)	50,000	(2)	40,000
(4)	5,500	(6)	2,700
(9)	1,000	(7)	400
(10)	22,000	(11)	2,100
Bal.	33,300		

Accounts Payable

| (7) | 400 | (3) | 500 |
| | | Bal. | 100 |

Common Stock

| | | (1) | 50,000 |
| | | Bal. | 50,000 |

REVENUE

Service Revenue

	(4)	5,500
	(5)	3,000
	Bal.	8,500

EXPENSES

Rent Expense

| (6) | 1,100 |
| Bal. | 1,100 |

Accounts Receivable

| (5) | 3,000 | (9) | 1,000 |
| Bal. | 2,000 | | |

Dividends

| (11) | 2,100 |
| Bal. | 2,100 |

Salary Expense

| (6) | 1,200 |
| Bal. | 1,200 |

Office Supplies

| (3) | 500 |
| Bal. | 500 |

Utilities Expense

| (6) | 400 |
| Bal. | 400 |

Land

| (2) | 40,000 | (10) | 22,000 |
| Bal. | 18,000 | | |

accounts, so we set an account balance apart from the individual amounts by horizontal lines.

If the sum of an account's debits is greater than the sum of its credits, that account has a debit balance, as the Cash account does here. If the sum of its credits is greater, that account has a credit balance, as Accounts Payable does.

FINANCIAL REPORTS AND THE FISCAL YEAR

At the end of the year, all the accounts in the ledger are totaled, and the firm's financial status is assessed. This summation is the basis for annual financial reports. With the preparation of the firm's financial reports, the old accounting cycle ends and a new one begins. The timing of the annual accounting cycle is called the fiscal year, which is the 12-month period used for financial reporting purposes. Although most companies adopt a normal calendar year of January to December, many companies use 12-month periods that reflect the seasonal nature of their industries. For example, to close its fiscal year at the completion of harvesting, a fruit orchard may select the period from September 1, 1997, to August 31, 1998.

The Trial Balance

A **trial balance** is a list of all accounts with their balances—assets first, followed by liabilities and then stockholders' equity. It provides a check on accuracy by showing whether the total debits equal the total credits. A trial balance may be taken at any time the postings are up to date, but the most common time is at the end of the period. Exhibit 2-6 is the trial balance of the ledger of Air & Sea Travel, Inc. after its first eleven transactions have been journalized and posted.

Do not confuse the trial balance with the balance sheet. Accountants prepare a trial balance for their internal records. The company reports its financial position on the balance sheet, which is a formal financial statement. And remember that the financial statements are the focal point of the accounting process; the trial balance is merely a step in the preparation of the financial statements.

Exhibit 2-6   Air & Sea Travel, Inc.

Trial Balance, April 30, 19X1

Account Title	Balance	
	Debit	Credit
Cash	$33,300	
Accounts receivable	2,000	
Office supplies	500	
Land	18,000	
Accounts payable		$ 100
Common stock		50,000
Dividends	2,100	
Service revenue		8,500
Rent expense	1,100	
Salary expense	1,200	
Utilities expense	400	
Total	$58,600	$58,600

An organization's chart of accounts lists all its accounts by their account numbers. These account numbers make it easy to locate individual accounts in the ledger. Companies may start with a relatively small number of accounts and add new accounts as the business grows.

Preparing the Financial Statements

After all the business entity transaction data have been analyzed, recorded, and balanced this information will be used to create a firm's current financial statements. Exhibit 2-7 shows all the data that will be used to create these financial statements. The data for the **statement of cash flows** are aligned under the Cash account. Cash receipts show up as increases in cash, and cash payments appear as decreases. **Income statement** data appear as revenues and expenses under Retained Earnings. The revenues increase retained earnings; the expenses decrease retained earnings. The **balance sheet** data are composed of the ending balances of the assets, liabilities, and stockholders' equities shown at the bottom of the exhibit. The accounting equation shows that total assets ($53,800) equal total liabilities plus stockholders' equity ($53,800). The **statement of retained earnings,** which shows net income (or net loss) and dividends, can be prepared from the income statement data.

Exhibit 2-7 shows Air & Sea Travel's financial statements at the end of April, the business's first month of operations. Follow the flow of data to observe that:

1. The income statement reports revenues, expenses, and either a net income or a net loss for the period. During April, Air & Sea Travel earned net income of $5,800.

2. The statement of retained earnings starts with the beginning balance of retained earnings, which for a new business is zero. Add net income for the period (arrow 1), subtract dividends, and obtain the ending balance of retained earnings ($3,700).

3. The balance sheet lists the assets, liabilities, and stockholders' equity of the business at the end of the period. Included in stockholders' equity is retained earnings, which comes from the statement of retained earnings (arrow 2).

4. The statement of cash flows summarizes cash receipts and cash payments under three categories of activities: operating, investing, and financing. The result is an increase or a decrease in cash during the period. Add the beginning cash balance to the change in cash and obtain the ending cash balance, which is reported on the balance sheet (arrow 3). The transaction analysis we've just examined can be used to prepare the financial statements. However, the analysis in Exhibit 2-7 can become cumbersome for even the smallest of organizations.

Consider the Coca-Cola Company with its hundreds of accounts and thousands of transactions. The spreadsheet to account for Coca-Cola's transactions would be too large to use. For this reason, accountants use a different accounting system called double-entry accounting to create the financial statements.

SUMMARY

Assets = Liabilities + Owners' Equity

An account is the detailed record of the changes that have occurred in a particular asset, liability, or stockholders' equity during a period. Assets are the economic resources that benefit the business and will continue to do so in the future. Liabilities are debts payable to outsiders. Stockholders' equity (sometimes called shareholders' equity or simply owners' equity) are the owners' claims to the assets of a corporation. Revenues are increases in stockholders' equity created by delivering goods or services to customers. Expenses are the costs of doing business that decrease stockholders' equity.

Exhibit 2-7 Financial Statements of Air & Sea Travel, Inc.

Income Statement, Month Ended April 30, 19X1

Revenue:		
Service revenue ($5,500 + $3,000)		$8,500
Expenses:		
Salary expense	$1,200	
Rent expense	1,100	
Utilities expense	400	
Total expenses		2,700
Net income		$5,800

Statement of Retained Earnings, Month Ended April 30, 19X1

Retained earnings, April 1, 19X1	$ 0
Add: Net income for the month	5,800
	5,800
Less: Dividends	2,100
Retained earnings, April 30, 19X1	$3,700

①

Balance Sheet, April 30, 19X1

Assets		Liabilities	
Cash	$33,300	Accounts payable	$ 100
Accounts receivable	2,000		
Office supplies	500	**Stockholders' Equity**	
Land	18,000	Common stock	50,000
		Retained earnings	3,700
		Total stockholders' equity	53,700
		Total liabilities and	
Total assets	$53,800	stockholders' equity	$53,800

②

Statement of Cash Flows, Month Ended April 30, 19X1

Cash flows from operating activities:		
Receipts:		
Collections from customers ($5,500 + $1,000)		$ 6,500
Payments:		
To suppliers and employees ($2,700 + $400)		(3,100)
Net cash inflow from operating activities		3,400
Cash flows from investing activities:		
Acquisition of land	$(40,000)	
Sale of land	22,000	
Net cash outflow from investing activities		(18,000)
Cash flows from financing activities:		
Issuance (sale) of stock to owners	$ 50,000	
Dividends	(2,100)	
Net cash inflow from financing activities		47,900
Net increase in cash		$33,300
Cash balance, April 1, 19X1		0
Cash balance, April 30, 19X1		$33,300

③

A transaction is any event that both affects the financial position of the business entity and can be reliably recorded. Analyzing business transactions involves determining, each transaction's effects on the accounting equation: assets = liabilities + stockholder's equity. The summary of all the business's transactions over a period forms the basis for its financial statements.

Double-entry accounting is an accounting system that uses debits and credits to record the dual effects of each business transaction. Every transaction involves both a debit and a credit, and the total amount debited must equal the total amount credited for each transaction. Debits are simply the left side of an account; credits are the right side of an account. Assets and expenses are increased by debits and decreased by credits. Liabilities, stockholders' equity, and revenues are increased by credits and decreased by debits.

Accountants record business transactions first in a journal, a chronological record of the entity's transactions. Each journal entry includes a date, the titles of the accounts debited and credited, the dollar amounts debited and credited, and a short explanation of the transaction. This information is then posted (transferred) to the ledger, a grouping of all the individual accounts and their balances. The balance of each account in the ledger may be taken after all posting is done.

QUESTIONS

1. Name the three basic accounts in the accounting equation.
2. Is the following statement true or false? "Debit means decrease and credit means increase." Explain your answer.
3. What role do transactions play in accounting?
4. Briefly describe the flow of accounting information from the business transaction to the ledger.
5. Label each of the following transactions as increasing stockholders' equity (+), decreasing stockholders equity (–), or having no effect on stockholders' equity (0).
   a. Investment by owner
   b. Revenue transaction
   c. Purchase of supplies on credit
   d. Expense transaction
   e. Cash payment on account
   f. Dividends
   g. Borrowing money on a note payable
   h. Sale of service on account
6. Rearrange the following accounts in their logical sequence in the ledger:

Notes Payable	Cash
Accounts Receivable	Common Stock
Sales Revenue	Salary Expense

7. Why do accountants prepare a trial balance?

PROBLEM

1. The analysis of the transactions in which Mossimo Leasing Corporation engaged during its first month of operations follows in their order of occurrence. The company buys equipment that it leases out to earn revenue. Mossimo Leasing paid no dividends during the period.

	Cash	+	Accounts Receivable	+	Lease Equipment	=	Note Payable	+	Common Stock	+	Retained Earnings
(a)	+50,000								+50,000		
(b)					+100,000		+100,000				
(c)			+500								+ 500
(d)	− 750				+750						
(e)	+ 150		−150								
(f)	− 1,000										−1,000
(g)	+ 2,500										+2,500
(h)	−10,000						− 10,000				

Required

A. Describe each transaction.
B. If these transactions fully describe the operations of Mossimo Leasing during the month, what was the amount of net income or net loss?

INTERNET EXERCISE

Select one of the following companies or a company of your choice and locate its current annual report. The annual report is usually located in the Investor Information Section of the company's web site.

Corporation	WWW Page Location
Xerox	www.xerox.com
Ben & Jerrys	www.benjerry.com
Microsoft	www.microsoft.com (go to the index)
Compaq	www.compaq.com (go to overview)
Eli Lilly	www.lilly.com

Required

Obtain the following information on the corporation's

a. Total Assets
b. Total Liabilities
c. Total Shareholders' Equity
d. Net Income

SECTION II
FINANCIAL STATEMENT ANALYSIS

CHAPTER 3

FINANCIAL STATEMENTS

The end product of the accounting process is a set of financial statements that portrays the company in financial terms. Each financial statement relates to a specific date or covers a specific period of business activity, such as a year. What would managers and investors want to know about a company at the end of a period? Exhibit 3-1 summarizes the four basic questions that decision makers are likely to ask. The answer to each question is given by one of the financial statements: the income statement, the statement of retained earnings, the balance sheet, and the statement of cash flows.

To examine what the financial statements include and how to read them, let's look at the Lands' End financial statements for fiscal year 1996. Our goal is an understanding of the four basic financial statements and the information they provide for decision makers. Let's begin with the income statement, also referred to as the statement of operations.

INCOME STATEMENT (STATEMENT OF OPERATIONS)

The **income statement,** or statement of operations, reports the company's revenues, expenses, and net income or net loss for the period. At the top of Exhibit 3-2 is the company's name, Lands' End, Inc. & Subsidiaries. Lands' End, the parent company, owns other companies that are its subsidiaries. The amounts reported on the statements include figures for both Lands' End and its subsidiaries to give a full picture of all the resources that Lands' End controls. Most companies' financial statements show the consolidation of the parent company and one or more subsidiaries.

The date of the income statement is "For the fiscal years ended February 27, 1996 and January 27, 1995." A fiscal year is the year used for accounting purposes.

Exhibit 3-1 Information Reported on the Financial Statement

Question	Answer	Financial Statement
How well did the company perform (or operate) during the period?	Revenues – Expenses ——— Net income (or Net loss)	Income statement (also called the Statement of operations)
Why did the company's retained earnings change during the period?	Beginning retained earnings + Net income (or – Net loss) – Dividends ——— Ending retained earnings	Statement of retained earnings (or Statement of stockholders' equity)
What is the company's financial position at the end of the period?	Assets = Liabilities + Owners' Equity	Balance sheet (also called the Statement of financial position)
How much cash did the company generate and spend during the period?	Operating cash flows ± Investing cash flows ± Financing cash flows ——— Increase (or Decrease) in cash during the period	Statement of cash flows

The Lands' End fiscal year ends on the Friday closest to January 31 of each year. If Lands' End followed the calendar year, its accounting year would end on December 31, and its income statement would be dated "For the year ended December 31, 1995." Lands' End uses a fiscal year that ends around January 31 because the company's big

Exhibit 3-2 Consolidated Income Statement (Statement of Operations) (adapted)

Lands's End, Inc. & Subsidiaries
Consolidated Statement of Operations

	(In thousands)	For the fiscal years ended	
		February 2, 1996	January 27, 1995
1	Net sales	$1,031,548	$992,106
2	Cost of sales	588,017	571,265
3	Gross profit	443,531	420,841
4	Selling, general, and administrative expenses	392,484	357,516
5	Charges from sale of subsidiary	1,882	3,500
6	Income from operations	49,165	59,825
7	Other income (expense):		
8	Interest expense	(2,771)	(1,769)
9	Interest income	253	307
10	Other	4,278	1,300
11	Total other income (expense), net	1,760	(162)
12	Income before income taxes	50,925	59,663
13	Income tax provision	20,370	23,567
14	Net income	$ 30,555	$ 36,096

selling period winds down about a month after Christmas. Most retailers use a fiscal year that ends on January 31. Most companies adopt an accounting year that ends with the low point in their annual operations. For 60% of large companies, the low point in their operation is December 31.

The Lands' End income statement reports operating results for two fiscal years, 1996 and 1995. The income statement includes more than one year's data to let owners and creditors examine the company's sales and net income trends.

To avoid cluttering the statement with zeros, Lands' End reports its figures in thousands of dollars. Some companies report their financial statement amounts in millions. During 1996, Lands' End increased net sales from $992 million to over $1 billion (line 1), but net income dropped from $36 million to under $31 million (line 14). Continuation of this downward trend in net income would concern the company's managers and investors.

The income statement is divided into two main categories:

- Revenues (also called income, such as interest income) and gains
- Expenses and losses

Net Income = Total Revenues and Gains − Total Expenses and Losses

Revenues Revenues and expenses do not always carry the terms "revenue" and "expense" in their titles. For example, net sales is really net sales revenue, but the term "revenue" is often omitted. During fiscal year 1996, Lands' End had net sales of $1,031,548,000 (line 1). The term "net sales" means that the company has subtracted from its total sales the sales value of the goods that Lands' End customers returned to the company.

Expenses Cost of sales (or cost of goods sold, line 2) represents the cost to Lands' End of the goods it sold to customers during the year. For example, when Lands' End buys a shirt for $16 and sells the shirt for $30, its sales revenue is $30, and cost of goods sold is $16.

On the Lands' End income statement, Net Sales − Cost of Sales = Gross Profit (line 3). **Gross profit** is profit before operating expenses have been deducted. To earn its revenue, Lands' End incurs expenses in addition to cost of sales. For catalog merchants such as Lands' End and L. L. Bean, the second highest major expense (behind cost of sales) is selling expense, which includes the cost of producing and mailing catalogs to prospective customers nationwide. All companies, Lands' End included, have general expenses such as utilities, maintenance, and property taxes, as well as administrative expenses for the home office and for executive and other employee salaries. Most companies combine all three expense categories and report a single amount for selling, general, and administrative expenses (line 4, often abbreviated as SG&A expense). During fiscal year 1996, Lands' End incurred SG&A expenses of just over $392,484 million (line 4).

Income before income taxes totaled $50.9 million (line 12), and income tax expense (here labeled as "Income tax provision") absorbed $20.4 million of the company's pre-tax income (line 13). For fiscal year 1996, Lands' End earned net income of $30.555 million after covering all expenses including income tax. The net income will now be fed into the statement of retained earnings.

Statement of Retained Earnings

Lands' End's retained earnings represent exactly what the words imply: that portion of net income the company has retained, or kept for use in the business. As we can see from the income statement, during 1996, the company earned net income of $30.555 million. This number will also appear on the **statement of retained earnings** (line 2 in Exhibit 3-3).

Exhibit 3-3 Consolidated Statement of Retained Earnings

Lands' End, Inc. & Subsidiaries
Consolidated Statement of Retained Earnings

(In thousands)	For the fiscal years ended	
	February 2, 1996	January 27, 1995
Retained Earnings		
1 Beginning balance	$229,554	$193,460
2 Net income	30,555	36,096
3 Cash dividends paid	—	—
4 Issuance of treasury stock	—	(2)
5 Ending balance	$260,109	$229,554

Thus, net income is the link between these two financial statements. After Lands' End earns net income, the board of directors must decide whether to retain the income for use in the business or to pay a dividend to the stockholders. In both 1996 and 1995, Lands' End decided not to pay dividends (line 3). Rather, it kept all its net income as retained earnings.

Note the $2,000 decrease in retained earnings due to the issuance of treasury stock in fiscal year 1995 (line 4). This item illustrates a general rule in financial reporting:

- Positive amounts in tabular displays usually appear with no sign—neither a plus (+) nor a minus (–).
- Negative amounts often appear in parentheses.

On the statement of retained earnings, net income (line 2) has no sign, which means that it is positive and thus added to the beginning balance of retained earnings (line 1). The issuance of treasury stock during fiscal year 1995 decreased retained earnings, so the ending balance for 1995 is computed as follows

$$\$193{,}460 + \$36{,}096 - \$2 = \$229{,}554$$

During fiscal years 1996 and 1995, Lands' End paid no dividends, so the statement of retained earnings shows no subtraction for dividends. During 1996, Lands' End's retained earnings grew from $229.6 million to $260.1 million because net income increased retained earnings by $30.6 million in 1996. This means that the company had $30 million more to work with in 1996 than it had in 1995.

Balance Sheet

The Lands' End balance sheet appears in Exhibit 3-4. Notice that the balance sheet is dated February 2, 1996, the end of the company's fiscal year. The balance sheet gives a picture (a snapshot) of the company's financial position at a moment in time—specifically at the stroke of midnight on that day. This is in contrast to the dates of the other three statements, for the fiscal year ended February 2, 1996. The income statement, the statement of retained earnings, and the statement of cash flows (which we discuss in the next section) report on events that occurred throughout the year, from beginning to end. A company's balance sheet, sometimes called its statement of financial position, reports three main categories of items: assets, liabilities, and owners' equity (which Lands' End calls "shareholders' investment").

Assets. Assets are subdivided into two categories: current assets and long-term assets. Current assets are those assets that the company expects to convert to cash, sell, or consume during the next 12 months or within the business's normal operating cycle if longer than a year. The operating cycle is the time span during which (1) cash is used to acquire goods and services, and (2) these goods and services are sold to customers, from whom the business collects cash.

Exhibit 3-4 Consolidated Balance Sheet (adapted)

Lands' End, Inc. & Subsidiaries
Consolidated Balance

(In thousands)	February 2, 1996	January 27, 1995
ASSETS		
Current assets:		
1 Cash	$ 17,176	$ 5,426
2 Receivables	8,064	4,459
3 Inventory	164,816	168,652
4 Prepaid advertising and other expenses	32,033	19,631
5 Total current assets	222,089	198,168
Property, plant, and equipment, at cost:		
6 Land and buildings	72,248	69,798
7 Fixtures and equipment	83,880	74,745
8 Leasehold improvements	2,912	1,862
9 Total property, plant, and equipment	159,040	146,405
10 Less accumulated depreciation and amortization	60,055	49,414
11 Property, plant, and equipment, net	98,985	96,991
12 Intangibles, net	2,423	2,453
13 Total assets	$323,497	$297,612
LIABILITIES AND SHAREHOLDERS' INVESTMENT		
Current liabilities:		
14 Lines of credit	$ 9,319	$ 7,539
15 Accounts payable	62,380	52,762
16 Reserve for returns	4,555	5,011
17 Accrued liabilities	23,751	25,959
18 Accrued profit sharing	1,483	1,679
19 Income taxes payable	13,256	9,727
20 Current maturities of long-term debt	—	40
21 Total current liabilities	114,744	102,717
22 **Deferred income taxes**	7,212	5,379
23 **Long-term liabilities**	349	388
Shareholders' investment:		
24 Common stock, 40,221 shares issued	26,567	26,219
25 Retained earnings	260,109	229,554
26 Other	(85,484)	(66,645)
27 Total shareholders' investment	201,192	189,128
28 Total liabilities and shareholders' investment	$323,497	$297,612

Current assets for Lands' End consist of cash, receivables, inventory, and prepaid advertising and other expenses (lines 1–4). Total current assets (line 5) were $222 million at the close of business on February 2, 1996. Lands' End had over $17 million of cash in the bank. The company sells to customers on credit, which explains the $8 million in receivables that Lands' End expects to collect within a short time. Inventory is the company's largest asset, totaling almost $165 million. Inventory is an abbreviation for merchandise inventory—the shirts, slacks, and other goods the company sells as its core operations. Because the company markets its products through catalogs, advertising is important. Prepaid advertising represents prepayments for advertisements that have not yet run. Prepaid expenses are assets because the company expects to benefit from these expenditures in the future.

The main category of long-term assets is property, plant, and equipment (lines 6–8). These assets cost a total of $159 million (line 9). The property, plant, and equipment are partially used up, as indicated by the accumulated depreciation of $60 million (line 10). Depreciation is the accounting process of allocating an asset's cost to expense; we discuss this concept in detail at the end of this chapter. The net amount of property, plant, and equipment is 99 million (cost 159 million – accumulated depreciation of $60 million = net of $99 million, line 11).

At the end of fiscal year 1996, Lands' End had total assets of more than $323 million (line 13).

Liabilities. Liabilities are also divided into current and long-term categories. Current liabilities (lines 14–20) are debts due to be paid within the year or within the entity's normal operating cycle if longer than a year. Chief among the current liabilities for Lands' End are accounts payable, accrued liabilities, income taxes payable, and lines of credit. Long-term liabilities are payable after one year.

Accounts payable (line 15) represents amounts owed for goods and services that Lands' End has purchased but not yet paid for. (The word payable always indicates a liability.) Accounts payable exceeded $62 million on February 2, 1996. The company's second largest current liability is accrued liabilities (line 17)—almost $24 million. Included among the accrued liabilities are salaries payable to Lands' End employees, payroll taxes the company owes to the government, and interest owed on borrowed money. Income taxes payable (line 19) are amounts the company owes the federal government for income taxes. The lines of credit (line 14) are short-term notes payable to banks.

On February 2, 1996, Lands' End owed current liabilities of almost $115 million that will be paid within a few months (line 21). How will the company pay this huge amount? They will pay it with cash generated from selling inventory and collecting cash from customers. Recall that current assets totaled $222 million. Would you feel safe if you had $222 million of current assets to pay $115 million of current liabilities within a year? Most managers of large businesses would feel safe because of the high proportion of current assets to current liabilities.

Lands' End is in the enviable position of having almost no long-term liabilities. This is unusual because most companies finance their operations with larger amounts of long-term debt. The company's long-term liabilities of $7.5 million consist of deferred income taxes (line 22 $7.2 million), tax debts whose payment can be deferred beyond a year, and other long-term liabilities (line 23, $0.3 million). In sum, Lands' End has total liabilities of around $122 million (current liabilities of $115 million + long-term liabilities of $7 million), which is quite low relative to total assets of $323 million.

The accounting equation states that

$$\text{Assets} - \text{Liabilities} = \text{Owners' Equity}$$

The assets (resources) and the liabilities (debts) of Lands' End are fairly easy to understand. Owners' equity is harder to pin down.

Owners' Equity. At a purely mathematical level, owners' equity is simple to calculate:

But what does owners' equity really mean? Lands' End labels its owners' equity as total shareholders' investment (line 27), and this title is descriptive. Remember that a company's owners' equity represents the shareholders' investment in the assets of the business. Owners' equity for Lands' End consists of common stock, represented by 40.2 million shares that the company has sold to stockholders for approximately $26.6 million (line 24). The largest part of the owners' equity is retained earnings of $260 million (line 25). This large amount may explain why long-term liabilities are so low: profitable operations, not long-term debt, have financed the company's operations. You should trace the $260 million ending balance of retained earnings from the statement of retained earnings in Exhibit 3-3 to the balance sheet. This is the link between these two financial statements.

On February 2, 1996, total shareholders' investment (owners' equity) for Lands' End was $201 million (line 27). For now you may ignore the "Other equity" in line 26 (negative amount of $85 million). We will explain the components of this item as we move through the text.

The bottom line of the balance sheet shows total liabilities and shareholders' investment of $323 million, which, as the accounting equation tells us, must equal the company's total assets ($323 million). The balance sheet thus reports that Lands' End, Inc. has $323 million of assets with which to work. Of this amount, the company owes $122 million, and the company's stockholders own $201 million of the company's assets free and clear of any debt.

STATEMENT OF CASH FLOWS

To examine the statement of cash flows, we return to the discussion with which we began the chapter. Managers engage in the following basic activities: they finance the organization to obtain the funds needed to invest in assets and operate the company. The statement of cash flows is organized around these activities.

The Lands' End statement of cash flows appears in Exhibit 3-6. Each of the three main categories of cash flows includes cash receipts and cash payments. Cash receipts are positive amounts with no signs. Cash payments are negative amounts indicated by parentheses.

Operating activities generate the lion's share of the company's cash (over $41 million in fiscal year 1996; see line 6). Investing activities include more cash payments than cash receipts, for a net cash outflow of $12 million (line 9). Financing activities resulted in a net cash outflow of $17 million (line 15). Overall, the company increased its cash balance by $11.75 million during 1996 (line 16) to end the year with cash of $17.2 million (line 18). Note that you can trace the ending cash balance to the balance sheet. The cash balance is the link between the statement of cash flows and the balance sheet.

Let's now examine the three major sections of the statement of cash flows more closely.

Cash Flows from Operating Activities. The bulk of the operating cash flows at Lands' End took the form of cash received from customers (line 1). This is a strong positive indicator because core operations are a company's largest source of cash for paying the bills and expanding the business. Consider an alternative: suppose the company's main source of cash is borrowing. This would suggest that operations are not very successful and that borrowing is necessary to keep the company afloat. This is clearly not the case at Lands' End. The largest cash payments went to Lands' End suppliers and to the company's 7,900 employees (line 3). Since Lands' End buys worldwide, the suppliers are scattered around the globe. Most company employees live in Wisconsin, Illinois, or Iowa.

Exhibit 3-6   Consolidated Statement of Cash Flows (adapted)

Lands' End, Inc. & Subsidiaries
Consolidated Statement of Cash Flows

		For the fiscal years ended	
	(In thousands)	February 2, 1996	January 27, 1995
	Cash flows from operating activities:		
1	Cash received from customers	$1,027,943	$991,291
2	Cash received from interest	253	307
3	Cash paid to suppliers and employees	(967,075)	(926,714)
4	Cash paid for interest	(2,833)	(2,828)
5	Cash paid for income taxes	(16,896)	(27,595)
6	Net cash flows from operating activities	41,392	34,461
	Cash flows from investing activities:		
7	Cash paid for capital additions and businesses acquired	(13,904)	(32,102)
8	Proceeds from divestiture	1,665	—
9	Net cash flows used for investing activities	(12,239)	(32,102)
	Cash flows from financing activities:		
10	Proceeds from short-term and long-term debt	1,780	7,539
11	Payment of long-term debt	(40)	(40)
12	Purchases of treasury stock	(20,001)	(27,979)
13	Issuance of treasury stock	858	1,978
14	Cash dividends paid	—	—
15	Net cash flows used for financing activities	(17,403)	(18,502)
16	**Net increase (decrease) in cash**	11,750	(16,143)
17	**Beginning cash**	5,426	21,569
18	**Ending cash**	$ 17,176	$ 5,426

What does management expect regarding the adequacy of cash flows from operations in the future? The company's annual report includes a section titled, "Management Discussion and Analysis," which states on page 11 that "The company believes that its cash flow from operations and borrowings under its current credit facilities will provide adequate resources to meet its [investment] requirements and operational needs for the foreseeable future."

Cash Flows from Investing Activities. During 1996, Lands' End spent $13.9 million to purchase new computer hardware and merchandise-handling equipment (capital additions) and to acquire new businesses (line 7). The company also sold property, plant, and equipment (divestitures) for $1.665 million (line 8), a relatively small amount. The net cash outflows from investing activities thus totaled $12.2 million over the course of fiscal year 1996 (line 9). A net cash outflow from investing activities is generally healthy because it indicates that the business is buying new assets. Again, consider the alternative: What would you think of a company that year after year had a net cash inflow from investing activities? This would reveal that the company is shrinking as it sells off its long-term assets. The outlook would be cloudy.

What investing activities was Lands' End planning for 1997 and beyond? The 1996 Management Discussion and Analysis states that "In the coming year, the company plans to invest about $16 million in capital improvements [same as long-term assets]." Also, "the company continues to explore investment opportunities arising from the expansion of its international businesses and the development of new businesses."

Cash Flows from Financing Activities. Borrowing is labeled "proceeds" from short-term and long-term debt on the Lands' End statement of cash flows. During the year the company borrowed a modest amount of cash, only $1.78 million (line 10).

The largest financing cash flow was a $20 million payment for the purchase of treasury stock (line 12). This means that Lands' End bought back some of its own stock that it had issued earlier to its stockholders. Consistent with the information provided by the statement of retained earnings, the cash flow statement reports no dividend payments during fiscal year 1996 (line 14). The overall effect of financing activities on the Lands' End cash position during fiscal 1996 was a net cash outflow of $17.4 million (line 15).

RELATIONSHIPS AMONG FINANCIAL STATEMENTS

Exhibit 3-7 summarizes the relationships among the financial statements. Study this exhibit carefully because you will use these relationships throughout your business career.

Specifically, note the following:

1. The Income Statement for the fiscal year ended February 2, 1996

    a. Reports all revenues and all expenses during the period. Revenues and expenses are reported only on the income statement.

    b. Reports net income of the period if total revenues exceed total expenses, as in the case of Lands' End, Inc.'s operations for fiscal year 1996. If total expenses exceed total revenues, a net loss is reported instead.

2. The Statement of Retained Earnings for the fiscal year ended February 2, 1996

    a. Opens with the retained earnings balance at the beginning of the period.

    b. Adds net income (or subtracts net loss, as the case may be). Net income (or net loss) comes directly from the income statement (see arrow 1 in Exhibit 3-6).

    c. Subtracts dividends, if appropriate. (There are no dividends in this example.)

    d. Ends with the retained earnings balance at the end of the period.

3. The Balance Sheet at February 2, 1996, the end of the fiscal year

    a. Reports all assets, all liabilities, and stockholders' equity of the business at the end of the period. No other financial statement reports assets and liabilities.

    b. Reports that total assets equal the sum of total liabilities plus total stockholders' equity. This balancing feature gives the balance sheet its name; it is based on the accounting equation.

    c. Reports the ending retained earnings, taken directly from the statement of retained earnings (see arrow 2).

4. The Statement of Cash Flows for the fiscal year ended February 2, 1996

    a. Reports cash flows from three types of business activities (operating, investing, and financing activities) during the year. Each category results in a net cash inflow or a net cash outflow for the period.

    b. Reports a net increase (or a net decrease) in cash during the year and ends with the cash balance on February 2, 1996. This is the amount of cash reported on the balance sheet (see arrow 3).

The Decision Guidelines Exhibit 3-8 summarizes how stockholders and creditors use the financial statements to make key decisions.

Exhibit 3-7 Relationships Among the Lands' End Financial Statements
(Amounts in thousands)

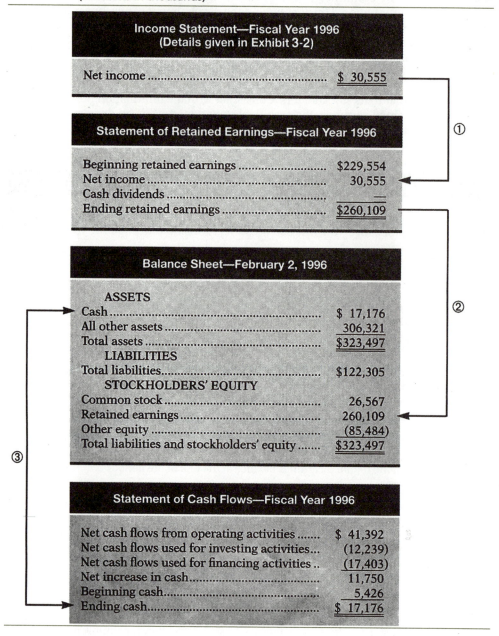

Income Statement—Fiscal Year 1996
(Details given in Exhibit 3-2)

Net income .... $ 30,555

Statement of Retained Earnings—Fiscal Year 1996

Beginning retained earnings $229,554
Net income 30,555
Cash dividends .... —
Ending retained earnings $260,109

Balance Sheet—February 2, 1996

ASSETS
Cash .... $ 17,176
All other assets 306,321
Total assets $323,497
LIABILITIES
Total liabilities $122,305
STOCKHOLDERS' EQUITY
Common stock 26,567
Retained earnings 260,109
Other equity .... (85,484)
Total liabilities and stockholders' equity $323,497

Statement of Cash Flows—Fiscal Year 1996

Net cash flows from operating activities .... $ 41,392
Net cash flows used for investing activities ... (12,239)
Net cash flows used for financing activities .. (17,403)
Net increase in cash 11,750
Beginning cash 5,426
Ending cash .... $ 17,176

① ② ③

Exhibit 3-8   The Decision Guidelines

How Stockholders and Creditors Use the Financial Statements

Group	Mainly Interested In	Reason	What They Look For
Stockholders	Net income	*Net income* means the company is profitable. Stockholders enhance their personal wealth through (a) an increase in the market price of the company's stock and (b) dividends received. Net income affects both stock prices and dividends.	Steadily rising level of net income over time means the company's profits look solid.
	Cash flows	*Cash flows* report how the company generates and uses its cash. Wise use of cash produces net income and more cash.	Operating activities should be the main source of cash.
Bankers and other creditors	Assets and liabilities	*Liabilities* indicate how much the company owes other creditors. *Assets* show what the company can pledge as collateral that a creditor can take if the company fails to pay its debts.	Assets far in excess of liabilities, or assets increasing faster than liabilities over time.
	Net income	Profitable companies can usually pay their debts.	Same as for stockholders.
	Cash flows	Same as for stockholders.	Same as for stockholders.

INVENTORY COSTING METHODS

Determining the unit cost of inventory is easy when the unit cost remains constant during the period, but the unit cost often changes. For example, during times of inflation, prices rise. The chair that cost Huntington Galleries $300 in January may cost $315 in June and $322 in October. Suppose Huntington sells 40 chairs in November. How many of them cost $300, how many cost $315, and how many cost $322? To compute the cost of goods sold and cost of inventory on hand, the accountant must have some way to assign the business's cost to each item sold. The four costing methods that GAAP allows are

1. Specific unit cost
2. Weighted-average cost
3. First-in, first-out (FIFO) cost
4. Last-in, first-out (LIFO) cost

A company can use any of these methods. Many companies use different methods for different categories of inventory. Here we use the periodic inventory system to illustrate the four inventory costing methods.

Specific Unit Cost. Some businesses deal in inventory items that may be identified individually, such as automobiles, jewels, and real estate. These businesses usually cost their inventory at the specific unit cost of the particular unit. For instance, a Chevrolet dealer may have two vehicles in the showroom—a "stripped-down" model that costs $14,000 and a "loaded" model that costs $17,000. If the dealer sells the loaded model for $19,700, cost of goods sold is $17,000, the cost of the specific unit. The gross margin on this sale is $2,700 ($19,700–$17,000). If the stripped-down auto is the only unit left in inventory at the end of the period, ending inventory is $14,000, the dealer's cost of the specific unit on hand.

The specific-unit-cost method is also called the specific identification method. This method is not practical for inventory items that have common characteristics, such as bushels of wheat, gallons of paint, or boxes of laundry detergent.

The weighted-average cost, FIFO (first-in, first-out) cost, and LIFO (last-in, first-out) cost methods are fundamentally different from the specific-unit-cost method. These methods do not assign to inventory the specific cost of particular units. Instead, they assume different flows of costs into and out of inventory.

Weighted-Average Cost. The weighted-average cost method, often called the average-cost method, is based on the weighted-average cost of inventory during the period. Weighted-average cost is determined as follows: divide the cost of goods available for sale (beginning inventory plus purchases) by the number of units available for sale (beginning inventory plus purchases). Compute the ending inventory and cost of goods sold by multiplying the number of units by the weighted-average cost per unit.

Suppose the business has 60 units of inventory available for sale during the period. Ending inventory consists of 20 units, and cost of goods sold is based on 40 units. Panel A of Exhibit 3-9 gives the data for computing ending inventory and cost of goods sold. Panel B shows the weighted-average cost computations.

First-In, First-Out (FIFO) Cost. Under the first-in, first-out (FIFO) method, the company must keep a record of the cost of each inventory unit purchased. The unit costs used in computing the ending inventory may then be different from the unit costs used in computing the cost of goods sold. Under FIFO, the first costs into inventory are the first costs out to cost of goods sold—hence the name first-in, first-out. Ending inventory is based on the costs of the most recent purchases. In our example in Exhibit 3-9, the FIFO cost of ending inventory is $36,000. Cost of goods sold is $54,000. Panel A gives the data, and Panel B shows the FIFO computations.

Last-In, First-Out (LIFO) Cost. The last-in, first-out (LIFO) method also depends on the costs of particular inventory purchases. LIFO is the opposite of FIFO. Under LIFO, the last costs into inventory are the first costs out to cost of goods sold. This method leaves the oldest costs—those of beginning inventory and plus the earliest purchases of the period—in ending inventory. In our example in Exhibit 3-9, the LIFO cost of ending inventory is $24,000. Cost of goods sold is $66,000. Again, Panel A gives the data, and Panel B shows the LIFO computations.

Income Effects of FIFO, LIFO, and Weighted-Average Cost

In our discussion and examples, the cost of inventory rose during the accounting period. When inventory unit costs change, the different costing methods produce different cost of goods sold and ending inventory figures, as Exhibit 3-9 shows. When inventory unit costs are increasing, FIFO ending inventory is highest because it is priced at the most recent costs, which are the highest. LIFO ending inventory is lowest because it is priced at the oldest costs, which are the lowest. When inventory unit costs are decreasing, FIFO ending inventory is lowest and LIFO is highest.

Exhibit 3-10 summarizes the income effects of the three inventory methods, using the data from Exhibit 3-9. Study the exhibit carefully, focusing on ending inventory, cost of goods sold, and gross margin.

The Income Tax Advantage of LIFO

When prices are rising, applying the LIFO method results in the lowest taxable income and thus the lowest income taxes. Let's use the gross margin data of Exhibit 3-10.

Exhibit 3-9 Inventory and Cost of Goods Sold under Weighted-Average, FIFO, and LIFO Inventory Costing Methods

PANEL A—Illustrative Data

Beginning inventory (10 units @ $1,000 per unit)..................		$10,000
Purchases:		
No. 1 (25 units @ $1,400 per unit).....................................	$35,000	
No. 2 (25 units @ $1,800 per unit).....................................	45,000	
Total purchases..		80,000
Cost of goods available for sale (60 units)		90,000
Ending inventory (20 units @ $? per unit).............................		?
Cost of goods sold (40 units @ $? per unit)...........................		$?

PANEL B—Ending Inventory and Cost of Goods Sold

Weighted-Average Cost Method

Cost of goods available for sale—see Panel A (60 units @ average cost of $1,500* per unit)...		$90,000
Ending inventory (20 units @ $1,500 per unit).......................		(30,000)
Cost of goods sold (40 units @ $1,500 per unit)		$60,000

$$*\ \frac{\text{Cost of goods available for sale, \$90,000}}{\text{Number of units available for sale, 60}} = \text{Average cost per unit, \$1,500}$$

FIFO Cost Method

Cost of goods available for sale (60 units—see Panel A)		$90,000
Ending inventory (cost of the *last* 20 units available):		
20 units @ $1,800 per unit (from purchase No. 2)..............		(36,000)
Cost of goods sold (cost of the *first* 40 units available):		
10 units @ $1,000 per unit (all of beginning inventory)	$10,000	
25 units @ $1,400 per unit (all of purchase No. 1)..............	35,000	
5 units @ $1,800 per unit (from purchase No. 2)..............	9,000	
Cost of goods sold		$54,000

LIFO Cost Method

Cost of goods available for sale (60 units—see Panel A)		$90,000
Ending inventory (cost of the *first* 20 units available):		
10 units @ $1,000 per unit (all of beginning inventory)	$10,000	
10 units @ $1,400 per unit (from purchase No. 1)..............	14,000	
Ending inventory...		(24,000)
Cost of goods sold (cost of the *last* 40 units available):		
25 units @ $1,800 per unit (all of purchase No. 2)..............	$45,000	
15 units @ $1,400 per unit (from purchase No. 1)..............	21,000	
Cost of goods sold..		$66,000

Exhibit 3-10 Income Effects of FIFO, LIFO, and Weighted-Average Inventory Methods

	FIFO		LIFO		Weighted-Average	
Sales revenue (assumed)........................		$100,000		$100,000		$100,000
Cost of goods sold:						
Goods available for sale						
(assumed)..	$90,000		$90,000		$90,000	
Ending inventory	36,000		24,000		30,000	
Cost of goods sold..............................		54,000		66,000		60,000
Gross margin		$ 46,000		$ 34,000		$ 40,000

Summary of Income Effects—When inventory unit costs are increasing

FIFO—Highest ending inventory	LIFO—Lowest ending inventory	Weighted-average—Results fall between
Lowest cost of goods sold	Highest cost of goods sold	the extremes of
Highest gross margin	Lowest gross margin	FIFO and LIFO

Summary of Income Effects—When inventory unit costs are decreasing

FIFO—Lowest ending inventory	LIFO—Highest ending inventory	Weighted-average—Results fall between
Highest cost of goods sold	Lowest cost of goods sold	the extremes of
Lowest gross margin	Highest gross margin	FIFO and LIFO

Exhibit 3-11

	FIFO	LIFO	Weighted-Average
Gross margin	$46,000	$34,000	$40,000
Operating expenses (assumed)	26,000	26,000	26,000
Income before income tax...............	$20,000	$ 8,000	$14,000
Income tax expense (40%)	$ 8,000	$ 3,200	$ 5,600

Income tax expense is lowest under LIFO ($3,200) and highest under FIFO ($8,000). The most attractive feature of LIFO is reduced income tax payments. The 1970s and early 1980s were marked by high inflation, so many companies changed to LIFO for its tax advantage based on an American institute of Certified Public Accountants (AICPA) survey of 600 companies, indicating that FIFO and LIFO are the most popular inventory costing methods.

GAAP and Practical Considerations: A Comparison of Inventory Methods

We may ask three questions to judge the three major inventory costing methods.

1. How well does each method match inventory expense—the cost of goods sold—to sales revenue on the income statement?
2. Which method reports the most up-to-date inventory amount on the balance sheet?
3. What effects do the methods have on income taxes?

LIFO better matches the current value of cost of goods sold with current revenue by assigning to this expense the most recent inventory costs. Therefore, LIFO produces the cost of goods sold figure that is closest to what it would cost the company to replace the goods that were sold. In this sense, LIFO produces the best measure of net income. In contrast, FIFO matches the oldest inventory costs against the period's revenue—a poor matching of current expense with current revenue.

FIFO reports the most current inventory costs on the balance sheet. LIFO can result in misleading inventory costs on the balance sheet because the oldest prices are left in ending inventory.

As shown earlier LIFO results in the lowest income tax payments when prices are rising. Tax payments are highest under FIFO. When inventory prices are decreasing, tax payments are highest under LIFO and lowest under FIFO. The weighted-average cost method produces amounts between the extremes of LIFO and FIFO,

FIFO Produces Inventory Profits. FIFO is sometimes criticized because it overstates income by so-called inventory profit during periods of inflation. Briefly, inventory profit is the difference between gross margin figured on the FIFO basis and gross margin figured on the LIFO basis. Exhibit 3-11 illustrates inventory profit. The $12,000 difference between FIFO and LIFO gross margins ($46,000–$34,000) results from the difference in cost of goods sold. This $12,000 amount is called FIFO inventory profit, phantom profit, or illusory profit. Why? Because to stay in business, the company must replace the inventory it has sold. The replacement cost of the merchandise is more closely approximated by the cost of goods sold under LIFO ($66,000) than by the FIFO amount ($54,000).

LIFO Allows Managers to Manage Reported Income—Up or Down. LIFO is often criticized because it allows managers to manage net income. When inventory prices are rising rapidly and a company wants to show less income for the year (in order to pay less in taxes), managers can buy a large amount of inventory near the end of the year. Under LIFO, these high inventory costs immediately become expenses—as cost of goods sold. As a result, the income statement reports a lower net income. Conversely, if the business is having a bad year, management may wish to increase reported income. To do so, managers can delay a large purchase of high-cost inventory until the next period.

This high-cost inventory is not expensed as cost of goods sold in the current year. Thus, management avoids decreasing the current year's reported income. In the process, the company draws down inventory quantities, a practice known as inventory liquidation.

LIFO Liquidation. When the LIFO method is used and inventory quantities fall below the level of the previous period, the situation is called LIFO liquidation. To compute cost of goods sold, the company must dip into older layers of inventory cost. Under LIFO and during a period of rising inventory costs, that action shifts older, lower costs into cost of goods sold. The result is higher net income than the company would have reported if no LIFO liquidation had occurred. Managers try to avoid LIFO liquidation because it increases reported income and income taxes. Owens-Corning, the world's leading supplier of glass fiber materials, reported that LIFO liquidations added $2.7 million to its net income.

International Perspective. Many companies manufacture their inventory in foreign countries, and companies that value inventory by the LIFO method often must use another accounting method for their inventories in foreign countries. Why? LIFO is allowed in the United States, but other countries are not bound by U.S. accounting practices. Australia and the United Kingdom, for example, do not permit the use of LIFO. Virtually all countries permit FIFO and the weighted-average cost method. Exhibit 3-12 lists a sampling of countries and whether or not they permit LIFO.

Higher Income or Lower Taxes? A company may want to report the highest income, and (as we've seen) FIFO meets this need when prices are rising. But the company also pays the highest income taxes under FIFO. When prices are falling, LIFO reports the highest income. Which inventory method is better, LIFO or FIFO? There is no single answer to this question. Different companies have different motives for the inventory method they choose. Polaroid Corporation uses FIFO, JC Penney Company uses LIFO, and Motorola, Inc., uses weighted-average cost. Still other companies use more than one method. The Black & Decker Corporation, best known for its power tools and small appliances, uses both LIFO and FIFO.

Exhibit 3-12   LIFO Use by Country

Country	LIFO Permitted?	Country	LIFO Permitted?
Australia	No	Netherlands	Yes
Brazil	Yes	Nigeria	No
Canada	Yes	Singapore	No
France	Yes	South Africa	Yes
Germany	Yes	Sweden	No
Hong Kong	No	Switzerland	No
Japan	Yes	United Kingdom	No
Mexico	Yes	United States	Yes

DEPRECIATION METHODS

Four methods exist for computing depreciation: straight-line, units-of-production, declining-balance, and sum-of-years'-digits. These four methods allocate different amounts of depreciation expense to each period. However, they all result in the same total amount of depreciation, the asset's depreciable cost over the life of the asset. Exhibit 3-13 presents the data we will use to illustrate depreciation computations by the three most widely used methods for a Home Depot truck. We omit the sum-of-years'-digits method because so few companies use it.

Exhibit 3-13   Data for Depreciation Computations for a Home Depot Truck

Data Item	Amount
Cost of truck	$41,000
Estimated residual value	1,000
Depreciable cost	$40,000
Estimated useful life:	
Years	5 years
Units of production	100,000 units [miles]

Straight-Line Method.   In the straight-line (SL) method, an equal amount of depreciation expense is assigned to each year (or period) of asset use. Depreciable cost is divided by useful life in years to determine the annual depreciation expense. The equation for SL depreciation, applied to the Home Depot truck data from Exhibit 3-13 is

$$\text{Straight-line depreciation per year} = \frac{\text{Cost} - \text{Residual value}}{\text{Useful life, in years}}$$

$$= \frac{\$41,000 - \$1,000}{5}$$

$$= \$8,000$$

The entry to record this depreciation is

Depreciation Expense	8,000	
Accumulated Depreciation		8,000

The impact on the accounting equation is

Assets	=	Liabilities	+	Stockholders' Equity	–	Expenses
–8,000	=	-0-				8,000

Assume that the truck was purchased on January 1, 19X1, and that Home Depot's fiscal year ends on December 31. A straight-line depreciation schedule is presented in Exhibit 3-14. The final column in Exhibit 3-14 shows the asset's book value, which is its cost less accumulated depreciation. Book value is also called carrying amount or carrying value.

As an asset is used, accumulated depreciation increases, and the book value decreases. Compare the Accumulated Depreciation column and the Book Value column. An asset's final book value is its residual value ($1,000 in Exhibit 3-12). At the end of its useful life, the asset is said to be fully depreciated.

Units-of-Production Method. In the units-of-production (UOP) method, a fixed amount of depreciation is assigned to each unit of output, or service, produced by the plant asset. Depreciable cost is divided by useful life, in units of production, to determine this amount. This per-unit depreciation expense is then multiplied by the number of units produced each period to compute depreciation for the period. The UOP depreciation equation for the Home Depot truck data in Exhibit 3-13, in which the units are miles, is

$$\text{Units-of-production depreciation Per unit of output} = \frac{\text{Cost} - \text{Residual value}}{\text{Useful life, in units of production}}$$

$$= \frac{\$41,000 - \$1,000}{100,000 \text{ miles}}$$

$$= \$0.40 \text{ per mile}$$

The truck is expected to be driven 20,000 miles during the first year, 30,000 during the second, 25,000 during the third, 15,000 during the fourth, and 10,000 during the fifth. The UOP depreciation schedule for this asset is shown in Exhibit 3-15.

The amount of UOP depreciation each period varies with the number of units the asset produces. In our example, the total number of units produced is 100,000, the measure of this asset's useful life. Therefore, UOP depreciation does not depend directly on time as do the other methods.

Exhibit 3-14 Straight-Line Depreciation Schedule for a Home Depot Truck

Date	Asset Cost	Depreciation for the Year			Accumulated Depreciation	Asset Book Value
		Depreciation Rate	Depreciable Cost	Depreciation Expense		
1- 1-19X1	$41,000					$41,000
12-31-19X1		0.20* ×	$40,000 =	$8,000	$ 8,000	33,000
12-31-19X2		0.20 ×	40,000 =	8,000	16,000	25,000
12-31-19X3		0.20 ×	40,000 =	8,000	24,000	17,000
12-31-19X4		0.20 ×	40,000 =	8,000	32,000	9,000
12-31-19X5		0.20 ×	40,000 =	8,000	40,000	1,000

* 1/5 years = 0.20 per year.

Exhibit 3-15 Units-of-Production Depreciation Schedule for a Home Depot Truck

Date	Asset Cost	Depreciation for the Year Depreciation Per Unit		Number of Units		Depreciation Expense	Accumulated Depreciation	Asset Book Value
1- 1-19X1	$41,000							$41,000
12-31-19X1		$0.40	×	20,000	=	$ 8,000	$ 8,000	33,000
12-31-19X2		0.40	×	30,000	=	12,000	20,000	21,000
12-31-19X3		0.40	×	25,000	=	10,000	30,000	11,000
12-31-19X4		0.40	×	15,000	=	6,000	36,000	5,000
12-31-19X5		0.40	×	10,000	=	4,000	40,000	1,000

Double-Declining-Balance Method. An accelerated depreciation method writes off a relatively larger amount of the asset's cost nearer the start of its useful life than the straight-line method does. Double-declining-balance is one of the accelerated depreciation methods. Double-declining-balance (DDB) depreciation computes annual depreciation by multiplying the asset's book value by a constant percentage, which is 2 times the straight-line depreciation rate. DDB amounts are computed as follows.

First, compute the straight-line depreciation rate per year. For example, a five-year truck has a straight-line depreciation rate of 1/5, or 20 percent. A ten-year asset has a straight-line rate of 1/10, or 10%, and so on.

Second, multiply the straight-line rate by 2 to compute the DDB rate. The DDB rate for a ten-year asset is 20% per year (10% × 2 = 20%). For a five-year asset, such as the Home Depot truck in Exhibit 3-13, the DDB rate is 40% (20% × 2 = 40%).

Third, multiply the DDB rate by the period's beginning asset book value (cost less accumulated depreciation). Ignore the residual value of the asset in computing depreciation by the DDB method, except during the last year. The DDB rate for the truck in Exhibit 3-13 is:

$$\text{DDB depreciation rate per year} = \frac{1}{\text{Useful life, in years}} \times 2$$

$$= \frac{1}{5 \text{ years}} \times 2$$

$$= 20\% \times 2 = 40\%$$

Fourth, determine the final year's depreciation amount, the amount needed to reduce the asset's book value to its residual value. In the DDB depreciation schedule in Exhibit 3-16, the fifth and final year's depreciation is $4,314—the $5,314 book value less the $1,000 residual value. The residual value should not be depreciated but should remain on the books until the asset's disposal.

Many companies change to the straight-line method during the next-to-last year of the asset's life. Under this plan, annual depreciation for 19X4 and 19X5 is $3,928. Look at Exhibit 3-16. Depreciable cost at the end of 19X3 is $7,856 (book value of $8,856 less residual value of $1,000). Depreciable cost can be spread evenly over the last two years of the asset's life ($7,856 / 2 remaining years = $3,928 per year).

The DDB method differs from the other methods in two ways. (1) The asset's residual value is ignored initially. In the first year, depreciation is computed on the asset's full cost. (2) The final year's calculation is changed in order to bring the asset's book value to the residual value.

Exhibit 3-16 Double-Declining-Balance Depreciation Schedule for a Home Depot Truck

Date	Asset Cost	DDB Rate	Asset Book Value		Depreciation Expense	Accumulated Depreciation	Asset Book Value
			Depreciation for the Year				
1- 1-19X1	$41,000						$41,000
12-31-19X1		0.40 ×	$41,000	=	$16,400	$16,400	24,600
12-31-19X2		0.40 ×	24,600	=	9,840	26,240	14,760
12-31-19X3		0.40 ×	14,760	=	5,904	32,144	8,856
12-31-19X4		0.40 ×	8,856	=	3,542	35,686	5,314
12-31-19X5					4,314*	40,000	1,000

*Last-year depreciation is the amount needed to reduce asset book value to the residual value ($5,314 – $1,000 = $4,314).

Comparing the Depreciation Methods

Let's compare the three methods we've just discussed in terms of the yearly amount of depreciation:

			Accelerated Method
	Amount of Depreciation Per Year		
Year	Straight-Line	Units-of-Production	Double-Declining-Balance
1	$ 8,000	$ 8,000	$16,400
2	8,000	12,000	9,840
3	8,000	10,000	5,904
4	8,000	6,000	3,542
5	8,000	4,000	4,314
Total	$40,000	$40,000	$40,000

The yearly amount of depreciation varies by method, but the total $40,000 depreciable cost is the same under all the methods.

Generally accepted accounting principles (GAAP) direct a business to match an asset's expense against the revenue that asset produces. For a plant asset that generates revenue evenly over time, the straight-line method best meets the matching principle. During each period the asset is used, an equal amount of depreciation is recorded. A recent survey of 600 companies, conducted by the AICPA, indicated that the straight-line method is most popular.

The units-of-production method best fits those assets that wear out because of physical use, not obsolescence. Depreciation is recorded only when the asset is used, and the more units the asset generates in a given year, the greater the depreciation expense.

The accelerated method (DDB) applies best to those assets that generate greater revenue earlier in their useful lives. The greater expense recorded under the accelerated methods in the earlier periods is matched against those periods' greater revenue.

The Relationship Between Depreciation and Income Taxes

Most companies use the straight-line depreciation method for reporting to their stockholders and creditors on their financial statements. But companies keep a separate set of depreciation records for computing their income taxes. For income tax purposes, most companies use an accelerated depreciation method.

You are a business manager. The IRS allows an accelerated depreciation method, which most managers prefer to straight-line depreciation. Why? Because it provides the most depreciation expense as quickly as possible, thus decreasing your immediate tax payments. You can then apply the cash you save to fit your business needs. This is the strategy most businesses follow.

To understand the relationships between cash flow (cash provided by operations), depreciation, and income tax, recall our earlier depreciation example for a Home Depot truck: first-year depreciation is $8,000 under straight-line and $16,400 under double-declining-balance. Now for illustrative purposes, let's assume that DDB is permitted for income tax reporting. Let's apply this to a Home Depot store that has a truck with the same depreciation schedule as before. This store has $400,000 in cash sales and $300,000 in cash operating expenses during the truck's first year and an income tax rate of 30 percent. The cash flow analysis appears in Exhibit 3-17.

Exhibit 3-17 highlights several important business relationships. Compare the amount of cash provided by operations before income tax. Both columns show $100,000. If there were no income taxes, the total cash provided by operations would be the same regardless of the depreciation method used. Depreciation is a noncash expense (an expense that requires no outlay of cash) and thus does not affect cash from operations.

Depreciation, however, is a tax-deductible expense. The higher the depreciation expense, the lower the before-tax income and, thus, the lower the income tax payment. Therefore, accelerated depreciation helps conserve cash for use in the business. Exhibit 3-17 indicates that the business will have $2,520 more cash at the end of the first year if it uses accelerated depreciation instead of straight line ($74,920 versus $72,400). If the company invests this money to earn a return of 10% during the second year, it will be better off by $252 ($2,520 × 10% = $252). The cash advantage of using the accelerated method is the $252 additional revenue.

The Tax Reform Act of 1986 created a special depreciation method—used only for income tax purposes—called the Modified Accelerated Cost Recovery System (MACRS). Under this method, assets are grouped into one of eight classes identified by asset life, as shown in Exhibit 3-18. Depreciation for the first four classes is computed by the

Exhibit 3-17 Cash-Flow Advantage of Accelerated Depreciation over Straight-Line Depreciation for Income Tax Purposes

	Income Tax Rate (30%)	
	SL	Accelerated
Cash revenues	$400,000	$400,000
Cash operating expenses	300,000	300,000
Cash provided by operations before income tax	100,000	100,000
Depreciation expense (a noncash expense)	8,000	16,400
Income before income tax	92,000	83,600
Income tax expense (30%)	27,600	25,080
Net income	$ 64,400	$ 58,520
Cash-flow analysis:		
Cash provided by operations before income tax	$100,000	$100,000
Income tax expense	27,600	25,080
Cash provided by operations	$ 72,400	$ 74,920
Extra cash available for investment if DDB is used ($74,920 − $72,400)		$2,520
Assumed earnings rate on investment of extra cash		× 0.10
Cash advantage of using DDB over SL		$ 252

Exhibit 3-18 Details of the Modified Accelerated Cost Recovery System (MACRS)
Depreciation Method

Class Identified by Asset Life (years)	Representative Assets	Depreciation Method
3	Race horses	DDB
5	Automobiles, light trucks	DDB
7	Equipment	DDB
10	Equipment	DDB
15	Sewage-treatment plants	150% DB
20	Certain real estate	150% DB
27½	Residential rental property	SL
39	Nonresidential rental property	SL

double-declining-balance method. Depreciation for 15-year assets and 20-year assets is computed by the double-declining-balance method.

Under this method, the annual depreciation rate is computed by multiplying the straight-line rate by 1.50 (rather than by 2.00, as for DDB). For a 20-year asset, the straight-line rate is 0.05 (1/20 = 0.05), so the annual MACRS depreciation rate is 0.075 (0.05 × 1.50 = 0.075). Most real estate is depreciated by the straight-line method.

Depreciation for Partial Years

Companies purchase plant assets as needed. They do not wait until the beginning of a year or a month. Therefore, companies must develop policies to compute depreciation for partial years. A company purchases a building on April 1 for $500,000. The building's estimated life is 20 years, and its estimated residual value is $80,000. The restaurant company's fiscal year ends on December 31. Let's consider how the company computes depreciation for the year ended December 31.

Many companies compute partial-year depreciation by first computing a full year's depreciation. They then multiply that amount by the fraction of the year that they held the asset. Assuming the straight-line method, the year's depreciation for the restaurant building is $15,750, computed as follows:

$$\text{Full-year depreciation} = \frac{\$500{,}000 - \$80{,}000}{20} = \$21{,}000$$

Partial year depreciation = $21,000 x 9/12 = $15,750

What if the company bought the asset on April 18? A widely used policy directs businesses to record no depreciation on assets purchased after the 15th of the month and to record a full month's depreciation on an asset bought on or before the 15th. Thus, the company would record no depreciation for April on an April 18 purchase. In that case, the year's depreciation would be $14,000 ($21,000 × 8/12).

How is partial-year depreciation computed under the other depreciation methods? Suppose the company acquires the building on October 4 and uses the double-declining-balance method. For a 20-year-asset, the DDB rate is 10% (1/20 = 5%; 5% × 2 = 10%). The annual depreciation computations for 19X1, 19X2, and 19X3 are shown in Exhibit 3-19.

Most companies use computerized systems to account for fixed assets. They identify each asset with a unique identification number and indicate the asset's cost, estimated life, residual value, and depreciation method. The system will automatically calculate the depreciation expense for each period. Both accumulated depreciation and book value are automatically updated.

Exhibit 3-19   Annual DDB Depreciation for Partial Years

Date	Asset Cost	DDB Rate	Asset Book Value, Beginning	Fraction of the Year	Depreciation Expense	Accumulated Depreciation	Asset Book Value, Ending
		Depreciation for the Year					
10- 4-19X1	$500,000						$500,000
12-31-19X1		$1/20 \times 2 = 0.10$ ×	$500,000 ×	3/12 =	$12,500	$ 12,500	487,500
12-31-19X2		0.10 ×	487,500 ×	12/12 =	48,750	61,250	438,750
12-31-19X3		0.10 ×	438,750 ×	12/12 =	43,875	105,125	394,875

SUMMARY

Use a company's financial statements to evaluate its operating performance and financial position. The financial statements communicate financial information about a business entity to decision makers. The income statement reports the company's revenues, expenses, and net income or net loss for a period. The statement of retained earnings summarizes the changes in a corporation's retained earnings during the period. The balance sheet is a snapshot of a business on a particular day; it reports on three main categories of items: assets, liabilities, and owners' equity. The statement of cash flows reports cash receipts and disbursements over a period, classified according to the entity's major activities: operating, investing, and financing.

Understand the relationships among the financial statements. The bottom line of the income statement, net income, feeds into the statement of retained earnings. The final value of retained earnings then appears on the balance sheet. The final cash balance on the statement of cash flows also appears on the balance sheet.

Apply the inventory costing methods: specific unit cost, weighted-average cost, FIFO, and LIFO. Businesses multiply the quantity of inventory items by their unit cost to determine inventory cost. Only businesses that sell items that may be identified individually such as automobiles and jewels, use the specific identification method. Most companies use the other methods. FIFO reports ending inventory at the most current cost. LIFO reports cost of goods sold at the most current cost.

Identify the income effects and the tax effects of the inventory costing methods. When inventory costs are increasing, LIFO produces the highest cost of goods sold and the lowest income, thus minimizing income taxes. FIFO results in the highest income. The weighted-average cost method gives results between the extremes of FIFO and LIFO.

Determine the cost of a plant asset. Plant assets are long-lived tangible assets, such as land, buildings, and equipment, used in the operation of a business. The cost of a plant asset is the purchase price plus applicable taxes, purchase commissions, and all other amounts paid to acquire the asset and to prepare it for its intended use.

Account for depreciation. Businesses may account for depreciation (the allocation of a plant asset's cost to expense over its useful life) by three methods: the straight-line method, the units-of-production method, or the double-declining-balance method. All these methods require accountants to estimate the asset's useful life and residual value.

Select the best depreciation method for income tax purposes. Most companies use an accelerated depreciation method for income tax purposes. Accelerated depreciation results in higher expenses, lower taxable income, and lower tax payments early in the asset's life.

QUESTIONS

1. Explain the difference between an account receivable and an account payable.
2. In what two ways can a business use its net income?
3. Give a more descriptive title for the balance sheet.
4. What feature of the balance sheet gives this financial statement its name?
5. Give another title for the income statement.
6. Which financial statement is like a snapshot of the entity at a specific time?
7. What information does the statement of retained earnings report?
8. What information flows from the income statement to the statement of retained earnings?
9. What information flows from the statement of retained earnings to the balance sheet?
10. List the cash flow activities in the order they are likely to occur for a new business. Rank the activities in the order of their importance to investors.

PROBLEMS

1. Sal and Sophia Molnari want to open an Italian restaurant in Los Angeles. In need of cash, they ask City Bank & Trust for a loan. The bank's procedures require borrowers to submit financial statements to show likely results of their operations for the first year and their likely financial position at the end of the first year. With little knowledge of accounting, Sal and Sophia don't know how to proceed. Explain to them the information provided by the statement of operations (the income statement) and the statement of financial position (the balance sheet). Indicate why a lender would require this information.

2. Lang Enterprises is being formed to develop web sites on the Internet for other companies. Lang needs funds and Alden Lang, the president, has asked you to consider investing in the business. Answer the following questions about the different ways that Lang might organize the business. Explain each of your answers.
   a. What form of business organization will give Lang the most freedom to manage the business as he wishes?
   b. What form of organization will give creditors the maximum protection in the event that Lang Enterprises fails and cannot pay its liabilities?
   c. What form of organization will enable the owners of Lang Enterprises to limit their risk of loss to the amount they have invested in the business?
   d. Under what form of organization will Lang Enterprises be likely to have the longest life?
   e. What form of organization will probably enable Lang Enterprises to raise the most money from owners' equity over the life of the business?

3. If you were Lang and could organize the business as you wish, what form of organization would you choose for Lang Enterprises? Explain your reasoning.

4. Compute the missing amount in the accounting equation for each entity:

	Assets	Liabilities	Owners' Equity
Entity A	$?	$81,800	$84,400
Entity B	85,900	?	$34,000
Entity C	81,700	49,800	?

5. Pepsi Co, Inc. has current assets of $5,072 million; property, plant, and equipment of $9,883 million; and other assets totaling $9,837 million. Current liabilities are $5,270 million, long-term debt is $8,841 million, and other long-term liabilities add up to $3,825 million.

Required

1. Use these data to write Pepsi Co's accounting equation.
2. How much in resources does Pepsi Co have to work with?
3. How much does Pepsi Co owe?
4. How much of the company's assets do the Pepsi Co stockholders actually own?
5. Managers at The Coca-Cola Company are planning an expansion of their bottling operations in Canada. They must decide where to locate the bottling plant, how much to spend on the building, and how to finance its construction. Of central importance is the level of net income they can expect to earn from operating the new plant. Identify the financial statement where these decision makers can find the following information about The Coca-Cola Company. (In some cases, more than one statement will report the needed data.)
   a. Liabilities that must be paid next year. (Long-term debt)
   b. Net income
   c. Total assets
   d. Cash spent to acquire the building
   e. Selling, general, and administrative expenses
   f. Cash collections from customers
   g. Ending cash balance
   h. Revenue
   i. Common stock
   j. Cash spent for income tax
   k. Dividends
   l. Income tax expense
   m. Ending balance of retained earnings
   n. Cost of goods sold
6. Apply your understanding of the relationships among the financial statements to answer these questions.
   a. Give two reasons why a business can have a steady stream of net income over a five-year period and still experience a shortage of cash.
   b. How can a business lose money several years in a row and still have plenty of cash?
   c. How can a business earn large profits but have a small balance of retained earnings?
   d. Suppose your business has $100,000 of current liabilities that must be paid within the next three months. Your current assets total only $70,000, and your sales and collections from customers are slow. Identify two ways to finance the extra $30,000 you will need to pay your current liabilities when they come due.
   e. If you could pick a single source of cash for your business, what would it be? Why?
7. A travel agency, Air & Sea Travel, Inc., began operations on April 1, 19X1 when the business received $50,000 and issued common stock to Gary and Monica Lyon, the stockholders. During April, the business provided travel services for clients. It is now April 30, and the Lyons wonder how well Air & Sea Travel performed during its first month. They also want to know the business's financial position at the end of April and its cash flows during the month.

They have assembled the following data, listed in alphabetical order. They have requested your help in preparing the Air & Sea Travel financial statements at the end of April 19X1.

Accounts payable	$100	Office supplies $500	
Accounts receivable	2,000	Payments of cash:	
Cash balance at beginning of April	-0-	Acquisition of land	40,000
Cash balance at end of April	33,300	Dividends	2,100
Cash receipts:		To suppliers and employees	3,100
Collections from customers	6,500	Rent expense	1,100
Issuance (sale) of stock to		Retained earnings at beginning	
owners	50,000	of April	-0-
Sale of land	22,000	Retained earnings at end of April	
Common stock	50,000	Salary expense	1,200
Dividends	2,100	Service revenue	8,500
Land	18,000	Utilities expense	400

Required

1. Prepare the income statement, the statement of retained earnings, and the statement of cash flows for the month ended April 30, 19X1, and the balance sheet at April 30, 19X1. Draw arrows linking the pertinent items in the statements.

2. Answer the owners' underlying questions.

   a. How well did Air & Sea Travel perform during its first month of operations?

   b. Where does Air & Sea Travel stand financially at the end of the first month?

3. If you were a banker, would you be willing to lend money to Air & Sea Travel, Inc.?

INTERNET EXERCISE

Lands' End, Inc.

The Internet and its multimedia component, the World Wide Web, contain a wealth of information at the click of a mouse. The Internet exercises are designed to help you explore the opportunities and information available on the Net. This first exercise builds on the book's annual report example (Lands' End) and is designed to get you acquainted with the Net.

From the Lands' End home page, the web site's starting point, you can view the company's on-line catalog, get gift ideas, place orders, or e-mail the company. Lands' End also uses its web site to give visitors a sense of the company's history, vision, and values. Finally much of the information in the Lands' End annual report is available.

Required

1. Go to http://www.landsend.com/. There you will find the Lands' End welcome page.

2. At the bottom of the page (you may have to scroll down), click on the "Home" button. Doing so takes you to a list of Lands' End sites on the Internet (Internet Store, Catalogs, Services, and so forth).

3. Answer the following questions by exploring the section labeled "The Company Inside and Out," where the firm's history and corporate information are presented with its annual report.

   a. What are Lands' End's principles of doing business?

b. Describe the typical Lands' End customer.
c. Why do the people at Lands' End consider themselves direct merchants instead of direct marketers?
d. Why is the apostrophe in Lands' End in the wrong place?
e. What is the Lands' End Guarantee?
f. How does the president and CEO of Lands' End describe last year's performance?
g. How much cash was generated (or used) by Lands' End operations?

ANALYSIS OF
FINANCIAL STATEMENTS

Financial statement analysis focuses on the techniques used by internal managers and by analysts external to the organization. Outside analysts rely on publicly available information. A major source of such information is the annual report. In addition to the financial statements (income statement, balance sheet, and statement of cash flows), annual reports usually contain the following:

1. Notes to the financial statements
2. A summary of the accounting methods used
3. Management's discussion and analysis of the financial results
4. The auditor's report
5. Comparative financial data for a series of years

Management's discussion and analysis (MD&A) of financial results is especially important because top management is in the best position to know how well or how poorly the company is performing. The SEC requires the MD&A from public corporations. For example, the 1995 annual report of Bristol-Myers Squibb Company includes six pages of MD&A. The report's financial review begins as follows:

> In 1995, Bristol-Myers Squibb achieved record sales, with all four of the company's segments reporting sales increases. Sales increased 15% over the prior year to $13.8 billion. Domestic sales increased 10% to $7.7 billion, while international sales increased 22% to $6.1 billion.
>
> Bristol-Myers Squibb management also discusses its sales and profits in various industry segments—pharmaceuticals, medical devices, toiletries, and beauty aids. The MD&A offers glimpses into the company's future from the viewpoint of people in the know—top management. Investors and creditors are, after all, primarily interested in where the business is headed.

THE OBJECTIVES OF FINANCIAL STATEMENT ANALYSIS

Investors who purchase a company's stock expect that they will receive dividends and that the stock's value will increase. Creditors make loans with the expectation of receiving interest and principal. Both groups bear the risk that they will not receive their expected returns. They use financial statement analysis to (1) predict the amount of expected returns and (2) assess the risks associated with those returns.

Creditors generally expect to receive specific fixed amounts and have the first claim on a company's assets, so they are most concerned with assessing short-term liquidity and long-term solvency. Short-term liquidity is an organization's ability to meet current payments as they become due. Long-term solvency is the ability to generate enough cash to pay long-term debts as they mature.

In contrast, investors are more concerned with profitability, dividends, and future security prices. Why? Because dividend payments depend on profitable operations, and stock-price appreciation depends on the market's assessment of the company's prospects. Creditors also assess profitability because profitable operations are the company's main source of cash to repay loans.

The tools and techniques that the business community uses in evaluating financial statement information can be divided into three broad categories: horizontal analysis, vertical analysis, and ratio analysis.

HORIZONTAL ANALYSIS

Many managerial decisions hinge on whether the numbers, in sales, income, expenses, and so on, are increasing or decreasing over time. Has the sales figure risen from last year? From two years ago? By how much? We may find that the net sales figure has risen by $20,000. This fact may be interesting, but considered alone it is not very useful for decision making. An analysis of the percentage change in the net sales figure over time improves our ability to make decisions. It is more useful to know that sales have increased by 20% than to know that the increase in sales is $20,000.

The study of percentage changes in comparative statements is called horizontal analysis. Computing a percentage change in comparative statements requires two steps:

1. Compute the dollar amount of the change from the base (earlier) period to the later period.
2. Divide the dollar amount of change by the base-period amount.

Horizontal analysis is illustrated for Bristol-Myers Squibb as follows (dollar amounts in millions):

	1995	1994	Increase (Decrease) Amount	Increase (Decrease) Percent
Sales	$13,767	$11,984	$1,783	14.9%
Net income.	1,812	1,842	(30)	(1.6%)

The percentage change in Bristol-Myers Squibb's sales during 1995 is computed as follows:

Step 1. Compute the dollar amount of change in sales from 19X4 to 19X5:

$$\underset{\$13,767}{1995} - \underset{\$11,984}{1994} = \underset{\$1,783}{\text{Increase}}$$

Step 2. Divide the dollar amount of change by the base-period amount to compute the percentage change during the later period:

$$\text{Percentage change} = \frac{\text{Dollar amount of change}}{\text{Base-year amount}}$$

$$= \frac{\$1,783}{\$11,984} = 14.9\%$$

During 1995, Bristol-Myers Squibb's sales increased by 14.9 percent.

Detailed horizontal analysis of comparative income statements and comparative balance sheets are shown in the two right-hand columns of Exhibits 4-1 and 4-2, the financial statements of Bristol-Myers Squibb Company. The income statements (statements of earnings) reveal that net sales increased by 14.9% during 1995. But cost of goods sold and the two largest operating expenses grew even more. As a result, net income decreased slightly—a bad sign.

Other analysts would take a different view of Bristol-Myers Squibb's operations during 1995. The provision for restructuring—a one-time expense that is not expected to repeat from year to year—was the main reason that net income decreased in 1995. Without the restructuring expense, 1995 would have been a better year than 1994.

The comparative balance sheet in Exhibit 4-2 shows that 1995 was a year of expansion for Bristol-Myers Squibb. Total assets increased by $1,019 million, or 7.9%. The bulk of this growth occurred as a result of increases in current assets, other assets, and goodwill. Total liabilities increased by 12.5%, and total stockholders' equity grew by 2.1%.

Trend Percentages

Trend percentages are a form of horizontal analysis. Trends are important indicators of the direction a business is taking. How have sales changed over a five-year period? What

Exhibit 4-1 Comparative Income Statement—Horizontal Analysis

Bristol-Myers Squibb Company
Statement of Earnings (Adapted)
Years Ended December 31, 1995 and 1994

(Dollar amounts in millions)	1995	1994	Increase (Decrease) Amount	Percent
Net sales	$13,767	$11,984	$1,783	14.9%
Cost of products sold	3,637	3,122	515	16.5
Gross profit	10,130	8,862	1,268	14.3
Operating expenses:				
Marketing, selling, and administrative	3,670	3,166	504	15.9
Advertising and product promotion	1,646	1,367	279	20.4
Research and development	1,199	1,108	91	8.2
Special charge	950	750	200	26.7
Provision for restructuring	310	—	310	100.0*
Other	(47)	(84)	(37)	(44.0)
Earnings before income taxes	2,402	2,555	(153)	(6.0)
Provision for income taxes	590	713	(123)	(17.3)
Net earnings	$ 1,812	$ 1,842	$ (30)	(1.6)

*An increase from zero to any positive number is treated as an increase of 100 percent.

Exhibit 4-2 Comparative Balance Sheet—Horizontal Analysis

Bristol-Myers Squibb Company
Statement of Earnings (Adapted)
Years Ended December 31, 1995 and 1994

(Dollar amounts in millions)	1995	1994	Increase (Decrease) Amount	Percent
Assets				
Current Assets:				
Cash and cash equivalents	$ 1,645	$ 1,642	$ 3	0.2%
Time deposits and marketable securities	533	781	(248)	(31.8)
Receivables, net of allowances	2,356	2,043	313	15.3
Inventories	1,451	1,397	54	3.9
Prepaid expenses	1,033	847	186	22.0
Total Current Assets	7,018	6,710	308	4.6
Property, Plant, and Equipment—net	3,760	3,666	94	2.6
Insurance Recoverable	959	968	(9)	(0.9)
Other Assets	973	627	346	55.2
Excess of cost over net tangible assets received in business acquisitions [Goodwill]	1,219	939	280	29.8
	$13,929	$12,910	$1,019	7.9%
Liabilities				
Current Liabilities:				
Short-term borrowings	$ 575	$ 725	$ (150)	(20.7)%
Accounts payable	848	693	155	22.4
Accrued expenses [payable]	1,939	1,481	458	30.9
U.S. and foreign income taxes payable	744	740	4	0.5
Product liability*	700	635	65	10.2
Total Current Liabilities	4,806	4,274	532	12.4
Product Liability [Long-term]	1,645	1,201	444	37.0
Other Liabilities	1,021	1,087	(66)	(6.1)
Long-Term Debt	635	644	(9)	(1.4)
Total Liabilities	8,107	7,206	901	12.5
Stockholders' Equity				
Common stock	54	54	-0-	0.0
Capital in excess of par value of stock	375	397	(22)	(5.5)
Cumulative translation adjustments	(327)	(301)	(26)	(8.6)
Retained earnings	7,917	7,600	317	4.2
Less cost of treasury stock	(2,197)	(2,046)	(151)	(7.4)
Total Stockholders' Equity	5,822	5,704	118	2.1
	$13,929	$12,910	$1,019	7.9%

*Warranties, guarantees, and the like.

trend does gross profit show? These questions can be answered by an analysis of trend percentages over a representative period, such as the most recent five or ten years. To gain a realistic view of the company, we often must examine more than just a two- or three-year period.

Trend percentages are computed by selecting a base year whose amounts are set equal to 100 percent. The amounts of each following year are expressed as a percentage of the base amount. To compute trend percentages, divide each item for following years by the corresponding amount during the base year:

$$\text{Trend \%} = \frac{\text{Any year \$}}{\text{Base year \$}}$$

Bristol-Myers Squibb Company showed sales, cost of goods sold, and gross profit for the past six years as follows:

(In millions)	1995	1994	1993	1992	1991	1990
Net Sales..	$13,767	$11,984	$11,413	$11,156	$10,571	$9,741
Cost of products sold..............................	3,637	3,122	3,029	2,857	2,717	2,665
Gross profit..	10,130	8,862	8,384	8,299	7,854	7,076

We want trend percentages for a five-year period starting with 1991. We use 1990 as the base year. Trend percentages for net sales are computed by dividing each net sales amount by the 1990 amount of $9,741 million. Trend percentages for cost of products sold are calculated by dividing each cost of products sold amount by $2,665 (the base-year amount), and trend percentages for gross profit are calculated by dividing each gross profit amount by $7,076 (the base-year amount). The resulting trend percentages follow (1990, the base year = 100%):

	1995	1994	1993	1992	1991	1990
Net Sales......................................	141%	123%	117%	115%	109%	100%
Cost of products sold	136	117	114	107	102	100%
Gross profit.................................	143	125	118	117	111	100%

Bristol-Myers Squibb's sales and cost of goods sold have trended upward. Gross profit has increased steadily, with the most dramatic growth during 1991 and 1995. This information suggests that gross profit is increasing steadily.

VERTICAL ANALYSIS

Horizontal analysis highlights changes in an item over time. However, no single financial analysis technique provides a complete picture of a business. Another method of analyzing a company is vertical analysis. Vertical analysis of a financial statement reveals the relationship of each statement item to a specified base, which is the 100% figure. Every other item on the financial statement is then reported as a percentage of that base. For example, when an income statement is subjected to vertical analysis, net sales is usually the base. Suppose under normal conditions a company's gross profit is 70% of net sales. A drop in gross profit to 60% of net sales may cause the company to report a net loss on the income statement. Management, investors, and creditors view a large decline in gross profit with alarm. Exhibit 4-3 shows the vertical analysis of Bristol-Myers Squibb's income statement as a percentage of net sales.

So, for example, the vertical analysis percentage for cost of products sold for 1995 equals 26.4% ($3,637/$13,767 = 0.264). Exhibit 4-4 shows the vertical analysis of the balance sheet amounts as a percentage of total assets.

The vertical analysis of Bristol-Myers Squibb's income statement (Exhibit 4-3) shows no unusual relationships. The gross profit percentage declined a bit in 1995, as did net income's percentage of sales. However, there is no cause for alarm. The vertical analysis of Bristol-Myers Squibb's balance sheet (Exhibit 4-4) also yields few surprises. Current assets' percentage of total assets declined in 1995, while current liabilities' percentage rose a little. The worst news on the balance sheet is the increase in product liability. The MD&A explained that the company's product liability resulted from claims

Exhibit 4-3   Comparative Income Statement—Vertical Analysis

Bristol-Myers Squibb Company
Statement of Earnings (Adapted)
Years Ended December 31, 1995 and 1994

(Dollar amounts in millions)	1995		1994	
	Amount	Percent	Amount	Percent
Net sales..	$13,767	100.0%	$11,984	100.0%
Cost of products sold	3,637	26.4	3,122	26.1
Gross profit...	10,130	73.6	8,862	73.9
Operating expenses:				
Marketing, selling, and administrative......	3,670	26.7	3,166	26.4
Advertising and product promotion..........	1,646	12.0	1,367	11.4
Research and development........................	1,199	8.7	1,108	9.2
Special charge..	950	6.9	750	6.3
Provision for restructuring	310	2.2	—	
Other	(47)	(0.3)	(84)	(0.7)
Earnings before income taxes....................	2,402	17.4	2,555	21.3
Provision for income taxes	590	4.2	713	(5.9)
Net earnings..	$ 1,812	13.2%	$ 1,842	15.4%

against the company for its former breast-implant products. Bristol-Myers Squibb disposed of the subsidiary that manufactured the breast-implant products.

Despite the ongoing litigation, the company's financial position remains strong. For example, the current ratio is 1.46 ($7,018 million/$4,806 million). The company has very little long-term debt, and retained earnings (profit from operations) is the largest single source of financing.

Common-Size Statements

The percentages in Exhibits 4-3 and 4-4 can be presented as a separate statement that reports only percentages (no dollar amounts). Such a statement is called a common-size statement.

On a common-size income statement, each item is expressed as a percentage of the net sales amount. Net sales is the common size to which we relate the statement's other amounts. In the balance sheet, the common size is the total on each side of the accounting equation (total assets or the sum of total liabilities and stockholders' equity). A common-size statement eases the comparison of different companies because their amounts are stated in percentages.

Common-size statements may identify the need for corrective action. Exhibit 4-5 is the common-size analysis of current assets taken from Exhibit 4-4. Exhibit 4-5 shows cash as a relatively high percentage of total assets at the end of each year. Receivables are a growing percentage of total assets. What could have caused the increase in receivables? Bristol-Myers Squibb may have been lax in collecting accounts receivable, a policy that may lead to a cash shortage. The company may need to pursue collection more vigorously. Or, the company may have sold to less-creditworthy customers. In any event, the company should monitor its cash position and collection of receivables to avoid a cash shortage. Common-size statements provide information useful for this purpose.

Exhibit 4-4   Comparative Balance Sheet—Vertical Analysis

Bristol-Myers Squibb Company
Balance Sheet
December 31, 1995 and 1994

(Dollar amounts in millions)	1995 Amount	1995 Percent	1994 Amount	1994 Percent
Assets				
Current Assets:				
Cash and cash equivalents.................................	$ 1,645	11.8%	$ 1,642	12.7%
Time deposits and marketable securities	533	3.8	781	6.0
Receivables, net of allowances.............................	2,356	16.9	2,043	15.8
Inventories	1,451	10.4	1,397	10.8
Prepaid expenses...	1,033	7.4	847	6.7
Total Current Assets	7,018	50.3	6,710	52.0
Property, Plant, and Equipment—net	3,760	27.0	3,666	28.4
Insurance Recoverable	959	6.9	968	7.5
Other Assets..	973	7.0	627	4.8
Excess of cost over net tangible assets received in business acquisitions [Goodwill]...	1,219	8.8	939	7.3
	$13,929	100.0%	$12,910	100.0%
Liabilities				
Current Liabilities:				
Short-term borrowings.....................................	$ 575	4.1%	$ 725	5.6%
Accounts payable	848	6.1	693	5.4
Accrued expenses [payable]	1,939	13.9	1,481	11.5
U.S. and foreign income taxes payable.................	744	5.4	740	5.7
Product liability	700	5.0	635	4.9
Total Current Liabilities................................	4,806	34.5	4,274	33.1
Product Liability [Long-term]	1,645	11.8	1,201	9.3
Other Liabilities...	1,021	7.3	1,087	8.4
Long-Term Debt	635	4.6	644	5.0
Total Liabilities..	8,107	58.2	7,206	55.8
Stockholders' Equity				
Common stock	54	0.4	54	0.4
Capital in excess of par value of stock.................	375	2.7	397	3.1
Cumulative translation adjustments....................	(327)	(2.3)	(301)	(2.3)
Retained earnings	7,917	56.8	7,600	58.9
Less cost of treasury stock...............................	(2,197)	(15.8)	(2,046)	(15.9)
Total Stockholders' Equity............................	5,822	41.8	5,704	44.2
	$13,929	100.0%	$12,910	100.0%

BENCHMARKING

Benchmarking is the practice of comparing a company to a standard set by other companies, with a view towards improvement.

Benchmarking Against the Industry Average

We study a company's records to help us understand past results and predict future performance. Still, the knowledge that we can develop from a company's records is

Exhibit 4-5   Common-Size Analysis of Current Assets

Bristol-Myers Squibb Company
Analysis of Current Assets
December 31, 1995 and 1994

	Percent of Total Assets	
	1995	**1994**
Current Assets:		
Cash and cash equivalents............................	11.8%	12.7%
Time deposits and marketable securities......	3.8	6.0
Receivables, net of allowances......................	16.9	15.8
Inventories...	10.4	10.8
Prepaid expenses	7.4	6.7
Total Current Assets................................	50.3	52.0
Long-Term Assets...	49.7	48.0
Total Assets	100.0%	100.0%

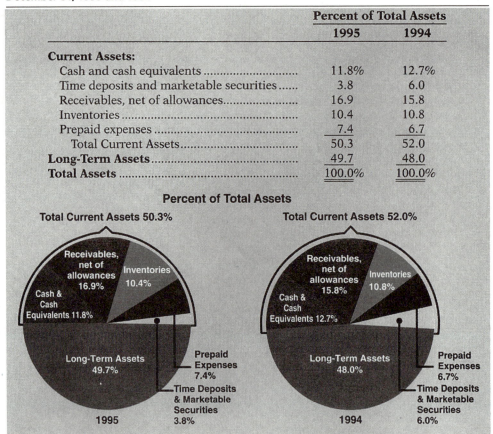

Percent of Total Assets

limited to that one company. We may learn that gross profit has decreased and that net income has increased steadily for the last ten years. This information is helpful, but it does not consider how businesses in the same industry have fared over the same time period. Have other companies in the same line of business increased their sales? Is there an industry wide decline in gross profit? Has cost of goods sold risen steeply for other businesses that sell the same products? Managers, investors, creditors, and other interested parties need to know how one company compares with other companies in the same line of business. For example, Apple Computer's gross margin has steadily declined in relation to its competitors'.

Exhibit 4-6 gives the common-size income statement of Bristol-Myers Squibb Company compared with the average for the pharmaceuticals (health-care) industry. This analysis compares Bristol-Myers Squibb with all other companies in its line of business. The industry averages were adapted from Robert Morris Associates' Annual Statement Studies. Analysts at Merrill Lynch and other companies specialize in a particular industry and make such comparisons in deciding which companies' stocks to buy or sell. For example, financial service companies such as Merrill Lynch have health-care industry specialists, airline-industry specialists, and so on. Boards of directors evaluate top managers on the basis of how well the company compares with other companies in the industry. Exhibit 4-6 shows that Bristol-Myers Squibb compares favorably with com-

Bristol-Myers Squibb Company
Common-Size Income Statement for Comparison with Industry Average
Year Ended December 31, 1995

	Bristol-Myers Squibb	Industry Average
Net sales	100.0%	100.0%
Cost of products sold	26.4	55.3
Gross profit	73.6	44.7
Operating expenses	56.2	37.7
Earnings from continuing operations before income tax	17.4	7.0
Income tax expense	4.2	1.7
Earnings from continuing operations	13.2	5.3
Special items (discontinued operations, extraordinary gains and losses, and effects of accounting changes)	—	1.1
Net earnings	13.2%	4.2%

Percent of Net Sales

Bristol-Myers
Squibb Company

Industry Average

peting companies in its industry. Its gross profit percentage is much higher than the industry average. The company does a good job of controlling total expenses, and as a result, its percentage of income from continuing operations and net income percentage are significantly higher than the industry average.

Benchmarking Against a Key Competitor

Common-size statements are also used to compare the company to another specific company. Suppose you are a member of Angela Lane's team at Baer & Foster. You are considering an investment in the stock of a manufacturer of health-care and other consumer products, and you are choosing between Bristol-Myers Squibb and Procter & Gamble. A direct comparison of their financial statements in dollar amounts is not meaningful because the amounts are so different.

However, you can convert the two companies' income statements to common size and compare the percentages. Exhibit 4-7 presents the common-size income statements of Bristol-Myers Squibb and Procter & Gamble. Procter & Gamble serves as an excellent benchmark because most of its products are market leaders. In this comparison, Bristol-Myers Squibb has higher percentages of gross profit, earnings from continuing operations, and net earnings.

Exhibit 4-7 Common-Size Income Statement Compared with a Key Competitor

Bristol-Myers Squibb Company
Common-Size Income Statement for Comparison with Key Competitor
Year Ended December 31, 1995

	Bristol-Myers Squibb	Procter & Gamble
Net sales	100.0%	100.0%
Cost of products sold	26.4	58.4
Gross profit	73.6	41.6
Operating expenses	56.2	29.6
Earnings from continuing operations, before income tax	17.4	12.0
Income tax expense	4.2	4.0
Earnings from continuing operations	13.2	8.0
Special items (discontinued operations, extraordinary gains and losses, and effects of accounting changes)	—	—
Net earnings	13.2%	8.0%

Percent of Net Sales

Bristol-Myers
Squibb Company

Procter & Gamble

Using the Statement of Cash Flows in Decision Making

Some analysts use cash-flow analysis to identify danger signals about a company's financial situation. For example, the statement in Exhibit 4-8 reveals what may be a weakness in DeMaris Corporation.

First, operations provided a net cash inflow of $52,000, which is much less than the $91,000 generated by the sale of fixed assets. An important question arises: Can the company remain in business by generating the majority of its cash by selling its property, plant, and equipment? No, because these assets are needed to manufacture the company's products in the future. Note also that borrowing by issuance of bonds payable brought in $72,000. No company can long survive by living on borrowed funds. DeMaris must eventually pay off the bonds. Indeed, the company paid $170,000 on older debt. Successful companies such as General Mills, DuPont, and Colgate-Palmolive generate the greatest percentage of their cash from operations, not from selling their fixed assets or from borrowing money. These conditions may be only temporary for DeMaris Corporation, but they are worth investigating.

The most important information that the statement of cash flows provides is a summary of the company's sources and uses of cash. How a company spends its cash today determines its sources of cash in the future. The company may wisely use its cash to

Exhibit 4-8   Statement of Cash Flows

DeMaris Corporation
Statement of Cash Flows
Year Ended December 31, 19X5

Operating activities:		
Income from operations		$ 35,000
Add (subtract) noncash items:		
Depreciation	$ 14,000	
Net increase in current assets other than cash.....	(5,000)	
Net increase in current liabilities........................	8,000	17,000
Net cash inflow from operating activities		52,000
Investing activities:		
Sale of property, plant, and equipment......................	$ 91,000	
Net cash inflow from investing activities		91,000
Financing activities:		
Issuance of bonds payable	$ 72,000	
Payment of long-term debt	(170,000)	
Purchase of treasury stock...	(9,000)	
Payment of dividends...	(33,000)	
Net cash outflow from financing activities..............		(140,000)
Increase in cash...		$ 3,000

purchase assets that will generate income in the years ahead. If a company invests unwisely, however, cash will eventually run short.

DeMaris' statement of cash flows reveals problems. Exhibit 4-8 indicates that DeMaris invested in no fixed assets to replace those that it sold. The company may in fact be going out of business. Also, DeMaris paid dividends of $33,000, an amount very close to its net income. Is the company retaining enough cash to finance future operations—especially in light of the large amount of long-term debt that DeMaris paid off? Analysts seek answers to questions such as this. They analyze the information from the statement of cash flows along with the information from the balance sheet and the income statement to form a well-rounded picture of the business.

SUMMARY PROBLEM FOR REVIEW

Perform a horizontal analysis and a vertical analysis of the comparative income statement of TRE Corporation, which makes metal detectors. State whether 19X3 was a good year or a bad year, and give your reasons.

The horizontal analysis shows that total revenues increased 22.2 percent. This percentage increase was greater than the 19.5% increase in total expenses, resulting in a 140% increase in net earnings.

The vertical analysis shows decreases in the percentages of net sales consumed by the cost of products sold (from 73.3% to 70.5%) and by the engineering, selling, and administrative expenses (from 21.3% to 19.6%). These two items are TRE's largest dollar expenses, so their percentage decreases are quite important. The relative reduction in expenses raised December 19X3 net earnings to 4.4% of sales, compared with 2.2% the preceding December. The overall analysis indicates that December 19X3 was significantly better than December 19X2.

TRE Corporation

Comparative Income Statement
Months Ended December 31, 19X3 and 19X2

	19X3	19X2
Total revenues	$275,000	$225,000
Expenses:		
Cost of products sold	$194,000	$165,000
Engineering, selling, and administrative expenses	54,000	48,000
Interest expense	5,000	5,000
Income tax expense	9,000	3,000
Other expense (income)	1,000	(1,000)
Total expenses	263,000	220,000
Net earnings	$ 12,000	$ 5,000

TRE Corporation

Horizontal Analysis of Comparative Income Statement
Months Ended December 31, 19X3 and 19X2

	19X3	19X2	Increase (Decrease) Amount	Increase (Decrease) Percent
Total revenues	$275,000	$225,000	$50,000	22.2%
Expenses:				
Cost of products sold	$194,000	$165,000	$29,000	17.6
Engineering, selling, and administrative expenses	54,000	48,000	6,000	12.5
Interest expense	5,000	5,000	—	—
Income tax expense	9,000	3,000	6,000	200.0
Other expense (income)	1,000	(1,000)	2,000	—*
Total expenses	263,000	220,000	43,000	19.5
Net earnings	$ 12,000	$ 5,000	$ 7,000	140.0%

*Percentage changes are typically not computed for shifts from a negative amount to a positive amount, and vice versa.

USING RATIOS TO MAKE BUSINESS DECISIONS

An important part of financial analysis is the calculation and interpretation of ratios. A ratio expresses the relationship of one number to another number. For example, if the balance sheet shows current assets of $100,000 and current liabilities of $25,000, the ratio of current assets to current liabilities is $100,000 to $25,000. We simplify this numerical expression to the ratio of 4 to 1, which may also be written 4:1 and 4/1. Other acceptable ways of expressing this ratio include (1) "current assets are 400% of current liabilities," (2) "the business has four dollars in current assets for every one dollar in current liabilities," or simply, (3) "the current ratio is 4.0."

We often reduce the ratio fraction by writing the ratio as one figure over the other (for example, 4/1), and then dividing the numerator by the denominator. In this way, the ratio 4/1 may be expressed simply as 4. The 1 that represents the denominator of the fraction is understood, not written. Consider the ratio $175,000:$165,000. After dividing the first figure by the second, we come to 1.06: 1, which we state as 1.06. The second part of the ratio, the 1, again is understood. Ratios provide a convenient and useful way of expressing a relationship between numbers. For example, the ratio of current assets to current liabilities—the current ratio—gives information about a company's ability to pay its current debts with existing current assets.

A manager, lender, or financial analyst may use any ratio that is relevant to a particular decision. Many companies include ratios in a special section of their annual financial reports. This information can also be found in Moody's, Standard & Poor's, Robert Morris Associates, and other investment services that report these ratios for companies and industries.

The Decision Guidelines

The Decision Guidelines summarize the widely used ratios that we will discuss in this chapter. The ratios may be classified as follows:

1. Ratios that measure the company's ability to pay current liabilities
2. Ratios that measure the company's ability to sell inventory and collect receivables
3. Ratios that measure the company's ability to pay long-term debt
4. Ratios that measure the company's profitability
5. Ratios used to analyze the company's stock as an investment

Online financial databases, such as Lexis/Nexis and the Dow Jones News Retrieval Service, offer quarterly financial figures for thousands of public corporations going back as far as ten years.

Measuring a Company's Ability to Pay Current Liabilities

Working capital is defined as follows:

Working capital = Current assets – Current Liabilities

Working capital is widely used to measure a business's ability to meet its short-term obligations with its current assets. In general, the larger the working capital, the better able is the business to pay its debt. Recall that capital, or owners' equity, is total assets minus total liabilities. Working capital is like a "current" version of total capital. The working capital amount considered alone does not give a complete picture of the entity's working capital position, however. Consider two companies with equal working capital:

	Company A	Company B
Current assets	$100,000	$200,000
Current liabilities	50,000	150,000
Working capital	50,000	50,000

Both companies have working capital of $50,000, but Company A's working capital is as large as its current liabilities. Company B's working capital is only one-third as large as its current liabilities. Which business has a better working capital position? Company A because its working capital is a higher percentage of current assets and current liabilities. To use working-capital data in decision making, it is helpful to develop ratios. Two decision-making tools based on working capital data are the current ratio and the acid-test ratio.

Current Ratio. The most common ratio using current-asset and current-liability data is the current ratio, which is current assets divided by current liabilities. Recall the makeup of current assets and current liabilities. Inventory is converted to receivables through sales, the receivables are collected in cash, and the cash is used to buy invento-

Decision Guidelines

Using Ratios in Financial Statement Analysis

Ratio	Computation	Information Provided
Measuring the company's ability to pay current liabilities:		
1. Current ratio	$\dfrac{\text{Current assets}}{\text{Current liabilities}}$	Measures ability to pay current liabilities with current assets.
2. Acid-test (quick) ratio	$\dfrac{\text{Cash} + \text{Short-term investments} + \text{Net current receivables}}{\text{Current liabilities}}$	Shows ability to pay all current liabilities if they come due immediately.
Measuring the company's ability to sell inventory and collect receivables:		
3. Inventory turnover	$\dfrac{\text{Cost of goods sold}}{\text{Average inventory}}$	Indicates saleability of inventory— the number of times a company sells its average inventory level during a year.
4. Accounts receivable turnover	$\dfrac{\text{Net credit sales}}{\text{Average net accounts receivable}}$	Measures ability to collect cash from credit customers.
5. Days' sales in receivables	$\dfrac{\text{Average net accounts receivable}}{\text{One day's sales}}$	Shows how many days' sales remain in Accounts Receivable—how many days it takes to collect the average level of receivables.
Measuring the company's ability to pay long-term debt:		
6. Debt ratio	$\dfrac{\text{Total liabilities}}{\text{Total assets}}$	Indicates percentage of assets financed with debt.
7. Times-interest-earned ratio	$\dfrac{\text{Income from operations}}{\text{Interest expense}}$	Measures the number of times operating income can cover interest expense.

ry and pay current liabilities. A company's current assets and current liabilities represent the core of its day-to-day operations. The current ratio measures the company's ability to pay current assets with current liabilities.

Exhibit 4-9 gives the comparative income statement and balance sheet of Palisades Furniture, Inc. The current ratios of Palisades Furniture, Inc., at December 31, 19X7 and 19X6, follow, along with the average for the retail furniture industry:

		Palisades' Current Ratio		Industry Average
Formula		**19X7**	**19X6**	
Current ratio =	$\dfrac{\text{Current assets}}{\text{Current liabilities}}$	$\dfrac{\$262,000}{\$142,000} = 1.85$	$\dfrac{\$236,000}{\$126,000} = 1.87$	1.80

The current ratio decreased slightly during 19X7. Lenders, stockholders, and managers closely monitor changes in a company's current ratio. In general, a higher current

Exhibit 4-9 Comparative Financial Statements

Palisades Furniture, Inc.
Comparative Income Statement
Years Ended December 31, 19X7 and 19X6

	19X7	19X6
Net sales	$858,000	$803,000
Cost of goods sold............................	513,000	509,000
Gross profit	345,000	294,000
Operating expenses:		
Selling expenses	126,000	114,000
General expenses...........................	118,000	123,000
Total operating expenses	244,000	237,000
Income from operations....................	101,000	57,000
Interest revenue	4,000	—
Interest expense	24,000	14,000
Income before income taxes	81,000	43,000
Income tax expense	33,000	17,000
Net income..	$ 48,000	$ 26,000

ratio indicates a stronger financial position. A higher current ratio suggests that the business has sufficient liquid assets to maintain normal business operations.

What is an acceptable current ratio? The answer depends on the nature of the industry. The norm for companies in most industries is between 1.60 and 1.90, as reported by Robert Morris Associates. Palisades Furniture's current ratio of 1.85 is within the range of those values. In most industries, a current ratio of 2.0 is considered good.

Acid-Test Ratio. The acid-test (or quick) ratio tells us whether the entity could pay all its current liabilities if they came due immediately. That is, could the company pass this acid test? To do so, the company would have to convert its most liquid assets to cash. To compute the acid-test ratio, we add cash, short-term investments, and net current receivables (accounts and notes receivable, net of allowances) and divide by current liabilities. Inventory and prepaid expenses are the two current assets not included in the acid-test computations because they are the least liquid of the current assets. A business may not be able to convert them to cash immediately to pay current liabilities. The acid-test ratio uses a narrower asset base to measure liquidity than the current ratio does. Palisades Furniture acid-test ratios for 19X7 and 19X6 are below.

The company's acid-test ratio improved considerably during 19X7 and is significantly better than the industry average.

Measuring a Company's Ability to Sell Inventory and Collect Receivables

The ability to sell inventory and collect receivables is fundamental to business success. Recall the operating cycle of a merchandiser: cash to inventory to receivables and back

		Palisades' Acid-Test Ratio		Industry Average
	Formula	**19X7**	**19X6**	
Acid-test ratio	=	$\dfrac{\text{Cash} + \text{short-term investments} + \text{net current receivables}}{\text{Current liabilities}}$	$\dfrac{\$29,000 + \$0 + \$114,000}{\$142,000} = 1.01$	$\dfrac{\$32,000 + \$0 + \$85,000}{\$126,000} = 0.93$	0.60

Exhibit 4-10 Comparative Financial Statements (continued)

	19X7	19X6
Assets		
Current assets:		
Cash	$ 29,000	$ 32,000
Accounts receivable, net	114,000	85,000
Inventories	113,000	111,000
Prepaid expenses	6,000	8,000
Total current assets	262,000	236,000
Long-term investments	18,000	9,000
Property, plant, and equipment, net	507,000	399,000
Total assets	$787,000	$644,000
Liabilities		
Current liabilities:		
Notes payable	$ 42,000	$ 27,000
Accounts payable	73,000	68,000
Accrued liabilities	27,000	31,000
Total current liabilities	142,000	126,000
Long-term debt	289,000	198,000
Total liabilities	431,000	324,000
Stockholders' Equity		
Common stock, no par	186,000	186,000
Retained earnings	170,000	134,000
Total stockholders' equity	356,000	320,000
Total liabilities and stockholders' equity	$787,000	$644,000

to cash. In this section we discuss three ratios that measure the company's ability to sell inventory and collect receivables.

Inventory Turnover. Companies generally seek to achieve the quickest possible return on their investments, including their investments in inventory. The faster inventory sells, the sooner the business creates accounts receivable, and the sooner it collects cash.

Inventory turnover is a measure of the number of times a company sells its average level of inventory during a year. A high rate of turnover indicates relative ease in selling inventory; a low turnover indicates difficulty in selling. In general, companies prefer a high inventory turnover. A value of 6 means that the company's average level of inventory has been sold six times during the year. This is generally better than a turnover of 3 or 4. However, a high value can mean that the business is not keeping enough inventory on hand, and inadequate inventory can result in lost sales if the company cannot fill a customer's order. Therefore, a business strives for the most profitable rate of inventory turnover, not necessarily the highest rate.

To compute the inventory turnover ratio, we divide cost of goods sold by the average inventory for the period. We use the cost of goods sold—not sales—in the computation because both cost of goods sold and inventory are stated at cost. Sales is stated at the sales value of inventory and, therefore, is not comparable with inventory cost. Palisades Furniture's inventory turnover for 19X7 is

Formula	Palisades' Inventory Turnover	Industry Average
Inventory turnover = $\dfrac{\text{Cost of goods sold}}{\text{Average inventory}}$	$\dfrac{\$513,000}{\$112,000} = 4.58$	2.70

Cost of goods sold appears in the income statement (Exhibit 4-9). Average inventory is figured by averaging the beginning inventory ($111,000) and ending inventory ($113,000). (See the balance sheet, Exhibit 4-9.) If inventory levels vary greatly from month to month, compute the average by adding the 12 monthly balances and dividing the sum by 12. Inventory turnover varies widely with the nature of the business. For example, most manufacturers of farm machinery have an inventory turnover close to three times a year. In contrast, companies that remove natural gas from the ground hold their inventory for a very short period of time and have an average turnover of 30. Palisades Furniture's turnover of 4.58 times a year is high for its industry, which has an average turnover of 2.70. Palisades' high inventory turnover results from its policy of keeping little inventory on hand. The company takes customer orders and has its suppliers ship directly to some customers. To evaluate fully a company's inventory turnover, we must compare the ratio over time. A sudden sharp decline or a steady decline over a long period suggests the need for corrective action.

Accounts Receivable Turnover. Accounts receivable turnover measures a company's ability to collect cash from credit customers. In general, the higher the ratio, the more successfully the business collects cash, and the better off its operations are. However, a receivable turnover that is too high may indicate that credit is too tight, causing the loss of sales to good customers. To compute the accounts receivable turnover, we divide net credit sales by average net accounts receivable. The resulting ratio indicates how many times during the year the average level of receivables was turned into cash.

Palisades Furniture's accounts receivable turnover ratio for 19X7 is computed as follows:

Formula	Palisades' Accounts Receivable Turnover	Industry Average
Accounts receivable turnover = $\dfrac{\text{Net credit sales}}{\text{Average net accounts receivable}}$	$\dfrac{\$858,000}{\$99,500} = 8.62$	22.2

The net credit sales figure comes from the income statement. Palisades Furniture makes all sales on credit. If the company makes both cash and credit sales, this ratio is best computed by using only net credit sales. Average net accounts receivable is figured by adding the beginning accounts receivable balance ($85,000) and the ending balance ($114,000), then dividing by 2. If the accounts receivable balances exhibit a seasonal pattern, compute the average by using the 12 monthly balances. Palisades' receivable turnover of 8.62 is much lower than the industry average. The explanation is simple: the company is a home-town store that sells to local people who tend to pay their bills over a period of time. Many larger furniture stores sell their receivables to other companies called factors, a practice that keeps receivables low and receivable turnover high. But companies that factor (sell) their receivables receive less than face value of the receivables. Palisades Furniture follows a different strategy.

Days' Sales in Receivables. Businesses must convert accounts receivable to cash. All else equal, the lower the accounts receivable balance, the more successful the business has been in converting receivables into cash, and the better off the business is.

The days'-sales-in-receivables ratio tells us how many days' sales remain in accounts receivable. To compute the ratio, we follow a two-step process. First, divide net sales by 365 days to figure the average sales amount for one day. Second, divide this average day's sales amount into the average net accounts receivable.

The data to compute this ratio for Palisades Furniture, Inc. for 19X7 are taken from the income statement and the balance sheet (Exhibit 4-9):

The days'-sales-in-receivables ratio

Formula	Palisades' Days' Sales in Accounts Receivables	Industry Average
Days' Sales in AVERAGE Accounts Receivable:		
1. One day's sales $= \dfrac{\text{Net sales}}{\text{365 days}}$	$\dfrac{\$858,000}{\text{365 days}} = \$2,351$	
2. $\begin{array}{l}\text{Days' sales in}\\ \text{average accounts} \\ \text{receivable}\end{array} = \dfrac{\begin{array}{c}\text{Average net} \\ \text{accounts receivable}\end{array}}{\text{One day's sales}}$	$\dfrac{\$99,500}{\$2,351} = 42 \text{ days}$	16 days

Days' sales in average receivables can also be computed in a single step:

$$\$99,500/(\$858,000/365 \text{ days}) = 42 \text{ days.}$$

Palisades' ratio tells us that 42 average days' sales remain in accounts receivable and need to be collected. The company will increase its cash inflow if it can decrease this ratio. To detect any changes over time in the firm's ability to collect its receivables, let's compute the days'-sales-in-receivables ratio at the beginning and the end of 19X7:

Days' Sales in ENDING 19X7 Accounts Receivable:

One day's sales $= \dfrac{\$803,000}{\text{365 days}} = \$2,200$ $\begin{array}{c}\text{Days's sales in}\\ \text{ENDING 19X6}\\ \text{accounts receivable}\end{array} = \dfrac{\$85,000}{\$2,200} = \begin{array}{c}39 \text{ days at}\\ \text{beginning of 19X7}\end{array}$

Days' Sales in ENDING 19X7 Accounts Receivable:

One day's sales $= \dfrac{\$858,000}{\text{365 days}} = \$2,351$ $\begin{array}{c}\text{Days's sales in}\\ \text{ENDING 19X7}\\ \text{accounts receivable}\end{array} = \dfrac{\$114,000}{\$2.351} = \begin{array}{c}49 \text{ days at}\\ \text{end of 19X7}\end{array}$

This analysis shows a drop in Palisades Furniture's collection of receivables; days'-sales-in-receivables has increased from 39 at the beginning of the year to 48 at year end. The credit and collection department should strengthen its collection efforts. Otherwise, the company may experience a cash shortage in 19X8 and beyond.

The days-sales-in-receivables for Palisades is higher (worse) than the industry average because the company collects its own receivables. Many other furniture stores sell their receivables and carry fewer days-sales-in-receivables. Palisades Furniture remains competitive because of its personal relationship with its customers. Without their good paying habits, the company's cash now would suffer.

Measuring a Company's Ability to Pay Long-Term Debt

The ratios discussed so far give us insight into current assets and current liabilities. They help us measure a business's ability to sell inventory, to collect receivables, and to pay current liabilities. Most businesses also have long-term debts. Bondholders and banks that loan money on long-term notes payable and bonds payable take special interest in the ability of a business to meet its long-term obligations. Two key indicators of a business's ability to pay long-term liabilities are the debt ratio and the times-interest-earned ratio.

Debt Ratio. The debt ratio indicates the proportion of the company's assets that it has financed with debt. If the debt ratio is 1, then debt has been used to finance all the assets. A debt ratio of 0.50 means that the company has used debt to finance half its assets and that the owners of the business have financed the other half. The higher the debt ratio, the higher the strain of paying interest each year and the principal amount at maturity. The lower the ratio, the lower the business's future obligations. Creditors view a high debt ratio with caution. If a business seeking financing already has large liabilities, then additional debt payments may be too much for the business to handle. To help protect themselves, creditors generally charge higher interest rates on new borrowing to companies with an already high debt ratio.

Calculation of the debt ratios for Palisades Furniture at the end of 19X7 and 19X6 is as follows:

	Formula	Palisades' Debt Ratio		Industry Average
		19X7	19X6	
Debt ratio =	$\dfrac{\text{Total liabilities}}{\text{Total assets}}$	$\dfrac{\$431,000}{\$787,000} = 0.55$	$\dfrac{\$324,000}{\$644,000} = 0.50$	0.61

Palisades Furniture expanded operations by financing the purchase of property, plant, and equipment through borrowing, which is common. This expansion explains the firm's increased debt ratio. Even after the increase in 19X7, the company's debt is not very high. Robert Morris Associates reports that the average debt ratio for most companies ranges around 0.57–0.67, with relatively little variation from company to company. Palisades' 0.55 debt ratio indicates a fairly low-risk debt position compared to the retail furniture industry average of 0.61.

Times-Interest-Earned Ratio. The debt ratio measures the effect of debt on the company's financial position (balance sheet) but says nothing about its ability to pay interest expense. Analysts use a second ratio, the times-interest-earned ratio, to relate income to interest expense. To compute this ratio, we divide income from operations by interest expense. This ratio measures the number of times that operating income can cover interest expense. For this reason, the ratio is also called the interest-coverage ratio. A high times-interest-earned ratio indicates ease in paying interest expense; a low value suggests difficulty.

Calculation of Palisades' times-interest-earned ratios is as follows:

	Formula	Palisades' Times-Interest-Earned Ratio		Industry Average
		19X7	19X6	
Times-interest-earned ratio =	$\dfrac{\text{Income from operations}}{\text{Interest expense}}$	$\dfrac{\$101,000}{\$24,000} = 4.21$	$\dfrac{\$57,000}{\$14,000} = 4.07$	2.00

The company's times-interest-earned ratio increased in 19X7. This is a favorable sign, especially since the company's short-term notes payable and long-term debt rose substantially during the year. Palisades Furniture's new plant assets, we conclude, have earned more in operating income than they have cost the business in interest expense. The company's times-interest-earned ratio of around 4.00 is significantly better than the 2.00 average for furniture retailers. The norm for U.S. business, as reported by Robert Morris Associates, falls in the range of 2.0 to 3.0 for most companies.

On the basis of its debt ratio and its times-interest-earned ratio, Palisades Furniture appears to have little difficulty servicing its debt, that is, paying its liabilities.

Measuring a Company's Profitability

The fundamental goal of business is to earn a profit. Ratios that measure profitability play a large role in decision making. These ratios are reported in the business press, by investment services, and in companies' annual financial reports.

Rate of Return on Net Sales. In business, the term "return" is used broadly and loosely as an evaluation of profitability. Consider a ratio called the rate of return on net sales, or simply return on sales. (The word net is usually omitted for convenience, even though the net sales figure is used to compute the ratio.) This ratio shows the percentage of each sales dollar earned as net income. The rate-of-return-on-net-sales ratios for Palisades Furniture are calculated as follows:

| | | Palisades' Rate of Return on Sales | | Industry Average |
Formula		19X7	19X6	
Rate of return on sales =	$\dfrac{\text{Net income}}{\text{Net sales}}$	$\dfrac{\$48,000}{\$858,000} = 0.056$	$\dfrac{\$26,000}{\$803,000} = 0.032$	0.008

Companies strive for a high rate of return. The higher the rate of return, the more net sales dollars are providing income to the business and the fewer net sales dollars are absorbed by expenses. The increase in Palisades Furniture's return on sales is significant and identifies the company as more successful than the average furniture store.

A return measure can be computed on any revenue and sales amount. Return on net sales, as we have seen, is net income divided by net sales. Return on total revenues is net income divided by total revenues. A company can compute a return on other specific portions of revenue as its information needs dictate.

Rate of Return on Total Assets. The rate of return on total assets, or simply return on assets, measures a company's success in using its assets to earn a profit. Creditors have loaned money to the company, and the interest they receive is the return on their investment. Shareholders have invested in the company's stock, and net income is their return. The sum of interest expense and net income is thus the return to the two groups that have financed the company's operations, and this amount is the numerator of the return-on-assets ratio. Average total assets is the denominator. Computation of the return-on-assets ratio for Palisades Furniture is as follows:

| | | Palisades' 19X7 Rate of Return on Total Assets | Industry Average |
Formula			
Rate of return on assets =	$\dfrac{\text{Net income} + \text{Interest expense}}{\text{Average total assets}}$	$\dfrac{\$48,000 + \$24,000}{\$715,500} = 0.101$	0.049

Net income and interest expense are taken from the income statement (Exhibit 4-9). To compute average total assets, we take the average of beginning and ending total assets from the comparative balance sheet.

Rate of Return on Common Stockholders' Equity. A popular measure of profitability is rate of return on common stockholders' equity, which is often shortened to return on stockholders' equity, or simply return on equity.

This ratio shows the relationship between net income and common stockholders' investment in the company—how much income is earned for every $1 invested by the common shareholders. To compute this ratio, we first subtract preferred dividends from net income. This calculation provides net income available to the common stockholders, which we need to compute the ratio. We then divide net income available to common stockholders by the average stockholders' equity during the year. Common stockholders' equity is total stockholders' equity minus preferred equity. The 19X7 rate of return on common stockholders' equity for Palisades Furniture is calculated as follows:

Formula		Palisades' 19X7 Rate of Return on Common Stockholders' Equity	Industry Average
Rate of return on common stockholders' equity	$= \dfrac{\text{Net income} - \text{Preferred dividends}}{\text{Average common stockholders' equity}}$	$\dfrac{\$48,000 - \$0}{\$338,000} = 0.142$	0.093

We compute average equity by using the beginning and ending balances [($356,000 + $320,000)/2 = $338,000]. Common stockholders' equity is total equity minus preferred equity.

Observe that Palisades' return on equity (0.142) is higher than its return on assets (0.101). This difference results from borrowing at one rate—say, 0.08, or 80% and investing the funds to earn a higher rate, such as the firm's 0.142, or 14.2%, return on stockholders' equity. This practice is called trading on the equity, or using leverage. It is directly related to the debt ratio. The higher the debt ratio, the higher the leverage. Companies that finance operations with debt are said to leverage their positions. Leverage increases the risk to common stockholders.

For Palisades Furniture and for many other companies, leverage increases profitability. This is not always the case, however. Leverage can have a negative impact on profitability. If revenues drop, debt and interest expense still must be paid. Therefore, leverage is a double-edged sword, increasing profits during good times but compounding losses during bad times.

Earnings per Share of Common Stock. Earnings per share of common stock, or simply earnings per share (EPS), is perhaps the most widely quoted of all financial statistics. EPS is the only ratio that must appear on the face of the income statement. EPS is the amount of net income per share of the company's outstanding common stock. Earnings per share is computed by dividing net income available to common stockholders by the number of common shares outstanding during the year. Preferred dividends are subtracted from net income because the preferred stockholders have a prior claim to their dividends. Palisades Furniture, Inc. has no preferred stock outstanding and, thus, has no preferred dividends. Computation of the firm's EPS for 19X7 and 19X6 follows (the company had 10,000 shares of common stock outstanding throughout 19X6 and 19X7):

Formula		Palisades' Earnings per Share	
		19X7	19X6
Earnings per share of common stock	$= \dfrac{\text{Net income} - \text{Preferred dividends}}{\text{Number of shares of common stock outstanding}}$	$\dfrac{\$48,000 - \$0}{10,000} = \$4.80$	$\dfrac{\$26,000 - \$0}{10,000} = \$2.60$

Palisades Furniture's EPS increased 85 percent. Its stockholders should not expect such a significant boost in EPS every year. Most companies strive to increase EPS by 10–15% annually, and the more successful companies do so. But even the most dramatic upward trends include an occasional bad year.

Analyzing a Company's Stock as an Investment

Investors purchase stock to earn a return on their investment. This return consists of two parts: (1) gains (or losses) from selling the stock at a price that differs from the investors' purchase price and (2) dividends, the periodic distributions to stockholders.

The ratios we examine in this section help analysts evaluate stock in terms of market price or dividend payments.

Price/Earnings Ratio. The price/earnings ratio is the ratio of the market price of a share of common stock to the company's earnings per share. This ratio, abbreviated P/E, appears in the *Wall Street Journal* stock listings. P/E ratios play an important part in decisions to buy, hold, and sell stocks. They indicate the market price of $1 of earnings.

Calculations for the P/E ratios of Palisades Furniture, Inc., follow. The market price of its common stock was $50 at the end of 19X7 and $35 at the end of 19X6. These prices can be obtained from a financial publication, a stockbroker, or some other source outside the accounting records.

	Formula	Palisades' Price/Earnings Ratio	
		19X7	**19X6**
P/E ratio =	$\dfrac{\text{Market price per share of common stock}}{\text{Earnings per share}}$	$\dfrac{\$50.00}{\$4.80} = 10.4$	$\dfrac{\$35.00}{\$2.60} = 13.5$

Given Palisades Furniture's 19X7 P/E ratio of 10.4, we would say that the company's stock is selling at 10.4 times earnings. The decline from the 19X6 P/E ratio of 13.5 is not a cause for alarm because the market price of the stock is not under Palisades Furniture's control. Net income is more controllable and it increased during 19X7.

Like most other ratios, P/E ratios vary from industry to industry. The higher a stock's P/E ratio the higher its downside risk—the risk that the stock's market price will fall. Many investors interpret a sharp increase in a stock's P/E ratio as a signal to sell the stock.

Dividend Yield. Dividend yield is the ratio of dividends per share of stock to the stock's market price per share. This ratio measures the percentage of a stock's market value that is returned annually as dividends, an important concern of stockholders. Preferred stockholders, who invest primarily to receive dividends, pay special attention to this ratio.

Palisades Furniture paid annual cash dividends of $1.20 per share of common stock in 19X7 and $1.00 in 19X6, and market prices of the company's common stock were $50 in 19X7 and $35 in 19X6. Calculation of the firm's dividend yields on common stock is as follows:

	Formula	Dividend Yield on Palisades' Common Stock	
		19X7	**19X6**
Dividend yield on common stock[1]	=	$\dfrac{\text{Dividend per share of common stock}}{\text{Market price per share of common stock}}$	$\dfrac{\$1.20}{\$50.00} = 0.024$	$\dfrac{\$1.00}{\$35.00} = \$0.029$

[1] Dividend yields may also be calculated for preferred stock.

An investor who buys Palisades Furniture common stock for $50 can expect to receive almost 2.5% of the investment annually in the form of cash dividends. Dividend yields vary widely, from 5% to 8% for older, established companies down to the range of 0–3% for young, growth-oriented companies. Palisades Furniture's dividend yield places the company in the second group.

Book Value per Share of Common Stock. Book value per share of common stock is simply common stockholders' equity divided by the number of shares of common stock outstanding. Common shareholders' equity equals total stockholders' equity less preferred equity. Palisades Furniture has no preferred stock outstanding.

Calculations of its book-value-per-share-of-common-stock ratio follows. Recall that 10,000 shares of common stock were outstanding at the end of years 19X7 and 19X6.

Formula	Book Value per Share of Palisades' Common Stock	
	19X7	19X6
Book value per share of common stock $= \dfrac{\text{Total stockholders' equity} - \text{Preferred equity}}{\text{Number of shares of common stock outstanding}}$	$\dfrac{\$356,000 - \$0}{10,000} = \$35.60$	$\dfrac{\$320,000 - \$0}{10,000} = \$32.00$

Book value indicates the recorded accounting amount for each share of common stock outstanding. Many experts argue that book value is not useful for investment analysis. It bears no relationship to market value and provides little information beyond stockholders' equity reported on the balance sheet. But some investors base their investment decisions on book value. For example, some investors rank stocks on the basis of the ratio of market price to book value. To these investors, the lower the ratio, the more attractive the stock. These investors are called "value" investors, as contrasted with "growth" investors, who focus more on trends in a company's net income.

LIMITATIONS OF FINANCIAL ANALYSIS: THE COMPLEXITY OF BUSINESS DECISIONS

Business decisions are made in a world of uncertainty. As useful as ratios are, they have limitations. We may liken their use in decision making to a physician's use of a thermometer. A reading of 101.6° Fahrenheit indicates that something is wrong with the patient, but the temperature alone does not indicate what the problem is or how to cure it.

In financial analysis, a sudden drop in a company's current ratio signals that something is wrong, but this change does not identify the problem or show how to correct it. The business manager must analyze the figures that go into the ratio to determine whether current assets have decreased, current liabilities have increased, or both. If current assets have dropped, is the problem a cash shortage? Are accounts receivable down? Are inventories too low? Only by analyzing the individual items that make up the ratio can the manager determine how to solve the problem. The manager must evaluate data on all ratios in the light of other information about the company and about its particular line of business, such as increased competition or a slowdown in the economy.

Legislation, international affairs, competition, scandals, and many other factors can turn profits into losses, and vice versa. To be most useful, ratios should be analyzed over a period of years to take into account a representative group of these factors. Any one year, or even any two years, may not be representative of the company's performance over the long term.

ECONOMIC VALUE ADDED— A NEW MEASURE OF PERFORMANCE

The top managers of Coca-Cola, Quaker Oats, AT&T, and other leading companies use **economic value added (EVA)** to evaluate a company's operating performance. EVA combines the concepts of accounting income and corporate finance to measure whether the company's operations have increased stockholder wealth. EVA can be computed as follows:

$$\text{EVA} = \text{Net income} + \text{Interest expense} - \text{Capital charge}$$

where

$$\text{Capital charge} = \left(\begin{array}{c} \text{Notes} \\ \text{payable} \end{array} + \begin{array}{c} \text{Loans} \\ \text{payable} \end{array} + \begin{array}{c} \text{Long-term} \\ \text{debt} \end{array} + \begin{array}{c} \text{Stockholders'} \\ \text{equity} \end{array} \right) \times \begin{array}{c} \text{Cost of} \\ \text{capital} \end{array}$$

All amounts for the EVA computation, except the cost of capital, are taken from the financial statements. The **cost of capital** is a weighted average of the returns demanded by the company's stockholders and lenders. The cost of capital varies with the company's level of risk. For example, stockholders would demand a higher return from a start-up computer software company than from AT&T because the new company is untested and therefore more risky. Lenders would also charge the new company a higher interest rate because of this greater risk. Thus, the new company has a higher cost of capital than AT&T. The cost of capital is a major topic in finance classes. In the following discussions we merely assume a value for the cost of capital (such as 10%, 12%, or 15%) to illustrate the computation of EVA and its use in decision making.

The idea behind EVA is that the returns to the company's stockholders (net income) and to its creditors (interest expense) should exceed the company's capital charge. The **capital charge** is the amount that stockholders and lenders charge a company for the use of their money. A positive EVA amount indicates an increase in stockholder wealth, and the company's stock should remain attractive to investors. If the EVA measure is negative, the stockholders will probably be unhappy with the company's progress and sell its stock, resulting in a decrease in the stock's price. Different companies tailor the EVA computation to meet their own needs.

The Coca-Cola Company is a leading user of EVA. Coca-Cola's EVA for 1995 can be computed as follows, assuming a 12% cost of capital for the company (dollar amounts in millions):

$$
\begin{array}{lcccccccccc}
\text{Coca-Cola's EVA} & = & \begin{array}{c}\text{Net}\\\text{income}\end{array} & + & \begin{array}{c}\text{Interest}\\\text{expense}\end{array} & - & \left[\left(\begin{array}{c}\text{Loans and}\\\text{notes payable}\end{array}\right. & + & \begin{array}{c}\text{Long-term}\\\text{debt}\end{array} & + & \left.\begin{array}{c}\text{Stockholders'}\\\text{equity}\end{array}\right) \times \left.\begin{array}{c}\text{Cost of}\\\text{capital}\end{array}\right]
\end{array}
$$

$$
= \quad \$2,986 \; + \; \$272 \quad - \quad [(\$2,371 \; + \; \$1,141 \; + \; \$5,392) \quad \times \quad 0.12]
$$

$$
= \quad \$3,258 \quad - \quad \$8,904 \quad \times \quad 0.12
$$

$$
= \quad \$3,258 \quad - \quad \$1,068
$$

$$
= \quad \$2,190
$$

By this measure, Coca-Cola's operations during 1995 added $2.19 billion ($2,190 million) of value to its stockholders' wealth after meeting the company's capital charge. This performance is outstanding. Coca-Cola's positive EVA measures explain why the company's stock price increased an average of 29% per year over the ten-year period from 1985 to 1995. A $100 investment in Coca-Cola stock in 1985 had grown to a value of $1,287 in 1995.

Banks loan money, investors buy stocks, and managers make decisions on the basis of accounting information. Horizontal analysis is the study of percentage changes in financial statement items from one period to the next. To compute these percentage changes (1) calculate the dollar amount of the change from the base (earlier) period to the later period and (2) divide the dollar amount of change by the base-period amount. Trend percentages are a form of horizontal analysis.

Vertical analysis of a financial statement reveals the relationship of each statement item to a specified base, which is the 100% figure. In an income statement, net sales is usually the base. On a balance sheet, total assets is usually the base.

A form of vertical analysis, common-size statements report only percentages, no dollar amounts. Common-size statements ease the comparison of different companies and may signal the need for corrective action. Benchmarking is the practice of comparing a company to a standard set by other companies, with a view toward improvement.

The statement of cash flows can be very useful in decision making. Analysts use cash-flow analysis to identify danger signals about a company's financial situation. The most important information provided by the cash-flow statement is a summary of the company's sources and uses of cash.

An important part of financial analysis is the calculation and interpretation of financial ratios. A ratio expresses the relationship of one item to another. The most important financial ratios measure a company's ability to pay current liabilities (current ratio, acid-test ratio); its ability to sell inventory and collect receivables (inventory turnover, accounts receivable turnover, days' sales in receivables); its ability to pay long-term debt (debt ratio, times-interest-earned ratio); its profitability (rate of return on net sales, rate of return on total assets, rate of return on common stockholders' equity, earnings per share of common stock); and its value as an investment (price/earnings ratio, dividend yield, book value per share of common stock).

Analysis of financial ratios over time is an important way to track a company's progress. A change in one of the ratios over time may signal the existence of a problem. It is up to the company's managers to find the source of this problem and take actions to correct it.

Economic value added (EVA) measures whether a company's operations have increased its stockholders' wealth. EVA can be defined as the excess of net income and interest expense over the company's capital charge, which is the amount that the company's stockholders and lenders charge for the use of their money. A positive amount of EVA indicates an increase in stockholder wealth; a negative amount indicates a decrease.

QUESTIONS

1. Identify two groups who use accounting information and the decisions they base on this information.
2. Name the three broad categories of analytical tools that are based on accounting information.
3. Briefly describe horizontal analysis. How do decision makers use this analytical tool?
4. What is vertical analysis, and what is its purpose?
5. What is the purpose of common-size statements?
6. State how an investor might analyze the statement of cash flows. How might the investor analyze investing-activities data?
7. Why are ratios important tools of financial analysis? Give an example of an important financial ratio.

8. Identify two ratios used to measure a company's ability to pay current liabilities. Show how they are computed.

9. Why is the acid-test ratio given that name?

10. What does the inventory turnover ratio measure?

11. Suppose the days'-sales-in-receivables ratio of Gomez, Inc. increased from 36 at January 1 to 43 at December 31. Is this a good sign or a bad sign? What might Gomez management do in response to this change?

12. Company A's debt ratio has increased from 0.50 to 0.70. Identify a decision maker to whom this increase is important and state how the increase affects this party's decisions about the company.

13. Which ratio measures the effect of debt on (a) financial position (the balance sheet) and (b) the company's ability to pay interest expense (the income statement)?

14. Company A is a chain of grocery stores, and Company B is a computer manufacturer. Which company is likely to have the higher (a) current ratio, (b) inventory turnover, and (c) rate of return on sales? Explain your answers.

15. Identify four ratios used to measure a company's profitability. Show how to compute these ratios and state what information each one provides.

16. The price/earnings ratio of General Motors was 6, and the price/earnings ratio of American Express was 45. Which company did the stock market favor? Explain.

17. McDonald's Corporation paid cash dividends of $0.78 2/3 (78 and 2/3 cents) per share when the market price of the company's stock was $58. What was the dividend yield on McDonald's stock? What does dividend yield measure?

INTERNET EXERCISE

Bristol-Myers Squibb

Financial statement analysis is as much art as it is science. There is no single "correct" way to analyze a firm; rather, the company's circumstances guide the analyst in determining which of the many analytical tools to employ and emphasize. Remember: The objective of financial statement analysis is to better understand the company by evaluating its current position, where it is headed, and how it is going to get there.

Bristol-Myers Squibb recently replaced its chief executive officer (CEO). The new CEO established some tough financial goals for Bristol-Myers Squibb to achieve by the turn of the century. An analysis of Bristol-Myers Squibb's financial statements will indicate whether the firm is on its way to meeting those goals.

Required

1. Go to http://www.bms.com, the home page of Bristol-Myers Squibb. This site provides information regarding the company's history, mission, and businesses (It is also the home of its headache center and links to a women's cyberclub.)

2. Find the company's latest annual report by clicking on "For Our Investors."

3. Click on the most recent "Annual Report" and answer the following questions.
   a. In the Letter to Stockholders, what does the CEO identify as the financial goals of Bristol-Myers Squibb? Which financial ratios would most likely reflect the results of these goals?
   b. Compute the ratios from your answer in (a) above for the past two years. Does it appear that Bristol-Myers Squibb is achieving its goals?

c. Bristol-Myers Squibb is a conglomerate of numerous companies competing in various lines of business. What are Bristol-Myers Squibb's lines of business?

d. Do Bristol-Myers Squibb's various business lines have similar levels of profitability, capital intensity, size, and international markets? How does the answer to this question affect your financial analysis of the firm as a whole?

SECTION III
COST MANAGEMENT SYSTEMS

CHAPTER 5

Introduction to Cost Management Systems

Managers rely on accountants to measure the cost of the goods and services the company produces. Consider the following commentaries on the modern role of management accountants:

> We (cost accountants) had to understand what the numbers mean, relate the numbers to business activity, and recommend alternative courses of action. Finally, we had to evaluate alternatives and make decisions to maximize business efficiency.
>
> —South Central Bell

> Because the ABC (Activity-Based Costing) system now mirrors the manufacturing process, the engineers and production staff believe the cost data produced by the accounting system. Engineering and production regularly ask accounting to help find the product design combination that will optimize costs. . . . The accountants now participate in product design decisions. They help engineering and production understand how costs behave. . . . The ABC system makes the professional lives of the accountants more rewarding.
>
> —Hewlett-Packard Company

As you can see, all kinds of organizations—manufacturing firms, service companies, and nonprofit organizations—need some form of **cost accounting,** that part of the accounting system that measures costs for the purposes of management decision making and financial reporting. Because it is the most general case, embracing production, marketing, and general administration functions, we will focus on cost accounting in a manufacturing setting. Remember, though, that you can apply this framework to any organization.

In this chapter we introduce the concepts of cost and management accounting appropriate to any manufacturing company. We also consider recent changes that have led to what is called the *new manufacturing environment*. Manufacturing companies are in the midst of great changes. The need to compete in global markets has changed the types of information useful to managers. At the same time technology has changed both the manufacturing processes and information-processing capabilities. Although the basic *concepts* of management accounting have not changed, their *application* is significantly different in many companies than it was a decade ago. Management accountants today must be able to develop systems to support globally oriented, technology-intensive companies, often called the *world-class manufacturing companies.*

In addition, we discuss how cost accounting affects and is affected by financial reporting, and how the need to use costs for reported income statements and balance sheets influences the way cost accounting systems are structured.

CLASSIFICATIONS OF COSTS

Costs may be classified in many ways—far too many to be covered in a single chapter. This chapter concentrates on the big picture of how manufacturing costs are accumulated and classified.

Cost Accumulation and Cost Objectives

A **cost** may be defined as a sacrifice or giving up of resources for a particular purpose. Costs are frequently measured by the monetary units (for example, dollars or francs) that must be paid for goods and services. Costs are initially recorded in elementary form (for example, repairs or advertising). Then these costs are grouped in different ways to help managers make decisions, such as evaluating subordinates and subunits of the organization, expanding or deleting products or territories, and replacing equipment.

To aid decisions, managers want to know the cost of something. This "something" is called a **cost objective** or **cost object,** defined as *any activity or resource for which a separate measurement of costs is desired.* Examples of cost objectives include departments, products, territories, miles driven, bricks laid, patients seen, tax bills sent, checks processed, student hours taught, and library books shelved.

The cost accounting system typically includes two processes:

1. **Cost accumulation:** Collecting costs by some "natural" classification such as materials or labor.
2. **Cost allocation:** Tracing and reassigning costs to one or more cost objectives such as departments, customers, or products.

Exhibit 5-1 illustrates these processes. First, the costs of all raw materials are *accumulated.* Then they are *allocated* to the departments that use them and further to the specific items made by these departments. The total raw materials cost of a particular product is the sum of the raw materials costs allocated to it in the various departments.

To make intelligent decisions, managers want reliable measurements. An extremely large U.S. grocery chain, A&P, ran into profit difficulties. It began retrenching by closing many stores. Management's lack of adequate cost information about individual store operations made the closing program a hit-or-miss affair. A news story reported the following:

> Because of the absence of detailed profit-and-loss statements, and a cost-allocation system that did not reflect true costs, A&P's strategists could not be sure whether an individual store was really unprofitable. For example, distribution costs were shared equally among all the stores in a marketing area without regard to such factors as a store's distance from the warehouse. Says one close observer of the company: "When they wanted to close a store, they had to wing it. They could not make rational decisions because they did not have a fact basis."

Exhibit 5-1   Cost Accumulation and Allocation

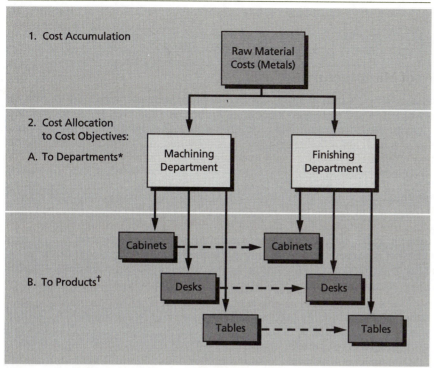

1. Cost Accumulation

    Raw Material Costs (Metals)

2. Cost Allocation to Cost Objectives:

   A. To Departments*

      Machining Department

      Finishing Department

   B. To Products†

      Cabinets → Cabinets

      Desks → Desks

      Tables → Tables

* Purpose: to evaluate performance of manufacturing departments.
† Purpose: to obtain costs of various products for valuing inventory, determining income, and judging product profitability.

Direct and Indirect Costs

A major feature of costs in both manufacturing and nonmanufacturing activities is whether the costs have a direct or an indirect relationship to a particular cost objective. **Direct costs** can be identified specifically and exclusively with a given cost objective in an economically feasible way. In contrast, **indirect costs** cannot be identified specifically and exclusively with a given cost objective in an economically feasible way.

Whenever it is "economically feasible," managers prefer to classify costs as direct rather than indirect. In this way, managers have greater confidence in the reported costs of products and services. "Economically feasible" means "cost effective," in the sense that managers do not want cost accounting to be too expensive in relation to expected benefits. For example, it may be economically feasible to trace the exact cost of steel and fabric (direct cost) to a specific lot of desk chairs, but it may be economically infeasible to trace the exact cost of rivets or thread (indirect costs) to the chairs.

Other factors also influence whether a cost is considered direct or indirect. The key is the particular cost objective. For example, consider a supervisor's salary in the maintenance department of a telephone company. If the cost objective is the department, the supervisor's salary is a direct cost. In contrast, if the cost objective is a service (the "product" of the company) such as a telephone call, the supervisor's salary is an indirect cost. In general, many more costs are direct when a department is the cost objective than when a service (a telephone call) or a physical product (a razor blade) is the cost objective.

Frequently managers want to know both the costs of running departments and the costs of products, services, activities, or resources. Costs are inevitably allocated to more than one cost objective. Thus, a particular cost may simultaneously be direct and indirect. As you have just seen, a supervisor's salary can be both direct (with respect to his or her department) and indirect (with respect to the department's individual products or services).

Categories of Manufacturing Costs

Any raw material, labor, or other input used by any organization could, in theory, be identified as a direct or indirect cost, depending on the cost objective. In manufacturing operations, which transform materials into other goods through the use of labor and factory facilities, products are frequently the cost objective. As a result, manufacturing costs are most often divided into three major categories: (1) direct materials, (2) direct labor, and (3) factory overhead.

1. **Direct-material costs** include the acquisition costs of all materials that are physically identified as a part of the manufactured goods and that may be traced to the manufactured goods in an economically feasible way. Examples are iron castings, lumber, aluminum sheets, and subassemblies. Direct materials often do not include minor items such as tacks or glue because the costs of tracing these items are greater than the possible benefits of having more precise product costs. Such items are usually called *supplies* or *indirect materials,* which are classified as a part of the factory overhead described in this list.

2. **Direct-labor costs** include the wages of all labor that can be traced specifically and exclusively to the manufactured goods in an economically feasible way. Examples are the wages of machine operators and assemblers. Much labor, such as that of janitors, forklift truck operators, plant guards, and storeroom clerks, is considered to be indirect labor because it is impossible or economically infeasible to trace such activity to specific products. Such indirect labor is classified as a part of factory overhead. In highly automated factories, there may be no direct labor costs. Why? Because it may be economically infeasible to physically trace any labor cost directly to specific products.

3. **Factory-overhead costs** include all costs associated with the manufacturing process that are not classified as direct material or direct labor. Other terms used to describe this category are **factory burden** and **manufacturing overhead.** Examples are power, supplies, indirect labor, supervisory salaries, property taxes, rent, insurance, and depreciation.

In traditional accounting systems, all manufacturing overhead costs are considered to be indirect. However, computers have allowed modern systems to physically trace many overhead costs to products in an economically feasible manner. For example, meters wired to computers can monitor the electricity used to produce each product, and costs of setting up a batch production run can be traced to the items produced in the run. In general, the more overhead costs that can be traced directly to products, the more accurate the product cost.

Prime Costs, Conversion Costs, and Direct-Labor Costs

Exhibit 5-2 shows that direct labor is sometimes combined with one of the other types of manufacturing costs. The combined categories are **prime costs**—direct labor plus direct materials—or **conversion costs**—direct labor plus factory overhead.

The twofold categorization, direct materials and conversion costs, has replaced the threefold categorization, direct materials, direct labor, and factory overhead, in many modern, automated manufacturing companies. Why? Because direct labor in such a company is a small part of costs and not worth tracing directly to the products. In fact, some companies call their two categories direct materials and factory overhead, and simply include direct labor costs in the factory overhead category.

Exhibit 5-2   Relationships of Key Categories of Manufacturing Costs for
Product-Costing Purposes

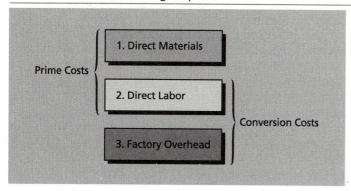

Why so many different systems? As mentioned earlier, accountants and managers weigh the costs and benefits of additional categories when they design their cost accounting systems. When the costs of any single category or item become relatively insignificant, separate tracking may no longer be desirable. For example, in highly automated factories direct labor is often less than 5% of total manufacturing costs. In such cases, it may make economic sense to combine direct-labor costs with one of the other major cost categories. Such is the case at several Hewlett-Packard plants, which collect direct labor as just another subpart of factory overhead.

To recap, the three major categories for manufacturing product costs are direct material, direct labor, and factory overhead. Some companies, however, have only two categories: direct materials and conversion costs. As information technology improves, some companies may have four or more. For instance, a company might have direct materials, direct labor, other direct costs (such as specifically metered power), and factory overhead.

In addition to direct-material, direct-labor, and factory-overhead costs, all manufacturing companies also incur selling and administrative costs. These costs are accumulated by departments such as advertising and sales departments. However, as you will see later in this chapter, most firm's *financial statements* do not allocate these costs to the physical units produced. In short, these costs do not become a part of the reported inventory cost of the manufactured products. To aid in decisions, however, managers often want to know the selling and administrative costs associated with each product. Therefore, *management reports* often include such costs as product costs.

COST ACCOUNTING FOR FINANCIAL REPORTING

Regardless of the type of cost accounting system used, the resulting costs are used in a company's financial statements. This section discusses how financial reporting requirements influence the design of cost accounting systems.

Costs are reported on both the income statement, as cost of goods sold, and the balance sheet, as inventory amounts.

Product Costs and Period Costs

When preparing both income statements and balance sheets, accountants frequently distinguish between *product costs* and *period costs*. **Product costs** are costs identified with goods produced or purchased for resale. Product costs are initially identified as part of the inventory on hand. These product costs (inventoriable costs) become expenses (in the form of *cost of goods sold*) only when the inventory is sold. In contrast, period costs are costs that are deducted as expenses during the current period without going through an inventory stage.

For example, look at the top half of Exhibit 5-3. A merchandising company (retailer or wholesaler) acquires goods for resale without changing their basic form. The only product cost is the purchase cost of the merchandise. Unsold goods are held as mer-

Exhibit 5-3   Relationships of Product Costs and Period Costs

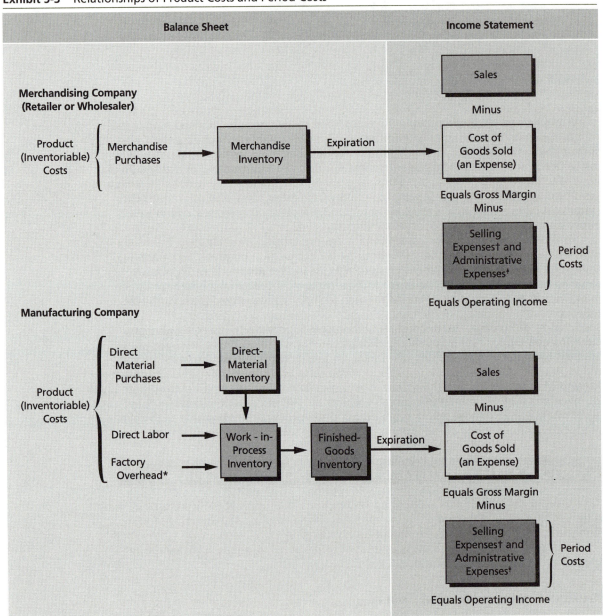

* Examples: indirect labor, factory supplies, insurance, and depreciation on plant.
† Examples: insurance on salespersons' cars, depreciation on salespersons' cars, salespersons's salaries.
‡ Examples: insurance on corporate headquarters building, depreciation on office equipment, clerical salaries.
Note particularly that when insurance and depreciation relate to the manufacturing function, they are inventoriable, but when they relate to selling and administration, they are not inventoriable.

chandise inventory cost and are shown as an asset on a balance sheet. As the goods are sold, their costs become expenses in the form of "cost of goods sold."

A merchandising company also has a variety of selling and administrative expenses. These costs are period costs because they are deducted from revenue as expenses without ever being regarded as a part of inventory.

The bottom half of Exhibit 5-3 illustrates product and period costs in a manufacturing firm. Note that direct materials are transformed into salable form with the help of direct labor and factory overhead. All these costs are product costs because they are allocated to inventory until the goods are sold. As in merchandising accounting, the selling and administrative expenses are not regarded as product costs but are treated as period costs.[1]

Be sure you are clear on the differences between merchandising accounting and manufacturing accounting for such costs as insurance, depreciation, and wages. In merchandising accounting, all such items are period costs (expenses of the current period). In manufacturing accounting, many of these items are related to production activities and thus, as factory overhead, are product costs (become expenses in the form of cost of goods sold as the inventory is sold).

In both merchandising and manufacturing accounting, selling and general administrative costs are period costs. Thus the inventory cost of a manufactured product excludes sales salaries, sales commissions, advertising, legal, public relations, and the president's salary. *Manufacturing overhead* is traditionally regarded as a part of finished-goods inventory cost, whereas *selling* expenses and *general administrative* expenses are not.

Balance Sheet Presentation

Examining both halves of Exhibit 5-3 together, you can see that the balance sheets of manufacturers and merchandisers differ with respect to inventories. The merchandiser's "inventory account" is supplanted in a manufacturing concern by three inventory classes that help managers trace all product costs through the production process to the time of sales.

These classes are:

- *Direct-materials inventory:* Materials on hand and awaiting use in the production process.
- *Work-in-process inventory:* Goods undergoing the production process but not yet fully completed. Costs include appropriate amounts of the three major manufacturing costs (direct material, direct labor, and factory overhead).
- *Finished-goods inventory:* Goods fully completed but not yet sold.

The only essential difference between the structure of the balance sheet of a manufacturer and that of a retailer or wholesaler would appear in their respective current asset sections:

Current Asset Sections of Balance Sheet

Manufacturer			Retailer or Wholesaler	
Cash		$ 4,000	Cash	$ 4,000
Receivables		25,000	Receivables	25,000
Finished goods	$32,000			
Work in process	22,000			
Direct material	23,000			
Total inventories		77,000	Merchandise inventories	77,000
Other current assets		1,000	Other current assets	1,000
Total current assets		$107,000	Total current assets	$107,000

Unit Costs for Product Costing

Reporting cost of goods sold or inventory values requires costs to be assigned to units of product. Assume the following:

Total cost of goods manufactured	$40,000,000
Total units manufactured	10,000,000
Unit cost of product for inventory purposes ($40,000,000 ÷ 10,000,000)	$ 4

If some of the 10 million units manufactured are still unsold at the end of the period, a part of the $40 million cost of goods manufactured will be "held back" as a cost of the ending inventory of finished goods (and shown as an asset on a balance sheet). The remainder becomes "cost of goods sold" for the current period and is shown as an expense on the income statement.

Costs and Income Statements

In income statements, the detailed reporting of selling and administrative expenses is typically the same for manufacturing and merchandising organizations, but the cost of goods sold is different:

Manufacturer	**Retailer or Wholesaler**
Manufacturing cost of goods produced and then sold, usually composed of the three major categories of cost: direct materials, direct labor, and factory overhead.	Merchandise cost of goods sold, usually composed of the purchase cost of items, including freight in, that are acquired and then resold.

Consider the additional details as they are presented in the model income statement of a manufacturing company in Exhibit 5-4. The $40 million cost of goods manufactured is subdivided into the major components of direct materials, direct labor, and factory overhead. In contrast, a wholesale or retail company would replace the entire "cost-of-goods-manufactured" section with a single line, "cost of goods purchased."

The terms "costs" and "expenses" are often used loosely by accountants and managers. "Expenses" denotes all costs deducted from (matched against) revenue in a given period. On the other hand, "costs" is a much broader term and is used to describe both an asset (the cost of inventory) and an expense (the cost of goods sold). Thus, manufacturing costs are funneled into an income statement as an expense (in the form of cost of goods sold) via the multistep inventory procedure shown earlier in Exhibit 5-3. In contrast, selling and general administrative costs are commonly deemed expenses immediately as they are incurred.

Transactions Affecting Inventories

The three manufacturing inventory accounts are affected by the following transactions:

- Direct Materials Inventory
  Increased by purchases of direct materials
  Decreased by use of direct materials
- Work-in-Process Inventory
  Increased by use of direct materials, direct labor, or factory overhead
  Decreased by transfer of completed goods to finished-goods inventory

Exhibit 5-4 Model Income Statement, Manufacturing Company

Sales (8,000,000 units @ $10)			$80,000,000
Cost of goods manufactured and sold			
Beginning finished-goods inventory			$ –0–
Cost of goods manufactured			
Direct materials used	$20,000,000		
Direct labor	12,000,000		
Factory overhead	8,000,000	40,000,000	
Cost of goods available for sale		$40,000,000	
Ending finished-goods inventory,			
2,000,000 units @ $4		8,000,000	
Cost of goods sold (an expense)			32,000,000
Gross margin or gross profit			$48,000,000
Less: other expenses			
Selling costs (an expense)		$30,000,000	
General and administrative costs			
(an expense)		8,000,000	38,000,000
Operating income*			**$10,000,000**

*Also net income in this example because other expenses such as interest and income taxes are ignored here for simplicity.

- Finished-Goods Inventory
  Increased by transfers of completed goods from work-in-process inventory
  Decreased by the amount of cost of goods sold at time of sale

Direct labor and factory overhead are used at the same time they are acquired. Therefore, they are entered directly into work-in-process inventory and have no separate inventory account. In contrast, direct materials are often purchased in advance of their use and held in inventory for some time.

Exhibit 5-5 traces the effects of each transaction. It uses the dollar amounts from Exhibit 5-4, with one exception. Purchases of direct materials totaled $30 million, with $20 million used in production (as shown in Exhibit 5-4) and $10 million left in inventory at the end of the period. As the bottom of Exhibit 5-5 indicates, the ending balance sheet amounts would be:

Direct-material inventory $10,000,000	
Work-in-process inventory	0
Finished-goods inventory	8,000,000
Total inventories	$18,000,000

Cost Behavior and Income Statements

In addition to differences between manufacturing and merchandising firms, manufacturers differ among themselves in accounting for costs on income statements, with some favoring an *absorption* approach and others using a *contribution* approach. To highlight the different effects of these approaches, we will assume that in 19X2 the Samson Company has direct-material costs of $7 million and direct-labor costs of $4 million. Assume also that the company incurred the factory overhead illustrated in Exhibit 5-6 and the selling and administrative expenses illustrated in Exhibit 5-7. Total sales were $20 million. Finally, assume that the units produced are equal to the units sold. That is, there is no change in inventory levels.

Note that Exhibits 5-6 and 5-7 subdivide costs as variable or fixed. Many companies do not make such subdivisions in their income statements. Furthermore, when such subdivisions are made, sometimes arbitrary decisions are necessary as to whether a

Exhibit 5-5   Inventory Transactions (in millions)

Inventory	Direct Materials Transaction	Work-in-Process Inventory	Finished-Goods Inventory
Beginning balance	$ 0	$ 0	$ 0
Purchase direct materials	+30	—	—
Use direct materials	−20	+20	—
Acquire and use direct labor	—	+12	—
Acquire and use factory overhead	—	+8	—
Complete production	—	−40	+40
Sell goods and record cost of goods sold	—	—	$−32
Ending balance	$ 10	$ 0	$ 8

Exhibit 5-6   Samson Company Schedules of Factory Overhead (Product Costs) for the Year Ended December 31, 19X2 (thousands of dollars)

Schedule 1: Variable Costs

Supplies (lubricants, expendable tools, coolants, sandpaper)	$ 150	
Material-handling labor (forklift operators)	700	
Repairs	100	
Power	50	$1,000

Schedule 2: Fixed Costs

Managers' salaries	$ 200	
Employee training	90	
Factory picnic and holiday party	10	
Supervisory salaries	700	
Depreciation, plant and equipment	1,800	
Property taxes	150	
Insurance	50	3,000
Total manufacturing overhead		$4,000

given cost is variable, fixed, or partially fixed (for example, repairs). Nevertheless, to aid decision making, many companies are attempting to report the extent to which their costs are approximately variable or fixed.

Absorption Approach

Exhibit 5-8 presents Samson's income statement using the **absorption approach** *(absorption costing)*, the approach used by most companies. Firms that take this approach consider all factory overhead (both variable and fixed) to be product (inventoriable) costs that become an expense in the form of manufacturing cost of goods sold only as sales occur.

Note in Exhibit 5-8 that gross profit or gross margin is the difference between sales and the *manufacturing* cost of goods sold. Note too that the *primary classifications* of costs on the income statement are by three major management *functions:* manufacturing, selling, and administrative.

Exhibit 5-7 Samson Company Schedules of Selling and Administrative Expenses (Period Costs) for the Year Ended December 31, 19X2 (thousands of dollars)

Schedule 3: Selling Expenses

Variable		
Sales commissions	$ 700	
Shipping expenses for products sold	300	$1,000
Fixed		
Advertising	$ 700	
Sales salaries	1,000	
Other	300	2,000
Total selling expenses		**$3,000**

Schedule 4: Administrative Expenses

Variable		
Some clerical wages	$ 80	
Computer time rented	20	$ 100
Fixed		
Office salaries	$ 100	
Other salaries	200	
Depreciation on office facilities	100	
Public-accounting fees	40	
Legal fees	100	
Other	360	900
Total administrative expenses		**$1,000**

Exhibit 5-8 Samson Company Absorption Income Statement for the Year Ended December 31, 19X2 (thousands of dollars)

Sales		$20,000
Less: manufacturing costs of goods sold		
Direct material	$7,000	
Direct labor	4,000	
Factory overhead (Schedules 1 plus 2)*	4,000	15,000
Gross margin or gross profit		$ 5,000
Selling expenses (Schedule 3)	$3,000	
Administrative expenses (Schedule 4)	1,000	
Total selling and administrative expenses		4,000
Operating income		$ 1,000

* Note: Schedules I and 2 are in Exhibit 5-6. Schedules 3 and 4 are in Exhibit 5-7.

Contribution Approach

In contrast, Exhibit 5-9 presents Samson's income statement using the **contribution approach** (*variable costing* or *direct costing*). The contribution approach is not allowed for external financial reporting. However, many companies use this approach for internal (management accounting) purposes and an absorption format for external purposes because they expect the benefits of making better decisions to exceed the extra costs of using different reporting systems simultaneously.

For decision purposes, the major difference between the contribution approach and the absorption approach is that the former emphasizes the distinction between variable and fixed costs. Its primary classifications of costs are by *variable and fixed cost behavior patterns,* not by *business functions.*

Exhibit 5-9 Samson Company Contribution Income Statement for the Year Ended December 31, 19X2 (thousands of dollars)

Sales		$20,000
Less: variable expenses		
Direct material	$ 7,000	
Direct labor	4,000	
Variable indirect manufacturing costs (Schedule 1)*	1,000	
Total variable manufacturing cost of goods sold	$12,000	
Variable selling expenses (Schedule 3)	1,000	
Variable administrative expenses (Schedule 4)	100	
Total variable expenses		13,100
Contribution margin		$ 6,900
Less: fixed expenses		
Manufacturing (Schedule 2)	$ 3,000	
Selling (Schedule 3)	2,000	
Administrative (Schedule 4)	900	5,900
Operating income		$ 1,000

* Note: Schedules I and 2 are in Exhibit 5-6. Schedules 3 and 4 are in Exhibit 5-7.

The contribution income statement provides a *contribution margin,* which is computed after deducting from revenue all variable costs including variable selling and administrative costs. This approach makes it easier to understand the impact of changes in sales demand on operating income.

The contribution approach stresses the lump-sum amount of fixed costs to be recouped before net income emerges. This highlighting of total fixed costs focuses management attention on fixed-cost behavior and control in making both short-run and long-run plans. Remember that advocates of the contribution approach do not maintain that fixed costs are unimportant or irrelevant. They do stress, however, that the distinctions between behaviors of variable and fixed costs are crucial for certain decisions.

The difference between the gross margin (from the absorption approach) and the contribution margin (from the contribution approach) is striking in manufacturing companies. Why? Because fixed manufacturing costs are regarded as a part of cost of goods sold, and these fixed costs reduce the gross margin accordingly. However, fixed manufacturing costs do not reduce the contribution margin, which is affected solely by revenues and *variable* costs.

The implications of the *absorption approach* and the *contribution approach* for decision making are discussed in the next chapter.

ACTIVITY-BASED ACCOUNTING, VALUE-ADDED COSTING, AND JUST-IN-TIME PRODUCTION

In the past decade, many companies in the United States, struggling to keep up with competitors from Japan, Germany, and other countries, adopted new management philosophies and developed new production technologies. In many cases, these changes prompted corresponding changes in accounting systems.

For example, Borg-Warner's Automotive Chain Systems Operation transformed its manufacturing operation to a just-in-time manufacturing system with work cells. This change in the way manufacturing was done made the traditional accounting system obsolete. A new cost accounting system coupled with the new production systems "improved the overall reporting, controls, and efficiency dramatically."[2]

Activity-Based Accounting

The primary focus of the changes in operations and accounting has been an increased attention to the cost of the *activities* undertaken to design, produce, sell, and deliver a company's products or services. **Activity-based accounting (ABA)** or **activity-based costing (ABC)** systems first accumulate overhead costs for each of the *activities* of an organization and then assign the costs of activities to the products, services, or other cost objects that caused that activity.

Consider the Salem manufacturing plant of a major appliance producer. Exhibit 5-10 contrasts the traditional costing system with an ABC system. In the traditional cost system, the portion of total *overhead* allocated to a product depends on the proportion of *total direct-labor-hours* consumed in making the product. In the ABC system, significant overhead activities (machining, assembly, quality inspection, etc.) and related resources are separately identified and traced to products using cost drivers—machine hours, number of parts, number of inspections, etc. In the ABC system, the amount of overhead costs allocated to a product depends on the proportion of total machine hours, total parts, total inspections, and so on, consumed in making the product. One large overhead cost pool has been broken into several pools, each associated with a key activity. We now consider a more in-depth illustration of the design of an ABC system.

Illustration of Activity-Based Costing[3]

Consider the Billing Department at Portland Power Company (PPC), an electric utility. The Billing Department (BD) at PPC provides account inquiry and bill printing services for two major classes of customers—residential and commercial. Currently, the BD services 120,000 residential and 20,000 commercial customer accounts.

Two factors are having a significant impact on PPC's profitability. First, deregulation of the power industry has led to increased competition and lower rates, so PPC must find ways of reducing its operating costs. Second, the demand for power in PPC's area will increase due to the addition of a large housing development and a shopping center. The marketing department estimates that residential demand will increase by almost 50% and commercial demand will increase by 10% during the next year. Since the BD is currently operating at full capacity, it needs to find ways to create capacity to service the expected increase in demand. A local service bureau has offered to take over the BD functions at an attractive lower cost (compared to the current cost). The service bureau's proposal is to provide all the functions of the BD at $3.50 per account regardless of the type of account.

Exhibit 5-11 depicts the residential and commercial customer classes (cost objects) and the resources used to support the BD. The costs associated with the BD are all indirect—they cannot be identified specifically and exclusively with either customer class in an economically feasible way. The BD used a traditional costing system that allocated all support costs based on the number of account inquiries of the two customer classes. Exhibit 5-11 shows that the cost of the resources used in the BD last month was $565,340. BD received 23,000 account inquiries during the month, so the cost per inquiry was $565,340 ÷ 23,000 = $24.58. There were 18,000 residential account inquiries, 78.26% of the total. Thus, residential accounts were charged with 78.26% of the support costs while commercial accounts were charged with 21.74%. The resulting cost per account is $3.69 and $6.15 for residential and commercial accounts, respectively.

Management believed that the actual consumption of support resources was much greater than 22% for commercial accounts because of their complexity. For example, commercial accounts average 50 lines per bill compared with only 12 for residential accounts. Management was also concerned about activities such as correspondence (and supporting labor) resulting from customer inquiries because these activities are costly but do not add value to PPC's services from the customer's perspective. However, management wanted a more thorough understanding of key BD activities and their

Exhibit 5-10   Traditional and Activity-Based Cost Systems

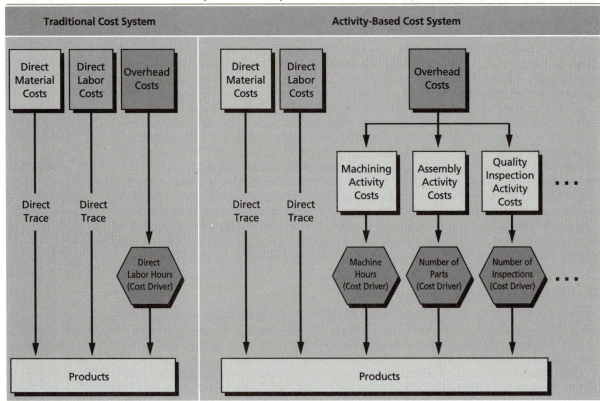

interrelationships before making important decisions that would impact PPC's profitability. The company decided to perform a study of the BD using activity-based costing. The following is a description of the study and its results.

The activity-based-costing study was performed by a team of managers from the BD and the chief financial officer from PPC. The team followed a four-step procedure to conduct the study.

Step 1: Determine cost objectives, key activities centers, resources, and related cost drivers. Management had set the objective for the study—determine the BD cost per account for each customer class. The team identified the following activities and related cost drivers for the BD through interviews with appropriate personnel.

Activity Centers	Cost Drivers
Account billing	Number of lines
Bill verification	Number of accounts
Account inquiry	Number of labor hours
Correspondence	Number of letters

The four key BD activity centers are *account billing, bill verification, account inquiry,* and *correspondence.* The resources shown in Exhibit 5-11 support these major activity centers. Cost drivers were selected based on two criteria:

1. There had to be a reasonable cause-effect relationship between the driver unit and the consumption of resources and/or the occurrence of supporting activities.
2. Data on the cost-driver units had to be available.

Exhibit 5-11 Current (Traditional) Costing System: Portland Power—
Billing Department

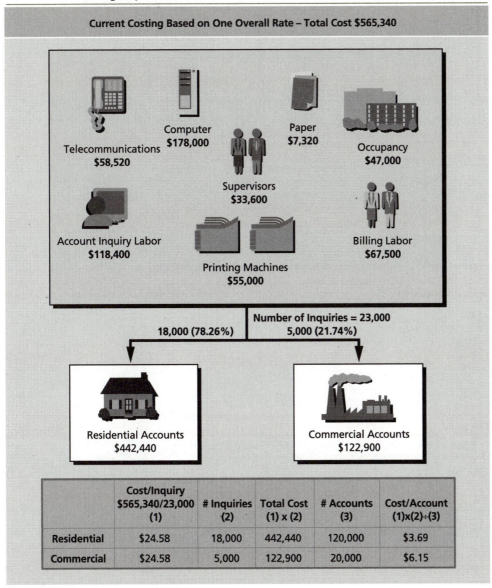

Current Costing Based on One Overall Rate – Total Cost $565,340

Telecommunications
$58,520

Computer
$178,000

Paper
$7,320

Occupancy
$47,000

Supervisors
$33,600

Account Inquiry Labor
$118,400

Printing Machines
$55,000

Billing Labor
$67,500

Number of Inquiries = 23,000

18,000 (78.26%)   5,000 (21.74%)

Residential Accounts
$442,440

Commercial Accounts
$122,900

	Cost/Inquiry $565,340/23,000 (1)	# Inquiries (2)	Total Cost (1) x (2)	# Accounts (3)	Cost/Account (1)x(2)÷(3)
Residential	$24.58	18,000	442,440	120,000	$3.69
Commercial	$24.58	5,000	122,900	20,000	$6.15

Step 2: Develop a process-based map representing the flow of activities, resources, and their interrelationships. An important phase of any activity-based analysis is identifying the interrelationships between key activities and the resources consumed. This is typically done by interviewing key personnel. Once the linkages between activities and resources are identified, a process map is drawn that provides a visual representation of the operations of the BD.

Exhibit 5-12 is a process map that depicts the flow of activities and resources at the BD.[4] Note that there are no costs on Exhibit 5-12. The management team first focused on understanding business processes. Costs were not considered until Step 3, after the key interrelationships of the business were understood.

Exhibit 5-12   Process Map of Billing Department Activities

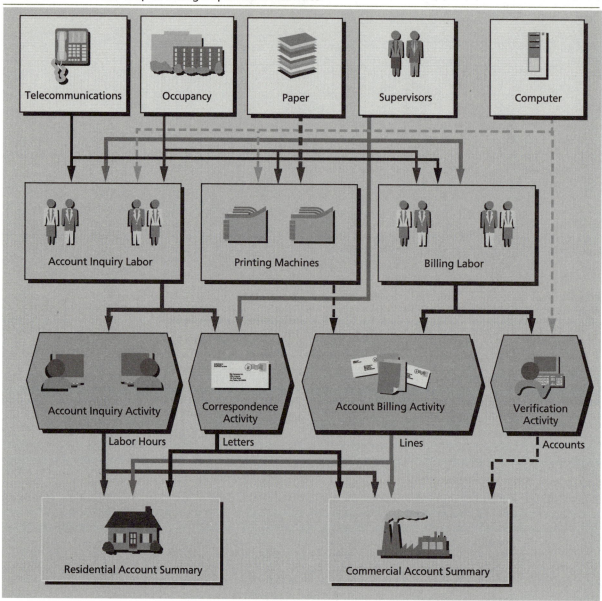

Consider residential accounts. Three key activities support these accounts: account inquiry, correspondence, and account billing. Account inquiry activity consumes account inquiry labor time. Account inquiry laborers, in turn, use telecommunication and computer resources, occupy space, and are supervised. Correspondence is sometimes necessary as a result of inquiries. This activity requires account inquiry laborers who are supervised. The account billing activity is performed by billing laborers using printing machines. The printing machines occupy space and require paper and computer resources. Billing laborers also occupy space, use telecommunications, and are supervised. The costs of each of the resources consumed were determined during Step 3—data collection.

Step 3: Collect relevant data concerning costs and the physical flow of the cost-driver units among resources and activities. Using the process map as a guide, BD accountants collected the required cost and operational data by further interviews with relevant personnel. Sources of data include the accounting records, special studies, and sometimes "best estimates of managers."

Exhibit 5-13 is a graphical representation of the data collected for the four activity centers identified in Step 1. For each activity center, data collected included traceable costs and the physical flow of cost-driver units. For example, Exhibit 5-13 shows traceable costs of $235,777 for the account billing activity. Traceable costs include the costs of the printing machines ($55,000 from Exhibit 5-11) plus portions of the costs of all other resources that support the billing activity (paper, occupancy, computer, and billing labor). Notice that the total traceable costs of $205,332 + $35,384 + $235,777 + $88,847 = $563,340 in Exhibit 5-13 equals the total indirect costs in Exhibit 5-11. Next, the physical flow of cost-driver units was determined for each activity or cost object. For each activity center, the traceable costs were divided by the sum of the physical flows to establish a cost per cost-driver unit.

Step 4: Calculate and interpret the new activity-based information. The activity-based cost per account for each customer class can be determined from the data in Step 3. Exhibit 5-14 shows the computations.

Examine the last two items in Exhibit 5-14. Notice that traditional costing overcosted the high-volume residential accounts and substantially undercosted the low-volume, complex commercial accounts. The cost per account for residential accounts using ABC is $2.28, which is $1.41 (or 38%) less than the $3.69 cost generated by the traditional costing system. The cost per account for commercial accounts is $14.57, which is $8.42 (or 137%) more than the $6.15 cost from the traditional cost system. Management's belief that traditional costing was undercosting commercial accounts was confirmed. PPC's management now has more accurate cost information for planning and decision-making purposes.

These results are common when companies perform activity-based-costing studies—high volume cost objects with simple processes are overcosted when only one volume-based cost-driver is used. In the BD, this volume-based cost-driver was the number of inquiries. Which system makes more sense—the existing allocation system that "spreads" all support costs to customer classes based solely on the number of inquiries, or the activity-based-costing system that identifies key activities and assigns costs based on the consumption of units of cost-drivers chosen for each key activity? For PPC, the probable benefits of the new activity-based-costing system appear to outweigh the costs of implementing and maintaining the new cost system. However, the cost-benefit balance must be assessed on a case-by-case basis.

Summary of Activity-Based Costing

Activity-based accounting systems can turn many indirect manufacturing overhead costs into direct costs, costs identified specifically with given cost objectives. Appropriate selection of activities and cost drivers allows managers to trace many manufacturing overhead costs to cost objectives just as specifically as they have traced direct-material and direct-labor costs. Because activity-based accounting systems classify more costs as direct than do traditional systems, managers have greater confidence in the accuracy of the costs of products and services reported by activity-based systems.

Activity-based accounting systems are more complex and costly than traditional systems, so not all companies use them. But more and more organizations in both manufacturing and nonmanufacturing industries are adopting activity-based systems for a variety of reasons:

- Fierce competitive pressure has resulted in shrinking profit margins. Companies may know their overall margin, but they often do not believe in the accuracy of the

Exhibit 5-13   ABC System: Portland Power Company—Billing Department

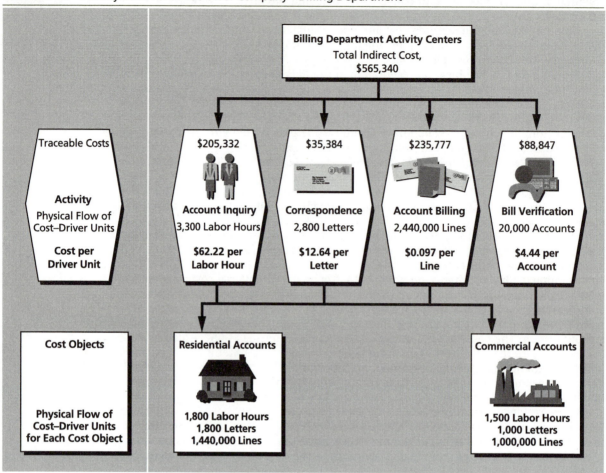

margins for *individual* products or services. Some are winners and some are losers—but which ones? Accurate costs are essential for answering this question.

- Business complexity has increased, which results in greater diversity in the types of products and services as well as customer classes. Therefore, the consumption of a company's shared resources also varies substantially across products and customers.

- New production techniques have increased the proportion of indirect costs—that is, indirect costs are far more important in today's world-class manufacturing environment. In many industries direct labor is being replaced by automated equipment. Indirect costs are sometimes over 50% of total cost.

- The rapid pace of technological change has shortened product life cycles. Hence, companies do not have time to make price or cost adjustments once costing errors are discovered.

- The costs associated with bad decisions that result from inaccurate cost determinations are substantial (bids lost due to overcosted products, hidden losses from undercosted products, failure to detect activities that are not cost effective, etc.). Companies with accurate costs have a huge advantage over those with inaccurate costs.

- Computer technology has reduced the costs of developing and operating cost systems that track many activities.

Figure 5-14 Key Results of Activity-Based-Costing Study

Driver Costs

Activity/Resource (Driver Units)	Traceable Costs (From Exhibit 5-13) (1)	Total Physical Flow of Driver Units (From Exhibit 5-13) (2)	Cost per Driver Unit (1)÷(2)
Account inquiry (labor hours)	$205,332	3,300 Hours	$62.2218
Correspondence (letters)	35,384	2,800 Letters	12.6371
Account billing (lines)	235,777	2,440,000 Lines	0.09663
Bill verification (accounts)	88,847	20,000 Accounts	4.44235

Cost per Customer Class

		Residential		Commercial	
	Cost per Driver Unit	Physical Flow of Driver Units	Cost	Physical Flow of Driver Units	Cost
Account inquiry	$62.2218	1,800 Hrs.	$111,999	1,500 Hrs.	$ 93,333
Correspondence	$12.6371	1,800 Ltrs.	22,747	1,000 Ltrs.	12,637
Account billing	$0.09663	1,440,000 Lines	139,147	1,000,000 Lines	96,630
Bill verification	$4.44235	0	0	20,000 Accts.	88,847
Total cost			$273,893		$291,447
Number of accounts			120,000		20,000
Cost per account			$ 2.28		$ 14.57
Cost per account, traditional system from Exhibit 5-11			$ 3.69		$ 6.15

Cost-Management Systems and Value-Added Costing

To support managers' decisions better, accountants go beyond simply determining the cost of products and services. They develop cost-management systems. A **cost-management system** identifies how management's decisions affect costs. To do so, it first measures the resources used in performing the organization's activities and then assesses the effects on costs of changes in those activities.

The cornerstone of cost management is distinguishing between value-added costs and non-value-added costs. A **value-added cost** is the cost of an activity that cannot be eliminated without affecting a product's value to the customer. Value-added costs are necessary (as long as the activity that drives such costs is performed efficiently). In contrast, companies try to minimize **non-value-added costs**, costs that *can* be eliminated without affecting a product's value to the customer. Activities such as handling and storing inventories, transporting partly finished products from one part of the plant to another, and changing the setup of production-line operations to produce a different model of the product are all non-value-adding activities that can be reduced, if not eliminated, by careful redesign of the plant layout and the production process. Often accounting is regarded as a non-value-adding activity. Although it cannot be eliminated, organizations should be sure that the benefits derived from accounting information exceed the costs.

JIT Systems

Attempts to minimize non-value-added costs have led many organizations to adopt JIT systems to eliminate waste and improve quality. In a **just-in-time (JIT) production system**, an organization purchases materials and parts and produces components just when they are needed in the production process. Goods are not produced until it is time for them to be shipped to a customer. The goal is to have zero inventory because holding inventory is a non-value-added activity.

JIT companies are customer-oriented because customer orders drive the production process. An order triggers the immediate delivery of materials, followed by production and delivery of the goods. Instead of producing inventory and hoping an order will come, a JIT system produces products directly for received orders. Several factors are crucial to the success of JIT systems:

1. *Focus on quality:* JIT companies try to involve all employees in controlling quality. Although any system can seek quality improvements, JIT systems emphasize total quality control (TQC) and continuous improvement in quality. Having all employees striving for zero defects minimizes non-value-added activities such as inspection and rework for defective items.

2. *Short **production cycle times**, the time from initiating production to delivering the goods to the customer:* Keeping production cycle times short allows timely response to customer orders and reduces the level of inventories. Many JIT companies have achieved remarkable reductions in production cycle times. For example, applying JIT methods in one AT&T division cut production cycle time by a factor of 12.

3. *Smooth flow of production:* Fluctuations in production rates inevitably lead to delays in delivery to customers and excess inventories. To achieve smooth production flow, JIT companies simplify the production process to reduce the possibilities of delay, develop close relationships with suppliers to assure timely delivery and high quality of purchased materials, and perform routine maintenance on equipment to prevent costly breakdowns.

Many companies help achieve these objectives by improving the physical layout of their plants. In conventional manufacturing, similar machines (lathes, molding machines, drilling machines, etc.) are grouped together. Workers specialize in only one machine operation (operating either the molding or the drilling machine). There are at least two negative effects of such a layout. First, products must be moved from one area of the plant to another for required processing. This increases material handling costs and results in work-in-process inventories that can be substantial. These are non-value-added activities and costs. Second, the specialized labor resource is often idle—waiting for work-in-process. This wasted resource—labor time—is also non-value-added.

In a JIT production system, machines are often organized in cells according to the specific requirements of a product family. This is called **cellular manufacturing**. Only the machines that are needed for the product family are in the cell, and these machines are located as close to each other as possible. Workers are trained to use all the cellular machines. Each cell (often shaped in the form of a "U") is a mini-factory or focused factory. Many problems associated with the conventional production layout are eliminated in cellular manufacturing. Work-in-process inventories are reduced or eliminated because there is no need for moving and storing inventory. Idle time is reduced or eliminated because workers are capable of moving from idle machine activity to needed activities. As a result, cycle times are reduced.

4. *Flexible production operations:* Two dimensions are important: facilities flexibility and employee flexibility. Facilities should be able to produce a variety of components and products to provide extra capacity when a particular product is in high demand and to avoid shut-down when a unique facility breaks down. Facilities should also require

short setup times, the time it takes to switch from producing one product to another. Cross-training employees—training employees to do a variety of jobs—provides further flexibility. Multiskilled workers can fill in when a particular operation is overloaded and can reduce setup time. One company reported a reduction in setup time from 45 minutes to 1 minute by training production workers to perform the setup operations.

Accounting for a JIT system is often simpler than for other systems. Most cost accounting systems focus on determining product costs for inventory valuation. But JIT systems have minimal inventories, so there is less benefit from an elaborate inventory costing system. In true JIT systems, material, labor, and overhead costs can be charged directly to cost of goods sold because inventories are small enough to be ignored. All costs of production are assumed to apply to products that have already been sold.

SUMMARY

Many new terms were introduced in this chapter. Review these terms to make sure you know their exact meaning. Basic terms, such as cost, cost objective, cost accumulation, and cost allocation are especially important.

A major feature of costs for both manufacturing and nonmanufacturing organizations is whether the costs have a direct or an indirect relationship to cost objectives such as a department or product. Manufacturing costs (direct material, direct labor, and factory overhead) are traditionally regarded as product costs (inventoriable costs). In contrast, selling and administrative costs are period costs; hence, they are typically deducted from revenue as expenses in the period incurred.

Financial statements for manufacturers differ from those of merchandisers. Costs such as utilities, wages, and depreciation, which are treated as period costs by a merchandising company, are product costs (part of factory overhead) for a manufacturing company if they are related to the manufacturing process. Balance sheets of manufacturers may include three inventory accounts: direct materials, work in process, and finished goods.

The contribution approach to preparing an income statement emphasizes the distinction between fixed and variable costs and is a natural extension of the CVP analysis used in decisions. In contrast, the absorption approach emphasizes the distinction between manufacturing costs and selling and administrative costs.

Activity-based costing (ABC) and just-in-time (JIT) production systems are two approaches used by modern companies to improve their competitiveness. The focus of activity-based costing is on more accurate product or service costing. Management can then use ABC information to manage costs better. To manage costs, they try to eliminate non-value-added activities. The JIT approach focuses on improving operating efficiencies by reducing waste. JIT and ABC can be used separately or together—many modern companies use both.

SELF-CORRECTION PROBLEMS

1. Review the illustrations in Exhibits 5-6 through 5-9. Suppose that all variable costs fluctuate in direct proportion to units produced and sold, and that all fixed costs are unaffected over a wide range of production and sales. What would operating income have been if sales (at normal selling prices) had been $20.9 million instead of $20.0 million? Which statement, the absorption income statement or the contribution income statement, did you use as a framework for your answer? Why?

2. Suppose employee training (Exhibit 5-6) was regarded as a variable rather than a fixed cost at a rate of $90,000 ÷ 1,000,000 units, or $.09 per unit. How would your answer in question 1 change?

1. Operating income would increase from $1,000,000 to $1,310,500, computed as follows:

Increase in revenue	**$ 900,000**
Increase in total contribution margin:	
Contribution-margin ratio in contribution income statement	
(Exhibit 5–9) is $6,900,000 ÷ $20,000,000 = .345	
Ratio times revenue increase is .345 × $900,000	$ 310,500
Increase in fixed expenses	–0–
Operating income before increase	1,000,000
New operating income	**$1,310,500**

   Computations are easily made by using data from the contribution income statement. In contrast, the traditional absorption costing income statement must be analyzed and divided into variable and fixed categories before the effect on operating income can be estimated.

2. The original contribution-margin ratio would be lower because the variable costs would be higher by $.09 per unit: ($6,900,000 - $90,000) ÷ $20,000,000 = .3405.

	Given Level	Higher Level	Difference
Revenue	$20,000,000	$20,900,000	$900,000
Variable expense ($13,100,000 + $90,000)	13,190,000	13,783,550	593,550
Contribution margin at .3405	$ 6,810,000	$ 7,116,450	$306,450
Fixed expenses ($5,900,000 – $90,000)	5,810,000	5,810,000	—
Operating income	$ 1,000,000	$1,306,450	$306,450

QUESTIONS

1. Name four cost objectives or cost objects.
2. "Departments are not cost objects or objects of costing." Do you agree? Explain.
3. What is the major purpose of detailed cost-accounting systems?
4. "The same cost can be direct and indirect." Do you agree? Explain.
5. "Economic feasibility is an important guideline in designing cost-accounting systems." Do you agree? Explain.
6. How does the idea of economic feasibility relate to the distinction between direct and indirect costs?
7. "The typical accounting system does not allocate selling and administrative costs to units produced." Do you agree? Explain.
8. Distinguish between prime costs and conversion costs.
9. "For a furniture manufacturer, glue or tacks become an integral part of the finished product, so they would be direct material." Do you agree? Explain.
10. Many cost-accounting systems have a twofold instead of a threefold category of manufacturing costs. What are the items in the twofold category?
11. "Depreciation is an expense for financial statement purposes." Do you agree? Explain.
12. Distinguish between "costs" and "expenses."
13. "Unexpired costs are always inventory costs." Do you agree? Explain.
14. "Advertising is noninventoriable." Explain.

15. Why is there no direct-labor inventory account on a manufacturing company's balance sheet?

16. What is the advantage of the contribution approach as compared with the absorption approach?

17. Distinguish between manufacturing and merchandising companies.

18. "The primary classifications of costs are by variable- and fixed-cost behavior patterns, not by business functions." Name three commonly used terms that describe this type of income statement.

19. Name four steps in the design and implementation of an activity-based-costing system.

20. Refer to the Portland Power Company illustration in Exhibit 5-11. Which BD resource costs depicted in Exhibit 5-11 would have variable cost behavior?

21. Why are more and more organizations adopting activity-based-costing systems?

22. Why do managers want to distinguish between value-added activities and non-value-added activities?

23. Name four factors crucial to the success of JIT production systems.

24. "ABC and JIT are alternative techniques for achieving competitiveness." Do you agree?

PROBLEMS

1. **Straightforward Income Statement.** The Goldsmith Company had the following manufacturing data for the year 19X6 (in thousands of dollars):

Beginning and ending inventories	None
Direct material used	$425
Direct labor	350
Supplies	20
Utilities—variable portion	45
Utilities—fixed portion	15
Indirect labor—variable portion	100
Indirect labor—fixed portion	50
Depreciation	110
Property taxes	20
Supervisory salaries	50

Selling expenses were $325,000 (including $70,000 that were variable) and general administrative expenses were $148,000 (including $24,000 that were variable). Sales were $1.9 million.

Direct labor and supplies are regarded as variable costs.

a. Prepare two income statements, one using the contribution approach and one using the absorption approach.

b. Suppose that all variable costs fluctuate directly in proportion to sales, and that fixed costs are unaffected over a very wide range of sales. What would operating income have been if sales had been $2.2 million instead of $1.9 million? Which income statement did you use to help obtain your answer? Why?

2. **Meaning of Technical Terms.** Refer to the absorption income statement of your solution to the preceding problem. Give the amounts of the following: (a) prime cost, (b) conversion cost, (c) factory burden, (d) factory overhead, and (e) manufacturing overhead.

3. **Activity-Based Costing.** Quality Machining Products (QMP) is an automotive component supplier. QMP has been approached by General Motors to consider expanding its production of part G108 to a total annual quantity of 2,000 units. This part is a low-volume, complex product with a high gross margin that is based on a proposed (quoted) unit sales price of $7.50. QMP uses a traditional costing system that allocates factory-overhead costs based on direct-labor costs. The rate currently used to allocate factory-overhead costs is 400% of direct-labor cost. This rate is based on the $3,300,000 annual factory overhead divided by $825,000 annual direct-labor cost. To produce 2,000 units of G108 requires $5,000 of direct materials and $1,000 of direct labor. The unit cost and gross margin percentage for part G108 based on the traditional cost system are computed as follows:

	Total	Per Unit (÷ 2,000)
Direct material	$5,000	$2.50
Direct labor	1,000	.50
Factory overhead:		
[400% × direct labor]	4,000	2.00
Total cost	$10,000	$5.00
Sales price quoted		7.50
Gross margin		$2.50
Gross margin percentage		33.3%

The management of QMP decided to examine the effectiveness of their traditional costing system versus an activity-based-costing system. The following data have been collected by a team consisting of accounting and engineering analysts:

Activity Center	Traceable Factory Overhead Costs (Annual)
Quality	$ 800,000
Production scheduling	50,000
Setup	600,000
Shipping	300,000
Shipping administration	50,000
Production	1,500,000
Total factory overhead cost	$3,300,000

Activity Center: Cost Drivers	Annual Cost-Driver Quantity
Quality: number of pieces scrapped	10,000
Production scheduling and setup:	
number of setups	500
Shipping: number of containers shipped	60,000
Shipping administration: number of shipments	1,000
Production: number of machine hours	10,000

The accounting and engineering team has performed activity analysis and provides the following estimates for the total quantity of cost drivers to be used to produce 2,000 units of part G108:

Cost Driver	Cost-Driver Consumption
Pieces scrapped	120
Setups	4
Containers shipped	10
Shipments	5
Machine hours	15

a. Prepare a schedule calculating the unit cost and gross margin of part G108 using the activity-based-costing approach.

b. Based on the ABC results, which course of action would you recommend regarding the proposal by General Motors? List the benefits and costs associated with implementing an activity-based-costing system at QMP.

4. **Contribution and Absorption Income Statements.** The following information is taken from the records of the Queensland Company for the year ending December 31, 19X5. There were no beginning or ending inventories.

Sales	$11,000,000	Long-term rent, factory	$ 110,000
Sales commissions	550,000	Factory superintendent's	
Advertising	225,000	salary	32,000
Shipping expenses	310,000	Supervisors' salaries	105,000
Administrative executive		Direct material used	4,100,000
salaries	100,000	Direct labor	2,200,000
Administrative clerical		Cutting bits used	60,000
salaries (variable)	450,000	Factory methods research	40,000
Fire insurance on		Abrasives for machining	100,000
factory equipment	2,000	Indirect labor	810,000
Property taxes on		Depreciation on	
factory equipment	10,000	equipment	300,000

a. Prepare a contribution income statement and an absorption income statement. If you are in doubt about any cost behavior pattern, decide on the basis of whether the total cost in question will fluctuate substantially over a wide range of volume. Prepare a separate supporting schedule of indirect manufacturing costs subdivided between variable and fixed costs.

b. Suppose that all variable costs fluctuate directly in proportion to sales and that fixed costs are unaffected over a wide range of sales. What would operating income have been if sales had been $12.5 million instead of $11 million? Which income statement did you use to help get your answer? Why?

5. **JIT and Non-Value-Added Activities.** A motorcycle manufacturer was concerned with declining market share because of foreign competition. To become more efficient, the company was considering changing to a JIT production system. As a first step in analyzing the feasibility of the change, the company identified its major activities. Among the 120 activities were the following:

Materials receiving and inspection
Production scheduling

Production setup

Rear-wheel assembly

Movement of engine from fabrication to assembly building

Assembly of handlebars

Paint inspection

Reworking of defective brake assemblies

Installation of speedometer

Placement of completed motorcycle in finished goods storage

a. From the preceding list of 10 activities, prepare two lists: one of value-added activities and one of non-value-added activities.

b. For each non-value-added activity, explain how a JIT production system might eliminate, or at least reduce, the cost of the activity.

6. **Activity-Based Costing.** The cordless phone manufacturing division of a consumer electronics company uses activity-based accounting. For simplicity, assume that its accountants have identified only the following three activities and related cost drivers for manufacturing overhead:

Activity	Cost Driver
Materials handling	Direct-materials cost
Engineering	Engineering change notices
Power	Kilowatt hours

Three types of cordless phones are produced: CL3, CL5, and CL9. Direct costs and cost-driver activity for each product for a recent month are as follows:

	CL3	CL5	CL9
Direct-materials cost	$25,000	$ 50,000	$125,000
Direct-labor cost	$4,000	$1,000	$3,000
Kilowatt hours	50,000	200,000	150,000
Engineering change notices	13	5	2

Manufacturing overhead for the month was:

Materials handling	$10,000
Engineering	30,000
Power	24,000
Total manufacturing overhead	$64,000

a. Compute the manufacturing overhead allocated to each product with the activity-based accounting system.

b. Suppose all manufacturing overhead costs had been allocated to products in proportion to their direct-labor costs. Compute the manufacturing overhead allocated to each product.

c. In which product costs, those in part a or those in part b, do you have the most confidence? Why?

ADDENDUM 5: MORE ON LABOR COSTS

Classifications of Labor Costs

The terms used to classify labor costs are often confusing. Each organization seems to develop its own interpretation of various labor-cost classifications. We begin by considering some commonly encountered labor-cost terms:

- Direct labor (already defined)
- Factory overhead (examples of prominent labor components of these indirect manufacturing costs follow)
  - Indirect labor (wages)
    - Forklift truck operators (internal handling of materials)
    - Maintenance (to set up for production runs)
    - Janitors
    - Expediting (overseeing special orders, usually on a rush basis)
    - Plant guards
    - Rework labor (time spent by direct laborers redoing defective work)
    - Overtime premium paid to all factory workers
    - Idle time
  - Managers' salaries
  - Payroll fringe costs (for example, health care premiums, pension costs)

All factory labor wages, other than those for direct labor and manager salaries, are usually classified as **indirect labor** costs, a major component of factory overhead. The term *indirect labor* is usually divided into many subsidiary classifications. The wages of forklift truck operators are generally not commingled with janitors' salaries, for example, although both are regarded as indirect labor.

Costs are classified in a detailed fashion primarily to associate a specific cost with its specific cost driver. Two classes of indirect labor deserve special mention: overtime premium and idle time.

Overtime premium paid to all factory workers is usually considered a part of overhead. If a lathe operator earns $8 per hour for straight time and time and one-half for overtime, the premium is $4 per overtime hour. If the operator works 44 hours, including 4 overtime hours, in one week, the gross earnings are classified as follows:

Direct labor: 44 hours × $8	$352
Overtime premium (factory overhead): 4 hours × $4	16
Total earnings for 44 hours	**$368**

Why is overtime premium considered an indirect cost rather than direct? After all, it can usually be traced to specific batches of work. It is usually not considered a direct charge because the scheduling of production jobs is generally random. Suppose that at 8:00 A.M. you bring your automobile to a shop for repair. Through random scheduling, your auto is repaired between 5:00 and 6:00 P.M., when technicians receive overtime pay. Then, when you come to get your car, you learn that all the overtime premium had been added to your bill. You probably would not be overjoyed.

Thus, in most companies, the overtime premium is not allocated to any specific job. Instead, the overtime premium is considered to be attributable to the heavy overall volume of work, and its cost is thus regarded as part of the indirect manufacturing costs (factory overhead). The latter approach does not penalize a particular batch of work solely because it happened to be worked on during the overtime hours.

Another subsidiary classification of indirect-labor costs is **idle time.** This cost typically represents wages paid for unproductive time caused by machine breakdowns, material shortages, sloppy production scheduling, and the like. For example, if the same lathe operator's machine broke down for 3 hours during the week, the operator's earnings would be classified as follows:

Direct labor: 41 hours × $8	$328
Overtime premium (factory overhead): 4 hours × $4	16
Idle time (factory overhead): 3 hours × $8	24
Total earnings for 44 hours	**$368**

Manager salaries usually are not classified as a part of indirect labor. Instead, the compensation of supervisors, department heads, and all others who are regarded as part of manufacturing management are placed in a separate classification of factory overhead.

Payroll Fringe Costs

A type of labor cost that is growing in importance is **payroll fringe costs** such as employer contributions to employee benefits such as social security, life insurance, health insurance, and pensions. Most companies classify these as factory overhead. In some companies, however, fringe benefits related to direct labor are charged as an additional direct-labor cost. For instance, a direct laborer, such as a lathe operator or an auto mechanic, whose gross wages are computed on the basis of $10 an hour, may enjoy fringe benefits totaling $4 per hour. Most companies classify the $10 as direct-labor cost and the $4 as factory overhead. Other companies classify the entire $14 as direct-labor cost. The latter approach is conceptually preferable because these costs are a fundamental part of acquiring labor services.

Accountants and managers need to pinpoint exactly what direct labor includes and excludes. Such clarity may avoid disputes regarding cost reimbursement contracts, income tax payments, and labor union matters. For example, some countries offer substantial income tax savings to companies that locate factories there. To qualify, these companies' "direct labor" in that country must equal at least a specified percentage of the total manufacturing costs of their products. Disputes have arisen regarding how to calculate the direct-labor percentage for qualifying for such tax relief. Are payroll fringe benefits on direct labor an integral part of direct labor, or are they a part of factory overhead? Depending on how companies classify costs, you can readily see that the two identical firms may show different percentages of total manufacturing costs. Consider a company with $10,000 of payroll fringe costs:

Classification A			Classification B		
Direct materials	$ 80,000	40%	Direct materials	$ 80,000	40%
Direct labor	40,000	20	Direct labor	50,000	25
Factory overhead	80,000	40	Factory overhead	70,000	35
Total manufacturing costs	**$200,000**	**100%**	Total manufacturing costs	**$200,000**	**100%**

Classification A assumes that payroll fringe costs are part of factory overhead. In contrast, Classification B assumes that payroll fringe costs are part of direct labor.

Notes

[1] This distinction between product and period costs has a long tradition for both internal and external reporting. During the late 1980s new U.S. income tax requirements forced companies to treat many selling and administrative costs as product instead of period costs. These special requirements, however, are confined to reporting to income tax authorities only.

[2] A. Phillips and Don Collins, "How Borg-Warner Made the Transition From Pile Accounting to JIT," *Management Accounting,* October 1990, pp. 32–35.

[3] Much of the discussion in this section is based on an illustration used in "Implementing Activity-Based Costing—The Modeling Approach," a workshop sponsored by the Institute of Management Accountants and Sapling Corporation.

[4] This example illustrates the process-based modeling approach to activity-based costing. For a more detailed description of the process modeling approach see Raef A. Lawson, "Beyond ABC: Process-Based Costing," *Journal of Cost Management,* Vol. 8, No. 3 (Fall 1994), pp. 33–3. Also, for a discussion of how one major firm used process-based costing to implement ABC in its billing center, see T. Hobdy, J. Thomson, and P. Sharman, "Activity-Based Management at AT&T," *Management Accounting* (April 1994), pp. 35–39.

CHAPTER 6

ANALYZING COST BEHAVIOR

How do the costs and revenues of a hospital change as one more patient is admitted for a 4-day stay? How are the costs and revenues of an airline affected when one more passenger is boarded at the last moment, or when one more flight is added to the schedule? How should the budget request by the Arizona Department of Motor Vehicles be affected by the predicted increase in the state's population? These questions introduce one common question: What will happen to financial results if a specified level of activity or volume fluctuates? Answering this question is the first step in analyzing **cost behavior**—how the activities of an organization affect its costs. A knowledge of the patterns of cost behavior offers valuable insights in planning and controlling short-and long-run operations. While this lesson is emphasized throughout this book, in this introductory chapter, our goal is to provide perspective rather than to impart an intimate knowledge of the complexities of cost behavior.

COST DRIVERS

Activities that affect costs are often called **cost drivers.** An organization may have many cost drivers. Consider the costs of running a warehouse that receives and stores material and supplies. The costs of operating the warehouse may be driven by the total dollar value of items handled, the weight of the items handled, the number of different orders received, the number of different items handled, the number of different suppliers, the fragility of the items handled, and possibly several other cost drivers. A major task in specifying cost behavior is to identify the cost drivers—that is, to determine the activities that cause costs to be incurred.

To examine cost behavior without undue complexity, this chapter focuses on *volume-related cost drivers.* Later chapters will introduce cost drivers that are not related to volume. Volume-related cost drivers include the number of orders processed, the number of items billed in a billing department, the number of admissions to a theater, the number of pounds handled in a warehouse, the hours of labor worked in an assembly department, the number of rides in an amusement park, the seat-miles on an airline, and the dollar sales in a retail business. All of these cost drivers can serve either directly or indirectly as a measure of the volume of output of goods or services. Of course, when only one product is being produced, the units of production is the most obvious volume-related cost driver for production-related costs.

COMPARISON OF VARIABLE AND FIXED COSTS

A key to understanding cost behavior is distinguishing *variable costs* from *fixed costs*. Costs are classified as variable or fixed depending on how much they change as the level of a particular cost driver changes. A **variable cost** is a cost that changes in direct proportion to changes in the cost driver. In contrast, a **fixed cost** is not immediately affected by changes in the cost driver. Suppose units of production is the cost driver of interest. A 10% increase in the units of production would produce a 10% increase in variable costs. However, the fixed costs would remain unchanged.

Some examples may clarify the differences between fixed and variable costs. The costs of most merchandise, materials, parts, supplies, commissions, and many types of labor are generally variable with respect to most volume-related cost drivers. Real estate taxes, real estate insurance, many executive salaries, and space rentals tend to be fixed with respect to any volume-related cost driver.

Consider some variable costs. Suppose Watkins Products pays its door-to-door sales personnel a 40% straight commission on sales. The total cost of sales commissions to Watkins is 40% of sales dollars—a variable cost with respect to sales revenues. Or suppose Dan's Bait Shop buys bags of fish bait for $2 each. The total cost of fish bait is $2 times the number of bags purchased—a variable cost with respect to units (number of bags) purchased. Notice that variable costs are uniform *per unit*, but that the *total* fluctuates in direct proportion to the cost-driver activity. Exhibit 6-1 depicts these relationships between cost and cost-driver activity graphically.

Now consider a fixed cost. Suppose Sony rents a factory to produce picture tubes for color television sets for $500,000 per year. The *total* cost of $500,000 is not affected by the number of picture tubes produced. The *unit cost* of rent applicable to each tube, however, does depend on the total number of tubes produced. If 100,000 tubes are produced, the unit cost will be $500,000 ÷ 100,000 = $5. If 50,000 tubes are produced, the

Exhibit 6-1   Variable-Cost Behavior

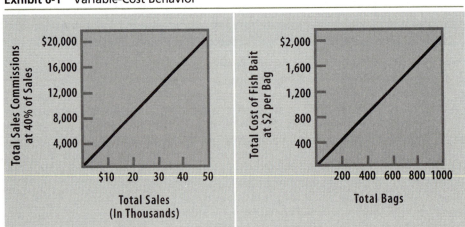

unit cost will be $500,000 ÷ 50,000 = $10. Therefore, a fixed cost does not change *in total*, but it becomes progressively smaller on a *per-unit* basis as the volume increases.

Note carefully from these examples that the "variable" or "fixed" characteristic of a cost relates to its *total dollar amount* and not to its per-unit amount. The following table summarizes these relationships.

	If Cost-Driver Activity Level Increases (or Decreases):	
Type of Cost	**Total Cost**	**Cost Per Unit***
Fixed Costs	No change	Decrease (or increase)
Variable costs	Increase (or decrease)	No change

*Per unit of activity volume, for example, product units, passenger-miles, sales dollars.

When predicting costs, two rules of thumb are useful:

1. Think of fixed costs as a *total*. Total fixed costs remain unchanged regardless of changes in cost-driver activity.
2. Think of variable costs on a *per-unit* basis. The *per-unit* variable cost remains unchanged, regardless of changes in cost-driver activity.

Relevant Range

Although we have just described fixed costs as unchanging regardless of cost-driver activity, this rule of thumb holds true only within reasonable limits. For example, rent costs will rise if increased production requires a larger or additional building—or if the landlord just decides to raise the rent. Conversely, rent costs may go down if decreased production causes the company to move to a smaller plant. The **relevant range** is the limit of cost-driver activity within which a specific relationship between costs and the cost driver is valid. In addition, remember that even within the relevant range, a fixed cost remains fixed only over a given period of time—usually the budget period. Fixed costs may change from budget year to budget year solely because of changes in insurance and property tax rates, executive salary levels, or rent levels. But these items are unlikely to change within a given year.

For example, suppose that a General Electric plant has a relevant range of between 40,000 and 85,000 cases of light bulbs per month and that total monthly fixed costs within the relevant range are $100,000. Within the relevant range, fixed costs will remain the same. If production falls below 40,000 cases, changes in personnel and salaries would slash fixed costs to $60,000. If operations rise above 85,000 cases, increases in personnel and salaries would boost fixed costs to $115,000.

These assumptions—a given period and a given activity range—are shown graphically at the top of Exhibit 6-2. It is highly unusual, however, for monthly operations to be outside the relevant range. Therefore, the three-level refinement at the top of Exhibit 6-2 is usually not graphed. Instead, a single horizontal line is typically extended through the plotted activity levels, as at the bottom of the exhibit. Often a dashed line is used outside the relevant range.

The basic idea of a relevant range also applies to variable costs. That is, outside a relevant range, some variable costs, such as fuel consumed, may behave differently per unit of cost-driver activity. For example, the efficiency of motors is affected if they are used too much or too little.

Exhibit 6-2 Fixed Costs and Relevant Range

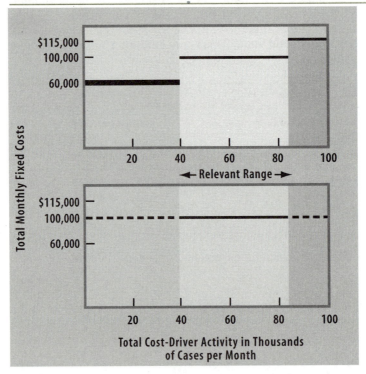

Differences in Classifying Costs

As you may suspect, it is often difficult to classify a cost as exactly variable or exactly fixed. Many complications arise including the possibility of costs behaving in some non-linear way (not producing a straight line graph). For example, as tax preparers learn to process the new year's tax forms, their productivity rises. This means that total costs may actually behave as in Panel A that follows, not as in Panel B.

Moreover, costs may simultaneously be affected by more than one cost driver. For example, the costs of shipping labor may be affected by both the weight and the number of units handled. We shall investigate various facets of this problem in succeeding chapters; for now, we shall assume that any cost may be classified as either variable or fixed. We assume also that a given variable cost is associated with only one volume-related cost driver, and that relationship is linear.

Finally, in the real world, classifying costs as fixed or variable depends on the decision situation. More costs are fixed and fewer are variable when decisions involve very short time spans and very small changes in activity level. Suppose a United Airlines plane with

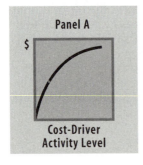

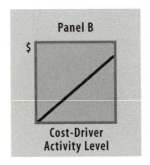

several empty seats will depart from its gate in 2 minutes. A potential passenger is running down a corridor bearing a transferable ticket from a competing airline. Unless the airplane is held for an extra 30 seconds, the passenger will miss the departure and will not switch to United for the planned trip. What are the variable costs to United of delaying the departure and placing one more passenger in an otherwise empty seat? Variable costs (for example, one more meal) are negligible. Virtually all the costs in that decision situation are fixed. Now in contrast, suppose United's decision is whether to add another flight, acquire another gate, add another city to its routes, or acquire another airplane. Many more costs would be regarded as variable and fewer as fixed.

These examples underscore the importance of how the decision affects the analysis of cost behavior. Whether costs are really "fixed" depends heavily on the relevant range, the length of the planning period in question, and the specific decision situation.

COST-VOLUME-PROFIT ANALYSIS

Managers often classify costs as fixed or variable when making decisions that affect the volume of output. The managers want to know how such decisions will affect costs and revenues. They realize that many factors in addition to the volume of output will affect costs. Yet, a useful starting point in their decision process is to specify the relationship between the volume of output and costs and revenues.

The managers of profit-seeking organizations usually study the effects of output volume on revenue (sales), expenses (costs), and net income (net profit). This study is commonly called **cost-volume-profit (CVP) analysis**. The managers of nonprofit organizations also benefit from the study of CVP relationships. Why? No organization has unlimited resources, and knowledge of how costs fluctuate as volume changes helps managers to understand how to control costs. For example, administrators of nonprofit hospitals are constantly concerned about the behavior of costs as the volume of patients fluctuates.

To apply CVP analysis, managers usually resort to some simplifying assumptions. The major simplification is to classify costs as either variable or fixed with respect to a single measure of the volume of output activity. This chapter focuses on such a simplified relationship.

CVP Scenario

Amy Winston, the manager of food services for Middletown Community College, is trying to decide whether to rent a line of food vending machines. Although individual snack items have various acquisition costs and selling prices, Winston has decided that an average selling price of 50¢ per unit and an average acquisition cost of 40¢ per unit will suffice for purposes of this analysis. She predicts the following revenue and expense relationships.

We will next use these data to illustrate several applications of CVP analysis.

	Per Unit	Percentage of Sales
Selling price	$ .50	100%
Variable cost of each item	.40	80
Selling price less variable cost	$ .10	20%
Monthly fixed expenses		
Rent	$1,000	
Wages for replenishing and servicing	4,500	
Other fixed expenses	500	
Total fixed expenses per month	$6,000	

Breakeven Point—Contribution Margin and Equation Techniques

The most basic CVP analysis computes the monthly breakeven point in number of units and in dollar sales. The **breakeven point** is the level of sales at which revenue equals expenses and net income is zero. The business press frequently refers to breakeven points. For example, a news story on hotel occupancy rates in San Francisco in 1994 stated that "seventy percent [occupancy] is considered a breakeven for hoteliers." Another news story stated that "the Big Three auto makers have slashed their sales breakeven point in North America from 12.2 million cars and trucks to only 9.1 million this year." Finally, an article on Outboard Marine Corporation reported that, as a result of restructuring, the company's "breakeven point will be $250 million lower than it was in 1993."

The study of cost-volume-profit relationships is often called breakeven analysis. This term is misleading because finding the breakeven point is often just the first step in a planning decision. Managers usually concentrate on how the decision will affect sales, costs, and net income.

One direct use of the breakeven point, however, is to assess possible risks. By comparing planned sales with the breakeven point, managers can determine a **margin of safety**:

margin of safety = planned unit sales – breakeven unit sales

The margin of safety shows how far sales can fall below the planned level before losses occur.

We next explore two basic techniques for computing a breakeven point: contribution margin and equation.

Contribution-margin technique. Consider the following common sense arithmetic approach. Every unit sold generates a **contribution margin** or **marginal income**, which is the sales price minus the variable cost per unit. For the vending machine snack items, the contribution margin per unit is $.10:

Unit sales price	$.50
Unit variable cost	.40
Unit contribution margin to fixed costs and net income	**$.10**

When is the breakeven point reached? When enough units have been sold to generate a *total* contribution margin (total number of units sold x contribution margin per unit) equal to the total fixed costs. Divide the $6,000 in fixed costs by the $.10 unit contribution margin. The number of units that must be sold to break even is $6,000 ÷ $.10 = 60,000 units. The sales revenue at the breakeven point is 60,000 units × $.50 per unit, or $30,000.

Think about the contribution margin of the snack items. Each unit purchased and sold generates *extra* revenue of $.50 and *extra* cost of $.40. Fixed costs are unaffected. If zero units were sold, a loss equal to the fixed cost of $6,000 would be incurred. Each unit reduces the loss by $.10 until sales reach the breakeven point of 60,000 units. After that point, each unit adds (or *contributes*) $.10 to profit.

The condensed income statement at the breakeven point is

	Total	Per Unit	Percentage
Units	60,000		
Sales	$30,000	$.50	100%
Variable costs	24,000	.40	80
Contribution margin*	$ 6,000	**$.10**	20%
Fixed costs	6,000		
Net income	$ 0		

*Sales less variable costs.

Sometimes the unit price and unit variable costs are not known. This situation is common at companies that sell more than one product because no single price or variable cost applies to all products. For example, a grocery store sells hundreds of products at many different prices. A breakeven point *in units* would not be meaningful. In such cases, you can use total sales and total variable costs to calculate variable costs as a *percentage of each sales dollar.*

Consider our ending machine example:

Sales price	100%
Variable expenses as a percentage of dollar sales	80
Contribution-margin percentage	**20%**

Therefore, 20% of each sales dollar is available for the recovery of fixed expenses and the making of net income: $6,000 ÷ .20 = $30,000 sales are needed to break even. The contribution-margin percentage is based on dollar sales and is often expressed as a ratio (.20 instead of 20%). Using the contribution-margin percentage, you can compute the breakeven volume in dollar sales without determining the breakeven point in units.

Equation technique. The equation technique is the most general form of analysis, the one that may be adapted to any conceivable cost-volume-profit situation. You are familiar with a typical income statement. Any income statement can be expressed in equation form, or as a *mathematical model,* as follows:

$$\text{sales} - \text{variable expenses} - \text{fixed expenses} = \text{net income} \qquad (1)$$

That is,

$$\left(\begin{array}{c} \text{unit} \\ \text{sales} \\ \text{price} \end{array} \times \begin{array}{c} \text{number} \\ \text{of} \\ \text{units} \end{array} \right) - \left(\begin{array}{c} \text{unit} \\ \text{variable} \\ \text{cost} \end{array} \times \begin{array}{c} \text{number} \\ \text{of} \\ \text{units} \end{array} \right) - \begin{array}{c} \text{fixed} \\ \text{expenses} \end{array} = \begin{array}{c} \text{net} \\ \text{income} \end{array}$$

At the breakeven point net income is zero:

$$\text{sales} - \text{variable expenses} - \text{fixed expenses} = 0$$

Let N = number of units to be sold to break even. Then, for the vending machine example,

$$\begin{aligned} \$.50N - \$.40N - \$6.000 &= 0 \\ \$.10N &= \$6,000 \\ N &= \$6,000 \div \$.10 \\ N &= 60,000 \text{ units} \end{aligned}$$

Total sales in the equation is a price-times-quantity relationship, which was expressed in our example as $.50N. To find the *dollar* sales, multiply 60,000 *units* by $.50, which would yield the breakeven dollar sales of $30,000.

You can also solve the equation for sales dollars without computing the unit breakeven point by using the relationship of variable costs and profits as a *percentage* of sales:

$$\begin{aligned} \text{variable-cost ratio or percentage} &= \frac{\text{variable cost per unit}}{\text{sales price per unit}} \\ &= \frac{\$.40}{\$.50} \\ &= .80 \text{ or } 80\% \end{aligned}$$

Let S = sales in dollars needed to break even. Then

$$S - .80S - \$6,000 = 0$$

$$.20S = \$60,000$$

$$S = \$6,000 \div .20$$

$$S = \$30,000$$

Relationship between the two techniques. You may have noticed that the contribution-margin technique is merely a shortcut version of the equation technique. Look at the last three lines in the two solutions given for equation 1. They read

Breakeven Volume	
Units	*Dollars*
$\$.10N = \$6,000$	$.20S = \$6,000$
$N = \dfrac{\$6,000}{\$.10}$	$S = \dfrac{\$6,000}{.20}$
$N = 60,000$ units	$S = \$30,000$

From these equations, we can derive the following general shortcut formulas:

$$\frac{\text{breakeven volume}}{\text{in units}} = \frac{\text{fixed expenses}}{\text{contribution margin per unit}} \qquad (2)$$

$$\frac{\text{breakeven volume}}{\text{in dollars}} = \frac{\text{fixed expenses}}{\text{contribution-margin ratio}} \qquad (3)$$

Which should you use, the equation or the contribution-margin technique? Use either. The choice is a matter of personal preference or convenience within a particular case.

Breakeven point—graphical techniques. Exhibit 6-3 is a graph of the cost-volume-profit relationship in our vending machine example. Study the graph as you read the procedure for constructing it.

1. Draw the axes. The horizontal axis is the sales volume, and the vertical axis is dollars of cost and revenue.
2. Plot sales volume. Select a convenient sales volume, say, 100,000 units, and plot point A for total sales dollars at that volume: 100,000 × $.50 = $50,000. Draw the revenue (i.e., sales) line from point A to the origin, point 0.
3. Plot fixed expenses. Draw the line showing the $6,000 fixed portion of expenses. It should be a horizontal line, intersecting the vertical axis at $6,000, point B.
4. Plot variable expenses. Determine the variable portion of expenses at a convenient level of activity: 100,000 units × $.40 = $40,000. Add this to the fixed expenses: 540,000 + $6,000 = $46,000. Plot point C for 100,000 units and $46,000. Then draw a line between this point and point B. This is the total expenses line.
5. Locate the breakeven point. The breakeven point is where the total expenses line crosses the sales line, 60,000 units or $30,000, namely, where total sales revenues exactly equal total costs, point D.

Exhibit 6-3 Cost-Volume-Profit Graph

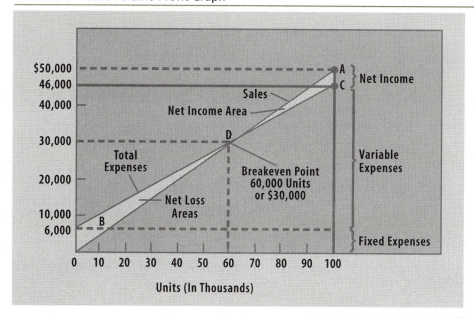

The breakeven point is only one facet of this cost-volume-profit graph. More generally, the graph shows the profit or loss at *any* rate of activity. At any given volume, the vertical distance between the sales line and the total expenses line measures the net income or net loss.

Managers often use breakeven graphs because they show potential profits over a wide range of volume more easily than numerical exhibits. Whether graphs or other types of exhibits are used depends largely on management's preference.

Note that the concept of relevant range is applicable to the entire breakeven graph. Almost all breakeven graphs show revenue and cost lines extending back to the vertical axis as shown in Exhibit 6-4(A). This approach is misleading because the relationships depicted in such graphs are valid only within the relevant range that underlies the construction of the graph. Exhibit 6-4(B), a modification of the conventional breakeven graph, partially demonstrates the multitude of assumptions that must be made in constructing the typical breakeven graph. Some of these assumptions follow:

1. Expenses may be classified into variable and fixed categories. Total variable expenses vary directly with activity level. Total fixed expenses do not change with activity level.
2. The behavior of revenues and expenses is accurately portrayed and is linear over the relevant range. The principal differences between the accountant's breakeven chart and the economist's are that (1) the accountant's sales line is drawn on the assumption that selling prices do not change with production or sales, and the economist assumes that reduced selling prices are normally associated with increased sales volume; and (2) the accountant usually assumes a constant variable expense per unit, and the economist assumes that variable expense per unit changes with production levels. Within the relevant range, the accountant's and the economist's sales and expense lines are usually close to one another, although the lines may diverge greatly outside the range.
3. Efficiency and productivity will be unchanged.
4. Sales mix will be constant. The **sales mix** is the relative proportions or combinations of quantities of products that constitute total sales. (See Addendum 6A for more on sales mixes.)

Exhibit 6-4   Conventional and Modified breakeven Graphs

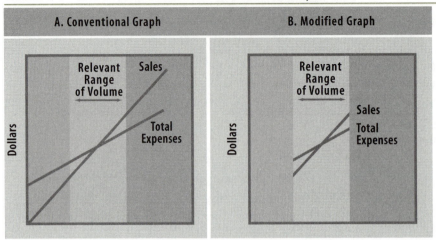

5. The difference in inventory level at the beginning and at the end of a period is insignificant.

Changes in Fixed Expenses

Changes in fixed expenses cause changes in the breakeven point. For example, if the $1,000 monthly rent of the vending machines were doubled, what would be the monthly breakeven point in number of units and dollar sales?

The fixed expenses would increase from $6,000 to $7,000, so

$$\frac{\text{breakeven volume}}{\text{in units}} = \frac{\text{fixed expenses}}{\text{contribution margin per unit}} = \frac{\$7,000}{\$.10} = 70,000 \text{ units} \qquad (2)$$

$$\frac{\text{breakeven volume}}{\text{in dollars}} = \frac{\text{fixed expenses}}{\text{contribution-margin ratio}} = \frac{\$7,000}{\$.20} = \$35,000 \qquad (3)$$

Note that a one-sixth increase in fixed expenses altered the breakeven point by one-sixth: from 60,000 to 70,000 units and from $30,000 to $35,000. This type of relationship always exists if everything else remains constant.

Companies frequently lower their breakeven points by reducing their total fixed costs. For example, closing or selling factories decreases property taxes, insurance, depreciation, and managers' salaries.

Changes in Contribution Margin per Unit

Changes in variable costs also cause the breakeven point to shift. Companies can reduce their breakeven points by increasing their contribution margins per unit of product through either increases in sales prices or decreases in unit variable costs, or both.

For example, assume that the fixed rent is still $1,000. (1) If the owner is paid 1¢ rental per unit sold in addition to the fixed rent, find the monthly breakeven point in number of units and in dollar sales. (2) If the selling price falls from 50¢ to 45¢ per unit, and the original variable expenses per unit are unchanged, find the monthly breakeven point in number of units and in dollar sales.

Here's what happens to the breakeven point:

1. The variable expenses would increase from 40¢ to 41¢, the unit contribution margin would decline from 10¢ to 9¢, and the contribution-margin ratio would become .18 ($.09 ÷ $.50).

   The original fixed expenses of $6,000 would be unaffected, but the denominators would change from those previously used. Thus,

$$\text{breakeven point in units} = \frac{\$6,000}{\$.09} = 66,667 \text{ units} \tag{2}$$

$$\text{breakeven points in dollars} = \frac{\$6,000}{.18} = \$33,333 \tag{3}$$

2. If the selling price fell from 50¢ to 45¢, and the original variable expenses were unchanged, the unit contribution would be reduced from 10¢ to 5¢ (i.e., 45¢–40¢), and the breakeven point would soar to 120,000 units ($6,000 ÷ $.05). The breakeven point in dollars would also change because the selling price and contribution-margin ratio change. The contribution-margin ratio would be. 1111 ($.05 ÷ $.45). The breakeven point, in dollars, would be $54,000 (120,000 units x $.45) or, using the formula:

$$\text{breakeven points in dollars} = \frac{\$6,000}{.1111} = \$54,00 \tag{3}$$

Target Net Profit and an Incremental Approach

Managers can also use CVP analysis to determine the total sales, in units and dollars, needed to reach a target profit. For example, in our snack-vending example, suppose Winston considers $480 per month the minimum acceptable net income. How many units will have to be sold to justify the adoption of the vending machine plan? How does this figure "translate" into dollar sales?

The method for computing desired or target sales volume in units and the desired or target net income is the same as was used in our earlier breakeven computations. Now the targets, however, are expressed in the equations:

$$\text{target sales} - \text{variable expenses} - \text{fixed expenses} = \text{target net income} \tag{4}$$

or

$$\text{target sales volume in units} = \frac{\text{fixed expenses} + \text{target net income}}{\text{contribution margin per unit}} \tag{5}$$

$$= \frac{\$6,000 + \$480}{\$.10} = 64,800 \text{ units}$$

Another way of getting the same answer is to use your knowledge of the breakeven point and adopt an incremental approach. The term **incremental** is widely used in accounting. It refers to the *change* in total results (such as revenue, expenses, or income) under a new condition in comparison with some given or known condition.

In this instance, the given condition is assumed to be the 60,000-unit breakeven point. All expenses would be recovered at that volume. Therefore, the *change* or *increment* in net income for every unit beyond 60,000 would be equal to the contribution margin of $.50 –$.40 = $.10. If $480 were the target net profit, 5480 ÷ $.10 would show that the target volume must exceed the breakeven volume by 4,800 units; it would therefore be 60,000 + 4,800 = 64,800 units.

To find the answer in terms of *dollar* sales, multiply 64,800 units by $.50 or use the formula:

$$\text{target sales volume in dollars} = \frac{\text{fixed expenses} + \text{target net income}}{\text{contribution margin per unit}} \qquad (6)$$

$$= \frac{\$6,000 + \$480}{.20} = \$32,400$$

To solve directly for sales dollars with the alternative incremental approach, the breakeven point, in dollar sales of $30,000, becomes the frame of reference. Every sales dollar beyond that point contributes $.20 to net profit. Divide $480 by .20. Dollar sales must exceed the breakeven volume by $2,400 to produce a net profit of $480; thus, the total dollar sales would be $30,000 + $2,400 = $32,400.

The following table summarizes these computations:

	Breakeven Point	Increment	New Condition
Volume in units	60,000	4,800	64,800
Sales	$30,000	$2,400	$32,400
Variable expenses	24,000	1,920	25,920
Contribution margin	$ 6,000	$ 480	$ 6,480
Fixed expenses	6,000	—	6,000
Net income	$0	$ 480	$ 480

Multiple Changes in Key Factors

In the real world, managers often must make decisions about the probable effects of multiple factor changes. For instance, suppose that after the vending machines have been in place a while, Winston is considering locking them from 6:00 P.M. to 6:00 A.M., which she estimates will save $820 in wages monthly. The cutback from 24-hour service would hurt volume substantially because many nighttime employees use the machines. Employees could find food elsewhere, however, so not too many complaints are expected.[1] Should the machines remain available 24 hours per day? Assume that monthly sales would decline by 10,000 units from current sales of (1) 62,000 units and (2) 90,000 units. Consider two approaches. One approach is to construct and solve equations for conditions that prevail under each alternative and select the volume level that yields the highest net income.

Regardless of the current volume level, be it 62,000 or 90,000 units, if we accept the prediction that sales will decline by 10,000 units as accurate, the closing from 6:00 P.M. to 6:00 A.M. will decrease net income by $180.

	62,000 to 52,000 Units		90,000 to 80,000 Units	
Units	62,000	52,000	90,000	80,000
Sales	$31,000	$26,000	$45,000	$40,000
Variable expenses	24,800	20,800	36,000	32,000
Contribution margin	$ 6,200	$ 5,200	$ 9,000	$ 8,000
Fixed expenses	6,000	5,180	6,000	5,180
Net income	$ 200	$ 20	$ 3,000	$ 2,820
Change in net income		($180)		($180)

A second approach—an incremental approach—is quicker and simpler. Simplicity is important to managers because it keeps the analysis from being cluttered by irrelevant and potentially confusing data.

What does the insightful manager see in this situation? First, whether 62,000 or 90,000 units are being sold is irrelevant to the decision at hand. The issue is the decline in volume, which would be 10,000 units in either case. The essence of this decision is whether the prospective savings in cost exceed the prospective loss in total contribution-margin dollars.

Lost total contribution margin, 10,000 units @.10	$1,000
Savings in fixed expenses	$ 820
Prospective decline in net income	$ 180

Locking the vending machines from 6:00 P.M. to 6:00 A.M. would cause a $180 decrease in monthly net income. Whichever way you analyze it, locking the machines is not a sound financial decision.

CVP Analysis in the Computer Age

As we have seen, cost-volume-profit analysis is based on a mathematical model, the equation

$$\text{sales} - \text{variable expenses} - \text{fixed expenses} = \text{net income}$$

The CVP model is widely used as a *planning model*. Managers in a variety of organizations use a personal computer and a CVP modeling program to study combinations of changes in selling prices, unit variable costs, fixed costs, and desired profits. Many nonprofit organizations also use computerized CVP modeling. For example, some private universities have models that help measure how decisions such as raising tuition, adding programs, and closing dormitories during winter holidays will affect financial results. The computer quickly calculates the results of changes and can display them both numerically and graphically.

Exhibit 6-5 is a sample spreadsheet that shows what the sales level would have to be at three different fixed expense levels and three different variable expense levels to reach three different income levels. The computer calculates the 27 different sales levels rapidly and without error. Managers can insert any numbers they want for fixed expenses (column A), variable expense percentage (column B), target net income (row 3 of columns C, D, and E), or combinations thereof, and the computer will compute the required sales level.

In addition to speed and convenience, computers allow a more sophisticated approach to CVP analysis than the one illustrated in this chapter. The assumptions listed above are necessary to simplify the analysis enough for most managers to construct a CVP model by hand. Computer analysts, however, can construct a model that does not require all the simplifications. Computer models can include multiple cost drivers, non-linear relationships between costs and cost drivers, varying sales mixes, and analyses that need not be restricted to a relevant range.

Use of computer models is a cost-benefit issue. Sometimes the costs of modeling are exceeded by the value of better decisions made using the models. However, the reliability of these models depends on the accuracy of their underlying assumptions about how revenues and costs will actually be affected. Moreover, in small organizations, simplified CVP models often are accurate enough that more sophisticated modeling is unwarranted.

Exhibit 6-5   Spreadsheet Analysis of CVP Relationships

	A	B	C	D	E
1			Sales Required to Earn		
2	Fixed	Variable	Annual Net Income of		
3	Expenses	Expense %	$2,000	$4,000	$6,000
4					
5	$4,000	0.40	$10,000*	$13,333	$16,667
6	$4,000	0.44	$10,714*	$14,286	$17,857
7	$4,000	0.48	$11,538*	$15,385	$19,231
8	$6,000	0.40	$13,333	$16,667	$20,000
9	$6,000	0.44	$14,286	$17,857	$21,429
10	$6,000	0.48	$15,385	$19,231	$23,077
11	$8,000	0.40	$16,667	$20,000	$23,333
12	$8,000	0.44	$17,857	$21,429	$25,000
13	$8,000	0.48	$19,231	$23,077	$26,923
15					
16	*(A5 + C3)/(1 − B5) = ($4,000 + $2,000)/(1 − $.40)				
17	(A6 + C3)/(1 − B6) = ($4,000 + $2,000)/(1 − $.44)				
18	(A7 + C3)/(1 − B7) = ($4,000 + $2,000)/(1 − $.48)				
19					

ADDITIONAL USES OF COST-VOLUME ANALYSIS

Best Combination of Factors

The analysis of cost-volume-profit relationships is an important management responsibility. Managers usually try to obtain the most profitable combination of variable and fixed-cost factors. For example, purchasing automated machinery may raise fixed costs but reduce labor cost per unit. Conversely, it may be wise to reduce fixed costs to obtain a more favorable combination. Thus, direct selling by a salaried sales force (a fixed cost) may be supplanted by the use of manufacturer's agents who are compensated via sales commissions (variable costs). Generally, companies that spend heavily for advertising are willing to do so because they have high contribution-margin percentages (airlines, cigarette, and cosmetic companies). Conversely, companies with low contribution-margin percentages usually spend less for advertising and promotion (manufacturers of industrial equipment). Obviously, two companies with the same unit sales volumes at the same unit prices could have different attitudes toward risking an advertising outlay. Assume the following:

	Perfume Company	Janitorial Service Company
Unit sales volume	100,000 bottles	100,000 square feet
Dollar sales at $20 per unit	$2,000,000	$2,000,000
Variable costs	200,000	1,700,000
Contribution margin	$1,800,000	$ 300,000
Contribution-margin percentage	90%	15%

Suppose each company wants to increase sales volume by 10%:

	Perfume Company	Janitorial Service Company
Increase in sales volume, 10,000 × $20	$200,000	$200,000
Increase in contribution margin, 90%, 15%	180,000	30,000

The perfume company would be inclined to increase advertising considerably to boost the contribution margin by $180,000. In contrast, the janitorial service company would be foolhardy to spend large amounts to increase the contribution margin by $30,000.

Note that when the contribution-margin percentage of sales is low, great increases in volume are necessary before significant increases in net profits can occur. As sales exceed the breakeven point, a high contribution-margin percentage increases profits faster than does a small contribution-margin percentage.

Operating Leverage

In addition to weighing the varied effects of changes in fixed and variable costs, managers need to consider their firm's ratio of fixed to variable costs, called **operating leverage.** In highly leveraged companies—those with high fixed costs and low variable costs—small changes in sales volume result in large changes in net income. Companies with less leverage (that is, lower fixed costs and higher variable costs) are not affected as much by changes in sales volume.

Exhibit 6-6 shows cost behavior relationships at two firms, one highly leveraged and one with low leverage. The firm with higher leverage has fixed costs of $14,000 and variable cost per unit of $.10. The firm with lower leverage has fixed costs of only $2,000 but variable costs of $.25 per unit. Expected sales at both companies are 80,000 units at $.30 per unit. At this sales level, both alternatives would have net incomes of $2,000. If sales fall short of 80,000 units, profits *drop* most sharply for the highly leveraged business. If sales exceed 80,000 units, however, profits *increase* most sharply for the highly leveraged concern.

The highly leveraged alternative is more risky. Why? Because it provides the highest possible net income and the highest possible losses. In other words, net income is highly variable, depending on the actual level of sales. The low-leverage alternative is less risky because variations in sales lead to only small variability in net income. At sales of 90,000 units, net income is $4,000 for the higher-leveraged firm but only $2,500 for the lower-leveraged firm. At sales of 70,000 units, however, the higher-leveraged firm has zero profits, compared to $1,500 for the lower-leveraged firm.

Exhibit 6-6   High Versus Low Leverage

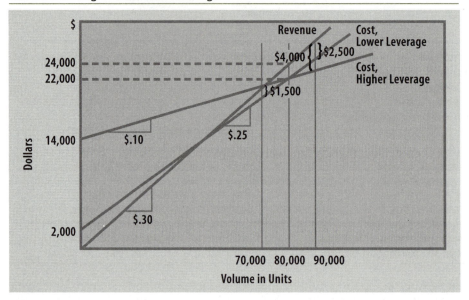

Contribution Margin and Gross Margin

Contribution margin may be expressed as a *total* absolute amount, a *unit* absolute amount, a *ratio,* and a *percentage.* The **variable-cost ratio** or **variable-cost percentage** is defined as all variable costs divided by sales. Thus, a contribution-margin ratio of 20% means that the variable-cost ratio is 80%.

Too often people confuse the terms *contribution margin* and *gross margin.* **Gross margin** (which is also called **gross profit**) is the excess of sales over the **cost of goods sold** (that is, the cost of the merchandise that is acquired or manufactured and then sold). It is a widely used concept, particularly in the retailing industry.

Compare the gross margin with the contribution margin:

gross margin = sales price – cost of goods sold
contribution margin = sales price – all variable expenses

The following comparisons from our vending machine illustration show the similarities and differences between the contribution margin and the gross margin in a retail store:

Sales	$.50
Variable costs: acquisition cost of unit sold	.40
Contribution margin and gross margin are equal	**$.10**

Thus, the original data resulted in no difference between the measure of contribution margin and gross margin. There would be a difference between the two, however, if the firm had to pay additional rent of 1¢ per unit sold:

	Contribution Margin	Gross Margin
Sales	$.50	$.50
Acquisition cost of unit sold	$.40	.40
Variable rent	.01	
Total variable expense	.41	
Contribution margin	$.09	
Gross margin		$.10

As the preceding tabulation indicates, contribution margin and gross margin are not the same concepts. Contribution margin focuses on sales in relation to *all variable costs,* whereas gross margin focuses on sales in relation to cost of goods sold. For example, consider MascoTech, a Detroit-based auto parts supplier. A newspaper article reported that MascoTech's "gross profit margin on sales is about 21% today, but for each additional sales dollar the contribution margin is more like 30%."

NONPROFIT APPLICATION

Consider how cost-volume-profit relationships apply to nonprofit organizations. Suppose a city has a $100,000 lump-sum budget appropriation for a government agency to conduct a counseling program for drug addicts. The variable costs for drug prescriptions are $400 per patient per year. Fixed costs are $60,000 in the relevant range of 50 to 150 patients. If all of the budget appropriation is spent, how many patients can be served in a year?

Let N be the number of patients.

$$
\begin{aligned}
\text{revenue} - \text{variable expenses} - \text{fixed expenses} &= 0 \text{ if budget is completely spent} \\
\$100.000 \text{ lump sum} - \$400N - \$60,000 &= 0 \\
\$400N &= \$100,000 - \$60,000 \\
N &= \$40,000 \div 400 \\
N &= 100 \text{ patients}
\end{aligned}
$$

Suppose the total budget appropriation for the following year is cut by 10%. Fixed costs will be unaffected, but service will decline:

$$
\begin{aligned}
\text{revenue} - \text{variable expenses} - \text{fixed expenses} &= 0 \\
\$90,000 - \$400N - \$60,000 &= 0 \\
\$400N &= \$90,000 - \$60,000 \\
N &= \$30,000 \div \$400 \\
N &= 75 \text{ patients}
\end{aligned}
$$

The reduction in service is more than the 10% reduction in the budget. Without restructuring operations, the service volume must be reduced 25% (from 100 to 75 patients) to stay within budget. Note that lump-sum revenue is a horizontal line on the following graph.

SUMMARY

Understanding cost behavior patterns and cost-volume-profit (CVP) relationships can help guide a manager's decisions. The first step in assessing cost behavior is to identify cost drivers. Variable costs and fixed costs have contrasting behavior patterns with respect to a particular cost driver—variable costs change in proportion to changes in the cost driver, whereas fixed costs are unaffected by cost-driver activity.

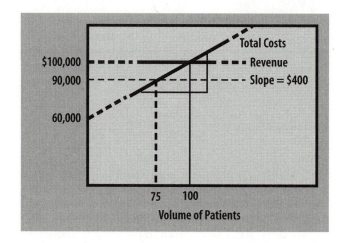

CVP analysis (sometimes called breakeven analysis) can be approached graphically or with equations. Managers use CVP analysis to compute a breakeven point, to compute a target net income, or to examine the effects on income of changes in factors such as fixed costs, variable costs, or volume. CVP analysis is used in nonprofit organizations as well as in profit-seeking companies.

Be sure to recognize the limitations of CVP analysis. Most important, it relies on the ability to separate costs into fixed and variable categories. Therefore, it is applicable only over a relevant range of activity. In addition, it assumes constant efficiency, sales mix, and inventory levels.

The contribution margin—the difference between sales price and variable costs—is an important concept. Do not confuse it with gross margin, the difference between sales price and cost of goods sold.

SELF-CORRECTION PROBLEM

1. The budgeted income statement of Port Williams Gift Shop is summarized as follows:

Net revenue	$800,000
Less: expenses, including $400,000 of fixed expenses	880,000
Net loss	$(80,000)

The manager believes that an increase of $200,000 on advertising outlays will increase sales substantially.

a. At what sales volume will the store break even after spending $200,000 on advertising?

b. What sales volume will result in a net profit of $40,000?

SOLUTION TO SELF-CORRECTION PROBLEM

1. a. Note that all data are expressed in dollars. No unit data are given. Most companies have many products, so the overall breakeven analysis deals with dollar sales, not units. The variable expenses are $880,000 − $400,000, or $480,000. The variable-expense ratio is $480,000 ÷ $800,000, or 60. Therefore, the contribution-margin ratio is .40. Let S = breakeven sales in dollars. Then

$$S - \text{variable expenses} - \text{fixed expenses} = \text{net profit}$$

$$S - .60S - (\$400,000 + \$200,00) = 0$$

$$.40S = \$600,000$$

$$S = \frac{\$600,000}{.40} = \frac{\text{fixed expenses}}{\text{contribution-margin ratio}}$$

$$S = \$1,500,000$$

b.

$$\text{required sales} = \frac{\text{fixed expenses} + \text{target net profit}}{\text{contribution-margin ratio}}$$

$$\text{required sales} = \frac{\$600,000 + \$40,000}{.40} = \frac{\$640,000}{.40}$$

$$\text{required sales} = \$1,600,000$$

Alternatively, we can use an incremental approach and reason that all dollar sales beyond the $1.5 million breakeven point will result in a 40% contribution to net profit. Divide $40,000 by .40. Sales must therefore be $100,000 beyond the $1.5 million breakeven point to produce a net profit of $40,000.

QUESTIONS

1. "Cost behavior is simply identification of cost drivers and their relationships to costs." Comment.
2. Give three examples each of variable costs and of fixed costs.
3. "Fixed costs decline as volume increases." Do you agree? Explain.
4. "It is confusing to think of fixed costs on a per-unit basis." Do you agree? Why or why not?
5. "The relevant range pertains to fixed costs, not variable costs." Do you agree? Explain.
6. Identify two simplifying assumptions that underlie CVP analysis.
7. "Classification of costs into variable and fixed categories depends on the decision situation." Explain.
8. "Contribution margin is the excess of sales over fixed costs." Do you agree? Explain.
9. Why is "breakeven analysis" a misnomer?
10. "Companies in the same industry generally have about the same breakeven point." Do you agree? Explain.
11. Distinguish between the equation technique of CVP analysis and the unit contribution-margin technique.
12. Describe three ways of lowering a breakeven point.
13. "Incremental analysis is quicker, but it has no other advantage over an analysis of all costs and revenues associated with each alternative." Do you agree? Why or why not?
14. Explain operating leverage and why a highly leveraged company is risky.
15. "CVP analysis is a common management use of personal computers." Do you agree? Explain.
16. "The contribution margin and gross margin are always equal." Do you agree? Explain.
17. "CVP relationships are unimportant in nonprofit organizations." Do you agree? Explain.

18. "Two products were sold. Total budgeted and actual total sales in number of units were identical to the units budgeted. Actual unit variable costs and sales prices were the same as budgeted. Actual contribution margin was lower than budgeted." What could be the reason for the lower contribution margin?

19. Present the CVP formula for computing the target income before income taxes.

20. Present the CVP formula for computing the effects of a change in volume on after-tax income.

PROBLEMS

1. **Cost-Volume-Profits and Vending Machines.** Delgado Food Services Company operates and services snack vending machines located in restaurants, gas stations, factories, etc., in four Midwestern states. The machines are rented from the manufacturer. In addition, Delgado must rent the space occupied by its machines. The following expense and revenue relationships pertain to a contemplated expansion program of 20 machines.

Fixed monthly expenses follow:

Machine rental: 20 machines @ $21.75	$ 435
Space rental: 20 locations @ $14.40	288
Part-time wages to service the additional 20 machines	727
Other fixed costs	50
Total monthly fixed costs	$1,500

Other data follow:

	Per Unit	Per $100 of Sales
Selling price	$.50	100%
Cost of snack	.40	80
Contribution margin	$.10	20%

These questions relate to the above data unless otherwise noted. **Consider each question independently.**

a. What is the monthly breakeven point in number of units? In dollar sales?

b. If 18,000 units were sold, what would be the company's net income?

c. If the space rental cost were doubled, what would be the monthly breakeven point in number of units? In dollar sales?

d. If, in addition to the fixed rent, Delgado Food Services Company paid the vending machine manufacturer 1¢ per unit sold, what would be the monthly breakeven point in number of units? In dollar sales? Refer to the original data.

e. If, in addition to the fixed rent, Delgado paid the machine manufacturer 2¢ for each unit sold in excess of the breakeven point, what would the new net income be if 18,000 units were sold? Refer to the original data.

2. **Exercises in Cost-Volume-Profit Relationships.** The MacKenzie-Hawkins Transportation Company specializes in hauling heavy goods over long distances. The company's revenues and expenses depend on revenue miles, a measure that combines both weights and mileage. Summarized budget data for next year are based on predicted total revenue miles of 800,000.

	Per Revenue Mile
Average selling price (revenue)	$1.50
Average variable expenses	1.30
Fixed expenses, $110,000	

   a. Compute the budgeted net income. Ignore income taxes.
   b. Management is trying to decide how various possible conditions or decisions might affect net income. Compute the new net income for each of the following changes. Consider each case independently.
      (1)   A 10% increase in revenue miles
      (2)   A 10% increase in sales price
      (3)   A 10% increase in variable expenses
      (4)   A 10% increase in fixed expenses
      (5)   An average decrease in selling price of 3¢ per mile and a 5% increase in revenue miles. Refer to the original data
      (6)   An average increase in selling price of 5% and a 10% decrease in revenue miles
      (7)   A 10% increase in fixed expenses in the form of more advertising and a 5% increase in revenue miles

3. **Basic CVP Exercises.** Each problem is *unrelated* to the others.
   a. Given: Selling price per unit, $20; total fixed expenses, $5,000; variable expenses per unit, $15. Find breakeven sales in units.
   b. Given: Sales, $40,000; variable expenses, $30,000; fixed expenses, $7,500; net income, $2,500. Find breakeven sales.
   c. Given: Selling price per unit, $30; total fixed expenses, $33,000; variable expenses per unit, $14. Find total sales in units to achieve a profit of $7,000, assuming no change in selling price.
   d. Given: Sales, $50,000; variable expenses, $20,000; fixed expenses, $20,000; net income, $10,000. Assume no change in selling price; find net income if activity volume increases 10%.
   e. Given: Selling price per unit, $40; total fixed expenses, $80,000; variable expenses per unit, $30. Assume that variable expenses are reduced by 20% per unit, and the total fixed expenses are increased by 10%. Find the sales in units to achieve a profit of $20,000, assuming no change in selling price.

4. **Basic CVP Analysis.** Peter Landis opened his own small day care facility, Toys 'N Tots (TNT), just over 2 years ago. After a rocky start, TNT has been thriving. Peter is now preparing a budget for November 19X6.

Rent	$ 800
Salaries	1,400
Other fixed costs	100
Total fixed costs	**$2,300**

The salary is for Lynn McGraw, the only employee, who works with Peter in caring for the children. Peter does not pay himself a salary, but he receives the excess of revenues over costs each month.

The cost driver for variable costs is "child-days." One child-day is one day in day care for one child, and the variable cost is $10 per child-day. The facility is open 6:00 A.M. to 6:00 P.M. weekdays (i.e., Monday through Friday), and there are 22 weekdays in November 19X6. An average day has 8 children attending TNT. State law prohibits TNT from having more than 14 children, a limit it has never reached. Peter charges $30 per day per child, regardless of how long the child is at TNT.

a. Suppose attendance for November 19X6 is equal to the average, resulting in 22 × 8 = 176 child-days. What amount will Peter have left after paying all his expenses?

b. Suppose both costs and attendance are difficult to predict. Compute the amount Peter will have left after paying all his expenses for each of the following situations. Consider each case independently.

    (1) Average attendance is 9 children per day instead of 8, generating 198 child-days.

    (2) Variable costs increase to $11 per child-day.

    (3) Rent is increased by $200 per month.

    (4) Peter spends $300 on advertising (a fixed cost) in November, which increases average daily attendance to 9.5 children.

    (5) Peter begins charging $33 per day on November 1, and average daily attendance slips to 7 children.

ADDENDUM 6A: SALES-MIX ANALYSIS

To emphasize fundamental ideas, the cost-volume-profit analysis in this chapter has focused on a single product. Nearly all companies, however, sell more than one product. *Sales mix* is defined as the relative proportions or combinations of quantities of products that comprise total sales. If the proportions of the mix change, the cost-volume-profit relationships also change.

    Suppose Ramos Company has two products, wallets (W) and key cases (K). The income budget follows:

	Wallets (W)	Key Cases (K)	Total
Sales in units	300,000	75,000	375,000
Sales @ $8 and $5	$2,400,000	$375,000	$2,775,000
Variable expenses @ $7 and $3	2,100,000	225,000	2,325,000
Contribution margins @ $1 and $2	$300,000	$150,000	$ 450,000
Fixed expenses			180,000
Net income			$ 270,000

    For simplicity, ignore income taxes. What would be the breakeven point? The typical answer assumes a constant mix of 4 units of W for every unit of K. Therefore, let K = number of units of product K to break even, and 4K = number of units of product W to break even:

$$\text{sales} - \text{variable expenses} - \text{fixed expenses} = \text{zero net income}$$
$$\$8(4K) + \$5(K) - \$7(4K) - \$3(K) - \$180,000 = 0$$
$$\$32K + \$5K - \$28K - \$3K - \$180,000 = 0$$
$$\$6K = \$180,000$$
$$K = 30,000$$
$$4K = 120,000 = W$$

The breakeven point is 30,000K + 120,000W = 150,000 units.

    This is the only breakeven point for a sales mix of four wallets for every key case. Clearly, however, there are other breakeven points for other sales mixes. For instance, suppose only key cases were sold, fixed expenses being unchanged:

$$\text{breakeven point} = \frac{\text{fixed expenses}}{\text{contribution margin per unit}}$$

$$= \frac{\$180,000}{\$2}$$

$$= 90,000 \text{ key cases}$$

If only wallets were sold:

$$\text{breakeven point} = \frac{180,000}{\$1}$$

$$= 180,000 \text{ wallets}$$

Managers are not primarily interested in the breakeven point for its own sake. Instead, they want to know how changes in a planned sales mix will affect net income. When the sales mix changes, the breakeven point and the expected net income at various sales levels are altered. For example, suppose overall actual total sales were equal to the budget of 375,000 units. However, only 50,000 key cases were sold:

	Wallets (W)	Key Cases (K)	Total
Sales in units	325,000	50,000	375,000
Sales @ $8 and $5	$2,600,000	$250,000	$2,850,000
Variable expenses @ $7 and $3	2,275,000	150,000	2,425,000
Contribution margins @ $1 and $2	$ 325,000	$100,000	$ 425,000
Fixed expenses			180,000
Net income			$ 245,000

The change in sales mix has resulted in a $245,000 actual net income rather than the $270,000 budgeted net income, an unfavorable difference of $25,000. The budgeted and actual sales in number of units were identical, but the proportion of the product bearing the higher unit contribution margin declined.

Different advertising strategies may also affect the sales mix. Clearly, if a sales budget is not actually attained, the budgeted net income will be affected by the individual sales volume of each product. The fewer the units sold, the lower the profit, and vice versa. All other factors being equal, the higher the proportion of the more profitable products, the higher the profit. For example, Reynolds Industries sells highly profitable cigarettes (such as the Winston brand) and less profitable canned goods (such as the Del Monte brand). For any given level of total sales, the greater the proportion of the cigarettes, the greater the total profit.

Managers usually want to maximize the sales of all their products. Faced with limited resources and time, however, executives prefer to generate the most profitable sales mix achievable. For example, consider a recent annual report of Deere & Co., a manufacturer of farm equipment: "The increase in the ratio of cost of goods sold to net sales resulted from higher production costs [and] a less favorable mix of products sold."

Profitability of a given product helps guide executives who must decide to emphasize or de-emphasize particular products. For example, given limited production facilities or limited time of sales personnel, should we emphasize wallets or key cases? These decisions may be affected by other factors beyond the contribution margin per unit of product.

ADDENDUM 6B: IMPACT OF INCOME TAXES

Thus far we have (as so many people would like to) ignored income taxes\. In most nations, however, private enterprises are subject to income taxes. Reconsider the vending machine example in the chapter. As part of our CVP analysis, we discussed the sales necessary to achieve a target income before income taxes of $480. If an income tax were levied at 40%, the new result would be

Income before income tax	$480	100%
Income tax	192	40
Net income	**$288**	60%

Note that

$$\text{net income} = \text{income before income taxes} - .40 \,(\text{income before income taxes})$$

$$\text{net income} = .60 \,(\text{income before income taxes})$$

$$\text{income before income taxes} = \frac{\text{net income}}{.60}$$

or

$$\text{target income before income taxes} = \frac{\text{target after-tax net income}}{1 - \text{tax rate}}$$

$$\text{target income before income taxes} = \frac{\$288}{1 - .40} = \frac{\$288}{.60} = \$480$$

Suppose the target net income after taxes was $288. The only change in the general equation approach would be on the right-hand side of the following equation:

$$\text{target sales} - \text{variable expenses} - \text{fixed expenses} = \frac{\text{target after-tax net income}}{1 - \text{tax rate}}$$

Thus, letting N be the number of units to be sold at $.50 each with a variable cost of $.40 each and total fixed costs of $6,000,

$$\$.50N - \$.40N - \$6,000 = \frac{\$288}{1 - .4}$$

$$\$.10N = \$6,000 + \frac{\$288}{.6}$$

$$\$.06N = \$3,600 + \$288 = \$3,888$$

$$N = \$3,888 \div \$.06 = 64,800 \text{ units}$$

Sales of 64,800 units produce an *after-tax* profit of $288 as shown here and a *before-tax* profit of $480 as shown in the chapter.

Suppose the target net income after taxes was $480. The volume needed would rise to 68,000 units, as follows:

$$\$.50N - \$.40N - \$6,000 = \frac{\$480}{1-.4}$$

$$\$.10N = \$6,000 + \frac{\$480}{.6}$$

$$\$.06N = \$3,600 + \$480 = \$4,080$$

$$N = \$4,080 \div \$.06 = 68,000 \text{ units}$$

As a shortcut to computing the effects of volume on the change in after-tax income, use the formula

$$\begin{pmatrix} \text{change} \\ \text{in net} \\ \text{income} \end{pmatrix} = \begin{pmatrix} \text{change in volume} \\ \text{in units} \end{pmatrix} \times \begin{pmatrix} \text{contribution margin} \\ \text{per unit} \end{pmatrix} \times (1 - \text{tax rate})$$

In our example, suppose operations were at a level of 64,800 units and $288 after-tax net income. The manager is wondering how much after-tax net income would increase if sales became 68,000 units.

$$\begin{aligned} \text{change in net income} &= (68,000 - 64,800) \times \$.10 \times (1 - .4) \\ &= 3,200 \times \$.10 \times .60 = 3,200 \times \$.06 \\ &= \$192 \end{aligned}$$

In brief, each unit beyond the break-even point adds to after-tax net profit at the unit contribution margin multiplied by (1 – income tax rate).

Throughout our illustration, the break-even point itself does not change. Why? Because there is *no income tax at a level of zero profits.*

Note

[1] The quality of overall working conditions might affect these decisions, even though such factors are difficult to quantify. In particular, if costs or profits do not differ much between alternatives. the nonquantifiable, subjective aspects may be the deciding factors.

SECTION IV
FINANCIAL PLANNING

CHAPTER 7: The Formal Budgeting Process

CHAPTER 8: Flexible Budgets and Standard Cost Systems

THE FORMAL BUDGETING PROCESS

Planning is the key to good management. This is true for individuals, small family-owned companies, new high-technology companies, large corporations, government agencies, and nonprofit organizations. For example, most successful students—who earn good grades, finance their education, and finish their degrees in a reasonable amount of time do so because they plan their time, their work, and their recreation. These students are *budgeting* their scarce resources to make the best use of their time, money, and energy. Likewise, owners of successful small companies who survive and grow even in difficult economic times carefully plan or budget their inventory purchases and their expansion of facilities so that they do not overextend themselves financially but are still able to meet customers' needs.

High-technology firms are often started by highly intelligent scientists and engineers who have valuable product ideas, but the high-technology firms that thrive are those whose managers also have superior planning and budgeting skills. Coordinating the use of scarce resources in a large, diverse corporation is an extremely complex and vital activity. Budgeting in these large corporations usually is ongoing throughout the year. Taxpayers demand that governments plan for the effective use of their hard-earned dollars, so government budgeting is especially important in difficult economic times, when tax dollars could otherwise have been spent for private purposes. Nonprofit organizations must develop more effective plans to achieve their objectives as they compete for scarce donations or grant monies. Not only are budgets critical to good planning in any endeavor, budgets are necessary for evaluation of performance. Keeping score is an American tradition, whether on the football field or in the boardroom. A *budget*— a formal, quantitative expression of plans (whether for an individual, business, or other organization)—provides a benchmark against which to measure actual performance.

As you will see in this chapter, a budget can be much more than a limit on expenditures. Although government agencies too often use a budget merely as a limit on their spending, businesses and other organizations generally use budgets to focus on operating or financial problems early, so that managers can take steps to avoid or remedy the problems. Thus, a budget is a tool that helps managers both *plan* and *control* operations.

Surveys of company practices indicate the importance of budgeting. For example, in a recent survey of manufacturing companies, the top ranked technique for cost reduction and control was budgetary planning and control. Advocates of budgeting maintain that the process of budgeting *forces a manager to become a better administrator and puts planning in the forefront of the manager's mind*. Indeed, failure to draw up, monitor, and adjust budgets to changing conditions is one of the primary reasons behind the collapse of many businesses.

In this chapter we will look at the uses and benefits of budgets and consider the construction of the master budget.

BUDGETS: WHAT THEY ARE AND HOW THEY BENEFIT THE ORGANIZATION

Another way to describe a budget is as a condensed business plan for the forthcoming year (or less). Few investors or bank loan officers today will provide funds for the would-be entrepreneur without a credible business plan. Similarly, within a firm, managers need budgets to guide them in allocating resources and maintaining control and to enable them to measure and reward progress.

Budgeting over Time

The planning horizon for budgeting may vary from one day to many years, depending on the organization's objectives and the uncertainties involved. The most forward-looking budget is the **strategic plan,** which sets the overall goals and objectives of the organization. (Note, though, that some business analysts do not call a strategic plan a budget because it covers no specific period and does not produce forecasted financial statements.)

Long-range planning produces forecasted financial statements for 5- or 10-year periods. Decisions made during long-range planning include addition or deletion of product lines, design and location of new plants, acquisition of buildings and equipment, and other long-term commitments. Long-range plans are coordinated with **capital budgets,** which detail the planned expenditures for facilities, equipment, new products, and other long-term investments,

A master budget is essentially a more extensive analysis of the first year of the long-range plan. A *budget* is a formal, quantitative expression of management plans. A **master budget** summarizes the planned activities of all subunits of an organization—sales, production, distribution, and finance. The master budget quantifies targets for sales, cost-driver activity, purchases, production, net income, cash position, and any other objective that management specifies. *Thus, the master budget is a periodic business plan that includes a coordinated set of detailed operating schedules and financial statements*. It includes forecasts of sales, expenses, cash receipts and disbursements, and balance sheets. Master budgets are also called **pro forma statements,** another term for forecasted financial statements. Management might prepare monthly budgets for the year or perhaps monthly budgets for only the first quarter and quarterly budgets for the three remaining quarters. The master budget is the most detailed budget that is coordinated across the whole organization, but individual managers may also prepare daily or weekly task-oriented budgets to help them carry out their particular functions and meet operating and financial goals.

Continuous budgets or **rolling budgets** are a very common form of master budgets that add a month in the future as the month just ended is dropped. Continuous budgets compel mangers to think specifically about the forthcoming 12 months and, thus, maintain a stable planning horizon. As they add a new 12th month to a continuous budget, managers may update the other 11 months as well. Then they can compare actual monthly results with both the original plan and the most recently revised plan.

Components of Master Budget

The terms used to describe assorted budget schedules vary from organization to organization; however, most master budgets have common elements. The usual master budget for a nonmanufacturing company has the following components:

A. Operating budget
    1. Sales budget (and other cost-driver budgets as necessary)
    2. Purchases budget
    3. Cost-of-goods-sold budget
    4. Operating expenses budget
    5. Budgeted income statement
B. Financial budget
    1. Capital budget
    2. Cash budget
    3. Budgeted balance sheet

Exhibit 7-1 presents a condensed diagram of the relationships among the various parts of a master budget for a nonmanufacturing company. In addition to these categories, manufacturing companies that maintain physical product inventories prepare ending inventory budgets and additional budgets for each type of resource activity (such as labor, materials, and factory overhead).

The two major parts of a master budget are the operating budget and the financial budget. The **operating budget** focuses on the income statement and its supporting schedules. Though sometimes called the **profit plan,** an operating budget may show a budgeted *loss,* or even be used to budget expenses in an organization or agency with no sales revenues. In contrast, the **financial budget** focuses on the effects that the operating budget and other plans (such as capital budgets and repayments of debt) will have on cash.

In addition to the master budget, there are countless forms of special budgets and related reports. For example, a report might detail goals and objectives for improvements in quality or customer satisfaction during the budget period.

Advantages of Budgets

All managers do some kind of planning or budgeting. Sometimes plans and budgets are unwritten, especially in small organizations. This might work in a small organization, but as an organization grows, informal, seat-of-the-pants planning is not enough. A more formal budgetary system becomes more than an attractive alternative—it is a necessity.

Skeptical managers have claimed, "I face too many uncertainties and complications to make budgeting worthwhile for me." Be wary of such claims. Planning and budgeting are especially important in uncertain environment. A budget allows *systematic rather than chaotic reaction to change.* For example, the Natural Resources Group of

Exhibit 7-1 Preparation of Master Budget for Nonmanufacturing Company

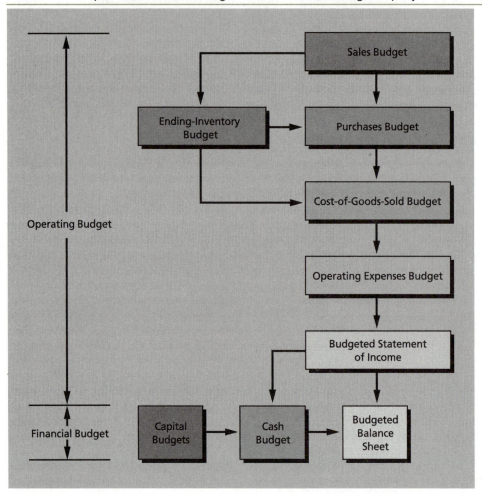

W. R. Grace & Co. greatly reduced a planned expansion in reaction to a worldwide abundance of oil and gas. A top executive, quoted in the company's annual report, stated that "management used the business planning process to adjust to changes in operating conditions."

Three major benefits of budgeting are as follows:

1. Budgeting compels managers to think ahead by formalizing their responsibilities for planning.
2. Budgeting provides definite expectations that are the best framework for judging subsequent performance.
3. Budgeting aids managers in coordinating their efforts, so that the objectives of the organization as a whole match the objectives of its parts.

Let's look more closely at each of these benefits.

Formalization of planning. Budgeting forces managers to think ahead—to anticipate and prepare for changing conditions. The budgeting process makes planning an *explicit* management responsibility. Too often, managers operate from day to day, extinguishing one business brush fire after another. They simply have "no time" for any tough-minded thinking beyond the next day's problems. Planning takes a back seat to or is actually obliterated by daily pressures.

The trouble with the day-to-day approach to managing an organization is that objectives are never crystallized. Managers react to current events rather than plan for the future. To prepare a budget, a manager should set goals and objectives, and establish policies to aid their achievement. The objectives are the destination points, and budgets are the road maps guiding us to those destinations. Without goals and objectives, company operations lack direction; problems are not foreseen; and results are difficult to interpret afterward.

Expectations: framework for judging performance. Budgeted goals and performance are generally a better basis for judging actual results than is past performance. The news that a company had sales of $100 million this year, as compared with $80 million the previous year, may or may not indicate that the company has been effective and has met company objectives. Perhaps sales should have been $110 million this year. The major drawback of using historical results for judging current performance is that inefficiencies may be concealed in the past performance. Intervening changes in economic conditions, technology, maneuvers by competitors, personnel, and so forth also limit the usefulness of comparisons with the past.

Communication and coordination. Another benefit of budgeting is that personnel are informed of what is expected of them. Nobody likes to drift along, not knowing what "the boss" expects or hopes to achieve. A good budget process communicates both from the top down and from the bottom up. Top management makes clear the goals and objectives of the organization in its budgetary directives to middle- and lower-level managers, and increasingly to all employees. Employees and lower-level managers then inform higher-level managers how they plan to achieve the goals and objectives.

Budgets also help managers coordinate objectives. For example, a budget forces purchasing personnel to integrate their plans with production requirements, while production managers use the sales budget and delivery schedule to help them anticipate and plan for the employees and physical facilities they will require. Similarly, financial officers use the sales budget, purchasing requirements, and so forth to anticipate the company's need for cash. Thus, the budgetary process forces managers to visualize the relationship of their department's activities to other departments and to the company as a whole.

ILLUSTRATION OF MASTER BUDGET PREPARATION

Now that you know what budgets are and why they are important, we can return to Exhibit 7-1 and trace the preparation of the master budget components. *Do not rush; follow each step carefully and completely.* Although the process may seem largely mechanical, remember that the master-budgeting process generates key decisions regarding pricing, product lines, capital expenditures, research and development, personnel assignments, and so forth. Therefore, the first draft of the budget leads to decisions that prompt subsequent drafts before a final budget is chosen. Because budget preparation is somewhat mechanical, many organizations use powerful spreadsheet or modeling software to prepare and modify budget drafts. Addendum 7 discusses using personal computer spreadsheets for budgeting.

Description of a Problem

To illustrate the budgeting process we will use as an example the Cooking Hut Company (CHC), a local retailer of a wide variety of kitchen and dining room items. The company rents a retail store in a midsized community near a large metropolitan area. CHC's management prepares a continuous budget to aid financial and operating decisions. For simplicity in this illustration, the planning horizon is only 4 months, April through July. In the past, sales have increased during this season. Collections lag behind sales, and cash is needed for purchases, wages, and other operating outlays. In the past, the company has met this cash squeeze with the help of short-term loans from a local bank and will continue to do so, repaying those loans as cash is available.

Exhibit 7-2 is the closing balance sheet for the fiscal year just ended. Sales in March were $40,000. Monthly sales are forecasted as follows:

April	$50,000
May	$80,000
June	$60,000
July	$50,000
August	$40,000

Management expects future sales collections to follow past experience: 60% of the sales should be in cash and 40% on credit. All credit accounts are collected in the month following the sales. The $16,000 of accounts receivable on March 31 represents credit sales made in March (40% of $40,000). Uncollectable accounts are negligible and are to be ignored. Also ignore all local, state, and federal taxes for this illustration.

Because deliveries from suppliers and customer demands are uncertain, at the end of each month, CHC wants to have on hand a basic inventory of items valued at $20,000 plus 80% of the expected cost of goods sold for the following month. The cost of merchandise sold averages 70% of sales. Therefore, the inventory on March 31 is $20,000 + .7(.8 × April sales of $50,000) = $20,000 + $28,000 = $48,000. The purchase terms available to CHC are net, 30 days. CHC pays for each month's purchases as follows: 50% during that month and 50% during the next month. Therefore, the accounts payable balance on March 31 is 50% of March's purchases, or $33,600 × .5 = $16,800.

Exhibit 7-2   The Cooking Hut Company Balance Sheet March 31, 19X1

Assets		
Current assets		
Cash	$ 10,000	
Accounts receivable, net (.4 x March sales of $40,000)	16,000	
Merchandise inventory, $20,000 + .7 (.8 x April sales of $50,000)	48,000	
Unexpired insurance	1,800	$ 75,800
Plant assets		
Equipment, fixtures, and other	$ 37,000	
Accumulated depreciation	12,800	24,200
Total assets		$100,000

Liabilities and Owners' Equity		
Current liabilities		
Accounts payable (.5 x March purchases of $33,600)	$ 16,000	
Accrued wages and commisions payable ($1,250 + $3,000)	4,250	$ 21,050
Owners' equity		78,950
Total liabilities and owners' equity		$100,000

CHC pays wages and commissions semimonthly, half a month after they are earned. They are divided into two portions: monthly fixed wages of $2,500 and commissions, equal to 15% of sales, which we will assume are uniform throughout each month. Therefore, the

March 31 balance of accrued wages and commissions payable is $(.5 \times \$2,500) + .5(.15 \times \$40,000) = \$1,250 + \$3,000 = \$4,250$. CHC will pay this $4,250 on April 15.

In addition to buying new fixtures for $3,000 cash in April, CHC's other monthly expenses are as follows:

Miscellaneous expenses	5% of sales, paid as incurred
Rent	$2,000, paid as incurred
Insurance	$200 expiration per month
Depreciation, including new fixtures	$500 per month

The company wants a minimum of $10,000 as a cash balance at the end of each month. To keep this simple, we will assume that CHC can borrow or repay loans in multiples of $1,000. Management plans to borrow no more cash than necessary and to repay as promptly as possible. Assume that borrowing occurs at the beginning and repayment at the end of the months in question. Interest is paid, under the terms of this credit arrangement, when the related loan is repaid. The interest rate is 18% per year.

Steps in Preparation of Master Budget

The principal steps in preparing the master budget are:

Operating Budget

1. Using the data given, prepare the following detailed schedules for each of the months of the planning horizon:
   a. Sales budget
   b. Cash collections from customers
   c. Purchases budget
   d. Disbursements for purchases
   e. Operating expense budget
   f. Disbursements for operating expenses
2. Using these schedules, prepare a budgeted income statement for the 4 months ending July 31, 19X1 (Exhibit 7-3).

Financial Budget

3. Using the data given and the supporting schedules, prepare the following forecasted financial statements:
   a. Cash budget including details of borrowings, repayments, and interest for each month of the planning horizon (Exhibit 7-4)
   b. Budgeted balance sheet as of July 31, 19X1 (Exhibit 7-5)

You will need schedules la, 1c, and le to prepare the budgeted income statement (Exhibit 7-3), and schedules 1b, 1d, and 1f to prepare the cash budget (Exhibit 7-4).

Organizations with effective budget systems have specific guidelines for the steps and timing of budget preparation. Although the details differ, the guidelines invariably include the preceding steps. As we follow these steps to examine the schedules of this illustrative problem, be sure that you understand the source of each figure in each schedule and budget. The logic of this manual example is identical to the logic used to prepare computerized budgeting models and systems (see the Addendum).

Step 1: Preparation of Operating Budget

You should now be ready to trace the budgeting process.

Step 1a: Sales budget. The sales budget (schedule a in the table below) is the starting point for budgeting because inventory levels, purchases, and operating expenses are geared to the rate of sales activities (and other cost drivers that are not present in this example). Accurate sales and cost-driver activity forecasting is essential to effective budgeting; sales forecasting is considered in a later section of this chapter. March sales are included in schedule a because they affect cash collections in April. Trace the final column in schedule a to the first row of Exhibit 7-3. In nonprofit organizations, forecasts of revenue or some level of services are also the focal points for budgeting. Examples are patient revenues and government reimbursement expected by hospitals and donations expected by churches. If no revenues are generated, as in the case of municipal fire protection, a desired level of service is predetermined.

Step 1b: Cash collections. It is easiest to prepare schedule b, cash collections, at the same time as preparing the sales budget. Cash collections include the current month's cash sales plus the previous month's credit sales. We will use total collections in preparing the cash budget—see Exhibit 7-4.

Step 1c: Purchases budget. After sales are budgeted, prepare the purchases budget (schedule c). The total merchandise needed will be the sum of the desired ending inventory plus the amount needed to fulfill budgeted sales demand. The total need will be

	March	April	May	June	July	April–July Total
Schedule a: Sales Budget						
Credit sales, 40%	$16,000	$20,000	$32,000	$24,000	$20,000	
Plus cash sales, 60%	24,000	30,000	48,000	36,000	30,000	
Total sales	$40,000	$50,000	$80,000	$60,000	$50,000	$240,000
Schedule b: Cash Collections						
Cash sales this month		$30,000	$48,000	$36,000	$30,000	
Plus 100% of last month's credit sales		16,000	20,000	32,000	24,000	
Total collections		$46,000	$68,000	$68,000	$54,000	

	March	April	May	June	July	April–July Total
Schedule c: Purchases Budget						
Desired ending inventory	$48,000*	$64,800	$ 53,600	$48,000	$42,400	
Plus cost of goods sold†	28,000	35,000	56,000	42,000	35,000	$168,000
Total needed	$76,000	$99,800	$109,600	$90,000	$77,400	
Less beginning inventory	42,400‡	48,000	64,800	53,600	48,000	
Purchases	$33,600	$51,800	$ 44,800	$36,400	$29,400	
Schedule d: Disbursements for Purchases						
50% of last month's purchases		$16,800	$ 25,900	$22,400	$18,200	
Plus 50% of this month's purchases		25,900	22,400	18,200	14,700	
Disbursements for purchases		$42,700	$ 48,300	$40,600	$32,900	

*$20,000 + (.8 × April cost of goods sold) = $20,000 + .8($35,000) = $48,000.
†.7 × March sales of $40,000 = $28,000; .7 × April sales of $50,000 = $35,000, and so on.
‡$20,000 + (.8 × March cost of goods sold of $28,000) = $20,000 + $22,400 = $42,400.

partially met by the beginning inventory; the remainder must come from planned purchases. These purchases are computed as follows:

budgeted purchases = desired ending inventory + cost of goods sold – beginning inventory

Trace the total purchases figure in the final column of schedule c to the second row of Exhibit 7-7.

Step 1d: Disbursements for purchases. Schedule d, disbursements for purchases, is based on the purchases budget. Disbursements include 50% of the current month's purchases and 50% of the previous month's purchases. We will use total disbursements in preparing the cash budget, Exhibit 7-4, for the financial budget.

Step 1e: Operating expense budget. The budgeting of operating expenses depends on various factors. Month-to-month fluctuations in sales volume and other cost-driver activities directly influence many operating expenses. Examples of expenses driven by sales volume include sales commissions and many delivery expenses. Other expenses are not influenced by sales or other cost-driver activity (such as rent, insurance, depreciation, and salaries) within appropriate relevant ranges and are regarded as fixed. Trace the total operating expenses in the final column of schedule e, which summarizes these expenses, to the budgeted income statement, Exhibit 7-3.

	March	April	May	June	July	April-July Total
Schedule e: Operating Expense Budget						
Wages (fixed)	$2,500	$ 2,500	$ 2,500	$ 2,500	$ 2,500	
Commissions (15% of current month's sales)	6,000	7,500	12,000	9,000	7,500	
Total wages and commissions	$8,500	$10,000	$14,500	$11,500	$10,000	$46,000
Miscellaneous expenses (5% of current sales)		2,500	4,000	3,000	2,500	12,000
Rent (fixed)		2,000	2,000	2,000	2,000	8,000
Insurance (fixed)		200	200	200	200	800
Depreciation (fixed)		500	500	500	500	2,000
Total operating expenses		$15,200	$21,200	$17,200	$15,200	$68,800

Exhibit 7-3 The Cooking Hut Company Budgeted Income Statement for 4 months Ending July 31, 19X1

	Data		Source of Data
Sales		$240,000	Schedule a
Cost of goods sold		168,000	Schedule c
Gross margin		$ 72,000	
Operating expenses:			
Wages and commissions	$46,000		Schedule e
Rent	8,000		Schedule e
Miscellaneous	12,000		Schedule e
Insurance	800		Schedule e
Depreciation	2,000	68,800	Schedule e
Income from operations		$ 3,200	
Interest expense		675	Figure 7-4
Net income		$ 2,525	

Exhibit 7-4   The Cooking Hut Company Cash Budget for 4 Months Ending July 31, 19X1

	April	May	June	July
Beginning cash balance	$ 10,000	$10,550	$10,970	$ 10,965
Cash receipts				
Collections from customers (schedule b)	46,000	68,000	68,000	54,000
Total cash available, before financing (w)	$ 56,000	$78,550	$78,970	$ 64,965
Cash disbursements				
Merchandise (schedule d)	42,700	48,300	40,600	32,900
Operating expenses (schedule f)	13,750	18,250	18,000	15,250
Purchase of new fixtures (given)	3,000	—	—	—
Total disbursements (x)	$ 59,450	$66,550	$58,600	$ 48,150
Minimum cash balance desired (y)	10,000	10,000	10,000	10,000
Total cash needed	$ 69,450	$76,550	$68,600	$ 58,150
Excess (deficiency) of total cash available over total cash needed before financing (w − x − y)	$(13,450)	$ 2,000	$10,370	$ 6,815
Financing				
Borrowing (at beginning of month)	$ 14,000†			
Repayments (at end of month)	—	$ (1,000)	$ (9,000)	$ (4,000)
Interest (at 18% per year)‡	—	(30)	(405)	(240)
Total cash increase (decrease) from financing (z)	$ 14,000	$ (1,030)	$ (9,405)	$ (4,240)
Ending cash balance (w − x + z)	$ 10,550	$10,970	$10,965	$ 12,575

*Letters are keyed to the explanation in the text.
†Borrowing and repayment of principal are made in multiples of $1,000, at an interest rate of 18% per year.
‡Interest computations: $.18 \times \$1,000 \times 2/12$; $.18 \times \$9,000 \times 3/12$; $.18 \times \$4,000 \times 4/12$.

Step 1f: Operating expense disbursements. Disbursements for operating expenses are based on the operating expense budget. Disbursements include 50% of last month's and this month's wages and commissions, and miscellaneous and rent expenses. We will use the total of these disbursements in preparing the cash budget, Exhibit 7-4.

Step 2: Preparation of Budgeted Income Statement

Steps 1a through 1f provide enough information to construct a budgeted income statement *from operations* (Exhibit 7-3). The income statement will be complete after addi-

	March	April	May	June	July	April-July Total
Schedule f: Disbursements for Operating Expenses						
Wages and commission						
50% of last month's expenses		$ 4,250	$ 5,000	$ 7,250	$ 5,750	
50% of this month's expenses		5,000	7,250	5,750	5,000	
Total wages and commissions		$ 9,250	$12,250	$13,000	$10,750	
Miscellaneous expenses		2,500	4,000	3,000	2,500	
Rent		2,000	2,000	2,000	2,000	
Total disbursements		$13,750	$18,250	$18,000	$15,250	

tion of the interest expense, which is computed after the cash budget has been prepared. Budgeted income from operations is often a benchmark for judging management performance.

Step 3: Preparation of Financial Budget

The second major part of the master budget is the financial budget, which consists of the capital budget, cash budget, and ending balance sheet. This chapter focuses on the cash budget and the ending balance sheet. In our illustration, the $3,000 purchase of new fixtures would be included in the capital budget.

Step 3a: Cash budget. The **cash budget** is a statement of planned cash receipts and disbursements. The cash budget is heavily affected by the level of operations summarized in the budgeted income statement. The cash budget has the following major sections, where the letters **w, x, y,** and **z** refer to the lines in Exhibit 7-4 that summarize the effects of that section.

The *total cash available before financing* (**w**) equals the beginning cash balance plus cash receipts. Cash receipts depend on collections from customers' accounts receivable and cash sales and on other operating income sources. Trace total collections from schedule b to Exhibit 7-4.

Cash disbursements (**x**) for

1. Purchases depend on the credit terms extended by suppliers and the bill-paying habits of the buyer (disbursements for merchandise from schedule d should be traced to Exhibit 7-4.

2. Payroll depends on wage, salary, and commission terms and on payroll dates (wages and commissions from schedule f should be traced to Exhibit 7-4).

3. Some costs and expenses depend on contractual terms for installment payments, mortgage payments, rents, leases, and miscellaneous items (miscellaneous and rent from schedule f should be traced to Exhibit 7-4).

4. Other disbursements include outlays for fixed assets, long-term investments, dividends, and the like (the $3,000 expenditure for new fixtures).

Management determines the minimum cash balance desired (**y**) depending on the nature of the business and credit arrangements.

Financing requirements (**z**) depend on how the total cash available, **w** in Exhibit 7-4, compares with the *total cash needed*. Needs include the disbursements, **x,** plus the desired ending cash balance, **y**. If the total cash available is less than the cash needed, borrowing is necessary—Exhibit 7-4 shows that CHC will borrow $14,000 in April to cover the planned *deficiency*. If there is an excess, loans may be repaid—$1,000, $9,000, and $4,000 are repaid in May, June, and July, respectively. The pertinent outlays for interest expenses are usually contained in this section of the cash budget. Trace the calculated interest expense to Exhibit 7-3, which then will be complete.

The *ending cash balance* is **w − x + z**. Financing, **z,** has either a positive (borrowing) or a negative (repayment) effect on the cash balance. The illustrative cash budget shows the pattern of short-term, "self-liquidating" financing. Seasonal peaks often result in heavy drains on cash—for merchandise purchases and operating expenses—before the sales are made and cash is collected from customers. The resulting loan is "self-liquidating"—that is, the borrowed money is used to acquire merchandise for sale, and the proceeds from sales are used to repay the loan. This "working capital cycle" moves from cash to inventory to receivables and back to cash.

Cash budgets help management to avoid having unnecessary idle cash, on the one hand, and unnecessary cash deficiencies, on the other. A well-managed financing program keeps cash balances from becoming too large or too small.

Step 3b: Budgeted balance sheet. The final step in preparing the master budget is to construct the budgeted balance sheet (Exhibit 7-5) that projects each balance sheet item in accordance with the business plan as expressed in the previous schedules. Specifically, the beginning balances at March 31 would be increased or decreased in light of the expected cash receipts and cash disbursements in Exhibit 7-4 and in light of the effects of noncash items appearing on the income statement in Exhibit 7-3. For example, unexpired insurance would decrease from its balance of $1,800 on March 31 to $1,000 on July 31, even though it is a noncash item.

When the complete master budget is formulated, management can consider all the major financial statements as a basis for changing the course of events. For example, the initial formulation may prompt management to try new sales strategies to generate more demand. Alternatively, management may explore the effects of various adjustments in the timing of receipts and disbursements. The large cash deficiency in April, for example, may lead to an emphasis on cash sales or an attempt to speed up collection of accounts receivable. In any event, the first draft of the master budget is rarely the final draft. As it is reworked, the budgeting process becomes an integral part of the management process itself—budgeting is planning and communicating.

DIFFICULTIES OF SALES FORECASTING

As you have seen in the foregoing illustration, the sales budget is the foundation of the entire master budget. The accuracy of estimated purchases budgets, production schedules, and costs depends on the detail and accuracy (in dollars, units, and mix) of the budgeted sales.

Sales forecasting is a key to preparing the sales budget, but a forecast and a budget are not necessarily identical. A **sales forecast** is a *prediction* of sales under a given set of conditions. A **sales budget** is the result of *decisions* to create the conditions that will generate a *desired* level of sales. For example, you may have forecasts of sales at various levels of advertising. The forecast for the one level you decide to implement becomes the budget.

Sales forecasts are usually prepared under the direction of the top sales executive. Important factors considered by sales forecasters include the following:

1. *Past patterns of sales:* Past experience combined with detailed past sales by product line, geographical region, and type of customer can help predict future sales.

2. *Estimates made by the sales force:* A company's sales force is often the best source of information about the desires and plans of customers.

Exhibit 7-5 The Cooking Hut Company Budgeted Balance Sheet, July 31, 19X1

Assets		
Current assets		
Cash (Exhibit 7-4)	$12,575	
Accounts receivable, net (.4 × July sales of $50,000, schedule a)	20,000	
Merchandise inventory (schedule c)	42,400	
Unexpired insurance ($1,800 – $800)	1,000	$ 75,975
Plant assets		
Equipment, fixtures, and other ($37,000 + $3,000 fixtures)	$40,000	
Accumulated depreciation ($12,800 + $2,000 depreciation expense)	(14,800)	25,200
Total assets		$101,175

Exhibit 7-5   The Cooking Hut Company Budgeted Balance Sheet, July 31, 19X1 (cont.)

Liabilities and Owners' Equity

Current liabilities		
Accounts payable (.5 × July purchases of $29,400, schedule c)	$14,700	
Accrued wages and commissions payable (.5 x $10,000, schedule e)	5,000	$ 19,700
Owners' equity ($78,950 + $2,525 net income)		81,475
Total liabilities and owners' equity		$101,175

Note: Beginning balances are used as a start for the computations of unexpired insurance, plant, and owners' equity.

3. *General economic conditions:* Predictions for many economic indicators, such as gross domestic product and industrial production indexes (local and foreign), are published regularly. Knowledge of how sales relate to these indicators can aid sales forecasting.

4. *Competitors' actions:* Sales depend on the strength and actions of competitors. To forecast sales, a company should consider the likely strategies and reactions of competitors, such as changes in their prices, product quality, or services.

5. *Changes in the firm's prices:* Sales can be increased by decreasing prices and vice versa. A company should consider the effects of price changes on customer demand.

6. *Changes in product mix:* Changing the mix of products often can affect not only sales levels but also overall contribution margin. Identifying the most profitable products and devising methods to increase their sales is a key part of successful management.

7. *Market research studies:* Some companies hire market experts to gather information about market conditions and customer preferences. Such information is useful to managers making sales forecasts and product mix decisions.

8. *Advertising and sales promotion plans:* Advertising and other promotional costs affect sales levels. A sales forecast should be based on anticipated effects of promotional activities.

Sales forecasting usually combines various techniques. In addition to the opinions of the sales staff, statistical analysis of correlations between sales and economic indicators (prepared by economists and members of the market research staff) provide valuable help. The opinions of line management also heavily influence the final sales forecasts. Ultimately, no matter how many technical experts are used in forecasting, the *sales budget* is the responsibility of line management.

Sales forecasting is still somewhat mystical, but its procedures are becoming more formalized and are being reviewed more seriously because of the intensity of global competitive pressures. Although this book does not include a detailed discussion of the preparation of the sales budget, the importance of an accurate sales forecast cannot be overstressed.

Governments and other nonprofit organizations also face a problem similar to sales forecasting. For example, the budget for city revenues may depend on a variety of factors, such as predicted property taxes, traffic fines, parking fees, license fees, and city income taxes. In turn, property taxes depend on the extent of new construction and, in most localities, general increases in real estate values. Thus, a municipal budget may require forecasting that is just as sophisticated as that required by a private firm.

MAKING A BUDGET WORK

No matter how accurate sales forecasts are, if budgets are to benefit an organization, they need the support of all the firm's employees. Lower-level workers and managers attitudes toward budgets will be heavily influenced by the attitude of top management. Even with the support of top management, however, budgets—and the managers who implement them—can run into opposition.

Managers often compare actual results with budgets in evaluating subordinates. Few individuals are immediately ecstatic about techniques used to check their performance. Lower-level managers sometimes regard budgets as embodiments of restrictive, negative top-management attitudes. Accountants reinforce this view if they use a budget only to point out managers' failings. Such negative attitudes are even greater when the budget's primary purpose is to limit spending. For example, budgets are generally unpopular in government agencies where their only use is to request and authorize funding. To avoid negative attitudes toward budgets, accountants and top management must demonstrate how budgets can *help each manager and employee* achieve better results. Only then will the budgets become a positive aid in motivating employees at all levels to work toward goals, set objectives, measure results accurately, and direct attention to the areas that need investigation.

Another serious human relations problem, which may preclude some of these benefits of budgeting, can result if budgets stress one set of performance goals, but employees and managers are rewarded for performance on other dimensions. For example, a budget may concentrate on current costs of production, but managers and employees may be rewarded on quality of production and on timely delivery of products to customers. These dimensions of performance could be in direct conflict.

The overriding importance of the human aspects of budgeting cannot be overemphasized. Too often, top management and accountants are overly concerned with the mechanics of budgets, ignoring the fact that the effectiveness of any budgeting system depends directly on whether the affected managers and employees understand and accept the budget. Budgets formulated with the active participation of all affected employees are generally more effective than budgets imposed on subordinates. This involvement is usually called **participative budgeting**.

FINANCIAL PLANNING MODELS

Properly constructed and implemented, the master budget is the best practical approximation to a formal *model* of the total organization: its objectives, inputs, constraints, and outputs. Managers try to predict how various decisions will affect the master budget. This is a step-by-step process whereby tentative plans are revised as managers exchange views on various aspects of expected activities.

Today, most large companies have developed **financial planning models**, mathematical models of the master budget that can react to any set of assumptions about sales, costs, product mix, and so on. For instance, Dow Chemical's model uses 140 separate, constantly revised cost inputs that are based on several different cost drivers.

By mathematically describing the relationships among all the operating and financial activities and among the other major internal and external factors that can affect the results of management decisions, financial planning models allow managers alternatives before final decisions are selected. For example, a manager might want to predict the consequences of changing the mix of products offered for sale to emphasize several products with the highest prospects for growth. A financial planning model would provide operational and financial budgets well into the future under alternative assumptions about the product mix, sales levels, production constraints, quality levels, scheduling, and so on. Most important, managers can get answers to "what if" questions, such as "What if sales are 10% below forecasts? What if material prices increase 8% instead of 4% as expected? What if the new union contract grants a 6% raise in consideration for productivity improvements?" Building models that can help answer "what if" questions is the subject of Addendum 7.

Financial planning models have shortened managers' reaction times dramatically. A revised plan for a large company that took many accountants many days to prepare by hand can be prepared in minutes. Public Service Electric & Gas, a New Jersey utility, can run its total master budget several times a day, if necessary.

Warning: The use of spreadsheet software on personal computers has put financial planning models within reach of even the smallest organizations. The ready access to powerful modeling, however, does not guarantee plausible or reliable results. Financial planning models are only as good as the assumptions and the inputs used to build and manipulate them—what computer specialists call GIGO (garbage in, garbage out). Nearly every chief financial officer has a horror story to tell about following bad advice from a faulty financial planning model.

SUMMARY

A budget outlines an organization's objectives and possible steps for achieving them. The budgetary process compels managers to think and to prepare for changing conditions. Budgets are aids in planning, communicating, setting standards of performance, motivating personnel toward goals, measuring results, and directing attention to the areas that need investigation.

Master budgets typically cover relatively short periods—usually 1 month to 1 year. Long-range plans, however, may extend over a much longer time horizon, up to 10 years ahead. Because the future is uncertain, long-range plans focus on strategic considerations. The master budget is more detailed and offers specific guidance over the immediate budget period. Within the master budget are operating budgets, which detail resource requirements, and financial budgets, which are forecasted financial plans. The steps involved in preparing a master budget vary across organizations but follow the general outline given above. Invariably, the first step is to forecast sales or service levels, which can be quite difficult. The next step should be to forecast cost-driver activity levels, given expected sales and service. From these forecasts and knowledge of cost behavior, collection patterns, and so on, the operating and financing budgets can be prepared.

One of the most crucial determinants of successful budgeting is how the organization includes and considers the people who are directly affected by the budget. Negative attitudes toward budgets usually prevent realization of many of the benefits of budgeting. Such attitudes are usually caused by managers who use budgets to force behavior or to punish substandard performance. Budgets generally are more useful when they are formulated with the willing participation of all affected parties.

Financial planning models are mathematical representations of the organization's master budget. Most large companies use financial planning models, and many small companies are beginning to use them. These models usually are prepared with computer spreadsheet software that allows powerful budget analysis and flexible planning (see Addendum 7).

SELF-CORRECTION PROBLEM

Do not attempt to solve this problem until you understand the *step-by-step* illustration in this chapter.

1. The Country Store is a retail outlet for a variety of hardware and homewares. The owner of the Country Store is anxious to prepare a budget for the next quarter, which is typically quite busy. She is most concerned with her cash position because she expects that she will have to borrow to finance purchases in anticipation of sales. She has gathered all the data necessary to prepare a simplified budget. Exhibit 7-6 shows these data in tabular form. In addition, equipment will be purchased in April for $19,750 cash, and dividends of $4,000 will be paid in June. Review the structure of the example in the chapter and then prepare the Country Store's master budget for the months of April, May, and June. The solution follows after the budget data. Note that there are a few minor differences between this example and the one in the chapter. These are identified in Exhibit 7-6 and in the solution. The primary difference is in the payment of interest on borrowing. Borrowing occurs at the end of a month when cash is needed. Repayments (if appropriate) occur at the end of a month when cash is available. Interest also is paid in cash at the end of the month at an annual rate of 12% on the amount of note payable outstanding during that month.

Exhibit 7-6   The Country Store Budget Data Balance Sheet as of March 31, 19X4

Assets		Budgeted Sales	
Cash	$ 9,000	March (actual)	$60,000
Accounts receivable	48,000	April	70,000
Inventory	12,600	May	85,000
Plant and equipment (net)	200,000	June	90,000
Total assets	$269,600	July	50,000
Liabilities and equities		Required minimum cash balance	$ 8,000
Interest payable	0	Sales mix, cash/credit:	
Note payable	0	Cash sales	20%
Accounts payable	18,300	Credit sales (collected the following	
Capital stock	180,000	month)	80%
Retained earnings	71,300	Gross profit rate	40%
Total liabilities and equities	$269,600	Loan interest rate (interest paid in cash	
Budgeted expenses (per month)		monthly)	12%
Wages and salaries	$ 7,500	Inventory paid for in:	
Freight out as a % of sales	6%	Month purchased	50%
Advertising	$ 6,000	Month after purchase	50%
Depreciation	$ 2,000		
Other expense as a % of sales	4%		
Minimum inventory policy as a %			
of next month's cost of goods sold	30%		

SOLUTION TO SELF-CORRECTION PROBLEM

Schedule a: Sales budget

	April	May	June	Total
Credit sales, 80%	$56,000	$68,000	$72,000	$196,000
Cash sales, 20%	14,000	17,000	18,000	49,000
Total sales	$70,000	$85,000	$90,000	$245,000

Schedule b: Cash collections

	April	May	June	Total
Cash sales	$14,000	$17,000	$18,000	$ 49,000
Collections from prior month	48,000	56,000	68,000	172,000
Total collections	$62,000	$73,000	$86,000	$221,000

Schedule c: Purchases budget

	April	May	June	Total
Desired ending inventory	$15,300	$16,200	$ 9,000	$ 40,500
Plus cost of goods sold	42,000	51,000	54,000	147,000
Total needed	$57,300	$67,200	$ 63,000	$187,500
Less beginning inventory	12,600	15,300	16,200	44,100
Total purchases	$44,700	$51,900	$46,800	$143,400

Schedule d: Cash disbursements for purchases

	April	May	June	Total
For March*	$18,300			$ 18,300
For April	22,350	$22,350		44,700
For May		25,950	$25,950	51,900
For June			23,400	23,400
Total disbursements	$40,650	$48,300	$49,350	$138,300

*The amount payable from the previous month.

Schedules e and f: Operating expenses and disbursements for expenses (except interest)

	April	May	June	Total
Cash expenses				
Salaries & wages	$ 7,500	$ 7,500	$ 7,500	$22,500
Freight-out	4,200	5,100	5,400	14,700
Advertising	6,000	6,000	6,000	18,000
Other expenses	2,800	3,400	3,600	9,800
Total disbursements for expenses	$20,500	$22,000	$22,500	$65,000
Noncash expenses				
Depreciation	2,000	2,000	2,000	6,000
Total expenses	$22,500	$24,000	$24,500	$71,000

The Country Store Cash Budget April-June, 19X4

	April	May	June
Beginning cash balance	$ 9,000	$ 8,000	$ 8,000
Cash collections	62,000	73,000	86,000
Total cash available	71,000	81,000	94,000
Cash disbursements			
Inventory purchases	40,650	48,300	49,350
Operating expenses	20,500	22,000	22,500
Equipment purchases	19,750	0	0
Dividends	0	0	4,000
Interest*	0	179	154
Total disbursements	80,900	70,479	76,004
Minimum cash balance	8,000	8,000	8,000
Total cash needed	$ 88,900	$78,479	$84,004
Cash excess (deficit)	$(17,900)	$ 2,521	$ 9,996
Financing			
Borrowing†	17,900	0	0
Repayments	0	(2,521)	(9,996)
Total cash from financing	17,900	(2,521)	(9,996)
Ending cash balance	$ 8,000	$ 8,000	$ 8,000

*In this example interest is paid on the loan amounts outstanding during the month; May: (0.12 ÷ 12) × ($17,900) = $179; June: (0.12 ÷ 12) × ($17,900 − $2,521) = $154.

†In this example, borrowings are at the end of the month in the amounts needed. Repayments also are made at the end of the month as excess cash permits.

The Country Store Budgeted Income Statement April-June, 19X4

	April	May	June	April-June Total
Sales	$70,000	$85,000	$90,000	$245,000
Cost of goods sold	42,000	51,000	54,000	147,000
Gross margin	28,000	34,000	36,000	98,000
Operating expenses				
Salaries and wages	7,500	7,500	7,500	22,500
Freight-out	4,200	5,100	5,400	14,700
Advertising	6,000	6,000	6,000	18,000
Other	2,800	3,400	3,600	9,800
Interest*	—	179	154	333
Depreciation	2,000	2,000	2,000	6,000
Total expense	$22,500	$24,179	$24,654	$71,333
Net operating income	$ 5,500	$ 9,821	$11,346	$26,667

*Note that interest expense is the monthly interest rate times the borrowed amount held for the month: May (0.12 ÷ 12) × $17,900 = $179; June: (0.12 ÷ 12) × $15,379 = $154.

The Country Store Budgeted Balance Sheets as of the End of April-June, 19X4

Assets	April	May	June*
Current assets			
Cash	$ 8,000	$ 8,000	$ 8,000
Accounts receivable	56,000	68,000	72,000
Inventory	15,300	16,200	9,000
Total current assets	79,300	92,200	89,000
Plant, less accumulated depreciation[†]	217,750	215,750	213,750
Total assets	$297,050	$307,950	$302,750

Liabilities and Equities			
Liabilities			
Accounts payable	$ 22,350	$ 25,950	$ 23,400
Notes payable	17,900	15,379	5,383
Total liabilities	40,250	41,329	28,783
Stockholders' equity			
Capital stock	180,000	180,000	180,000
Retained earnings	76,800	86,621	93,967
Total equities	256,800	266,621	273,967
Total liabilities & equities	$297,050	$307,950	$302,750

*The June 30, 19X4 balance sheet is the ending balance sheet for the entire three-month period.
[†]$200,000 + $19,750 − $2,000 = $217,750.

QUESTIONS

1. Is budgeting used primarily for scorekeeping, attention directing, or problem solving?
2. "Budgets are okay in relatively certain environments. But everything changes so quickly in the electronics industry that budgeting is a waste of time." Comment on this statement.
3. What are the major benefits of budgeting?
4. Why is budgeted performance better than past performance as a basis for judging actual results?
5. What is the major technical difference between historical and budgeted financial statements?
6. "Budgets are primarily a tool used to limit expenditures." Do you agree? Explain.
7. How do strategic planning, long-range planning, and budgeting differ?
8. "Capital budgets are plans for managing long-term debt and common stock." Do you agree? Explain.
9. "I oppose continuous budgets because they provide a moving target. Managers never know what to aim at." Discuss.
10. "Pro forma statements are those statements prepared in conjunction with continuous budgets." Do you agree? Explain.
11. Differentiate between an operating budget and a financial budget.
12. Why is the sales forecast the starting point for budgeting?
13. What is the principal objective of a cash budget?
14. Differentiate between a sales forecast and a sales budget.
15. What factors influence the sales forecast?
16. "Education and salesmanship are key features of budgeting." Explain.
17. What are financial planning models?
18. "Budgeting for a manufacturing firm is fundamentally different from budgeting for a retail firm." Do you agree? Explain.
19. "I cannot be bothered with setting up my monthly budget on a spreadsheet. It just takes too long to be worth the effort." Comment.
20. Explain the importance of understanding cost behavior to preparing the master budget.
21. Explain the relationship between the sales (or service) forecast and cost-driver activity.

PROBLEMS

1. **Prepare Master Budget.** A wholesaling subsidiary of Paul Lamb Industries has a strong belief in using highly decentralized management. You are the new manager of one of its small "Apex" stores (Store No. 82). You know much about how to buy, how to display, how to sell, and how to reduce shoplifting. You know little about accounting and finance, however.

    Top management is convinced that training for higher management should include the active participation of store managers in the budgeting process. You have been asked to prepare a complete master budget for your store for June, July, and August. You are responsible for its actual full preparation. All accounting is done centrally, so you have no expert help on the premises. In addition, tomorrow the branch manager and the assistant controller will be here to examine your work; at that time they will assist you in formulating the final budget document. The idea is to have you prepare the budget a few times so that you gain more confidence about accounting matters. You want to make a favorable impression on your superiors, so you gather the following data as of May 31, 19X6:

		Recent and Projected Sales	
Cash	$ 29,000		
Inventory	420,000	April	$300,000
Accounts receivable	369,000	May	350,000
Net furniture and fixtures	168,000	June	700,000
Total assets	$986,000	July	400,000
Accounts payable	$475,000	August	400,000
Owners' equity	511,000	September	300,000
Total liabilities and owners' equities	$986,000		

Credit sales are 90% of total sales. Credit accounts are collected 80% in the month following the sale and 20% in the following month. Assume that bad debts are negligible and can be ignored. The accounts receivable on May 31 are the result of the credit sales for April and May: (.20 × .90 x $300,000 = $54,000) + (1.00 × .90 × $350,000 = $315,000) = $369,000. The average gross profit on sales is 40%.

The policy is to acquire enough inventory each month to equal the following month's projected sales. All purchases are paid for in the month following purchase.

Salaries, wages, and commissions average 20% of sales; all other variable expenses are 4% of sales. Fixed expenses for rent, property taxes, and miscellaneous payroll and other items are $55,000 monthly. Assume that these variable and fixed expenses require cash disbursements each month. Depreciation is $2,500 monthly.

In June, $55,000 is going to be disbursed for fixtures acquired in May. The May 31 balance of accounts payable includes this amount.

Assume that a minimum cash balance of $25,000 is to be maintained. Also assume that all borrowings are effective at the beginning of the month and all repayments are made at the end of the month of repayment. Interest is paid only at the time of repaying principal. The interest rate is 12% per annum; round interest computations to the nearest ten dollars. All loans and repayments of principal must be made in multiples of a thousand dollars.

a. Prepare a budgeted income statement for the coming quarter, a budgeted statement of monthly cash receipts and disbursements (for the next 3 months), and a budgeted balance sheet for August 30, 19X6. All operations are evaluated on a before-income tax basis. Also, because income taxes are disbursed from corporate headquarters, they may be ignored here.

b. Explain why there is a need for a bank loan and what operating sources supply cash for repaying the bank loan.

2. **Prepare Master Budget.** The Little Teddy Company wants a master budget for the next 3 months, beginning January 1, 19X7. It desires an ending minimum cash balance of 55,000 each month. Sales are forecasted at an average selling price of $4 per miniature teddy bear. In January, Little Teddy is beginning JIT deliveries from suppliers, which means that purchases equal expected sales. On January 1, purchases will cease until inventory reaches $6,000, after which time purchases will equal sales. Merchandise costs are $2 per bear. Purchases during any given month are paid in full during the following month. All sales are on credit, payable within 30 days, but experience has shown that 60% of current sales is collected in the current month, 30% in the next month, and 10% in the month thereafter. Bad debts are negligible.

Monthly operating expenses are as follows:

Wages and salaries	$15,000
Insurance expired	125
Depreciation	250
Miscellaneous	2,500
Rent	250/month + 10% of quarterly sales over $10,000

Cash dividends of $1,500 are to be paid quarterly, beginning January 15, and are declared on the 15th of the previous month. All operating expenses are paid as incurred, except insurance, depreciation, and rent. Rent of $250 is paid at the beginning of each month, and the additional 10% of sales is paid quarterly on the 10th of the month following the end of the quarter. The next settlement is due January 10.

The company plans to buy some new fixtures for $3,000 cash in March.

Money can be borrowed and repaid in multiples of $500 at an interest rate of 12% per annum. Management wants to minimize borrowing and repay rapidly. Interest is computed and paid when the principal is repaid. Assume that borrowing occurs at the beginning, and repayments at the end, of the months in question. Money is never borrowed at the beginning and repaid at the end of the *same* month. Compute interest to the nearest dollar.

Assets as of December 31, 19X6		Liabilities as of December 31, 19X6	
Cash	$ 5,000	Accounts payable (merchandise)	$35,550
Accounts receivable	12,500	Dividends payable	1,500
Inventory*	39,050	Rent payable	7,800
Unexpired insurance	1,500		$44,850
Fixed assets, net	12,500		
	$70,550		

*November 30 inventory balance = $16,000

Recent and forecasted sales:

October	$38,000	December	$25,000	February	$75,000	April	$45,000
November	25,000	January	62,000	March	38,000		

a. Prepare a master budget including a budgeted income statement, balance sheet, statement of cash receipts and disbursements, and supporting schedules for the months January through March 19X7.

b. Explain why there is a need for a bank loan and what operating sources provide the cash for the repayment of the bank loan.

ADDENDUM 7: USING SPREADSHEETS FOR BUDGETING

Spreadsheet software for personal computers is an extremely powerful and flexible tool for budgeting. An obvious advantage of the spreadsheet is that arithmetic errors are virtually nonexistent. The real value of spreadsheets, however, is that they can be used to make a mathematical model (a financial planning model) of the organization. This model can be used repeatedly at a very low cost and can be altered to reflect possible changes in expected sales, cost drivers, cost functions, and so on. The objective of this appendix is to illustrate *sensitivity analysis*, one aspect of the power and flexibility of spreadsheet software that has made this software an indispensable budgeting tool.

Recall the chapter's master budgeting example. Suppose CHC has prepared its master budget using spreadsheet software. To simplify making changes to the budget, the relevant forecasts and other budgeting details have been placed in Exhibit 7-7. Note that for simplification, only the data necessary for the purchases budget have been shown here; the full master budget would require a larger table with all the data given in the chapter. Each part of the table can be identified by its column and row intersection or "cell address." For example, the beginning inventory for the budget period can be located with the cell address "D4," which is shown as $48,000.

By referencing. the budget data's cell addresses, you can generate the purchases budget (Exhibit 7-8) within the same spreadsheet by entering *formulas* instead of numbers into the schedule. Consider Exhibit 7-8. Instead of typing $48,000 as April's beginning inventory in the purchases budget at cell D17, type a "formula" with the cell address for the beginning inventory from the preceding *table*, + D4 (the cell address preceded by a "+" sign—a spreadsheet rule to identify a formula; some spreadsheets use "=" to indi-

Exhibit 7-7 The Cooking Hut Company Budget Data
(Column and row labels are given by the spreadsheet)

	A	B	C	D	E	F	6
1	Budget data						
2	Sales forecasts		Other information				
3							
4	March (actual)	$40,000	Beginning inventory	$48,000			
5	April	50,000	Desired ending inventory: Base amount	$20,000			
6	May	80,000	Plus percent of next				
7	June	60,000	month's cost of				
8	July	50,000	goods sold	80%			
9	August	40,000	Cost of goods sold				
10			as percent of sales	70%			

Exhibit 7-8 The Cooking Hut Company Purchases Budget Formulas

	A	B	C	D	E	F	G
11	Schedule c						
12	Purchases budget			April	May	June	July
13	Desired ending inventory			+D5+D8 D10*B6	+D5+D8 D10*B7	+D5+D8 D10*B8	+D5+D8 D10*B9
14	Plus cost of goods sold			+D10*B5	+D10*B6	+D10*B7	+D10*B8
15							
16	Total needed			+D13+ D14	+E13+E14	+F13+F14	+G13+G14
17	Less beginning inventory			+D4	+D13	+E13	+F13
18							
19	Purchases			+D16–D17	+E16–E17	+F16–F17	+G16–G17
20							

cate a formula). Likewise, all the cells of the purchases budget will be composed of formulas containing cell addresses instead of numbers. The *total needed* in April (D16) is + D13 + D14, and *purchases* in April (D19) are budgeted to be + D16 – D17. The figures for May, June, and July are computed similarly within the respective columns. This approach gives the spreadsheet the most flexibility because you could change any number in the budget data in Exhibit 7-7 (e.g., a sales forecast), and the software automatically recalculates the numbers in the entire purchases budget. Exhibit 7-8 shows the formulas used for the purchases budget. Exhibit 7-9 is the purchases budget displaying the numbers generated by the formulas in Exhibit 7-8.

Now, what if sales could be 10% higher than initially forecasted during April through August? What effect will this alternative forecast have on budgeted purchases? Even to revise this simple purchases budget would require a considerable number of manual recalculations. Merely changing the sales forecasts in spreadsheet Exhibit 7-7, however, results in a nearly instantaneous revision of the purchases budget. Exhibit 7-10 shows the alternative sales forecasts and other unchanged data along with the revised purchases budget. We could alter every piece of budget data in the table and easily view or print out the effects on purchases. This sort of analysis, assessing the effects of varying one of the budget inputs, up or down, is called *sensitivity analysis.* **Sensitivity analysis** for budgeting is the systematic varying of budget data input to determine the effects of each change on the budget. This type of "what if" analysis is one of the most powerful uses of spreadsheets for financial planning models. Note, though, that it is not generally a good idea to vary more than one of the types of budget inputs at a time, unless they are obviously related, because doing so makes it difficult to isolate the effect of each change.

Every schedule, operating budget, and financial budget of the master budget can be prepared on the spreadsheet. Each schedule would be linked by the appropriate cell addresses just as the budget input data (Exhibit 7-7) are linked to the purchases budget (Exhibits 7-8 and 7-9). As in the purchases budget, ideally all cells in the master budget

Exhibit 7-9 The Cooking Hut Company Purchases Budget

	A	B	C	D	E	F	G
11	Schedule c						
12	Purchases budget			April	May	June	July
13	Desired ending inventory			$64,800	$53,600	$48,000	$42,400
14	Plus cost of goods sold			35,000	56,000	42,000	35,000
15							
16	Total needed			99,800	109,600	90,000	77,400
17	Less beginning inventory			48,000	64,800	53,600	48,000
18							
19	Purchases			$51,800	$44,800	$36,400	$29,400
20							

are formulas, not numbers. That way, every budget input can be the subject of sensitivity analysis, if desired, by simply changing the budget data in Exhibit 7-7.

Preparing the master budget on a spreadsheet is time-consuming—the first time. After that, the time savings and planning capabilities through sensitivity analysis are enormous compared with a manual approach. A problem can occur, however, if the master budget model is not well documented when a person other than the author attempts to modify the spreadsheet model. Any assumptions that are made should be described either within the spreadsheet or in a separate budget preparation document.

Exhibit 7-10   The Cooking Hut Company Purchases Budget

	A	B	C	D	E	F	G
1	Budgeted data						
2	Sales forecasts		Other information				
3							
4	March (actual)	$40,000	Beginning inventory	$48,000			
5	April	55,000	Desired ending inventory: Base amount	$20,000			
6	May	88,000	Plus percent of next				
7	June	66,000	month's cost of				
8	July	55,000	goods sold	80%			
9	August	44,000	Cost of goods sold				
10			as percent of sales	70%			
11	Schedule c						
12	Purchases budget			April	May	June	July
13	Desired ending inventory			$69,280	$56,960	$50,800	$44,640
14	Plus cost of goods sold			38,500	61,600	46,200	38,500
15							
16	Total needed			107,780	118,560	97,000	83,140
17	Beginning inventory			48,000	69,280	56,960	50,800
18							
19	Purchases			59,780	49,280	$40,040	$32,340
20							

CHAPTER 8

FLEXIBLE BUDGETS AND STANDARD COST SYSTEMS

Formal budgeting procedures result in comprehensive operational and financial plans for future periods. These budgets guide managers and employees as they make their daily decisions and as they try to anticipate future problems and opportunities. As the budget period unfolds, it is only natural that employees and managers want to know, "How did we do?" Employees and their supervisors at the shop floor or at the customer service desk should know how they are doing in meeting their nonfinancial objectives (such as making on-time deliveries and resolving customer problems). Upper-level managers also want to know how the organization is meeting its financial objectives as spelled out in the master budget. Managers obtain feedback on how effectively economic conditions were forecast and how well plans were executed by comparing budgets to actual results. Knowing what went right and what went wrong should help managers plan and manage more effectively in future periods. The accounting system in most organizations is designed to record transactions continuously and report actual financial results at designated intervals. The way budgets and actual results are compared, however, determines the value of financial feedback.

This chapter introduces flexible budgets, which are budgets designed to direct management to areas of actual financial performance that deserve attention. Managers can apply this same basic process to control of other important areas of performance such as quality or customer service.) After discussing flexible budgets and basic budget variances that are applicable to all organizations, we take a detailed look at variances for traditional manufacturing inputs such as material, labor, and overhead.

BRIDGING STATIC BUDGETS AND ACTUAL RESULTS

Static Budgets

All *master budgets* are *static* or inflexible because even though they may be easily revised, the budgets as accepted assume fixed levels of future activity. A master budget is prepared for only one level of activity (for example, one volume of sales activity). To illustrate, a typical master budget is a plan tailored to a single target sales level of, say, 9,000 units. The terms *static budget* and *master budget* are usually regarded as synonyms.

All *actual* results could be compared with the original plan, regardless of changes in ensuing conditions—even though, for example, sales volume turned out to be only 7,000 units instead of the originally planned 9,000 units. Suppose the Dominion Company, a one-department firm in Toronto, manufactures and sells a wheeled, collapsible suitcase carrier that is popular with airline flight crews. Manufacture of this suitcase carrier requires several manual and machine operations. The product has some variations, but may be viewed for our purposes essentially as a single product bearing one selling price.

The master (static) budget for June 19X4 included the condensed income statement shown in Exhibit 8-1, column 2. The actual results for June 19X4 are in column 1. Differences or variances between actual results and the master budget are in column 3. The master budget called for production and sales of 9,000 units, but only 7,000 units were actually produced and sold. There were no beginning or ending inventories, so the units made in June were sold in June.

The master budget was based on carefully forecasted sales and operations. The performance report in Exhibit 8-1 compares the actual results with the master budget. *Performance report* is a generic term that usually means a comparison of actual results with some budget. A helpful performance report will include *variances* that direct upper management's attention to significant deviations from expected results, allowing *management by exception.* Recall that a *variance* is a deviation of an actual amount from the expected or budgeted amount. Exhibit 8-1 shows variances of actual results from the master budget; these are called **master (static) budget variances.** Actual revenues that exceed expected revenues result in favorable revenue variances; when actual revenues are below expected revenues, variances are unfavorable. Similarly, actual expenses that exceed budgeted expenses result in **unfavorable expense variances;** actual expenses that are less than budgeted expenses result in **favorable expense variances.** Each significant variance should cause a manager to ask "Why?" By explaining why a variance occurs, managers are forced to recognize changes that have affected costs and that might affect future decisions.

Suppose the president of Dominion Company asks you to explain *why* there was an operating loss of $11,570 when a profit of $12,800 was budgeted. Clearly, sales were below expectations, but the favorable variances for the variable costs are misleading. Considering the lower-than-projected level of sales activity, was cost control really satisfactory? The comparison of actual results with a master budget does not give much help in answering that question. Master budget variances are not very useful for management by exception.

Flexible Budgets

In contrast to the performance report based only on comparing the master budget to actual results, a more helpful benchmark for analysis is the *flexible budget.* A **flexible budget** (sometimes called **variable budget**) is a budget that adjusts for changes in sales volume and other cost-driver activities. The flexible budget is identical to the master budget in format, but managers may prepare it for any level of activity. For performance

Exhibit 8-1 Dominion Company Performance Report Using Master Budget for the Month Ended June 30, 19X3

	Actual (1)	Master Budget (2)	Master Budget Variances (3)
Units	7,000	9,000	2,000
Sales	$217,000	$279,000	$62,000 U
Variable expenses			
Variable manufacturing expenses	$151,270	$189,000	$37,730 F
Shipping expenses (selling)	5,000	5,400	400 F
Administrative expenses	2,000	1,800	200 U
Total variable expenses	$158,270	$196,200	$37,930 F
Contribution margin	$ 58,730	$ 82,800	$24,070 U
Fixed expenses			
Fixed manufacturing expenses	$ 37,300	$ 37,000	$300 U
Fixed selling and administrative expenses	33,000	33,000	—
Total fixed expenses	$ 70,300	$ 70,000	$ 300 U
Operating income (loss)	$ (11,570)	$ 12,800	$24,370 U

U = **Unfavorable expense variances** occur when actual expenses are more than budgeted expenses.

F = **Favorable expense variances** occur when actual expenses are less than budgeted expenses.

volume and other cost-driver activities. The flexible budget is identical to the master budget in format, but managers may prepare it for any level of activity. For performance evaluation, the flexible budget would be prepared at the actual levels of activity achieved. In contrast, the master budget is kept fixed or static to serve as the primary benchmark for evaluating performance. It shows revenues and costs at only the originally *planned* levels of activity.

To reiterate, flexible budgets have the following distinguishing features (1) they may be prepared for a range of activity (as shown in Addendum 7, this is a natural use of financial planning software), and (2) they provide a dynamic basis for comparison with the actual results because they are automatically matched to changes in activities.

The flexible-budget approach says, "Give me any activity level you choose, and I'll provide a budget tailored to that particular level." Many companies routinely "flex" their budgets to help evaluate recent financial performance. For example, Procter & Gamble evaluates monthly financial performance of all its business units by comparing actual results to new, flexible budgets that are prepared for actual levels of activity.

Flexible-Budget Formulas

The flexible budget is based on the same assumptions of revenue and cost behavior (within the relevant range) as the master budget. It is based on knowledge of cost behavior regarding appropriate cost drivers—*cost functions* or *flexible-budget formulas*. Cost functions can be used as flexible-budget formulas. Recall that these cost functions had units of volume as the single cost driver. The flexible budget incorporates effects on each cost and revenue caused by changes in activity. Exhibits 8-2 and 8-3 show Dominion Company's simple flexible budget, which has a single cost driver, units of output. Dominion Company's cost functions or flexible budget formulas are believed to be valid within the relevant range of 7,000 to 9,000 units. Be sure that you understand that each column of Exhibit 8-2 (7,000, 8,000, and 9,000 units, respectively) is prepared

Exhibit 8-2 Dominion Company Flexible Budget

		Flexible Budgets for Various Levels of Sales/Production Activity		
BUDGET FORMULA PER UNIT				
Units		7,000	8,000	9,000
Sales	$31.00	$217,000	$248,000	$279,000
Variable costs/expense				
Variable manufacturing costs	$21.00	$147,000	$168,000	$189,000
Shipping expenses (selling)	.60	4,200	4,800	5,400
Administrative	.20	1,400	1,600	1,800
Total variable costs/expenses	$21.80	$152,600	$174,400	$196,200
Contribution margin	$ 9.20	$ 64,400	$ 73,600	$ 82,800
BUDGET FORMULA PER MONTH				
Fixed costs				
Fixed manufacturing costs	$37,000	$37,000	$37,000	$37,000
Fixed selling and administrative costs	33,000	33,000	33,000	33,000
Total fixed costs	$70,000	$70,000	$70,000	$70,000
Operating income (loss)		$ (5,600)	$ 3,600	$12,800

using the same flexible-budget formulas—and any activity level within this range could be used, as shown in the graph in Exhibit 8-3. Note that fixed costs are expected to be constant across this range of activity.

Evaluation of Financial Performance Using Flexible Budgets

Comparing the flexible budget to actual results accomplishes an important performance evaluation purpose. There are basically two reasons why actual results might not have conformed to the master budget. One is that sales and other cost-driver activities were not the same as originally forecasted. The second is that revenues or variable costs per unit of activity and fixed costs per period were not as expected. Though these reasons may not be completely independent (for example, higher sales prices may have caused lower sales levels), it is useful to separate these effects because different people may be responsible for them and because different management actions may be indicated. The intent of using the flexible budget for performance evaluation is to isolate unexpected effects on actual results that can be corrected if adverse or enhanced if beneficial. Because the flexible budget is prepared at the actual levels of activity (in our example, sales volume), any variances between the flexible budget and actual results cannot be due to activity levels (again, assuming cost and revenue functions are valid). These variances between the flexible budget and actual results are called **flexible-budget variances** and must be due to departures of actual costs or revenues from flexible-budget formula amounts—because of pricing or cost control. In contrast, any differences or variances between the master budget and the flexible budget are due to activity levels, not cost control. These latter differences between the master budget amounts and the amounts in the flexible budget are called **activity-level variances.**

Consider Exhibit 8-4. The flexible budget (column 3) taken from Exhibit 8-2 (and simplified) provides an explanatory bridge between the master budget (column 5) and the actual results (column 1). The variances for operating income are summarized at the bottom of Exhibit 8-4. Note that the sum of the activity-level variances (here sales-activity variances because sales is the only activity used as a cost driver) and the flexible-

Exhibit 8-3 Dominion Company: Graph of Flexible Budget of Costs

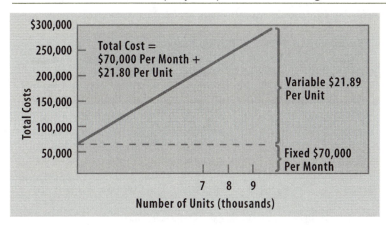

budget variances equals the total of the master budget variances. The difference between actual results and the original master budget has two components: the sales-activity variances and the flexible-budget variances.

Isolation of Budget Variances and Their Causes

Managers use comparisons between actual results, master budgets, and flexible budgets to evaluate organizational performance. When evaluating performance, it is useful to distinguish between **effectiveness**—the degree to which a goal, objective, or target is met—and **efficiency**—the degree to which inputs are used in relation to a given level of outputs.

Performance may be effective, efficient, both, or neither. For example, Dominion Company set a master budget objective of manufacturing and selling 9,000 units. Only 7,000 units were actually made and sold, however. Performance, as measured by sales-activity variances, was ineffective because the sales objective was not met.

Was Dominion's performance efficient? Managers judge the degree of efficiency by comparing actual outputs achieved (7,000 units) with actual inputs (such as the costs of direct materials and direct labor). *The less input used to produce a given output, the more efficient the operation.* As indicated by the flexible-budget variances, Dominion was inefficient in its use of a number of inputs. Later in this chapter we consider in detail direct material, direct labor, and variable overhead flexible-budget variances.

Flexible-Budget Variances

Flexible-budget variances measure the efficiency of operations at the actual level of activity. The first three columns of Exhibit 8-4 compare the actual results with the flexible-budget amounts. The flexible-budget variances are the differences between columns 1 and 3, which total $5,970 unfavorable because:

total flexible-budget variance = total actual results – total flexible budget, planned results
= (–$11,570) – (–$5,600)
= $–5,970, or $5,970 unfavorable[1]

The total flexible-budget variance arises from sales prices received and the variable and fixed costs incurred. Dominion Company had no difference between actual sales price and the flexible-budgeted sales price, so the focus is on the differences between actual costs and flexible-budgeted costs at the actual 7,000-unit level of activity. Without the flexible budget in column 3, we cannot separate the effects of differences in cost behav-

Exhibit 8-4 Dominion Company Summary of Performance for the Month Ended June 30, 19X4

	Actual Results at Actual Activity Level* (1)	Flexible-Budget Variances† (2) = (1) − (3)	Flexible-Budget for Actual Sales Activity‡ (3)	Sales-Activity Variances (4) = (3) − (5)	Master Budget (5)
Units	7,000	—	7,000	2,000 U	9,000
Sales	$217,000	—	$217,000	$62,000 U	$279,000
Variable costs	158,270	5,670 U	152,600	43,600 F	196,200
Contribution margin	$ 58,730	$5,670 U	$ 64,400	$18,400 U	$ 82,800
Fixed costs	70,300	300 U	70,000	—	70,000
Operating income	$ (11,570)	$5,970 U	$ (5,600)	$18,400 U	$ 12,800

Total flexible-budget variances, $5,970 U

Total sales-activity variances, $18,400 U

Total master budget variances, $24,370 U

U = Unfavorable, F = Favorable.
* Figures are from Exhibit 8-1.
† Figures are shown in more detail in Exhibit 8-5.
‡ Figures are from the 7,000-unit column in Exhibit 8-2.

ior from the effects of changes in sales activity. The flexible-budget variances indicate whether operations were efficient or not, and may form the basis for periodic performance evaluation. Operations managers are in the best position to explain flexible-budget variances.

Companies that use variances primarily to fix blame, however, often find that managers resort to cheating and subversion to beat the system. Managers of operations usually have more information about those operations than higher-level managers. If that information is used against them, lower-level managers can be expected to withhold or misstate valuable information for their own protection. For example, one manufacturing firm actually *reduced* the next period's departmental budget by the amount of the department's unfavorable variances in the current period. If a division had a $50,000 expense budget and experienced a $2,000 unfavorable variance, the following period's budget would be set at $48,000. This system led managers to cheat and to falsify reports to avoid unfavorable variances. We can criticize departmental managers' ethics, but the system was as much at fault as the managers.

Exhibit 8-5 gives an expanded, line-by-line computation of variances for all master budget items at Dominion. Note how most of the costs that had seemingly favorable variances when a master budget was used as a basis for comparison have, in reality, unfavorable variances. Do not conclude automatically that favorable flexible-budget variances are good and unfavorable flexible-budget variances are bad. Instead, *interpret all variances as signals that actual operations have not occurred exactly as anticipated* when the flexible-budget formulas were set. Any cost that differs significantly from the flexible budget deserves an explanation. The last column of Exhibit 8-5 gives possible explanations for Dominion Company's variances.

Exhibit 8-5   Dominion Company Cost-Control Performance Report
for the Month Ended June 30, 19x4

	Actual Costs Incurred	Flexible Budget*	Flexible Budget Variances†	Explanation
Units	7,000	7,000	—	
Variable costs				
Direct material	$ 69,920	$ 70,000	$ 80 F	Lower prices but higher usage
Direct labor	61,500	56,000	5,500 U	Higher wage rates and higher usage
Indirect labor	9,100	11,900	2,800 F	Decreased setup time
Idle time	3,550	2,800	750 U	Excessive machine breakdowns
Cleanup time	2,500	2,100	400 U	Cleanup of spilled solvent
Supplies	4,700	4,200	500 U	Higher prices and higher usage
Variable manufacturing costs	$151,270	$147,000	$4,270 U	
Shipping	5,000	4,200	800 U	Use of air freight to meet delivery
Administration	2,000	1,400	600 U	Excessive copying and long distance calls
Total variable costs	$158,270	$152,600	$5,670 U	
Fixed costs				
Factory supervision	$ 14,700	$ 14,400	$ 300 U	Salary increase
Factory rent	5,000	5,000	—	
Equipment depreciation	15,000	15,000	—	
Other fixed factory costs	2,600	2,600	—	
Fixed manufacturing costs	$ 37,300	$ 37,000	$ 300 U	
Fixed selling and administrative costs	33,000	33,000	—	
Total fixed costs	$ 70,300	$ 70,000	$ 300 U	
Total variable and fixed costs	$228,570	$222,600	$5,970 U	

* From 7,000-unit column of Exhibit 8-2.

† This is a line-by-line breakout of the variances in column 2 of Exhibit 8-4.

Sales-Activity Variances

Sales-activity variances measure how effective managers have been in meeting the planned sales objective. In Dominion Company, sales activity fell 2,000 units short of the planned level. The final three columns of Exhibit 8-4 clearly show how the sales-activity variances (totaling $18,400 U) are unaffected by any changes in unit prices or variable costs. Why? Because the same budgeted unit prices and variable costs are used in constructing both the flexible and master budgets. Therefore, all unit prices and variable costs are held constant in columns 3 through 5.

The total of the sales-activity variances informs the manager that falling short of the sales target by 2,000 units caused operating income to be $18,400 lower than initially budgeted (a $5,600 loss instead of a $12,800 profit). In summary, the shortfall of sales by 2,000 units caused Dominion Company to incur a total sales activity variance of 2,000 units at a contribution margin of $9.20 per unit (from the first column of Exhibit 8-2).

$$\text{total sales-activity variance} = \left(\begin{array}{c} \text{actual sales units} - \\ \text{master budget sales units} \end{array} \right) \times \left(\begin{array}{c} \text{budgeted contribution} \\ \text{margin per unit} \end{array} \right)$$

$$= (9,000 - 7.000) \times \$9.20$$
$$= \$18,400 \text{ Unfavorable}$$

Who has responsibility for the sales-activity variance? Marketing managers usually have the primary responsibility for reaching the sales level specified in the static budget. Of course variations in sales may be attributable to many factors.[2] Nevertheless, marketing managers are typically in the best position to explain why sales activities attained differed from plans.

Expectations, Standard Costs, and Standard Cost Systems

Expectations or *standard costs* are the building blocks of a planning and control system. An **expected cost** is the cost that is most likely to be attained. A standard cost is a carefully developed cost per unit that *should* be attained. It is often synonymous with the expected cost, but some companies intentionally set standards above or below expected costs to create desired incentives. Do not confuse having expectations or standards with having a *standard cost system*. **Standard cost systems** value products according to standard costs only.[3] These inventory valuation systems simplify financial reporting, but in most companies they are expensive to install and to maintain. Therefore, standard costs may not be revised often enough to be useful for management decision making regarding specific products or services. (Ideally, only one cost system should be necessary in any organization, but in practice many organizations have developed multiple cost systems.) The expected costs used in flexible budgets also may be called standards because they are benchmarks or objectives to be attained. The fact that they are called standards does not imply that the organization also must have a *standard cost system* for inventory valuation or that it must use the standard cost system for planning and control.

Current Attainability: Most Widely Used Standard

What standard of expected performance should be used in flexible budgets? Should it be so strict that it is rarely, if ever, attained? Should it be attainable 50% of the time? 90%? 20%? Individuals who have worked a lifetime setting and evaluating standards for performance disagree, so there are no universal answers to this question.

Perfection standards (also called **ideal standards**) are expressions of the most efficient performance possible under the best conceivable conditions, using existing specifications and equipment. No provision is made for waste, spoilage, machine breakdowns, and the like. Those who favor using perfection standards maintain that the resulting unfavorable variances will constantly remind personnel of the continuous need for improvement in all phases of operations. Though concern for continuous improvement is widespread, these standards are not widely used because they have an adverse effect on employee motivation. Employees tend to ignore unreasonable goals, especially if they would not share the gains from meeting imposed perfection standards. Organizations that apply the JIT philosophy attempt to achieve continuous improvement from "the bottom up," not by prescribing what should be achieved via perfection standards.

Currently attainable standards are levels of performance that can be achieved by realistic levels of effort. Allowances are made for normal defectives, spoilage, waste, and nonproductive time. There are at least two popular interpretations of the meaning of currently attainable standards. The first interpretation has standards set just tightly enough that employees regard their attainment as highly probable if normal effort and diligence are exercised. That is, variances should be random and negligible. Hence, the standards are predictions of what will indeed occur, anticipating some inefficiencies. Managers accept the standards as being reasonable goals. The major reasons for "reasonable" standards, then, are:

1. The resulting standards serve multiple purposes. For example, the same cost can be used for financial budgeting, inventory valuation, and budgeting departmental perfor-

mance. In contrast, perfection standards cannot be used for inventory valuation or financial budgeting, because the costs are known to be inaccurate.

2. Reasonable standards have a desirable motivational impact on employees, especially when combined with incentives for continuous improvement. The standard represents reasonable future performance, not fanciful goals. Therefore, unfavorable variances direct attention to performance that is not meeting reasonable expectations.

A second interpretation of currently attainable standards is that standards are set tightly. That is, employees regard their fulfillment as possible, though unlikely. Standards can be achieved only by very efficient operations. Variances tend to be unfavorable; nevertheless, employees accept the standards as being tough but not unreasonable goals. Is it possible to achieve continuous improvement using currently attainable standards? Yes, but expectations must reflect improved productivity and must be tied to incentive systems that reward continuous improvement.

Trade-offs Among Variances

Because the operations of organizations are linked, the level of performance in one area of operations will affect performance in other areas. Nearly any combination of effects is possible: Improvements in one area could lead to improvements in others and vice versa. Likewise, substandard performance in one area may be balanced by superior performance in others. For example, a service organization may generate favorable labor variances by hiring less-skilled customer representatives, but this favorable variance may lead to unfavorable customer satisfaction and future unfavorable sales-activity variances. In another situation, a manufacturer may experience unfavorable materials variances by purchasing higher-quality materials at a higher than planned price, but this variance may be more than offset by the favorable variances caused by lower inventory handling costs (e.g., inspections) and higher-quality products (such as favorable scrap and rework variances).

Because of the many interdependencies among activities, an "unfavorable" or "favorable" label should not lead the manager to jump to conclusions. By themselves, such labels merely raise questions and provide clues to the causes of performance. *They are attention directors, not problem solvers.* Furthermore, the cause of variances might be faulty expectations rather than the execution of plans by managers. One of the first questions a manager should consider when explaining a large variance is whether expectations were valid.

When to Investigate Variances

When should variances be investigated? Frequently the answer is based on subjective judgments, hunches, guesses, and rules of thumb that have proved to be useful. The most troublesome aspect of using the feedback from flexible budgeting is deciding when a variance is large enough to warrant management's attention. The master and flexible budgets imply that the standard cost is the only permissible outcome. Practically speaking, the accountant (and everybody else) realizes that the standard is one of the many possible acceptable cost outcomes. Consequently, the accountant expects variances to fluctuate randomly within some normal limits. Of course, an activity that allows wildly fluctuating variances as "normal" may be a poorly designed activity. A random variance from a well-designed activity, by definition, is not caused by controllable actions and calls for no corrective action. In short, a random variance is attributable to chance rather than to management's implementation of plans. Consequently, the more a variance randomly fluctuates, the larger the variance required to make investigation worthwhile. There are two questions: First, what is a large versus a small variance? Second, is a large variance random or controllable? Usually, the second question is answered only after an investigation, so answering the first question is critical.

Managers recognize that, even if everything operates as planned, variances are unlikely to be exactly zero. They predict a range of "normal" variances; this range may be based on economic criteria (i.e., how big a variance must be before investigation could be worth the effort) or on statistical criteria. For some critical items, any deviation may prompt a follow-up. For most items, a minimum dollar or percentage deviation from budget may be necessary before investigations are expected to be worthwhile. For example, a 4% variance in a $1 million material cost may deserve more attention than a 20% variance in a $10,000 repair cost. Because knowing exactly when to investigate is difficult, many organizations have developed such rules of thumb as, "Investigate all variances exceeding $5,000 or 25% of expected cost, whichever is lower."

Comparisons with Prior Period's Results

Some organizations compare the most recent budget period's actual results with last year's results for the same period rather than use flexible budget benchmarks. For example, an organization might compare June 19X4's actual results to June 19X3's actual results. In general these comparisons are not as useful for evaluating performance of an organization as comparisons of actual outcomes with planned results for the same period. Why? Because many changes probably have occurred in the environment and in the organization that make a comparison across years invalid. Very few organizations and environments are so stable that the only difference between now and a year ago is merely the passage of time. Even comparisons with last month's actual results may not be as useful as comparisons with flexible budgets. Comparisons over time may be useful for analyzing *trends* in such key variables as sales volume, market share, and product mix, but they do not help answer questions such as "Why did we have a loss of $11,570 in June, when we expected a profit of $12,800?"

FLEXIBLE-BUDGET VARIANCES IN DETAIL

The rest of this chapter probes the analysis of variances in detail. The emphasis is on subdividing labor, material, and overhead cost variances into usage and price or spending components. Note that in companies where direct-labor costs are small in relation to total costs (that is, in highly automated companies) direct-labor costs may be treated as an overhead-cost item, so separate labor standards, budgets, or variances need not be analyzed.

Variances from Material and Labor Standards

Consider Dominion Company's $10 standard cost of direct materials and $8 standard cost of direct labor. These standards per unit are derived from two components: a standard quantity of an input and a standard price for the input.

	Standards		
	Standard Inputs Expected per Unit of Output	Standard Price Expected per Unit of Input	Standard Cost Expected per Unit of Output
Direct material	5 pounds	$2	$10
Direct labor	1/2 hour	16	8

Once standards are set and actual results are observed, we can measure variances from the flexible budget. To show how the analysis of variances can be pursued more fully, we will reconsider Dominion's direct-material and direct-labor costs, as shown in Exhibit 8-5, and assume that the following actually occurred for the production of 7,000 units of output:

- *Direct material:* 36,800 pounds of material were purchased and *used* at an actual unit price of $1.90 for a total actual cost of $69,920.
- *Direct labor:* 3,750 hours of labor were *used* at an actual hourly *price* (rate) of $16.40, for a total cost of $61,500.

Note that the flexible-budget variances for direct labor and direct material can be attributed to (1) using more or less of the resource than planned and (2) spending more or less for the resource than planned at the actual level of output achieved. These additional data enable us to subdivide the flexible-budget variances (column 3) from Exhibit 8-5 into the separate *usage* and *price* components, which are shown below in columns 4 and 5.

	(1) Actual Costs	(2) Flexible-Budget	(3) Flexible-Budget Variance	(4) Price Variance*	(5) Usage Variance'
Direct material	$69,920	$70,000	$ 80 F	$ 3,680 F	$3,600 U
Direct labor	61,500	56,000	5,500 U	1,500 U	4,000 U

*Computations to be explained shortly.

The flexible-budget totals for direct materials and direct labor are the amounts that would have been spent with expected efficiency. They are often labeled total *standard costs allowed*, computed as follows:

flexible budget or total standard cost allowed	=	units of good output achieved	x	input allowed per unit of output	x	standard unit of output

standard direct-materials cost allowed = 7,000 units x 5 pounds x $2.00 per pound = $70,000

standard direct-labor cost allowed = 7,000 units x 1/2 hour x $16.00 per hour = $56,000

Before reading on, note particularly that the flexible-budget amounts (i.e., the standard costs allowed) are tied to an initial question: What was the output achieved? Always ask yourself: What was the good output? Then proceed with your computations of the total standard cost allowed for the good output achieved.

Price and Usage Variances

As noted earlier, we computed the flexible-budget amounts using the flexible-budget formulas, or currently attainable standards. Flexible-budget variances measure the relative efficiency of achieving the actual output. Price and usage variances subdivide each flexible-budget variance into the following:

1. **Price variance**—difference between actual input prices and standard input prices multiplied by the actual quantity of inputs used.

2. **Usage variance**—difference between the quantity of inputs actually used and the quantity of inputs that should have been used to achieve the actual quantity of output multiplied by the expected price of the input (also called a **quantity variance** or **efficiency variance**).

When feasible, you should separate the variances that are subject to a manager's direct influence from those that are not. This aids scorekeeping, attention directing, and problem solving. The usual approach is to separate price factors from usage factors. Price factors are less subject to immediate control than are usage factors, principally because of external forces, such as general economic conditions, that can influence prices. Even when price factors are regarded as being outside management control, isolating them helps to focus on the efficient usage of inputs. For example, the commodity prices of wheat, oats, corn, and rice are outside the control of General Mills. By separating price variances from usage variances, the breakfast cereal maker can focus on whether grain was used efficiently.

Price and usage variances are helpful because they provide feedback to those responsible for inputs. These variances should not be the only information used for decision making, control, or evaluation, however. Exclusive focus on material price variances by purchasing agents or buyers, for example, can work against an organization's JIT and total quality management goals. A buyer may be motivated to earn favorable material price variances by buying in large quantities and by buying low-quality material. The result could then be excessive inventory-handling and opportunity costs and increased manufacturing defects owing to faulty material. Similarly, exclusive focus on labor price and usage variances could motivate supervisors to use lower-skilled workers or to rush workers through critical tasks, both of which could impair quality of products and services.

Price and Usage Variance Computations

We now consider the detailed calculation of price and usage variances. The objective of these variance calculations is to hold either price or usage constant so that the effect of the other can be isolated. When calculating the price variance, you hold use of inputs constant at the actual level of usage. When calculating the usage variance, you hold price constant at the standard price. For Dominion Company the price variances are:

Direct-material price variance = (actual price – standard price) x actual quantity
= ($1.90 – $2.00) per pound x 36,800 pounds
= $3,680 favorable

Direct-labor price variance = (actual price – standard price) x actual quantity
= ($16.40 – $16.00) per hour x 3,750 hours
= $1,500 unfavorable

The usage variances are:

Direct-material usage variance = (actual quantity used – standard quantity allowed) x standard price
= [36,800 – (7,000 x 5)] pounds x $2.00 per pound
= (36,800 – 35,000) x $2 = $3,600 unfavorable

Direct-labor usage variance = (actual quantity used – standard quantity allowed) x standard price
= [3,750 – (7,000 x 1/2)] hours x $16 per hour
= (3,750 – 3,500) x $16
= $4,000 unfavorable

To determine whether a variance is favorable or unfavorable, use logic rather than memorizing a formula. A price variance is favorable if the actual price is less than the standard. A usage variance is favorable if the actual quantity used is less than the standard quantity allowed. The opposite relationships imply unfavorable variances.

Exhibit 8-6   Graphical Representation of Price and Usage Variances for Labor

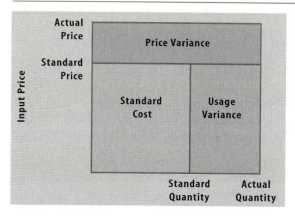

Note that the sum of the direct-labor price and usage variances equals the direct labor flexible-budget variance. Furthermore, the sum of the direct-material price and usage variances equals the total direct-material flexible-budget variance.

Direct-materials flexible-budget variance = $80 favorable = $3,680 favorable + $3,600 unfavorable

Direct-labor flexible-budget variance = $5,500 unfavorable = $1,500 unfavorable + $4,000 unfavorable

Variances themselves do not show why the budgeted operating income was not achieved. They raise questions, provide clues, and direct attention, however. For instance, one possible explanation for this set of variances is that a manager might have made a trade-off—the manager might have purchased at a favorable price some materials that were substandard quality, saving $3,680 (the materials price variance). Excessive waste might have nearly offset this savings, as indicated by the $3,600 unfavorable material usage variance and net flexible-budget variance of $80 favorable. The material waste also might have caused at least part of the excess use of direct labor. Suppose more than $80 of the $4,000 unfavorable direct-labor usage variance was caused by reworking units with defective materials. Then the manager's tradeoff was not successful. The cost inefficiencies caused by using substandard materials exceeded the savings from the favorable price.

Exhibit 8-6 shows the price and usage variance computations for labor graphically. The standard cost (or flexible budget) is the standard quantity multiplied by the standard price—the square shaded light gray. The price variance is the difference between the unit prices, actual and standard, multiplied by actual quantity used—the rectangle shaded dark gray. The usage variance is the standard price multiplied by the difference between the actual quantity used and the standard quantity allowed for the good output achieved—the area of the shaded rectangle on the lower right. (Note that for clarity the graph portrays only unfavorable variances.)

Effects of Inventories

Analysis of Dominion Company was simplified because (1) there were no finished goods inventories—any units produced were sold in the same period—and (2) there was no direct-material inventory—the materials were purchased and used in the same period.

What if production does not equal sales? The sales-activity variance then is the difference between the static budget and the flexible budget for the number of units *sold*. In contrast, the flexible-budget cost variances compare actual costs with flexible-budgeted costs for the number of units *produced*.

Generally managers want quick feedback and want variances to be identified as early as is practical. In the case of direct materials, that time is when the materials are purchased rather than when they are used, which may be much later. Therefore, the material price variance is usually based on the quantity purchased, measured at the time of purchase. The material usage variance remains based on the quantity used. Suppose Dominion Company purchased 40,000 pounds of material (rather than the 36,800 pounds used) at $1.90 per pound. The material price variance would be (actual price – standard price) x material *purchased* = ($1.90 – $2.00) per pound x 40,000 pounds = $4,000 favorable. The material usage variance would remain at $3,600 unfavorable because it is based on the material *used*.

OVERHEAD VARIANCES

Direct-material and direct-labor variances are often subdivided into price and usage components. In contrast, many organizations believe that it is not worthwhile to monitor individual overhead items to the same extent. Therefore, overhead variances often are not subdivided beyond the flexible-budget variances—the complexity of the analysis may not be worth the effort.

But in some cases, it may be worthwhile to subdivide the flexible-budget overhead variances, especially those for variable overhead. Part of the variable overhead flexible-budget variance is related to control of the cost driver and part to the control of overhead spending itself. When actual cost-driver activity differs from the standard amount allowed for the actual output achieved, a **variable-overhead efficiency variance** will occur. Suppose that Dominion Company's cost of supplies, a variable-overhead cost, is driven by direct-labor hours. A variable-overhead cost rate of $.60 per unit at Dominion would be equivalent to $1.20 per direct-labor hour (because 1/2 hour is allowed per unit of output). Of the $500 unfavorable variance, $300 unfavorable is due to using 3,750 direct-labor hours rather than the 3,500 allowed by the flexible budget, as calculated below:

$$\text{Variable-overhead efficiency variance for supplies} = \left(\begin{array}{c} \text{actual direct} \\ \text{labor hours} \end{array} - \begin{array}{c} \text{standard direct} \\ \text{labor hours allowed} \end{array} \right) \times \begin{array}{c} \text{standard} \\ \text{variable-overhead} \\ \text{rate per hour} \end{array}$$

$$= \left(3{,}750 \text{ actual hours} - \begin{array}{c} 3{,}500 \text{ standard hours} \\ \text{allowed} \end{array} \right) \times \$1.20 \text{ per hour}$$

$$= \$300 \text{ unfavorable}$$

This $300 excess usage of supplies is attributable to inefficient use of cost-driver activity, direct-labor hours. Whenever actual cost-driver activity exceeds that allowed for the actual output achieved, overhead efficiency variances will be unfavorable and vice versa. In essence this efficiency variance tells management the cost of *not* controlling the use of cost-driver activity. The remainder of the flexible-budget variance measures control of overhead spending itself, given actual cost-driver activity.

$$\text{Variable-overhead spending variance for supplies} = \begin{array}{c} \text{actual variable} \\ \text{overhead} \end{array} - \left(\begin{array}{c} \text{expected variable} \\ \text{overhead rate} \end{array} \times \begin{array}{c} \text{actual} \\ \text{direct labor} \\ \text{hours used} \end{array} \right)$$

$$= 4{,}700 - (\$1.20 \times 3{,}750 \text{ hours})$$

$$\text{rs} = \$4{,}700 - \$4{,}500$$

$$= \$200 \text{ unfavorable}$$

Exhibit 8-7 General Approach to Analysis of Direct Labor and Direct Material Variances

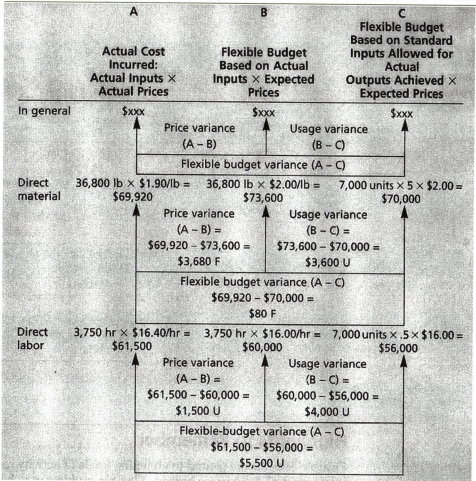

	A	B	C
	Actual Cost Incurred: Actual Inputs × Actual Prices	Flexible Budget Based on Actual Inputs × Expected Prices	Flexible Budget Based on Standard Inputs Allowed for Actual Outputs Achieved × Expected Prices
In general	$xxx	$xxx	$xxx

Price variance (A – B)   Usage variance (B – C)

Flexible budget variance (A – C)

| Direct material | 36,800 lb × $1.90/lb = $69,920 | 36,800 lb × $2.00/lb = $73,600 | 7,000 units × 5 × $2.00 = $70,000 |

Price variance (A – B) = $69,920 – $73,600 = $3,680 F

Usage variance (B – C) = $73,600 – $70,000 = $3,600 U

Flexible budget variance (A – C) $69,920 – $70,000 = $80 F

| Direct labor | 3,750 hr × $16.40/hr = $61,500 | 3,750 hr × $16.00/hr = $60,000 | 7,000 units × .5 × $16.00 = $56,000 |

Price variance (A – B) = $61,500 – $60,000 = $1,500 U

Usage variance (B – C) = $60,000 – $56,000 = $4,000 U

Flexible-budget variance (A – C) $61,500 – $56,000 = $5,500 U

That is, the **variable-overhead spending variance** is the difference between the actual variable overhead and the amount of variable overhead budgeted for the actual level of cost-driver activity.

Like other variances, the overhead variances by themselves cannot identify causes for results that differ from the static and flexible budgets. The only way for management to discover why overhead performance did not agree with the budget is to investigate possible causes. The distinction between spending and usage variances provides a springboard for more investigation, however.

GENERAL APPROACH

Exhibit 8-7 presents the analysis of direct material and direct labor in a format that deserves close study. The general approach is at the top of the figure; the specific applications then follow. Even though the figure may seem unnecessarily complex at first, its repeated use will solidify your understanding of variance analysis. Of course, the other flexible-budget variances in Exhibit 8-5 could be further analyzed in the same manner in which direct labor and direct material are analyzed in Exhibit 8-7. Such a detailed investigation depends on the manager's perception of whether the extra benefits will exceed the extra costs of the analysis.

Exhibit 8-8   General Approach to Analysis of Overhead Variances

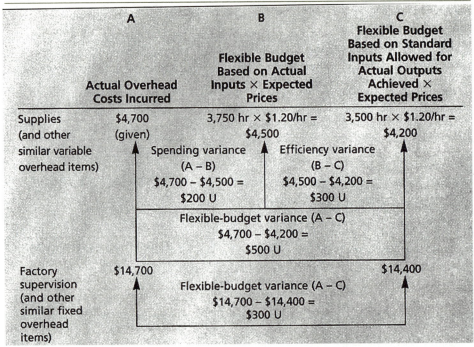

	A	B	C
	Actual Overhead Costs Incurred	**Flexible Budget Based on Actual Inputs × Expected Prices**	**Flexible Budget Based on Standard Inputs Allowed for Actual Outputs Achieved × Expected Prices**
Supplies (and other similar variable overhead items)	$4,700 (given)	3,750 hr × $1.20/hr = $4,500	3,500 hr × $1.20/hr = $4,200

Spending variance (A – B)
$4,700 – $4,500 =
$200 U

Efficiency variance (B – C)
$4,500 – $4,200 =
$300 U

Flexible-budget variance (A – C)
$4,700 – $4,200 =
$500 U

| Factory supervision (and other similar fixed overhead items) | $14,700 | | $14,400 |

Flexible-budget variance (A – C)
$14,700 – $14,400 =
$300 U

Column A of Exhibit 8-7 contains the actual costs incurred for the inputs during the budget period being evaluated. Column B is the flexible-budgeted costs for the inputs *given the actual inputs used,* using expected prices but actual usage. Column C is the flexible budget amount using both expected prices and expected usage for the outputs actually achieved. (This is the flexible budget amount from Exhibit 8-5 for 7,000 units.) Column B is inserted between A and C by using *expected* prices and *actual* usage. The difference between columns A and B is attributed to changing prices because usage is held constant between A and B at actual levels. The difference between columns B and C is attributed to changing usage because price is held constant between B and C at expected levels.

Actual output achieved in Column C is measured in units of product. However, most organizations manufacture a variety of products. When the variety of units are added together, the sum is frequently a nonsensical number (such as apples and oranges). Therefore, all units of output are often expressed in terms of the standard inputs allowed for their production, such as pounds of fruit. Labor hours may also become the common denominator for measuring total output volume. Thus, production, instead of being expressed as 12,000 chairs and 3,000 sofas, could be expressed as 20,000 standard hours allowed (or more accurately as *standard hours of input allowed for outputs achieved*). Remember that *standard hours allowed* is a measure of actual *output* achieved. A key idea illustrated in Exhibit 8-7 is the versatility of the flexible budget. A flexible budget is geared to activity volume, and Exhibit 8-7 shows that activity volume can be measured in terms of either actual inputs used (columns A and B) or *standard inputs allowed for actual outputs achieved* (column C).

Exhibit 8-8 summarizes the general approach to overhead variances. The flexible-budget variances for fixed-overhead items are not subdivided here. Note that the sales activity variance for fixed overhead is zero because as long as activities remain within relevant ranges, the fixed-overhead budget is the same at both planned and actual levels of activity.

SUMMARY

Flexible budgets are geared to changing levels of activity rather than to the single, static level of the master budget. Flexible budgets may be tailored to particular levels of sales or cost-driver activity—before or after the fact. They tell how much revenue and cost to expect for any level of activity.

Cost functions, or flexible-budget formulas, reflect fixed- and variable-cost behavior and allow managers to compute budgets for any desired output or cost-driver activity level. The flexible budget amounts are computed by multiplying the variable cost per unit of activity times the level of activity expected for the actual outputs achieved.

The evaluation of performance is aided by feedback that compares actual results with budgeted expectations. The flexible-budget approach helps managers explain why the master budget was not achieved. Master budget variances are divided into (sales) activity and flexible-budget variances. Activity variances reflect the organization's effectiveness in meeting financial plans. Flexible-budget variances reflect the organization's efficiency at actual levels of activity.

Expectations form the basis for budgeting and performance evaluation. Expectations may be formalized as standard costs and may be incorporated into standard cost systems, but only expectations (which may be called standards) are required for master and flexible budgets. The most commonly used standards are considered to be attainable with reasonable effort.

Flexible-budget variances for variable inputs can be further broken down into price (or spending) and usage (or efficiency) variances. Price variances reflect the effects of changing input prices, holding usage of inputs constant at actual use. Usage variances reflect the effects of different levels of input usage, holding prices constant at expected prices.

SELF-CORRECTION PROBLEMS

1. Refer to the data contained in Exhibits 8-1 and 8-2. Suppose actual production and sales were 8,500 units instead of 7,000 units; actual variable costs were $188,800; and actual fixed costs were $71,200. The selling price remained at $31 per unit.

   a. Compute the master budget variance. What does this tell you about the efficiency of operations? The effectiveness of operations?

   b. Compute the sales-activity variance. Is the performance of the marketing function the sole explanation for this variance? Why?

   c. Using a flexible budget at the actual activity level, compute the budgeted contribution margin, budgeted operating income, and flexible-budget variance. What do you learn from this variance?

2. The following questions are based on the data contained in the Dominion Company illustration used in this chapter.

   • Direct materials: standard, 5 pounds per unit @ $2 per pound

   • Direct labor: standard, 1/2 hour @ $16 per hour

   Suppose the following were the actual results for production of 8,500 units:

   • Direct material: 46,000 pounds purchased and used at an actual unit price of $1.85 per pound, for an actual total cost of $85,100

   • Direct labor: 4,125 hours of labor used at an actual hourly rate of $16.80, for a total actual cost of $69,300

   a. Compute the flexible-budget variance and the price and usage variances for direct labor and direct material.

b. Suppose the company is organized so that the purchasing manager bears the primary responsibility for purchasing materials, and the production manager is responsible for the use of materials. Assume the same facts as in question 1 except that the purchasing manager bought 60,000 pounds of material. This means that there is an ending inventory of 14,000 pounds of material. Recompute the materials variances.

SOLUTIONS TO SELF-CORRECTION PROBLEMS

1. a.
   actual operating income = (8,500 x $31) – $188,800 – $71,200 = $3,500

   master budget operating income = $12,800 (from Figure 8-1)

   master budget variance = $12,800–$3,500=$9,300 U

   Three factors affect the master budget variance: sales activity, efficiency, and price changes. There is no way to tell from the master budget variance alone how much of the $9,300 U was caused by any of these separate factors.

   b.
   sales-activity variance = budgeted unit contribution margin x difference between the master budget unit sales and the actual unit sales

   = $9.20 per unit CM x (9,000 – 8,500)

   = $4,600 U

   This variance is labeled as a sales-activity variance because it quantifies the impact on operating income of the deviation from an original sales target while holding price and efficiency factors constant. This is a measure of the effectiveness of the operations—Dominion was ineffective in meeting its sales objective. Of course, the failure to reach target sales may be traceable to several causes beyond the control of marketing personnel including material shortages, factory breakdowns, and so on.

   c. The budget formulas in Exhibit 8-2 are the basis for the following answers:

   flexible-budget contribution margin = $9.20 x 8,500 = $78,200

   flexible-budget operating income = $78,200 – $70,000 fixed costs = $8,200

   actual operating income = $3,500 (from requirement 1)

   flexible-budget variance = $8,200 – $3,500 = $4,700 U

   The flexible-budget variance shows that the company spent $4,700 more to produce and sell the 8,500 units than it should have if operations had been efficient and unit costs had not changed. Note that this variance plus the $4,600 U sales-activity variance total to the $9,300 U master budget variance.

2. a. The variances are on the facing page.
   b. Price variances are isolated at the most logical control point—time of purchase rather than time of use. In turn, the operating departments that later use the materials are generally charged at some predetermined budget, expected, or standard price rather than at actual prices. This represents a slight modification of the approach in part a as shown below.

   Note that this favorable price variance on balance may not be a good outcome—Dominion Company may not desire the extra inventory in excess of its immediate needs, and the favorable price variance may reflect that quality of the material is lower than planned. Note also that the usage variance is the same in parts a and b. Typically, the price and usage variances for materials now would be reported separately and not added together because they are based on different measures of volume. The price variance is based on inputs *purchased,* but the usage variance is based on inputs *used.*

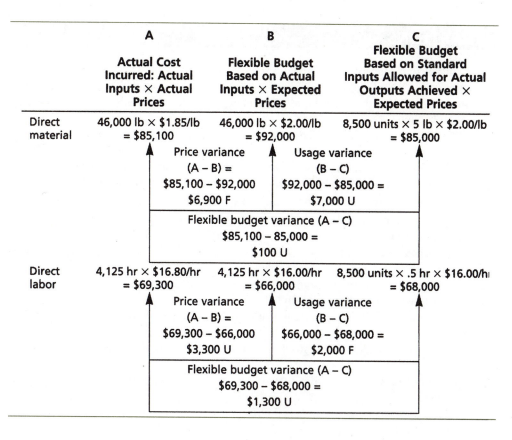

	A	B	C
	Actual Cost Incurred: Actual Inputs × Actual Prices	**Flexible Budget Based on Actual Inputs × Expected Prices**	**Flexible Budget Based on Standard Inputs Allowed for Actual Outputs Achieved × Expected Prices**
Direct material	46,000 lb × $1.85/lb = $85,100	46,000 lb × $2.00/lb = $92,000	8,500 units × 5 lb × $2.00/lb = $85,000

Price variance
(A – B) =
$85,100 – $92,000
$6,900 F

Usage variance
(B – C)
$92,000 – $85,000 =
$7,000 U

Flexible budget variance (A – C)
$85,100 – 85,000 =
$100 U

| Direct labor | 4,125 hr × $16.80/hr = $69,300 | 4,125 hr × $16.00/hr = $66,000 | 8,500 units × .5 hr × $16.00/hr = $68,000 |

Price variance
(A – B) =
$69,300 – $66,000
$3,300 U

Usage variance
(B – C)
$66,000 – $68,000 =
$2,000 F

Flexible budget variance (A – C)
$69,300 – $68,000 =
$1,300 U

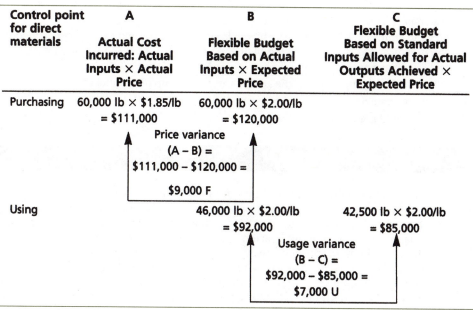

Control point for direct materials	A	B	C
	Actual Cost Incurred: Actual Inputs × Actual Price	**Flexible Budget Based on Actual Inputs × Expected Price**	**Flexible Budget Based on Standard Inputs Allowed for Actual Outputs Achieved × Expected Price**
Purchasing	60,000 lb × $1.85/lb = $111,000	60,000 lb × $2.00/lb = $120,000	

Price variance
(A – B) =
$111,000 – $120,000 =
$9,000 F

| Using | | 46,000 lb × $2.00/lb = $92,000 | 42,500 lb × $2.00/lb = $85,000 |

Usage variance
(B – C) =
$92,000 – $85,000 =
$7,000 U

1. "The flex in the flexible budget relates solely to variable costs." Do you agree? Explain.
2. "We want a flexible budget because costs are difficult to predict. We need the flexibility to change budgeted costs as input prices change." Does a flexible budget serve this purpose? Explain.
3. "Effectiveness and efficiency go hand in hand. You can't have one without the other." Do you agree? Explain.
4. Differentiate between a master-budget variance and a flexible-budget variance.
5. Why do some companies classify direct-labor costs as part of factory overhead?
6. Differentiate between perfection standards and currently attainable standards.
7. What are two possible interpretations of "currently attainable standards"?
8. Why should a budgeted cost not be merely an extension of past experience?
9. "Price variances should be computed even if prices are regarded as being outside of company control." Do you agree? Explain.
10. Are direct-material price variances generally recognized when the materials are purchased or when they are used? Why?
11. Explain the role of understanding cost behavior and cost-driver activities for flexible budgeting.
12. Why do the techniques for controlling overhead differ from those for controlling direct materials?
13. How does the variable-overhead spending variance differ from the direct-labor price variance?
14. "Failure to meet price standards is the responsibility of the purchasing officer." Do you agree? Explain.
15. "A standard is one point in a band or range of acceptable outcomes." Evaluate this statement.
16. "A good control system places the blame for every unfavorable variance on someone in the organization. Without affixing blame, no one will take responsibility for cost control." Do you agree? Explain.
17. What are the key questions in the analysis and follow-up of variances?
18. What are some common causes of usage variances?
19. When should managers investigate variances?

PROBLEMS

1. **Flexible and Static Budgets.** RDC Transportation Company's manager has had trouble interpreting operating performance for several years. The company has used a budget based on detailed expectations for the forthcoming quarter. For example, the condensed performance report for a recent quarter is shown on the next page.

   Although the manager was upset about not obtaining enough revenue, she was happy that her cost performance was favorable, otherwise her net operating income would be even worse.

   The president was totally unhappy and remarked: "I can see some merit in comparing actual performance with budgeted performance because we can see whether actual revenue coincided with our best guess for budget purposes. But I can't see how this performance report helps me evaluate cost control performance."

a. Prepare a columnar flexible budget for RDC at revenue levels of $7,000,000, $8,000,000 and $9,000,000. Use the format of the last three columns of Exhibit 8-2. Assume that the prices and mix of products sold are equal to the budgeted prices and mix.

b. Express the flexible budget for costs in formula form.

c. Prepare a condensed table showing the static (master) budget variance, the sales activity variance, and the flexible-budget variance. Use the format of Exhibit 8-4.

	Budget	Actual	Variance
Net revenue	$8,000,000	$7,600,000	$400,000 U
Fuel	$ 160,000	$ 157,000	$ 3,000 F
Repairs and maintenance	80,000	78,000	2,000 F
Supplies and miscellaneous	800,000	788,000	12,000 F
Variable payroll	5,360,000	5,200,000	160,000 F
Total variable costs*	$6,400,000	$6,223,000	$177,000 F
Supervision	$ 160,000	$ 160,000	—
Rent	160,000	160,000	—
Depreciation	480,000	480,000	—
Other fixed costs	160,000	160,000	—
Total fixed costs	$ 960,000	$ 960,000	—
Total costs charged against revenue	$7,360,000	$7,183,000	$177,000 F
Operating income	$ 640,000	$ 417,000	$223,000 U

U = Unfavorable. F = Favorable.

*For purposes of this analysis, assume that all these costs are totally variable with respect to sales revenue. In practice, many are mixed and have to be subdivided into variable and fixed components before a meaningful analysis can be made. Also assume that the prices and mix of services sold remain unchanged.

2. **Direct-Material and Direct-Labor Variances.** The Handy Dandy Company manufactures metal giftware that is hand-shaped and hand-finished. The following standards were developed for a line of vases:

	Standard Inputs Expected for Each Unit of Output Achieved	Standard Price per Unit of Input
Direct materials	10 pounds	$ 6 per pound
Direct labor	5 hours	$ 25 per hour

During April, 550 vases were scheduled for production. However, only 525 were actually produced.

Direct materials purchased and used amounted to 5,500 pounds at a unit price of $5.25 per pound. Direct labor was actually paid $26.00 per hour, and 2,850 hours were used.

a. Compute the standard cost per vase for direct materials and direct labor.

b. Compute the price variances and usage variances for direct materials and direct labor.

c. Based on these sketchy data, what clues for investigation are provided by the variances?

3. **Activity Level Variances**. DataTech Company provides information systems services to local businesses. The costs of these services are driven by customer demand. One important cost is the cost of systems consultants who design data collecting, encoding, and reporting systems to fit customers' special needs. An overall cost driver is believed to be the number of these requests made to the systems consulting department. The expected variable cost of handling a request for June 19X7 was $60, and the number of requests expected was 75. Monthly fixed costs for the department (salaries, equipment depreciation, space costs) were budgeted at $7,000.

   The actual number of requests serviced by systems consulting in June 19X7 was 90, and the total costs incurred by the department was $12,300. Of that amount, $7,800 was for fixed costs.

   Compute the master (static) budget variances and the flexible-budget variances for the systems consulting department for June 19X7.

4. **Summary Performance Reports**. Consider the following data for Monarch Escrow Company:

   - Master budget data: sales, 2,500 clients at $35 each; variable costs, $25 per client; fixed costs, $15,000.

   - Actual results at actual prices: sales, 3,000 clients at $36 per client; variable costs, $80,000; fixed costs, $15,750.

   a. Prepare a summary performance report similar to Exhibit 8-4.
   b. Fill in the blanks:

Master budget operating income	$_____	
Variances		
Sales-activity variances	$_____	
Flexible-budget variances	===========	===========
Actual operating income	$_____	

5. **Material and Labor Variances**. Consider the following data:

	Direct Material	Direct Labor
Actual price per unit of input (lb and hr)	$ 18	$ 12
Standard price per unit of input	$ 14	$ 13
Standard inputs allowed per unit of output	5	2
Actual units of input	56,000	30,000
Actual units of output (product)	14,400	14,400

   a. Compute the price, usage, and flexible-budget variances for direct material and direct labor. Use U or F to indicate whether the variances are unfavorable or favorable.
   b. Prepare a plausible explanation for the performance.

6. **Variable-Overhead Variances**. You have been asked to prepare an analysis of the overhead costs in the billing department of a hospital. As an initial step, you prepare a summary of some events that bear on overhead for the most recent period. The variable-overhead flexible-budget variance was $5,000 unfavorable. The standard variable-overhead price per billing was $.06. Ten bills per hour is regarded as standard productivity per clerk. The total overhead incurred was $202,200, of which $134,500 was fixed. There were no variances for fixed overhead. The variable-overhead spending variance was $2,500 favorable.

Find the following:

a. Variable-overhead efficiency variance
b. Actual hours of input
c. Standard hours allowed for output achieve

Notes

[1] What if the total flexible budget results were positive—say $4,000? The total flexible-budget variance would be (–$11,570) – ($4,000) = S–15,570, or $15,570 unfavorable

[2] For example, sales-activity variances can be subdivided into sales quantity, sales mix, market size, and market share variances. This more advanced treatment of sales activity variances is covered in Charles T. Horngren, George Foster, and Srikant M. Datar, *Cost Accounting: A Managerial Emphasis* (Englewood Cliffs, NJ: Prentice Hall, 1994), pp. 758–763. These sales activity variances might result from changes in the product, changes in customer demand, effective advertising, and so on.

[3] Details of standard cost systems for financial reporting are covered in Charles T. Horngren, George Foster, and Srikant M. Datar, *Cost Accounting: A Managerial Emphasis* (Upper Saddle River, NJ: Prentice Hall, 1994), Chapters 7 and 8. pp. 225–296.

SECTION V
MANAGEMENT CONTROL SYSTEMS

CHAPTER 9: Internal Management Control Systems

INTERNAL MANAGEMENT CONTROL SYSTEMS

Internal control requirements were extended to managers in the public sector by the Federal Managers' Financial Integrity Act. Briefly, the act requires each executive agency to establish a system of internal accounting and administrative control that meets prescribed standards. They must also report annually, based on an evaluation conducted in accordance with established guidelines, to the president, Congress, and the public on the extent to which the agency's systems comply with the standards.

The documentation of internal control should systematically refer to (1) management's cost-benefit choices regarding the system and (2) management's evaluation of how well the internal control system is working. Documentation includes memos, minutes of meetings discussing internal control concepts with all affected individuals, written statements of compliance, flowcharts, procedures manuals, and the like. Moreover, there should be a written program for ongoing review and evaluation of the system. Finally, there should be letters from independent auditors stating that they found no material weaknesses in internal control during their audit, or that necessary improvements have been made.

THE AUDIT COMMITTEE

The first objective of internal accounting control is authorization; transactions should be executed in accordance with management's intentions. Moreover, management bears primary responsibility for the entity's financial statements. This authority and responsibility extends upward to the board of directors. Most boards have an **audit committee,** which oversees the internal accounting controls, financial statements, and financial affairs of the corporation. Indeed, such committees are required of companies whose shares are listed on the New York Stock Exchange.

Audit committees typically have three or more "outside" board members. Not everyday employees of the company, they are considered to be more independent than the "inside" directors—employees who serve as part of the corporation's management.[1] The committee provides contact and communication among the board, the external auditors, the internal auditors, the financial executives, and the operating executives. These relationships are depicted in Exhibit 9-1.

Exhibit 9-1 shows only one of many possible arrangements. Above all, note how the audit committee serves as the main pipeline to the board of directors, especially for individuals responsible for the accounting function. In Exhibit 9-1, the internal audit manager is directly responsible (solid line) through the controller on up to the board. The dashed lines indicate that the audit committee should communicate with and gather information directly from the internal auditors as well as the external auditors.

These relationships are evolving. For example, the internal auditing department sometimes is directly responsible to the executive vice-president. But increasingly the internal audit department is directly responsible to the audit committee itself and is totally independent of the financial officers.

The audit committee meets at least twice annually. The first meeting is typically to review the annual external audit plan; the second, to review the audited financial statements before their publication. Additional meetings may be held (1) to consider the retention or replacement of the independent external auditors; (2) to review the company's accounting system, particularly the internal controls; and (3) to review any special matters raised by internal audits. At least once a year, the committee should discuss with the independent auditors their evaluation of corporate management (without the presence of the latter). Similarly, the committee should obtain management's evaluation of the independent auditors.

Many companies include an audit committee report in their annual report. Merck & Co., the pharmaceutical firm, included the report shown in Exhibit 9-2.

CHECKLIST OF INTERNAL CONTROL

All good systems of internal control have certain features in common. These features can be summarized in a **checklist of internal control**, which may be used to appraise any specific procedures for cash, purchases, sales, payroll, and the like. This checklist is sometimes called **principles** or **rules** or **characteristics** or **features** or **elements**. The following checklist summarizes the guidance that is found in much of the systems and auditing literature.[2]

1. Reliable Personnel with Clear Responsibilities

The most important element of successful control is personnel. Incompetent or dishonest individuals can undermine a system, no matter how well it meets the other items on the checklist. Procedures to hire, train, motivate, and supervise employees are essential. Individuals must be given authority, responsibility, and duties commensurate with their abilities, interests, experience, and reliability. Yet many employers use low-cost talent that may prove exceedingly expensive in the long run, not only because of fraud but because of poor productivity.

Assessing responsibility means tracking actions as far down in the organization as is feasible, so that results can be related to individuals. It means having sales clerks sign sales slips, inspectors initial packing slips, and workers sign time cards and requisitions. Grocery stores often assign each cashier a separate money tray; therefore, shortages can easily be traced to the person responsible. The psychological impact of fixing responsibility tends to promote care and efficiency. Employees often perform better when they must explain deviations from required procedures.

Exhibit 9–1 Organization Chart Showing Position of Audit Committee

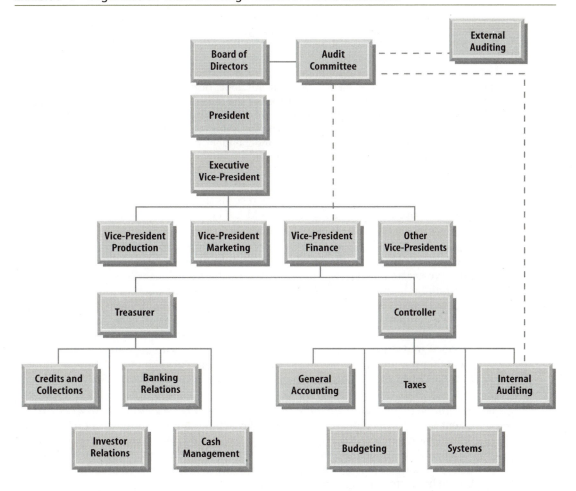

The possibility of employee theft is distasteful to most managers, but it must be taken seriously. The National Mass Retailing Institute estimates that retailers lose about 2% of sales to theft and mistakes. Shoplifting accounts for part of this, but employee theft causes much larger losses than shoplifting. The institute estimates that an average retail store loses $10 per shift per clerk. Convenience stores and fast-food restaurants are especially vulnerable to employee theft. Such businesses need to be especially concerned with internal control systems.

2. Separation of Duties

The separation of duties not only helps ensure accurate compilation of data but also limits the chances for fraud that would require the collusion of two or more persons. This extremely important and often neglected element can be subdivided into four parts:

1. *Separation of operational responsibility from recordkeeping responsibility.* The entire accounting function should be divorced from operating departments. For example, product inspectors, not machine operators, should count units produced; inventory records clerks or computers, not material handlers, should keep perpetual inventory

The Audit Committee of the Board of DIrectors is comprised of five outside directors. The members of the Committee are Charles E. Exley, Jr., Chairman; Carolyn K. Davis, Ph.D., Vice Chair; Sir Derek Birkin; William N. Kelley, M.D.; and Dennis Weatherstone. The committee held three meetings during 1993.

The Audit Committee meets with independent public accountants, management, and internal auditors to assure that all are carrying out their respective responsibilities. The Audit Committee reviews the performance and fees of the independent public accountants prior to recommending their appointment and meets with them, without management present, to discuss the scope and results of their audit work, including the adequacy of internal controls and the quality of financial reporting. Both the independent public accountants and the internal auditors have full access to the Audit Committee.

records. Why? Because those keeping the records should have nothing to gain by falsifying the records. A material handler should not be able to steal materials and cover up the theft by recording the issue of the materials to production.

2. *Separation of the custody of assets from accounting.* This practice reduces temptation and fraud. For example, the bookkeeper should not handle cash, and the cashier should not have access to ledger accounts such as the individual records of customers. A person with both accounting and cash-handling duties could pocket cash that is received and make a false entry in the accounting records.

    In a computer system, a person with custody of assets should not have access to programming or any input of records. In a classic example, a programmer in a bank rounded transactions to the next lower cent rather than the nearest cent and had the computer put the fraction of a cent into his account. For example, a customer amount of $10.057 became $10.05, and the programmer's account received $0.007. With millions of transactions, the programmer's account became very large.

3. *Separation of the authorization of transactions from the custody of related assets.* To the extent feasible, persons who authorize transactions should not have control over the related asset. For instance, the same individual should not authorize the payment of a supplier's invoice and also sign the check in payment of the bill. Nor should an individual who handles cash receipts have the authority to indicate which accounts receivable should be written off as uncollectible.

    The latter separation of powers prevents such embezzlement as the following: a bookkeeper opens the mail, removes a $1,000 check from a customer, and somehow cashes it. To hide the theft, the bookkeeper prepares the following journal entry:

Allowance for bad debts 1,000	
Accounts receivable 1,000	
To write off an amount owed by a customer.	

4. *Separation of duties within the accounting function.* An employee should not be able to record a transaction from its origin to its ultimate posting in a ledger. Independent performance of various phases will help ensure control over errors. Even a small company should have some separation of duties. For example, if there is only one bookkeeper who writes checks and keeps the accounting records, the owner can at least sign the checks and reconcile the monthly bank statement.

    A main goal of the separation of duties is to make sure that one person, acting alone, cannot defraud the company. It is more difficult, although not impossible, for two or more employees to collude in a fraud. This is why movie theaters have a cashier selling tickets and an usher taking them. The cashier takes in cash, the usher keeps the ticket stubs, and in an audit step performed by a third person, the cash is compared with the number of stubs. But suppose they do collude. The ticket seller pockets the cash and issues a fake ticket. The usher accepts the fake ticket and allows entry. Separation of duties alone will not prevent collusive theft.

3. Proper Authorization

The Foreign Corrupt Practices Act stresses proper authorization. Authorization can be either *general* or *specific*. General authorization is usually found in writing. It often sets definite limits on what price to pay (whether to fly economy or first class), on what price to receive (whether to offer a sales discount), on what credit limits to grant to customers, and so forth. There may also be complete prohibitions (against paying extra fees or bribes or overtime premiums).

Specific authorization usually means that a superior manager must permit (typically in writing) any particular deviations from the limits set by general authorization. For example, the plant manager, rather than the lathe supervisor, may have to approve any overtime. Another example is the need for approval from the board of directors regarding expenditures for capital assets in excess of a specific limit.

4. Adequate Documents

Documents and records vary considerably, from source documents such as sales invoices and purchase orders to journals and ledgers. Immediate, complete, and tamper-proof recording is the aim. It is encouraged by optical scanning of bar-coded data, by having all source documents prenumbered and accounted for, by using devices such as cash registers, and by designing forms for ease of recording.

Immediate recording is especially important for handling cash sales. Devices used to ensure immediate recording include "rewards" to customers if they are not offered a receipt at the time of sale and forcing clerks to make change by pricing items at $1.99, $2.99, and $3.99 rather than at $2, $3, and $4. (Historically, such pricing was originally adopted to force clerks to make change as well as for its psychological impact on potential customers.) The need to access the change drawer forces the clerk to ring up the sale so the drawer will open.

5. Proper Procedures

Most organizations have **procedures manuals**, which specify the flow of documents and provide information and instructions to facilitate adequate recordkeeping.

Routine and automatic checks are major ways of attaining proper procedures. In a phrase, this means doing things "by the numbers." Repetitive procedures may be prescribed for order taking, order filling, collating, and inspecting. The use of general routines permits specialization of effort, division of duties, and automatic checks on previous steps in the routine.

6. Physical Safeguards

Obviously, losses of cash, inventories, and records are minimized by safes, locks, guards, and limited access. For example, many companies (such as Boeing and Hewlett-Packard) require all *visitors* to sign a register and wear a name tag. Often *employees* will also wear name tags that are coded to show the facilities to which they have access. Doors to research areas or computer rooms often may be opened only with special keys or by use of a specific code.

Sometimes small businesses are especially vulnerable to theft of physical assets. For example, retail stores use alarm systems, guard dogs, security guards, special lighting, and many other safeguards to protect their property.

7. Bonding, Vacations, and Rotation of Duties

Key people may be subject to excessive temptation. Thus, top executives, branch managers, and individuals who handle cash or inventories should have understudies, be required to take vacations, and be bonded.

Rotating employees and requiring them to take vacations ensures that at least two employees know how to do each job so that an absence due to illness or a sudden resignation does not create major problems. Further, the practice of having another employee periodically perform their duties discourages employees from engaging in fraudulent activities that might be discovered when someone else has access to their records.

Rotation of duties is illustrated by the common practice of having employees such as receivables and payables clerks periodically exchange duties. Or a receivables clerk may handle accounts from A to C for three months and then be rotated to accounts M to P for three months, and so forth.

Incidentally, the act of **bonding**—that is, buying insurance against embezzlement—is not a substitute for vacations, rotation of duties, and similar precautions. Insurance companies will pay only when a loss is proved; establishing proof is often difficult and costly in itself.

8. Independent Check

All phases of the system should be subjected to periodic review by outsiders (for example, by independent public accountants) and by internal auditors. Auditors have a degree of objectivity that allows them to spot weaknesses overlooked by managers immersed in day-to-day operations. It is too costly for external auditors to examine all transactions, so they inspect a sample of the transactions. By first evaluating the system of internal control and testing the extent to which it is being followed, the auditor decides on the likelihood of undetected errors. If internal controls are weak, there is a greater probability of significant errors in the accounting records. Then the auditor must examine many transactions to provide reasonable assurance that existing errors will be found. If internal controls are strong, the auditor can use a smaller sample to develop confidence in the accuracy of the accounting records.

Internal auditors are company employees who help design control systems and assess the degree of compliance with the existing systems. Their main goal is to enhance efficiency of operations by promoting adherence to both administrative and accounting controls and to continuously improve the system.

The idea of an independent check extends beyond the work performed by professional auditors. For example, bank statements should be reconciled with book balances. The bank provides an independent record of cash. Furthermore, the monthly bank reconciliations should be conducted by some clerk other than the cash, receivables, or payables clerks. Other examples of independent checks include monthly statements sent to credit customers and physical counts of inventory to check against perpetual records.

9. Cost-Benefit Analysis

Highly complex systems tend to strangle people in red tape, impeding rather than promoting efficiency. Besides, the "cost of keeping the costs" sometimes gets out of hand. Investments in more costly systems must be compared with the expected benefits. Unfortunately, it is easier to relate new lathes or production methods to cost savings in manufacturing than to link a new computer to cost savings in inventory control. Yet efforts must be made. For example, the accounting firm of KPMG Peat Marwick completed a study of office automation for a client. After examining the jobs of 2,600 white-collar workers, KPMG Peat Marwick quantified a cost-benefit relationship: "A single investment of $10 million would result in a productivity savings equal to $8.4 million every year."

Although many companies implement more complex procedures to improve internal control, a few have taken a reverse course. They have decided that the increased costs of additional scrutiny are not worth the expected savings from catching mistakes or crooks. For example, an aerospace manufacturer routinely pays the invoice amounts without checking supporting documentation except on a random-sampling basis. An aluminum company sends out a blank check with its purchase orders, and then the supplier fills out the check and deposits it.

No framework for internal control is perfect in the sense that it can prevent some shrewd individual from "beating the system" either by outright embezzlement or by producing inaccurate records. The task is not total prevention of fraud, nor is it implementation of operating perfection; rather, the task is the designing of a *cost-effective* tool that will help achieve efficient operations and reduce temptation.

EFFECTS OF COMPUTERS ON INTERNAL CONTROL

The nine items in the preceding checklist apply to both computer and manual accounting systems. However, computers change the focus of internal control in two ways:

1. The computer can accomplish traditional internal control functions more efficiently.
2. But, additional controls must be put in place to ensure the accuracy and reliability of computer-processed data.

Computers Change the Control Environment

The computer has allowed relatively inexpensive processing of huge volumes of accounting data. However, internal control over computerized operations is essential. Consider an error that a human might make once a month. Such an error would be repeated thousands of times a day in a computer program for processing vast quantities of data. Further, errors that would be obvious by scanning journal entries could go undetected because data are "invisible," stored on tape or disks. Input and output data transmitted over phone lines may be vulnerable to unauthorized access. Thus, the installation of internal control systems must accompany computerization.

Computers are amazingly accurate. The focus of internal control is not *computer* errors. Invariably, the computer has done exactly what it was told (or programmed) to do. Errors usually result because someone entered the wrong data, programmed the computer incorrectly, ran the wrong program, or asked for the wrong output.

Types of Control for Computer Systems

The greatest source of errors in computerized systems is the data input. Both the original recording (for example, key-punching cards or direct entry from a remote terminal) are frequent sources of error. Other possible sources of errors are managed by processing, output, and general controls.

Input controls can help guard against the entry of false or erroneous data, especially those due to multiple steps in handling the data when human processing is involved. Such controls include using standardized forms and verifying data input. Accountants also program the computer to verify that all required data are included on each input document, identify key numbers outside a range of reasonableness, and conduct other such checks. Use of optical scanning equipment can also limit data-recording errors.

Processing controls start with the design and programming of the system, including complete documentation. They also include control of operations, including normal separation and rotation of duties. For example, programmers should not be allowed to operate the computers. A computer consultant commented that he had immense stealing opportunities when he ran computer operations for a large bank: "I alone designed the dividend-payment operation, wrote the program for it, and ran the job on the machine. The operation was so big that it had a mistake tolerance of nearly $100,000. I could have paid at least half that much to myself, in small checks, and the money wouldn't even have been missed."

Output controls check output against input, possibly by random manual processing of data. Output controls should also ensure that only authorized persons receive the reports. Computers often generate literally tons of printed output. A paper shredder can be an important control tool to safeguard privileged information.

General controls focus on the organization and operation of the data-processing activity. Good internal control requires well-defined procedures for developing, testing, and approving new systems and programs or changing old ones. Access to equipment and files should be restricted. But most important, as in any system, manual or computerized, are personnel controls. Hiring reliable personnel and keeping temptation from their doorsteps through common-sense controls are important goals of any internal control system.

EXAMPLES OF INTERNAL CONTROL

This section discusses specific internal control considerations for cash and inventories. Additional details are provided in Addendum 9.

Internal Control of Cash

Cash is almost always the most enticing asset for potential thieves and embezzlers. Therefore, internal controls are far more elaborate for cash than for, say, the paper clips and desks on the premises. The following points are especially noteworthy:

1. As previously mentioned, the function of receiving cash should be separated from the function of disbursing cash. Moreover, individuals who handle cash or checks should not have access to the accounting records.

2. All receipts should be deposited intact daily. That is, none of the currency and checks received each day should be used directly for any other purposes. For example, sales in retail establishments are recorded in a cash register. A supervisor compares the locked cash register tape with the actual cash in the register drawer. Then the cash receipts are deposited, and the tape is forwarded to the accounting department as a basis for accounting entries. If cash from the till is sometimes used to pay suppliers, there is a serious internal control weakness.

3. All major disbursements should be made by serially numbered checks. Gaps should be investigated. The *Wall Street Journal* cited an example of good controls used poorly: "A bookkeeping assistant [was] under strict orders to note every missing number. . . . But no one checked to see how many were missing or why."

4. Bank accounts should be reconciled monthly. (This recommendation also applies to personal banking accounts.) A **bank reconciliation** is an analysis that explains any difference between the cash balance shown by the depositor and that shown by the bank. It is surprising how many businesses (some of substantial size) do not reconcile their bank accounts regularly.

Control of cash requires procedures for handling both checks and currency. To control checks, many organizations use check protectors that perforate or otherwise establish an unalterable amount on the face of each check. Dual signatures are frequently required on large checks.

Currency is probably the most alluring form of cash. Businesses that handle much currency, such as gambling establishments, restaurants, and bars, are particularly subject to theft and false reporting. For example, many owners of small retail outlets do not record all of their cash receipts, a procedure known as *skimming*. Why? To save income taxes.

A recent news story reported: "Federal undercover agents in New York City opened an attack on the underground economy, which spawns billions of dollars yearly in untaxed income through off-the-books transactions." According to the affidavits, the establishments searched by the agents grossed more than $5 million while reporting on their tax returns only $3.6 million.

Tax authorities often use known gross profit margins for an industry to assess the reasonableness of the profits based on reported revenues and costs of goods sold for a particular company. Measures, such as industry average sales per square foot of store space, allow assessment of the adequacy of reported revenue.

Comparing reported results with averages is not foolproof. An exclusive clothing store in San Francisco paid a percentage of sales for rent. Reported sales for a recent year were $11.2 million; an independent audit later disclosed actual sales of $20.5 million. The lessor always compared sales per square foot of floor space with those of similar stores. No clue to any impropriety arose. In fact, the lessor termed the reported sales per square foot "extraordinary" and the actual results as "unheard of."

Internal Control of Inventories

In many organizations, inventories are more easily accessible than cash. Therefore, they become a favorite target for thieves.

Retail merchants must contend with inventory shrinkage, a polite term for shoplifting by customers and embezzling by employees. *Inventory shrinkage* is the difference between (1) the value of inventory that would occur if there were no pilferage, misclassifications, breakage, or clerical errors and (2) the value of inventory when it is physically counted. Consider the following footnote from a recent annual report of Associated Dry Goods, one of the largest operators of department and discount stores in the country: "Physical inventories are taken twice each year. Department store inventory shrinkage at retail, as a percent of retail sales, was 2.4% this year compared with 2.1% last year. Discount store inventory shrinkage as a percent of retail sales was 0.4% and 0.3%, respectively." Some department stores have suffered shrinkage losses of 4% to 5% of their sales volume. Compare this with the typical net profit margin of 5% to 6%.

A management consulting firm has demonstrated how widespread shoplifting has become. The firm concentrated on a midtown New York City department store. Five hundred shoppers, picked at random, were followed from the moment they entered the store to the time they departed. Forty-two shoppers, or one out of every twelve, took something. They stole $300 worth of merchandise, an average of $7.15 each. Similar experiments were conducted in Boston (1 of 20 shoplifted), Philadelphia (1 of 10), and again in New York (1 of 12).

Experts on controlling inventory shrinkage generally agree that the best deterrent is an alert employee at the point of sale. Retail stores use sensitized tags on merchandise; if not detached or neutralized by a salesclerk, these miniature transmitters trip an alarm as the culprit begins to leave the store. Many libraries use a similar system to safeguard their books. Macy's in New York has continuous surveillance with over fifty television cameras.

Retailers must also scrutinize their own personnel because they account for at least 30% to 40% of inventory shortages. Some stores have actors pose as shoplifters, who are then subjected to fake arrests. If potential thieves see the arrests, they may be deterred. Such ploys have helped reduce thefts by employees at major retail chains.

The problem of stealing is not confined to profit-seeking entities. According to the student newspaper at Northwestern University, $14,000 worth of silverware, glasses, and china was stolen from the university dining halls annually. That amounts to $4.71 for every regular customer. Signs posted at the end of each school term requesting the return of "borrowed" goods have had little success. The food service director commented: "Two years ago, we put up really nice signs and set out boxes for returns. Kids saw the boxes and stole them for packing."

The imposing magnitude of retail inventory shrinkage demonstrates how management objectives may differ among industries. For example, consider the grocery business, where net income is about 1% of sales. You can readily see why a prime responsibility of the store manager is to control inventory shrinkage rather than boost gross sales volume. The trade-off is clear: if the operating profit is 2% of sales, to offset a $1,000 increase in shrinkage requires a $50,000 boost in gross sales.

Shrinkage in Perpetual and Periodic Inventory Systems

Measuring inventory shrinkage is straightforward for companies that use a perpetual inventory system. Shrinkage is simply the difference between the cost of inventory identified by a physical count and the clerical inventory balance. Consider the following example:

Sales	$100,000
Cost of goods sold (perpetual inventory system)	$ 80,000
Beginning inventory	$ 15,000
Purchases	$ 85,000
Ending inventory, per clerical records	$ 20,000
Ending inventory, per physical count	$ 18,000

Shrinkage is $20,000 – $18,000 = $2,000. The journal entries under a perpetual inventory system would be:

Inventory shrinkage	2,000	
Inventory		2,000
To adjust ending inventory to its balance per physical count.		
Cost of goods sold	2,000	
Inventory shrinkage		2,000
To close inventory shrinkage to cost of goods sold.		

The total cost of goods sold would be $80,000 + $2,000 = $82,000.

By definition, a periodic inventory system has no clerical balance of the inventory account. Inventory shrinkage is automatically included in cost of goods sold. Why? Because beginning inventory plus purchases less ending inventory measures all inventory that has flowed out, whether it went to customers, shoplifters, or embezzlers, or was simply lost or broken. Our example would show:

Beginning inventory	$ 15,000
Plus: Purchases	85,000
Goods available for sale	$100,000
Less: Ending inventory, per physical count	18,000
Cost of goods sold	$ 82,000

To assess shrinkage, we need some way to *estimate* what the ending inventory *should be*. The difference between this *estimate* and the physical count is inventory shrinkage. No journal entries are necessary.

SUMMARY

It is tempting to delegate internal control decisions to accountants. However, managers at all levels have a major responsibility for the success of internal controls. In fact, in the United States there is a federal law that explicitly places the ultimate responsibility for the adequacy of internal controls of publicly held companies on top management. To help monitor internal control, boards of directors appoint audit committees, which oversee accounting controls, the financial statements, and general financial affairs of the company.

The following general characteristics form a checklist that can be used as a starting point for judging the effectiveness of internal control:

1. Reliable personnel with clear responsibilities
2. Separation of duties
3. Proper authorization
4. Adequate documents
5. Proper procedures
6. Physical safeguards
7. Bonding, vacations, and rotation of duties
8. Independent check
9. Cost-benefit analysis

Managers and accountants should recognize that the role of an internal control system is as much a positive one (enhancing efficiency) as a negative one (reducing errors and fraud).

The checklist of internal controls applies to both computerized and manual systems. However, computerized systems change the emphasis of internal controls. Although computers process data exactly as instructed, controls over programming and data input are especially important.

Control systems for cash and inventories are usually well developed because these assets are often the targets of theft or embezzlement.

SELF-CORRECTION PROBLEMS

1. Identify the internal control weaknesses in each of the following situations:

   a. Mike Reynolds performs all purchasing functions for Bayside Marine. He orders merchandise, oversees its delivery, and approves invoices for payment.

   b. The Winthrop Mudhens, a minor league baseball team, is struggling financially. To save costs, and because all seating is general admission, the team has eliminated ticket takers. The ticket seller simply lets fans go through the gate when they pay the admission fee.

   c. Cash and checks received by mail from customers who purchased items on open account are opened by an accounts receivable clerk, who deposits the cash and checks in the bank and prepares the appropriate accounting journal entry.

   d. Ruth Ann Kilstrom is a trusted and dedicated employee. In fact, she is so dedicated that she has not taken a vacation in five years. Her boss appreciates her dedication because no one could do her job if she were gone.

   e. Employees in Wing Point Grocery do a variety of jobs. When business is slack, they stock shelves and perform other necessary tasks. When the checkout stands are busy, everyone is expected to help with checkouts by operating whatever cash register is available. Each employee works at an average of four different checkout stands in an average shift, and every checkout stand is manned by an average of six different persons each day.

2. A news story reported:

    A federal grand jury indicted seven former Cenco, Inc. officials, accusing them of an inventory overstatement scheme that led the concern to report about $25 million in false profits. The indictment charged that the overstatement was accomplished by increasing the number of products shown on inventory tabulating cards and making up new cards. The inflation of inventory lessened the reported cost of sales and, thereby, resulted in a greater reported profit figure.

    Given this description, were any assets stolen? What is the major feature in the chapter checklist of internal control that is aimed at preventing such dishonesty? Indicate how such dishonest acts could be accomplished and how the dishonest officials might have expected to benefit from those acts.

SOLUTIONS TO SELF-CORRECTION PROBLEMS

1. a. A single person should not perform all these functions. Reynolds could order fictitious merchandise, record its delivery, and authorize payment to his own (or a confederate's) account.

    b. There is no control against the ticket seller's letting friends in free or pocketing cash without issuing a ticket, by simply letting the fans go through the gate.

    c. The accounts receivable clerk performs too many functions. The clerk could keep cash (or forge an endorsement of a check) and make a false entry in the accounts, such as writing off the account as a bad debt.

    d. There are at least two problems with Kilstrom's dedication. First, because no one else could do her job, the company would be in dire straits if something happened to her or if she resigned suddenly. Second, she has too great an opportunity to perpetuate a fraud without anyone discovering it. If someone replaced her periodically, he or she might be in a position to discover any fraud.

    e. Responsibility is not well defined. If a shortage of cash occurs at any checkout stand, it will be impossible to identify the employees responsible.

2. Assets in the form of inventories were probably not stolen. Overstatement of ending inventory also causes overstatement of net income in the current period. Major motives were job security (by means of a display of higher net income) and greed (by means of management bonuses and raises in future salaries). Indeed, the manager who began the scheme was hired on a four-year contract with Cenco, giving him a modest annual base salary of $40,000 plus a bonus that added 1% to his salary for every 1% increase in the Cenco Medical Health (CMH) Group's net income. Net profits soared during the life of the manager's contract. The manager reaped total compensation far in excess of his base salary.

    Two subordinate managers had no incentive bonus plans, but they played along with the inventory scheme to please their boss. A variety of ways were used to overstate inventories. For example, three boxes of gauze pads would become twenty-three. The auditors were fooled with the help of fake invoices and lies. The scheme was uncovered when a subordinate informed the company treasurer. Three executives were given prison terms ranging from one to three years.

    The major feature that should prevent such dishonesty is *separation of duties*. Collusion makes dishonest acts harder to accomplish. Nevertheless, as the Cenco case illustrates, separation of duties is not enough to detect fictitious inventories when there is collusion.

    Reliable personnel with clear responsibilities is an additional feature on the checklist that is illustrated by this case. Personnel must be not only competent and honest, but also adequately instructed and supervised. Immediate supervisors should know enough about underlying operations so that they can sense any significant unauthorized conduct. Independent check is another feature that helps. That is why outside auditors conduct their own counts and observe management's counts.

QUESTIONS

1. "The words *internal control* are commonly misunderstood to refer only to those facets of the accounting system that are supposed to prevent embezzling." Comment.

2. What are the responsiblities of the audit commitee?

3. Into what four categories of transactions can the most repetitive, voluminous transactions in most organizations be divided?

4. "Business operations would be a hopeless tangle without the paperwork that is often regarded with disdain." Explain.

5. "The primary responsibility for internal controls rests with the outside auditors." Do you agree? Explain.

6. Give three examples of documentation of an internal accounting control system.

7. What is the primary responsibility of the audit committee?

8. "Internal control systems have both negative and positive objectives." Do you agree? Explain.

9. Prepare a checklist of important factors to consider in judging an internal control system.

10. "The most important element of successful control is personnel." Explain.

11. What is the essential idea of separation of duties?

12. Authorization can be general or specific. Give an example of each.

13. Internal control of a computerized system consists of applications controls and general controls. What are the three types of applications controls?

14. Briefly describe how a bottler of soda water might compile data regarding control of breakage of bottles at the plant, where normal breakage can be expected.

15. The branch manager of a national retail grocery chain has stated: "My managers are judged more heavily on the basis of their merchandise-shrinkage control than on their overall sales volume." Why? Explain.

16. "It is easy to be ethical. Just identify the ethical choice and then do it." Do you agree? Explain.

17. "Our managers know they are expected to meet budgeted profit targets. We do not take excuses. Good managers find a way to make budget." Discuss the possible consequences of this policy.

18. Pressure for profits extends beyond managers in profit-seeking companies. A news story reported: "The profit motive, even in nonprofit hospitals, is steadily eroding the traditional concern to provide care to the medically indigent." Why does the profit motive affect even nonprofit organizations?

ADDENDUM 9: INTERNAL CONTROL OF CASH

This appendix describes how organizations control cash. Most cash is kept in bank accounts. Therefore, the focus is on understanding bank statements and transactions.

The Bank Statement

Exhibit 9-3 displays a bank statement for account number 96848602, one of thousands of the bank's deposits. Together, these accounts form the subsidiary ledger that supports the bank's general ledger account *Deposits*, a liability.

The supporting documents for the detailed checks on the statement are canceled checks; for additional deposits, deposit slips. Notice that the minimum balance, $–33.39, is negative. This indicates an *overdraft*, which is a negative account balance arising from the bank's paying a check even though the depositor had insufficient funds available at the instant the check was presented.

Overdrafts are permitted as an occasional courtesy by the bank. However, the depositor is rarely given more than a day or two to eliminate the overdraft by making a deposit. Moreover, the bank may levy a fee (e.g., $10 or $30) for each overdraft.

Banks often provide (for a fee plus interest) "automatic" loan privileges, short-term loans (from ten to thirty days or more) to cover overdrafts. That is, when a depositor has insufficient funds, the bank increases the depositor's account with an "automatic" loan. The depositor avoids any embarrassment or risks of a bank's delaying payment of a check to await an additional deposit.

Bank Reconciliations

Exhibit 9-4 demonstrates how an independent check of cash balances works for any bank depositor (individual or business entity). First, note how parallel records are kept. The balance on December 31 is an asset (Cash) on the depositor's books and a liability (Deposits) on the bank's books. The terms *debit* and *credit* as used by banks may seem strange. Banks *credit* the depositor's account for additional deposits because the bank has a liability to the depositor. Banks *debit* the account for checks cleared and canceled (paid) by the bank. When the $2,000 check drawn by the depositor on January 5 is paid by the bank on January 8, the bank's journal entry would be:

Jan. 8 Deposits	$2,000	
Cash		$2,000
To decrease the depositor's account.		

A credit balance on the bank's books means that the bank owes money to the depositor.

A monthly *bank reconciliation* is conducted by the depositor to make sure that all cash receipts and disbursements are accounted for. Bank reconciliations take many forms, but the objective is unchanged: to explain all differences in the cash balances shown on the bank statement and in the depositor's general ledger at a given date. Using the data in Exhibit 9-4:

Bank Reconciliation January 31, 19X2

Balance per books (also called *balance per check register, register balance*)	$ 8,000
Deduct: Bank service charges for January not recorded on the books	
(also include any other charges by the bank not yet deducted)*	20
Adjusted (corrected) balance per books	$ 7,980
Balance per bank (also called *bank statement balance, statement balance*)	$10,980
Add: Deposits not recorded by bank(also called	
unrecorded deposits, deposits in transit), deposit of 1/31	7,000
Total	$17,980
Deduct: Outstanding checks, check of 1/29	10,000
Adjusted (corrected) balance per bank	$ 7,980

---

* Note that new entries on the depository's books are required for all previously unrecorded additions and deductions made to achieve the adjusted balance per books.

Exhibit 9-3 An Actual Bank Statement

SEAFIRST BANK

University Branch
4701 University Way NE
Seattle WA 98145

		Account Number
Richard B. Sandstrom	777	96848602
2420 Highline Rd.		Statement Period
Redmond WA 98110		11-21-95 to 12-20-95

SUMMARY OF YOUR ACCOUNTS

CHECKING

First Choice Minimum Balance	96848602
Beginning Balance	368.56
Deposits	5,074.00
Withdrawals	3,232.92
Service Charges/Fees	16.00
Ending Balance	2,193.64
Minimum Balance on 12-9-95	**– 33.39**

CHECKING ACTIVITY

Deposits

Posted	Amount	Description
11-21	700.00	Deposit
11-25	1,810.00	Payroll Deposit
12-10	1,810.00	Payroll Deposit
12-16	754.00	Deposit

Withdrawals

Ck No	Paid	Amount
1606	12-02	1134.00
1607	11-28	561.00
1609*	12-09	12.00
1617*	12-05	7.00
1629*	11-26	10.00
1630	11-25	16.95
1639*	12-02	96.00
1641*	12-09	1025.00
1642	12-05	50.00
1643	12-15	236.25
1644	12-17	84.72

* = Gap in check sequence
Total number of checks = 10

Exhibit 9-4   Comparative Cash Balances, January 19X2

Depositor's Records

Cash in Bank
(receivable from bank)

1/1/X2 Bal.	11,000	1/5	2,000
		1/15	3,000
1/10	4,000		
		1/19	5,000
1/24	6,000		
1/31	7,000	1/29	10,000
	28,000		20,000
1/31/X2 Bal.	8,000		

Bank's Records

Deposits (payable)

1/8	2,000	1/1/X2 Bal.	11,000
1/20	3,000		
		1/11	4,000
1/28	5,000	1/26	6,000
1/31	20*		
	10,020		21,000
		1/31/X2 Bal.	10,980

*Service charge for printing checks.

Date	Depositor's General Journal	Debit	Credit
1/5	Accounts payable	2,000	
	Cash		2,000
	Check No. 1.		
1/10	Cash	4,000	
	Accounts receivable		4 000
	Deposit slip No. 1.		
1/15	Income taxes payable	3,000	
	Cash		3,000
	Check No. 2.		
1/19	Accounts payable	5,000	
	Cash		5,000
	Check No. 3.		
1/24	Cash	6,000	
	Accounts receivable		6,000
	Deposit No. 2.		
1/29	Accounts payable	10,000	
	Cash		10,000
	Check No. 4.		
1/31	Cash	7,000	
	Accounts receivable		7,000
	Deposit No. 3.		

As the bank reconciliation indicates, an adjustment is necessary on the books of the depositor:

```
Jan. 31 Bank service charge expense  . . . . . . .  20
            Cash  . . . . . . . . . . . . . . . . . . . . . . . . . . .        20
        To record bank charges for printing checks.
```

This popular format has two major sections. The first section begins with the balance per books (that is, the balance in the Cash T-account). Adjustments are made for items not entered on the books but already entered by the *bank,* such as deduction of the $20 service charge. No additions are shown in the illustrated section, but an illustrative addition would be the bank's collection of a customer receivable on behalf of the company. The second section begins with the balance per bank. Adjustments are made for items not entered by the *bank* but already entered in the books. After adjustments, each section should end with identical adjusted cash balances. This is the amount that should appear as cash in bank on the depositor's balance sheet.

Paperless Bank Transactions

Each passing year brings us closer to so-called paperless banking. For example, many employees never see their payroll checks. Instead the employer deposits the "checks" in the employees' bank accounts. This is an example of an "automatic" deposit. If the employee forgets to add the amount to his or her check register, the bank's books would show a higher balance than the depositor's books. Similarly, some 75% of transactions in "branch banking" offices occur at automatic teller machines (ATM). Many depositors may forget to record these, but will find them when they reconcile their bank statement with their books (check register).

Petty Cash

Every organization desires to minimize red tape—for example, avoiding unjustifiably complicated procedures for minor disbursements. Consequently, petty cash funds are usually created and accounted for on an **imprest basis**. An imprest petty cash fund is initiated with a fixed amount of currency and coins. As the currency is used, petty cash receipts or vouchers are prepared to show the purposes of the disbursements. When the balance of currency gets low, the fund is restored to its original level by drawing and cashing a single check for the exact amount of the needed cash replenishment. The following are typical journal entries:

```
Petty cash  . . . . . . . . . . . . . . . . . . . . . . . . . . .  100
        Cash in bank . . . . . . . . . . . . . . . . . . . . .           100
    To set up a fund for miscellaneous minor
    office disbursements. (A check is drawn,
    cashed, and proceeds placed with some
    responsible person.)
Postage  . . . . . . . . . . . . . . . . . . . . . . . . . . . .   10
Freight in  . . . . . . . . . . . . . . . . . . . . . . . . . . .   40
Miscellaneous office expenses . . . . . . . . . . . . .   35
        Cash in bank . . . . . . . . . . . . . . . . . . . . .            85
    To replenish the petty cash fund and record
    expenses paid therefrom.
```

Examples of petty cash outlays include special post-office charges for certifying or insuring mail, collections by delivery personnel, and dinner money given to an employee when working overtime.

Note that after inception, the petty cash account itself is never directly charged or credited unless the $100 initial amount is increased or decreased. Further, the cash on hand plus the receipts (or vouchers) should always equal the $100 amount of the petty cash fund.

Notes

1 Mobil Corporation, the oil company, has a typical board composition. Of sixteen directors, six are also members of management and ten are "outside" directors. Five of the outside directors form the audit committee.

2 For an expanded discussion, see A. Arens and J. Loebbecke, *Auditing*, 5th ed. (Upper Saddle River, NJ: Prentice Hall, 1991), Chap. 9.

SECTION VI
THE FINANCIAL MANAGEMENT
ENVIRONMENT

CHAPTER 10

INTRODUCTION TO FINANCIAL MANAGEMENT

Do you intend to make a career in marketing, purchasing, production, or human resources management? Possibly you want to be an economist, an attorney, a tax expert, a public relations specialist, or your goal is your own communications firm. No matter which field you choose, you will be involved with finance in one way or another. Let's look at a few of these careers to see how each may incorporate finance. Decisions by marketing managers influence growth in sales; as a result, there may be a need for increased funds to support further investment in plant and equipment. Purchasing managers must know whether sufficient funds exist to take advantage of volume discounts. Lower material costs increase profits, and increased profits may result in higher value of the firm. Public relations specialists must know about the financial strengths and weaknesses of the business so they can carry on informed discussions with inquiring reporters and investors. Attorneys are involved in corporate fund raising or in litigation in which the value of a company may be at stake. As an owner of a small business, an entrepreneur has complete financial responsibility and must closely manage money and credit.

An understanding of finance can do more than enhance your career. It can also sharpen your day-to-day grasp of current events and give you a better handle on your personal finances. How much of today's morning business broadcast or financial page of the newspaper did you understand? Chances are you found the glut of facts too much to absorb in one sitting. If you did make the effort to comprehend the material about "bulls and bears," the Dow Jones Industrial Average, interest rates, money supply, and so on, you possibly came away wondering how the information will affect you. This is a typical reaction. Most people have difficulty applying the meaning of financial data to their own situations. For instance, they do not know:

- How actions of the Federal Reserve affect the level of interest rates.
- How interest rates affect investments.
- How to calculate effective interest rates charged on their credit cards.

- How to evaluate the risk of an investment.
- How bonds or stocks are valued, or how to buy them.
- How to read annual reports issued by companies.

And so people often make decisions about financial matters without really understanding what financial news means and how finance operates.

Let's begin the study of finance by discussing the origins of the finance discipline. The meaning of the word "finance" is derived from the Latin word *finis*. During Roman times, *finis* meant the completion of a contract between parties with either a transfer of money or barter (exchange) or a credit agreement. The word "finance" has much the same meaning today. However, we must conceptualize the discipline of finance in broader terms. Finance encompasses the analysis of, issuance of, distribution of, and purchase of financial contracts written against real assets. Implicit in these activities is the determination of value; finance involves a process of deciding what something is worth.

The issuers, or suppliers, of financial contracts include individuals, business corporations, and government agencies located worldwide. The issuers must use the funds efficiently to provide satisfactory returns to investors who buy the contracts in financial markets. The efficient use of funds requires that the issuers administrate and manage investors' funds efficiently; they must practice sound financial decision making.

This brief introduction to finance illustrates that it is a multifaceted discipline, international in scope, and bound together by contracts. It includes the areas of managerial finance, investments, and financial markets. These areas are closely related for a very simple reason: the most widely accepted financial objective of a company is maximization of its market value. Management's actions can influence the market value, but they are unable to determine the value completely. The simultaneous interplay of supply and demand for financial securities (ownership claims) in financial markets determines market value. Through the mechanism of these financial markets, other companies also participate as suppliers of securities, and a great number of investors participate as demanders for these securities. The study of finance provides an explanation of how securities are valued and how investors behave by taking into account the relationships among these investors' decisions. The interactions of the demands of all investors determine market values.

Finance in its broadest terms is an integrated body of knowledge built around the guiding principles of wealth maximization, time value of money, expected return versus risk, leverage, and diversification. You will see how they help to integrate the areas of managerial finance, investments, and financial markets.

When you have completed this chapter, you should understand:

- Some of the differences and similarities among managerial finance, investments, and financial markets.
- The dominant guiding principles of finance.
- Common elements of finance that cross all the subareas of the discipline.
- How finance is integrated with and depends on other areas of business.
- Ethical issues that are important to finance.

TRADITIONAL AREAS OF FINANCE

Finance and many other business disciplines were originally part of the field of economics. By the turn of the century, as a result of the growth of industry engendered by the Industrial Revolution, a greater need for studying detailed business problems and processes arose. About this time business schools were established and managerial finance, or corporate finance, as it was called more generally, was one of the first specialties to be taught separately from economics. The principal emphasis in economics first was on institutions and institutional arrangements. The economics of the individual firm had not yet been developed as a focal point of economic inquiry. Within this general context, the purpose of the newly defined area of managerial finance was to describe and document the rapidly evolving, complex nature of financial market institutions, instruments, and practices. Rather than correspond to managerial finance as we know it today, these studies precede the modern-day finance subareas of financial markets and investments. Thus, managerial finance began as a descriptive, legalistic, and institutional subject with little focus on financial decision making within the firm.

The study of finance changed little until the 1940s, when critics questioned the lack of interest in day-to-day problems of financial management such as those pertaining to cash, accounts receivable, and inventory. However, it was not until the late 1950s and early 1960s that finance began to evolve into the dynamic field of study called financial economics. Academicians in economics and mathematics, namely, Harry Markowitz, Merton Miller, Franco Modigliani, and William Sharpe, provided the impetus for this change. Each of these founders of modern finance has received the Nobel Prize in economics in recognition for their contributions. Their insights and research contributions are the basis for today's valuation concepts.

The areas of managerial finance, investments, and financial markets are used frequently to classify financial topics. Managerial finance deals with financial decisions in the business organization. It is usually the area that receives the most emphasis in the finance class required of all business students. The area of investments primarily relates to the valuation of financial securities and their grouping to satisfy an investor's objectives. Financial markets represent the channels for transferring funds from savings into investment. Taken together, a study of managerial finance, investments, and financial markets provides a strong understanding of the financial system.

Managerial Finance

Managerial finance has evolved from its early beginning as a descriptive, institutional subject to the dynamic study of decision making on financial issues pertaining to the firm. Specifically, managerial finance addresses the following issues:

- What investments should the firm make?
- What type of financing should be used to pay for the investments?
- How should daily financial activities be managed to satisfy cash requirements?

We can classify the first two issues, which pertain to investment and financing alternatives, as strategic decisions. These decisions select from among investment and financing alternatives that offer long-term opportunities for management to increase the value of the firm. An example is General Motors Corporation's decision in early 1990's to close several assembly plants in an effort to return to profitability. Another example is Ford Motor Company's decision of whether to build a new assembly plant or buy an existing plant that GM abandons. The third issue, concerning daily financial activities, such as management of cash, accounts receivable, inventories, and short-term liabilities, applies to tactical decisions. These decisions concern managing resources, including cash, to ensure the firm meets customer demand.

The financial manager must worry about the interrelationships between strategic and tactical decisions and the effect these decisions may have on the value of the firm. For example, if Ford buys a plant from GM, can Ford generate enough cash from operations to pay back any debt borrowed to finance the acquisition?

There is little difference in most types of decisions domestic and international financial managers face. However, two significant financial problems confront firms competing in foreign markets. Managers cannot ignore two constant risks: currency risks and political risks. An unexpected currency devaluation or expropriation of the company's foreign facilities by an unfriendly government can wipe out profit margins on sales to foreign clients.

A major difference exists between financial management practices in developed countries and in developing countries. In the major developed countries, financial markets are very sophisticated and market participants usually engage in independent corporate financial decision making. However, even within the leading world economies, significant differences exist. For example, investment and financing decisions by German and Japanese firms often involve more communications between bankers and firms' managers than do similar decisions in Britain, Canada, or the United States. In less developed economies, the governments and financial institutions play a significant role in corporate financial decision making.

Investments

The financial area of investments includes investors' activities and decision rules about the selection and management of assets, such as stocks, bonds, gold, and real estate. When a group of assets is held by an investor, the collection is called a portfolio. The portfolio can be arranged to lessen total risk for a targeted expected return.

The expected return versus risk concept is central. An underlying assumption of this concept is the existence of efficient financial markets; that is, markets in which competition is as fierce and extreme as possible. Investors act quickly and efficiently to incorporate any new information in the determination of each asset's price. Since all investors respond in a similar manner, no investor can consistently earn excess profits—returns more than necessary to compensate for risk. In finance, we call such markets informational efficient markets. Asset prices set in informational efficient financial markets reflect the market's assessment of managerial performance. The broadest measure of a firm's achievements over time is the extent to which the firm develops its future earnings potential while controlling the risk.

Sometimes the amount and quality of information in financial markets can be a problem. Often there is a scarcity of information about young firms or foreign firms. Also, accounting philosophies vary among countries, and this can result in difficulty interpreting information about companies. Regulatory monitoring of financial markets also varies drastically from one country to another. The protection afforded investors in the United States does not exist in every financial market in the world.

Investment decisions involve asset selection and portfolio formation with respect to longer-term risk and return relationships. Another important aspect of investments is the art of trading assets. Trading is a complex activity separate from investing. Trading involves the implementation of investment decisions and buying and selling assets in an attempt to profit from weekly, daily, hourly, or shorter, price swings. The New York Stock Exchange (NYSE) is the most renowned securities marketplace in the world for trading shares of over 1800 companies from around the world.

Financial Markets

Financial markets consist of money markets and capital markets. If financial contracts are for one year or less, they have a short-term duration and trade in money markets. The most important money markets are in New York and London. Financial contracts with durations in excess of one year are long term and trade in capital markets, with the largest markets located in Tokyo and New York. Financial markets are the channels whereby savings are translated into investment—into accumulation of assets. There are three broad ways in which investment takes place:

- Households (individuals and families) buy assets.
- Firms buy assets and finance them by selling stocks and bonds to households.
- Firms buy assets and finance them by loans from financial intermediaries, who in turn take in households' savings.

Financial intermediaries are firms whose principal business is taking deposits, making loans, and buying securities. The best known type of financial intermediary is a commercial bank, such as Citibank. The financial markets for stocks and bonds coordinate the actions of households, firms, and financial intermediaries. Stock markets, like the New York Stock Exchange, are markets in which shares (commonly called stocks) representing ownership of firms, such as Home Shopping Network, Inc., trade. The bond market is the market in which debts issued by firms like CSX Corporation and local, state, or national governments trade.

GUIDING PRINCIPLES OF FINANCE

Managerial finance, investments, and financial markets are integrated under the broad heading of finance through shared principles. These important principles are maximization of wealth, time value of money, expected return versus risk trade-off, leverage, and diversification. We will review each principle and how it affects financial decision making.

Maximization of Wealth

The most important guiding principle is maximization of wealth, which is the creation of as much wealth as possible with the resources available. A wealth-maximizing goal looks beyond the short run and explicitly seeks to incorporate the entire future stream of cash flows that will be generated by the decision. Needless to say, the principle assumes that wealth is created lawfully and ethically.

Many people would temper a goal of wealth maximization to include a goal of social responsibility, which is generally defined as a consciousness for the good of all people in society and a respect for the environment on the part of the corporation. Social responsibility can extend as far as the role of corporations in funding social programs. While many individuals may see this as a noble goal to embrace, we must remember that we are dealing with the role of the business entity. Nobel laureate economist Milton Friedman argues that when investors bring a corporation into existence through buying stock, they do so on the condition that corporate managers will follow their wishes—usually, to make a profit[1]. A moral obligation is thus generated for managers, namely, to serve as agents for profit-seeking investors. It follows that using the investors' money otherwise is equivalent to stealing. Theodore Levitt states that if business were to become a protector of the welfare society, the result could be disastrous[2]. Levitt argues that because corporate officials are not democratically elected business should stick to business. It has no holy mission and it ought not become a new "church." Yet there are some business managers, such as those of Ben and Jerry's Ice Cream, who disagree with this position and take active roles to promote through financial incentives the opening of franchises in minority urban neighborhoods. We will come to see that there is room for much firm-specific decision making—on all levels—within the financial discipline.

The wealth-maximization goal has broad applicability to the areas of managerial finance, investments, and financial markets. For the financial manager, maximization of wealth means operating the firm with the goal of increasing shareholders' wealth. Financial management decisions, such as buying new equipment or extending credit to customers, are all subject to decision rules whose aim it is to maximize shareholders' wealth, that is, to maximize the long-run stock price.

From an investment perspective, it is clear that investors choose financial contracts expecting to increase wealth. The decision to invest in different types of assets or combinations of assets into a portfolio is a simple example. Deciding whether to invest in low-risk, low-expected-return assets versus high-risk, high-expected-return assets is another case.

Financial markets provide individuals and firms with the means to make wealth increasing decisions by efficiently transacting financial contracts. Efficient financial markets provide buyers and sellers with more opportunities to select securities that satisfy their needs.

Time Value of Money

The principle of time value of money is central to financial decision making. Time value of money means that funds have an opportunity cost because alternative uses for the funds exist. Should opportunity number one or opportunity number two be taken?

Managers and investors evaluate potential wealth-increasing decisions using an interest rate called the opportunity cost of money to value all future cash flows. A technique called future value analysis finds the value of funds to be received in the future. If the opportunity rate is 8%, $1 received two periods from now is worth $1 \times (1 + 0.08) \times (1 + 0.08) = \$1.166$. Because interest paid on money can itself earn interest, there is a multiplicative growth dimension to the future amount. The growth dimension is called compounding. As the interest rate increases, a dollar invested today appreciates faster to some future value. For example, if the Native Americans who sold Manhattan for $24 had invested this money at 6% compounded annually, it would have been worth about $74 billion at the end of 1994.

We can also use the opportunity rate to convert future cash flows into a present value to determine if the wealth-maximization goal is satisfied. More present value dollars are sought rather than fewer. The present value process is called discounted cash flow analysis. For example, $1 received one year from now is worth $0.926 today if the opportunity cost of money is 8%: $1 t (1 + 0.08) = $0.926. If the opportunity cost of money is 10%, the value of that same $1 is about $0.909 today. Check this number. The present worth declines as the interest rate, or opportunity cost of money, increases.

Expected Return versus Risk Trade-off

The principle that ties finance together is the expected return versus risk concept. The expected return-risk principle states that if investments A and B have the same risk, the investment with the greater expected return, B, should be chosen. Or consider a firm that issues additional debt, which causes risk to increase. Investors' expected return must increase to compensate for the higher risk. Exhibit 10-1 shows these relationships.

The cornerstone of managerial finance and investments is the application of discounted cash flow analysis and expected return and risk concepts to the valuation (that is, finding the present value) of financial claims. The opportunity rate used to discount cash flows is the same rate we could have expected to earn from alternative investments of equal risk.

A necessary assumption of the expected return-risk principle is that market equilibrium prices exist in financial markets. A market equilibrium price is the price at which the quantity demanded of financial instruments equals the quantity supplied. At the equilibrium price, opposing forces exactly balance each other. Trust officers at Wells Fargo & Company, investment officers employed by Metropolitan Life Insurance Company, money managers hired by CalPERS to invest pension funds, specialized dealers on the floor of the stock exchange, individual investors, and thousands of other organizations constantly trade financial securities, thereby maintaining equality between demand and supply.

Exhibit 10-1 Expected Return–Risk Trade-Off

Investment *B* is better than investment *A* because for equal risk, *B* offers higher return. When risk increases, the risk-return relationship moves to point *C*. The basic formulation states that a positive relationship exists between risk and expected return. Any additional expected return accompanies additional risk.

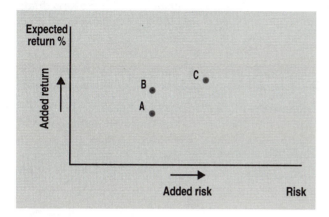

Leverage

Some costs are constant, or fixed, over a range of business activity. Other costs are variable and change in direct response to changes in business activity. The linkage, or leverage, between the fixed and variable costs offers significant financial gains or losses. There are two types of leverage: operating and financial. The particular choice of fixed and variable operating costs existing within a firm is a result of the production technology chosen by management to compete in the industry. Operating costs are the necessary outlays incurred in producing the product or service. A business like Intel Corporation uses highly advanced technology to produce state-of-the-art computer chips. The result is relatively high fixed operating costs, which result in relatively high operating leverage. Operating leverage is favorable if sales (the activity) expand faster than additional fixed costs. Operating leverage is unfavorable if sales decline faster than any reduction in fixed costs. Financial leverage is the use of debt financing to support income-earning investments. The commitment of the firm or investor to pay interest on borrowed funds (that is, the leverage portion) is not (usually) related to the amount of product or services produced by the assets financed. As business activity improves without any changes in fixed costs, financial leverage causes profits to increase. A change in the opposite direction causes losses. Profits improve if debt-financed investments earn more than the cost of debt. Conversely, losses increase if the cost of debt exceeds the return earned by the assets. The financial leverage relationship holds true for all participants in the financial system, whether they be managers, individuals, or financial institutions.

Diversification

The principle of diversification is based on the need for the firm or investor to reduce risk. Diversification means to introduce variety into the portfolio. The maxim stating "Don't put all your eggs in one basket" describes the concept of diversification.

Too much or too little of one type of investment can be detrimental at any time. For example, Artisoft, Inc. produces and sells local area networks (LANS). Artisoft's LANS may be very profitable when that product is in demand. However, if consumers stop buying LANS, Artisoft may become unprofitable and eventually cease to exist. A similar result can happen if competitors take market share away from an undiversified firm selling a product or service that is similar to many other firms. Casualties in the airline industry in recent years provide an example. America West, Eastern, TWA, and Continental airlines filed bankruptcy. Likewise, if an investor's retirement income is dependent on a single financial security, say IBM stock, that person is more likely to find that not enough money exists in the retirement account upon reaching retirement age than if he or she invested in several securities. A prudent person invests in several different assets to diversify risk. The finance terminology is that the person seeks an efficient portfolio.

ELEMENTS COMMON TO THE THREE AREAS OF FINANCE

Common elements are woven throughout the areas of managerial finance, investments, and financial markets helping to integrate the discipline. These elements include: investment decision rules, financial analysis, organizational form, taxes, and politics. We examine each of these elements in the following sections.

Investment Decision Rules

Investment decision rules specify the desired standards of financial decision making. The most widely accepted investment decision standard is the maximization of wealth. From an investment perspective, the investor seeks to invest in and trade securities that result in the greatest appreciation in long-term value of the portfolio.

From a managerial finance perspective, shareholders are the owners of the firm and the investment rule states that a financial decision that adds to the net wealth position of shareholders is a good decision. An unwise decision is one that knowingly causes shareholders' wealth to deteriorate. If several actions increase shareholders' wealth, the more desirable action is the one that results in greater wealth with equal or less risk. Sales maximization, profit maximization, and firm size maximization, among others, are sometimes used as investment decision standards. These standards are inferior to maximization of shareholders' wealth; generally, they tend to make managers more happy than they do shareholders.

Financial Analysis

Managerial finance relies on economic and quantitative analysis to fulfill the goal of increasing wealth of shareholders. The financial manager must have the analytical skills and insights that reveal ways to reduce costs and increase revenues and, thus, lead to improved profitability for the company. In the areas of investments and financial markets, financial analysis helps investors by providing guidelines for evaluating the risk versus expected return trade-off.

Financial analysis takes its meaning from the study of the financial interrelationships that exist in a particular problem. You cannot assume that these relationships are constant from problem to problem. For example, common stock issued by Bank America Corporation, a financial institution, is more sensitive to interest rate changes than is common stock issued by Cincinnati Milacron Inc., a manufacturer. The reason is that financial institutions have significant investments in debt securities (financial assets) whose values move inversely to interest rates. Manufacturing firms invest heavily in physical, or real, assets such as plant and equipment. Values of investments in physical assets are less affected by changes in interest rates. Ignoring expected changes in interest rates when analyzing stock prices of financial institutions will result in questionable conclusions.

Techniques we use to explore financial interrelationships are the basic mathematical tools of financial analysis. The dominant analytical tools are financial ratio analysis, statistical models to analyze expected return versus risk, and operations research models to determine the acceptability of investments. Imagination and ability are proving the only limits to recently developed techniques for financial analysis.

Organizational Form

Economic organizations are entities through which people interact to reach individual and collective economic goals. The economic system consists of networks of people and organizations linked together. The highest-level organization is the economy as a whole. At the next level are entities more traditionally regarded as organizations: business organizations, labor unions, and government agencies. A key characteristic of an organization at this level is its legal identity. For example, consider the definition of a business organization in a broad context. It means the set of contracts between an entity, called the firm (for example, Club Med, Inc.), and its stakeholders. Stakeholders are those who have an interest in the welfare of the firm, including the firm's creditors, customers, employees, governments, managers, shareholders, and suppliers. Laws and legal remedies help to enforce the contracts between stakeholders.

Three primary forms of business organizations exist: the sole proprietorship, the partnership, and the corporation. Most firms operating in the world are proprietorships. However, most of the dollar value of sales is attributed to corporations like Exxon and The Home Depot. State governments charter corporations to do business. In chartering a corporation, the state grants to it certain rights and privileges and imposes certain duties and obligations. By demanding that corporations act responsibly and in a legal manner, states attempt, through the chartering process, to bring any corporate abuse under control. A problem arises if one state decides to impose more stringent duties upon corporations chartered in its state. The corporations could move to a state where the laws are less demanding. Today, most of the major corporations are established in Delaware, a state with the least restrictive chartering laws.

The issue of ownership versus control is an important topic in finance. When ownership and control in the corporation are separate, a principal-agent problem exists. The important issue centers on whether corporate managers (agents) have the proper incentives for them to act in the interests of stakeholders (principals). The principal-agent problem assumes that managers, if left alone, will operate in their own interest, not in the interest of the stakeholders. Critics make the following claims:

- Managers invest a firm's earnings in low-value projects to expand their empires when the funds would be better distributed to the shareholders to invest for themselves.
- Managers supposedly hang on to badly performing operations when new managers could run them more profitably.
- Managers pay themselves exorbitantly and lavish expensive perquisites upon themselves.
- Managers resist attempts to force more profitable operations, especially by resisting takeovers that threaten their jobs.

All these alleged misdeeds serve the interests of the managers themselves, not the interests of the firm's owners. Agents' actions may be detrimental to the wealth of principals.

Management is protecting its own future even if its actions result in bankruptcy of the firm. As a shareholder your stock would lose much of its value, as a supplier or creditor you would likely not receive full value on your claims, and as an employee you could lose your job. The need for a sense of trust is an integral part of the business relationship. Ethical decisions (or unethical ones) affect the world of finance as much as they do any aspect of business. Hence, an awareness of the principal-agent problem should improve our study of finance.

Taxes

Tax rules legislated by governments affect the rates of return investments earn both before and after any taxes. Before-tax rates of return differ because domestic and foreign federal, state, and local taxing authorities are not consistent in their application of taxes. They tax returns to different types of investments differently. Different jurisdictions tax similar investments differently. We will also find that returns to similar investments within the same jurisdiction are taxed differently depending upon the organizational form; corporations are taxed differently than partnerships. Finally, returns to similar investments located in the same jurisdiction and owned by the same type of organization receive differential tax treatment if the operating histories of the organizations differ.

As an example of the problem managers face, consider the Italian federal corporate tax system. Italian tax authorities assume that no corporation operating in Italy would submit a tax return showing its true profits. The presumption is that firms understate actual profits 30 to 70%. They are essentially correct. Thus, about six months after the deadline for filing tax returns, the tax authorities issue an "invitation to discuss" the tax return to each corporation. At the meeting, the Italian revenue authorities state the amount of corporate income tax which it believes is due. The authorities and the corporation then proceed through several rounds of bargaining until they reach a settlement. The area of taxes is a highly specialized topic and subjected to frequent changes by governmental attempts to raise revenues to fund government programs or stimulate the economy.

Politics

Most discussions about finance leave politics to the politicians. However, it can be said that politics is an inseparable facet of many financial decisions. Historically, times of business depression and social unrest have periodically given rise to attacks upon "big corporations" by those who hope to gain public support and political office. Yet surprisingly little has been done to inhibit the use of the corporate form of business. Many corporations maintain offices in a country's capital city not only to influence legislation, but also to help management predict changes in government policy.

Financial markets, via the buying and selling actions of investors, are constantly responding to either real or anticipated changes in legislation. The attitudes of government can seriously affect certain business segments. For instance:

- Expectations of decreased demand for defense contributed to General Dynamics Corporation, Northrop Corporation, and other American firms cutting back on making investment decisions in their defense businesses.
- The Tax Reform Act of 1986 reversed some incentives given to real estate investors a few years earlier. The new act greatly reduced the attractiveness of investing in real estate.

Politics and economic policy are more complex when we consider international financial markets. Actions of many governments become part of the decision-making process. Integrating political considerations into managerial finance is particularly appropriate in multinational firms, such as PepsiCo, Inc., Motorola, Inc., and Caterpillar, Inc., which build facilities in both domestic and foreign markets. The development of multinational firms is partially a response to world conditions that do not allow free movement of labor, materials, goods, and services between countries. The

Exhibit 10-2   Relationship of Finance with Other Disciplines

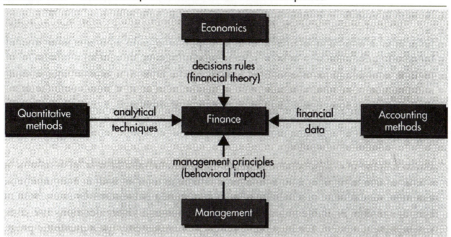

reason for many of the barriers is understandable from a political perspective. For instance, international trade agreements between countries exist because of import restrictions and other politically motivated arguments.

RELATIONSHIP OF FINANCE TO OTHER DISCIPLINES

Finance incorporates information from the disciplines of economics, management, accounting, and quantitative methods. Figure 10-2 depicts the relationships. Economics provides the underlying theory for financial decision making, whereas accounting provides a form for much of the data used to analyze financial decisions through various quantitative techniques. The field of management provides an understanding of organizational psychology that enhances decision making.

Economics

Finance is said to represent applied micro-economics. For example, the rule a financial manager uses to decide to accept or reject a proposed project or investment is essentially the same as the economist's marginal revenue versus marginal cost rule. The financial decision rule says: Accept all projects whose expected rates of return are greater than the opportunity cost of capital; or simply, accept projects whose marginal revenues exceed marginal costs.

Another interplay between economics and finance has to do with the economic concept of an efficient market. The basis for modern financial theory is a belief in efficient financial markets, which is adapted from the economist's concept of perfect competition. As stated earlier, an efficient financial market is one in which investors cannot consistently earn excess returns because essentially everyone has access to the same information, which is reflected in security prices.

Management

In all areas of finance, decisions are unmistakably affected by behavioral issues, both on the parts of individuals and as a consequence of organizational form. A key element of managerial finance is decision making, and decisions are made by people who are managers. Financial managers oversee the efficient use of resources within the firm. A manager's understanding of organizational psychology can be an important factor in motivating employees to produce quality products and improving the firm's performance.

From an investor's perspective, knowledge of the psychology of behavior applied to an aggregation of investors can influence decisions about buying and selling securities. This knowledge may entail anything from a "sense" or "feel" some investors might have to large-scale predictions about behavior. For example, many professional investors take the position that when most investors see "good times" ahead, it is time to sell securities. The idea is that the euphoria about the financial market is likely wrong and securities soon may decline significantly in value.

Accounting

Good accounting data are necessary for both the financial manager and the investor to make informed financial decisions. Financial statements accompanied by complete notes explaining the accounting rules followed allow a better understanding of how management derived items like sales, profits, and assets. However, comparison of accounting information from one firm to another can often be difficult because generally accepted accounting principles (GAAP) allow alternative methods for management to choose from to record transactions.

Institutions such as the American Institute of Certified Public Accountants (AICPA) and the United States Securities and Exchange Commission (SEC) provide guidance or legal monitoring of financial markets. These actions improve the quality of financial information available to investors in the United States. However, accounting philosophies and practices vary internationally. When the financial analyst works with foreign data, these variations sometimes lead to poor-quality information.

Quantitative Methods

Finance draws heavily on quantitative methods for analysis of financial decisions. Some decisions use fairly straightforward quantitative approaches such as ratio analysis. For example, we calculate profitability of sales by dividing net income by sales. Both numbers are readily available in a firm's income statement. Other decisions use complex mathematical models. For instance, a portfolio manager may use a quadratic programming model to decide on the allocation of funds among several securities to be included in a portfolio. In another case, a financial analyst for a manufacturing firm may use a linear programming model to recommend which of several projects to select, given future cash flows and a limited amount of money to invest.

ETHICS AND FINANCE

A theoretical discussion of finance implicitly assumes that participants conduct activities and relationships in an ethical manner. Unfortunately, this is not always the case. In 1980, Fortune magazine surveyed 1,043 large companies.[3] A total of 117 of the corporations satisfied Fortune's definition of law violation-conviction on criminal charges or consent decrees for bribery, criminal fraud, illegal political contributions, tax evasion, and criminal antitrust.

In some cases, it is easy to understand why corporate managers may act unethically. Consider a company on the brink of bankruptcy. Can the president be expected to reject an ethically objectionable but potentially lucrative last-minute gamble to save the company on the grounds that, because it is unethical, it will be unprofitable in the long run? The president may reason that unless the gamble is taken, there will be no long run. Or consider the many activities of securities brokers. They execute transactions in financial markets for clients, examine the securities of various companies as possible investments, and recommend securities to individual clients. Financial institutions with brokerage offices may also be in the business of investment banking. Investment bankers help companies sell their financial securities to investors. As brokers try to perform all these functions, especially the provision of financial advice, there is room for serious questions of professional ethics. One legitimate ethics question involves the objectivity of research about a public company. Consider what can happen when an investment banking division of a large financial institution such Merrill Lynch & Company takes a firm public in an initial public offering of stock (called an IPO) and then passes its research on to the brokers. The investment banking division receives a large fee for taking the firm public. The brokers, in turn, try to convince investors to buy the public company's securities. Brokerages are typically reluctant to issue sell recommendations about stocks. What does this imply about the investment banking brokerage relationship?

Another question about ethics in securities markets addresses the distinction between investments, speculation, and gambling. Is the only distinction the degree of risk involved in a particular transaction? Stock exchange officials react in horror to the commonly voiced opinion that Wall Street is "the biggest casino in the world." Yet, some say, the grounds for distinction are not clear. There are relatively safe bets available to gamblers and extremely risky propositions in securities markets, such as the new issues of a young firm.

Of the many ethical issues surrounding financial markets, the most intriguing and publicized in recent years is insider trading. The common definition of insider trading is trading in which someone buys or sells securities using information that is not publicly available to all investors. Thus, instead of the financial markets being efficient in the sense that all investors have equal access to information, a significant market imperfection exists. Asymmetric information exists; information is known only to certain people. The presence of asymmetric information inhibits the accurate valuation of assets.

Insider trading is extremely difficult to define legally, however. Securities and Exchange Commission (SEC) officials have frequently refused to define the term. Former SEC Commissioner Irving Pollock said at a Congressional hearing: "I see it in the same way the Supreme Court Justice Stewart saw pornography. You can't define insider trading, but you know it when you see it."

Another very contentious issue is the responsibility that management has to shareholders of the company; this is the principal-agent problem that we discussed earlier. Managers have been known to use many tactics to protect their positions, including issuance of voting stock to friendly shareholders, the nomination of a board of directors that is friendly to management, and the use of golden parachutes, or employment contracts that provide large severance pay if senior managers lose their jobs because of an unfriendly takeover by another firm. For instance, the chief executive officer of Pinnacle West Corporation has a severance agreement calling for severance benefits of about three times his average annual compensation over the preceding five years if there is change of control of the company.

SUMMARY

Traditional Finance Areas
- The traditional finance areas are managerial finance, investments, and financial markets.
- Managerial finance addresses what investments to make, how these investments should be financed, and how daily financial activities should be managed.

- Investments relate to activities and decision rules about selecting, managing, and trading assets, such as stocks and bonds. The underlying theory is that assets trade in perfect markets so that investors earn profits consistent with their risk exposure.
- Financial markets—money and capital markets—are the channels which direct funds to their most profitable use. These markets determine the appropriate risk-adjusted rate to evaluate investments.

Guiding Principles of Finance

- Five guiding principles integrate the three areas of finance:
  1. Maximization of wealth
  2. Time value of money
  3. Expected return versus risk trade-off
  4. Leverage
  5. Diversification

- Maximization of wealth principle provides the necessary focus for evaluating decisions.
- The principles of time value of money and expected return versus risk tradeoff are critical for determining value and maximizing wealth.
- Leverage allows output or wealth to expand for a fixed input.
- The principle of diversification is investing in more than one asset to reduce risk.

Elements Common to the Three Areas of Finance

- The subject of finance uses the common elements of financial analysis, investment decision rules, organizational form, taxes, and politics.
- Finance, as a quantitative subject, relies on insightful analysis to make wealth maximization decisions.
- Organizational form influences these decisions. Proprietors, as owners, are responsible for creating their own wealth. At the other extreme, nonowner managers' decisions affect the wealth of the stakeholders of the business, including the shareholders, who are the real owners of the corporation. In this latter case, principal-agent problems can arise.
- Investors and managers make decisions based on both taxes and legal concerns.

Relationship of Finance to Other Disciplines

- The discipline of finance relies on economics, accounting, quantitative methods, and management.
- Economics provides theoretical foundations for assessing wealth—creating decisions.
- Accounting provides much of the data necessary to evaluate decisions.
- Quantitative methods offer several techniques for analyzing the data. The area of management provides skills for understanding people, as they behave in organizations, who ultimately carry out the wealth-creating decisions.

Ethics and Finance

- The role of ethics in finance is significant in several areas. Investment in securities is a major area of concern, and managers also can make decisions that are ethically objectionable.
- Insider stock trading clearly is unethical. There are several gray areas a student of finance must evaluate as well, such as corporate decisions that injure local economies in the interest of short-term profit and unrealistically high executive compensation or severance packages.

1. What is the most widely accepted objective of a company's management?
2. What three areas does managerial finance address?
3. What two constant risks must a financial manager be concerned with?
4. How many ways can investment take place and what are they?
5. What does wealth maximization mean to the financial manager?
6. Define "Time Value of Money."
7. Explain the "expected return principle."
8. What are three primary forms of business organization?
9. Define the four principal agent problems.
10. Identify the disciplines used by finance managers.

Notes

[1] Milton Friedman, "The Social Responsibility of Business Is to Increase Its Profits," New York. *Time* Magazine, September 13, 1970, p. 33.

[2] Theodore Levitt, "The Dangers of Social Responsibility," *Harvard Business Review* (September–October 1958), p. 4.

[3] "How Lawless Are Big Companies?," *Fortune*, December 1, 1980, p. 57.

CHAPTER 11

FINANCIAL MARKETS AND RATES OF RETURN

At times internally generated funds will not be sufficient to finance all of the firm's proposed expenditures. In these situations, the corporation may find it necessary to attract large amounts of financial capital externally. By externally generated, we mean that the funds are obtained by means other than through retention or depreciation. Funds from these latter two sources are commonly called internally generated funds. This chapter focuses on the market environment in which long-term capital is raised. It also introduces and covers the logic behind the determination of interest rates and required rates of return in the capital markets. We will explore interest rate levels and risk differentials over recent time periods and will study several theories that attempt to explain the shape of the term structure of interest rates. Long-term funds are raised in the capital market. By the term capital market, we mean all institutions and procedures that facilitate transactions in long-term financial instruments (like common stocks and bonds).

CORPORATE SECURITIES IN THE CAPITAL MARKET

When corporations decide to raise cash in the capital market, what type of financing vehicle is most favored? Many individual investors think that common stock is the answer to this question. This is understandable, given the coverage of the level of common stock prices by the popular news media. All the major television networks, for instance, quote the closing price of the Dow Jones Industrial Average on their nightly news broadcasts. Common stock, though, is not the financing method relied on most heavily by corporations. The answer to this question is corporate bonds. The corporate debt markets clearly dominate the corporate equity markets when funds are being raised.

When financial executives responsible for raising corporate cash have a choice between marketing new bonds and marketing new preferred stock, the outcome is usually in favor of bonds. The after-tax cost of capital on the debt is less than that incurred on the preferred stock. Likewise, if the firm has unused debt capacity and the general level of equity prices is depressed, financial executives favor the issuance of debt securities over the issuance of new common stock.

In this chapter we cover material that introduces the manager to the processes involved in raising funds in the nation's capital markets and also cover the logic that lies behind the determination of interest rates and required rates of return in those capital markets.

We will see that the United States has a highly developed, complex, and competitive system of financial markets that allows for the quick transfer of savings from those economic units with a surplus of savings to those economic units with a savings deficit. Such a system of highly developed financial markets allows great ideas (like the personal computer) to be financed and increases the overall wealth of the economy. Consider your wealth, for example, compared to that of the average family in Russia. Russia lacks a complex system of financial markets to facilitate transactions in financial claims (securities). As a result, real capital formation there has suffered.

WHY FINANCIAL MARKETS EXIST

Financial markets are institutions and procedures that facilitate transactions in all types of financial claims. The purchase of your home, the common stock you may own, and your life insurance policy all took place in some type of financial market. Why do financial markets exist? What would the economy lose if our complex system of financial markets were not developed? We will address these questions here.

Some economic units, such as households, firms, or governments, spend more during a given period than they earn. Other economic units spend less on current consumption than they earn. For example, business firms in the aggregate usually spend more during a specific period than they earn. Households in the aggregate spend less on current consumption than they earn. As a result, some mechanism is needed to facilitate the transfer of savings from those economic units with a surplus to those with a deficit. That is precisely the function of financial markets. Financial markets exist in order to allocate the supply or savings in the economy to the demanders of those savings. The central characteristic of a financial market is that it acts as the vehicle through which the forces of demand and supply for a specific type of financial claim (such as a corporate bond) are brought together.

Now, why would the economy suffer without a developed financial market system? The answer is that the wealth of the economy would be less without the financial markets. The rate of capital formation would not be as high if financial markets did not exist. This means that the net additions during a specific period to the stocks of (l) dwellings, (2) productive plant and equipment, (3) inventory, and (4) consumer durables would occur at lower rates. Exhibit 11-1 helps clarify the rationale behind this assertion. The abbreviated balance sheets in the figure refer to firms or any other type of economic units that operate in the private as opposed to governmental sectors of the economy. This means that such units cannot issue money to finance their own activities.

At stage l in Exhibit 11-1 only real assets exist in the hypothetical economy. Real assets are tangible assets like houses, equipment, and inventories. They are distinguished from financial assets, which represent claims for future payment on other economic units. Common and preferred stocks, bonds, bills, and notes all are types of financial assets. If only real assets exist, then savings for a given economic unit, such as a firm, must be accumulated in the form of real assets. If the firm has a great idea for a new product, that new product can be developed, produced, and distributed only out of company savings (retained earnings). Furthermore, all investment in the new product must occur simultaneously as the savings are generated. If you have the idea, and we

Exhibit 11-1 Development of a Financial Market System

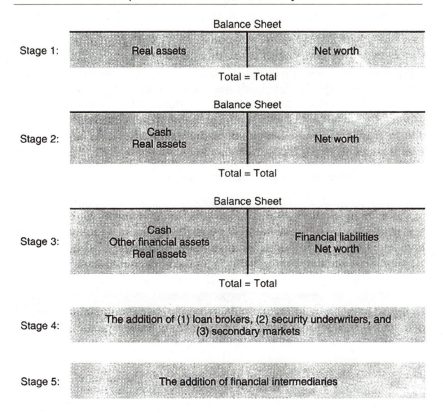

have the savings, there is no mechanism to transfer our savings to you. This is not a good situation.

At stage 2, paper money (cash) comes into existence in the economy. Here, at least, you can store your own savings in the form of money. Thus, you can finance your great idea by drawing down your cash balances. This is an improvement over stage 1, but there is still no effective mechanism to transfer our savings to you. You see, we will not just hand you our dollar bills. We will want a receipt. The concept of a receipt that represents the transfer of savings from one economic unit to another is a monumental advancement. The economic unit with excess savings can lend the savings to an economic unit that needs them. To the lending unit these receipts are identified as "other financial assets" in stage 3 of Exhibit 11-1. To the borrowing unit, the issuance of financial claims (receipts) shows up as "financial liabilities" on the stage 3 balance sheet. The economic unit with surplus savings will earn a rate of return on those funds. The borrowing unit will pay that rate of return, but it has been able to finance its great idea.

In stage 4 the financial market system moves further toward full development. Loan brokers come into existence. These brokers help locate pockets of excess savings and channel such savings to economic units needing the funds. Some economic units will actually purchase the financial claims of borrowing units and sell them at a higher price to other investors; this process is called underwriting. Underwriting will be discussed in more detail later in this chapter. In addition, secondary markets develop. Secondary markets simply represent trading in already existing financial claims. If you buy your brother's General Motors common stock, you have made a secondary market transaction. Secondary markets reduce the risk of investing in financial claims. Should you need cash, you can liquidate your claims in the secondary market. This induces savers to invest in securities.

The progression toward a developed and complex system of financial markets ends with stage 5. Here, financial intermediaries come into existence. You can think of financial intermediaries as the major financial institutions with which you are used to dealing. These include commercial banks, savings and loan associations, credit unions, life insurance companies, and mutual funds. Financial intermediaries share a common characteristic: they offer their own financial claims, called indirect securities, to economic units with excess savings. The proceeds from selling their indirect securities are then used to purchase the financial claims of other economic units. These latter claims can be called direct securities. Thus, a mutual fund might sell mutual fund shares (their indirect security) and purchase the common stocks (direct securities) of some major corporations. A life insurance company sells life insurance policies and purchases huge quantities of corporate bonds. Financial intermediaries thereby involve many small savers in the process of capital formation. This means there are more "good things" for everybody to buy.

A developed financial market system provides for a greater level of wealth in the economy. In the absence of financial markets, savings are not transferred to the economic units most in need of those funds. It is difficult, after all, for a household to build its own automobile. The financial market system makes it easier for the economy to build automobiles and all the other goods that economic units like to accumulate.

FLOW OF FUNDS IN THE ECONOMY

The Financing Process

We now understand the crucial role that financial markets play in a capitalist economy. At this point we will take a brief look at how funds flow across some selected sectors of the U.S. economy. In addition, we will focus a little more closely on the process of financial intermediation that was introduced in the preceding section. Some actual data are used to sharpen our knowledge of the financing process. We will see that financial institutions play a major role in bridging the gap between savers and borrowers in the economy. Nonfinancial corporations, we already know, are significant borrowers of financial capital.

Exhibit 11-2 shows how funds were supplied and raised by the major sectors of our economy in 1993. Households were the largest net suppliers of funds to the financial markets. This is the case, by the way, year in and year out. In 1993, households made available $155.0 billion in funds to other sectors. That was the excess of their funds supplied over their funds raised in the markets. In the jargon of economics, the household sector is a savings-surplus sector.

By contrast, the nonfinancial business sector is a savings-deficit sector. In 1993, nonfinancial corporations raised $11.0 billion more in the financial markets than they supplied to the markets. This too is a consistent long-term relationship. The nonfinancial business sector is typically a savings-deficit sector.

Next, it can also be seen that the U.S. government sector was a savings-deficit sector for 1993. In 1993 the federal government raised $285.0 billion in excess of the funds it supplied to the financial markets. This highlights a serious problem for the entire economy and for the financial manager. Persistent federal deficits have increased the role of the federal government in the market for borrowed funds. The last time the federal government posted a budget surplus was 1980; the last time prior to that was 1969. The federal government has thus become a "quasi-permanent" savings-deficit sector. Most financial economists agree that this tendency puts upward pressure on interest rates in the financial market and thereby raises the general (overall) cost of capital to corporations. This phenomenon has become known as crowding-out: the private borrower is pushed out of the financial markets in favor of the government borrower.

Exhibit 11-2   Sector View of Flow of Funds in U.S. Financial Markets for 1993
(in Billions of Dollars)

SECTOR	[1] FUNDS RAISED	[2] FUNDS SUPPLIED	[2] − [1] NET FUNDS SUPPLIED
Households[a]	$325.4	$480.4	$155.0
Nonfinancial corporate business	94.0	83.0	−11.0
U.S. government	286.0	1.0	−285.0
State and local governments	60.1	15.9	−44.2
Foreign	187.2	270.0	82.8

[a]Includes personal trusts and nonprofit organizations.
Source: Flow of Funds Accounts, Second Quarter 1994, Flow of Funds Section (Washington, DC: Board of Governors of the Federal Reserve System, September 20, 1994).

Exhibit 11-2 further highlights how important foreign financial investment is to the activity of the U.S. economy. As the federal government has become more of a "confirmed" savings-deficit sector, the need for funds has been increasingly supplied by foreign interests. Thus, in 1993, the foreign sector supplied a net $82.8 billion to the domestic capital markets. As recently as 1982, the foreign sector raised, rather than supplied, $30.8 billion in the U.S. financial markets. This illustrates the dynamic nature of financial management.

Exhibit 11-2 demonstrates that the financial market system must exist to facilitate the orderly and efficient flow of savings from the surplus sectors to the deficit sectors of the economy. The result during long periods is that the nonfinancial business sector is typically dependent on the household sector to finance its investment needs.

The governmental sectors—especially the federal government—are quite reliant on foreign financing.

As we noted in the preceding section, the financial market system includes a complex network of intermediaries that assist in the transfer of savings among economic units. Two intermediaries will be highlighted here: life insurance companies and pension funds. They are especially important participants in the capital market of the country.

Because of the nature of their business, life insurance firms can invest heavily in long-term financial instruments. This investment tendency arises for two key reasons: (1) life insurance policies usually include a savings element in them, and (2) their liabilities liquidate at a very predictable rate. Thus, life insurance companies invest in the "long end" of the securities markets. This means that they favor (1) mortgages and (2) corporate bonds as investment vehicles rather than shorter-term-to-maturity financial instruments like U.S. Treasury bills (T-bills). To a lesser extent, they acquire corporate stocks for their portfolios.

Over recent years, about 47 percent of the financial assets of life insurance firms are represented by corporate stocks and bonds. We see that life insurance companies are an important financial intermediary. By issuing life insurance policies (indirect securities), they can acquire direct securities (corporate stocks and bonds) for their investment portfolios. Their preference, by far, is for bonds over stocks.

Let us now direct our attention to another financial intermediary, private pension funds. In comparison with life insurance companies, three factors are emphasized. First, since 1960, private pension funds have grown at a much faster rate than have the insurance companies. Second, a greater proportion of the financial asset mix of the pension funds is devoted to corporate stocks and bonds. Third, the pension funds invest more heavily in corporate stocks than they do in corporate bonds. Over recent years, about 62 percent of the financial assets of private pension funds have been tied up in corporate stocks and bonds. These financial institutions also are significant sources of business financing in this country. The pension funds play the same intermediary role as does the life insurance sub-sector of the economy.

U.S. FINANCIAL MARKETS SYSTEM

Numerous approaches exist for classifying the securities markets. At times, the array can be confusing. An examination of four sets of dichotomous terms can help provide a basic understanding of the structure of the U.S. financial markets.

Public Offerings and Private Placements

When a corporation decides to raise external capital, those funds can be obtained by making a public offering or a private placement. In a public offering both individual and institutional investors have the opportunity to purchase the securities. The securities are usually made available to the public at large by a managing investment banking firm and its underwriting (risk-taking) syndicate. The firm does not meet the ultimate purchasers of the securities in the public offering. The public market is an impersonal market.

In a private placement, also called a direct placement, the securities are offered and sold to a limited number of investors. The firm will usually hammer out, on a face-to-face basis with the prospective buyers, the details of the offering. In this setting the investment-banking firm may act as a finder by bringing together potential lenders and borrowers. The private placement market is a more personal market than its public counterpart.

Primary Markets and Secondary Markets

Primary markets are those in which securities are offered for the first time to potential investors. A new issue of common stock by AT&T is a primary market transaction. This type of transaction increases the total stock of financial assets outstanding in the economy.

As mentioned in our discussion of the development of the financial market system, secondary markets represent transactions in currently outstanding securities. If the first buyer of the AT&T stock subsequently sells it, he or she does so in the secondary market. All transactions after the initial purchase take place in the secondary market. The sales do not affect the total stock of financial assets that exist in the economy. Both the money market and the capital market, described next, have primary and secondary sides.

Money Market and Capital Market

Money market. The key distinguishing feature between the money and capital markets is the maturity period of the securities traded in them. The money market refers to all institutions and procedures that provide for transactions in short-term debt instruments generally issued by borrowers with very high credit ratings. By financial convention, short term means maturity periods of one year or less. Notice that equity instruments, either common or preferred, are not traded in the money market. The major instruments issued and traded are U.S. Treasury bills, various federal agency securities, bankers' acceptances, negotiable certificates of deposit, and commercial paper. Keep in mind that the money market is an intangible market. You do not walk into a building on Wall Street that has the words "Money Market" etched in stone over its arches. Rather, the money market is primarily a telephone market.

Capital market. The capital market refers to all institutions and procedures that provide for transactions in long-term financial instruments. Long-term here means having maturity periods that extend beyond one year. In the broad sense this encompasses term loans and financial leases, corporate equities, and bonds. The funds that comprise the firm's capital structure are raised in the capital market. Important elements of the capital market are the organized security exchanges and the over-the-counter markets.

Organized Security Exchanges and Over-the-Counter Markets

Organized security exchanges are tangible entities; they physically occupy space (such as a building or part of a building), and financial instruments are traded on their premises. The over-the-counter markets include all security markets except the organized exchanges. The money market, then, is an over-the-counter market. Since both markets are important to financial officers concerned with raising long-term capital, some additional discussion is warranted.

Organized security exchanges. For practical purposes there are seven major security exchanges in the United States[1]. These are the (1) New York Stock Exchange, (2) American Stock Exchange, (3) Midwest Stock Exchange, (4) Pacific Stock Exchange, (5) Philadelphia Stock Exchange, (6) Boston Stock Exchange, and (7) Cincinnati Stock Exchange. The New York Stock Exchange (NYSE) and the American Stock Exchange (AMEX) are called national exchanges, whereas the others are loosely described as regional. All of these seven active exchanges are registered with the Securities and Exchange Commission (SEC). Firms whose securities are traded on the registered exchanges must comply with reporting requirements of both the specific exchange and the SEC.

An indication of the importance of the NYSE to our financial market system is reflected in something known as "consolidated tape volume." The Consolidated Tape prints all of the transactions on stocks that are listed on the NYSE and are traded on other organized markets. These markets include the exchanges mentioned earlier plus over-the-counter markets. In 1991, the NYSE accounted for 82.3% of consolidated volume[2].

The business of an exchange, including securities transactions, is conducted by its members. Members are said to occupy "seats." There are 1,366 seats on the NYSE, a number that has remained constant since 1953. Major brokerage firms own seats on the exchanges. An officer of the firm is designated to be the member of the exchange, and this membership permits the brokerage house to use the facilities of the exchange to effect trades. During 1991 the prices of seats that were exchanged for cash ranged from a low of $345,000 to a high of $440,000[3]. The record price, by the way, was $1.15 million paid on September 21, 1987—just prior to the October 19 market debacle. Both corporations and investors enjoy several benefits provided by the existence of organized security exchanges. These include the following:

1. **Providing a continuous market**. This may be the most important function of an organized security exchange. A continuous market provides a series of continuous security prices. Price changes from trade to trade tend to be smaller than they would be in the absence of organized markets. The reasons are that there is a relatively large sales volume in each security, trading orders are executed quickly, and the range between the price asked for a security and the offered price tends to be narrow. The result is that price volatility is reduced.

2. **Establishing and publicizing fair security prices**. An organized exchange permits security prices to be set by competitive forces. They are not set by negotiations off the floor of the exchange, where one party might have a bargaining advantage. The bidding process flows from the supply and demand underlying each security. This means the specific price of a security is determined in the manner of an auction. In addition, the security prices determined at each exchange are widely publicized.

Exhibit 11-3 NYSE Listing Requirements

Profitability
Earnings before taxes (EBT) for the most recent year must be at least $2.5 million. For the two years preceding that, EBT must be at least $2.0 million.

Size
Net tangible assets must be at least $18.0 million.

Market Value[a]
The market value of publicly held stock must be at least $18.0 million.

Public Ownership
There must be at least 1.1 million publicly held common shares. There must be at least 2000 holders of 100 shares or more.

---

[a] The market values tied to the level of common stock prices prevailing in the marketplace at the time of the listing application. From time to time the $18.0 million requirement noted above may be lessened. Under current regulations of the NYSE the requirement can never be less than $9.0 million.

3. **Helping business raise new capital**. Because a continuous secondary market exists where prices are competitively determined, it is easier for firms to float new security offerings successfully. This continuous pricing mechanism also facilitates the determination of the offering price of a new issue. This means that comparative values are easily observed.

To receive the benefits provided by an organized exchange, the firm must seek to have its securities listed on the exchange. An application for listing must be filed and a fee paid. The requirements for listing vary from exchange to exchange; those of the NYSE are the most stringent. The general criteria for listing fall into these categories: (1) profitability, (2) size, (3) market value, and (4) public ownership. To give you the flavor of an actual set of listing requirements, those set forth by the NYSE are displayed in Exhibit 11-3[4].

Over-the-counter markets. Many publicly held firms do not meet the listing requirements of major stock exchanges. Others may want to avoid the reporting requirements and fees required to maintain listing. As an alternative their securities may trade in the over-the-counter markets. On the basis of sheer numbers (not dollar volume), more stocks are traded over-the-counter than on organized exchanges. As far as secondary trading in corporate bonds is concerned, the over-the-counter markets are where the action is. In a typical year, more than 90% of corporate bond business takes place over-the-counter.

Most over-the-counter transactions are done through a loose network of security traders who are known as broker-dealers and brokers. Brokers do not purchase securities for their own account, whereas dealers do. Broker-dealers stand ready to buy and sell specific securities at selected prices. They are said to "make a market" in those securities. Their profit is the spread or difference between the price they will pay for a security (bid price) and the price at which they will sell the security (asked price).

The availability of prices is not as continuous in the over-the-counter market as it is on an organized exchange. Since February 8, 1971, however, when a computerized network called NASDAQ came into existence, the availability of prices in this market has improved substantially. NASDAQ stands for National Association of Security Dealers Automated Quotation System. It is a telecommunications system that provides a national information link among the brokers and dealers operating in the over-the-counter markets. Subscribing traders have a terminal that allows them to obtain representative bids and ask prices for thousands of securities traded over-the-counter. NASDAQ is a quotation system, not a transactions system. The final trade is still consummated by direct negotiation between traders. NASDAQ price quotes for many stocks

Exhibit 11-4 Financial Management in Practice

Reading a Bond Quote in the *Wall Street Journal*

Below is shown a section of the *Wall Street Journal* that gives the quotes on July 1, 1996, for some of the corporate bonds traded on the New York Stock Exchange on that date.

BONDS	CUR YLD	VOL	CLOSE	NET CHG
CaterpInc 6s07	6.8	49	$88\frac{3}{8}$	$+\frac{3}{8}$
ChsCp 8s04	7.9	1	101	$-\frac{5}{8}$
ChsCp $6\frac{1}{8}$08	6.8	8	$89\frac{1}{2}$	$-\frac{1}{2}$
CPWV $7\frac{1}{4}$13	7.8	30	$93\frac{1}{2}$	$-\frac{5}{8}$
Chiquta $10\frac{1}{2}$04	10.5	3	100	-1
ChckFul 7s12	cv	65	84	-1
Chryslr 10.4s99	10.0	61	$104\frac{1}{8}$	$-\frac{3}{8}$
Chryslr 10.95s17	10.0	8	109	...
ChryF $6\frac{1}{2}$98	6.4	6	101	...
Clardge $11\frac{3}{4}$02	13.6	341	$86\frac{3}{8}$	...
ClrkOil $9\frac{1}{2}$04	9.3	51	$102\frac{1}{8}$	$+\frac{1}{8}$
ClevEl $8\frac{3}{4}$05	9.0	25	$97\frac{1}{4}$	$+\frac{1}{4}$

The bonds shown in the list above as "CaterpInc 6s07" were issued by Caterpillar, Inc.; they pay a 6 percent coupon interest rate (indicated by the "6s"), or $60 interest paid annually (actually $30 paid semiannually) on a par value of $1,000; and they mature in 2007 (07 is the last two digits of the year the bonds mature). The closing price of the bonds on July 1, 1996, was $88\frac{3}{8}$, which is stated as a percent of the bond's $1,000 par value; thus, the bond's closing price on July 1 was $883.75 = .88375 × $1,000. The current yield on the bonds is 6.8 percent, calculated as the annual interest divided by the closing price, or $60 ÷ $883.75 = 6.8%. During the trading day, 49 bonds were traded on the exchange, as reflected by the "Vol" heading.[1] Finally, the net change "Net Chg" in the price of the bond from the previous day's close was an increase of $\frac{3}{8}$ of 1 percent.

[1]There may have been a lot more than 49 bonds changing hands on July 1, 1996. Many bond trades are negotiated directly between institutional investors or through bankers and are not listed in the *Wall Street Journal*.

are published daily in the Wall Street Journal. This same financial newspaper also publishes prices on hundreds of other stocks traded over-the-counter. Local papers supply prices on stocks of regional interest. Finally, the National Quotation Bureau publishes daily "pink sheets," which contain prices on about 8,000 securities; these sheets are available in the offices of most security dealers.

READING THE BOND AND STOCK TABLES

Many newspapers worldwide report the stock and bond transactions that occur on the New York Stock Exchange and the American Stock Exchange. Exhibit 11-4 is a sample of some of the information reported in the Wall Street Journal on the bonds traded on July 1, 1996.

Stock quotations represent a large portion of the financial pages. Exhibit 11-5 shows a sample of NYSE quotations for February 12, 1994. The table provides daily information on share prices, yields, and trading volume of both preferred and common stocks of many companies that trade on the exchange. Prices are in dollars and a dollar fraction. The fractions are in sixteenth or a "sixteenth point." Every sixteenth of a dollar has a value of 6.25 cents. The exhibit also provides some explanatory notes.

THE INVESTMENT BANKER

Most corporations do not raise long-term capital frequently. The activities of working-capital management go on daily, but attracting long-term capital is, by comparison, episodic. The sums involved can be huge, so these situations are considered of great

Exhibit 11-5   Financial Management in Practice

Reading a Stock Quote in the *Wall Street Journal*

Below is shown a section of the *Wall Street Journal* that gives the quotes on February 12, 1997 for some of the stocks traded on the New York Stock Exchange on that date.

52 Weeks					Yld		Vol				Net
Hi	Lo	Stock	Sym	Div	%	PE	100s	Hi	Lo	Close	Chg
$107\frac{7}{8}$	$73\frac{5}{8}$	GenElec	GE	2.08	2.0	24	28140	$106\frac{1}{8}$	$104\frac{1}{4}$	$105\frac{7}{8}$	$+1\frac{1}{4}$
$32\frac{7}{8}$	$21\frac{1}{8}$	GenGrowProp	GGP	1.72	5.5	14	1498	$31\frac{1}{2}$	$31\frac{1}{4}$	$31\frac{1}{4}$	$-\frac{1}{4}$
$4\frac{1}{4}$	$2\frac{3}{8}$	GenHost	GH	⋯	dd	439	$3\frac{1}{2}$	$3\frac{1}{8}$	$3\frac{1}{8}$	$-\frac{1}{4}$	
$14\frac{1}{8}$	8	GenHouse	GHW	.32	3.1	dd	65	$10\frac{5}{8}$	$10\frac{3}{8}$	$10\frac{3}{8}$	$-\frac{1}{8}$
$34\frac{3}{8}$	$18\frac{1}{8}$	GenInstrCp	GIC	⋯	dd	7091	$23\frac{5}{8}$	$23\frac{1}{4}$	$23\frac{1}{2}$	$+\frac{1}{4}$	
$68\frac{3}{4}$	52	GenMills	GIS	2.00	2.9	24	5591	$68\frac{1}{4}$	$67\frac{3}{8}$	$67\frac{7}{8}$	$-\frac{3}{4}$
$63\frac{3}{4}$	$45\frac{3}{4}$	GenMotor	GM	2.00f	3.5	10	29880	$57\frac{7}{8}$	$56\frac{3}{4}$	$57\frac{5}{8}$	$+\frac{7}{8}$

The stocks listed above include some familiar companies, such as General Electric (GE), General Mills, and General Motors, that are listed in the *Wall Street Journal* on a daily basis. To help us understand how to read the quotes, consider General Electric:

- The 52 week *high* column shows that General Electric stock reached a high of $107\frac{7}{8}$ ($107.88) during the past year
- The 52 week *low* column shows that General Electric sold for a low of $73\frac{5}{8}$ ($73.63) during the past year
- The *stock* (GenElec) & *sym* (GE) columns give an abbreviated version of the corporation's name and the ticker symbol, respectively

- *Div*, the dividend column, gives the amount of dividend that General Electric paid its common stockholder's in the last year; $2.08 per share
- *Yld* % (2.0) is the stock's dividend yield—the amount of the dividend divided by the day's closing price ($2.08 ÷ $105.88)
- *PE* (24) gives the current market price ($105\frac{7}{8}$) divided by the firm's earnings per share
- The amount of General Electric stock traded on February 12, 1997 is represented in the *Vol 100s* column, or 2,814,000 shares
- General Electric stock traded at a high price (Hi - $106\frac{1}{8}$) and a low price (Lo - $104\frac{1}{4}$) during the day
- The previous day's closing price is subtracted from the closing price (Close) of $105\frac{7}{8}$ for February 12, 1997 for a net change (Net Chg) of $+1\frac{1}{4}$

importance to financial managers. Because most managers are unfamiliar with the subtleties of raising long-term funds, they enlist the help of an expert. That expert is an investment banker.

Definition

The investment banker is a financial specialist involved as an intermediary in the merchandising of securities. He or she acts as a "middle person" by facilitating the flow of savings from those economic units that want to invest to those units that want to raise funds. We use the term investment banker to refer both to a given individual and to the organization for which such a person works, variously known as an investment-banking firm or an investment-banking house. Although these firms are called investment bankers, they perform no depository or lending functions. The activities of commercial banking and investment banking as we know them today were separated by the Banking Act of 1933 (also known as the Glass-Steagall Act of 1933). Just what does this middleman role involve? That is most easily understood in terms of the basic functions of investment banking.

Functions

The investment banker performs three basic functions: (1) underwriting, (2) distributing, and (3) advising.

Underwriting

The term underwriting is borrowed from the field of insurance. It means assuming a risk. The investment banker assumes the risk of selling a security issue at a satisfactory price. A satisfactory price is one that will generate a profit for the investment-banking house.

The procedure goes like this. The managing investment banker and its syndicate will buy the security issue from the corporation in need of funds. The syndicate is a group of other investment bankers who are invited to help buy and resell the issue. The managing house is the investment-banking firm that originated the business because its corporate client decided to raise external funds. On a specific day, the firm that is raising capital is presented with a check in exchange for the securities being issued. At this point the investment-banking syndicate owns the securities. The corporation has its cash and can proceed to use it. The firm is now immune from the possibility that the securities markets might turn sour. If the price of the newly issued security falls below that paid to the firm by the syndicate, the syndicate will suffer a loss. The syndicate, of course, hopes that the opposite situation will result. Its objective is to sell the new issue to the investing public at a price per security greater than its cost.

Distributing

Once the syndicate owns the new securities, it must get them into the hands of the ultimate investors. This is the distribution or selling function of investment banking. The investment banker may have branch offices across the United States, or it may have an informal arrangement with several security dealers who regularly buy a portion of each new offering for final sale. It is not unusual to have 300 to 400 dealers involved in the selling effort. The syndicate can properly be viewed as the security wholesaler, and the dealer organization can be viewed as the security retailer.

Advising

The investment banker is an expert in the issuance and marketing of securities. A sound investment-banking house will be aware of prevailing market conditions and can relate those conditions to the particular type of security that should be sold at a given time. Business conditions may be pointing to a future increase in interest rates. The investment banker might advise the firm to issue its bonds in a timely fashion to avoid the higher yields that are forthcoming. The banker can analyze the firm's capital structure and make recommendations as to what general source of capital should be issued. In many instances the firm will invite its investment banker to sit on the board of directors. This permits the banker to observe corporate activity and make recommendations on a regular basis.

Industry Leaders

All industries have their leaders, and investment banking is no exception. We have discussed investment bankers in general at some length in this chapter. Exhibit 11-6 gives us some idea who the major players are within the investment-banking industry. It lists the top 10 houses in 1995 based on the dollar volume of security issues that were managed. The number of issues the house participated in as lead manager is also identified, along with its share of the market.

PRIVATE PLACEMENT

Private placements are an alternative to the sale of securities to the public or to a restricted group of investors through a privileged subscription. Any type of security can be privately placed (directly placed). This market, however, is clearly dominated by debt issues. Thus, we restrict this discussion to debt securities. From year to year the volume of private placements will vary greatly.

Exhibit 11-6 Leading U.S. Investment Bankers, 1995
(Domestic Debt and Equity Issues)

	FIRM	UNDERWRITING VOLUME (BILLIONS OF DOLLARS)	PERCENT OF MARKET
1.	Merrill Lynch	$122.3	17.9%
2.	Lehman Brothers	70.3	9.9
3.	Goldman Sachs	68.5	9.7
3.	Morgan Stanley	68.5	9.7
5.	Salomon Brothers	68.1	9.6
6.	CS First Boston	64.6	9.1
7.	J.P. Morgan	40.2	5.7
8.	Bear, Sterns	25.4	3.6
9.	Donaldson, Lufkin & Jenrette	22.2	3.1
10.	Smith Barney	20.7	2.9

Source: Securities Data Co., as reported in the *Wall Street Journal,* January 2, 1996, p. R-38.

The major investors in private placements are large financial institutions. Based on the volume of securities purchased, the three most important investor groups are (1) life insurance companies, (2) state and local retirement funds, and (3) private pension funds.

In arranging a private placement the firm may (1) avoid the use of an investment banker and work directly with the investing institutions or (2) engage the services of an investment banker. If the firm does not use an investment banker, of course, it does not have to pay a fee. Conversely, investment bankers can provide valuable advice in the private placement process. They are usually in contact with several major institutional investors; thus, they will know if a firm is in a position to invest in its proposed offering, and they can help the firm evaluate the terms of the new issue.

Private placements have advantages and disadvantages compared with public offerings. The financial manager must carefully evaluate both sides of the question. The advantages associated with private placements are these:

1. Speed. The firm usually obtains funds more quickly through a private placement than a public offering. The major reason is that registration of the issue with the SEC is not required.

2. Reduced flotation costs. These savings result because the lengthy registration statement for the SEC does not have to be prepared, and the investment-banking underwriting and distribution costs do not have to be absorbed.

3. Financing flexibility. In a private placement the firm deals on a face-to-face basis with a small number of investors. This means that the terms of the issue can be tailored to meet the specific needs of the company. For example, all of the funds need not be taken by the firm at once. In exchange for a commitment fee the firm can "draw down" against the established amount of credit with the investors. This provides some insurance against capital market uncertainties, and the firm does not have to borrow the funds if the need does not arise. There is also the possibility of renegotiation. The terms of the debt issue can be altered. The term to maturity, the interest rate, or any restrictive covenants can be discussed among the affected parties.

The following disadvantages of private placements must be evaluated:

1. Interest costs. It is generally conceded that interest costs on private placements exceed those of public issues. Whether this disadvantage is enough to offset the reduced flotation costs associated with a private placement is a determination the financial manager

must make. There is some evidence that on smaller issues, say $500,000 as opposed to $30 million, the private placement alternative would be preferable.

2. Restrictive covenants. Dividend policy, working-capital levels, and the raising of additional debt capital may all be affected by provisions in the private-placement debt contract. That is not to say that such restrictions are always absent in public debt contracts. Rather, the financial officer must be alert to the tendency for these covenants to be especially burdensome in private contracts.

3. The possibility of future SEC registration. If the lender (investor) should decide to sell the issue to a public buyer before maturity, the issue must be registered with the SEC. Some lenders, then, require that the issuing firm agree to a future registration at their option.

Flotation Cost

The firm raising long-term capital incurs two types of flotation costs: (1) the underwriter's spread and (2) issuing costs. Of these two costs, the underwriter's spread is the larger. The underwriter's spread is simply the difference between the gross and net proceeds from a given security issue expressed as a percent of the gross proceeds. The issue costs include (1) printing and engraving, (2) legal fees, (3) accounting fees, (4) trustee fees, and (5) several other miscellaneous components. The two most significant issue costs are printing and engraving and legal fees.

Data published by the SEC have consistently revealed two relationships about flotation costs. First, the costs associated with issuing common stock are notably greater than the costs associated with preferred stock offerings. In turn, preferred stock costs exceed those of bonds. Second, flotation costs (expressed as a percent of gross proceeds) decrease as the size of the security issue increases.

In the first instance, the stated relationship reflects the fact that issue costs are sensitive to the risks involved in successfully distributing a security issue. Common stock is riskier to own than corporate bonds. Underwriting risk is, therefore, greater with common stock than with bonds. Thus, flotation costs just mirror these risk relationships. In the second case, a portion of the issue costs is fixed. Legal fees and accounting costs are good examples. So, as the size of the security issue rises, the fixed component is spread over a larger gross proceeds base. As a consequence, average flotation costs vary inversely with the size of the issue.

REGULATION

Following the severe economic downturn of 1929–1932, congressional action was taken to provide for federal regulation of the securities markets. State statutes (blue laws) also govern the securities markets where applicable, but the federal regulations are clearly more pressing and important.

Primary Market Regulations

The new issues market is governed by the Securities Act of 1933. The intent of the act is important. It aims to provide potential investors with accurate, truthful disclosure about the firm and the new securities being offered to the public. This does not prevent firms from issuing highly speculative securities. The SEC says nothing whatsoever about the possible investment worth of a given offering. It is up to the investor to separate the junk from the jewels. The SEC does have the legal power and responsibility to enforce the 1933 act.

Full public disclosure is achieved by the requirement that the issuing firm file a registration statement with the SEC containing requisite information. The statement details particulars about the firm and the new security being issued. During a minimum 20-day waiting period, the SEC examines the submitted document. In numerous instances the 20-day wait has been extended by several weeks. The SEC can ask for additional information that was omitted in order to clarify the original document. The SEC can also order that the offering be stopped. During the registration process a preliminary prospectus (the red herring) may be distributed to potential investors. When the registration is approved, the final prospectus must be made available to the prospective investors. The prospectus is actually a condensed version of the full registration statement. If, at a later date, the information in the registration statement and the prospectus is found to be lacking, purchasers of the new issue who incurred a loss can sue for damages. Officers of the issuing firm and others who took part in the registration and marketing of the issue may suffer both civil and criminal penalties.

Generally, the SEC defines public issues as those that are sold to more than 25 investors. Some public issues need not be registered. These include

1. Relatively small issues where the firm sells less than $1.5 million of new securities per year.
2. Issues that are sold entirely intrastate.
3. Issues that are basically short-term instruments. This translates into maturity periods of 270 days or less.
4. Issues that are already regulated or controlled by some other federal agency. Examples here are the Federal Power Commission (public utilities) and the Interstate Commerce Commission (railroads).

Secondary Market Regulations

Secondary market trading is regulated by the Securities Exchange Act of 1934. This act created the SEC to enforce federal securities laws. The Federal Trade Commission enforced the 1933 act for one year. The major aspects of the 1934 act can be best presented in outline form:

1. Major security exchanges must register with the SEC. This regulates the exchanges and places reporting requirements on the firms whose securities are listed on them.
2. Insider trading is regulated. Insiders can be officers, directors, employees, relatives, major investors, or anyone having information about the operation of the firm that is not public knowledge. If an investor purchases the security of the firm in which the investor is an insider, he or she must hold it for at least six months before disposing of it. Otherwise, profits made from trading the stock within a period of less than six months must be returned to the firm. Furthermore, insiders must file with the SEC a monthly statement of holdings and transactions in the stock of their corporation.
3. Manipulative trading of securities by investors to affect stock prices is prohibited.
4. The SEC is given control over proxy procedures.
5. The Board of Governors of the Federal Reserve System is given responsibility for setting margin requirements. This affects the flow of credit into the securities markets. Buying securities on margin simply means using credit to acquire a portion of the subject financial instruments.

RATE OF RETURN IN FINANCIAL MARKETS

To obtain financing for projects that will benefit the firm's stockholders, the firm must offer the supplier of capital a rate of return competitive with the next best investment alternative available to that (investor). This rate of return on the next best investment alternative is known as the supplier's of capital opportunity cost of funds. The opportunity cost concept is crucial in financial management because it impacts how much the firm must pay to the supplier capital financing decisions.

The investor rate of return, thus the firm's cost of funds, is affected by four factors:

1. Inflation Rate
2. Default Risk of the investment
3. The maturity date of the investment
4. The investment liquidity

To see how these four risk factors impact interest rates, we can develop a simple equation to determine the nominal (i.e., observed) rate of interest. The nominal interest rate, also called the "quoted" rate, is the interest rate paid on debt securities without an adjustment for any loss in purchasing power. It is the rate that you would read about in the Wall Street Journal for a specific fixed-income security. That equation follows:

$$k = k^* + IRP + DRP + t\,MP + LP \qquad\qquad (1)$$

where:

k   = the nominal or observed rate of interest on a specific fixed-income security.

k^* = the real risk-free rate of interest; it is the required rate of interest on a fixed-income security that has no risk and in an economic environment of zero inflation. This can be reasonably thought of as the rate of interest demanded by investors in U.S. Treasury securities during periods of no inflation.

IRP   = the inflation-risk premium.

DRP = the default-risk premium.

MP   = the maturity premium.

LP   = the liquidity premium.

Sometimes in analyzing interest rate relationships over time it is of use to focus on what is called the "nominal risk-free rate of interest." Again, by nominal we mean "observed." So let us designate the nominal risk-free interest rate as k(rf). Drawing, then, on our discussions and notation from above we can write this expression for k(rf):

$$k(rf) = k^* + IRP \qquad\qquad (2)$$

This equation just says that the nominal risk-free rate of interest is equal to the real risk-free interest rate plus the inflation-risk premium. It also provides a quick and approximate way of estimating the risk-free rate of interest, k^*, by solving directly for this rate. This basic relationship in equation (2) contains important information for the financial decision maker. It has also for years been the subject of fascinating and lengthy discussions among financial economists. We will look more at the substance of the real rate of interest in the next section. In this following section we will improve on equation (2) by making it more precise.

The Effects of Inflation on Rates of Return and the Fisher Effect

When a rate of interest is quoted, it is generally the nominal, or observed rate. The real rate of interest, on the other hand, represents the rate of increase in actual purchasing power, after adjusting for inflation. For example, if you have $100 today and lend it to someone for a year at a nominal rate of interest of 11.3 percent, you will get back $111.30 in one year. But if during the year prices of goods and services rise by 5 percent, it will take $105 at year end to purchase the same goods and services that $100 purchased the beginning of the year. What was your increase in purchasing power over the year? The quick and dirty answer is found by subtracting the inflation rate from the nominal rate, 11.3% – 5% = 6.3%, but this is not exactly correct. To be more precise, let the nominal rate of interest be represented by k(rf), the anticipated rate of inflation by IRP, and the real rate of interest by k*. Using these notations, we can express the relationship among the nominal interest rate, the rate of inflation, and the real rate of interest as follows.

$$1 + k(rf), = (1 + k^*)(1 + IRP) \qquad (3)$$

$$k \cdot (rf) = k^* + IRP + (k^* \bullet IRP)$$

Consequently, the nominal rate of interest k(rf) is equal to the sum of the real rate of interest (k*), the inflation rate (IRP), and the product of the real rate and the inflation rate. This relationship among nominal rates, real rates, and the rate of inflation has come to be called the Fisher effect.** It means that the observed nominal rate of interest includes both the real rate and an inflation premium as noted in the previous section.

Substituting into equation (2-3) using a nominal rate of 11.3% and an inflation rate of 5 percent, we can calculate the real rate of interest, k*, as follows:

$$.113 = k^* + .05 + (k^* \bullet .05)$$
$$.113 = k^* (1 + .05) + .05$$
$$.113 - .05 = k^* (1 + .05)$$
$$.08 = k^* (1.05)$$
$$k^* = .08/1.05$$
$$k^* = .06 \text{ or } 6\%$$

Thus, at the new higher prices, your purchasing power will have increased by only 6%, although you have $11.30 more than you had at the start of the year. To see why, let's assume that at the outset of the year one unit of the market basket of goods and services costs $1, so you could purchase 100 units with your $100. At the end of the year you have $11.30 more, but each unit now costs 1.05 (remember the 5% rate of inflation). How many units can you buy at the end of the year? The answer is $111.30/$1.05 = 106, which represents a 6% increase in real purchasing power.

TERM STRUCTURE OF INTEREST RATES

The relationship between a debt security's rate of return and the length of time until the debt matures is known as the term structure of interest rates or the yield to maturity. For the relationship to be meaningful to us, all the factors other than maturity, meaning factors such as the chance of the bond defaulting, must be held constant. Thus, the term structure reflects observed rates or yields on similar securities, except for the length of time until maturity, at a particular moment in time. Exhibit 11-7 shows an example of the term structure of interest rates. The curve is upward sloping, indicating that longer terms to maturity command higher returns, or yields. In this hypothetical term structure, the rate of interest on a 5-year note or bond is 11.5%, whereas the comparable rate on a 20-year bond is 13%.

Trying to Explain the Shape of the Term Structure

A number of theories may explain the shape of the term structure of interest rates at any point. Three possible explanations are prominent: (1) the unbiased expectations theory, (2) the liquidity preference theory, and (3) the market segmentation theory[5].
Let's look at each in turn.

The Unbiased Expectations Theory

The unbiased expectations theory says that the term structure is determined by an investor's expectations about future interest rates. To see how this works, consider the following investment problem faced by Mary Maxell. Mary has $10,000 that she wants to

Exhibit 11-7 Term Structure of Interest Rates

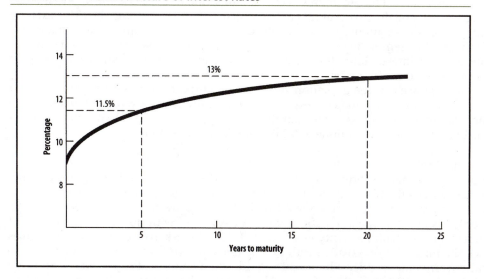

invest for two years, at which time she plans to use her savings to make a down payment on a new home. Wanting not to take any risk of losing her savings, she decides to invest in U.S. government securities. She has two choices. First, she can purchase a government security that matures in two years, which offers her an interest rate of 9%, per year. If she does this, she will have $11,881 in two years, calculated as follows:ment security that matures in two years, which offers her an interest rate of 9%, per year. If she does this, she will have $11,881 in two years, calculated as follows:

Principal amount	$10,000
Plus: Year 1 interest (.09 x $10,000)	900
Principal plus interest at the end of year 1	$10,900
Plus: Year 2 interest (.09 x $10,900)	981
Principal plus interest at the end of year 2	$11,881

Alternatively, Mary could buy a government security maturing in one year that pays an 8% rate of interest. She would then need to purchase another one-year security at the end of the first year. Which alternative Mary will prefer obviously depends in part on the rate of interest she expects to receive on the government security she will purchase a year from now.

We cannot tell Mary what the interest rate will be in a year; however, we can at least calculate the rate that will give her the same two-year total savings she would get from her first choice, or $11,881. The interest rate can be calculated as follows:

Savings needed in two years	$11,881
Savings at the end of the first year	
$10,000 (1 + .08)	$10,800
Interest needed in year two	$ 1,081

For Mary to receive $1,081 in the second year, she would have to earn about 10% on her second-year investment, computed as follows:

$$\frac{\text{interest received in year 2}}{\text{investment made at}} = \frac{\$\ 1,081}{\$10,800} = 10\%$$

So the term structure of interest rates for our example consists of the one-year interest rate of 8%, and the two-year rate of 9%, which is shown in Exhibit 11-7. This exercise also gives us information about the expected one-year rate for investments made one year hence. In a sense, the term structure contains implications about investor expectations of future interest rates; thus, this explains the unbiased expectations theory of the term structure of interest rates.

Although we can see a relationship between current interest rates with different maturities and the investor's expectations about future interest rates, is this the whole story? Are there influences other than the investor's expectations about future interest rates? Probably, so let's continue to think about Mary's dilemma.

Liquidity Preference Theory

In presenting Mary's choices, we have suggested that she would be indifferent to a choice between the two-year government security offering a 9% return and two consecutive one-year investments offering 8% and 10%, respectively. However, that would be so only if she is unconcerned about the risk associated with not knowing the rate of interest on the second security as of today. If Mary is risk averse (that is, she dislikes risk), she might not be satisfied with expectations of a 10% return on the second one-year government security. She might require some additional expected return to be truly indifferent. Mary might in fact decide that she will expose herself to the uncertainty of future interest rates only if she can reasonably expect to earn an additional .5% in interest, or 10.5%, on the second one-year investment. This risk premium (additional required interest rate) to compensate for the risk of changing future interest rates is nothing more than the maturity premium (MP) introduced earlier, and this concept underlies the liquidity preference theory of the term structure.[7] In the liquidity preference theory, investors require maturity premiums to compensate them for buying securities that expose them to the risks of fluctuating interest rates.

Market Segmentation Theory

The market segmentation theory is the third popular theory of the term structure of interest rates. This concept is built on the notion that legal restrictions and personal preferences limit choices for investors to certain ranges of maturities. For example, commercial banks prefer short- to medium-term securities as a result of the short-term nature of their deposit liabilities. They prefer not to invest in long-term securities. Life insurance companies, on the other hand, have longer-term liabilities, so they prefer longer maturities in investments. At the extreme, the market segmentation theory implies that the rate of interest for a particular maturity is determined solely by demand and supply for a given maturity and that it is independent of the demand and supply for securities having different maturities. A more moderate version of the theory allows investors strong maturity preferences, but it also allows them to modify their feelings and preferences if significant yield inducements occur.

SUMMARY

This chapter centers on the market environment in which corporations raise long-term funds, including the structure of the U.S. financial markets, the institution of investment banking, and the various methods for distributing securities. It also discusses the role of interest rates in allocating savings to ultimate investment.

Mix of Corporate Securities Sold

When corporations go to the capital market for cash, the most favored financing method is debt. The corporate debt markets clearly dominate the equity markets when new funds are raised. The U.S. tax system inherently favors debt capital as a fund raising method. In an average year over the past decade, bonds and notes made up 72% of external cash that was raised.

Why Financial Markets Exist

The function of financial markets is to allocate savings efficiently in the economy to the ultimate demander (user) of the savings. In a financial market the forces of supply and demand for a specific financial instrument are brought together. The wealth of an economy would not be as great as it is without a fully developed financial market system.

Financing of Business

Every year households are a net supplier of funds to the financial markets. The nonfinancial business sector is always a net borrower of funds. Both life insurance companies and private pension funds are important buyers of corporate securities. Savings are ultimately transferred to the business firm seeking cash by means of (1) the direct transfer, (2) the indirect transfer using the investment banker, or (3) the indirect transfer using the financial intermediary.

Components of U.S. Financial Market System

Corporations can raise funds through public offerings or private placements. The public market is impersonal in that the security issuer does not meet the ultimate investors in the financial instruments. In a private placement, the securities are sold directly to a limited number of institutional investors. The primary market is the market for new issues. The secondary market represents transactions in currently outstanding securities. Both the money and capital markets have primary and secondary sides. The money market refers to transactions in short-term debt instruments. The capital market, on the other hand, refers to transactions in long-term financial instruments. Trading in the money and capital markets can occur in either the organized security exchanges or the over-the-counter market. The money market is exclusively an over-the-counter market.

Investment Banker

The investment banker is a financial specialist involved as an intermediary in the merchandising of securities. He or she performs the functions of (1) underwriting, (2) distributing, and (3) advising. Major methods for the public distribution of securities include (1) the negotiated purchase, (2) the competitive bid purchase, (3) the commission or best-efforts basis, (4) privileged subscriptions, and (5) direct sales. The direct sale bypasses the use of an investment banker. The negotiated purchase is the most profitable distribution method to the investment banker. It also provides the greatest amount of investment banking services to the corporate client.

Private Placements

Privately placed debt provides an important market outlet for corporate bonds. Major investors in this market are (1) life insurance firms, (2) state and local retirement funds, and (3) private pension funds. Several advantages and disadvantages are associated with private placements. The financial officer must weigh these attributes and decide if a private placement is preferable to a public offering.

Flotation Costs

Flotation costs consist of the underwriter's spread and issuing costs. The flotation costs of common stock exceed those of preferred stock, which, in turn, exceed those of debt.

Moreover, flotation costs as a percent of gross proceeds are inversely related to the size of the security issue.

Regulation

The new issues market is regulated at the federal level by the Securities Act of 1933. It provides for the registration of new issues with the SEC. Secondary market trading is regulated by the Securities Exchange Act of 1934.

The Logic of Rates of Return and Interest Rate Determination

The financial markets give managers an informed indication of investors' opportunity costs. The more efficient the market, the more informed the indication. This information is a useful input about the rates of return that investors require on financial claims. In turn, this will become useful to financial managers as they estimate the overall cost of capital used as a screening rate in the capital budgeting process.

Rates of return on various securities are based on the underlying supply of loanable funds (savings) and demand for those loanable funds. In addition to a risk-free return, investors will want to be compensated for the potential loss of purchasing power resulting from inflation. Moreover, investors require a greater return the greater the default-risk, maturity premium, and liquidity premium are on the securities being analyzed.

QUESTIONS

1. What are financial markets? What function do they perform? How would an economy be worse off without them?
2. Define in a technical sense what we mean by "financial intermediary." Give an example of your definition.
3. Distinguish between the money and capital markets.
4. What major benefits do corporations and investors enjoy because of the existence of organized security exchanges?
5. What are the general categories examined by an organized exchange in determining whether an applicant firm's securities can be listed on it? (Areas of investigation rather than specific numbers are needed.)
6. What is an investment banker and what major functions does he or she perform?
7. What is the major difference between a negotiated purchase and a competitive bid purchase?
8. Why is an investment banking syndicate formed?
9. Why might a large corporation want to raise long-term capital through a private placement rather than a public offering?
10. As a recent business school graduate, you work directly for the corporate treasurer. Your corporation is going to issue a new security and is concerned with the probable flotation costs. What tendencies about flotation costs can you relate to the treasurer?
11. What is the major (most significant) savings-surplus sector in the U.S. economy?
12. Identify three distinct ways that savings are ultimately transferred to business firms in need of cash.
13. Explain the term "opportunity cost" with respect to cost of funds to the firm.
14. Explain the impact of inflation on rates of return.
15. Define the term structure of interest rates.
16. Explain the popular theories for the rationale of the term structure of interest rates.

PROBLEMS

1. What would you expect the nominal rate of interest to be if the real rate is 4% and the expected inflation rate is 7%?
2. Assume the expected inflation rate to be 4%. If the current real rate of interest is 6%, what ought the nominal rate of interest be?
3. Assume the expected inflation rate to be 5%. If the current real rate of interest is 7%, what would you expect the nominal rate of interest to be?

Notes

[1] Others include (1) The Honolulu Stock Exchange, which is unregistered; (2) the Board of Trade of the City of Chicago, which does not now trade stocks, and (3) the Chicago Board Options Exchange, Inc., which deals in options rather than stocks. The cities of Colorado Springs, Salt Lake City, and Spokane also have small exchanges. From time to time you may hear of the New York Futures Exchange (NYFE). This subsidiary of the NYSE was incorporated on April 5, 1979. Trading on the NYFE is in futures contracts and options contracts.

[2] New York Stock Exchange, Fact Book (New York, 1992), p. 24.

[3] New York Stock Exchange, Fact Book (New York, 1992), p. 74

[4] New York Stock Exchange, Fact Book (New York, 1992), p. 32

[5] See Richard Roll, *The Behavior of Interest Rates: An Application of the Efficient Market Model to U.S. Treasury Bills* (New York: Basic Books, 1970).

[6] Irving Fisher thought of this idea in 1896. The theory was later refined by J. R. Hicks in *Value and Capital* (London: Oxford University Press, 1946) and F. A. Lutz and V. C. Lutz in *The Theory of Investment in the Firm* (Princeton, NJ: Princeton University Press, 1951).

[7] We could also calculate the principal plus interest for Mary's investment using the following compound interest equation: $\$10,000 (1 + 09)^2 = \$11,881$.

SECTION VII
TIME VALUE OF MONEY AND THE PRINCIPLES OF CAPITAL BUDGETING

CHAPTER 12

TIME VALUE OF MONEY

In evaluating and comparing investment proposals, we need to examine how dollar values might accrue from accepting these proposals. To do this, all dollar values must first be comparable; since a dollar received today is worth more than a dollar received in the future, we must move all dollar flows back to the present or out to a common future date. An understanding of the time value of money is essential, therefore, to an understanding of financial management, whether basic or advanced.

COMPOUND INTEREST

Most of us encounter the concept of compound interest at an early age. Anyone who has ever had a savings account or purchased a government savings bond has received compound interest. Compound interest occurs when interest paid on the investment during the first period is added to the principal and then, during the second period, interest is earned on this new sum.

For example, suppose we place $100 in a savings account that pays 6% interest, compounded annually. How will our savings grow? At the end of the first year, we have earned 6% or $6 on our initial deposit of $100, giving us a total of $106 in our savings account. The mathematical formula illustrating this phenomenon is

$$FV_1 = PV(1 + i) \tag{1}$$

where FV_1 = the future value of the investment at the end of one year
      i = the annual interest (or discount) rate
   PV = the present value, or original amount invested at the beginning of the first year

In our example

$$FV_1 = PV(1 + i) \qquad (1)$$
$$= \$100(1 + .06)$$
$$= \$100(1.06)$$
$$= \$106$$

Carrying these calculations one period further, we find that we now earn the 6% interest on a principal of $106, which means we earn $6.36 in interest during the second year. Why do we earn more interest during the second year than we did during the first? Simply because we now earn interest on the sum of the original principal, or present value, and the interest we earned in the first year. In effect we are now earning interest on interest; this is the concept of compound interest. Examining the mathematical formula illustrating the earning of interest in the second year, we find

$$FV_2 = FV(1)(1 + i) \qquad (2)$$

which, for our example, gives

$$FV_2 = \$106(1.06)$$
$$= \$112.36$$

Looking back at equation (1), we can see that $FV(1)$ or $106, is actually equal to $PV(1+i)$, or $100 (1 + 0.6). If we substitute these values into equation (2), we get

$$FV_2 = PV(1 + i)(1 + i) \qquad (3)$$
$$= PV(1 + i)^2$$

Carrying this forward into the third year, we find that we enter the year with $112.36 and we earn 6%, or $6.74 in interest, giving us a total of $119.10 in our savings account. Expressing this mathematically:

$$FV_3 = FV_,(1 + i) \qquad (4)$$
$$= \$112.36(1.06)$$
$$= \$119.10$$

If we substitute the value in equation (3) for FV, into equation (4), we find

$$FV_3 = PV(1 + i)(1 + 1)(1 + i) \qquad (5)$$
$$= PV(1 + i)^3$$

By now a pattern is beginning to be evident. We can generalize this formula to illustrate the value of our investment if it is compounded annually at a rate of i for n years to be

$$FV_n = PV(1 + i)n \qquad (a)$$

where FV_n = the future value of the investment at the end of n years
         n = the number of years during which the compounding occurs
         i = the annual interest (or discount) rate
       PV = the present value or original amount invested at the beginning of the first year

Exhibit 12-1 illustrates how this investment of $100 would continue to grow for the first 10 years at a compound interest rate of 6%. Notice how the amount of interest earned annually increases each year. Again, the reason is that each year interest is received on the sum of the original investment plus any interest earned in the past.

Exhibit 12-1 Illustration of Compound Interest Calculations

Year	Beginning Value	Interest Earned	Ending Value
1	$100.00	$ 6.00	$106.00
2	106.00	6.36	112.36
3	112.36	6.74	119.10
4	119.10	7.15	126.25
5	126.25	7.57	133.82
6	133.82	8.03	141.85
7	141.85	8.51	150.36
8	150.36	9.02	159.38
9	159.38	9.57	168.95
10	168.95	10.13	179.08

When we examine the relationship between the number of years an initial invest-ment is compounded for and its future value graphically, as shown in Exhibit 12-2, we see that we can increase the future value of an investment by either increasing the num-ber of years for which we let it compound or by compounding it at a higher interest rate. We can also see this from equation (6), since an increase in either i or n while PV is held constant will result in an increase in FV.

For example, if we place $1,000 in a savings account paying 5% interest compound-ed annually, how much will our account accrue in 10 years? Substituting PV = $1000, $i = 50/0$, and $n = 10$ years into equation (6), we get

$$FV_n = PV(1 + i)^n \qquad\qquad (6)$$
$$= \$1,000(1 + .05)^{10}$$
$$= \$1,000(1.62889)$$
$$= \$1,628.89$$

Thus at the end of 10 years we will have $1,628.89 in our savings account.

Exhibit 12-2 Future Value of $100 Initially Deposited and Compounded at 0, 5, and 10%

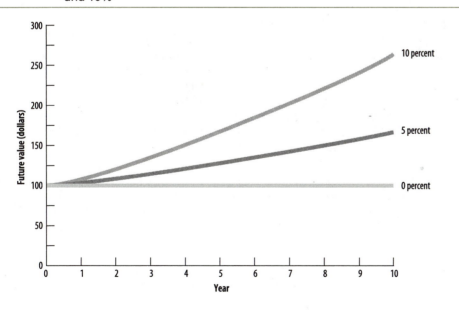

As the determination of future value can be quite time consuming when an investment is held for a number of years, the future-value interest factor for i and n $(FVIF_{i,n})$, defined as $(1 + i)^n$, has been compiled for various values of i and n. An abbreviated compound interest or future-value interest factor table appears in Exhibit 12-3, with a more comprehensive version of this appearing in Appendix B. Alternatively, the $(FVIF_{i,n})$ values could easily be determined using a calculator. Note that the compounding factors given in these tables represent the value of \$1 compounded at rate i at the end of the nth year. Thus, to calculate the future value of an initial investment we need only determine the $(FVIF_{i,n})$ using a calculator or the appendices and multiply this times the initial investment. In effect, we can rewrite equation (6) as follows:

$$FV_n = PV(FVIF_{i,n}) \qquad (6a)$$

As an example, if we invest \$500 in a bank where it will earn 8% compounded annually, how much will it be worth at the end of seven years? Looking at Exhibit 12-3 in the row $n = 7$ and column $i = 8\%$, we find that $(FVIF_{8\%,\ 7\ yr})$ has a value of 1.714.

Substituting this in equation (6a), we find

$$\begin{aligned} FV_n &= PV(FVIF8\%,\ 7\ yr) \qquad (6a)\\ &= \$500(1.714)\\ &= \$857 \end{aligned}$$

Thus, we will have \$857 at the end of seven years.

In the future we will find several uses for equation (6); not only will we find the future value of an investment, but we can also solve for PV, i, or n. In any case, we will be given three of the four variables and will have to solve for the fourth. For instance, how many years will it take for an initial investment of \$300 to grow to \$774 if it is invested at 9% compounded annually? In this problem we know the initial investment, $PV = \$300$; the future value, $FV_n = \$774$; the compound growth rate, $i = 9\%$; and we are solving for the number of years it must compound for, $n = ?$

Substituting the known values in equation (6), we find

$$\begin{aligned} FV_n &= (1 + i)^n \qquad (6)\\ \$774 &= \$300(1 + .09)^n\\ 2.58 &= (1 + .09)^n \end{aligned}$$

Exhibit 12-3 $FVIF_{i,n}$ or the Compound Sum of \$1

n	1%	2%	3%	4%	5%	6%	7%	8%	9%	10%
1	1.010	1.020	1.030	1.040	1.050	1.060	1 070	1.080	1.090	1.100
2	1.020	1.040	1.061	1.082	1.102	1.124	ı 145	1.166	1.188	1.210
3	1.030	1.061	1.093	1.125	1.158	1.191	1.225	1.260	1.295	1.331
4	1.041	1.082	1.126	1.170	1.216	1.262	1.311	1.360	1.412	1.464
5	1.051	1.104	1.159	1.217	1.276	1.338	1.403	1.469	1.539	1.611
6	1.062	1.126	1.194	1.265	1.340	1.419	1.501	1.587	1.677	1.772
7	1.072	1.149	1.230	1.316	1.407	1.504	1.606	1.714	1.828	1.949
8	1.083	1.172	1.267	1.369	1.477	1.594	1.718	1.851	1.993	2.144
9	1.094	1.195	1.305	1.423	1.551	1.689	1.838	1.999	2.172	2.358
10	1.105	1.219	1.344	1.480	1.629	1.791	1.967	2.159	2.367	2.594
11	1.116	1.243	1.384	1.539	1.710	1.898	2.105	2.332	2.580	2.853
12	1.127	1.268	1.426	1.601	1.796	2.012	2.252	2.518	2.813	3.138
13	1.138	1.294	1.469	1.665	1.886	2.133	2.410	2.720	3.066	3.452
14	1.149	1.319	1.513	1.732	1.980	2.261	2.579	2.937	3.342	3.797
15	1.161	1.346	1.558	1.801	2.079	2.397	2.759	3.172	3.642	4.177

Thus we are looking for a value of 2.58 in the $FVIF_{i,n}$ tables, and we know it must be in the 9% column. Looking down the 9% column for the value closest to 2.58, we find that it occurs in the $n = 11$ row. Thus, it will take 11 years for an initial investment of $300 to grow to $774 if it is invested at 9% compounded annually.

At what rate must $100 be compounded annually for it to grow to $179.10 in 10 years? In this case we know the initial investment, $PV = \$100$; the future value of this investment at the end of n years, $FV_n = \$179.10$; and the number of years that the initial investment will compound for, $n = 10$ years. Substituting into equation (6), we get

$$FV_n = PV(1 + i)^n \qquad (6)$$
$$\$179.10 = \$100(1 + i)^{10}$$
$$1.791 = (1 + i)^{10}$$

We know that we are looking in the $n = 10$ row of the $FVIF_{i,n}$ table for a value of 1.791, and we find this in the $i = 6\%$ column. Thus, if we want our initial investment of $100 to accrue to $179.10 in 10 years, we must invest it at 6%.

COMPOUND INTEREST WITH NON-ANNUAL PERIODS

Until now we have assumed that the compounding period is always annual; however, it need not be, as evidenced by savings and loan associations and commercial banks that compound on a quarterly, daily, and in some cases continuous basis. Fortunately, this adjustment of the compounding period follows the same format as that used for annual compounding. If we invest our money for five years at 8% interest compounded semi-annually, we are really investing our money for 10 six-month periods during which we receive 4% interest each period. If it is compounded quarterly, we receive 2% interest per period for 20 three-month periods. This process can easily be generalized, giving us the following formula for finding the future value of an investment for which interest is compounded in non-annual periods:

$$FV_n = PV\left(1 + \frac{i}{m}\right)^{mn} \qquad (7)$$

where
FV_n = the future value of the investment at the end of n years
n = the number of years during which the compounding occurs
i = the annual interest (or discount) rate
PV = the present value or original amount invested at the beginning of the first year
m = the number of times compounding occurs during the year

In the case of continuous compounding, the value of m in equation (7) is allowed to approach infinity. In effect, with continuous compounding, interest begins to earn interest immediately. As this happens, the value of $[1 + (i/m)]^{mn}$ approaches e^{in}, with e being defined as follows and having a value of approximately 2.71828:

$$e = \lim_{m \to \infty} \left(1 + \frac{1}{m}\right)^m \qquad (8)$$

where ∞ indicates infinity. Thus the future value of an investment compounded continuously for n years can be determined from the following formula:

$$FV_n = PV \times e^{in} \qquad (9)$$
where
FV_n = the future value of the investment at the end of n years

$$e = 2.71828$$
$$n = \text{the number of years during which the compounding occurs}$$
$$i = \text{the annual interest (or discount) rate}$$
$$PV = \text{the present value or original amount invested at the beginning of the first year}$$

Continuous compounding may appear complicated, but it is used frequently and is a valuable theoretical concept. Continuous compounding is important because it allows interest to be earned on interest more frequently than any other compounding method does. We can see the value of intrayear compounding by examining Exhibit 12-4. Since interest is earned on interest more frequently as the length of the compounding period declines, there is an inverse relationship between the length of the compounding period and the effective annual interest rate.

For example, if we place $100 in a savings account that yields 12% compounded quarterly, what will our investment grow to at the end of five years? Substituting $n = 5$, $m = 4$, $i = 12\%$, and $PV = \$100$ into equation (7), we find

$$FV_5 = \$100 \left(1 + \frac{.12}{4}\right)^{4 \cdot 5}$$

$$= \$100(1 + .03)^{20}$$
$$= \$100(1.806)$$
$$= \$180.60$$

Thus, we will have $180.60 at the end of five years. Notice that a calculator solution is slightly different because of rounding errors in the tables, as explained in the previous section, and that it also takes on a negative value.

Exhibit 12-4 The Value of $100 Compounded at Various Intervals

For One Year at *i* Percent				
i =	2%	5%	10%	15%
Compounded annually	$102.00	$105.00	$110.00	$115.00
Compounded semiannually	102.01	105.06	110.25	115.56
Compounded quarterly	102.02	105.09	110.38	115.87
Compounded monthly	102.02	105.12	110.47	116.08
Compounded weekly (52)	102.02	105.12	110.51	116.16
Compounded daily (365)	102.02	105.13	110.52	116.18
Compounded continuously	102.02	105.13	110.52	116.18

For Ten Years at *i* Percent				
i =	2%	5%	10%	15%
Compounded annually	$121.90	$162.89	$259.37	$404.56
Compounded semiannually	122.02	163.86	265.33	424.79
Compounded quarterly	122.08	164.36	268.51	436.04
Compounded monthly	122.12	164.70	270.70	444.02
Compounded weekly (52)	122.14	164.83	271.57	447.20
Compounded daily (365)	122.14	164.87	271.79	448.03
Compounded continuously	122.14	164.87	271.83	448.17

As another example, how much money will we have at the end of 20 years if we deposit $1,000 in a savings account yielding 10% interest continuously compounded? Substituting $n = 20$, $i = 10\%$, and $PV = \$1000$ into equation (9) yields

$$
\begin{aligned}
FV_{10} &= \$1,000(2.71828)^{.10 \times 20} \\
&= \$1,000(2.71828)^2 \\
&= \$1,000(7.38905) \\
&= \$7,389.05
\end{aligned}
$$

Thus, we will have $7,389.05 at the end of 20 years.

PRESENT VALUE

Up until this point we have been moving money forward in time; that is, we know how much we have to begin with and are trying to determine how much that sum will grow in a certain number of years when compounded at a specific rate. We are now going to look at the reverse question: what is the value in today's dollars of a sum of money to be received in the future? The answer to this question will help us determine the desirability of investment projects. In this case we are moving future money back to the present. We will be determining the **present value** of a lump sum, which in simple terms is the current value of a future payment. What we will be doing is, in fact, nothing other than inverse compounding. The differences in these techniques comes about merely from the investor's point of view. In compounding we talked about the compound interest rate and the initial investment; in determining the present value we will talk about the discount rate and present value. Determination of the discount rate can be defined as the rate of return available on an investment of equal risk to what is being discounted. Other than that, the technique and the terminology remain the same, and the mathematics are simply reversed. In equation (6) we were attempting to determine the future value of an initial investment. We now want to determine the initial investment or present value. By dividing both sides of equation (6) by $(1 + i)^n$, we get

$$
PV = FV_n \left(\frac{1}{(1+i)^n} \right)
$$

where FV_n = the future value of the investment at the end of n years
n = the number of years until the payment will be received
i = the annual discount (or interest) rate
PV = the present value of the future sum of money

Because the mathematical procedure for determining the present value is exactly the inverse of determining the future value, we also find that the relationships among n, i, and PV are just the opposite of those we observed in future value. The present value of a future sum of money is inversely related to both the number of years until the payment will be received and the discount rate. Graphically, this relationship can be seen in Exhibit 12-5.

Exhibit 12-5   Present Value of $100 to Be Received at a Future Date and Discounted Back
to the Present at 0, 5, and 10%

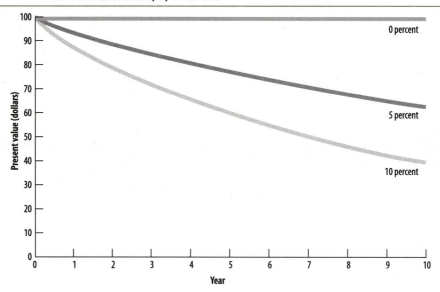

For example, what is the present value of $500 to be received 10 years from today if
our discount rate is 6%? Substituting $FV_{10} = \$500$, $n = 10$, and $i = 6\%$ into equation (10),
we find

$$PV = \$500 \left(\frac{1}{(1+.06)^{10}} \right)$$

$$= \$500 \left(\frac{1}{1.791} \right)$$

$$= \$500(.558)$$

$$= \$279$$

Thus, the present value of the $500 to be received in 10 years is $279.

To aid in the computation of present values, the **present-value interest factor** for i
and n ($PVIF_{i,n}$) defined as $[1/(1 + i)^n]$, has been compiled for various combinations of i
and n and appears in Appendix C. An abbreviated version of Appendix C appears in
Exhibit 12-6. A close examination shows that the values in Exhibit 12-6 are merely the
inverse of those found in Exhibit 12-3 and Appendix B. This, of course, is as it should be,
as the values in Appendix B are $(1 + i)^n$ and those in Appendix C are $[1/(1 + i)^n]$. Now, to
determine the present value of a sum of money to be received at some future date, we
need only determine the value of the appropriate $PVIF_{i,n}$, either by using a calculator or
consulting the tables, and multiply it by the future value. In effect we can use our new
notation and rewrite equation (10) as follows:

$$PV = FV_n(PVIF_{in}) \tag{10a}$$

For instance, what is the present value of $1,500 to be received at the end of 10 years
if our discount rate is 8%? By looking at the $n = 10$ row and $i = 8\%$ column of Exhibit
12-6, we find the $PVIF_{8\%, 10\,yr}$ is .463. Substituting this value into equation (10), we find

$$PV = \$1,500(.463)$$

$$= \$694.50$$

Exhibit 12-6 $PVIF_{i,n}$ or the Present Value of $1

n	1%	2%	3%	4%	5%	6%	7%	8%	9%	10%
1	.990	.980	.971	.962	.952	.943	.935	.926	.917	.909
2	.980	.961	.943	.925	.907	.890	.873	.857	.842	.826
3	.971	.942	.915	.889	.864	.840	.816	.794	.772	.751
4	.961	.924	.888	.855	.823	.792	.763	.735	.708	.683
5	.951	.906	.863	.822	.784	.747	.713	.681	.650	.621
6	.942	.888	.837	.790	.746	.705	.666	.630	.596	.564
7	.933	.871	.813	.760	.711	.655	.623	.583	.547	.513
8	.923	.853	.789	.731	.677	.627	.582	.540	.502	.467
9	.914	.837	.766	.703	.645	.592	.544	.500	.460	.424
10	.905	.820	.744	.676	.614	.558	.508	.463	.422	.386
11	.896	.804	.722	.650	.585	.527	.475	.429	.388	.350
12	.887	.789	.701	.625	.557	.497	.444	.397	.356	.319
13	.879	.773	.681	.601	.530	.469	.415	.368	.326	.290
14	.870	.758	.661	.577	.505	.442	.388	.340	.299	.263
15	.861	.743	.642	.555	.481	.417	.362	.315	.275	.239

Thus, the present value of this $1,500 payment is $694.50.

Again, we only have one present-value—future-value equation; that is, equations (6) and (10) are identical. We have introduced them as separate equations to simplify our calculations; in one case we are determining the value in future dollars and in the other case the value in today's dollars. In either case the reason is the same: to compare values on alternative investments and to recognize that the value of a dollar received today is not the same as that of a dollar received at some future date. We must measure the dollar values in dollars of the same time period. Because all present values are comparable (they are all measured in dollars of the same time period), we can add and subtract the present value of inflows and outflows to determine the net present value of an investment.

As another example, what is the present value of an investment that yields $500 to be received in five years and $1,000 to be received in 10 years if the discount rate is 4%? Substituting the values of $n = 5$, $i = 4\%$, and $FV_5 = \$500$; and $n = 10$, $i = 4\%$, and $FV_{10} = \$1000$ into equation (10) and adding these values together, we find

$$PV = \$500 \left(\frac{1}{(1+.04)^5} \right) + \$1,000 \left(\frac{1}{(1+.04)^{10}} \right)$$

$$= \$500(PVIF_{4\%,\ 5\ yr}) + \$1,000(PVIF_{4\%,\ 10\ yr})$$
$$= \$500(.822) + \$1,000(.676)$$
$$= \$411 + \$676$$
$$= \$1,087$$

Again, present values are comparable because they are measured in the same time period's dollars.

ANNUITIES

An **annuity** is a series of equal dollar payments for a specified number of years. Because annuities occur frequently in finance—for example, as bond interest payments—we will treat them specially. Although compounding and determining the present value of an annuity can be dealt with using the methods we have just described, these processes can be time consuming, especially for larger annuities. Thus, we have modified the formulas to deal directly with annuities.

Compound Annuities

A **compound annuity** involves depositing or investing an equal sum of money at the end of each year for a certain number of years and allowing it to grow. Perhaps we are saving money for education, a new car, or a vacation home. In any case we want to know how much our savings will have grown by some point in the future.

Actually, we can find the answer by using equation (6), our compounding equation, and compounding each of the individual deposits to its future value. For example, if to provide for a college education we are going to deposit $500 at the end of each year for the next five years in a bank where it will earn 6% interest, how much will we have at the end of five years? Compounding each of these values using equation (6), we find that we will have $2,818.50 at the end of five years.

$$
\begin{aligned}
FV_5 &= \$500(1 + .06)^4 + \$500(1 + .06)^3 + \$500(1 + .06)^2 + \$500(1 + .06) + \$500 \\
&= \$500(1.262) + \$500(1.191) + \$500(1.124) + \$500(1.060) + \$500 \\
&= \$631.00 + \$595.50 + \$562.00 + \$530.00 + \$500.00 \\
&= \$2,818.50
\end{aligned}
$$

From examining the mathematics involved and the graph of the movement of money through time in Exhibit 12-7, we can see that this procedure can be generalized to

$$
FV_n = PMT\left(\sum_{t=0}^{n-1}(1+i)^t\right) \tag{11}
$$

where

FV_n = the future value of the annuity at the end of the nth year
PMT = the annuity payment deposited or received at the end of each year
i = the annual interest (or discount) rate
n = the number of years for which the annuity will last

To aid in compounding annuities, the **future-value interest factor for an annuity** for i and n ($FVIFA_{i,n}$) defines as

$$
\left(\sum_{t=0}^{n-1}(1+i)^t\right)
$$

is provided in Appendix D for various combinations of n and i; an abbreviated version is shown in Exhibit 12-8.[1]

Using this new notation, we can rewrite equation (11) as follows:

$$
FV_n = PMT(FVIFA_{i,n}) \tag{12}
$$

Exhibit 12-7   Illustration of a Five-Year $500 Annuity Compounded at 6%

Year	0	1	2	3	4	5
Dollar deposits at end of year		500	500	500	500	500
						$ 500.00
						530.00
						562.00
						595.50
						631.00
Future value of the annuity						$2,818.50

Exhibit 12-8 $FVIFA_{i,n}$ or the Sum of an Annity of $1 for n Years

n	1%	2%	3%	4%	5%	6%	7%	8%	9%	10%
1	1.000	1.000	1.000	1.000	1.000	1.000	1.000	1.000	1.000	1.000
2	2.010	2.020	2.030	2.040	2.050	2.060	2.070	2.080	2.090	2.100
3	3.030	3.060	3.091	3.122	3.152	3.184	3.215	3.246	3.278	3.310
4	4.060	4.122	4.184	4.246	4.310	4.375	4.440	4.506	4.573	4.641
5	5.101	5.204	5.309	5.416	5.526	5.637	5.751	5.867	5.985	6.105
6	6.152	6.308	6.468	6.633	6.802	6.975	7.153	7.336	7.523	7.716
7	7.214	7.434	7.662	7.898	8.142	8.394	8.654	8.923	9.200	9.487
8	8.286	8.583	8.892	9.214	9.549	9.897	10.260	10.637	11.028	11.436
9	9.368	9.755	10.159	10.583	11.027	11.491	11.978	12.488	13.021	13.579
10	10.462	10.950	11.464	12.006	12.578	13.181	13.816	14.487	15.193	15.937
11	11.567	12.169	12.808	13.486	14.207	14.972	15.784	16.645	17.560	18.531
12	12.682	13.412	14.192	15.026	15.917	16.870	17.888	18.977	20.141	21.384
13	13.809	14.680	15.618	16.627	17.713	18.882	20.141	21.495	22.953	24.523
14	14.947	15.974	17.086	18.292	19.598	21.015	22.550	24.215	26.019	27.975
15	16.097	17.293	18.599	20.023	21.578	23.276	25.129	27.152	29.361	31.772

Re-examining the previous example, in which we determined the value after five years of $500 deposited at the end of each of the next five years in the bank at 6%, we would look in the $i = 6\%$ column and $n = 5$ year row and find the value of the $FVIFA_{6\%, 5\,yr}$ to be 5.637. Substituting this value into equation (11a), we get

$$FV_5 = \$500(5.637)$$
$$= \$2,818.50$$

This is the same answer we obtained earlier using equation (6).

Rather than asking how much we will accumulate if we deposit an equal sum in a savings account each year, a more common question is how much we must deposit each year to accumulate a certain amount of savings. This problem frequently occurs with respect to saving for large expenditures and pension funding obligations.

For example, we may know that we need $10,000 for education in eight years; how much must we deposit in the bank at the end of each year at 6% interest to have the college money ready? In this case we know the values of n, i, and FV_n in equation (11); what we do not know is the value of PMT. Substituting these example values in equation (11), we find

$$\$10,000 = PMT\left(\sum_{t=0}^{8-1}(1+.06)^t\right)$$
$$\$10,000 = PMT(FVIFA_{5\%, 8\,yr})$$
$$\$10,000 = PMT(9.897)$$
$$\frac{\$10,000}{9,897} = PMT$$

$$PMT = \$1,010.41$$

Thus, we must deposit $1,010.41 in the bank at the end of each year for eight years at 6% interest to accumulate $10,000 at the end of eight years.

How much must we deposit in an 8% savings account at the end of each year to accumulate $5,000 at the end of ten years? Substituting the values $FV_{10} = \$5,000$, $n = 10$, and $i = 8\%$ into equation (11), we find

$$\$5,000 = PMT\left(\sum_{t=0}^{10-1}(1+.08)^t\right) = PMT\left(FVIFA_{8\%, 10\,yr}\right)$$

$$\$5{,}000 = PMT(14.487)$$

$$\frac{\$5{,}000}{14.487} = PMT$$

$$PMT = \$345.14$$

Thus, we must deposit $345.14 per year for 10 years at 8% to accumulate $5,000.

Present Value of an Annuity

Pension funds, insurance obligations, and interest received from bonds all involve annuities. To compare them, we need to know the present value of each. While we can find this by using the present-value table in Appendix C, this can be time consuming, particularly when the annuity lasts for several years. For example, if we wish to know what $500 received at the end of the next five years is worth to us given the appropriate discount rate of 6%, we can simply substitute the appropriate values into equation (10), such that

$$PV = \$500\left(\frac{1}{(1+.06)}\right) + \$500\left(\frac{1}{(1+.06)^2}\right) + \$500\left(\frac{1}{(1+.06)^3}\right) + \$500\left(\frac{1}{(1+.06)^4}\right) + \$500\left(\frac{1}{(1+.06)^5}\right)$$

$$= \$500(.943) + \$500(.890) + \$500(.840) + \$500(.792) + \$500(.747)$$

$$= \$2{,}106$$

Thus, the present value of this annuity is $2,106.00. From examining the mathematics involved and the graph of the movement of these funds through time in Exhibit 12-9, we see that this procedure can be generalized to

$$PV = PMT\left(\sum_{t=0}^{n}\frac{1}{(1+i)^t}\right)$$

where PMT = the annuity payment deposited or received at the end of each year
  i = the annual discount (or interest) rate
  PV = the present value of the future annuity
  n = the number of years for which the annuity will last

To simplify the process of determining the present value of an annuity, the **present-value interest factor for an annuity** for i and n $(PVIFA_{i,n})$, defined as $\left(\sum_{t=1}^{n}\frac{1}{(1+i)^t}\right)$

has been compiled for various combinations of i and n in Appendix E with an abbreviated version provided in Exhibit 12-10.[2]

Exhibit 12-9   Illustration of a Five-Year $500 Annuity Discounted to the Present at 6%

Year	0	1	2	3	4	5
Dollars received at the end of year		500	500	500	500	500
	$ 471.50					
	445.00					
	420.00					
	396.00					
	373.50					
Present value of the annuity	$2,106.00					

Exhibit 12-10 $PVIFA_{i,n}$ or the Present Value of an Annuity of $1

n	1%	2%	3%	4%	5%	6%	7%	8%	9%	10%
1	0.990	0.980	0.971	0.962	0.952	0.943	0.935	0.926	0.917	0.909
2	1.970	1.942	1.913	1.886	1.859	1.833	1.808	1.783	1.759	1.736
3	2.941	2.884	2.829	2.775	2.723	2.673	2.624	2.577	2.531	2.487
4	3.902	3.808	3.717	3.630	3.546	3.465	3.387	3.312	3.240	3.170
5	4.853	4.713	4.580	4.452	4.329	4.212	4.100	3.993	3.890	3.791
6	5.795	5.601	5.417	5.242	5.076	4.917	4.767	4.623	4.486	4.355
7	6.728	6.472	6.230	6.002	5.786	5.582	5.389	5.206	5.033	4.868
8	7.652	7.326	7.020	6.733	6.463	6.210	5.971	5.747	5.535	5.335
9	8.566	8.162	7.786	7.435	7.108	6.802	6.515	6.247	5.995	5.759
10	9.471	8.983	8.530	8.111	7.722	7.360	7.024	6.710	6.418	6.145
11	10.368	9.787	9.253	8.760	8.306	7.887	7.499	7.139	6.805	6.495
12	11.255	10.575	9.954	9.385	8.863	8.384	7.943	7.536	7.161	6.814
13	12.134	11.348	10.635	9.986	9.394	8.853	8.358	7.904	7.487	7.103
14	13.004	12.106	11.296	10.563	9.899	9.295	8.746	8.244	7.786	7.367
15	13.865	12.849	11.938	11.118	10.380	9.712	9.108	8.560	8.061	7.606

Using this new notation we can rewrite equation (12) as follows:

$$PV = PMT(PVIFA_{i,n}) \qquad (12a)$$

Solving the previous example to find the present value of $500 received at the end of each of the next five years discounted back to the present at 6%, we look in the $i = 6\%$ column and $n = 5$ year row and find the $PVIFA_{6\%, 5\,yr}$ to be 4.212. Substituting the appropriate values into equation (12a), we find

$$PV = \$500(4.212)$$
$$= \$2,106$$

This, of course, is the same answer we calculated when we individually discounted each cash flow to the present. The reason is that we really only have *one* table; the Exhibit 12-10 value for an *n*-year annuity for any discount rate *i* is merely the sum of the first *n* values in Exhibit 12-6. We can see this by comparing the value in the present-value-of-an-annuity table (Exhibit 12-10) for $i = 8\%$ and $n = 6$ years, which is 4.623, with the sum of the values in the $i = 8\%$ column and $n = 1, \ldots , 6$ rows of the present-value table (Exhibit 12-6), which is equal to 4.623, as shown in Exhibit 12-11.

Exhibit 12-11 Present Value of a Six-Year Annuity Discounted at 8%

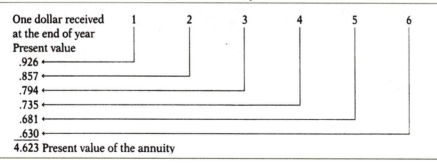

For example, what is the present value of a 10-year annuity discounted back to the present at 5%? Substituting $n = 10$ years, $i = 5\%$, and $PMT = \$1,000$ into equation (12), we find

$$PV = \$1,000 \left(\sum_{t=1}^{10} \frac{1}{(1+.05)^t} \right) = \$1,000 \left(PVIFA_{5\%, 10 \, yr} \right)$$

Determining the value for the $PVIFA_{5\%, 10 \, yr}$ from Exhibit 12-10, row $n = 10$, column $i = 5\%$, and substituting it in, we get

$$PV = \$1,000(7.722)$$
$$= \$7,722$$

Thus, the present value of this annuity is \$7,722.

As with our other compounding and present-value tables, given any three of the four unknowns in equation (12), we can solve for the fourth. In the case of the present-value-of-an-annuity table we may be interested in solving for PMT, if we know i, n, and PV. The financial interpretation of this action would be: how much can be withdrawn, perhaps as a pension or to make loan payments, from an account that earns i percent compounded annually for each of the next n years if we wish to have nothing left at the end of n years? For example, if we have \$5,000 in an account earning 8% interest, how large an annuity can we draw out each year if we want nothing left at the end of five years? In this case the present value, PV, of the annuity is \$5,000, $n = 5$ years, $i = 8\%$, and PMT is unknown. Substituting this into equation (12), we find

$$\$5,000 = PMT(3.993)$$
$$\$1,252.19 = PMT$$

Thus, this account will fall to zero at the end of five years if we withdraw \$1,252.19 at the end of each year.

AMORTIZED LOANS

This procedure of solving for PMT, the annuity payment value when i, n, and PV are known, is also used to determine what payments are associated with paying off a loan in equal installments over time. Loans that are paid off this way, in equal periodic payments, are called *amortized loans*. For example, suppose a firm wants to purchase a piece of machinery. To do this, it borrows \$6,000 to be repaid in four equal payments at the end of each of the next four years, and the interest rate that is paid to the lender is 15% on the outstanding portion of the loan. To determine what the annual payments associated with the repayment of this debt will be, we simply use equation (12) and solve for the value of PMT, the annual annuity. Again we know three of the four values in that equation, PV, i, and n. PV, the present value of the future annuity, is \$6,000; i, the annual interest rate, is 15%; and n, the number of years for which the annuity will last, is four years. PMT, the annuity payment received (by the lender and paid by the firm) at the end of each year, is unknown. Substituting these values into equation (12), we find

$$\$6,000 = PMT \left(\sum_{t=1}^{4} \frac{1}{(1+.15)^t} \right)$$
$$\$6,000 = PMT(PVIFA_{15\%, 4 \, yr})$$
$$\$6,000 = PMT(2.855)$$
$$\$2,101.58 = PMT$$

Exhibit 12-12 Loan Amortization Schedule Involving a $6,000 Loan at 15% to Be Repaid in Four Years

Year	Annuity	Interest Portion of the Annuity[a]	Repayments of the Principal Portion of the Annuity[b]	Outstanding Loan Balance after the Annuity Payment
1	$2,101.58	$900.00	$1,201.58	$4,798.42
2	2,101.58	719.76	1,381.82	3,416.60
3	2,101.58	512.49	1,589.09	1,827.51
4	2,101.58	274.07	1,827.51	

[a]The interest portion of the annuity is calculated by multiplying the outstanding loan balance at the beginning of the year by the interest rate of 15% Thus, for year 1 it was $6,000.00 × .15 = $900.00, for year 2 it was $4,798.42 × .15 = $719.76. and so on.
[b]Repayment of the principal portion of the annuity was calculated by subtracting the interest portion of the annuity (column 2) from the annuity (column 1).

To repay the principal and interest on the outstanding loan in four years the annual payments would be $2,101.58. The breakdown of interest and principal payments is given in the *loan amortization schedule* in Exhibit 12-12, with very minor rounding error. As you can see, the interest payment declines each year as the loan outstanding declines.

PRESENT VALUE OF AN UNEVEN STREAM

While some projects will involve a singe cash flow and some annuities, many projects will involve uneven cash flows over several years. There we will be comparing not only the present value of cash flows between projects but also the cash inflows and outflows within a particular project, trying to determine that project's present value. However, this will not be difficult because the present value of any cash flow is measured in today's dollars and, thus, can be compared, through addition for inflows and subtraction for outflows, to the present value of any other cash flow also measured in today's dollars. For example, if we wished to find the present value of the following cash flows given a 6% discount rate, we would merely discount the flows back to the present and total them by adding in the positive flows and subtracting the negative ones. However, this problem is complicated by the annuity of $500 that runs from years 4 through 10. To accommodate this, we can first discount the annuity back to the beginning of period 4 (or end of period 3) by multiplying it by the value of $PFIVA_{6\%, 7 \text{ yr}}$ and get its present value at that point in time. We then multiply this value times the $PVIF_{6\%, 3 \text{ yr}}$ in order to bring this single cash flow (which is the present value of the 7-year annuity) back to the present. This is shown graphically in Exhibit 12-13 and numerically in Exhibit 12-14. Thus, the present value of this uneven stream of cash flows is $2,657.94.

Year	Cash Flow	Year	Cash Flow
1	$500	6	500
2	200	7	500
3	−400	8	500
4	500	9	500
5	500	10	500

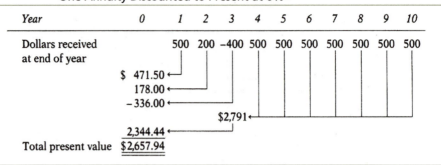

What, then, is the present value of an investment involving $200 received at the end of years 1 through 5, a $300 cash outflow at the end of year 6, and $500 received at the end of years 7 through 10, given a 5% discount rate? Here we have two annuities, one that can be discounted directly back to the present by multiplying it by the value of the $PVIFA_{5\%, 5 yr}$ and one that must be discounted twice to bring it back to the present. This second annuity, which is a four-year annuity, must first be discounted back to the beginning of period 7 (or end of period 6) by multiplying it by the value of the $PVIFA_{5\%, 4 yr}$. Then the present value of this annuity at the end of period 6 (which can be viewed as a single cash flow) must be discounted back to the present by multiplying it by the value of the $PVIF_{5\%, 6 yr}$.

To arrive at the total present value of this investment, we subtract the present value of the $300 cash outflow at the end of year 6 from the sum of the present value of the two annuities. Exhibit 12-15 shows this graphically; Exhibit 12-16 gives the calculations. Thus, the present value of this series of cash flows is $1,964.66.

PERPETUITIES

A **perpetuity** is an annuity that continues forever; that is, every year from its establishment this investment pays the same dollar amount. An example of a perpetuity is preferred stock that pays a constant dollar dividend infinitely. Determining the present value of a perpetuity is delightfully simple; we merely need to divide the constant flow by the discount rate. For example, the present value of a $100 perpetuity discounted

Exhibit 12-14   Determination of Present Value of an Example with Uneven Stream Involving One Annuity Discounted to Present at 6%

1. Present value of $500 received at the end of one year = $500(.943) = $ 471.50
2. Present value of $200 received at the end of two years = $200(.890) =   178.00
3. Present value of a $400 outflow at the end of three years = –400(.840) =   –336.00
4. (a) Value at the end of year 3 of a $500 annuity, years 4 through 10 =
        $500(5.582) = $2,791.00
    (b) Present value of $2,791.00 received at the end of year 3 =
        $2,791 (.840) =   2,344.44
5. Total present value =   **$2,657.94**

Exhibit 12-15 Illustration of an Example of Present Value of an Uneven Stream Involving Two Annuities Discounted to Present at 5%

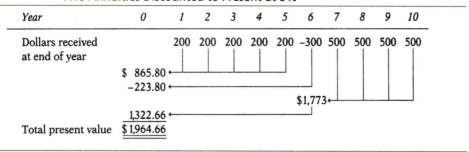

Year	0	1	2	3	4	5	6	7	8	9	10
Dollars received at end of year		200	200	200	200	200	–300	500	500	500	500

$ 865.80
–223.80
$1,773
1,322.66
Total present value $ 1,964.66

back to the present at 5% is $100/.05 = $2,000. Thus, the equation representing the present value of a perpetuity is

$$PV = \frac{PP}{i}$$ (13)

where
  PV = the present value of the perpetuity
  PP = the constant dollar amount provided by the perpetuity
  i = the annual interest (or discount) rate

What is the present value of a $500 perpetuity discounted back to the present at 8%? Substituting PP = $500 and i = .08 into equation (13), we find

Thus, the present value of this perpetuity is $6,250.

$$PV = \frac{\$500}{.08} = \$6,250$$

SUMMARY

To make decisions, financial managers must compare the costs and benefits of alternatives that do not occur during the same time period. Whether to make profitable investments or to take advantage of favorable interest rates, financial decision making requires an understanding of the time value of money. Managers who use the time value of money in all of their financial calculations assure themselves of more logical decisions. The time value process first makes all dollar values comparable; because money has a time value it moves all dollar flows either back to the present or out to a common future date. All time value formulas presented in this chapter actually stem from the single compounding formula $FV_n = PV(1 + i)^n$. The formulas are used to deal simply with common financial situations, for example, discounting single flows, compounding annuities, and discounting annuities. Exhibit 12-17 provides a summary of these calculations.

Exhibit 12-16 Determination of Present Value of an Example with Uneven Stream Involving Two Annuities Discounted to Present at 5%

1. Present value of first annuity, years 1 through 5 = $200(4.329) $ 865.80
2. Present value of $300 cash outflow = –$300(.746) = –223.80
3. (a) Value at end of year 6 of second annuity, years 7 through 10 = $500(3.546) = $1,773.00
   (b) Present value of $1,773.00 received at the end of year 6 = $1,773.00(.746) = 1,322.66
4. Total present value = $1,964.66

Exhibit 12-17   Summary of Time Value of Money Equations*

Future value of a single payment	$FV_n = PV(1 + i)^n = PV(FVIF_{i,n})$
Future value of a single payment with nonannual compounding	$FV_n = PV\left(1 + \dfrac{i}{m}\right)^{mn}$
Present value of a single payment	$PV = FV_n \left(\dfrac{1}{(1 + i)^n}\right) = FV_n\left(PVIF_{i,n}\right)$
Future value of an annuity	$FV_n = PMT\left(\displaystyle\sum_{t=0}^{n-1} (1 + i)^t\right) = PMT\left(FVIFA_{i,n}\right)$
Present value of an annuity	$PV = PMT\left(\displaystyle\sum_{t=1}^{n} \dfrac{1}{(1 + i)^t}\right) = PMT\left(PVIFA_{i,n}\right)$
Present value of a perpetuity	$PV = \dfrac{PP}{i}$

Notation:
- FV_n = the future value of the investment at the end of n years
- n = the number of years until payment will be received or during which compounding occurs
- i = the annual interest or discount rate
- PV = the present value of the future sum of money
- m = the number of times compounding occurs during the year
- PMT = the annuity payment deposited or received at the end of each year
- PP = the constant dollar amount provided by the perpetuity

* Related tables appear in Appendices B–E.

SELF-CORRECTION PROBLEMS

1. You place $25,000 in a savings account paying annual compound interest of 8% for three years and then move it into a savings account that pays 10% interest compounded annually. How much will your money have grown at the end of six years?

2. You purchase a boat for $35,000 and pay $5,000 down and agree to pay the rest over the next 10 years in 10 equal annual end-of-year payments that include principal payments plus 13% compound interest on the unpaid balance. What will be the amount of each payment?

3. For an investment to grow eightfold in nine years, at what rate would it have to grow?

SOLUTIONS TO SELF-CORRECTION PROBLEMS

1. This is a compound interest problem in which you must first find the future value of $25,000 growing at 8% compounded annually for 3 years and then allow that future value to grow for an additional three years at 10%. First, the value of the $25,000 after three years growing at 8% is

$$FV_3 = PV(1 + i)^n$$
$$FV_3 = \$25,000(1 + .08)^3$$
$$FV_3 = \$25,000(1.260)$$
$$FV_3 = \$31,500$$

Thus, after three years you have $31,500. Now this amount is allowed to grow for three years at 10%. Plugging this into equation (6), with $PV = \$31,500$, $i = 10\%$, n = 3 years, we solve for FV_3:

$$FV_3 = \$31,500(1 + .10)^3$$
$$FV_3 = \$31,500(1.331)$$
$$FV_3 = \$41,926.50$$

Thus, after six years the $25,000 will have grown to $41,926.50.

2. This loan amortization problem is actually just a present-value-of-an-annuity problem in which we know the values of i, n, and PV and are solving for PMT. In this case the value of i is 13%, n is 10 years, and PV is $30,000. Substituting these values into equation (12) we find

$$\$30,000 = PMT \left(\sum_{t=1}^{10} \frac{1}{(1+.13)^t} \right)$$
$$\$30,000 = PMT(5.426)$$
$$\$5,528.93 = PMT$$

3. This is a simple compound interest problem in which FV_9 is eight times larger than PV. Here again three of the four variables are known: $n = 9$ years, $FV_9 = 8$, and $PV = 1$, and we are solving for i. Substituting these values into equation (6) we find

$$FV_9 = PV(1 = i)^n$$
$$FV_9 = PV(FVIF_{i,n})$$
$$8 = 1(FVIF_{i,9 \text{ yr}})$$
$$8.00 = FVIF_{i,9 \text{ yr}}$$

Thus, we are looking for an $FVIF_{i,9 \text{ yr}}$ with a value of 8 in Appendix B, which occurs in the 9-year row. If we look in the 9-year row for a value of 8.00, we find it in the 26% column (8.004). Thus, the answer is 26%.

QUESTIONS

1. What is the time value of money? Why is it so important?
2. The processes of discounting and compounding are related. Explain this relationship.
3. How would an increase in the interest rate (i) or a decrease in the holding period (n) affect the future value (FV_n) of a sum of money? Explain why.
4. Suppose you were considering depositing your savings in one of three banks, all of which pay 5% interest; bank A compounds annually, bank B compounds semi-annually, and bank C compounds continuously. Which bank would you choose? Why?

5. What is the relationship between the $PVIF_{i,n}$ (Exhibit 12-6) and the $PVIFA_{i,n}$ (Exhibit 12-10)? What is the $PVIFA_{10\%,\ 10\ yr}$? Add up the values of the $PVIF_{10\%,\ n}$, for $n = 1, \ldots, 10$. What is this value? Why do these values have the relationship they do?

6. What is an annuity? Give some examples of annuities. Distinguish between an annuity and a perpetuity.

7. What does continuous compounding mean?

PROBLEMS

1. **Compound Interest**. To what amount will the following investments accumulate?
   a. $5,000 invested for 10 years at 10% compounded annually
   b. $8,000 invested for 7 years at 8% compounded annually
   c. $775 invested for 12 years at 12% compounded annually
   d. $21,000 invested for 5 years at 5% compounded annually

2. **Compound Value Solving for n**. How many years will the following take?
   a. $500 to grow to $1,039.50 if invested at 5% compounded annually
   b. $35 to grow to $53.87 if invested at 9% compounded annually
   c. $100 to grow to $298.60 if invested at 20% compounded annually
   d. $53 to grow to $78.76 if invested at 2% compounded annually

3. **Compound Value Solving for i**. At what annual rate would the following have to be invested?
   a. $500 to grow to $1,948.00 in 12 years
   b. $300 to grow to $422.10 in 7 years
   c. $50 to grow to $280.20 in 20 years
   d. $200 to grow to $497.60 in 5 years

4. **Present Value**. What is the present value of the following future amounts?
   a. $800 to be received 10 years from now discounted back to present at 10%
   b. $300 to be received 5 years from now discounted back to present at 5%
   c. $1,000 to be received 8 years from now discounted back to present at 3%
   d. $1,000 to be received 8 years from now discounted back to present at 20%

5. **Compound Annuity.** What is the accumulated sum of each of the following streams of payments?
   a. $500 a year for 10 years compounded annually at 5%
   b. $100 a year for 5 years compounded annually at 10%
   c. $35 a year for 7 years compounded annually at 7%
   d. $25 a year for 3 years compounded annually at 2%

6. **Present Value of an Annuity**. What is the present value of the following annuities?
   a. $2,500 a year for 10 years discounted back to the present at 7%
   b. $70 a year for 3 years discounted back to the present at 3%
   c. $280 a year for 7 years discounted back to the present at 6%
   d. $500 a year for 10 years discounted back to the present at 10%

Time Value of Money

If you need a calculator, you can use the web site maintained by Salem Five to calculate present value and future value amounts using http://www.salemfive.com (interactive calculator).

If you are leasing a car, buying a home, borrowing money, and many other time value of money related transactions, you can visit http://www.financenter.com for handy worksheets on mortgages, leases, loans, and so forth.

1. Try to use any of the above web site Internet calculators to calculate the following time-value problems.

    a. Assume you need to borrow $200,000 for 25 years at 8%. Using any of the above Internet sites, what would your monthly payment be?

    b. Using Salem Five's "savings and investment planner," find how much $4,000 saved at the end of the next 30 years will grow to be, assuming it earns a constant 10% per year.

    c. Utilize www.moneyadvisor.com web site amortization calculator. Amortize a $200,000 loan over 10 years at 9%. What is the remaining balance after the fifth payment?

Notes

[1] Another useful analytical relationship for FV_n is $FV_n = PMT[(1 + i)^n - 1]/i$.

[2] Another useful analytical relationship for PV is $PV = PMT[1 - [1/(1 + i)^n]]/i$.

CHAPTER 13

CAPITAL BUDGETING

Capital budgeting is the process used by managers to evaluate and select investment projects that will generate future benefits for the firm. Before any project is selected most firms screen all proposals at multiple levels of authority. For a proposal originating in the production area, the hierarchy of authority might run from (1) section chiefs to (2) plant managers to (3) the vice president for operations to (4) a capital expenditures committee under the financial manager to (5) the president to (6) the board of directors. How high a proposal must go before it is finally approved usually depends on its size. The greater the capital outlay, the greater the number of screens usually required. Plant managers may be able to approve moderate-sized projects on their own, but only higher levels of authority approve larger ones.

To select and successfully manage a capital budgeting project the management team must insure that the following events occur:

1. Generation of investment proposals
2. Estimation of cash flows for the proposals
3. Evaluation of cash flows
4. Selection of projects based on an acceptance criterion

Managers use many different capital-budgeting models in selecting investments. Each model summarizes facts and forecasts about an investment in a way that provides information for a decision maker. In this chapter we compare the uses and limitations of various capital-budgeting models.

For purposes of analysis, projects may be classified into one of five categories:

1. New products or expansion of existing products
2. Replacement of equipment or buildings
3. Research and development
4. Exploration
5. Others

The fifth category comprises miscellaneous items such as the expenditure of funds to comply with certain health standards or the acquisition of a pollution-control device. For a new product, the proposal usually originates in the marketing department. On the other hand, a proposal to replace a piece of equipment with a more sophisticated model usually emanates from the production area of the firm. In each case, efficient administrative procedures are needed for channeling investment requests.

CASH-FLOW FORECAST

One of the most important tasks in capital budgeting is estimating future cash flows for a project. The final results we obtain are really only as good as the accuracy of our estimates. Since cash, not income, is central to all decisions of the firm, we express whatever benefits we expect from a project in terms of cash flows rather than income. The firm invests cash now in the hope of receiving cash returns in a greater amount in the future. Only cash receipts can be reinvested in the firm or paid to stockholders in the form of dividends. In capital budgeting, good guys may get credit, but effective managers get cash. In setting up the cash flows for analysis, a computer spreadsheet program is invaluable. It allows one to change assumptions and quickly produce a new cash-flow stream.

Incremental Cash Flows. For each investment proposal, we need to provide information on expected future cash flows on an after-tax basis. In addition, the information must be provided on an incremental basis, so that we analyze only the difference between the cash flows of the firm with and without the project. For example, if a firm contemplates a new product that is likely to compete with existing products, it is not appropriate to express cash flows in terms of the estimated sales of the new product. We must take into account some probable "cannibalization" of existing products, and we must make our cash-flow estimates on the basis of incremental sales. The key is to analyze the situation with and without the new investment. Only incremental cash flows matter.

Ignore Sunk Costs. Because sunk costs have already been expended they must be ignored. Management is concerned with the project's incremental costs and benefits: the recovery of past costs is irrelevant. They are bygones and should not enter into the decision process. Also, we must be mindful that certain costs do not necessarily involve a dollar outlay. If we have allocated plant space to a project and this space can be used for something else, its opportunity cost must be included in the project's evaluation. If a presently unused building can be sold for $300,000, that amount should be treated as a cash outlay at the outset of the project. Thus, in deriving cash flows we must consider appropriate opportunity costs.

Illustration. To illustrate the information needed for a capital budgeting decision, consider the following situation. Dilly Duck Apparel Company is considering the introduction of a new clothing line. To launch the product line, the company will need to spend $150,000 for special equipment and the initial advertising campaign. The marketing department envisions the product life to be 6 years and expects incremental sales revenue to be

Year	1	2	3	4	5	6
Inflow	$60,000	$120,000	$160,000	$180,000	$110,000	$50,000

Cash outflows include labor and maintenance costs, material costs, and various other expenses associated with the product. As with sales, these costs must be estimated on an incremental basis. In addition to these outflows, the company will need to pay higher taxes if the new product generates higher profits, and this incremental outlay must be included. Cash outflows should not include interest costs on debt employed to finance the project. Such costs are embodied in the required rate of return to be discussed later. To deduct interest charges from net cash flows would result in double counting.

Suppose that on the basis of these considerations, Dilly Duck Apparel estimates total incremental cash outflows to be

Year	1	2	3	4	5	6
Outflow	$40,000	$70,000	$100,000	$100,000	$70,000	$40,000

Because depreciation is a noncash expense, it is not included in these outflows. The expected net cash flows from the project are

| | Initial Cost | Years | | | | | |
		1	2	3	4	5	6
Cash inflow		$60,000	$120,000	$160,000	$180,000	$110,000	$50,000
Cash outflow	150,000	40,000	70,000	100,000	100,000	70,000	40,000
Net cash flow	−$150,000	$20,000	$ 50,000	$ 60,000	$ 80,000	$ 40,000	$10,000

Thus, for an initial cash outflow of $150,000 the company expects to generate net cash flows of $20,000, $50,000, $60,000, $80,000, $40,000 and $10,000 over the next 6 years. These cash flows represent the relevant information we need in order to judge the attractiveness of the project. The development of cash-flow data of this sort is facilitated greatly by the use of a spreadsheet program.

REPLACEMENT DECISIONS AND DEPRECIATION

To go to a somewhat more complicated replacement decision example involving taxes, suppose we are considering the purchase of a new machine to replace an old one, and we need to obtain cash-flow information in order to evaluate the attractiveness of this project. The purchase price of the new machine is $18,500, and it will require an additional $1,500 to install, bringing the total cost to $20,000. We can sell the old machine for its depreciated book value of $2,000. The initial net cash outflow for the investment project, therefore, is $18,000. The new machine should cut labor and maintenance costs and effect other cash savings totaling $7,100 a year before taxes for each of the next 5 years, after which it will probably not provide any savings, nor will it have a salvage value. These savings represent the net savings to the firm if it replaces the old machine with the new. In other words, we are concerned with the difference between the cash flows resulting from the two alternatives: continuing with the old machine or replacing it with a new one.

Depreciation Effect. Because a machine of this sort has a useful life in excess of 1 year, we cannot charge its cost against income for tax purposes but must depreciate it. We then deduct depreciation from income in order to compute taxable income. Under the tax laws when this edition was written, capital assets fall into defined cost recovery classes depending on their nature. These classes of property have periods, or depreciable lives, of 3, 5, 7, 10, 15, 20, 27, and 39 years. A general description of the classes follows shortly. For now, suppose the machine we are considering falls into the 5-year property class for cost recovery (depreciation) purposes. Later in the chapter we consider the exact depreciation that may be deducted under existing tax law. For simplicity of illustration now, we assume straight-line depreciation.

As a result, the annual depreciation charge is 20% of the total depreciable cost of $20,000, or $4,000 a year. Assume additionally that the corporate income tax rate is 40%. Moreover, assume that the old machine has a remaining depreciable life of 5 years, that there is no expected salvage value at the end of this time, and that the machine also is subject to straight-line depreciation. Thus, the annual depreciation charge on the old machine is 20% of its depreciated book value of $2,000, or $400 a year. Because we are interested in the incremental impact of the project, we must subtract depreciation charges on the old machine from depreciation charges on the new one to obtain the incremental depreciation charges associated with the project. Given the information cited, we now are able to calculate the expected net cash flow (after taxes) resulting from the acceptance of the project.

	Book Account	Cash-Flow Account
Annual cash savings	$7,100	$7,100
Depreciation on new machine	4,000	
Less: Depreciation on old machine	400	
Additional depreciation charge	$3,600	
Additional income before taxes	3,500	
Income tax (40%)	1,400	1,400
Additional income after taxes	$2,100	
Annual net cash flow		$5,700

Putting It Together. In figuring the net cash flow, we simply deduct the additional cash outlay for federal income taxes from the annual cash savings. The expected annual net cash inflow for this replacement proposal is $5,700 for each of the next 5 years; this figure compares with additional income after taxes of $2,100 a year. The cash flow and net profit figures differ by the amount of additional depreciation. As our concern is not with income as such, but with cash flows, we are interested in the right-hand column. For an initial cash outlay of $18,000, then, we are able to replace an old machine with a new one that is expected to result in net cash savings of $5,700 a year over the next 5 years. As in the previous example, the relevant cash flow information for capital budgeting purposes is expressed on an incremental, after-tax basis.

VALUATION METHODS

Once we have collected the necessary information, we are able to evaluate the attractiveness of the various investment proposals under consideration. Because our purpose in this chapter is to examine the basic concepts of capital budgeting, we assume that the risk or quality of all investment proposals under consideration does not differ from the risk of existing investment projects of the firm and that the acceptance of any proposal or group of investment proposals does not change the relative business risk of the firm. The investment decision will be either to accept or to reject the proposal. In this section, we evaluate five methods used in capital budgeting:

1. Average rate of return
2. Payback
3. Internal rate of return
4. Net present value
5. Profitability Index

The first two are approximate methods for assessing the economic worth of a project. For simplicity, we assume throughout that the expected cash flows are realized at the end of each year.

Average Rate of Return

This accounting measure represents the ratio of the average annual profits after taxes to the investment in the project. In the previous example of the new machine, the average annual book earnings for the 5-year period are $2,100, and the initial investment in the project is $18,000. Therefore,

$$\text{Average rate of return} = \frac{\$\ 2,100}{\$18,000} = 11.67\%$$

If income were variable over the 5 years, an average would be calculated and employed in the numerator. Once the average rate of return for a proposal has been calculated, it may be compared with a required rate of return to determine if a particular proposal should be accepted or rejected.

The principal virtue of the average rate of return is its simplicity; it makes use of readily available accounting information. Once the average rate of return for a proposal has been calculated, it may be compared with a required, or cutoff, rate of return to determine if a particular proposal should be accepted or rejected. The principal shortcomings of the method are that it is based on accounting income rather than cash flows and that it fails to take account of the timing of cash inflows and outflows. The time value of money is ignored: benefits in the last year are valued the same as benefits in the first year.

Payback

The payback period of an investment project tells us the number of years required to recover our initial cash investment. It is the ratio of the initial fixed investment over the annual cash inflows for the recovery period. For our example

$$\text{Payback period} = \frac{\$18,000}{\$\ 5,700} = 3.16 \text{ years}$$

If the annual cash inflows are not equal, the job of calculation is somewhat more difficult. Suppose annual cash inflows are $4,000 in the first year, $6,000 in the second and third years, and $4,000 in the fourth and fifth years. In the first 3 years, $16,000 of the original investment will be recovered, followed by $4,000 in the fourth year. With an initial cash investment of $18,000, the payback period is 3 years + ($2,000/$4,000), or 3 1/2 years.

Shortcomings. If the payback period calculated is less than some maximum acceptable payback period, the proposal is accepted; if not, it is rejected. If the required payback period were 4 years, the project in our example would be accepted. The major shortcoming of the payback method is that it fails to consider cash flows after the payback period; consequently, it cannot be regarded as a measure of profitability. Two proposals costing $10,000 each would have the same payback period if they both had annual net cash inflows of $5,000 in the first 2 years; but, one project might be expected to provide no cash flows after 2 years, whereas the other might be expected to provide cash flows of $5,000 in each of the next 3 years. Thus, the payback method can be deceptive as a yardstick of profitability. In addition to this shortcoming, the method does not take account of the magnitude or timing of cash flows during the payback period. It considers only the recovery period as a whole.

Popularity of Payback. The payback method continues in use, nevertheless, frequently as a supplement to other, more sophisticated methods. It does afford management limited insight into the risk and liquidity of a project. The shorter the payback period, supposedly, the less risky the project and the greater its liquidity. The company that is cash poor may find the method to be very useful in gauging the early recovery of funds invested. There is some merit to its use in this regard, but the method does not take into account the dispersion of possible outcomes—only the magnitude and timing of the expected value of these outcomes relative to the original investment. Therefore, it cannot be considered an adequate indicator of risk. When the payback method is used, it is more appropriately treated as a constraint to be satisfied than as a profitability measure to be maximized.

Internal Rate of Return

Because of the various shortcomings in the average rate of return and payback methods, it generally is felt that discounted cash-flow methods provide a more objective basis for evaluating and selecting investment projects. These methods take account of both the magnitude and the timing of expected cash flows in each period of a project's life. The two discounted cash-flow methods are the internal rate-of-return (IRR) and the net present-value methods. The internal rate of return for an investment proposal is the discount rate that equates the present value of the expected cash outflows with the present value of the expected inflows.

There are two methods used to calculate the IRR:

1. The Annuity Method
2. The Interpolation Method

The annuity method is when a project's cash flows are received in equal amounts, and the interpolation method is used when the cash flows are received in uneven amounts. Using our example problem the IRR can be determined using the following:

1. The Annuity Method

$$PVIFA = \frac{Investment}{Cash\ Inflows} = \frac{\$18,000}{\$5,700} = 3.15$$

The *PVIFA* is then found in the present value of an annuity table where 3.15 is between the 17% and 18% columns on the 5 years line.

2. The Interpolation Method

Step 1. Find the average of the cash inflows.
Step 2. Divide this sum by the sum of digits.

The investment of $18,000 will generate cash inflows of

1. 5,100
2. 5,200
3. 5,400
4. 5,700
5. 5,700
   $27,100 / 5 = $5,420

The *PVIFA* is found by the following:

$$\frac{Investment}{Inflows} = \frac{\$18,000}{\$5,420} = 3.32\ PVIFA$$

Step 3. Refer to the Percent Value Annuity Table to find out where this factor falls.

In this case 3.32 is found between the PVIFA values for 15% and 16%. The actual rate of return will be higher because of the averaging. Therefore, we will start the interpolation process by trying 15%:

Step 4. Determine the present value for each sum.

Year   15%

1	$5,100	× .870	=	$ 4,437
2	5,200	× .756	=	3,931
3	5,400	× .658	=	3,553
4	5,700	× .572	=	3,260
5	5,700	× .497	=	2,833
				$18,014

$18,014   This sum is above the investment

Year   16%

1	$5,100	× .862	=	$4,396
2	5,200	× .743	=	3,834
3	5,400	× .641	=	3,461
4	5,700	× .552	=	3,146
5	5,700	× .476	=	2,713
				$17,550

$17,550   This sum is below the investment

This indicates that the actual IRR lies between 15% and 16%.

Step 5. Using interpolation the exact IRR can be found:

Rate	Present Value
15%	$18,014
*	$18,000
16%	$17,550

$$15\% + \left[\left(\frac{\$\ 14}{\$464} \right) \times 1\% \right] = 15.03\%$$

(16% − 15%) = 1%

The IRR for this project is 15.03%.

Acceptance Criterion. The acceptance criterion generally employed with the internal-rate-of-return method is to compare the internal rate-of-return with a required rate-of-return, known also as the cutoff, or hurdle, rate. If the internal rate-of-return exceeds the required rate, the project is accepted; if not, it is rejected. If the required rate-of-return is 12% and this criterion is used, the investment proposal being considered will be accepted. Accepting a project with an internal rate-of-return in excess of the required rate-of-return should result in an increase in the market price of the stock, because the firm accepts a project with a return greater than that required to maintain the present market price per share.

Recognize, however, that capacity-expanding investment projects may differ from cost-reduction projects and, hence, require a different return. Capital-expanding projects are highly related to the level of economic activity, producing sizable cash flows when the economy is prosperous. The systematic risk of this type of project would be high. Replacement projects, on the other hand, are cost reducing and would likely produce benefits across more states of the economy. As a result, they would possess lower systematic risk and require a lower return to satisfy investors.

Net Present Value

Like the internal-rate-of-return method, the net-present-value method is a discounted cash-flow approach to capital budgeting. With the net-present-value method, all cash flows are discounted to present value, using the required rate-of-return.

If the sum of these discounted cash flows is zero or more, the proposal is accepted; if not, it is rejected. Another way to express the acceptance criterion is to say that the project will be accepted if the present value of cash inflows exceeds the present value of cash outflows. The rationale behind the acceptance criterion is the same as that behind the internal-rate-of-return method. If the required rate of return is the return investors expect the firm to earn on the investment proposal, and the firm accepts a proposal with a net present value greater than zero, the market price of the stock should rise. Again, the firm is taking on a project with a return greater than that necessary to leave the market price of the stock unchanged.

Using our example we assume a required rate of return of 12%; the net present value can be calculated using the following methods:

1. The Annuity Method: when all the cash flows are equal

$$NPV = PV \text{ cash inflow} - \text{Investment}$$

$5,700	× 3.605 =	$20,549	
	Less	<$18,000>	
	NPV =	2,549	

2. The Uneven Cash Flow Method:

Determine the present value of the cash inflows:

1	$5,100	× .893 =	$4,554	
2	5,200	× .797 =	4,144	
3	5,400	× .712 =	3,845	
4	5,700	× .636 =	3,625	
5	5,700	× .567 =	3,232	
PV of cash inflows		=	$19,400	
Less the investment		=	<$18,000>	
	NPV	=	$1,400	

Because both values are greater than 0, the project should be accepted using the two net-present-value methods. With the internal-rate-of-return method, we are given the cash flows, and we solve for the rate of discount that equates the present value of the cash inflows with the present value of the outflows. We then compare the internal rate of return with the required rate of return to determine whether the proposal should be accepted. With the present-value method, we are given the cash flows and the required rate of return, and we solve for the net present value. The acceptability of the proposal depends on whether the net present value is zero or more.

The profitability index, or benefit/cost ratio, of a project is the present value of future net cash flows over the initial cash outlay. This index is used to rank investment projects in descending order of attractiveness. If the profitability index is greater than 1, then you should accept the project. It can be expressed as

$$\text{Profitability index} = \frac{\text{Present value of the inflows}}{\text{Present value of outflows}}$$

The present value of inflows in part two of the above example was used to compute the profitability index.

$$\text{Profitability index} = \frac{\$20,549}{\$18,000} = 1.14$$

The profitability index indicates that the investment generates $1.14 for every dollar invested.

As long as the profitability index is 1.00 or greater, the investment proposal is acceptable. For any given project, the net-present-value method and the profitability index give the same accept-reject signals. If we must choose between mutually exclusive projects, the net-present-value measure is preferred because it expresses in absolute terms the expected economic contribution of the project. In contrast, the profitability index expresses only the relative profitability.

Mutually Exclusive

In evaluating a group of investment proposals, we must determine whether the proposals are independent of each other. A proposal is mutually exclusive if the acceptance of it precludes the acceptance of one or more other proposals. For example, if the firm is considering investment in one of two temperature-control systems, acceptance of one system will rule out acceptance of the other. Two mutually exclusive proposals cannot both be accepted.

NET PRESENT VALUE VERSUS INTERNAL RATE OF RETURN

In general, the net-present-value and internal-rate-of-return methods lead to the same acceptance or rejection decision. In Exhibit 13-1, we illustrate graphically the two methods applied to a typical investment project. The figure shows the curvilinear relationship between the net present value of a project and the discount rate employed. When the discount rate is 0, net present value is simply the total cash inflows less the total cash outflows of the project. Assuming that total inflows exceed total outflows and that outflows are followed by inflows, the typical project will have the highest net present value when the discount rate is 0. As the discount rate increases, the present value of future cash inflows decreases relative to the present value of outflows. As a result, NPV declines. The crossing of the NPV line with the 0 line establishes the internal rate of return for the project.

If the required rate of return is less than the internal rate of return, we would accept the project, using either method. Suppose that the required rate were 10%. As seen in Exhibit 13-1, the net present value of the project then would be Y. Inasmuch as Y is greater than 0, we would accept the project, using the present-value method. Similarly, we would accept the project using the internal-rate-of-return method because the internal rate of return exceeds the required rate. For required rates greater than the internal rate of return, we would reject the project under either method. Thus, we see that the internal-rate-of-return and present-value methods give us identical answers with respect to the acceptance or rejection of an investment project.

DEPRECIATION AND OTHER REFINEMENTS IN CASH-FLOW INFORMATION

In our machine replacement example, we assumed straight-line depreciation, the depreciable life of the asset equaling its economic life, no salvage value, and no working capital requirement. Our purpose was to keep the example simple so that we could analyze the methods for evaluating expected profitability. We shall now digress for a while in order to examine the effect of these real-world considerations on the magnitude and timing of cash flows.

Depreciation Methods

In our earlier example, we assumed straight-line depreciation when computing cash flows. However, a more advantageous method of depreciation is available for tax purposes in the United States. Known as the modified accelerated cost recovery system

Exhibit 13-1   Relation Between Discount Rate and Net Present Value

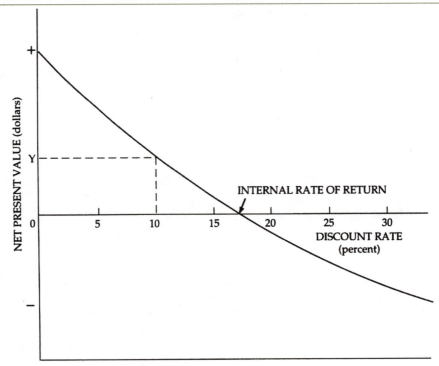

(MACRS), and pronounced "makers," there are eight property classes for depreciation purposes. The property category in which an asset falls determines its depreciable life for tax purposes.

- 3-Year class: includes property with a midpoint life of 4 years or less. The midpoint life of various types of assets is determined by the Treasury Department under the asset depreciation range (ADR) system.
- 5-Year class: includes property with an ADR midpoint life of 4 to 10 years. Included in this class are most machinery, automobiles, light trucks, most technological and semiconductor equipment, switching equipment, small power production facilities, and research and experimental equipment.
- 7-Year class: includes property with an ADR midpoint of 10 to 16 years and railroad track and single-purpose agriculture structures.
- 10-Year class: includes property with an ADR midpoint life of 16 to 20 years.
- 15-Year class: includes property with a midpoint of 20 to 25 years and telephone distribution plants.
- 20-Year class: includes property with an ADR midpoint of 25 years or more, other than real property described below.
- 27 1/2-Year class: includes residential rental property.
- 39-Year class: other real-estate.

For the 3-, 5-, 7-, and 10-year property classes, the method of depreciation is the 200% declining-balance method. This method switches to straight line in the year that provides the quickest write-off. Moreover, a half-year convention is used in the first year and in the year following the last year. For the 15-year and 20-year property classes, 150% declining-balance depreciation is used with subsequent switching to straight line.

Finally for the 27 1/2-year and 39-year classes, straight-line depreciation is used throughout.

Rather than having to make these calculations oneself, the Treasury publishes depreciation percentages of original cost for each property class. For the first four property categories, they are:

Recovery

Year	3-Year	5-Year	7-Year	10-Year
1	33.33%	20.00%	14.29%	10.00%
2	44.45	32.00	24.49	18.00
3	14.81	19.20	17.49	14.40
4	7.41	11.52	12.49	11.52
5		11.52	8.93	9.22
6		5.76	8.93	7.37
7			8.92	6.55
8			4.46	6.55
9				6.56
10				6.55
11				3.28

These percentages correspond to the principles taken up in our previous calculations, and they should be used for determining depreciation.

Setting Up the Cash Flow

In most cases, the capital recovery (depreciation) period is shorter than the economic life of the asset. To illustrate how we might go about using depreciation tables and setting up the cash flows for analysis, suppose a company were considering an asset costing $100,000 that fell in the 5-year property class. The asset was expected to produce annual before-tax cash savings of $32,000 in each of the first 2 years, $27,000 in each of the next 2 years, $22,000 in both the fifth and the sixth years, and $20,000 in the seventh and last year. Assume further a 40% tax rate (federal and state) and no salvage value. Setting up the cash flows is facilitated greatly with a spreadsheet program. The annual net cash flows are as follows:

	0	1	2	3	4	5	6	7
1. Cost	($100,000)							
2. Annual savings		$32,000	$32,000	$27,000	$27,000	$22,000	$22,000	$20,000
3. Depreciation (Minus)		20,000	32,000	9,200	1,520	11,520	5,760	-0-
4. Income		$12,000	-0-	$ 7,800	$15,480	$10,480	$16,240	$20,000
5. Taxes (40%)		4,800	-0-	3,120	6,192	4,192	6,496	8,000
6. Net cash flow	($100,000)	$27,200	$32,000	$23,880	$20,808	$17,808	$15,504	$12,000

We see that the tax shield occurs only in the first 6 years, after which the full cash savings are subject to taxation. As a result, the cash flow is lower. This shift in timing over what would occur with straight-line depreciation has a favorable present-value effect. To determine the net present value of the project, we discount the cash flows shown in row 6 by the required rate of return and sum them. If the required rate of return were 12%, the net present value would be $3,405 and the internal rate of return 13.25%, both measures indicating acceptance of the project. Cash flows for other projects can be set up similarly.

Salvage Value and Taxes

The cash-flow pattern will change toward the better if the asset is expected to have salvage, or scrap, value at the end of the project. As the asset will be fully depreciated at that time, the salvage value realized is subject to taxation at the ordinary income tax rate. Suppose the asset were sold for $10,000 at the end of year 7. With a 40% tax rate, the company will realize cash proceeds of $6,000 at the end of the last year. This amount then would be added to the net cash inflow previously determined to give the total cash flow in the last year.

If the asset is sold before it is fully depreciated, the tax treatment is different. In general, if an asset is sold for more than its depreciated book value but for less than its cost, the firm pays taxes at the full corporate rate. If the asset is sold for more than its cost, this excess is subject to the capital-gains tax treatment, which sometimes is more favorable. As such calculations are complicated, the reader is referred to the tax code and/or to a tax attorney when faced with the tax treatment of the sale of an asset.

Working Capital Requirement

In addition to the investment in a fixed asset, it is sometimes necessary to carry additional cash, receivables, or inventories. This investment in working capital is treated as a cash outflow at the time it occurs. For example, if $15,000 in working capital is required in connection with our example, there would be an additional cash outflow of $15,000 at time 0, bringing the total outflow to $115,000. At the end of the project's life, the working capital investment presumably is returned. Therefore, there would be a $15,000 cash inflow at the end of year 7. As a result, the cash inflow in that year would be $27,000 instead of $12,000.

This switching of cash flows obviously is adverse from a present-value standpoint: $15,000 is given up at time 0 and is not gotten back until 7 years later. Again using 12% as the required rate of return, the net present value of row 6 of our previous example, rearranged as suggested, is -$4,810. The IRR is now 10.57%. These figures compare with $3,405 and 13.25% determined before. Thus, an initial working capital investment of $15,000 causes the project to be unacceptable, whereas before it was acceptable. While total cash flows are not affected, their timing is affected.

Increases and decreases in working capital investment are not confined to the beginning and the end of the project. They can occur at any time. It is important that incremental working capital needs are treated as cash outflows when they occur and that any subsequent reductions in these needs are recorded as cash inflows.

CAPITAL RATIONING

Capital rationing occurs any time there is a budget ceiling, or constraint, on the amount of funds that can be invested during a specific period of time, such as a year. Such constraints are prevalent in a number of firms, particularly in those that have a policy of financing all capital expenditures internally. Another example of capital rationing occurs when a division of a large company is allowed to make capital expenditures only up to a specified budget ceiling, over which the division usually has no control. With a capital rationing constraint, the firm attempts to select the combination of investment proposals that will provide the greatest profitability.

Your firm may have the following investment opportunities, ranked in descending order of profitability indexes (the ratio of the present value of future net cash flows over the initial cash outlay):

	Proposal						
	4	**7**	**2**	**3**	**6**	**5**	**1**
Profitability index	1.25	1.19	1.16	1.14	1.09	1.05	0.97
Initial outlay	$400,000	$100,000	$175,000	$125,000	$200,000	$100,000	$150,000

If the budget ceiling for initial outlays during the present period is $1 million, and the proposals are independent of each other, you would select proposals in descending order of profitability until the budget was exhausted. With capital rationing, you would accept the first five proposals, totaling $1 million in initial outlays. In other words, you do not necessarily invest in all proposals that increase the net present value of the firm; you invest in an acceptable proposal only if the budget constraint allows such an investment. You will not invest in proposal 5, even though the profitability index in excess of 1.00 would suggest its acceptance. The critical aspect of the capital rationing constraint illustrated is that capital expenditures during a period are strictly limited by the budget ceiling, regardless of the number of attractive investment opportunities.

Selection Criterion

Under capital rationing, the objective is to select the combination of investment proposals that provides the highest net present value, subject to the budget constraint for the period. If this constraint is strictly enforced, it may be better to accept several smaller, less profitable proposals that allow full utilization of the budget than to accept one large proposal that results in part of the budget being unused. Admittedly, a fixed one-period constraint is highly artificial. Companies engaging in capital rationing seldom will set a budget so rigidly that it does not provide for some flexibility. In addition, the cost of certain investment projects may be spread over several years. Finally, a one-period analysis does not take account of intermediate cash flows generated by a project. Some projects provide relatively high net cash flows in the early years; these cash flows serve to reduce the budget constraints in the early years because they may be used to finance other investment projects. For the reasons discussed, when capital is rationed, management should consider more than one period in the allocation of limited capital to investment projects.

Problem Incurred

A budget ceiling carries its cost, too, when it bars us from taking advantage of an opportunity that provides a return in excess of that required. In our first example, the opportunity forgone by the $1 million budget ceiling is proposal 5, which has a profitability index of 1.05. Though all cash flows are discounted at the required rate of return, we do not necessarily accept proposals that provide positive net present values. We see which proposals we can accept before we exhaust the budget. In so doing, we may reject projects that provide positive net present values, as was shown with proposal 5.

Capital rationing usually results in an investment policy that is less than optimal. In some periods, the firm accepts projects down to its required rate of return; in others, it rejects projects that would provide returns substantially in excess of the required rate. If the required rate of return corresponds to the project's cost of capital, and the firm actually can raise capital at that approximate cost, should it not invest in all projects yielding more than the required rate of return? If it rations capital and does not invest in all projects yielding more than the required rate, is it not forgoing opportunities that would enhance the market price of its stock?

In the final analysis, the firm should accept all proposals yielding more than their required rates of return. By so doing, it will increase the market price per share because it is taking on projects that will provide a return higher than necessary to maintain the present market price per share. Certainly, there are circumstances that complicate the use of this rule. In general, however, this policy should tend to maximize the market price of the stock over the long run.

SUMMARY

Capital budgeting involves the outlay of current funds in anticipation of future cash-flow benefits. Collection of cash-flow information is essential for the evaluation of investment proposals. The key is to measure incremental cash flows with and without the investment proposal being analyzed. Depreciation under the accelerated cost recovery system has a significant effect on the pattern of cash flows and, hence, on present value. Also affecting the pattern of cash flows is the presence of salvage value and a working capital requirement.

Capital budgeting methods, including the average-rate-of-return and payback methods, were examined under the assumption that the acceptance of any investment proposal does not change the business-risk complexion of the firm as perceived by suppliers of capital. The two discounted cash-flow methods—internal rate of return and net present value—are the only appropriate means by which to judge the economic contribution of an investment proposal. The important distinctions between the internal-rate-of-return method and the present-value method involve the implied compounding rate, the scale of investment, and the possibility of multiple internal rates of return. Depending on the situation, contrary answers can be given with respect to the acceptance of mutually exclusive investment proposals. On theoretical grounds, a case can be made for the superiority of the present-value method, though in practice the IRR is popular.

SELF-CORRECTION PROBLEMS

1. Briarcliff Stove Company is considering a new product line to supplement its range line. It is anticipated that the new product line will involve cash investments of $700,000 at time 0 and $1.0 million in year 1. After-tax cash inflows of $250,000 are expected in year 2, $300,000 in year 3, $350,000 in year 4, and $400,000 each year thereafter through year 10. While the product line might be viable after year 10, the company prefers to be conservative and end all calculations at that time.
   a. If the required rate of return is 15%, what is the net present value of the project? Is it acceptable?
   b. What is its internal rate of return?
   c. What would be the case if the required rate of return were 10%?
   d. What is the project's payback period?

2. Carbide Chemical Company is considering the replacement of two old machines with a new, more efficient machine. The old machines could be sold for $70,000 in the secondary market. Their depreciated book value is $120,000 with a remaining useful and depreciable life of 8 years. Straight-line depreciation is used on these machines. The new machine can be purchased and installed for $480,000. It has a useful life of 8 years, at the end of which a salvage value of $40,000 is expected. The machine falls into the 5-year property class for accelerated cost recovery (depreciation) purposes. Due to its greater efficiency, the new machine is expected to result in an incremental annual savings of $120,000. The company's corporate tax rate is 34%, and if a loss occurs in any year on the project it is assumed that the company will receive a tax credit of 34% of such loss.

a. What are the incremental cash inflows over the 8 years and what is the incremental cash outflow at time 0?

b. What is the project's net present value if the required rate of return is 14%?

3. The Platte River Perfect Cooker Company is evaluating three investment situations: (1) produce a new line of aluminum skillets, (2) expand its existing cooker line to include several new sizes, and (3) develop a new higher-quality line of cookers. If only the project in question is undertaken, the expected present values and the amounts of investment required are

Project	Investment Required	Present Value of Future Cash Flows
1	$200,000	$290,000
2	115,000	185,000
3	270,000	400,000

If projects 1 and 2 are jointly undertaken, there will be no economies; the investments required and present values will simply be the sum of the parts. With projects 1 and 3, economies are possible in investment because one of the machines acquired can be used in both production processes. The total investment required for projects 1 and 3 combined is $440,000. If projects 2 and 3 are undertaken, there are economies to be achieved in marketing and producing the products but not in investment. The expected present value of future cash flows for projects 2 and 3 is $620,000. If all three projects are undertaken simultaneously, the economies noted will still hold. However, a $125,000 extension on the plant will be necessary, as space is not available for all three projects. Which project or projects should be chosen?

4. Insell Corporation is considering the acquisition of Fourier-Fox, Inc., which is in a related line of business. Fourier-Fox presently has a cash flow of $2 million per year. With a merger, synergism would be expected to result in a growth rate of this cash flow of 15% per year for 10 years, at the end of which level cash flows would be expected. To sustain the cash-flow stream, Insell will need to invest $1 million annually. For purposes of analysis and to be conservative, Insell limits its calculations of cash flows to 25 years.

a. What expected annual cash flows would Insell realize from this acquisition?

b. If its required rate of return is 18%, what is the maximum price Insell should pay?

SOLUTIONS TO SELF-CORRECTION PROBLEMS

1. a.

Year	Cash Flow	Discount Factor (15%)	Present Value
0	$ (700,000)	1.00000	$(700,000)
1	(1,000,000)	.86957	(869,570)
2	250,000	.75614	189,035
3	300,000	.65752	197,256
4	350,000	.57175	200,113
5–10	400,000	2.1638*	865,520
		Net present value =	$(117,646)

*5.0188 for 10 years (minus) 2.8550 for 4 years.

As the net present value is negative, the project is unacceptable.

b. IRR = 13.20%

c. The project would be acceptable.

d. Payback period = 6 years:

−$700,000 − $1,000,000 + $250,000 + $300,000 + $350,000 + $400,000 +$400,000 = 0

2. a. Incremental cash inflows:

1. Savings	$120,000	$120,000	$120,000	$120,000	$120,000	$120,000	$120,000	$120,000
2. Depreciation, new	96,000	153,600	92,160	55,296	55,296	27,648		
3. Depreciation, old	15,000	15,000	15,000	15,000	15,000	15,000	15,000	15,000
4. Incremental depreciation	$ 81,000	$138,600	$ 77,160	$ 40,296	$ 40,290	$ 12,648	$(15,000)	$(15,000)
5. Profit before tax (1)-(4)	39,000	(18,600)	42,840	79,704	79,704	107,352	135,000	135,000
6. Taxes (34%)	13,260	(6,324)	14,566	27,099	27,099	36,500	45,900	45,900
7. Operating cash flow (1)-(6)	$106,740	$126,324	$105,434	$92,901	$92,901	$83,500	$74,100	$74,100
8. Salvage value x (1 – .34)								26,400
9. Net cash flow	$106,740	$126,324	$105,434	$92,901	$92,901	$83,500	$74,100	$100,50

Incremental cash outflow:

Cost – Sale of old machines – Tax savings on book loss
$480,000 – $70,000 – .34 ($120,000 – $70,000) = $393,000

b. Net present value of $393,000 outflow and the cash inflows on line 9 above at 24% = $75,139. The project is acceptable.

3.

Project	Investment Required	Present Value of Future Cash Flows	Net Present Value
1	$200,000	$290,000	$ 90,000
2	115,000	185,000	70,000
3	270,000	400,000	130,000
1 and 2	315,500	475,000	160,000
1 and 3	440,000	690,000	250,000
2 and 3	385,000	620,000	235,000
1, 2, and 3	680,000	910,000	230,000

Projects 1 and 3 should be chosen, as they provide the highest net present value.

4. a.

Year	Cash Flow	Investment	Net Cash Flow	Present Value of Net Cash Flow (18%)
1	$2,300,000	$1,000,000	$1,300,000	$ 1,101,698
2	2,645,000	1,000,000	1,645,000	1,181,406
3	3,041,750	1,000,000	2,041,750	1,242,670
4	3,498,013	1,000,000	2,498,013	1,288,450
5	4,022,714	1,000,000	3,022,714	1,321,259
6	4,626,122	1,000,000	3,626,122	1,343,224
7	5,320,040	1,000,000	4,320,040	1,356,147
8	6,118,046	1,000,000	5,118,046	1,361,605
9	7,035,753	1,000,000	6,035,753	1,360,821
10–25	8,091,116	1,000,000	7,091,116	8,253,350
			Total present value =	$19,810,630

b. The maximum price that is justified is approximately $19.8 million. It should be noted that these calculations use present-value tables. For cash flows going from years 10 to 25, we subtract the discount factor for 9 years of annuity payments, 4.3030, in Table B at the back of the book from that for 25 years, 5.4669. The difference 5.4669 - 4.3030 = 1.1639 is the discount factor for cash flows for an annuity starting in year 10 and going through year 25. If a present-value function of a calculator is used, a slightly different total may be given due to rounding in the present-value tables.

PROBLEMS

Lobears, Inc. is considering two investment proposals, labeled project A and project B, with the characteristics shown in the accompanying table.

| | | Project A | | | Project B | |
| | | Profit | Net Cash | | Profit | Net Cash |
Period	Cost	after Taxes	Flow	Cost	after Taxes	Flow
0	$9,000	—	—	$12,000	—	—
1		$1,000	$5,000		$1,000	$5,000
2		1,000	4,000		1,000	5,000
3		1,000	3,000		4,000	8,000

1. For each project, compute its average rate of return, its payback period, and its net present value, using a discount rate of 15%.

   What criticisms may be offered against the average-rate-of-return method as a capital budgeting technique? What criticisms may be offered against the payback method

2. Zaire Electronics can make either of two investments at time 0. Assuming a required rate of return of 14%, determine for each project (a) the payback period; (b) the net present value; (c) the profitability index; and (d) the internal rate of return. Assume the accelerated cost recovery system for depreciation and that the asset falls in the 5-year property class and the corporate tax rate is 34%.

| | | | | | Period | | | |
Project	Cost	1	2	3	4	5	6	7
A	$28,000	$8,000	$8,000	$8,000	$8,000	$8,000	$8,000	$8,000
B	20,000	5,000	5,000	6,000	6,000	7,000	7,000	7,000

3. Two mutually exclusive projects have projected cash flows as follows:

| | | | Period | | |
Project	0	1	2	3	4
A	-$10,000	$5,000	$5,000	$5,000	$ 5,000
B	-10,000	0	0	0	30,000

   a. Determine the internal rate of return for each project.
   b. Assuming a required rate of return of 10%, determine the net present value for each project.
   c. Which project would you select? What assumptions are inherent in your decision?

4. The Lake Tahoe Ski Resort is studying a half-dozen capital improvement projects. It has allocated $1 million for capital budgeting purposes. The following proposals and associated profitability indexes have been determined. The projects themselves are independent of one another.

Project	Amount	Profitability Index
Extend ski lift 3	$500,000	1.21
Build a new sports shop	150,000	.95
Extend ski lift 4	350,000	1.20
Build a new restaurant	450,000	1.18
Add to housing complex	200,000	1.20
Build an indoor skating rink	400,000	1.05

a. With strict capital rationing, which of these investments should be undertaken?

b. Is this an optimal strategy?

5. An investment has an inflow of $200 today, an outflow of $300 at the end of 1 year, and an inflow of $400 at the end of 2 years. What is its internal rate of return? (Hint: Try calculating NPVs for a wide range of required returns.)

SECTION VIII
WORKING-CAPITAL MANAGEMENT

CHAPTER 14

WORKING-CAPITAL AND LIQUID ASSET MANAGEMENT

Traditionally, working capital has been defined as the firm's investment in current assets. Current assets comprise all assets that the firm expects to convert into cash within the year, including cash, marketable securities, accounts receivable, and inventories. Managing the firm's working capital, however, has come to mean more than simply managing the firm's investment in current assets. In fact, a more descriptive title for this chapter might be "Net Working-Capital Management," where net working capital refers to the difference in the firm's current assets and its current liabilities:

Net Working Capital = Current Assets – Current Liabilities

Thus, in managing the firm's net working capital, we are concerned with managing the firm's liquidity. This entails managing three important types of current assets:

1. Cash
2. Marketable securities
3. Accounts receivable and inventory.

This chapter provides the basic principles underlying the analysis of each of these assets

WORKING-CAPITAL MANAGEMENT

The importance of working-capital management cannot be overstated. As we will see, for many firms current assets represent over half of the total assets. Moreover, surveys of financial managers indicate that the majority of their time is taken by the management of the day-to-day operations of the firm. This is largely the management of current assets and liabilities. Managers must make sure the firm has enough working capital to operate the business cost effectively. For smaller firms, working-capital management takes on even greater importance. For smaller firms, access to capital markets, and the long-term sources of financing they supply, is limited. As such, smaller firms are forced to rely more heavily on short-term sources of financing, such as trade credit, accounts receivable, and inventory loans.

APPROPRIATE LEVEL OF WORKING CAPITAL

Managing the firm's net working capital (its liquidity) has been shown to involve simultaneous and interrelated decisions regarding investment in current assets and use of current liabilities. Fortunately, a guiding principle exists that can be used as a benchmark for the firm's working-capital policies: the hedging principle, or principle of self-liquidating debt.

Hedging Principle

Very simply, the hedging principle involves matching the cash-flow-generating characteristics of an asset with the maturity of the source of financing used to finance its acquisition. For example, a seasonal expansion in inventories, according to the hedging principle, should be financed with a short-term loan or current liability. The rationale underlying the rule is straightforward. Funds are needed for a limited period, and when that time has passed, the cash needed to repay the loan will be generated by the sale of the extra inventory items. Obtaining the needed funds from a long-term source (longer than one year) would mean that the firm would still have the funds after the inventories they helped finance had been sold. In this case the firm would have "excess" liquidity which it either holds in cash or invests in low-yield marketable securities until the seasonal increase in inventories occurs again and the funds are needed. The result of all this would be an overall lowering of firm profits.

Consider an example in which a firm purchases a new conveyor belt system, which is expected to produce cash savings to the firm by eliminating the need for two laborers and, consequently, their salaries. This amounts to an annual savings of $14,000, whereas the conveyor belt costs $150,000 to install and will last 20 years. If the firm chooses to finance this asset with a 1-year note, then it will not be able to repay the loan from the $14,000 cash flow generated by the asset. In accordance with the hedging principle, the firm should finance the asset with a source of financing that more nearly matches the expected life and cash-flow-generating characteristics of the asset. In this case, a 15- to 20-year loan would be more appropriate.

PERMANENT INVESTMENTS AND TEMPORARY ASSET INVESTMENTS

The notion of maturity matching in the hedging principle can be most easily understood when we think in terms of the distinction between permanent and temporary investments in assets as opposed to the more traditional fixed and current asset categories. A permanent investment in an asset is an investment that the firm expects to hold for a period longer than one year. Note that we are referring to the period the firm plans to hold an investment, not the useful life of the asset. For example, permanent investments are made in the firm's minimum level of current assets, as well as in its fixed assets. Temporary asset investments, on the other hand, are composed of current assets that will be liquidated and not replaced within the current year. Thus, some part of the firm's current assets is permanent and the remainder is temporary For example, a seasonal increase in level of inventories is a temporary investment; the buildup in inventories will be eliminated when it is no longer needed.

TEMPORARY, PERMANENT, AND SPONTANEOUS SOURCES OF FINANCING

Since total assets must always equal the sum of temporary, permanent, and spontaneous sources of financing, the hedging approach provides the financial manager with the basis for determining the sources of financing to use at any point.

Now, what constitutes a temporary, permanent, or spontaneous source of financing? Temporary sources of financing consist of current liabilities. Short-term notes payable constitute the most common example of a temporary source of financing. Examples of notes payable include unsecured bank loans, commercial paper, and loans secured by accounts receivable and inventories. Permanent sources of financing include intermediate-term loans, long-term debt, preferred stock, and common equity.

Spontaneous sources of financing consist of trade credit and other accounts payable that arise spontaneously in the firm's day-to-day operations. For example, as the firm acquires materials for its inventories, trade credit is often made available spontaneously or on demand from the firm's suppliers. Trade credit appears on the firm's balance sheet as accounts payable, and the size of the accounts payable balance varies directly with the firm's purchases of inventory items. In turn, inventory purchases are related to anticipated sales. Thus, part of the financing needed by the firm is spontaneously provided in the form of trade credit.

In addition to trade credit, wages and salaries payable, accrued interest, and accrued taxes also provide valuable sources of spontaneous financing. These expenses accrue throughout the period until they are paid. For example, if a firm has a wage expense of $10,000 a week and pays its employees monthly, then its employees effectively provide financing equal to $10,000 by the end of the first week following a payday, $20,000 by the end of the second week, and so forth. Since these expenses generally arise in direct conjunction with the firm's ongoing operations, they too are referred to as spontaneous.

Before proceeding to our discussion of liquid asset management, it will be helpful to distinguish among several terms. Cash is the currency and coin the firm has on hand in petty cash drawers, in cash registers, or in checking accounts (i.e., demand deposit accounts) at the various commercial banks. Marketable securities, also called near cash or near-cash assets, are security investments that the firm can quickly convert into cash balances. Generally, firms hold marketable securities with very short maturity periods (less than one year). Together, cash and marketable securities constitute the most liquid assets of a firm.

WHY A COMPANY HOLDS CASH

Companies hold cash for several reasons:

(1)   Transactions purposes
(2)   Precautionary purposes
(3)   Speculative purposes

The transactions purposes. Balances held for transactions purposes allow the firm to meet cash needs that arise in the ordinary course of doing business. Transactions balances would be used to meet the irregular outflows as well as the planned acquisition of fixed assets and inventories.

The relative amount of cash needed to satisfy transactions requirements is affected by a number of factors, such as the industry in which the firm operates. It is well known that utilities can forecast cash receipts quite accurately because of stable demand for their services. Computer software firms, however, have a more difficult time predicting their cash flows. New products are brought to market at a rapid pace, thereby making it difficult to project cash flows and balances precisely.

The precautionary purposes. Precautionary balances are a buffer stock of liquid assets. The purpose for holding these liquid assets relates to the maintenance of balances that can be used to satisfy possible, but as yet indefinite, needs.

Cash flow predictability also has a material influence on the firm's demand for cash through this precautionary motive. The airline industry provides a typical illustration. Air passenger carriers are plagued with a high degree of cash flow uncertainty. The weather, rising fuel costs, and continual strikes by operating personnel make cash forecasting difficult for any airline. The upshot of this problem is that because of all the things that might happen, the minimum cash balances desired by the management of the air carriers tend to be large.

In actual business practice, the precautionary motive is met to a large extent by the holding of a portfolio of liquid assets, not just cash. Notice in Exhibit 14-1 the two-way flow of funds between the company's holdings of cash and marketable securities. In large corporate organizations, funds may flow either into or out of the marketable securities portfolio on a daily basis.

The speculative purposes. Cash is held for speculative purposes in order to take advantage of potential profit-making situations. Construction firms that build private dwellings will at times accumulate cash in anticipation of a significant drop in lumber costs. If the price of building supplies does drop, the companies that built up their cash balances stand to profit by purchasing materials in large quantities. This will reduce their cost of goods sold and increase their net profit margin. Generally, the speculative motive is the least important component of a firm's preference for liquidity. The transactions and precautionary motives account for most of the reasons why a company holds cash balances.

CASH MANAGEMENT OBJECTIVES AND DECISIONS

The Risk-Return Tradeoff

A company-wide cash-management program must be concerned with minimizing the firm's risk of insolvency. In the context of cash management, the term insolvency describes the situation where the firm is unable to meet its maturing liabilities on time. In such a case the company is technically insolvent in that it lacks the necessary liquidity to make prompt payment on its current debt obligations. A firm could avoid this problem by carrying large cash balances to pay the bills that come due.

The financial manager must strike an acceptable balance between holding too much cash and too little cash. This is the focal point of the risk-return tradeoff. A large cash investment minimizes the chances of insolvency, but penalizes company profitability. A small cash investment frees excess balances for investment in both marketable securities and longer-lived assets; this enhances company profitability and the value of the firm's common shares, but increases the chances of running out of cash.

The Objectives

The risk-return tradeoff can be reduced to two prime objectives for the firm's cash-management system:

1. Enough cash must be on hand to meet the disbursal needs that arise in the course of doing business.
2. Investment in idle cash balances must be reduced to a minimum.

Evaluation of these operational objectives, and a conscious attempt on the part of management to meet them, gives rise to the need for some typical cash-management decisions.

THE DECISIONS

Two conditions or ideals would allow the firm to operate for extended periods with cash balances near or at a level of zero; (1) a completely accurate forecast of net cash flows over the planning horizon and (2) perfect synchronization of cash receipts and disbursements. Cash flow forecasting is the initial step in any effective cash-management program. Given that the firm will, as a matter of necessity, invest in some cash balances, certain types of decisions related to the size of those balances dominate the cash-management process. These include decisions that answer the following questions:

1. What can be done to speed up cash collections and slow down or better control cash outflows?
2. What should be the composition of a marketable securities portfolio?
   The remainder of this chapter dwells on these two questions.

COLLECTION AND DISBURSEMENT PROCEDURES

The efficiency of the firm's cash management program can be enhanced by knowledge and use of various procedures aimed at (1) accelerating cash receipts and (2) improving the methods used to disburse cash. We will see that greater opportunity for corporate profit improvement lies with the cash receipts side of the funds flow process, although it would be unwise to ignore opportunities for favorably affecting cash-disbursement practices.

Managing the Cash Inflow

The reduction of float lies at the center of the many approaches employed to speed up cash receipts. Float (or total float) has four elements:

1. **Mail float** is caused by the time lapse from the moment a customer mails a remittance check until the firm begins to process it.
2. **Processing float** is caused by the time required for the firm to process remittance checks before they can be deposited in the bank.
3. **Transit float** is caused by the time necessary for a deposited check to clear through the commercial banking system and become usable funds to the company. Credit is deferred for a maximum of two business days on checks that are cleared through the Federal Reserve System.
4. **Disbursing float** derives from the fact that funds are available in the company's bank account until its payment check has cleared through the banking system.

Float reduction can yield considerable benefits in terms of usable fluids that are released for company use and returns produced on such freed-up balances. For example, a major computer company reported total revenues of $64.8 billion. The amount of usable funds that would be released if IBM could achieve a one-day reduction in float can be approximated by dividing annual revenues (sales) by the number of days in a year. In this case one day's freed-up balances would be

$$\frac{\text{annual revenues}}{\text{days in years}} = \frac{\$64,800,000,000}{365} = \$177,534,247$$

If these released fluids, which represent one day's sales, of approximately $177.5 million could be invested to return 6% a year, then the annual value of the one-day float reduction would be

$$\text{(sales per day)} \times \text{(assumed yield)}$$
$$\$177,534,247 \times .06 = \$10,652,055$$

It is clear that effective cash management can yield impressive opportunities for profit improvement. Let us look now at specific techniques for reducing float.

The lock-box arrangement. The lock-box arrangement is the most widely used commercial banking service for expediting cash gathering. Banks have offered this service since 1946. Such a system speeds up the conversion of receipts into usable funds by reducing both mail and processing float. In addition, it is possible to reduce transit float if lock boxes are located near Federal Reserve Banks and their branches.

Exhibit 14-1 shows a simple lock-box arrangement. The firm's customers are instructed to mail their remittance checks not to company headquarters or regional offices, but to a numbered post office box. The bank that is providing the lock-box service is authorized to open the box, collect the mail, process the checks, and deposit the checks directly into the company's account. Typically a large bank will collect payments from the lock box at one- to two-hour intervals, 365 days of the year. During peak business hours, the bank may pick up mail every 30 minutes. Once the mail is received at the bank, the checks will be examined, totaled, photocopied, and microfilmed. A deposit

Exhibit 14-1   Ordinary Cash-Gathering System

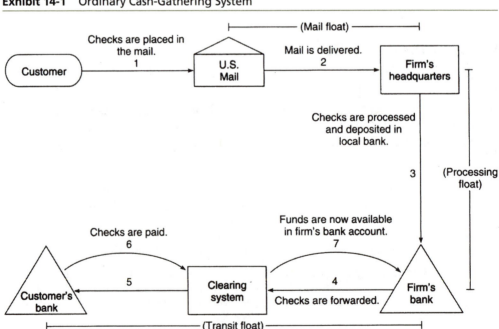

form is then prepared by the bank, and each batch of processed checks is forwarded to the collection department for clearance. Funds deposited in this manner are usually available for company use in one business day or less.

In our earlier example we determined that the company's sales per day were $177.5 million, now let's assume the firm could invest its excess cash in marketable securities to yield 6% annually. If the computer company could speed up its cash collections by four days, the results would be startling. The gross annual savings to the company (apart from the cost of operating the lock-box system) would amount to $42.6 million, as follows:

$$\text{(sales per day)} \times \text{(days of float reduction)} \times \text{(assumed yield)}$$
$$\$177,534,247 \times 4 \text{ days} \times .06 = \$42,608,219$$

As you might guess, the prospects for generating revenues of this magnitude are important not only to the firms involved, but also to commercial banks that offer lock-box services.

The benefits of a lock-box arrangement are these:

1. Increased working cash. The time required for converting receivables into available funds is reduced. This frees up cash for use elsewhere in the enterprise.

2. Elimination of clerical functions. The bank takes over the tasks of receiving, endorsing, totaling, and depositing checks. With less handling of receipts by employees, better audit control is achieved and the chance of documents becoming lost is reduced.

3. Early knowledge of dishonored checks. Should a customer's check be uncollectible because of lack of funds, it is returned, usually by special handling, to the firm.

These benefits are not free. Usually, the bank levies a charge for each check processed through the system. The benefits derived from the acceleration of receipts must exceed the incremental costs of the lock-box arrangement or the firm would be better off without it.

EVALUATING COSTS OF CASH-MANAGEMENT SERVICES

A form of breakeven analysis can help the financial officer decide whether a particular collection or disbursement service will provide an economic benefit to the firm. The evaluation process involves a very basic relationship in micro-economics:

$$\text{added costs} = \text{added benefits}$$

If this equation holds exactly, then the firm is no better or worse off for having adopted the given service. We will illustrate this procedure in terms of the desirability of installing an additional lock box. The above equation can be restated on a per-unit basis as follows:

$$P = (D) \times (S) \times (i)$$

where

P = increases in per-check processing cost if the new system is adopted
D = days saved in the collection process (float reduction)
S = average check size in dollars
i = the daily, before-tax opportunity cost (rate of return) of carrying cash

Assume now that check processing cost, P, will rise by $.18 a check if the lock box is used. The firm has determined that the average check size, S, that will be mailed to the lock-box location will be $900. If funds are freed by use of the lock box, they will be invested in marketable securities to yield an annual before-tax return of 6%. With these data it is possible to determine the reduction in check collection time, D, that is required to justify use of the lock box. That level of D is found to be

$$\$.18 = D \ (\$900) \ (06/365)$$
$$\$.18 = D \ \$900 \times .000164384$$
$$\$.18 = D \ .1479$$
$$\$.18/.1479 = D$$
$$1.217 \ days = D$$

Thus, the lock box is justified if the firm can speed up its collections by more than 1.217 days. This same style of analysis can be adapted to analyze the other tools of cash management.

Preauthorized checks (PACs). Whereas the lock-box arrangement can often reduce total float by two to four days, for some firms the use of PACs can be an even more effective way of converting receipts into working cash. A PAC resembles the ordinary check, but it does not contain nor require the signature of the person on whose account it is being drawn. A PAC is created only with the individual's legal authorization.

The PAC system is advantageous when the firm regularly receives a large volume of payments of a fixed amount from the same customers. This type of cash management service has proved useful to insurance companies, savings and loan associations, consumer credit firms, leasing enterprises, and charitable and religious organizations. The objective of this system is to reduce both mail and processing. The operation of a PAC system involves the following sequence of events:

1. The firm's customers authorize it to draw checks on their respective demand deposit accounts.
2. Indemnification agreements are signed by the customers and forwarded to the banks where they maintain their demand deposit accounts. These agreements authorize the banks to honor the PACs when they are presented for payment through the commercial bank clearing system.
3. The firm prepares a magnetic tape that contains all appropriate information about the regular payments.
4. At each processing cycle (monthly, weekly, semimonthly) the corporation retains a hard copy listing of all tape data for control purposes. Usually, the checks that are about to be printed will be deposited in the firm's demand deposit account, so a deposit ticket will also be forwarded to the bank.
5. Upon receipt of the tape the bank will produce the PACs, deposit them to the firm's account, forward them for clearing through the commercial banking system, and return a control report to the firm.

For firms that can take advantage of a PAC system, the benefits include the following:

1. Highly predictable cash flows.
2. Reduced expenses. Billing and postage costs are eliminated, and the clerical processing of customer payments is significantly reduced.
3. Customer preference. Many customers prefer not to be bothered with a regular billing. With a PAC system the check is actually written for the customer and the payment made even if he or she is on vacation or otherwise out of town.
4. Increased working cash. Mail float and processing float can be dramatically reduced in comparison with other payment processing systems.

Depository transfer checks. Both depository transfer checks and wire transfers are used in conjunction with what is known as concentration banking. A concentration bank is one where the firm maintains a major disbursing account.

In an effort to accelerate collections, many companies have established multiple collection centers. Rather than have funds sitting in these multiple bank accounts in different geographic regions of the country, most firms will regularly transfer the surplus balances to one or more concentration banks. Centralizing the firm's pool of cash provides the following benefits:

1. Lower levels of excess cash. Desired cash balance target levels are set for each regional bank. These target levels consider both compensating balance requirements and necessary working levels of cash. Cash in excess of the target levels can be transferred regularly to concentration banks for deployment by the firm's top-level management.

2. Better control. With more cash held in fewer accounts, stricter control over available cash is achieved. Quite simply, there are fewer problems. The concentration banks can prepare sophisticated reports that detail corporate wide movements of funds into and out of the central cash pool.

3. More efficient investments in near-cash assets. The coupling of information from the firm's cash forecast with data on available funds supplied by the concentration banks allows the firm to transfer cash quickly to the marketable securities portfolio.

Major banks claim that funds transferred by use of the automated depository transfer check system can become available for company use in one business day or less.

Wire Transfers. The fastest way to move cash between banks is by use of wire transfers, which eliminate transit float. Funds moved in this manner, then, immediately become usable funds or "good funds" to the firm at the receiving bank. The following two major communication facilities are used to accommodate wire transfers:

1. **Bank Wire.** Bank Wire is a private wire service used and supported by approximately 250 banks in the United States for transferring funds, exchanging credit information, or effecting securities transactions.

2. **Federal Reserve Wire System.** The Fed Wire is directly accessible to commercial banks that are members of the Federal Reserve System. A commercial bank that is not on the Bank Wire or is not a member of the Federal Reserve System can use the wire transfer through its correspondent bank.

Wire transfers are often initiated on a standing-order basis. By means of a written authorization from company headquarters, a local depository bank might be instructed to transfer funds regularly to the firm's concentration bank.

As might be expected, wire transfers are a relatively expensive method of marshaling funds through a firm's money management system. Generally, the movement of small amounts does not justify the use of wire transfers.

Management of Cash Outflow

Significant techniques and systems for improving the firm's management of cash disbursements include (1) zero balance accounts, (2) payable-through drafts, and (3) remote disbursing. The first two offer markedly better control over company wide payments, and as a secondary benefit they increase disbursement float. The last technique, remote disbursing, aims solely to increase disbursement float.

Zero balance accounts (ZBA) permit centralized control (at the headquarters level) over cash outflows while maintaining divisional disbursing authority. Under this system the firm's authorized employees, representing their various divisions, continue to write checks on their individual accounts. Note that the numerous individual disbursing accounts are now all located in the same concentration bank. Actually, these separate accounts contain no funds at all, thus their appropriate label, "zero balance." These accounts have all the characteristics of regular demand deposit accounts including separate titles, numbers, and statements.

Managing the cash outflow through use of a ZBA system offers the following benefits to the firm with many operating units:

1. Centralized control over disbursements is achieved, even though payment authority continues to rest with operating units.
2. Management time spent on superficial cash-management activities is reduced. Exercises, such as observing the balances held in numerous bank accounts, transferring funds to those accounts short of cash, and reconciling the accounts, demand less attention.
3. Excess balances held in outlying accounts can be reduced.
4. The costs of cash management can be reduced as wire transfers to build up funds in outlying disbursement accounts are eliminated.
5. Funds may be made available for company use through an increase in disbursement float. When local bank accounts are used to pay nearby suppliers, the checks clear rapidly. The same checks, if drawn on a ZBA located in a more distant concentration bank, will take more time to clear against the disbursing firm's account.

Payable-through drafts. Payable-through drafts are legal instruments that have the physical appearance of ordinary checks but are not drawn on a bank. Instead, payable-through drafts are drawn on and payment is authorized by the issuing firm against its demand deposit account. Like checks, the drafts are cleared through the banking system and are presented to the issuing firm's bank. The bank serves as a collection point and passes the drafts on to the firm. The corporate issuer usually has to return by the following business day all drafts it does not wish to cover (pay). Those documents not returned to the bank are automatically paid. The firm inspects the drafts for validity by checking signatures, amounts, and dates. Stop-payment orders can be initiated by the company on any drafts considered inappropriate.

The main purpose of using a payable-through draft system is to provide for effective control over field payments. Central office control over payments begun by regional units is provided as the drafts are reviewed in advance of final payment. Payable through drafts, for example, are used extensively in the insurance industry. The claims agent does not typically have check-signing authority against a corporate disbursement account. This agent can issue a draft, however, for quick settlement of a claim.

The Federal Reserve System requires transfer of available or "good" funds upon presentation of drafts to the payable-through bank. The payable-through bank will cover drafts but will be reluctant to absorb the float that would occur until the issuing firm authorized payment the next business day. Therefore, the drafts that are presented for payment will usually be charged in total against the corporate master demand deposit account. This is for purposes of measuring usable funds available to the firm on that day. Legal payment of the individual drafts will still take place after their review and approval by the firm.

Remote disbursing. A few banks will provide the corporate customer with a cash management service specifically designed to extend disbursing float. The firm's concentration bank may have a correspondent relationship with a smaller bank located in a distant city. In that remote city the Federal Reserve System is unable to maintain frequent clearings of checks drawn on local banks. For example, a firm that is located in Dallas and maintains its master account there may open an account with a bank situated in, say, Amarillo, Texas. The firm will write the bulk of its payment checks against the account in the Amarillo bank. The checks will probably take at least one business day longer to clear, so the firm can "play the float" to its advantage.

A firm must use this technique of remote disbursing with extreme care. If a key supplier of raw materials located in Dallas has to wait the extra day for funds drawn on the Amarillo account, the possibility of incurring ill will might outweigh the apparent gain from an increase in the disbursing float. The impact on the firm's reputation of using remote disbursing should be explicitly evaluated. The practice of remote disbursing is discouraged by the Federal Reserve System.

Before moving on to a discussion of the firm's marketable securities portfolio, it will be helpful to draw together the preceding material. Exhibit 14-2 summarizes the salient features of the cash-collection and disbursal techniques we have considered here.

Exhibit 14-2 Features of Selected Cash-Collection and Disbursal Techniques: Summary

1. Lock-box system	Reduce (1) mail float, (2) processing float, and (3) transit float.	Strategic location of lock boxes to reduce mail float and transit float. Firm's commercial bank has access to lock box to reduce processing float.
2. Preauthorized checks	Reduce (1) mail float and (2) processing float.	The firm writes the checks (the PACs) for its customers to be charged against their demand deposit accounts.
3. (Ordinary) Depository transfer checks	Eliminate excess funds in regional banks.	Used in conjunction with concentration banking whereby the firm maintains several collection centers. The transfer check authorizes movement of funds from a local bank to the concentration bank.
4. Automated depository transfer checks	Eliminate the mail float associated with the ordinary transfer check.	Telecommunications company transmits deposit data to the firm's concentration bank.
5. Wire transfers	Move funds immediately between banks. This eliminates transit float in that only "good funds" are transferred.	Use of Bank Wire or the Federal Reserve Wire System.
Cash-Disbursal Techniques		
1. Zero balance accounts	(1) Achieve better control over cash payments, (2) reduce excess cash balances held in regional banks, and (3) possibly increase disbursing float.	Establish zero balance accounts for all of the firm's disbursing units. These accounts are all in the same concentration bank. Checks are drawn against these accounts, with the balance in each account never exceeding $0. Divisional disbursing authority is thereby maintained at the local level of management.
2. Payable-through drafts	Achieve effective central office control over field-authorized payments.	Field office issues drafts rather than checks to settle up payables.
3. Remote disbursing	Extend disbursing float.	Write checks against demand deposit accounts held in distant banks.

MARKETABLE SECURITIES PORTFOLIO

Once the design of the firm's cash receipts and payments system has been determined, the financial manager faces the task of selecting appropriate financial assets for inclusion in the firm's marketable securities portfolio.

General Selection Criteria

Certain criteria can provide the financial manager with a useful framework for selecting a proper marketable securities mix. These considerations include evaluation of the following:

(1) financial risk

(2) interest rate risk

(3) liquidity

(4) taxability

(5) yields

We will briefly delineate these criteria from the investor's viewpoint.

Financial risk. Financial risk here refers to the uncertainty of expected returns from a security attributable to possible changes in the financial capacity of the security issuer to make future payments to the security owner. If the chance of default on the terms of the instrument is high (low), then the financial risk is said to be high (low).

In both financial practice and research, when estimates of risk-free returns are desired, the yields available on Treasury securities are consulted and the safety of other financial instruments is weighed against them.

Interest rate risk. Interest rate risk refers to the uncertainty of expected returns from a financial instrument attributable to changes in interest rates. Of particular concern to the corporate treasurer is the price volatility associated with instruments that have long, as opposed to short, terms to maturity. To hedge against the price volatility caused by interest rate risk, the firm's marketable securities portfolio will tend to be composed of instruments that mature over short periods.

Liquidity. In the present context of managing the marketable securities portfolio, liquidity refers to the ability to transform a security into cash. Should an unforeseen event require that a significant amount of cash be immediately available, then a sizable portion of the portfolio might have to be sold. The financial manager will want the cash quickly and will not want to accept a large price concession in order to convert the securities. Thus, in the formulation of preferences for the inclusion of particular instruments in the portfolio, the manager must consider (1) the period needed to sell the security and (2) the likelihood that the security can be sold at or near its prevailing market price.

Taxability. The tax treatment of the income a firm receives from its security investments does not affect the ultimate mix of the marketable securities portfolio as much as the criteria mentioned earlier. This is because the interest income from most instruments suitable for inclusion in the portfolio is taxable at the federal level. Still, some corporate treasurers seriously evaluate the taxability of interest income and capital gains.

The interest income from only one class of securities escapes the federal income tax. That class of securities is generally referred to as **municipal obligations,** or more simply as **municipals**. Because of the tax-exempt feature of interest income from state and local government securities, municipals sell at lower yields to maturity in the market than do securities that pay taxable interest. The after-tax yield on a municipal obligation, however, could be higher than the yield from a non-tax-exempt security. This would depend mainly on the purchasing firm's tax situation.

Consider Exhibit 14-3. A firm is assumed to be analyzing whether to invest in a one-year tax-free debt issue yielding 6% on a $1,000 outlay or a one-year taxable issue that yields 8% on a $1,000 outlay. The firm pays federal taxes at the rate of 34%. The yields quoted in the financial press and in the prospectuses that describe debt issues are before-tax returns. The actual after-tax return enjoyed by the investor depends on his or her tax bracket. Notice that the actual after-tax yield received by the firm is only 5.28% on the taxable issue versus 6% on the tax-exempt obligation. The lower portion of Exhibit 14-5 shows that the fully taxed bond must yield 9.091% to make it comparable with the tax-exempt issue.

Exhibit 14-3 Comparison of After-Tax Yields

	Tax-exempt Debt Issue (6% Coupon)	Taxable Debt Issue (8% Coupon)
Interest income	$ 60.00	$ 80.00
Income tax (.34)	0.00	27.20
After-tax interest income	$ 60.00	$ 52.80
After-tax yield	$ 60.00 = 6%	$ 52.80 = 5.28%
	$1,000.00	$1,000.00

Derivation of equivalent before-tax yield on a taxable debt issue:

$$r = \frac{r^*}{1-T} = \frac{.06}{1-.34} = 9.901\%$$

where r = equivalent before-tax yield,
r* = after-tax yield on tax-exempt security,
T = firm's marginal income tax rate.

Proof: Interest income [$1,000 × .09091]	= $90.91
Income tax (.34)	30.91
After-tax interest income	**$60.00**

Yields. The final selection criterion that we mention is a significant one—the yields that are available on the different financial assets suitable for inclusion in the near cash portfolio. By now it is probably obvious that the factors of (1) financial risk, (2) interest rate risk, (3) liquidity, and (4) taxability all influence the available yields on financial instruments. The yield criterion involves an evaluation of the risks and benefits inherent in all of these factors. If a given risk is assumed, such as lack of liquidity, a higher yield may be expected on the non-liquid instrument. Exhibit 14-4 summarizes our framework for designing the firm's marketable securities portfolio. These four basic considerations are shown to influence the yields available on securities. The financial manager must focus on the risk-return tradeoffs identified through analysis. Coming to grips with these tradeoffs will enable the financial manager to determine the proper marketable securities mix for the company.

Let us look now at the marketable securities prominent in firms' near-cash portfolios.

Marketable Security Alternatives

U.S. Treasury bills. U.S. Treasury bills, or T-bills, are the best known and most popular short-term investment outlet among firms. A T-bill is a direct obligation of the United States government sold on a regular basis by the U.S. Treasury. New T-bills are issued in denominations of $10,000, $15,000, $50,000, $100,000, $500,000, and $1,000,000. In

Exhibit 14-4 Designing the Marketable Securities Portfolio

Considerations	→	Influence	→	Focus Upon	→	Determine
Financial risk		Yields		Risk vs. return		Marketable
Interest rate risk				preferences		securities
Liquidity						mix
Taxability						

effect, therefore, one can buy bills in multiples of $5,000 above the smallest purchase price of $10,000 by combining $10,000 bills and $15,000 bills to reach the desired sum.

Bills currently are regularly offered with maturities of 91, 182, and 365 days. The three-month and six-month bills are auctioned weekly by the Treasury, and the one-year bills are offered every four weeks. Bids (orders to purchase) are accepted by the various Federal Reserve Banks and their branches, which perform the role of agents for the Treasury. Each Monday, bids are received until 1:30 P.M.; after that time they are opened, tabulated, and forwarded to the Treasury for allocation (filling the purchase orders).

Treasury bills are sold on a discount basis; for that reason, the investor does not receive an actual interest payment. The return is the difference between the purchase price and the face (par) value of the bill.

The bills are marketed by the Treasury only in bearer form. They are purchased, therefore, without the investor's name on them. This attribute makes them easily transferable from one investor to the next. Of prime importance to the corporate treasurer is the fact that a very active secondary market exists for bills. After a bill has been acquired by the firm, should the need arise to turn it into cash, a group of securities dealers stand ready to purchase it. This highly developed secondary market for bills not only makes them extremely liquid, but also allows the firm to buy bills with maturities of a week or even less.

As bills have the full financial backing of the United States government, they are, for all practical purposes, risk free. This negligible financial risk and high degree of liquidity makes the yields lower than those obtainable on other marketable securities. The income from T-bills is subject to federal income taxes, but not to state and local government income taxes.

Federal agency securities. Federal agency securities are debt obligations of corporations and agencies that have been created to effect the various lending programs of the United States government. Five such government-sponsored corporations account for the majority of outstanding agency debt. The "big five" agencies are

1. The Federal National Mortgage Association (FNMA)
2. The Federal Home Loan Banks (FHLB)
3. The Federal Land Banks
4. The Federal Intermediate Credit Banks
5. The Banks for Cooperatives

These five federally sponsored agencies are not owned nor are they fully guaranteed by the United States government. The five agencies are entirely owned by their member associations or the general public.

These agencies sell their securities in a variety of denominations and maturities. Obligations can at times be purchased with maturities as short as 30 days or as long as 15 years. Agency debt usually sells on a coupon basis and normally pays interest to the owner on a semiannual schedule.

The income from agency debt that the investor receives is subject to taxation at the federal level. Of the "big five" agencies, only the income from FNMA issues is taxed at the state and local level.

The yields available on agency obligations will always exceed those of Treasury securities of similar maturity. This yield differential is attributable to lesser marketability and greater default risk. The financial officer might keep in mind, however, that none of these agency issues has ever gone into default.

Bankers' acceptances. Bankers' acceptances are one of the least understood instruments suitable for inclusion in the firm's marketable securities portfolio. Their part in U.S. commerce today is largely concentrated in the financing of foreign transactions. Generally, an acceptance is a draft (order to pay) drawn on a specific bank by an exporter in order to obtain payment for goods shipped to a customer, who maintains an account with that specific bank.

The usual denominations range from $25,000 to $1 million. The maturities on acceptances run from 30 to 180 days, although longer periods are available from time to time. The most common period is 90 days.

Acceptances, like T-bills, are sold on a discount basis and are payable to the bearer of the paper. A secondary market for the acceptances of large banks does exist. The income generated from investing in acceptances is fully taxable at the federal, state, and local levels. Because of their greater financial risk and lesser liquidity, acceptances provide investors a yield advantage over T-bills and agency obligations. In fact, the acceptances of major banks are a very safe investment, making the yield advantage over T-bills worth looking at from the firm's vantage point.

Negotiable certificates of deposit. A negotiable certificate of deposit, CD, is a marketable receipt for funds that have been deposited in a bank for a fixed period. The deposited funds earn a fixed rate of interest. These are not the type of CDs offered to individuals with ordinary passbook savings accounts or nonmarketable time deposits offered by all commercial banks. These CDs are offered by key banks in a variety of denominations ranging from $25,000 to $10,000,000. The popular sizes are $100,000, $500,000, and $1,000,000. The original maturities on CDs can range from 1 to 18 months.

CDs are offered by banks on a basis differing from T-bills; that is, they are not sold at a discount. Rather, when the certificate matures, the owner receives the full amount deposited plus the earned interest.

A secondary market for CDs does exist, the heart of which is found in New York City. However it is harder to liquidate large blocks of CDs because a more specialized investor must be found. The securities dealers who "make" the secondary market in CDs mainly trade in $1 million units. Smaller denominations can be traded but will bring a relatively lower price. The income received from an investment in CDs is subject to taxation at all government levels. In recent years CD yields have been above those available on bankers' acceptances.

Commercial paper. Commercial paper refers to short-term, unsecured promissory notes sold by large businesses to raise cash. These are sometimes described in the popular financial press as short-term corporate IOUs. Because they are unsecured, the issuing side of the market is dominated by large corporations. The issuing (borrowing) firm can sell the paper to a dealer who sells it to the investing public or the paper can be sold directly to the ultimate investor. Commercial paper can be bought in a wide range of denominations from $5,000 to $5 million, or even more, with maturities that range from 3 to 270 days. Notes with maturities exceeding 270 days are very rare because they would have to be registered with the Securities and Exchange Commission—a task firms avoid, when possible, because it is time consuming and costly.

For practical purposes, there is no active trading in a secondary market for commercial paper. Thus, when the financial officer evaluates commercial paper for possible inclusion in its marketable securities portfolio, the firm should plan to hold it to maturity. The return on commercial paper is fully taxable to the investor at all levels of government.

Repurchase agreements. Repurchase agreements (repos) are legal contracts that involve the actual sale of securities by a borrower to the lender, with a commitment on the part of the borrower to repurchase the securities at the contract price plus a stated interest charge. The securities sold to the lender are U.S. government issues or other instruments of the money market such as those described above. The borrower is either a major financial institution—most important, a commercial bank—or a dealer in U.S. government securities.

These agreements are usually executed in sizes of $1 million or more. The maturities may be for a specified time period or may have no fixed maturity date. In the latter case either lender or borrower may terminate the contract without advance notice. The returns the lender receives on repurchase agreements are taxed at all governmental levels. Since the interest rates are set by direct negotiation between lender and borrower, no regular published series of yields is available for direct comparison with the other short-term investments. The rates available on repurchase agreements, however, are closely related to, but generally less than, Treasury bill rates of comparable maturities.

Money market mutual funds. The money market mutual funds sell their shares to raise cash, and by pooling the funds of large numbers of small savers, they can build their liquid-asset portfolios. Many of these funds allow the investor to start an account with as little as $1,000. This small initial investment, coupled with the fact that some liquid-asset funds permit subsequent investments in amounts as small as $100, makes this type of outlet for excess cash suited to the small firm and even the individual. Furthermore, the management of a small enterprise may not be highly versed in the details of short-term investments. By purchasing shares in a liquid-asset fund, the investor is also buying managerial expertise.

Money market mutual funds typically invest in a diversified portfolio of short-term, high-grade debt instruments such as those described above. Some such funds, however, will accept more interest rate risk in their portfolios and acquire some corporate bonds and notes. Money market mutual funds offer the investing firm a high degree of liquidity. By redeeming (selling) shares, the investor can obtain cash quickly. Procedures for liquidation vary among the funds, but shares can usually be redeemed by means of (1) special redemption checks supplied by the fund, (2) telephone instructions, (3) wire instructions, or (4) a letter. When liquidation is ordered by telephone or wire, the mutual fund can remit to the investor by the next business day.

The returns earned from owning shares in a money market fund are taxable at all governmental levels. The yields follow the returns the investor could receive by purchasing the marketable securities directly.

The discussion on designing the firm's marketable securities portfolio, touched on the essential elements of several near cash assets. At times it is difficult to sort out the distinguishing features among these short-term investments. To alleviate that problem, Exhibit 14-5 draws together their principal characteristics.

ACCOUNTS RECEIVABLE MANAGEMENT

We now turn from the most liquid of the firm's current assets (cash and marketable securities) to those which are less liquid—accounts receivable and inventories. All firms by their very nature are involved in selling either goods or services. Although some of these sales will be for cash, a large portion will involve credit. Whenever a sale is made on credit, it increases the firm's accounts receivable. Thus, the importance of how a firm manages its accounts receivable depends on the degree to which the firm sells on credit.

Accounts receivable typically comprise over 25% of a firm's assets. In effect, when we discuss management of accounts receivable, we are discussing the management of one-quarter of the firm's assets. Moreover, because cash flows from a sale cannot be invested until the account is collected, control of receivables takes on added importance; efficient collection determines both profitability and liquidity of the firm.

Size of Investment in Accounts Receivable

The size of the investment in accounts receivable is determined by several factors. First, the percentage of credit sales to total sales affects the level of accounts receivable held. Although this factor certainly plays a major role in determining a firm's investment in accounts receivable, it generally is not within the control of the financial manager. The nature of the business tends to determine the blend between credit sales and cash sales

Exhibit 14-5 Features of a Selected Marketable Securities Instrument

Instrument	Denominations	Maturities	Basis	Form	Liquidity	Taxability
U.S. Treasury bills—direct obligations of the U.S. government	$10,000 15,000 50,000 100,000 500,000 1,000,000	91 days 182 days 365 days 9-month not presently issued	Discount	Bearer	Excellent secondary market	Exempt from state and local income
Federal agency securities—obligations of corporations and agencies created to effect the federal government's lending programs	Wide variation; from $1,000 to $1 million	5 days (Farm Credit consolidated system-wide discount notes) to more than 10 years	Discount or coupon; usually on coupon	Bearer or registered	Good for issues of "big five" agencies	Generally exempt at local level; FNMA issues are *not*
Bankers' acceptances—drafts accepted for future payment by commercial banks	No set size; typically range from $25,000 to $1 million	Predominantly from 30 to 180 days	Discount	Bearer	Good for acceptances of large "money market" banks	Taxed at all levels of government
Negotiable certificates of deposit—marketable receipts for funds deposited in a bank for a fixed time period	$25,000 to $10 million	1 to 18 months	Accrued interest	Bearer or registered; bearer is preferable from liquidity standpoint	Fair to good	Taxed at all levels of government
Commercial paper—short-term unsecured promissory notes	$5,000 to $5 million; $1,000 and $5,000 multiples above the initial offering size are sometimes available	3 to 270 days	Discount	Bearer	Poor; no active secondary market in usual sense	Taxed at all levels of government
Repurchase agreements—legal contracts between a borrower (security seller) and lender (security buyer). The borrower will repurchase at the contract price plus an interest charge.	Typical sizes are $500,000 or more	According to terms of contract	Not applicable	Not applicable	Fixed by the agreement; that is, borrower will repurchase	Taxed at all levels of government
Money market mutual funds—holders of diversified portfolios of short-term, high-grade debt instruments	Some require an initial investment as small as $1,000	Your shares can be sold at any time	Net asset value	Registered	Good; provided by the fund itself	Taxed at all levels of government

A large grocery store tends to sell exclusively on a cash basis, whereas most construction-lumber supply firms make their sales primarily with credit.

The level of sales is also a factor in determining the size of the investment in accounts receivable. Very simply, the more sales, the greater accounts receivable. It is not a decision variable for the financial manager, however.

The final determinants of the level of investment in accounts receivable are the credit and collection policies—more specifically, the terms of sale, the quality of customer, and collection efforts. These policies are under the control of the financial manager. The terms of sale specify both the time period during which the customer must pay and the terms, such as penalties for late payments or discounts for early payments. The type of customer or credit policy also affects the level of investment in accounts receivable. For example, the acceptance of poorer credit risks and their subsequent delinquent payments may lead to an increase in accounts receivable. The strength and timing of the collection efforts can affect the period for which past-due accounts remain delinquent, which in turn affects the level of accounts receivable. Collection and credit policy decisions may further affect the level of investment in accounts receivable by causing changes in the sales level and the ratio of credit sales to total sales.

Terms of Sale—Decision Variable

The terms of sale identify the possible discount for early payment, the discount period, and the total credit period. They are generally stated in the form a/b net c, indicating that the customer can deduct a percent if the account is paid within b days; otherwise, the account must be paid within c days. Thus, for example, trade credit terms of 2/10, net 30 indicate that a 2% discount can be taken if the account is paid within 10 days; otherwise it must be paid within 30 days. Failure to take the discount represents a cost to the customer. For instance, if the terms are 2/10, net 30, the annualized opportunity cost of passing up this 2% discount in order to withhold payment for an additional 20 days is 36.73%. This is determined as follows:

$$\left(\begin{array}{c} \text{annualized opportunity cost} \\ \text{of foregoing the discount} \end{array} \right) = \frac{a}{1-a} \times \frac{360}{c-b}$$

Substituting the values from the example, we get

$$36.73\% = \frac{.02}{1-.02} \times \frac{360}{30-10}$$

In industry the typical discount ranges anywhere from one-half percent to 1%, whereas the discount period is generally 10 days and the total credit period varies from 30 to 90 days. Although the terms of sale vary radically from industry to industry, they tend to remain relatively uniform within any particular industry. Moreover, the terms tend to remain relatively constant over time, and they do not appear to be used frequently as a decision variable.

Type of Customer—Decision Variable

A second decision variable involves determining the type of customer who is to qualify for trade credit. Several costs always are associated with extending credit to less credit-worthy customers. First, as the probability of default increases, it becomes more important to identify which of the possible new customers would be a poor risk. When more time is spent investigating the less credit-worthy customer, the costs of credit investigation increase.

Default costs also vary directly with the quality of the customer. As the customer's credit rating declines, the chance that the account will not be paid on time increases. In the extreme case, payment never occurs. Thus, taking on less credit-worthy customers results in increases in default costs.

Collection costs also increase as the quality of the customer declines. More delinquent accounts force the firm to spend more time and money collecting them. Overall, the decline in customer quality results in increased costs of credit investigation, collection, and default.

In determining whether to grant credit to an individual customer, we are primarily interested in the customer's short-run welfare. Thus, liquidity ratios, other obligations, and the overall profitability of the firm become the focal point in this analysis. Credit-rating services, such as Dun & Bradstreet, provide information on the financial status, operations, and payment history for most firms. Other possible sources of information would include credit bureaus, trade associations, Chambers of Commerce, competitors, bank references, public financial statements, and, of course, the firm's past relationship with the customer.

One way in which both individuals and firms are often evaluated as credit risks is through the use of credit scoring. Credit scoring involves the numerical evaluation of each applicant. An applicant receives a score based on his or her answers to a simple set of questions. This score is then evaluated according to a predetermined standard, its level relative to the standard determining whether credit should be extended. The major advantage of credit scoring is that it is inexpensive and easy to perform. For example, once the standards are set, a computer or clerical worker without any specialized training could easily evaluate any applicant.

The techniques used for constructing credit-scoring indexes range from the simple approach of adding up default rates associated with the answers given to each question, to sophisticated evaluations using multiple discriminate analysis (MDA). MDA is a statistical technique for calculating the appropriate importance to assign each question used in evaluating the applicant.

Collection Efforts—Decision Variable

The key to maintaining control over collection of accounts receivable is the fact that the probability of default increases with the age of the account. Thus, control of accounts receivable focuses on the control and elimination of past-due receivables. One common way of evaluating the current situation is ratio analysis. The financial manager can determine whether accounts receivable are under control by examining the average collection period, the ratio of receivables to assets, the ratio of credit sales to receivables (called the accounts receivable turnover ratio), and the amount of bad debts relative to sales over time. In addition, the manager can perform what is called an aging of accounts receivable to provide a breakdown in both dollars and in percentages of the proportion of receivables that are past due. Comparing the current aging of receivables with past data offers even more control.

Once the delinquent accounts have been identified, the firm's accounts receivable group makes an effort to collect them. For example, a past-due letter, called a dunning letter, is sent if payment is not received on time, followed by an additional dunning letter in a more serious tone if the account becomes 3 weeks past due, followed after 6 weeks by a telephone call. Finally, if the account becomes 12 weeks past due, it might be turned over to a collection agency. Again, a direct tradeoff exists between collection expenses and lost goodwill on one hand and non-collection of accounts on the other, and this tradeoff is always part of making the decision.

INVENTORY MANAGEMENT

Inventory management involves the control of the assets that are produced to be sold in the normal course of the firm's operations. The general categories of inventory include raw materials inventory, work-in-process inventory, and finished goods inventory. The importance of inventory management to the firm depends on the extent of the inventory investment. For an average firm, approximately 4.88% of all assets are in the form of inventory. However, the percentage varies widely from industry to industry. Thus, the importance of inventory management and control varies from industry to industry also. For example, it is much more important in the automotive dealer and service station trade, where inventories make up 49.72% of total assets, than in the hotel business, where the average investment in inventory is only 1.56% of total assets.

Purposes and Types of Inventory

The purpose of carrying inventories is to make each function of the business independent of each other function, so that delays or shutdowns in one area do not affect the production and sale of the final product. Because production shutdowns result in increased costs, and because delays in delivery can lose customers, the management and control of inventory are important duties of the financial manager.

Decision making in inventory investment involves a basic tradeoff between risk and return. The risk is that if the level of inventory is too low, the various functions of business do not operate independently, and delays in production and customer delivery can result. The return results because reduced inventory investment saves money. As the size of inventory increases, storage and handling costs as well as the required return on capital invested in inventory rise. Therefore, as the inventory a firm holds is increased, the risk of running out of inventory is lessened, but inventory expenses rise.

Raw Materials Inventory

Raw materials inventory consists of basic materials purchased from other firms to be used in the firm's production operations. These goods may include steel, lumber, petroleum, or manufactured items such as wire, ball bearings, or tires that the firm does not produce itself. Regardless of the specific form of the raw materials inventory, all manufacturing firms by definition maintain a raw materials inventory. Its purpose is to separate the production function from the purchasing function, so that delays in shipment of raw materials do not cause production delays. In the event of a delay in shipment, the firm can satisfy its need for raw materials by liquidating its inventory.

Work-in-Process Inventory

Work-in-process inventory consists of partially finished goods requiring additional work before they become finished goods. The more complex and lengthy the production process, the larger the investment in work-in-process inventory. The purpose of work-in-process inventory is to uncouple the various operations in the production process so that machine failures and work stoppages in one operation will not affect the other operations. Assume, for example, there are ten different production operations, each one involving the piece of work produced in the previous operation. If the machine performing the first production operation breaks down, a firm with no work-in-process inventory will have to shut down all production operations. Yet if a firm has such inventory, the remaining nine operations can continue by drawing the input for the second operation from inventory.

Finished-Goods Inventory

Finished-goods inventory consists of goods on which production has been completed but that are not yet sold. The purpose of a finished-goods inventory is to uncouple the production and sales functions so that it is not necessary to produce the good before a sale can occur; sales can be made directly out of inventory. In the auto industry, for example, people would not buy from a dealer who made them wait weeks or months when another dealer could fill the order immediately.

Stock of Cash

Although we have already discussed cash management at some length, it is worthwhile to mention cash again in the light of inventory management. This is because the stock of cash carried by a firm is simply a special type of inventory. In terms of uncoupling the various operations of the firm, the purpose of holding a stock of cash is to make the payment of bills independent of the collection of accounts due. When cash is kept on hand, bills can be paid without prior collection of accounts.

Inventory-Management Techniques

The importance of effective inventory management is directly related to the size of the investment in inventory. Effective management of these assets is essential to the goal of shareholder wealth maximization. To control the investment in inventory, management must solve two problems: the order quantity problem and the order point problem.

Order Quantity Problem

The order quantity problem involves determining the optimal order size for an inventory item given its expected usage, carrying costs, and ordering costs.

The economic order quantity (EOQ) model attempts to determine the order size that will minimize total inventory costs. It assumes that

$$\text{total inventory costs} = \text{total carrying costs} + \text{total ordering costs}$$

Assuming that inventory is allowed to fall to zero and then is immediately replenished (this assumption will be lifted when we discuss the order point problem), the average inventory becomes $Q/2$, where Q is inventory order size in units. If the average inventory is $Q/2$ and the carrying cost per unit is C, then carrying costs become:

$$\text{total carrying costs} = (\text{average inventory}) \, (\text{carrying cost per unit})$$
$$= (Q/2) \, C$$

where
Q = the inventory order size in units
C = carrying costs per unit

The carrying costs on inventory include the required rate of return on investment in inventory, in addition to warehouse or storage costs, wages for those who operate the warehouse, and costs associated with inventory shrinkage. Thus, carrying costs include both real cash flows and opportunity costs associated with having funds tied up in inventory.

The ordering costs incurred are equal to the ordering costs per order times the number of orders. If we assume total demand over the planning period is S and we order in lot sizes of Q, then S/Q represents the number of orders over the planning period. If the ordering cost per order is O, then

$$\text{total ordering costs} = (\text{number of orders}) \, (\text{ordering cost per order})$$
$$= (S/Q) \, O$$

where
S = total demand in units over the planning period
O = ordering cost per order

Thus, the total costs equation becomes

$$\text{total costs} = (Q/2)C + (S/Q)O$$

What we are looking for is the ordering size, Q*, which provides the minimum total costs. By manipulating equation (11), we find that the optimal value of Q—that is, the economic ordering quantity (EOQ)—is

$$Q^{\cdot} = \sqrt{\frac{2SO}{C}}$$

The use of the EOQ model can best be illustrated through an example. Suppose a firm expects total demand (S) for its product over the planning period to be 5,000 units, whereas the ordering cost per order (O) is $200 and the carrying cost per unit (C) is $2. Substituting these values into the equation yields

$$Q^{\cdot} = \sqrt{\frac{2 \cdot (5000) \cdot (200)}{2}} = \sqrt{1,000,000} = 1,000 \text{ units}$$

Thus, if this firm orders in 1,000-unit lot sizes, it will minimize its total inventory costs.

Order Point Problem

The two most limiting assumptions—those of constant or uniform demand and instantaneous delivery—are dealt with through the inclusion of safety stock, which is the inventory held to accommodate any unusually large and unexpected usage during delivery time. The decision on how much safety stock to hold is generally referred to as the order point problem; that is, how low should inventory be depleted before it is reordered?

Two factors go into the determination of the appropriate order point; (1) the procurement or delivery-time stock and (2) the safety stock desired. We observe that the order point problem can be separated into its two components, the delivery-time stock—that is, the inventory needed between the order date and the receipt of the inventory ordered—and the safety stock. Thus, the order point is reached when inventory falls to a level equal to the delivery-time stock plus the safety stock.

inventory order point
[order new inventory when inventory = (delivery – time stock) (safety stock)
falls to this level]

As a result of constantly carrying safety stock, the average level of inventory increases. Whereas before the inclusion of safety stock the average level of inventory was equal to EOQ/2, now it will be

$$\text{average inventory} = \frac{EOQ}{2} + \text{safety stock}$$

In general, several factors simultaneously determine how much delivery-time stock and safety stock should be held. First, the efficiency of the replenishment system affects how much delivery-time stock is needed. Because the delivery-time stock is the expected inventory usage between ordering and receiving inventory, efficient replenishment of inventory would reduce the need for delivery-time stock. The uncertainty surrounding both the delivery time and the demand for the product affects the level of safety stock needed. The more certain the patterns of these inflows and outflows from the inventory, the less safety stock required. In effect, if these inflows and outflows are highly predictable, then there is little chance of any stock-out occurring. However, if they are unpredictable, it becomes necessary to carry additional safety stock to prevent unexpected stock-outs.

The safety margin desired also affects the level of safety stock held. If it is a costly experience to run out of inventory, the safety stock held will be larger than it would be otherwise. If running out of inventory and the subsequent delay in supplying customers result in strong customer dissatisfaction and the possibility of lost future sales, then additional safety stock is necessary. A final determinant is the cost of carrying additional inventory, in terms of both the handling and storage costs and the opportunity cost associated with the investment in additional inventory. Very simply, the greater the costs, the smaller the safety stock.

EXAMINATION OF EOQ ASSUMPTIONS

Despite the fact that the EOQ model tends to yield quite good results, there are weaknesses in the EOQ model associated with several of its assumptions. When its assumptions have been dramatically violated, the EOQ model can generally be modified to accommodate the situation. The model's assumptions are as follows:

1. Constant or uniform demand. Although the EOQ model assumes constant demand, demand may vary from day to day. If demand is stochastic—that is, not known in advance—the model must be modified through the inclusion of a safety stock.

2. Constant unit price. The inclusion of variable prices resulting from quantity discounts can be handled quite easily through a modification of the original EOQ model, redefining total costs and solving for the optimum order quantity.

3. Constant carrying costs. Unit carrying costs may vary substantially as the size of the inventory rises, perhaps decreasing because of economies of scale or storage efficiency or increasing as storage space runs out and new warehouses have to be rented. This situation can be handled through a modification in the original model similar to the one used for variable unit price.

4. Constant ordering costs. Although this assumption is generally valid, its violation can be accommodated by modifying the original EOQ model in a manner similar to the one used for variable unit price.

5. Instantaneous delivery. If delivery is not instantaneous, which is generally the case, the original EOQ model must be modified through the inclusion of a safety stock, that is, the inventory held to accommodate any unusually large and unexpected usage during the delivery time.

6. Independent orders. If multiple orders result in cost savings by reducing paperwork and transportation cost, the original EOQ model must be further modified.

Although this modification is somewhat complicated, special EOQ models have been developed to deal with it.

These assumptions illustrate the limitations of the basic EOQ model and the ways in which it can be modified to compensate for them. An understanding of the limitations and assumptions of the EOQ model provides the financial manager with a better base for making inventory decisions.

JUST-IN-TIME INVENTORY CONTROL

The just-in-time inventory control system is more than just an inventory control system, it is a production and management system. Not only is inventory cut down to a minimum, but the time and physical distance between the various production operations are also reduced. In addition, management is willing to trade off costs to develop close relationships with suppliers and promote speedy replenishment of inventory in return for the ability to hold less safety stock.

The just-in-time inventory control system was originally developed in Japan by Taiichi Okno, a vice-president of Toyota. The idea behind the system is that the firm should keep a minimum level of inventory on hand, relying on suppliers to furnish parts "just in time" for them to be assembled. This is in direct contrast to the traditional inventory philosophy of U.S. firms, which is sometimes referred to as a "just-in-case" system, which keeps healthy levels of safety stocks to ensure that production will not be interrupted. Although large inventories may not be a bad idea when interest rates are low, when interest rates are high they become very costly.

Although the just-in-time inventory system is intuitively appealing, it has not proved easy to implement. Long distances from suppliers and plants constructed with too much space for storage and not enough access (doors and loading docks) to receive inventory have limited successful implementation. But many firms' relationships with their suppliers have been forced to change. Because firms rely on suppliers to deliver high-quality parts and materials immediately, they must have a close long-term relationship with them. Despite the difficulties of implementation, many U.S. firms are committed to moving toward a just-in-time system.

The philosophy behind the just-in-time inventory system is that the benefits associated with reducing inventory and delivery time to a bare minimum through adjustment in the EOQ model will more than offset the costs associated with the increased possibility of stock-outs.

SUMMARY

In this chapter, we have developed many of the tools that a financial manager needs to manage the firm's cash and other current assets with the overall objective of ensuring that the firm has an appropriate level of liquidity or net working capital to carry out the goal of maximizing shareholder wealth. The hedging principle, or principle of self-liquidating debt, is a benchmark of working-capital decisions. Basically, this principle involves matching the cash-flow-generating characteristics of an asset with the cash flow requirements of the source of funds used to finance its acquisition. The firm experiences both regular and irregular cash flows. Once cash is obtained, the firm will have three motives for holding cash rather than investing it: to satisfy transactions, precautionary and speculative liquidity needs. To a certain extent, such needs can be satisfied by holding readily marketable securities rather than cash. A significant challenge of cash management, then, is dealing with the tradeoff between the firm's need to have cash on hand to pay liabilities that arise in the course of doing business and the objective of maximizing wealth by reducing to a minimum idle cash balances that earn no return.

Various procedures exist to improve the efficiency of a firm's cash management. Such procedures focus not only (although primarily) on accelerating the firm's cash receipts, but also on improving the methods for disbursing cash. Generally, at the heart of attempts to accelerate cash receipts is a significant effort to reduce the mail, processing and transit elements of the float. Often used in conjunction with concentration banking and a lock-box arrangement are depository transfer checks and wire transfers.

On the cash disbursements side, firms try to prolong the time cash stays in their own accounts by increasing the disbursement float through the use of zero balance accounts, payable-through drafts, and, especially, remote disbursing. The first two of these methods also offer much better central-office control over disbursements. Before any collection or disbursement procedure is introduced, however, a careful analysis should be performed to ensure that expected benefits outweigh the expected costs of such procedures.

Because idle cash earns no return, a financial manager will look for opportunities to invest such cash until it is required in the operations of the company. A variety of different readily marketable securities, which are described in the chapter, are available in the market today. The yields on such securities vary depending on four factors: the (1) financial risk, (2) interest rate risk, (3) liquidity, and (4) taxability of the security. By simultaneously taking into account these factors and the desired rate of return, the financial manager is able to determine the most suitable mix of cash and marketable securities for the firm.

When we consider that accounts receivable constitute approximately 25% of total assets for the typical firm, the importance of accounts receivable management becomes even more apparent. The size of a firm's investment in accounts receivable depends on three factors: the percentage of credit sales to total sales, the level of sales, and the credit and collection policies of the firm. The financial manager, however, generally only has control over the terms of sale, the quality of customer, and the collection efforts.

Although the level of investment in inventories by the typical firm is less than the investment in accounts receivable, inventory management and control remains an important function of the financial manager because inventories play a significant role in the operations of the firm. The purpose of holding inventory is to make each function of the business independent of the other functions. The primary issues related to inventory management are: How much inventory should be ordered and when the order should be placed. The EOQ model is used to answer the first of these questions. The order-point model, which depends on the desired levels of delivery-time stock and safety stock, is applied to answer the second question The just-in-time approach to inventory control is growing in popularity as an attempt to obtain additional cost savings by reducing the level of inventory a firm needs to have on hand. Instead of depending solely on its own inventories, the firm relies on its vendors to furnish supplies "just in time" to satisfy the firm's production requirements.

SELF-CORRECTION PROBLEMS

1. Mountaineer Outfitters has $2 million in excess cash that it might invest in marketable securities. To buy and sell the securities, however, the firm must pay a transactions fee of $45,000.

   a. Would you recommend purchasing the securities if they yield 12% annually and are held for
      (1) One month?
      (2) Two months?
      (3) Three months?
      (4) Six months?
      (5) One year?

   b. What minimum required yield would the securities have to return for the firm to hold them for three months? (What is the breakeven yield for a three-month holding period?)

2. Consider the following inventory information and relationships for the F. Beamer Corporation:
   - Orders can be placed only in multiples of 100 units.
   - Annual unit usage is 300,000. (Assume a 50-week year in your calculations.)
   - The carrying cost is 30% of the purchase price of the goods.
   - The purchase price is $10 per unit
   - The ordering cost is $50 per order.
   - The desired safety stock is 1,000 units. (This does not include delivery-time stock.)
   - Delivery time is two weeks.

Given this information
  a. What is the optimal EOQ level?
  b. How many orders will be placed annually?
  c. At what inventory level should a reorder be made?

SOLUTIONS TO SELF-CORRECTION PROBLEMS

1. a. Here we must calculate the dollar value of the estimated return for each holding period and compare it with the transactions fee to determine if a gain can be made by investing in the securities. Those calculations and the resultant recommendations follow:

Recommendation

(1)	$2,000,000(.12)(1/12)	= $20,000<$45,000	No
(2)	$2,000,000(.12)(2/12)	= $40,000<$45,000	No
(3)	$2,000,000(.12)(3/12)	= $60,000<$45,000	Yes
(4)	$2,000,000(.12)(6/12)	= 120,000<$45,000	Yes
(5)	$2,000,000(.12)(12/12)	= $240,000<$45,000	Yes

  b. Let (%) be the required yield. With $2 million to invest for three months we have

$2,000,000(%)(3/12)   = $ 45,000
$2,000,000(%)   = $180,000
                      = $180,000 / 2,000,000 = 9%

The breakeven yield, therefore, is 9%.

2. a.

$$EOQ = \sqrt{\frac{2SO}{C}}$$

$$= \sqrt{\frac{2(300,000)(50)}{3}}$$

$$= \sqrt{10,000,000}$$

$$= 3,162 \text{ units}$$

  b. Because orders must be placed in 100 unit lots, the effective EOQ becomes 3,200 units.

$$\frac{\text{Total usage}}{\text{EOQ}} = \frac{300,000}{3,200} = 93.75 \text{ orders per year}$$

  c.

Inventory order point = delivery time + safety stock

$$= \frac{2}{50} \times 300,000 + 1,000$$

$$= 12,000 + 1,000$$

$$= 13,000 \text{ units}$$

QUESTIONS

1. Define and contrast the terms "working capital" and "net working capital."
2. Discuss the risk-return relationship involved in the firm's asset investment decisions as that relationship pertains to working-capital management.
3. Define the hedging principle. How can this principle be used in the management of working capital?
4. Define the following terms:
   a. Permanent asset investments
   b. Temporary asset investments
   c. Permanent sources of financing
   d. Temporary sources of financing
   e. Spontaneous sources of financing
5. Identify the principal motives for holding cash and near-cash assets. Explain the purpose of each motive.
6. What is concentration banking and how may it be of value to the firm?
7. What are the two major objectives of the firm's cash-management system?
8. What three decisions dominate the cash-management process?
9. Distinguish between financial risk and interest rate risk as these terms are commonly used in discussions of cash management.
10. What key factors might induce a firm to invest in repurchase agreements rather than a specific security of the money market?
11. What factors determine the size of the investment a firm makes in accounts receivable? Which of these factors are under the control of the financial manager?
12. What are the risk-return tradeoffs associated with adopting a more liberal trade credit policy?
13. What is the purpose of holding inventory? Name several types of inventory and describe their purpose.
14. Can cash be considered a special type of inventory? If so, what functions does it attempt to uncouple?
15. What are the major assumptions made by the EOQ model?

PROBLEMS

1. **Concentration Banking.** Byron Sporting Goods operates in Miami, Florida. The firm produces and distributes a full line of athletic equipment on a nationwide basis. The firm currently uses a centralized billing system. Byron Sporting Goods has annual credit sales of $362 million. Austin National Bank has presented an offer to operate a concentration banking system for the company. Byron already has an established line of credit with Austin. Austin says it will operate the system on a flat-fee basis of $175,000 per year. The analysis done by the bank's cash-management services division suggests that three days in mail float and one day in processing float can be eliminated. Because Byron borrows almost continuously from Austin National, the value of the float reduction would be applied against the line of credit. The borrowing rate on the line of credit is set at an annual rate of 7%. Furthermore, because of the reduction in clerical help, the new system will save the firm $57,500 in processing costs. Byron uses a 365-day year in analyses of this sort. Should Byron accept the bank's offer to install the new system?

2. **Buying and Selling Marketable Securities.** Miami Dice & Card Company has generated $800,000 in excess cash that it could invest in marketable securities. In order to buy and sell the securities, the firm will pay total transactions fees of $20,000.

    a. Would you recommend purchasing the securities if they yield 10.5% annually and are held for

        (1) One month?

        (2) Two months?

        (3) Three months?

        (4) Six months?

        (5) One year?

    b. What minimum required yield would the securities have to return for the firm to hold them for two months? (What is the breakeven yield for a two-month holding period?)

3. **Costs of Service.** Mustang Ski-Wear, Inc. is investigating the possibility of adopting a lock-box system as a cash receipts acceleration device. In a typical year this firm receives remittances totaling $12 million by check. The firm will record and process 6,000 checks over this same period. The Colorado Springs Second National Bank has informed the management of Mustang that it will expedite checks and associated documents through the lock-box system for a unit cost of $.20 per check. Mustang's financial manager has projected that cash freed by adoption of the system can be invested in a portfolio of near-cash assets that will yield an annual before-tax return of 7%. Mustang financial analysts use a 365-day year in their procedures.

    a. What reduction in check collection time is necessary for Mustang to be neither better nor worse off for having adopted the proposed system?

    b. How would your solution to (a) be affected if Mustang could invest the freed balances only at an expected annual return of 4.5%?

    c. What is the logical explanation for the difference in your answers to (a) and (b)?

4. **Lock-Box System.** Penn Steelworks is a distributor of cold-rolled steel products to the automobile industry. All its sales are on a credit basis, net 30 days. Sales are evenly distributed over its 10 sales regions throughout the United States. Delinquent accounts are no problem. The company has recently undertaken an analysis aimed at improving its cash-management procedures. Penn determined that it takes an average of 3.2 days for customers' payments to reach the head office in Pittsburgh from the time they are mailed. It takes another full day in processing time prior to depositing the checks with a local bank. Annual sales average $4,800,000 for each regional office. Reasonable investment opportunities can be found yielding 7% per year. To alleviate the float problem confronting the firm, the use of a lock-box system in each of the 10 regions is being considered. This would reduce mail float by 1.2 days. One day in processing float would also be eliminated, plus a full day in transit float. The lock-box arrangement would cost each region $250 per month.

    a. What is the opportunity cost to Penn Steelworks of the funds tied up in mailing and processing? Use a 365-day year.

    b. What would the net cost or savings be from use of the proposed cash-acceleration technique? Should Penn adopt the system?

5. **Cash Receipts Acceleration System.** Peggy Pierce Designs, Inc. is a vertically integrated national manufacturer and retailer of women's clothing. Currently, the firm has no coordinated cash-management system. A proposal, however, from the First Pennsylvania Bank aimed at speeding up cash collections is being examined by several of Pierce's corporate executives.

    The firm currently uses a centralized billing procedure, which requires that all checks be mailed to the Philadelphia head office for processing and eventual deposit.

Under this arrangement all the customers' remittance checks take an average of five business days to reach the head office. Once in Philadelphia another two days are required to process the checks for ultimate deposit at the First Pennsylvania Bank.

The firm's daily remittances average $1 million. The average check size is $2,000. Pierce Designs currently earns 6% annually on its marketable securities portfolio.

The cash acceleration plan proposed by officers of First Pennsylvania involves both a lock-box system and concentration banking. First Pennsylvania would be the firm's only concentration bank. Lock boxes would be established in (1) San Francisco, (2) Dallas, (3) Chicago, and (4) Philadelphia. This would reduce funds tied up by mail float to three days, and processing float will be eliminated. Funds would then be transferred twice each business day by means of automated depository transfer checks from local banks in San Francisco, Dallas, and Chicago to the First Pennsylvania Bank. Each ADTC costs $15. These transfers will occur all 270 business days of the year. Each check processed through the lock-box system will cost $.18.

a. What amount of cash balances will be freed if Pierce Designs, Inc. adopts the system suggested by First Pennsylvania?

b. What is the opportunity cost of maintaining the current banking setup?

c. What is the projected annual cost of operating the proposed system?

d. Should Pierce adopt the new system? Compute the net annual gain or loss associated with adopting the system.

CHAPTER 15

SHORT-TERM LOANS AND LEASE FINANCING

The principal characteristic of short-term loans is that they are self-liquidating in less than a year. Frequently, they finance seasonal or temporary funds requirements. In examining the use of short-term liabilities, three major issues are involved in selecting a source of short-term financing: (1) the effective cost of credit, (2) the availability of financing in the amount and for the time needed, and (3) the effect of the use of credit from a particular source on the cost and availability of other sources of credit.

Term financing, on the other hand, finances more permanent funds requirements, such as those for fixed assets and underlying buildups in receivables and inventories. The loan is usually paid with the generation of cash flows over a period of years. As a result, most of these loans are paid in regular, periodic installments. We regard term financing as involving final maturities between 1 and 10 years. Although the 1-year boundary is rather commonly accepted, the 10-year upper limit is somewhat arbitrary. In this chapter we examine various types of term debt as well as lease financing.

ESTIMATING COST OF SHORT-TERM CREDIT

Approximate Cost-of-Credit Formula

The procedure for estimating the cost of short-term credit is a very simple one and relies on the basic interest equation:

$$\text{Interest} = \text{Principal} \times \text{Rate} \times \text{Time}$$

where interest is the dollar amount of interest on a principal that is borrowed at some annual rate for a fraction of a year (represented by time). For example, a six-month loan for $1,000 at 8% interest would require an interest payment of $40:

$$\text{Interest} = \$1,000 \times .08 \times (1/2) = \$40$$

We use this basic relationship to solve for the cost of a source of short-term financing or the annual percentage rate (APR) where the interest amount, the principal sum, and the time period for financing are known. Thus, solving the basic interest equation for APR produces:

$$APR = \frac{\text{interest}}{\text{principal} \times \text{time}}$$

or

$$APR = \frac{\text{interest}}{\text{principal}} \times \frac{1}{\text{time}}$$

This calculation, called the APR equation, is clarified with the following example. A company plans to borrow $1,000 for a 90-day period. At maturity the firm will repay the $1,000 principal amount plus $30 interest. The effective annual rate of interest for the loan can be estimated using the APR equation. A 30-day month and a 360-day year will be used for ease of computation throughout this chapter.

$$APR = \frac{\$30}{\$1,000} \times \frac{1}{90/360}$$

$$= .03 \times \frac{360}{90} = .12, \text{ or } 12\%$$

The effective annual cost of funds provided by the loan is therefore 12%.

Annual Percentage Yield Formula

The simple APR equation does not consider compound interest. To account for the influence of compounding, we can use the following equation:

$$APY = [1 + (i/m)]^m - 1$$

where APY is the annual percentage yield, I is the nominal rate of interest per year (12% in the above example), and m is the number of compounding periods within a year [$m = 1/\text{TIME} = 1/(90/365) = 4$ in the preceding example]. Thus, the effective rate of interest on the example problem, considering compounding, is

$$APY = [1 + (.12/4)]^4 - 1 = .126, \text{ or } 12.6\%$$

Compounding effectively raises the cost of short-term credit. Because the differences between APR and APY are usually small, we use the simple interest version of APR to compute the cost of short-term credit.

SOURCES OF SHORT-TERM CREDIT

Short-term credit sources can be classified into two basic groups: unsecured and secured. **Unsecured** loans include all those sources that have as their security only the lender's faith in the ability of the borrower to repay the funds when due. Major sources of unsecured short-term credit include accrued wages and taxes, trade credit, unsecured bank loans, and commercial paper. Secured loans involve the pledge of specific assets as collateral in the event the borrower defaults in payment of principal or interest. Commercial banks, finance companies, and factors are the primary suppliers of secured credit. The principal sources of collateral include accounts receivable and inventories.

Unsecured Sources: Accrued Wages and Taxes

Because most businesses pay their employees only periodically (weekly, biweekly, or monthly), firms accrue a wages payable account that is, in essence, a loan from their employees. For example, if the wage expense for the Appleton Manufacturing Company is $450,000 per week and it pays its employees monthly, then by the end of a four-week month the firm will owe its employees $1.8 million in wages for services they have already performed during the month. Consequently, the employees finance their own efforts through waiting a full month for payment.

Similarly, firms generally make quarterly income tax payments for their estimated quarterly tax liability. This means that the firm has the use of the tax moneys it owes based on quarterly profits up through the end of the quarter. In addition, the firm pays sales taxes and withholding (income) taxes for its employees on a deferred basis. The longer the period that the firm holds the tax payments, the greater the amount of financing they provide.

Note that these sources of financing rise and fall spontaneously with the level of firm sales. That is, as the firm's sales increase so do its labor expenses, sales taxes collected, and income tax. Consequently, these accrued expense items provide the firm with automatic or spontaneous sources of financing.

Unsecured Sources: Trade Credit

Trade credit provides one of the most flexible sources of short-term financing available to the firm. We previously noted that trade credit is a primary source of spontaneous, or on-demand, financing. That is, trade credit arises spontaneously with the firm's purchases. To arrange for credit the firm need only place an order with one of its suppliers. The supplier checks the firm's credit and, if it is good, sends the merchandise. The purchasing firm then pays for the goods in accordance with the supplier's credit terms.

Credit terms and cash discounts. Very often the credit terms offered with trade credit involve a cash discount for early payment. For example, a supplier might offer terms of 2/10, net 30, which means that a 2% discount is offered for payment within 10 days or the full amount is due in 30 days. Thus, a 2% penalty is involved for not paying within 10 days or for delaying from the 10th to the 30th day (that is, for 20 days). The effective annual cost of not taking the cash discount can be quite severe. Using a $1 invoice amount, the effective cost of passing up the discount period using the preceding credit terms and our APR equation can be estimated.

Note that the 2% cash discount is the interest cost of extending the payment period an additional 20 days. Note also that the principal amount of the credit is $.98. This amount constitutes the full principal amount as of the 10th day of the credit period, after which time the cash discount is lost. The effective cost of passing up the 2% discount for twenty days is quite expensive: 36.73%. Furthermore, once the discount period has passed, there is no reason to pay before the final due date (the 70th day). Exhibit 15-1 lists the effective annual cost of a number of alternative credit terms. Note that the cost of trade credit varies directly with the size of the cash discount and inversely with the length of time between the end of the discount period and the final due date.

Stretching of trade credit. Some firms that use trade credit engage in a practice called stretching of trade accounts. This practice involves delaying payments beyond the prescribed credit period. For example, a firm might purchase materials under credit terms of 3/10, net 60; however, when faced with a shortage of cash, the firm might extend payment to the 80th day. Continued violation of trade terms can eventually lead to a loss of credit. However, for short periods, and at infrequent intervals, stretching offers the firm an emergency source of short-term credit.

Advantages of trade credit. As a source of short-term financing, trade credit has a number of advantages. First, trade credit is conveniently obtained as a normal part of

Exhibit 15-1 Effective Rate of Interest on Selected Trade Credit Terms

Credit Terms	Effective Rate
2/10, net 60	14.69%
2/10, net 90	9.18%
3/20, net 60	27.84%
6/10, net 90	28.72%

$$APY = \frac{\$.02}{\$.98} \times \frac{1}{20/360} = .3673, \text{ or } 36.73\%$$

the firm's operations. Second, no formal agreements are generally involved in extending credit. Furthermore, the amount of credit extended expands and contracts with the needs of the firm; this is why it is classified as a spontaneous, or on-demand, source of financing.

Unsecured Sources: Bank Credit

Commercial banks provide unsecured short-term credit in two basic forms: lines of credit and transaction loans (notes payable). Maturities of both types of loans are usually one year or less, with rates of interest depending on the creditworthiness of the borrower and the level of interest rates in the economy as a whole.

Line of credit. A line of credit is generally an informal agreement or understanding between the borrower and the bank as to the maximum amount of credit that the bank will provide the borrower at any one time. Under this type of agreement there is no legal commitment on the part of the bank to provide the stated credit. In a revolving credit agreement, which is a variant of this form of financing, a legal obligation is involved. The line of credit agreement generally covers a period of one year corresponding to the borrower's fiscal year. Thus, if the borrower is on a July 31 fiscal year, its lines of credit will be based on the same annual period.

Lines of credit generally do not involve fixed rates of interest; instead they state that credit will be extended at 1/2% over prime or some other spread over the bank's prime rate.[1] Furthermore, the agreement usually does not spell out the specific use that will be made of the funds beyond a general statement, such as for working-capital purposes.

Lines of credit usually require that the borrower maintain a minimum balance in the bank throughout the loan period, called a compensating balance. This required balance (which can be stated as a percent of the line of credit or the loan amount) increases the effective cost of the loan to the borrower, unless a deposit balance equal to or greater than this balance requirement is ordinarily maintained in the bank. The effective cost of short-term bank credit can be estimated using the APR equation. Consider the following example: M & M Beverage Company has a $300,000 line of credit that requires a compensating balance equal to 10% of the loan amount. The rate paid on the loan is 12% per annum, $200,000 is borrowed for a six-month period, and the firm does not currently have a deposit with the lending bank. The dollar cost of the loan includes the interest expense and, in addition, the opportunity cost of maintaining an idle cash balance equal to the 10% compensating balance. To accommodate the cost of the compensating balance requirement, assume that the added funds will have to be borrowed and simply left idle in the firm's checking account. Thus, the amount actually borrowed (B) will be larger than the $200,000 needed. In fact, the needed $200,000 will constitute 90% of the total borrowed funds because of the 10% compensating balance requirement, hence .90B = $200,000, such that B = $222,222 ($200,000/.90). Thus, interest is paid on a $222,222 loan ($222,222 × .12 × 1/2 = $13,333.32), of which only $200,000 is available for use by the firm. The effective annual cost of credit therefore is

$$APR = \frac{\$13,333.32}{\$200,000} \times \frac{1}{180/360} = 13.33\%$$

The same answer would have been obtained by assuming a total loan of $200,000, of which only 90% or $180,000 was available for use by the firm; that is,

$$APR = \frac{\$12,000}{\$180,000} \times \frac{1}{180/360} = 13.33\%$$

Interest is now calculated on the $200,000 loan amount ($12,000 = $200,000 × .12 × 1/2).

In the M & M Beverage Company example the loan required the payment of principal ($222,222) plus interest ($13,333.32) at the end of the six-month loan period. Frequently, bank loans will be made on a discount basis. That is, the loan interest will be deducted from the loan amount before the funds are transferred to the borrower. Extending the M & M Beverage Company example to consider discounted interest involves reducing the loan proceeds ($200,000) in the previous example by the amount of interest for the full six months ($13,333.32). The effective rate of interest on the loan is now:

$$APR = \frac{\$13,333.32}{\$200,000 - \$13,333.32} \times \frac{1}{180/360}$$

$$= .1429, \text{ or } 14.29\%$$

The effect of discounting interest was to raise the cost of the loan from 13.33% to 14.29%. This results from the fact that the firm pays interest on the same amount of funds as before ($222,222); however, this time it gets the use of $13,333.32 less, or $200,000 − $13,333.32 = $186,666.68.[2]

Transaction loans. Still another form of unsecured short-term bank credit can be obtained in the form of transaction loans. Here the loan is made for a specific purpose. This is the type of loan that most individuals associate with bank credit and is obtained by signing a promissory note.

Unsecured transaction loans are very similar to a line of credit regarding cost, term to maturity, and compensating balance requirements. In both instances commercial banks often require that the borrower clean up its short-term loans for a 30- to 45-day period during the year. This means, very simply, that the borrower must be free of any bank debt for the stated period. The purpose of such a requirement is to ensure that the borrower is not using short-term bank credit to finance a part of its permanent needs for funds.

Unsecured Sources: Commercial Paper

Only the largest and most creditworthy companies are able to use commercial paper, which is simply a short-term promise to pay that is sold in the market for short-term debt securities.

Credit terms. The maturity of this credit source is generally six months or less, although some issues carry 270-day maturities. The interest rate on commercial paper is generally slightly lower (.5% to 1%) than the prime rate on commercial bank loans. Also, interest is usually discounted, although sometimes interest-bearing commercial paper is available.

New issues of commercial paper are either placed directly (sold by the issuing firm directly to the investing public) or dealer placed. Dealer placement involves the use of a commercial paper dealer, who sells the issue for the issuing firm. Many major finance companies, such as General Motors Acceptance Corporation, place their commercial paper directly. The volume of direct versus dealer placements is roughly 4 to 1 in favor of direct placements. Dealers are used primarily by industrial firms that either make only infrequent use of the commercial paper market or, owing to their small size, would have difficulty placing the issue without the help of a dealer.

Commercial paper as a source of short-term credit. Several advantages accrue to the user of commercial paper:

1. **Interest rate.** Commercial paper rates are generally lower than rates on bank loans and comparable sources of short-term financing.

2. **Compensating balance requirement.** No minimum balance requirements are associated with commercial paper. However, issuing firms usually find it desirable to maintain lines of credit agreements sufficient to back up their short-term financing needs in the event that a new issue of commercial paper cannot be sold or an outstanding issue cannot be repaid when due.

3. **Amount of credit.** Commercial paper offers the firm with very large credit needs a single source for all its short-term financing. Because of loan restrictions placed on the banks by the regulatory authorities, obtaining the necessary funds from a commercial bank might require dealing with a number of institutions.

4. **Prestige.** Because it is widely recognized that only the most creditworthy borrowers have access to the commercial paper market, its use signifies a firm's credit status.

It should be noted that member banks of the Federal Reserve System are limited to 10% of their total capital, surplus, and undivided profits when making loans to a single borrower. Thus, when a corporate borrower's needs for financing are very large it may have to deal with a group of participating banks to raise the needed funds.

Using commercial paper for short-term financing, however, involves a very important risk. That is, the commercial paper market is highly impersonal and denies even the most creditworthy borrower any flexibility in terms of repayment. When bank credit is used, the borrower has someone with whom he or she can work out any temporary difficulties that might be encountered in meeting a loan deadline. This flexibility simply does not exist for the user of commercial paper.

Estimation of the cost of commercial paper. The cost of commercial paper can be estimated using the simple effective cost-of-credit equation (APR). The key points to remember are that commercial paper interest is usually discounted and that if a dealer is used to place the issue, a fee is charged. Even if a dealer is not used, the issuing firm will incur costs associated with preparing and placing the issue, and these costs must be included in estimating the cost of credit.

For example, EPG Mfg. Company uses commercial paper regularly to support its needs for short-term financing. The firm plans to sell $100 million in 270-day-maturity paper on which it expects to have to pay discounted interest at a rate of 12% per annum ($9,000,000). In addition, EPG expects to incur a cost of approximately $100,000 in dealer placement fees and other expenses of issuing the paper. The effective cost of credit to EPG can be calculated as follows:

$$ APR = \frac{\$9,000,000 + \$100,000}{\$100,000,000 - \$100,000 - \$9,000,000} \times \frac{1}{270/360} = .1335, \text{ or } 13.35\% $$

where the interest cost is calculated as $100,000,000 \times .12 \times (270/360) = \$9,000,000$ plus the $100,000 dealer placement fee. Thus, the effective cost of credit to EPG is 13.35%.

Secured Sources: Accounts Receivable Loans

Secured sources of short-term credit have certain assets of the firm pledged as collateral to secure the loan. Upon default of the loan agreement, the lender has first claim to the pledged assets in addition to its claim as a general creditor of the firm. Hence, the secured credit agreement offers an added margin of safety to the lender. Generally, a firm's receivables are among its most liquid assets. For this reason they are considered by many lenders to be prime collateral for a secured loan. Two basic procedures can be used in arranging for financing based on receivables: pledging and factoring.

Pledging accounts receivable. Under the pledging arrangement the borrower simply pledges accounts receivable as collateral for a loan obtained from either a commercial bank or a finance company. The amount of the loan is stated as a percent of the face value of the receivables pledged. If the firm provides the lender with a general line on its receivables, then all of the borrower's accounts are pledged as security for the loan. This method of pledging is simple and inexpensive. However, because the lender has no control over the quality of the receivables being pledged, it will set the maximum loan at a relatively low percent of the total face value of the accounts, generally ranging downward from a maximum of around 75%.

Still another approach to pledging involves the borrower's presenting specific invoices to the lender as collateral for a loan. This method is somewhat more expensive in that the lender must assess the creditworthiness of each individual account pledged; however, given this added knowledge the lender will be willing to increase the loan as a percent of the face value of the invoices. In this case the loan might reach as high as 85% or 90% of the face value of the pledged receivables.

Accounts receivable loans generally carry an interest rate 2% to 5% higher than the bank's prime lending rate. Finance companies charge an even higher rate. In addition, the lender will usually charge a handling fee stated as a percent of the face value of the receivables processed, which may be as much as 1% to 2% of the face value. Consider the following example.

The A. B. Good Company sells electrical supplies to building contractors on terms of net 60. The firm's average monthly sales are $100,000; thus, given the firm's two-month credit terms, its average receivables balance is $200,000. The firm pledges all its receivables to a local bank, which in turn advances up to 70% of the face value of the receivables at 3% over prime and with a 1% processing charge on all receivables pledged. A. B. Good follows a practice of borrowing the maximum amount possible, and the current prime rate is 10%.

The APR of using this source of financing for a full year is computed as follows:

$$\text{APR} = \frac{\$18{,}200 + \$12{,}000}{\$140{,}000} \times \frac{1}{360/360} = .2157 \text{ or } 21.57\%$$

where the total dollar cost of the loan consists of both the annual interest expense (.13 $\times$ .70 $\times$ \$200,000 = \$18,200) and the annual processing fee (.01 x \$100,000 $\times$ 12 months = \$12,000). The amount of credit extended is .70 $\times$ \$200,000 = \$140,000. Note that the processing charge applies to all receivables pledged. Thus, the A. B. Good Company pledges \$100,000 each month, or \$1,200,000 during the year, on which a 1% fee must be paid, for a total annual charge of \$12,000.

One more point: the lender, in addition to making advances or loans, may be providing certain credit services to the borrower. For example, the lender may provide billing and collection services. The value of these services should be considered in computing the cost of credit. In the preceding example, A. B. Good Company may save credit department expenses of \$10,000 per year by pledging all its accounts and letting the lender provide those services. In this case, the cost of short-term credit is only

$$\text{APR} = \frac{\$18{,}200 + \$12{,}000 - \$10{,}000}{\$140{,}000} \times \frac{1}{360/360} = .1443 \text{ or } 14.43\%$$

The primary advantage of pledging as a source of short-term credit is the flexibility it provides the borrower. Financing is available on a continuous basis. The new accounts created through credit sales provide the collateral for the financing of new production. Furthermore, the lender may provide credit services that eliminate or at least reduce the need for similar services within the firm. The primary disadvantage associated with this method of financing is its cost, which can be relatively high compared with other sources of short-term credit, owing to the level of the interest rate charged on loans and the processing fee on pledged accounts.

Factoring accounts receivable. Factoring accounts involves the outright sale of a firm's accounts to a financial institution called a factor. A factor is a firm that acquires the receivables of other firms. The factoring institution may be a commercial finance company that engages solely in the factoring of receivables (known as an old-liner factor) or it may be a commercial bank. The factor, in turn, bears the risk of collection and, for a fee, services the accounts. The fee is stated as a percent of the face value of all receivables factored (usually from 1% to 3%). The factor firm typically does not make payment for factored accounts until the accounts have been collected or the credit terms have been met. Should the firm wish to receive immediate payment for its factored accounts, it can borrow from the factor, using the factored accounts as collateral. The maximum loan the firm can obtain is equal to the face value of its factored accounts less the factor's fee (1% to 3%) less a reserve (6% to 10%) less the interest on the loan. For example, if $100,000 in receivables is factored, carrying 60-day credit terms, a 2% factor's fee, a 6% reserve, and interest at 1% per month on advances, then the maximum loan or advance the firm can receive is computed as follows:

Face amount of receivables factored	$100,000
Less: Fee (.02 × $100,000)	(2,000)
Reserve (.06 × $100,000)	(6,000)
Interest (.01 × $92,000 × 2 months)	(1,840)
Maximum advance	$90,160

Note that interest is discounted and calculated based on a maximum amount of funds available for advance ($92,000 = $100,000 − $2,000 − $6,000). Thus, the effective cost of credit can be calculated as follows:

$$\text{APR} = \frac{\$1,840 + \$2,000}{\$90,160} \times \frac{1}{60/360} = .2555 \text{ or } 25.55\%$$

Secured Sources: Inventory Loans

Inventory loans provide a second source of security for short-term secured credit. The amount of the loan that can be obtained depends on both the marketability and perishability of the inventory. Some items, such as raw materials (grains, oil, lumber, and chemicals), are excellent sources of collateral because they can easily be liquidated. Other items, such as work-in-process inventories, provide very poor collateral because of their lack of marketability.

There are several methods by which inventory can be used to secure short-term financing. These include a floating or blanket lien, chattel mortgage, field warehouse receipt, and terminal warehouse receipt.

Under a **floating lien** agreement the borrower gives the lender a lien against all its inventories. This provides the simplest but least secure form of inventory collateral. The borrowing firm maintains full control of the inventories and continues to sell and replace them as it sees fit. Obviously, this lack of control over the collateral greatly dilutes the value of this type of security to the lender.

Under a **chattel mortgage agreement** the inventory is identified (by serial number or otherwise) in the security agreement and the borrower retains title to the inventory but cannot sell the items without the lender's consent.

Under a **field warehouse financing agreement**, inventories used as collateral are physically separated from the firm's other inventories and placed under the control of a third-party field warehousing firm.

The **terminal warehouse agreement** differs from the field warehouse agreement in only one respect. Here the inventories pledged as collateral are transported to a public warehouse that is physically removed from the borrower's premises. The lender has an added degree of safety or security because the inventory is totally removed from the borrower's control. Once again the cost of this type of agreement is increased because the warehouse firm must be paid by the borrower; in addition, the inventory must be transported to and eventually from the public warehouse.

TERM LOANS

Commercial banks are a primary source of term financing. Two features of a bank term loan distinguish it from other types of business loans. First, a term loan has a final maturity of more than one year. Second, it most often represents credit extended under a formal loan agreement. For the most part, these loans are repayable in periodic installments—quarterly, semiannually, or annually—that cover both interest and principal. The payment schedule of the loan is usually geared to the borrower's cash flow ability to service the debt. Typically, the repayment schedule calls for equal periodic installments, but it may specify irregular amounts or repayment in one lump sum at final maturity. Sometimes the loan is amortized (gradually extinguished) in equal periodic installments except for a final balloon payment (a payment much larger than any of the others). Most bank term loans are written with original maturities in the three- to five-year range.

Costs and Benefits

Generally the interest rate on a term loan is higher than the rate on a short-term loan to the same borrower. If a firm could borrow at the prime rate on a short-term basis, it might pay .25% to .50% more on a term loan. The higher interest rate helps to compensate for the more prolonged risk exposure of the lender. The interest rate on a term loan is generally set in two ways: (1) a fixed rate established at the outset that remains effective over the life of the loan or (2) a variable rate adjusted in keeping with changes in market rates. Sometimes a floor or a ceiling rate is established, limiting the range within which a variable rate may fluctuate. In addition to interest costs, the borrower is required to pay the legal expenses that the bank incurs in drawing up the loan agreement. Also, a commitment fee may be charged for the time during the commitment period when the loan is not "taken down." For an ordinary term loan, these additional costs are usually rather small in relation to the total interest cost of the loan. Typically fees on the unused portion of a commitment range between .25% and .75%. Suppose, for example, that the commitment fee was .50% on a commitment of $1 million and a company took down all of the loan three months after the commitment. The firm would owe the bank a ($1 million) $\times$ (.005) $\times$ (3 months/12 months) = $1,250 commitment fee.

The principal advantage of an ordinary term loan is flexibility. The borrower deals directly with the lender, and the loan can be tailored to the borrower's needs through direct negotiation. The bank usually has had previous experience with the borrower, so it is familiar with the company's situation. Should the firm's requirements change, the terms and conditions of the loan may be revised. In many instances, term loans are made to small businesses that do not have access to the capital markets and cannot readily float a public issue. The ability to float a public issue varies over time in keeping with the tone of the capital markets, whereas access to term loan financing is more dependable. Even large companies that are able to go to the public market may occasionally find it more convenient to seek a term loan than to float a public issue.

Revolving Credit Agreements

A revolving credit agreement is a formal commitment by a bank to lend up to a certain amount of money to a company over a specified period of time. The actual notes evidencing debt are short term, usually 90 days, but the company may renew them or borrow additionally, up to the specified maximum, throughout the duration of the commitment. Many revolving credit commitments are for three years, although it is possible for a firm to obtain a shorter commitment. As with an ordinary term loan, the interest rate is usually .25% to .50% higher than the rate at which the firm could borrow on a short-term basis under a line of credit. When a bank makes a revolving credit commitment, it is legally bound under the loan agreement to have funds available whenever the company wants to borrow. The borrower usually must pay for this availability in the form of a commitment fee, perhaps .50% per annum, on the difference between the amount borrowed and the specified maximum.

This borrowing arrangement is particularly useful at times when the firm is uncertain about its funds requirements. The borrower has flexible access to funds over a period of uncertainty and can make more definite credit arrangements when the uncertainty is resolved. Revolving credit agreements can be set up so that at the maturity of the commitment, borrowings then owing can be converted into a term loan at the option of the borrower. Suppose that the company you work for is introducing a new product and is facing a period of uncertainty over the next several years. To provide maximum financial flexibility, you might arrange a three-year revolving credit agreement that is convertible into a five-year term loan at the expiration of the revolving credit commitment. At the end of three years, the company should know its funds requirements better. If these requirements are permanent, or nearly so, the firm might wish to exercise its option and take down the term loan.

Insurance Company Term Loans

In addition to banks, life insurance companies and certain other institutional investors lend money on a term basis but with differences in the maturity of the loan extended and in the interest rate charged. In general, life insurance companies are interested in term loans with final maturities in excess of seven years. Because these companies do not have the benefit of compensating balances or other business from the borrower and because their loans usually have a longer maturity than bank term loans, the rate of interest is typically higher than a bank would charge. To the insurance company, the term loan represents an investment and must yield a return commensurate with the costs involved in making the loan, as well as the risk and the maturity of the loan and the prevailing yields on alternative investments. Because an insurance company is interested in keeping its funds employed without interruption, it normally has a prepayment penalty, whereas the bank usually does not. Insurance company term loans are generally not competitive with bank term loans. Indeed, they are complementary, for they serve different maturity ranges.

PROVISIONS OF LOAN AGREEMENTS

When a lender makes a term loan or revolving credit commitment, it provides the borrower with available funds for an extended period. Much can happen to the financial condition of the borrower during that period. To safeguard itself, the lender requires the borrower to maintain its financial condition and, in particular, its current position at a level at least as favorable as when the commitment was made. The provisions for protection contained in a loan agreement are known as protective **covenants**.

The **loan agreement** itself simply gives the lender legal authority to step in should the borrower default under any of the loan provisions. Otherwise, the lender would be locked into a commitment and would have to wait until maturity before being able to take corrective actions. The borrower who suffers losses or other adverse developments will default under a well-written loan agreement. The lender will then be able to act. The action usually takes the form of working with the company to straighten out its problems. Seldom will a lender demand immediate repayment, despite the legal right to do so in cases of default. More typically, the condition under which the borrower defaults is waived, or the loan agreement is amended. The point is that the lender has the authority to act, even though negotiation with the borrower may be instituted to resolve the problem.

Formulation of Provisions

The formulation of the different restrictive provisions should be tailored to the specific loan situation. The lender fashions these provisions for the overall protection of the loan. No one provision is able by itself to provide the necessary safeguard. Collectively, however, these provisions act to ensure the firm's overall liquidity and ability to repay a loan. The important protective covenants of a loan agreement may be classified as follows: (1) general provisions used in most loan agreements, which are usually variable to fit the situation; (2) routine provisions used in most agreements, which are usually not variable; and (3) specific provisions that are used according to the situation.

General provisions. The *working-capital requirement* is probably the most commonly used and most comprehensive provision in a loan agreement. Its purpose is to preserve the company's current position and ability to repay the loan. Frequently, a straight dollar amount, such as $6 million, is set as the minimum working capital the company must maintain during the duration of the commitment. When the lender feels that it is desirable for a specific company to build working capital, it may increase the minimum working-capital requirement throughout the duration of the loan. The establishment of a working-capital minimum is normally based on the amount of present working capital and projected working capital, allowing for seasonal fluctuations. The requirement should not unduly restrict the company in the ordinary generation of profit. Should the borrower incur sharp losses or spend too much for fixed assets, common stock repurchases, dividends, redemption of long-term debt, and so forth, it would probably breach the working capital requirement.

The *cash dividend and repurchase of common stock restriction* is another major provision in this category. Its purpose is to limit cash going outside the business, thus preserving the liquidity of the company. Most often, cash dividends and repurchases of common stock are limited to a percentage of net profits on a cumulative basis after a certain base date, frequently the last fiscal year end prior to the date of the term loan agreement. A less flexible method is to restrict dividends and repurchases of common stock to an absolute dollar amount each year. In most cases the prospective borrower must be willing to restrict cash dividends and repurchases of common stock. If tied to earnings, this restriction will still allow adequate dividends as long as the company is able to generate satisfactory profits.

The *capital expenditures limitation* is third in the category of general provisions. Capital expenditures may be limited to a yearly fixed dollar amount or, more commonly, either to an amount equal to current depreciation charges or to a certain percentage of current depreciation charges. The capital expenditures limitation is another tool the lender uses to ensure the maintenance of the borrower's current position. By directly limiting capital expenditures, the bank can be more sure that it will not have to look to liquidation of fixed assets for repayment of its loan. Again, the provision should not be so restrictive that it prevents adequate maintenance and improvement of facilities.

A *limitation on other indebtedness* is the last general provision. This limitation may take a number of forms, depending on the circumstances. Frequently, a loan agreement will prohibit a company from incurring any other long-term debt. This provision protects the lender, inasmuch as it prevents future lenders from obtaining a prior claim on the borrower's assets. Usually a company is permitted to borrow within reasonable limits for seasonal and other short-term purposes arising in the ordinary course of business.

Routine provisions. The second category of restrictions includes routine, usually inflexible, provisions found in most loan agreements. Ordinarily, the loan agreement requires the borrower to furnish the bank with financial statements and to maintain adequate insurance. Additionally, the borrower normally must not sell a significant portion of its assets and must pay, when due, all taxes and other liabilities, except those it contests in good faith. A provision forbidding the future pledging or mortgaging of any of the borrower's assets is almost always included in a loan agreement. This important provision is known as a **negative pledge clause**.

Ordinarily, the company is required not to discount or sell its receivables. Moreover, the borrower generally is prohibited from entering into any leasing arrangement of property, except up to a certain dollar amount of annual rental. The purpose of this provision is to prevent the borrower from taking on a substantial lease liability, which might endanger its ability to repay the loan. A lease restriction also prevents the firm from leasing property instead of purchasing it and thereby getting around the limitations on capital expenditures and debt. Usually, too, there is a restriction on other contingent liabilities. The provisions in this category appear as a matter of routine in most loan agreements. Although somewhat mechanical, they close many loopholes and provide a tight, comprehensive loan agreement.

Special provisions. In specific loan agreements, the lender uses special provisions to achieve a desired protection of its loan. A loan agreement may contain a definite understanding regarding the use of the loan proceeds, so that there will be no diversion of funds to purposes other than those contemplated when the loan was negotiated. A provision for limiting loans and advances is often found in a term loan agreement. Closely allied to this restriction is a limitation on investments, which is used to safeguard liquidity by preventing certain nonliquid investments.

If one or more key executives are essential to a firm's effective operation, a lender may insist that the company carry life insurance on them. Proceeds of the insurance may be payable to the company or directly to the lender, to be applied to the loan. An agreement may also contain a management clause, under which certain key individuals must remain actively employed in the company during the time the loan is outstanding. Aggregate executive salaries and bonuses are sometimes limited in the loan agreement to prevent excessive compensation of executives, which might reduce profits. This provision also closes another loophole. It prevents large shareholders who are officers of the company from increasing their own salaries in lieu of paying higher dividends, which are limited under the agreement.

Negotiation of Restrictions

The provisions just described represent the most frequently used protective covenants in a loan agreement. From the standpoint of the lender, the aggregate impact of these provisions should be to safeguard the financial position of the borrower and its ability to repay the loan. Under a well-written agreement, a borrower cannot get into serious financial difficulty without defaulting under an agreement, thereby giving the lender legal authority to take action. Although the lender is instrumental in establishing the restrictions, the restrictiveness of protective covenants is subject to negotiation between borrower and lender. The final result will depend on the bargaining power of each of the parties involved.

EQUIPMENT FINANCING

Equipment represents another asset of the firm that may be pledged to secure a loan. If the firm either has equipment that is marketable or is purchasing such equipment, it is usually able to obtain some sort of secured financing. Because the terms of such loans are usually more than a year, we take them up in this chapter rather than under short-term secured loans. As with other secured loans, the lender evaluates the marketability of the collateral and will advance a percentage of the market value, depending on the quality of the equipment. Frequently, the repayment schedule for the loan is set in keeping with the economic depreciation schedule of the equipment. In setting the repayment schedule, the lender wants to be sure that the market value of the equipment always exceeds the balance of the loan.

The excess of the expected market value of the equipment over the amount of the loan is the margin of safety, which will vary according to the specific situation. For example, the rolling stock of a trucking company is movable collateral and reasonably marketable. As a result, the advance may be as high as 80%. Less marketable equipment, such as that with a limited use, will not command as high an advance. A certain type of lathe may have a thin market, and a lender might not be willing to advance more than 50% of its reported market value. Some equipment is so specialized that it has no value as collateral.

Sources and Types of Equipment Financing

Commercial banks, finance companies, and the sellers of equipment are among the sources of equipment financing. Because the interest charged by a finance company on an equipment loan is usually higher than that charged by a commercial bank, a firm will turn to a finance company only if it is unable to obtain the loan from a bank. The seller of the equipment may finance the purchase either by holding a secured note itself or by selling the note to its captive finance subsidiary or some third party. The interest charge will depend on the extent to which the seller uses financing as a sales tool. The seller who uses financing extensively may charge only a moderate interest but may make up for part of the cost of carrying the notes by charging higher prices for the equipment. The borrower must consider this possibility in judging the true cost of financing. Equipment loans may be secured by either a chattel mortgage or by a conditional sale contract arrangement.

Chattel mortgage. A *chattel mortgage* is a **lien** on property other than real estate. The borrower signs a security agreement that gives the lender a lien on the equipment specified in the agreement. To *perfect* (make legally valid) the lien, the lender files a copy of the security agreement or a financing statement with a public office of the state in which the equipment is located. Given a valid lien, the lender can sell the equipment if the borrower defaults in the payment of principal or interest on the loan.

Conditional sales contract. With a **conditional sales contract** arrangement, the seller of the equipment retains the title to it until the purchaser has satisfied all the terms of the contract. The buyer signs a conditional sales contract security agreement to make periodic installment payments to the seller over a specified period of time. These payment are usually monthly or quarterly. Until the terms of the contract are completely satisfied, the seller retains title to the equipment. Thus, the seller receives a down payment and a **promissory note** for the balance of the purchase price upon the sale of the equipment. The note is secured by the contract, which gives the seller the authority to repossess the equipment if the buyer does not meet all of the terms of the contract.

The seller may either hold the contract or sell it, simply by endorsing it, to a commercial bank or finance company. The bank or finance company then becomes the lender and assumes the security interest in the equipment. If the buyer should default under the terms of the contract, the bank or finance company could repossess the equipment and sell it in satisfaction of its loan. Often, the vendor will sell the contract to a bank or finance company *with recourse*. Under this arrangement, the lender has the additional protection of recourse to the seller in case the buyer defaults and the lender realizes less than the loan balance from the sale of the equipment.

LEASE FINANCING

A **lease** is a contract. By its terms the owner of an asset (the lessor) gives another party (the lessee) the exclusive right to use the asset, usually for a specified period of time, in return for the payment of rent. Most of us are familiar with leases of houses, apartments, offices, or automobiles. Recent decades have seen an enormous growth in the leasing of business assets such as cars and trucks, computers, machinery, and even manufacturing plants. An obvious advantage to the lessee is the use of an asset without having to buy it. For this advantage, the lessee incurs several obligations. First and foremost is the obligation to make periodic lease payments, usually monthly or quarterly. Also, the lease contract specifies who is to maintain the asset. Under a *full-service* (or *maintenance*) *lease*, the lessor pays for maintenance, repairs, taxes, and insurance. Under a **net lease**, the lessee pays these costs.

The lease may be cancellable or noncancellable. When cancellable, there sometimes is a penalty. An **operating lease** for office space, for example, is relatively short term and is often cancellable at the option of the lessee with proper notice. The term of this type of lease is shorter than the asset's economic life. In other words, the lessor does not recover its investment during the first lease period. It is only in leasing the space over and over, either to the same party or to others, that the lessor recovers its costs. Other examples of operating leases include the leasing of copying machines, certain computer hardware, word processors, and automobiles. In contrast, a **financial lease** is longer term in nature and is noncancellable. The lessee is obligated to make lease payments until the lease's expiration, which generally corresponds to the useful life of the asset. These payments not only amortize the cost of the asset but provide the lessor an interest return. Our focus in this chapter is on financial as opposed to operating leases since it is this longer term arrangement that is employed when a lease is used as a source of intermediate- to long-term financing.

Finally, the lease contract typically specifies one or more options to the lessee at expiration. One option is to simply return the leased asset to the lessor. Another option may involve renewal, where the lessee has the right to renew the lease for another lease period, either at the same rent or at a different, usually lower, rent. A final option would be to purchase the asset at expiration. For tax reasons, the asset's purchase price must not be significantly lower than its **fair market value**. If the lessee does not exercise its option, the lessor takes possession of the asset and is entitled to any **residual value** associated with it.

Forms of Lease Financing

Virtually all financial lease arrangements fall into one of three main types of lease financing: a sale and leaseback arrangement, direct leasing, and leveraged leasing. In this section we briefly describe these categories. In the subsequent section we present a framework for the analysis of lease financing.

Sale and leaseback. Under a **sale and leaseback** arrangement a firm sells an asset to another party, and this party leases it back to the firm. Usually the asset is sold at approximately its market value. The firm receives the sales price in cash and the economic use of the asset during the basic lease period. In turn, it contracts to make periodic lease payments and give up title to the asset. As a result, the lessor realizes any residual value the asset might have at the end of the lease period, whereas before, this value would have been realized by the firm. The firm may realize an income tax advantage if the asset involves a building on owned land. Land is not depreciable if owned outright. However, since lease payments are tax deductible, the lessee is able to indirectly "depreciate" (or expense) the cost of the land. Lessors engaged in sale and leaseback arrangements include insurance companies, other institutional investors, finance companies, and independent leasing companies.

Direct leasing. Under *direct leasing*, a company acquires the use of an asset it did not own previously. A firm may lease an asset from the manufacturer. IBM leases computers. Xerox Corporation leases copiers. Indeed, capital goods are abundantly available today on a lease-financed basis. A wide variety of direct leasing arrangements meet various needs of firms. The major types of lessors are manufacturers, finance companies, banks, independent leasing companies, special-purpose leasing companies, and partnerships. For leasing arrangements involving all but manufacturers, the vendor sells the asset to the lessor who, in turn, leases it to the lessee. As in any lease arrangement, the lessee has use of the asset, along with a contractual obligation to make lease payments to the lessor.

Leverage leasing. A special form of leasing has become popular in the financing of big-ticket assets such as aircraft, oil rigs, and railway equipment. This device is known as **leveraged leasing**. In contrast to the two parties involved in a sale and leaseback or direct leasing, there are three parties involved in leveraged leasing: (1) the lessee, (2) the lessor (or equity participant), and (3) the lender. We examine each in turn.

From the standpoint of the lessee, there is no difference between a leveraged lease and any other type of lease. The lessee contracts to make periodic payments over the basic lease period and, in return, is entitled to the use of the asset over that period of time. The role of the lessor, however, is changed. The lessor acquires the asset in keeping with the terms of the lease arrangement and finances the acquisition in part by an equity investment of, say 20% (hence the term "equity participant"). The remaining 80% of the financing is provided by a long-term lender or lenders. Usually the loan is secured by a mortgage on the asset, as well as by the assignment of the lease and lease payments. The lessor, then, is itself a borrower.

As owner of the asset, the lessor is entitled to deduct all depreciation charges associated with the asset. The cash-flow pattern for the lessor typically involves (1) a cash outflow at the time the asset is acquired, which represents the lessor's equity participation; (2) a period of cash inflows represented by lease payments and tax benefits, less payments on the debt (interest and principal); and (3) a period of net cash outflows during which, because of declining tax benefits, the sum of lease payments and tax benefits falls below the debt payments due. If there is any *residual value* at the end of the lease period, this of course represents a cash inflow to the lessor. Although the leveraged lease may seem the most complicated of the three forms of lease financing we have described, it reduces to certain basic concepts. From the standpoint of the lessee, which is our stance, the leveraged lease can be analyzed in the same manner as any other lease. Therefore, we will not treat it separately in the rest of this chapter.

Accounting Treatment

Accounting for leases has changed dramatically over time. A number of years ago lease financing was attractive to some because the lease obligation did not appear on the company's financial statements. As a result, leasing was regarded as a "hidden" or " off-balance-sheet" method of financing. However, accounting requirements have changed so that now many long-term leases must be shown on the balance sheet as a "capitalized" asset with an associated liability being shown as well. For these leases, the reporting of earnings is affected. Other leases must be fully disclosed in footnotes to the financial statements. As the accounting treatment of leases is involved, we discuss it separately in the Addendum to this chapter in order to maintain the chapter's continuity. The main point is that it is no longer possible for a firm to "fool" informed investors and creditors by using a lease as opposed to debt financing. The full impact of the lease obligation is apparent to any supplier of capital who makes the effort to read the financial statements.

Tax Treatment

For tax purposes, the lessee can deduct the full amount of the lease payment in a properly structured lease. The Internal Revenue Service (IRS) wants to be sure that the lease contract truly represents a lease and not an installment purchase of the asset. To assure itself that a "true" lease is in fact involved, it may check on whether there is a meaningful *residual value* at the end of the lease term. Usually this is construed to mean that the term of the lease cannot exceed 90% of the useful life of the asset. In addition to this criterion, the lessee must not be given an option to purchase the asset or to release it at a nominal price at the end of the lease period. Any purchase option must be based on the asset's *fair market value* at the lease's expiration, such as would occur with an outside offer. The lease payments must be reasonable in that they provide the lessor not only a return of principal but a reasonable interest return as well. In addition, the lease term must be for less than 30 years; otherwise it will be construed as an installment purchase of the asset.

The IRS wants to assure itself that the lease contract is not, in effect, a purchase of the asset, for which the lease payments are much more rapid than would be allowed with depreciation under an outright purchase. As lease payments are deductible for tax purposes, such a contract would allow the lessor to effectively "depreciate" the asset more quickly than allowed with depreciation under a straight purchase. If the lease contract meets the conditions described, the full lease payment is deductible for tax purposes.

With leasing, the cost of any land is amortized in the lease payments. By deducting the lease payments as an expense for federal income tax purposes, the lessee is able to effectively write off the original cost of the land. If, instead, the land is purchased, the firm cannot depreciate it for tax purposes. When the value of land represents a significant portion of the asset acquired, lease financing can offer a tax advantage to the firm. Offsetting this tax advantage is the likely residual value of land at the end of the basic lease period. The firm may also gain certain tax advantages in a sale and leaseback arrangement when the assets are sold for less than their depreciated value.

Economic Rationale for Leasing

The principal reason for the existence of leasing is that companies, financial institutions, and individuals derive different tax benefits from owning assets. The marginally profitable company may not be able to reap the full benefit of accelerated depreciation, whereas the high-income taxable corporation or individual is able to realize such. The former may be able to obtain a greater portion of the overall tax benefits by leasing the asset from the latter party as opposed to buying it. Because of competition among lessors, part of the tax benefits may be passed on to the lessee in the form of lower lease payments than would otherwise be the case.

Another tax disparity has to do with the **alternative minimum tax (AMT)**. For a company subject to the AMT, accelerated depreciation is a "tax preference item," whereas a lease payment is not. Such a company may prefer to lease, particularly from another party that pays taxes at a higher effective rate. The greater the divergence in abilities of various parties to realize the tax benefits associated with owning an asset, the greater the attraction of lease financing overall. It is not the existence of taxes per se that gives rise to leasing but divergences in the abilities of various parties to realize the tax benefits.

Another consideration, albeit a minor one, is that lessors enjoy a somewhat superior position in bankruptcy proceedings over what would be the case if they were secured lenders. The riskier the firm that seeks financing, the greater the incentive for the supplier of capital to make the arrangement a lease rather than a loan.

In addition to these reasons, there may be others that explain the existence of lease financing. For one thing, the lessor may enjoy economies of scale in the purchase of assets that are not available to individual lessees. This is particularly true for the purchase of autos and trucks. Also, the lessor may have a different estimate of the life of the asset, its salvage value, or the opportunity cost of funds. Finally, the lessor may be able to provide expertise to its customers in equipment selection and maintenance. While all of these factors may give rise to leasing, we would not expect them to be nearly as important as the tax reason.

EVALUATING LEASE FINANCING IN RELATION TO DEBT FINANCING

To evaluate whether or not a proposal for lease financing makes economic sense, one should compare the proposal with financing the asset with debt. Whether leasing or borrowing is best will depend on the patterns of cash flows for each financing method and on the opportunity cost of funds. To illustrate a method of analysis, we compare lease financing with debt financing, using a hypothetical example. We assume that the investment worthiness of the project is evaluated separately from the specific method of financing to be employed. We also assume that the firm has determined an appropriate capital structure and has decided to finance the project with a fixed-cost type of instrument—either debt or lease financing. We turn now to examining the two alternatives.

Suppose that McNabb Electronics, Inc. has decided to acquire a piece of equipment costing $148,000 to be used in the fabrication of microprocessors. If it finances the equipment with a lease, the manufacturer will provide such financing over seven years. The terms of the lease call for an annual payment of $27,500. The lease payments are made in advance; that is, at the beginning of each of the seven years. The lessee is responsible for maintenance of the equipment, insurance, and taxes; in short, it is a *net lease*.

Embodied in the lease payments is an implied interest return to the lessor. If we ignore possible residual value, the before-tax return to the lessor can be found by solving the following for R:

$$\$148,000 = \sum_{t=0}^{6} \frac{\$27,500}{(1+R)^t} \tag{1}$$

$$= \$27,500 + \$27,500 \, (PVIFA_{R,6}) \tag{2}$$

Because these lease payments are made in advance, we solve for the internal rate of return, R, that equates the cost of the asset with one lease payment at time 0, plus the present value of an annuity consisting of six lease payments at the end of each of the next six years. When we solve for R, we find it to be 9.79%. If, instead of this return, the lessor wishes a before-tax return of 11%, it would need to obtain annual lease payments of X in the following equation:

$$\$148,000 = \sum_{t=0}^{6} \frac{X}{(1+.11)^t}$$

$$\$148,000 = X + X\,(PVIFA_{11\%,\,6})$$
$$\$148,000 = X + X\,(4.231) \qquad\qquad (3)$$
$$\$148,000 = X\,(5.231)$$
$$X = \$148,000/5.231$$
$$X = \mathbf{\$28,293}$$

In equation (3), 4.231 is the present value interest factor of an annuity at 11% for six years. Therefore, the annual lease payment would be $28,293.

If the asset is purchased, McNabb Electronics would finance it with a seven-year term loan at 12%. The company is in a 40% tax bracket. The asset falls in the five-year property class for modified accelerated cost recovery (depreciation) purposes. Accordingly, the depreciation schedule discussed earlier is used:

	YEAR					
	1	2	3	4	5	6
Depreciation	20.00%	32.00%	19.20%	11.52%	11.52%	5.76%

The cost of the asset is then depreciated at these rates, so that first-year depreciation is .20 × $148,000 = $29,600 and so forth. At the end of the seven years, the equipment is expected to have a salvage value of $15,000. McNabb Electronics is entitled to this residual value, as it would be the owner of the asset under the purchase alternative.

Present Value for Lease Alternative

By comparing the present values of cash outflows for leasing and borrowing, we are able to tell which method of financing should be used. It is simply the one with the *lowest* present value of cash outflows less inflows. Remember that the company will make annual lease payments of $27,500 if the asset is leased. Because these payments are an expense, they are deductible for tax purposes, but only in the year for which the payment applies. The $27,500 payment at the end of year 0 represents a prepaid expense and is not deductible for tax purposes until the end of year 1. Similarly, the other six payments are not deductible until the end of the following year.

As leasing is analogous to borrowing, an appropriate discount rate for discounting the after-tax cash flows might be the after-tax cost of borrowing. For our example, the after-tax cost of borrowing is 12% times (1 − .40), or 7.2%. The reason for using this rate as our discount rate is that the difference in cash flows between lease financing involves little risk. Therefore, it is not appropriate to use the company's overall cost of capital, which embodies a risk premium for the firm as a whole, as the discount rate.

Given the foregoing information, we are able to compute the present value of cash flows. The computed figures are shown in the last column of Exhibit 15-2. We see that the present value of the total cash flows under the leasing alternatives is $98,904. This figure must then be compared with the present value of cash flows under the borrowing alternative.

Present Value for Borrowing Alternative

If the asset is purchased, McNabb Electronics is assumed to finance it entirely with a 12% unsecured term loan with a payment schedule being of the same general configuration as the lease payment schedule. In other words, loan payments are assumed to be payable at the beginning, not the end, of each year. This assumption places the loan on a basis roughly equivalent with the lease in terms of the time pattern of cash flows. A loan of $148,000 is taken out at time 0 and is payable over seven years with annual payments of $28,955 at the beginning of each year.[3] The proportion of interest in each payment depends on the unpaid principal amount owing during the year. The principal amount owing during the first year is $148,000 minus the payment at the very start of the year of $28,955, or **$119,045**. The annual interest for the first year is $119,045 × .12 = **$14,285**.[4] As subsequent payments are made, the interest component decreases. Exhibit 15-3 shows these components over time.

To compute the cash outflows after taxes for the debt alternative, we must determine the tax effect.[5] This requires knowing the amounts of annual interest and annual depreciation. Using the modified accelerated cost recovery schedule for the five-year property class listed earlier, we show the annual depreciation charges in column (c) of Exhibit 15-4. Because both depreciation and interest are deductible expenses for tax purposes, they provide tax-shield benefits equal to their sum times the assumed tax rate of 40%. This is shown in column (d) of the table. When these benefits are deducted from the debt payment, we obtain the cash outflow after taxes at the end of each year, shown in column (e). At the end of the seventh year, the asset is expected to have a salvage value of $15,000. This *recapture of depreciation* is subject to the corporate tax rate of 40% for the company, which leaves an expected after-tax cash inflow of $9,000. Finally we compute the present value of all these cash flows at a 7.2% discount rate and find that they total $93,484.

This present value of cash outflow for the debt alternative, $93,484, is less than that for the lease alternative, which is $98,904. Therefore, the analysis suggests that the company use debt as opposed to lease financing in acquiring the use of the asset. This conclusion arises despite the fact that the implicit interest rate embodied in the lease payments, 9.79%, is less than the explicit cost of debt financing, 12%. However, if the asset

Exhibit 15-2 Schedule of Cash Flows for the Leasing Alternative

End of Year	(a) Lease Payment	(b) Tax-Shield Benefits $(a)_{t-1} \times (.40)$	(c) Cash Outflow after Taxes $(a) - (b)$	(d) Present Value of Cash Outflows (at 7.2%)
0	$27,500	—	$27,500	$27,500
1–6	27,500	$11,000	16,500	78,165*
7	—	11,000	(11,000)	(6,761)
				$98,904

*Total for years 1–6.

Exhibit 15-3 Schedule of Debt Payments

End of Year	(a) Loan Payment	(b) Principal Amount Owing at End of Year $(b)_{t-1} - (a) + (c)$	(c) Annual Interest $(b)_{t-1} \times (.12)$
0	$28,955	$119,045	$ 0
1	28,955	104,375	14,285
2	28,955	87,945	12,525
3	28,955	69,543	10,553
4	28,955	48,933	8,345
5	28,955	25,850	5,872
6	28,952	0	3,102

Exhibit 15-4   Schedule of Cash Flows for the Debt Alternative

End of Year	(a) Loan Payment	(b) Annual Interest	(c) Annual Depreciation	(d) Tax-Shield Benefits [(b) + (c)] × (.40)	(e) Cash Outflows after Taxes (a) – (d)	(f) Present Value of Cash Outflows (at 7.2%)
0	$ 28,955	$ 0	$ 0	$ 0	$28,955	$28,955
1	28,955	14,285	29,600	17,554	11,401	10,635
2	28,955	12,525	47,360	23,954	5,001	4,352
3	28,955	10,553	28,416	15,588	13,367	10,851
4	28,955	8,345	17,050	10,158	18,797	14,233
5	28,955	5,872	17,050	9,169	19,786	13,976
6	28,952	3,102	8,524	4,650	24,303	16,013
7	(15,000)*	0	0	(6,000)**	(9,000)	(5,532)
			$148,000			$93,484

*Salvage value.
**Tax due to recapture of depreciation, $15,000 × .40 = $6,000.

is bought, the company is able to avail itself of modified accelerated cost recovery depreciation, and this helps the situation from a present value standpoint. Moreover, the residual value at the end of the project is a favorable factor, whereas this value goes to the lessor with lease financing.

Another factor that favors the debt alternative is the deductibility of interest payments for tax purposes. Because the amount of interest embodied in a "mortgage-type" debt payment is higher at first and declines with successive payments, the tax benefits associated with these payments follow the same pattern over time. From a present value standpoint, this pattern benefits the firm relative to the pattern of lease payments, which are typically constant over time. These advantages of a debt-financed purchase more than offset the implied interest-rate advantage to lease financing. The lease payment terms are simply not attractive enough to give up the tax and other benefits associated with ownership.

Other Considerations

The decision to borrow rests on the relative timing and magnitude of cash flows under the two financing alternatives, as well as on the discount rate employed. We have assumed that the cash flows are known with certainty. While this is reasonable for the most part, there is some uncertainty that, on occasion, can be important. The estimated salvage (residual) value of an asset is usually subject to considerable uncertainty, for example.

As we can see, deciding between leasing and borrowing can involve some rather extensive calculations. Each situation requires a separate analysis. The analysis is complicated if the two alternatives involve different amounts of financing. If we finance less than the total cost of the asset by borrowing but finance 100% of the cost by leasing, we must consider the difference in the amount of financing, both from the standpoint of explicit as well as implicit costs. These considerations and the others mentioned throughout this chapter can make the evaluation of lease financing rather detailed.

The Importance of the Tax Rate

Lease-versus-borrow analyses are very sensitive to the tax rate of the potential lessee. If the effective tax rate is 20% instead of the 40% in our previous example, the present value comparison changes. The tax-shield benefits are lower and the discount rate—the after-tax cost of borrowing—higher, i.e., 12% (1 − .20) = 9.6%. By reworking the figures in Exhibits 15-2 and 15-4, we can determine that these two changes result in the present value of cash outflows for the lease alternative being $121,554 and for the debt alternative $118,577. The debt alternative still dominates, but by a lesser margin than before. At a zero tax rate and using the full 12% as the discount rate, the present value of cash outflows for the lease alternative is $140,564 versus $141,215 for the debt alternative. The lease alternative now dominates by a slight margin.

The important lesson of these examples is that the tax rate of the lessee matters a lot. In general, as the effective tax rate declines, the relative advantage of debt versus lease financing declines and may actually reverse, depending on the circumstances. This explains why lease financing usually is attractive only to those in low or zero tax brackets who are unable to enjoy the full tax benefits associated with owning an asset. By leasing from a party in a high tax bracket, the lessee may be able to get part of the tax benefits of ownership because lease payments are lower than they otherwise would be. How much lower depends on the supply and demand conditions in the leasing industry. The exact sharing of the tax benefits is negotiable, and it depends on the competitive situations at the time.

For all practical purposes, the leasing industry in the United States is an artifact of the tax laws. As these laws change, the industry is impacted, often in dramatic ways. Parties that financed via the leasing route may no longer do so, while others may find it attractive. Previous lessors may step out of the business, while others may be able to serve this role to advantage. The greater the change in laws affecting asset write-offs, tax rates, and alternative minimum taxes, the greater the disequilibrium, and the longer the equilibration process as parties exit or enter the market as either lessors or lessees. One thing is clear: taxes have a dominant influence on the leasing industry.

SUMMARY

Three basic factors provide the key considerations in selecting a source of short-term financing: (1) the effective cost of credit, (2) the availability of financing in the amount and for the time needed, and (3) the effect of the use of credit from a particular source on the cost and availability of other sources of credit.

The various sources of short-term credit can be categorized into two groups: unsecured and secured. Unsecured credit offers no specific assets as security for the loan agreement. The primary sources include trade credit, lines of credit, unsecured transaction loans from commercial banks, and commercial paper. Secured credit is generally provided to business firms by commercial banks, finance companies, and factors. The most popular sources of security involve the use of accounts receivable and inventories. Loans secured by accounts receivable include pledging agreements, in which a firm pledges its receivables as security for a loan, and factoring agreements, in which the firm sells the receivables to a factor. A primary difference in these two arrangements relates to the ability of the lender to seek payment from the borrower in the event the accounts used as collateral become uncollectable. In a pledging arrangement the lender retains the right of recourse in the event of default, whereas in factoring, a lender is generally without recourse.

Loans secured by inventories can be made using one of several types of security arrangements. Among the most widely used are the floating lien, chattel mortgage, field warehouse agreement, and terminal warehouse agreement. The form of agreement used will depend on the type of inventories pledged as collateral and the degree of control the lender wishes to exercise over the loan collateral.

- A term loan represents debt originally scheduled for repayment in more than 1 year but generally in less than 10 years.
- Commercial banks, insurance companies, and other institutional investors make term loans to business firms. Banks also provide financing under a revolving credit agreement, which represents a formal commitment on the part of the bank to lend up to a certain amount of money over a specified period of time.
- Lenders who offer unsecured credit usually impose restrictions on the borrower. These restrictions are called protective covenants and are contained in a loan agreement. If the borrower defaults under any of the provisions of the loan agreement, the lender may initiate immediate corrective measures.
- On a secured basis, firms can obtain intermediate-term financing by pledging equipment that they own or are purchasing. Banks, finance companies, and sellers of the equipment are active in providing this type of secured financing.
- In lease financing, the lessee (the renter) agrees to pay the lessor (the owner), periodically, for economic use of the lessor's asset. Because of this contractual obligation, leasing is regarded as a method of financing similar to borrowing.
- An operating lease is a short-term lease that is often cancelable, while a financial lease is a long-term lease that is not cancelable.
- A financial lease can involve the acquisition of an asset under a direct lease, a sale and lease-back arrangement, or a leveraged lease.
- One of the principal economic reasons for leasing is the inability of a firm to utilize all the tax benefits associated with the ownership of an asset. This can arise because of (1) unprofitable operations, (2) the provisions of the alternative minimum tax (AMT), or (3) insufficient earnings to effectively utilize all of the possible tax benefits.
- A common means used for analyzing lease financing in relation to debt financing is to discount to present value the after-tax net cash flows under each alternative, using the after-tax cost of borrowing as the discount rate. The preferred financing alternative is the one that provides the lower present value of cash outflows.

SELF-CORRECTION PROBLEMS

1. The Marilyn Sales Company is a wholesale machine tool broker that has gone through a recent expansion of its activities resulting in a doubling of its sales. The company has determined that it needs an additional $200 million in short-term funds to finance peak season sales during roughly six months of the year. Marilyn's treasurer has recommended that the firm use a commercial paper offering to raise the needed funds. Specifically, he has determined that a $200 million offering would require 10% interest (paid in advance or discounted) plus a $125,000 placement fee. The paper would carry a six-month (180-day) maturity. What is the effective cost of credit?

2. The treasurer of the Lights-a-Lot Mfg. Company is faced with three alternative bank loans. The firm wishes to select the one that minimizes its cost of credit on a $200,000 note that it plans to issue in the next 10 days. Relevant information for the three loan configurations is found below:

   a. An 18% rate of interest with interest paid at year-end and no compensating balance requirement.

   b. A 16% rate of interest but carrying a 20% compensating balance requirement. This loan also calls for interest to be paid at year-end.

   c. A 14% rate of interest that is discounted plus a 20% compensating balance requirement.

Analyze the cost of each of these alternatives. You may assume the firm would not normally maintain any bank balance that might be used to meet the 20% compensating balance requirements of alternatives (b) and (c).

3. Burger Rex is expanding its chain of fast-food outlets. This program will require a capital expenditure of $3 million, which must be financed. The company has settled on a three-year revolving credit of $3 million, which may be converted into a three-year term loan at the expiration of the revolving credit commitment. The commitment fee for both credit arrangements is .5% of the unused portions. The bank has quoted Burger Rex an interest rate of 1% over prime for the revolving credit and 1.5% over prime for the term loan, if that option is taken. The company expects to borrow $1.4 million at the outset and another $1.6 million at the very end of the first year. At the expiration of the revolving credit, the company expects to take down the full-term loan. At the end of each of the fourth, fifth, and sixth years, it expects to make principal payments of $1 million.

   a. For each of the next six years, what is the expected commitment fee in dollars?

   b. What is the expected dollar interest cost above the prime rate?

4. Assuming that annual lease payments are made in advance (an annuity due) and that there is no residual value, solve for the unknown in each of the following situations:

   a. For a purchase price of $46,000, an implicit interest rate of 11%, and a six-year lease period, solve for the annual lease payment.

   b. For a purchase price of $210,000, a five-year lease period, and annual lease payments of $47,030, solve for the implied interest rate.

   c. For an implied interest rate of 8%, a seven-year lease period, and annual lease payments of $16,000, solve for the purchase price.

   d. For a purchase price of $165,000, an implied interest rate of 10%, and annual lease payments of $24,412, solve for the lease period.

5. U.S. Blivet wishes to acquire a $100,000 blivet degreasing machine, which has a useful life of eight years. At the end of this time, the machine's scrap value will be $8,000. The asset falls into the five-year property class for cost recovery (depreciation) purposes. The company can use either lease or debt financing. Lease payments of $16,000 at the beginning of each of the eight years would be required. If debt financed, the interest rate would be 10%, and debt payments would be due at the beginning of each of the eight years. (Interest would be amortized as a mortgage-type of debt instrument.) The company is in a 40% tax bracket. Which method of financing has the lower present value of cash outflows?

SOLUTIONS TO SELF-CORRECTION PROBLEMS

1. The discounted interest cost of the commercial paper is calculated as follows:

$$\text{Interest expense} = .10 \times \$200,000,000 \times 180/360 = \$10,000,000$$

The effective cost of credit can now be calculated as follows:

$$\text{APR} = \frac{\$10,000,000 + \$125,000}{\$200,000,000 - \$125,000 - \$10,000,000} \times \frac{1}{180/360} = .1066 \text{ or } 10.66\%$$

2. a.

$$\text{APR} = \frac{.18 \times \$200,000}{\$200,000,000} \times \frac{1}{1} = .18, \text{ or } 18\%$$

b.

$$APR = \frac{.16 \times \$200,000}{\$200,000 - (.20 \times \$200,000)} \times \frac{1}{1} = .20 \text{ or } 20\%$$

c.

$$APR = \frac{.14 \times \$200,000}{\$200,000 - (.14 \times \$200,000) - (.2 \times \$200,000)} \times \frac{1}{1} = .2121 \text{ or } 21.21\%$$

Alternative (a) offers the lower-cost service of financing, although it carries the highest stated rate of interest. The reason for this is that there is no compensating balance requirement, nor is interest discounted for this alternative.

3. a. b. (in thousands)

	Year					
	Revolving Credit			Term Loan		
	1	2	3	4	5	6
Amount borrowed during year	$1,400	$3,000	$3,000	$3,000	$2,000	$1,000
Unused portion	1,600	0	0	0	1,000	2,000
Commitment fee (.005)	8	0	0	0	5	10
Interest cost above prime (1% first 3 years and 1.5% in last 3)	14	30	30	45	30	15

4. A generalized version of equation (2) as the formula is used throughout.

a. $46,000 = X + X(\text{PVIFA } 11\%, 5 \text{ yr})$
    $46,000 = X + X(3.696) = X(4.696)$
    $X = \$46,000/4.696 = \$9,796$

b. $\$210,000 = \$47,030/(1 + PVIFA_{X, 5 \text{ yr}})$
    $\$210,000/\$47,030 = (1 + PVIFA_{X, 5 \text{ yr}}) = 4.465$

Subtracting 1 from this gives $PVIFA_{X, 5} = 3.465$. Looking in Appendix E, across the *4-period row*, we find that 3.465 is the figure reported for 6%. Therefore, the implied interest rate, X, is 6%.

c.

$$X = \$16,000 (1 + PVIFA_{8\%, 6})$$
$$X = \$16,000 (1 + 4.623) = \mathbf{\$89,968}$$

d.

$$\$165,000 = \$24,412 (1 + PVIFA_{10\%, X})$$
$$\$165,000/\$24,412 = (1 + PVIFA_{10\%, X}) = 6.759$$

Subtracting 1 from this gives 5.759. Looking in Appendix E in the *10% column*, we find that 5.759 corresponds to the *9-period row*. Therefore, the lease period is 9 + 1, or *10 years*.

5. Schedule of cash flows for the leasing alternative

End of Year	(a) Lease Payment	(b) Tax-Shield Benefits $(a)_{t-1} \times (.40)$	(c) Cash Outflow after Taxes (a) – (b)	(d) Present Value of Cash Outflows (at 8.4%)
0	$16,000	—	$16,000	$16,000
1–7	16,000	$6,400	9,600	49,305*
8	—	6,400	(6,400)	(3,357)
				$61,948

*Total for years 1–7

The discount rate is the before-tax cost of borrowing times 1 minus the tax rate, or $(14\%)(1 - .40) = 8.4\%$.

Annual debt payment:

$$\$100,000 = X(1 + PVIFA_{14\%,\ 7})$$
$$\$100,000 = X(1 + 4.288) = X(5.288)$$
$$X = \$100,000/5.288 = \$18,910$$

Schedule of debt payments

End of Year	(a) Loan Payment	(b) Principal Amount Owing at End of Year $(b)_{t-1} - (a) + (c)$	(c) Annual Interest $(b)_{t-1} \times (.14)$
0	$18,910	$81,090	$ 0
1	18,910	73,533	11,353
2	18,910	64,917	10,295
3	18,910	55,096	9,088
4	18,910	43,899	7,713
5	18,910	31,135	6,146
6	18,910	16,584	4,359
7	18,906*	0	2,322

*The last payment is slightly lower due to rounding throughout.

Schedule of cash flows for the debt alternative

End of Year	(a) Debt Payment	(b) Annual Interest	(c) Annual Depreciation	(d) Tax-Shield Benefits (b + c) .40	(e) After-Tax Cash Flow (a) – (d)	(f) PV of Cash Flows (at 8.4%)
0	$18,910	$ 0	$ 0	$ 0	$18,910	$18,910
1	18,910	11,353	20,000	12,541	6,369	5,875
2	18,910	10,295	32,000	16,918	1,992	1,695
3	18,910	9,088	19,200	11,315	7,693	5,962
4	18,910	7,713	11,520	7,693	11,217	8,124
5	18,910	6,146	11,520	7,066	11,844	7,913
6	18,910	4,359	5,760	4,048	14,862	9,160
7	18,906	2,322		929	17,977	10,222
8	(8,000)*			(3,200)**	(4,800)	(2,518)
			$100,000			$65,344

*Salvage value.
**Tax due to recapture of depreciation, ($8,000) (.40) = $3,200.

As the lease alternative has the lower present value of cash outflows, it is preferred.

QUESTIONS

1. Identify and discuss the advantages and disadvantages generally associated with the use of short-term debt.
2. Explain what is meant by the statement, "The use of current liabilities as opposed to long-term debt subjects the firm to a greater risk of illiquidity."
3. What distinguishes short-term, intermediate-term, and long-term debt?
4. What considerations should be used in selecting a source of short-term credit?
5. How can we accommodate the effects of compounding in our calculation of the effective cost of short-term credit?
6. There are three major sources of unsecured short-term credit other than accrued wages and taxes. List and discuss the distinguishing characteristics of each.
7. What is meant by the following trade credit terms: 2/10, net 30; 4/30, net 60; 3/15, net 45?
8. Define the following:
   a. Line of credit
   b. Commercial paper
   c. Compensating balance
   d. Prime rate
9. What is the purpose of protective covenants in a term loan agreement?
10. How does a revolving credit agreement differ from a line of credit?
11. How should a lender go about setting (a) the working capital protective covenant in a loan agreement? (b) the capital expenditure covenant in a loan agreement?
12. As a borrower, how would you approach negotiating the working capital and capital expenditure restrictions a lender wished to impose?

13. What are the key financial institutions that provide intermediate-term financing to business firms?

14. How does a chattel mortgage differ from a conditional sales contract when it comes to financing equipment?

15. How does a financial lease differ from an operating lease? How does a full-service (or maintenance) lease differ from a net lease?

16. Contrast a sale and leaseback with direct leasing.

17. Some business people consider that the risk of obsolescence and inflexibility is being transferred from the lessee to the lessor. How is the lessor induced to accept higher risk and greater inflexibility?

18. In your opinion, would the following factors tend to favor borrowing or leasing as a financing alternative? Why?
   a. Increased corporate tax rate
   b. Faster accelerated depreciation
   c. Rising price level
   d. Increased residual value of the leased asset
   e. An increase in the risk-free interest rate

PROBLEMS

1. Estimating the Cost of Bank Credit. Paymaster Enterprises has arranged to finance its seasonal working-capital needs with a short-term bank loan. The loan will carry a rate of 12% per annum with interest paid in advance (discounted). In addition, Paymaster must maintain a minimum demand deposit with the bank of 10% of the loan balance throughout the term of the loan. If Paymaster plans to borrow $100,000 for a period of three months, what is the effective cost of the bank loan?

2. Estimating the Cost of Commercial Paper. On February 3, 199X, the Burlington Western Company plans a commercial paper issue of $20 million. The firm has never used commercial paper before but has been assured by the firm placing the issue that it will have no difficulty raising the funds. The commercial paper will carry a 270-day maturity and will require interest based on a rate of 11% per annum. In addition, the firm will have to pay fees totaling $200,000 in order to bring the issue to market and place it. What is the effective cost of the commercial paper issue to Burlington Western?

3. Cost of Trade Credit. Calculate the effective cost of the following trade credit terms where payment is made on the net due date: (a) 2/10, net 30; (b) 3/15, net 30; (c) 3/15, net 45; (d) 2/15, net 60.

4. Eva Forlines Fashions Corporation wishes to borrow $600,000 on a five-year term basis. Cattleperson's National Bank is willing to make such a loan at a 14% rate, provided the loan is completely amortized over the five-year period. Payments are due at the end of each of the five years. Set up an amortization schedule of equal annual loan payments that will satisfy these conditions. Be sure to show both the principal and interest components of each of the overall payments.

5. Given the following information, compute the annual lease payment (paid in advance) that a lessor will require:
   a. Purchase price of $260,000, interest rate of 13%, five-year lease period, and no residual value
   b. Purchase price of $138,000, interest rate of 6%, nine-year lease period, and a near-certain residual value of $20,000
   c. Purchase price of $773,000, interest rate of 9%, ten-year lease period, and no residual value

6. Volt Electronics Company is considering leasing one of its products in addition to selling it outright to customers. The product, the Volt Tester, sells for $18,600 and has an economic life of eight years.

   a. To earn 12% interest, what annual lease payment must Volt require as lessor? (Assume that lease payments are payable in advance.)

   b. If the product has a salvage value (known with certainty) of $4,000 at the end of eight years, what annual lease payment will be required?

7. Fez Fabulous Fabrics wishes to acquire a $100,000 multifacet cutting machine. The machine has a useful life of eight years, after which there is no expected salvage value. If Fez were to finance the cutting machine by signing an eight-year lease contract, annual lease payments of $16,000 would be required, payable in advance. The company could also finance the purchase of the machine with a 12% term loan having a payment schedule of the same general configuration as the lease payment schedule. The asset falls in the five-year property class for cost recovery (depreciation) purposes, and the company has a 35% tax rate. What is the present value of cash outflows for each of these alternatives, using the after-tax cost of debt as the discount rate? Which alternative is preferred?

8. Valequez Ranches, Inc. wishes to acquire a mechanized feed spreader that costs $80,000. The ranch company intends to operate the equipment for five years, at which time it will need to be replaced. However, it is expected to have a salvage value of $10,000 at the end of the fifth year. The asset will be depreciated on a straight-line basis ($16,000 per year) over the next five years, and Valequez Ranches is in a 30% tax bracket. Two means for financing the feed spreader are available. A lease arrangement calls for annual lease payments of $19,000, payable in advance. A debt alternative carries an interest cost of 10%. Debt payments will be made at the start of each of the five years using mortgage-type debt amortization. Using the present-value method, determine the best financing alternative.

9. The Locke Corporation has just leased a metal-bending machine that calls for annual lease payments of $30,000 payable in advance. The lease period is six years, and the lease is classified as a capital lease for accounting purposes. The company's incremental borrowing rate is 11%, whereas the lessor's implicit interest rate is 12%. Amortization of the lease in the first year amounts to $16,332. On the basis of this information, compute the following:

   a. The accounting lease liability that will be shown on the balance sheet immediately after the first lease payment.

   b. The annual lease expense (amortization plus interest) in the first year as it will appear on the accounting income statement. (The interest expense is based on the accounting value determined in a. above.)

   c. The annual lease expense for tax purposes.

ADDENDUM 15: ACCOUNTING FOR LEASES

The accounting treatment of leases has undergone sweeping change over the past three decades. At one time leases were not disclosed in financial statements at all. Gradually lease disclosure was required and appeared first in the footnotes to the financial statements. With only minimal disclosure, leasing was attractive to certain firms as an "off-balance-sheet" method of financing. There is, however, no evidence that such financing had a favorable effect on company valuation, all other things being the same. Nevertheless, many companies proceeded on the assumption that "off-balance-sheet" financing was a good thing. Then came the Financial Accounting Standards Board Statement No. 13 (called **FASB 13**) in 1976 with an explicit ruling which called for the capitalization on the balance sheet of certain types of leases.[6] In essence, this statement says that if the lessee acquires essentially all of the economic benefits and risks of the leased property, then the value of the asset along with the corresponding lease liability must be shown on the lessee's balance sheet.

Capital and Operating Leases

Leases that conform in principle to this definition are called *capital leases*. More specifically, a lease is regarded as a capital lease if it meets one or more of the following conditions:

1. The lease transfers ownership of the asset to the lessee by the end of the lease period.
2. The lease contains an option to purchase the asset at a bargain price.
3. The lease period equals 75% or more of the estimated economic life of the asset.
4. At the beginning of the lease, the present value of the minimum lease payment equals 90% or more of the fair market value of the leased asset.

If any of these conditions is met, the lessee is said to have acquired most of the economic benefits and risks associated with the leased property. Therefore, a capital lease is involved. If a lease does not meet any of these conditions, it is classified (for accounting purposes) as an *operating lease*.[7] Essentially, operating leases give the lessee the right to use the leased property over a period of time, but they do not give the lessee all of the benefits and risks that are associated with the asset.

Recording the value of a capital lease. With a capital lease, the lessee must report the value of the leased property on the asset side of the balance sheet. The amount reflected is the present value of the minimum lease payments over the lease period. If executory costs, such as insurance, maintenance, and taxes, are a part of the total lease payment, these are deducted, and only the remainder is used for purposes of calculating the present value. As required by the accounting rules, the discount rate employed is the lower of (1) the lessee's incremental borrowing rate or (2) the rate of interest implicit in the lease if, in fact, that rate can be determined.

The present value of the lease payments should be recorded as an asset on the lessee's balance sheet. (If the fair market value of the leased property is lower than the present value of the minimum lease payments, then the fair market value would be shown.) A corresponding liability is also recorded on the balance sheet, with the present value of payments due after one year being shown as noncurrent liabilities. Information on leased property may be combined with similar information on assets that are owned, but there must be a disclosure in a footnote with respect to the value of the leased property and its amortization. The capital-lease-related portions of a hypothetical balance sheet might look like the following:

Assets		Liabilities	
Gross fixed assets[a]	$3,000,000	Current	
Less: accumulated		Obligations under	
depreciation end		capital leases	$90,000
amortization	1,000,000	Noncurrent	
Net fixed assets	$2,000,000	Obligations under	
		capital leases	$270,000

[a]Gross fixed assets include leased property of $500,000. Accumulated depreciation and amortization includes $140,000 in amortization associated with such property

Here we see in the footnote to the balance sheet information that the capitalized value of leases of the company is $500,000 less $140,000 in amortization, or $360,000 in total. The liability is split between $90,000 in current liabilities and $270,000 due beyond one year. In addition to this information, more details are required in footnotes. Relevant information here includes the gross amounts of leased property by major property categories (these can be combined with categories of owned assets); the total future minimum lease payments; a schedule, by years, of future lease payments required over the next five years; the total minimum sublease rentals to be received; the existence and terms of purchase or renewal options and escalation clauses; rentals that are contingent on some factor other than the passage of time; and any restrictions imposed in the lease agreements.

Disclosure of operating leases. For operating leases, as for capital leases, some of the same disclosure is required, but it can be in footnotes. For noncancellable leases having remaining terms in excess of one year, the lessee must disclose total future minimum lease payments; a schedule, by year, for the next five years plus a total figure for all years thereafter; the total sublease rentals to be received; the basis for contingent rental payments; the existence and terms of purchase and renewal options and escalation clauses; and any lease agreement restrictions. The last two categories are included in a general description of the leasing arrangement.

Amortizing the Capital Lease and Reducing the Obligation

A capital lease must be amortized and the liability reduced over the lease period. The method of amortization can be the lessee's usual depreciation method for assets that are owned. It should be pointed out that the period of amortization is always the lease term even if the economic life of the asset is longer. If the economic life is longer, the asset would have an expected residual value, which would go to the lessor. FASB 13 also requires that the capital lease obligation be reduced and expensed over the lease period by the "interest method." Under this method, each lease payment is separated into two components—the payment of principal and the payment of interest. The obligation is reduced by just the amount of the principal payment.

Reporting earnings. For income reporting purposes, FASB 13 requires that both the amortization of the leased property and the annual interest embodied in the capital lease payment be treated as an expense. This expense is then deducted in the same way that any expense is to obtain net income. As you can appreciate, the accounting for leases can become quite complicated.

INTERNET EXERCISE

Short-Term, Intermediate-Term, and Long-Term Financing

1. Visit www.sb.gov.bc.ca for a small business workshop and complete the tutorials in short-term and long-term financing.

   Prepare a one-page business memo summarizing your findings.
2. Use the credit card calculator at www.moneyadvisor.com web site to analyze your credit card situation. Based on your findings, what changes (if any) should you make in your usage of credit cards?

Leasing

1. Use the lease-versus-buy calculator at www.moneyadvisor.com to determine whether to lease or buy your next car. Hand in a printout of the screen on which your average cost per year is calculated.

2. The Dorman Company has decided to build a 10-story office building and, just like many other companies, this company has decided to contract a professional lessor to build the building and then lease it to you on a 25-year lease. Using a major search engine, find three leasing companies that provide real estate leasing of this type.

Notes

[1] The *prime rate of interest* is the rate that a bank charges its most creditworthy customers.

[2] If M & M needs the use of a full $200,000 then it will have to borrow more than $222,222 to cover both the compensating balance requirement and the discounted interest. In fact, the firm will have to borrow some amount B such that

$$B - .10B - (.12 \times 1/2)B = \$200,000$$

$$.84B = \$200,000$$

$$B = \frac{\$200,000}{.84} = \$238,095$$

The cost of credit remains the same at 14.29%, as we see below:

$$APR = \frac{\$14,285.70}{\$238,095 - \$23,810 - \$14,285.70} \times \frac{1}{180/360}$$

$$= .1429, \text{ or } 14.29\%$$

[3] This amount is computed in the same manner as in equation (3), using 12% instead of 11%. However, rather than relying on Appendix E for (PVIFA12%, 7 yr) we chose to use the PVIFA formula in order to get a figure that was accurate to more significant digits.

[4] For ease of illustration, we round to the nearest dollar throughout. This results in the final debt payment in Exhibit 15-3 being slightly less than would otherwise be the case.

[5] We assume for ease of illustration that the firm's regularly determined tax is higher than its AMT. Therefore, the tax-shield benefits of depreciation (a "tax preference item") are not lost (or lowered) through a debt-financed purchase.

[6] *Statement of Financial Accounting Standards No. 13, Accounting for Leases* (Stamford, CT: Financial Accounting Standards Board, November 1976).

[7] Earlier in this chapter, we used the term *operating lease* to describe a short-term lease. Accountants, however, would also apply this term to any (long-term) financial lease that did not technically qualify to be considered a capital lease.

SECTION IX
COST OF CAPITAL AND VALUATION OF LONG-TERM DEBT AND EQUITY

Chapter 16: Introduction to Cost of Capital

Chapter 17: Valuing Long-Term Debt and Equity

INTRODUCTION TO COST OF CAPITAL

A firm's cost of capital is simply a weighted average of the rates of return required by investors in the firm's securities. Thus, the cost of capital serves as the linkage between a firm's investment and financing decisions. In this chapter we take an in-depth look at the cost of capital or hurdle rate for new investments. Specifically, we will discuss the following topics:

1. The cost-of-capital concept
2. The factors that determine investor-required rates of return
3. The assumptions underlying the measurement of a firm's cost of capital
4. The calculation of the weighted average cost of capital
5. An empirical study of large firms' estimates of their cost of capital

THE COST-OF-CAPITAL CONCEPT

The cost of capital is the opportunity cost of using funds to invest in new projects. This is appropriate because the cost of capital is that rate of return on the firm's total investment which earns the required rates of return of all the sources of financing. Furthermore, if the firm earns the required rates of return on all its sources of financing, including that of the common shareholders, then the value of its common stock will not be changed by the investment. By the same reasoning, if the firm earns a rate of return higher than the cost of capital, then the excess return will lead to an increase in the value of the firm's common stock and, consequently, an increase in shareholder wealth. The logic of using the cost of capital as the hurdle rate for new capital investment can be summarized as follows:

If the investment rate of return is:	Then shareholder wealth will
Less than Cost of Capital	Decrease
Equal to Cost of Capital	No Change
More than Cost of Capital	Increase

To illustrate the calculation of the cost of capital, consider the capital structure of the company found in Exhibit 16-1. The company has three sources of capital: debt, preferred stock, and common stock. Management is considering a $200,000 investment opportunity with an expected internal rate of return of 14%. The current cost of the firm's capital (i.e., its required rates of return) for each source of financing is as follows:

Cost of debt capital	10%
Cost of preferred stock	12
Cost of common stock	16

Given this information, should the firm make the investment? The debt holder and preferred stockholders would probably encourage us to undertake the project. However, because the 14% internal rate of return on the investment is less than the common stockholder's required rate of return, shareholders might argue that the investment should be forgone. What is the right choice?

To answer this question, we must first determine what percentage of the $200,000 is to be provided by each type of investor. If we intend to maintain the same capital structure mix as reflected in Exhibit 16-1 (30% debt, 10% preferred stock, and 60% common stock), we could compute a weighted cost of capital, where the weights equal the percentage of capital to be financed by each source. For our example, the weighted cost of the individual sources of capital as computed in Exhibit 16-2 is 13.8%. From this calculation we would conclude that an investment offering at least a 13.8% return would be acceptable to the company's investors. The investment should be undertaken, because the 14% rate of return more than satisfies all investors, as indicated by a 13.8% weighted cost of capital. Again, the weighted cost of capital is equal to the cost of each source of financing (debt, preferred stock, and common stock) multiplied by the percentage of the financing provided by that source.

Exhibit 16-1   The Company Capital Structure

	Amount	Percentage of Capital Structure
Debt	$ 600,000	30%
Preferred stock	200,000	10
Common stock	1,200,000	60
Total liabilities and equity	$2,000,000	100%

Exhibit 16-2   The Company's Weighted Cost of Capital

	Weights (Percentage of Financing)	×	Cost of Individual Sources	=	Weighted Cost
Debt	30%		10%		3.0%
Preferred stock	10		12		1.2
Common stock	60		16		9.6
	100%		Weighted cost of capital:		13.8%

FACTORS DETERMINING COST-OF-CAPITAL SOURCES

What are the elements in the business environment that cause a company's weighted cost of capital to be high or low? Exhibit 16-3 identifies four primary factors: general economic conditions, the marketability of the firm's securities (market conditions), operating and financing conditions within the company, and the amount of financing needed for new investments.

Factor 1: General Economic Conditions

General economic conditions determine the demand for and supply of capital within the economy, as well as the level of expected inflation. This economic variable is reflected in the riskless rate of return. This rate represents the rate of return on risk-free investments, such as the interest rate on short-term U.S. government securities. In

Exhibit 16-3   Primary Factors Influencing the Cost of Particular
Sources of Capital

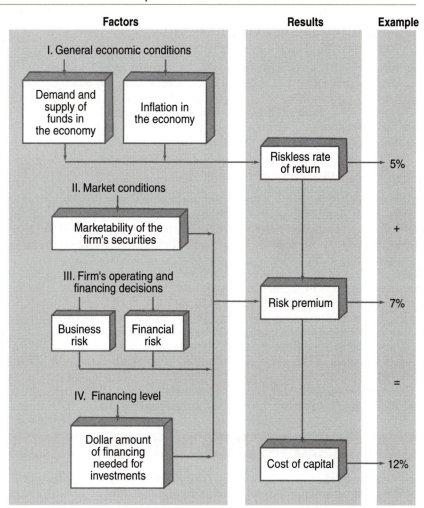

principle, as the demand for money in the economy changes relative to the supply, investors alter their required rate of return. For example, if the demand for money increases without an equivalent increase in the supply, lenders will raise their required interest rate. At the same time, if inflation is expected to deteriorate the purchasing power of the dollar, investors require a higher rate of return to compensate for this anticipated loss.

Factor 2: Market Conditions

When an investor purchases a security with a significant investment risk, an opportunity for additional returns is necessary to make the investment attractive. Essentially, as risk increases, the investor requires a higher rate of return. This increase is called a risk premium. When investors increase their required rate of return, the cost of capital rises simultaneously. Remember we have defined risk as the potential variability of return. If the security is not readily marketable when the investor wants to sell, or even if a continuous demand for the security exists but the price varies significantly, an investor will require a relatively high rate of return. Conversely, if a security is readily marketable and its price is reasonably stable, the investor will require a lower rate of return and the company's cost of capital will be lower.

Factor 3: Operating and Financing Decisions

Risk, or the variability of returns, also results from decisions made within the company. Risk resulting from these decisions is generally divided into two types: business risk and financial risk. Business risk is the variability in returns on assets and is affected by the company's investment decisions. Financial risk is the increased variability in returns to common stockholders as a result of financing with debt or preferred stock. As business risk and financial risk increase or decrease, the investors' required rate of return (and the cost of capital) will move in the same direction.

Factor 4: Amount of Financing

The last factor determining the corporation's cost of funds is the level of financing that the firm requires. As the financing requirements of the firm become larger, the weighted cost of capital increases for several reasons. For instance, as more securities are issued, additional flotation costs, or the costs incurred by the firm from issuing securities, will affect the percentage cost of the funds to the firm. Also, as management approaches the market for large amounts of capital relative to the firm's size, the investors' required rate of return may rise. Suppliers of capital become hesitant to grant relatively large sums without evidence of management's capability to absorb this capital into the business. This is typically "too much too soon." Also, as the size of the issue increases, there is greater difficulty in placing it in the market without reducing the price of the security, which also increases the firm's cost of capital.

The right-hand margin of Exhibit 16-3 presents an illustration of the cost of capital for a particular source. The risk-free rate, determined by the general economic conditions, is 5%. However, owing to the additional risks associated with the security, the firm has to earn an additional 7% to satisfy the investors' required return of 12%.

WEIGHTED COST-OF-CAPITAL MODEL ASSUMPTIONS

In a complex business world, difficulties quickly arise in computing a corporation's cost of capital. For this reason, we make several simplifying assumptions.

Constant Business Risk

Business risk is defined as the potential variability of returns on an investment, and the level of business risk within a firm is determined by management's investment policies. An investor's required rate of return for a company's securities—and therefore the firm's cost of capital—is a function of the firm's current business risk. If this risk level is altered, the corporation's investors will naturally change their required rates of return, which in turn will modify the cost of capital. However, the amount of change in the cost of capital resulting from a given increase or decrease in business risk is difficult to assess. For this reason, the cost of capital calculation assumes that any investment under consideration will not significantly change the firm's business risk. In other words, the corporation's cost of capital is an appropriate investment criterion only for an investment having a business risk level similar to that of existing assets.

Constant Financial Risk

Financial risk has been defined as the increased variability in returns on common stock resulting from the increased use of debt and preferred stock financing. Also, financial risk relates to the threat of bankruptcy. As the percentage of debt in the capital structure increases, the possibility that the firm will be unable to pay interest and the principal balance is also increased. As a result, the level of financial risk in a company has an impact on the investors' required rate of return. As the amount of debt rises, the common stockholders will increase their required rate of return. In other words, the costs of individual sources of capital are a function of the current financial structure. For this reason, the data used in computing the cost of capital are appropriate only if management continues to use the same financial mix. If the present capital structure consists of 40% debt, 10% preferred stock, and 50% common stock, this capital structure is assumed to be maintained in the financing of future investments.

Constant Dividend Policy

A third assumption required in estimating the cost of capital relates to the corporation's dividend policy. For ease of computation, we generally assume that a firm's dividends are increasing at a constant annual growth rate. Also, we assume this growth to be a function of the firm's earning capabilities and not merely the result of paying out a larger percentage of the company's earnings. Thus, it is implicitly assumed that the dividend payout ratio (dividends/net income) is constant. The aforementioned assumptions of the weighted cost-of-capital model are quite restrictive. In a practical investment analysis, the financial executive may need a range of possible cost of capital values rather than a single-point estimate. For example, it may be more appropriate to talk in terms of a 10% to 12% range as an estimate of the firm's cost of capital, rather than assuming that a precise number can be determined. In this chapter, however, our principal concern will be with calculating a single cost of capital figure.

COMPUTING THE WEIGHTED COST OF CAPITAL

A firm's weighted cost of capital is a composite of the individual costs of financing, weighted by the percentage of financing provided by each source. Therefore, a firm's weighted cost of capital is a function of (1) the individual costs of capital and (2) the makeup of the capital structure—the percentage of funds provided by debt, preferred stock, and common stock. Also, as we noted earlier, the amount of funds needed affects the cost of capital.

The three basic steps for computing a company's cost of capital are outlined in Exhibit 16-4. The computations are not difficult if we understand our purpose: we want

Exhibit 16-4　Computing the Weighted Cost of Capital: Basic Steps

To compute a firm's weighted cost of capital requires the following three things:

1. Identify the cost of capital for each and every source of financing (i.e., each source of debt, preferred stock, and common stock).
2. Determine the percentage of debt, preferred stock, and common stock to be used in the financing of future investments.
3. Calculate the firm's weighted average cost of capital using the percentage of financing as the weights.

to calculate the firm's weighted cost of capital. For a simple exercise, calculate the average age of students in a course where 40% are 19 years old, 50% are 20 years old, and 10% are 21 years old. We can easily find the average age to be 19.7 years by weighing each age by the percentage in each age category [(40%) (19) + (50%) (20) + (10%) (21)]. In a similar way, the weighted cost of capital is estimated by weighting the cost of each individual source by the percentage of financing it provides. If we finance an investment by 40% debt at a 10% cost and 60% common equity at a cost of 18%, the weighted cost of capital is 14.8% (.40 × 10% + .60 x 18% = 14.8%).

Although the details become somewhat involved, the basic approach which is summarized in Exhibit 16-4 is relatively simple.

Determining Individual Costs of Capital

Companies attempting to attract new investors have created a large variety of financing instruments. However, we will examine only three basic types of securities: debt, preferred stock, and common stock. In calculating their respective costs, the objective is to determine the rate of return the company must earn on its investments to satisfy investors' required rates of return after allowing for any flotation costs incurred in raising new funds. Also, because the cash flows used in capital-budgeting analysis (net present value, profitability index, and internal rate of return) are on an after-tax basis, the required rates of return should also be expressed on an after-tax basis.

Cost of Debt

The cost of debt may be defined as the rate that must be received from an investment to achieve the required rate of return for the creditors. The required rate of return for debt capital may be found by using the approximate yield to maturity or with the use of a financial calculator, where we solve the following equation:

$$\text{Before tax cost of debt} = \frac{\text{Interest payment} + \left[\dfrac{\begin{array}{c}\text{maturity value} \\ \text{(of the debt}\end{array} - \begin{array}{c}\text{market price} \\ \text{of the debt)}\end{array}}{\text{number of years to maturity}}\right]}{(\text{maturity value of the debt} + \text{market price of the debt})/2}$$

Assume that an investor is willing to pay $908 for a bond. The bond is worth $1,000, pays 8% annual interest, and matures in 20 years. Using the approximate yield to maturity equation, the investor's required rate of return is 8.86%.

$$= \frac{\$80 + [(\$1000 - \$908)/20]}{(\$1000 + \$908)/2}$$

$$= \frac{\$80 + \$4.60}{\$1908/2}$$

$$= \frac{\$84.60}{\$954}$$

$$= .0886 \text{ or } 8.86$$

The company's cost of debt, before recognizing the tax deductibility of interest expense, is 8.86%. Now we want to know the after-tax cost of the debt because interest paid on the debt is a tax-deductible expense. For every $1 paid in interest, the firm lowers its tax liability by $1 times the tax rate. Therefore, if the company has an effective tax rate, including all federal and state taxes, of 40%, then a dollar in interest means that we save $.40 in taxes. That is, the after-tax cost is only $.60 or $1(1–.40 tax rate). To determine the after-tax cost of debt, the before-tax interest rate is multiplied by (1 – tax rate).

After-tax cost of debt = cost of debt × (1 – tax rate)

If in the present example the corporation's tax rate is 40%, then the after-tax cost of debt is 5.32%:

8.86% × (1–.40)
8.86% × .60 = 5.32%

In summary, the firm must earn 5.32% on its borrowed capital after payment of taxes. In doing so, the investors will earn a 8.86% rate of return (their required rate) on their $908 investment (market price of the bond).

Cost of Preferred Stock

Determining the cost of preferred stock follows the same logic as the cost of debt computations. The objective is to find the rate of return that must be earned on money raised through the sale of preferred stock to satisfy their required rate of return.

The value of a preferred stock, P, that is non-maturing and promised a constant dividend per year can be determined using the following equation:

$$\text{cost of preferred stock} = \frac{\text{dividend paid}}{\text{market price}}$$

If a preferred stock pays $1.50 in annual dividends and sells for $15, the investors' required rate of return is 10%:

$$\text{cost of preferred stock} = \frac{\$1.50}{\$15.00} = 10\%$$

No adjustment for taxes is required, since preferred stock dividends are not tax deductible.

Cost of Common Stock

Although debt and preferred stock must be issued to receive any new money from these sources, common stockholders can provide additional capital in one of two ways. First, new common stock may be issued. Second, the earnings available to common stockholders can be retained, in whole or in part, within the company and used to finance future investments. Retained earnings represent the largest source of capital for most U.S. corporations. To distinguish between these two sources, we will use the term internal common equity to designate the profits retained within the business for investment purposes, and external common equity to represent a new issue of common stock.

Cost of internal common equity. When managers are considering the retention of earnings as a means for financing an investment, they are serving in a fiduciary capacity. That is, the stockholders have entrusted the company assets to management. If the company's objective is to maximize the wealth of its common stockholders, management should retain the profits only if the company investments within the firm are at least as attractive as the stockholders' next best investment opportunity.[1] Otherwise the profits should be paid out in dividends, permitting the investor to invest more profitably elsewhere.

How can management know the stockholders' alternative investment opportunities? Certainly identifying those specific investments is not feasible. However, the investors' required rate of return should be a function of competing investment opportunities. If the only other investment alternative of similar risk has a 12% return, one would expect a rational investor to set a minimum acceptable return on investment at 12%. In other words, the investors' required rate of return should be equal to the expected rate of the best competing investment available. Thus, if the common stockholders' required rate of return is used as a minimum return for investments financed by common stock investors, management may be assured that its investment policies are acceptable to the common stockholder.

There are three alternative approaches to determine the common stockholders' required rate of return:

(1)   Dividend-growth model

(2)   The Capital Asset Pricing Model

(3)   The Risk-Premium Approach

We will only discuss the dividend-growth model here because the remaining approaches are beyond the scope of this text.

Dividend-growth model. The value of a common stock is defined as the common stockholders' required rate of return on the firm's stock. The dividend-growth model is

$$\text{Required Rate of Return } = \frac{\text{dividend in 1 year}}{\text{market price}} + \text{ (annual growth rate in dividends)}$$

To demonstrate the computation, a corporation's common stockholders recently received a $2 dividend per share, and they expect dividends to grow at an annual rate of 10%. If the market price of the security is $50, the investors' required rate of return is

$$\text{Required Rate of Return } = \frac{\$2\,(1 + .10)}{\$50} + .10$$

$$= \frac{\$2.20}{\$50} + .10$$
$$= \ .044 + .10$$
$$= .144 \text{ or } 14.4\%$$

Note that the forthcoming dividend, dividend in 1 year is estimated by taking the past dividend of $2, and increasing it by 10%, the expected growth rate dividend = (1 + .10%) = $2 (1.10) = $2.20.

The dividend-growth model has been a relatively popular approach for calculating the cost of equity. The primary difficulty in using this model is estimating the expected growth rate in future dividends. One possible source of such expectations are investment advisory services such as Merrill Lynch and Value Line. There are even services that collect and publish the forecasts of a large number of analysts. For instance, Institutional Broker's Estimate System (IBES) publishes earnings per share forecasts made by about 2,000 analysts on a like number of stocks.

The cost of internal common equity. Dividends paid to the firm's common stockholders are not tax deductible; therefore, the cost is on an after-tax basis. There is no cost adjustment involved in computing the cost of internal common equity because the funds are already within the business. Thus, the investor's required rate of return is the same as the cost of internal common equity.

Cost of new common stock. If internal common equity does not provide all the equity capital needed for new investments, the firm may need to issue new common stock. Again, this capital should not be acquired from the investors unless the expected returns on the prospective investments exceed a rate sufficient to satisfy the stockholders' required rate of return. Returning to the dividend-growth model, the only significant adjustment necessary is to consider the potential flotation costs incurred from issuing the stock. The effect of the flotation costs on the cost of new common stock may be found by reducing the market price of the stock by the amount of these costs. Thus, the cost of new common stock equation is:

$$\text{Cost of new common stock} = \frac{\text{dividend in 1 year}}{\text{market price (1 - flotation cost)}} + \text{growth rate}$$

Computing the Weighted Cost of Capital

Let's now compute the weighted cost of capital for a firm, which is simply the weighted average of the individual costs, given the firm's financial mix. This calculation is best demonstrated with an example.

Assume a firm receives the following amounts of funds from the following three sources at the interest rates listed. The debt interest rate is the after-tax rate:

Source	Fund	Individual cost
Debt	$3,000	8% (after-tax rate)
Preferred	$1,000	5%
Common	$6,000	10%

If the $10,000 is invested, what rate of return must it earn in order to pay each source its stated interest rate?

(1) Source	(2) Funds	(3) Percentage of total	(4) Cost	(5) WACC = (2 x 4)
Debt	$ 3,000	$\frac{\$\ 3,000}{\$10,000}$ = .30	.08	.024
Preferred	$ 1,000	$\frac{\$\ 1,000}{\$10,000}$ = .10	.05	.005
Common	$ 6,000	$\frac{\$\ 6,000}{\$\ 10000}$ = .60	.10	.06
	$10,000	$10,000 1.0		.089 × 100 = 8.9%

To demonstrate the computation for a new stock issue with a market price of $50, a flotation cost of 15% of the stock's market price, with a projected dividend of $2.20 a share and a growth rate of 10%, the cost of capital for the new common stock is calculated as follows:

$$\text{Cost of new common stock} = \frac{\$2.20}{\$50.00\,(1 - 15\%)} + 10\%$$

$$= \frac{\$2.20}{\$50.00\,(.85)} + 10\%$$

$$= \frac{\$2.20}{\$42.50} = .1518$$

$$= 15.18\%$$

In this example, if management achieves a 15.18% return on the net capital received from common stockholders, it will satisfy the investors' required rate of return of 14%, as determined earlier.

The weighted cost of capital can also be determined by the aggregate interest cost for each source of funds.

Source	Funds	x	Interest Rate	=	Interest Paid
Bonds	$3,000		08%		$240
Preferred	$1,000		05%		$ 50
Common	$6,000		10%		$600
	$10,000				$890

$$\text{Weighted cost} = \frac{\$890}{\$10,000} = 8.9\%$$

As this example illustrates, the firm's weighted cost of capital is a very important part of a firm's capital structure mix (the source of funds). It can have a significant impact not only on the amount of leverage the firm has but the overall risk to the investor as well.

SUMMARY

Cost of capital is an important concept within financial management. In making an investment, the cost of capital is the rate of return that must be achieved on the company's projects in order to satisfy all the investors' required rates of return. If the rate of return from the corporation's investments equals the cost of capital, the price of the stock should remain unchanged. In other words, the firm's cost of capital may be defined as the rate of return from an investment that will leave the company's stock price unchanged. Therefore, the cost of capital, if certain assumptions are met, represents the minimum acceptable rate of return for new corporate investments. The factors that affect a firm's cost of capital consist of four components. First, general economic conditions (as reflected in the demand and supply of funds in the economy), as well as inflationary pressures, affect the general level of interest rates. Second, the marketability of the firm's securities has an impact on the cost of capital. Any change in the marketability of a firm's stock will affect investors' required rate of return. These changes directly influence the firm's cost of capital. Finally, a relationship exists between a firm's cost of capital and the dollar amount of financing needed for future investments.

Cost of Individual Sources of Financing

The cost of debt is equal to the effective interest rate on new debt adjusted for the tax deductibility of the interest expense. The cost of preferred stock is equal to the effective dividend yield on new preferred stock. In making this computation, we should use the net price received by the company from the new issue. Thus,

$$\text{cost of preferred stock} = \frac{\text{dividend paid}}{\text{market price}}$$

In calculating the cost of common equity, we distinguish between the cost of internally generated funds and the costs of new common stock. If historical data reasonably reflect the expectations of investors, the cost of internally generated capital is equal to the dividend yield on the common stock plus the anticipated percentage increase in dividends (and in the price of the stock) during the forthcoming year. If, however, the common equity is to be acquired by issuing new common stock, the cost of common stock should recognize the effect of flotation costs. This alteration results in the following equation for the cost of the new common stock:

$$\text{Cost of new common stock} = \frac{\text{dividend paid}}{\text{market price (1 - flotation cost)}} + \text{growth rate}$$

where (market price – flotation cost) is equivalent to the net market price.

Weighted Cost of Capital

A firm's weighted cost of capital is a composite of the individual costs of financing, weighted by the percentage of financing provided by each source. In this chapter we assume that the firm is to finance future investments in the same manner as past investments. Hence, the existing capital structure was used for developing the weighting scheme.

SELF-CORRECTION PROBLEM

1. Compute the cost for the following sources of financing:
   a. A $1,000 per value bond with a market price $970 and a coupon interest rate of 10%. The bonds mature in 10 years and the corporate tax rate is 34%.
   b. A preferred stock selling for $100 with an annual dividend payment of $8.
   c. The price of the common stock is $75 per share, and the dividend per share was $9.80 last year. The dividend is not expected to increase.
   d. New common stock where the most recent dividend was $2.80. The company's dividends per share should continue to increase at an 8% growth rate into the indefinite future. The market price of the stock is currently $53; however, flotation costs of $6 per share are expected if the new stock is issued.

1. a.

$$\text{Before tax cost of debt} = \frac{\text{interest payment} + \left[\dfrac{\begin{array}{cc}\text{maturity value} & \text{market price} \\ \text{(of the debt} & - \quad \text{of the debt)}\end{array}}{\text{number of years to maturity}}\right]}{(\text{maturity value of the debt} + \text{market price of the debt})/2}$$

$$= \frac{\$100 + [(\$1000 - \$970)/10]}{(\$1000 + \$970)/2}$$

$$= \frac{\$100 + \$3.00}{\$1970/2}$$

$$= \frac{\$103.00}{\$985}$$

$$= .1045 \text{ or } 10.45$$

After-tax cost of debt = cost of debt $\times$ (1 - tax rate).

$$10.45\% \times (1 - .34)$$
$$10.45\% \times .66 = 6.89\%$$

b.

$$\text{cost of preferred stock} = \frac{\text{dividend paid}}{\text{market price}}$$

$$\text{cost of preferred stock} = \frac{\$8.00}{\$100.00}$$

$$= .08\%$$

c.

$$\text{Required Rate of Return} = \frac{\text{dividend in 1 year}}{\text{market price} (1 - \text{flotation cost})} + \text{growth rate}$$

$$\text{Required Rate of Return} = \frac{\$9.80}{\$75} + 0 = 13.07$$

d.

$$\text{Cost of new common stock} = \frac{\text{dividend in 1 year} (1 + \text{growth rate})}{\text{market price} (1 - \text{flotation cost})} + \text{growth rate}$$

$$= \frac{\$2.80 (1 + 0.08)}{(\$53 - \$6)} + 0.08 = .1443 \text{ or } 14.43\%$$

$$= \frac{3.024}{\$47} + 0.08$$

$$= .064340 + .08 = 0.1443 \text{ or } 14.43\%$$

QUESTIONS

1. Define the term "cost of capital."
2. Why do we calculate a firm's cost of capital?
3. In computing the cost of capital, which sources of capital do we consider?
4. In general, what factors determine a firm's cost of capital? In answering this question, identify the factors that are within management's control and those that are not.
5. What limitations exist in using the firm's cost of capital as an investment hurdle rate?
6. How does a firm's tax rate affect its cost of capital? What is the effect of the flotation costs associated with a new security issue?
7. Distinguish between internal common equity and new common stock.

PROBLEMS

Individual or Component Costs of Capital. Compute the cost for the following sources of financing:

1. A bond worth $1,000 has a current market value $1,125 and an annual interest rate of 11%. The bond matures in 10 years. The firm's average tax rate is 34%.
2. A new common stock issue that paid a $1.80 dividend last year. The par value of the stock is $15, and earnings per share have grown at a rate of 7% per year. This growth rate is expected to continue into the foreseeable future. The company maintains a constant dividend/earnings ratio of 30%. The price of this stock is now $27.50, but 5% flotation costs are anticipated.
3. Internal common equity where the current market price of the common stock is $43. The expected dividend this coming year should be $3.50, increasing thereafter at a 7% annual growth rate. The corporation's tax rate is 34%.
4. A preferred stock paying a 9% dividend on a $150 par value. If a new issue is offered, flotation costs will be 12% of the current price of $175.
5. A bond selling to yield 12% prior to adjusting for the marginal corporate tax rate of 34%. What is the after-tax cost of this bond?

INTERNET EXERCISE

Cost of Capital

1. Access the web site at http://www.ibbotson.com/ccq2-sam.htm. Read the sample issue of the cost of capital quarterly. Find and report the median cost of equity capital for normal size firms and compare it to the cost for smaller firms. Does the difference seem excessive to you? Why?

Note

[1] Other factors may justify management's not adhering completely to this principle.

CHAPTER 17

VALUING LONG-TERM DEBT AND EQUITY

What determines the value or price of an asset, such as a bond or stock or land? Why does the value of an asset change so radically at times? For example, why did IBM common stock sell for $50 in early 1993 and $125 in 1998? Knowing the fair value or price of an asset is no easy matter. The maxims of the French writer La Rouchefoucauld, written over three centuries ago, still speak to us: "The greatest of all gifts is the power to estimate things at their true worth."

In this chapter we examine the concepts of and procedures for valuing an asset and apply these ideas to valuing bonds, preferred and common stock. Understanding how to value financial securities is essential if managers are to meet the objective of maximizing the value of the firm. If they are to maximize the investor's value, they must know what drives the value of an asset. Specifically, they need to understand how bonds and stocks are valued in the marketplace; otherwise, they cannot act in the best interest of the firm's investors.

DEFINITIONS OF VALUE

The term "value" is often used in different contexts, depending on its application. Examples of different uses of this term include the following:

Book value is the "value" of an asset as shown on a firm's balance sheet. It represents the historical cost of the asset rather than its current worth. For instance, the book value of a company's preferred stock is the amount the investors originally paid for the stock and, therefore, the amount the firm received when the stock was issued.

Liquidation value is the dollar sum that could be realized if an asset were sold individually and not as part of a going concern. For example, if a firm's operations were discontinued and its assets were divided up and sold, the sale price would represent the asset's liquidation value.

Market value of an asset is the observed value for the asset in the marketplace. This value is determined by supply and demand forces working together in the marketplace, where buyers and sellers negotiate a mutually acceptable price for the asset. For instance, the market price for Ford common stock on March 22, 1993, was $44. This price was reached by a large number of buyers and sellers working through the New York Stock Exchange. In theory, a market price exists for all assets. However, many assets have no readily observable market price because trading seldom occurs. For instance, the market price for the common stock of Blanks Engraving, a Dallas-based family-owned firm, would be more difficult to establish than the market value of J. C. Penney's common stock.

The intrinsic or economic value of an asset can be defined as the present value of the asset's expected future cash flows. This value is the amount the investor considers to be a fair value, given the amount, timing, and riskiness of future cash flows. Once the investor has estimated the intrinsic value of a security, this value could be compared with its market value when available.

If the intrinsic value is greater than the market value, then the security is undervalued in the eyes of the investor. Should the market value exceed the investor's intrinsic value, then the security is overvalued.

We hasten to add that if the securities market is working efficiently, the market value and the intrinsic value of a security will be equal. Whenever a security's intrinsic value differs from its current market price, the competition among investors seeking opportunities to make a profit will quickly drive the market price back to its intrinsic value. Thus, we may define an efficient market as one in which the values of all securities at any instant fully reflect all available public information, which results in the market value and the intrinsic value being the same. If the markets are efficient, it is extremely difficult for an investor to make extra profits from an ability to predict prices.

AN OVERVIEW OF VALUATION

For our purposes, the value of an asset is its intrinsic value or the present value of its expected future cash flows, where these cash flows are discounted back to the present using the investor's required rate of return. This statement is true for valuing all assets and serves as the basis of almost all that we do in finance. Thus, value is affected by three elements:

1. The amount and timing of the asset's expected cash flows
2. The riskiness of these cash flows
3. The investor's required rate of return for undertaking the investment

The first two factors are characteristics of the asset; the third one, the required rate of return, is the minimum rate of return necessary to attract an investor to purchase or hold a security. This rate must be high enough to compensate the investor for the risk perceived in the asset's future cash flows.

Exhibit 17-1 depicts the basic factors involved in valuation. As the figure shows, finding the value of an asset involves:

1. Assessing the asset's characteristics, which include the amount and timing of the expected cash flows and the riskiness of these cash flows;
2. Determining the investor's required rate of return, which embodies the investor's attitude about assuming risk and perception of the riskiness of the asset; and
3. Discounting the expected cash flows back to the present, using the investor's required rate of return as the discount rate.

Figure 17-1 Basic Factors Determining an Asset's Value

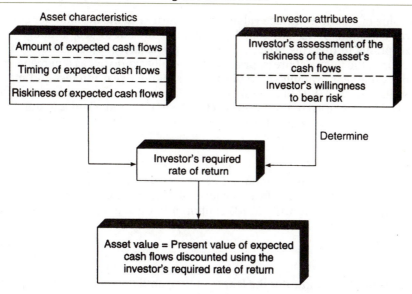

BONDS: TERMINOLOGY AND CHARACTERISTICS

Before applying our valuation expertise to valuing bonds, we first need to understand the terminology related to bonds. Also, we should be apprised of the different types of bonds that exist. Then we will be better prepared to determine the value of a bond.

When a firm or nonprofit institution needs financing, one source is bonds. This type of financing instrument is simply a long-term promissory note, issued by the borrower, promising to pay its holder a predetermined and fixed amount of interest each year. Some of the more important terms and characteristics that you might hear about bonds are as follows:

- Claims on assets and income
- Par value
- Coupon interest rate
- Maturity
- Indenture
- Current yield
- Bond ratings

Let's consider each in turn.

Claims on Assets and Income

In the case of insolvency claims of debt in general, including bonds, are honored before those of both common stock and preferred stock. However, different types of debt may also have a hierarchy among themselves as to the order of their claim on assets.

Bonds also have a claim on income that comes ahead of common and preferred stock. In general, if interest on bonds is not paid, the bond trustees can classify the firm insolvent and force it into bankruptcy. Thus, the bondholder's claim on income is more likely to be honored than that of common and preferred stockholders, whose dividends are paid at the discretion of the firm's management.

Par Value

The par value of a bond is its face value that is returned to the bondholder at maturity. In general, corporate bonds are issued in denominations of $1,000, although there are some exceptions to this rule. Also, when bond prices are quoted, either by financial managers or in the financial press, prices are generally expressed as a percentage of the bond's par value. For example, a bond that pays $90 per year interest and matures in 2009 is selling for 95 1/8 (1/8 = .125). That does not mean you can buy the bond for $95.125. The market price of this bond is actually $951.25, and when it matures in 2009, the bondholder will receive the $1,000.

Coupon Interest Rate

The coupon interest rate on a bond indicates the percentage of the par value of the bond that will be paid out annually in the form of interest. Thus, regardless of what happens to the price of a bond with an 8% coupon interest rate and a $1,000 par value, it will pay out $80 annually in interest until maturity (.08 × $1,000 = $80).

Maturity

The maturity of a bond indicates the length of time until the bond issuer returns the par value to the bondholder and terminates or redeems the bond.

Indenture

An indenture is the legal agreement between the firm issuing the bonds and the bond trustee who represents the bondholders. The indenture provides the specific terms of the loan agreement, including a description of the bonds, the rights of the bondholders, the rights of the issuing firm, and the responsibilities of the trustee. This legal document may run 100 pages or more in length, with the majority of it devoted to defining protective provisions for the bondholder. The bond trustee, usually a banking institution or trust company, is then assigned the task of overseeing the relationship between the bondholder and the issuing firm, protecting the bondholder, and seeing that the terms of the indenture are carried out.

Typically, the restrictive provisions included in the indenture attempt to protect the bondholder's financial position relative to that of other outstanding securities. Common provisions involve (1) prohibitions on the sale of accounts receivable, (2) constraints on the issuance of common stock dividends, (3) restrictions on the purchase or sale of fixed assets, and (4) constraints on additional borrowing. Prohibitions on the sale of accounts receivable are specified because such sales would benefit the firm's short-run liquidity position at the expense of its future liquidity position. Constraints on common stock dividends generally mean limiting their issuance when working capital falls below a specified level, or simply limiting the maximum dividend payout to some fraction, say 50% or 60% of earnings under any circumstance. Fixed-asset restrictions generally require lender permission before the liquidation of any fixed asset or prohibit the use of any existing fixed asset as collateral on new loans. Constraints on additional borrowing are usually in the form of restrictions or limitations on the amount and type of additional long-term debt that can be issued. All these restrictions have one thing in common: they attempt to prohibit action that would improve the status of other securities at the expense of bonds and to protect the status of bonds from being weakened by any managerial action.

Current Yield

The current yield on a bond refers to the ratio of the annual interest payment to the bond's current market price. If, for example, we have a bond with an 8% coupon interest rate, a par value of $1,000, and a market price of $700, it would have a current yield of

$$\text{current yield} = \frac{\text{annual interest payments}}{\text{market price of the bond}}$$

$$= \frac{.08 \times \$1,000}{\$700} = \frac{\$80}{\$700} = 0.114 = 11.4\%$$

Bond Ratings

John Moody first began to rate bonds in 1909; since that time three rating agencies—Moody's, Standard and Poor's, and Fitch Investor Services—have provided ratings on corporate bonds. These ratings involve a judgment about the future risk potential of the bond. Bond ratings are favorably affected by

(1) a greater reliance on equity than debt in financing the firm
(2) profitable operations
(3) a low variability in past earnings
(4) large firm size, and
(5) little use of subordinated debt. (Subordinated debt will be described shortly.)

The rating a bond receives affects the rate of return demanded on the bond by the investors. The poorer the bond rating, the higher the rate of return demanded in the capital markets. Exhibit 17-2 provides an example and description of these ratings. The bond ratings are extremely important to a financial manager. They provide an indicator of default risk that in turn affects the rate of return that must be paid on borrowed funds.

Having an understanding of the basic terms and characteristics of bonds in general, we can now consider the different types of bonds that companies use in funding their debt needs.

TYPES OF BONDS

Whereas the term "bond" may be defined simply as long-term debt, there are a variety of such creatures. Just to mention a few, we have

- debentures
- subordinated debentures
- mortgage bonds
- Eurobonds
- zero and very low coupon bonds
- junk bonds

We will briefly explain each of these types of bonds.

Debentures

The term "debenture" applies to any unsecured long-term debt. Since these bonds are unsecured, the earning ability of the issuing corporation is of great concern to the bondholder. They are also viewed as being more risky than secured bonds and, as a result,

Exhibit 17-2   Standard and Poor's Corporate Bond Ratings

AAA	This is the highest rating assigned by Standard and Poor's for debt obligation and indicates an extremely strong capacity to pay principal and interest.
AA	Bonds rated AA also qualify as high-quality debt obligations. Their capacity to pay principal and interest is very strong, and in the majority of instances they differ from AAA issues only in small degree.
A	Bonds rated A have a strong capacity to pay principal and interest, although they are somewhat more susceptible to the adverse effects of changes in circumstances and economic conditions.
BBB	Bonds rated BBB are regarded as having an adequate capacity to pay principal and interest. Whereas they normally exhibit adequate protection parameters, adverse economic conditions or changing circumstances are more likely to lead to a weakened capacity to pay principal and interest for bonds in this category than for bonds in the A category.
BB B CCC CC	Bonds rated BB, B, CCC, and CC are regarded, on balance, as predominantly speculative with respect to the issuer's capacity to pay interest and repay principal in accordance with the terms of the obligation. BB indicates the lowest degree of speculation and CC the highest. While such bonds will likely have some quality and protective characteristics, these are outweighed by large uncertainties or major risk exposures to adverse conditions.
C	The rating C is reserved for income bonds on which no interest is being paid.
D	Bonds rated D are in default, and payment of principal and/or interest is in arrears.

Plus (+) or Minus (–): To provide more detailed indications of credit quality, the ratings from "AA" to "BB" may be modified by the addition of a plus or minus sign to show relative standing within the major rating categories.

Source: *Standard and Poor's Fixed Income Investor,* Vol. 8 (1980). Reprinted by permission.

must provide investors with a higher yield than secured bonds provide. Often the issuing firm attempts to provide some protection to the holder through the prohibition of any additional encumbrance of assets. This prohibits the future issuance of secured long-term debt that would further tie up the firm's assets and leave the bondholders less protected. To the issuing firm, the major advantage of a debenture is that it is not secured by property. This allows the firm to issue debt and still preserve some future borrowing power.

Subordinated Debentures

Many firms have more than one issue of debentures outstanding. In this case a hierarchy may be specified, in which some debentures are given subordinated standing in case of insolvency. The claims of the subordinated debentures are honored only after the claims of secured debt and un-subordinated debentures have been satisfied.

Mortgage Bonds

A mortgage bond is a bond secured by a lien on real property. Typically, the value of the real property is greater than that of the mortgage bonds issued. This provides the mortgage bondholders with a margin of safety in the event the market value of the secured property declines. In the case of foreclosure, the trustees have the power to sell the secured property and use the proceeds to pay the bondholders. In the event that the proceeds from this sale do not cover the bonds, the bondholders become general creditors, similar to debenture bondholders, for the unpaid portion of the debt.

Eurobonds

Eurobonds are securities, in this case bonds, issued in a country different from the one in whose currency the bond is denominated. For example, a bond that is issued in Europe or in Asia by an American company and that pays interest and principal to the lender in U.S. dollars would be considered a Eurobond. Thus, even if the bond is not issued in Europe, it merely needs to be sold in a country different from the one in whose currency it is denominated to be considered a Eurobond. The Eurobond market actually had its roots in the 1950s and 1960s as the U.S. dollar became increasingly popular because of its role as the primary international reserve. In recent years, as the U.S. dollar has gained a reputation for being one of the most stable currencies, demand for Eurobonds has increased. The primary attractions to borrowers, aside from favorable rates, in the Eurobonds market are the relative lack of regulation (Eurobonds are not registered with the Securities and Exchange Commission), less rigorous disclosure requirements than those of the SEC, and the speed with which they can be issued. Interestingly, not only are Eurobonds not registered with the SEC, but U.S. citizens and residents may not be offered them during their initial distribution.

Zero and Very Low Coupon Bonds

Zero and very low coupon bonds allow the issuing firm to issue bonds at a substantial discount from their $1,000 face value with a zero or very low coupon rate. The investor receives a large part (or all on the zero coupon bond) of the return from the appreciation of the bond. For example, in April 1983 Homestead Savings issued $60 million of debt maturing in 1995 with a zero coupon rate. These bonds were sold at a 75% discount from their par value; that is, investors only paid $250 for a bond with a $1,000 par value. Investors who purchased these bonds for $250 and held them until they mature in 1995 received a 12.25% yield to maturity, at all of this yield came from appreciation of the bond. Homestead Savings, on the other hand, had no cash outflows until these bonds matured; however, at that time it had to pay back $60 million even though it only received $15 million when the bonds were first issued. As with any form of financing, there are both advantages and disadvantages of issuing zero or very low coupon bonds. The disadvantages are, first (as already mentioned), when the bonds matured Homestead Savings faced an extremely large cash outflow, much greater than the cash inflow it experienced when the bonds were first issued. Second, discount bonds are not callable and could only be retired at maturity. Thus, as interest rates fell, Homestead Savings could not benefit by requiring the investors to sell their bonds back to the company. The advantages of zero and low coupon bonds are, first, that annual cash outflows associated with interest payments do not occur with zero coupon bonds and are at a relatively low level with very low coupon bonds. Second, because there is relatively strong investor demand for this type of debt, prices tend to be bid up and yields tend to be bid down. That is to say, Homestead Savings was able to issue zero coupon bonds at about half a percent less than it would have been if they had been traditional coupon bonds. Finally, Homestead Savings was able to deduct the annual amortization of the discount from taxable income, which provided a positive annual cash flow to Homestead.

Junk Bonds

Junk or low-rated bonds are bonds rated BB or below. Originally, the term was used to describe bonds issued by "fallen angels," that is, firms with sound financial histories that were facing severe financial problems and suffering from poor credit ratings. Today, junk bonds refer to any bonds with a low rating. The major participants in this market are new firms that do not have an established record of performance, although junk bonds have been issued to finance corporate buyouts. Still, the backbone of the junk bond market involves young firms without established records of performance. Before the mid-1970s these new firms simply did not have access to the capital markets because of the reluctance of investors to accept speculative grade bonds. However, by the late 1980s, junk bonds grew to the point that they represented between 10% and 20% of the total public bond issuances by U.S. corporations.

Because junk bonds are of speculative grade, they carry a coupon interest rate of between 3% to 5% more than AAA grade long-term debt. Having an understanding of the basic characteristics of bonds, we will now turn our attention to valuing a bond.

BOND VALUATION

The valuation process for a bond, as depicted in Exhibit 17-4, requires knowledge of three essential elements: (1) the amount of the cash flows to be received by the investor, (2) the maturity date of the loan, and (3) the investor's required rate of return. The amount of cash flows is dictated by the periodic interest to be received and by the par value to be paid at maturity. Given these elements, we can compute the value of the bond, or the present value.

Consider a bond that was issued in 1984 and matures in 2008 with a par value of $1,000 and a coupon rate of 6%. Interest is paid annually and the bond matures in 10 years. The investor's required rate of return is 8%. We can calculate the value of the bond to an investor using the following simplified equation:

$$Po = I \, (PVIFA \, kd,n) + M(PVIF \, kd,n)$$

where
- Po = Bond value
- I = Annual interest payment
- M = Par value of bond
- kd = Investor required rate of return
- n = Years to maturity
- $PVIFA$ = Present value interest factor of an annuity
- $PVIF$ = Present value interest factor of a single sum

Substituting the values in the equation

- I = $60.00 (.06 × $1,000)
- M = $1,000
- kd = 8%
- n = 10 years

$$
\begin{aligned}
PV &= \$60.00 \, (PVIFA \ 8\%, 10 \ years) + \$1,000 \, (PV \ 8\%_2 \ 10 \ years) \\
&= \$60.00 \, (6.710) + \$1,000 \, (.463) \\
&= \$403.00 + \$463.00 \\
&= \$866.00
\end{aligned}
$$

the value of this bond is $866.00, which is the amount an investor would be willing to pay for this bond.

Semiannual Interest Payments

In the preceding illustration, the interest payments were assumed to be paid annually. However, companies typically pay interest to bondholders semiannually. For example, a company remits the interest to its bondholders on a semiannual basis, on January 15 and July 15. The value of this bond can be determined by restating the original bond valuation equation to:

$$Po = I/2 \, (PVIFA \, kd/2, 2n) + M(PVIF \, kd/2, 2n)$$

The calculation of semiannual interest payments is:

$$PV = \$60.00/2 \ (\text{PVIFA } 8\%/2, \ 2 \times 10 \text{ years}) + \$1,000 \ (\text{PVIF } 8\%/2, \ 2 \times 10 \text{ years})$$
$$PV = \$30.00 \ (\text{PVIFA } 4\%, \ 20 \text{ years}) + \$1,000 \ (\text{PVIF } 4\%, \ 20 \text{ years})$$
$$= \$30.00 \ (13.590) + \$1,000 \ (.456)$$
$$= \$407.00 + \$456.00$$
$$= \$863$$

Bond Valuation: Three Important Relationships

There are certain three important relationships that exist in bond valuation, these three key relationships are:

1. A decrease in interest rates (required rates of return) will cause the value of a bond to increase; an interest rate increase will cause a decrease in value. The change in value caused by changing interest rates is called interest-rate risk.
2. If the bondholder's required rate of return (current interest rate):
   a. Equals the coupon interest rate, the bond will sell at par, or maturity value.
   b. Exceeds the bond's coupon rate, the bond will sell below par value, or at a discount.
   c. Is less than the bond's coupon rate, the bond will sell above par value, or at a premium.
3. A bondholder owning a long-term bond is exposed to greater interest-rate risk than one owning a short-term bond.

Preferred Stock

Preferred stock is often referred to as a hybrid security because it has many characteristics of both common stock and bonds. Preferred stock is similar to common stock in that it has no fixed maturity date, the nonpayment of dividends does not bring on bankruptcy, and dividends are not deductible for tax purposes. On the other hand, preferred stock is similar to bonds in that dividends are limited in amount.

The size of the preferred stock dividend is generally fixed either as a dollar amount or as a percentage of the par value. For example, Texas Power and Light has issued $4 preferred stock, while Toledo Edison has some 4.25%, preferred stock outstanding. The par value on the Toledo Edison preferred stock is $100; hence, each share pays $4.25% x $100, or $4.25 in dividends annually. Because these dividends are fixed, preferred stockholders do not share in the residual earnings of the firm but are limited to their stated annual dividend.

In examining preferred stock we will first discuss several features common to almost all preferred stock. Next we will investigate features less frequently included and take a brief look at methods of retiring preferred stock. We will close by learning how to value preferred stock.

Features of Preferred Stock

Although each issue of preferred stock is unique, a number of characteristics are common to almost all issues. Some of these more frequent traits include:

- Multiple classes of preferred stock
- Preferred stock's claim on assets and income
- Cumulative dividends

- Protective provisions
- Convertibility

Other features that are less common include:

- Adjustable rates
- Participation
- Pay-in-kind (PIK) preferred

In addition, there are provisions frequently used to retire an issue of preferred stock, including the ability of the firm to call its preferred stock or to use a sinking-fund provision. All these features are presented in the discussion that follows.

Multiple classes. If a company desires, it can issue more than one series or class of preferred stock, and each class can have different characteristics. In fact, it is quite common for firms that issue preferred stock to issue more than one series. For example, Philadelphia Electric has 13 different issues of preferred stock outstanding. These issues can be further differentiated in that some are convertible into common stock and others are not, and they have varying priority status regarding assets in the event of bankruptcy.

Claim on assets and income. Preferred stock has priority over common stock with regard to claims on assets in the case of bankruptcy. The preferred stock claim is honored after that of bonds and before that of common stock. Multiple issues of preferred stock may be given an order of priority. Preferred stock also has a claim on income prior to common stock. That is, the firm must pay its preferred stock dividends before it pays common stock dividends. Thus, in terms of risk, preferred stock is safer than common stock because it has a prior claim on assets and income. However, it is riskier than long-term debt because its claims on assets and income come after those of bonds.

Cumulative feature. Most preferred stocks carry a cumulative feature that requires all past unpaid preferred stock dividends be paid before any common stock dividends are declared. The purpose is to provide some degree of protection for the preferred shareholder. Without a cumulative feature there would be no reason why preferred stock dividends would not be omitted or passed when common stock dividends were passed. Because preferred stock does not have the dividend enforcement power of interest from bonds, the cumulative feature is necessary to protect the rights of preferred stockholders.

Protective provisions. In addition to the cumulative feature, protective provisions are common to preferred stock. These protective provisions generally allow for voting rights in the event of nonpayment of dividends, or they restrict the payment of common stock dividends if sinking-fund payments are not met or if the firm is in financial difficulty. In effect, the protective features included with preferred stock are similar to the restrictive provisions included with long-term debt.

To examine typical protective provisions, consider Tenneco Corporation and Reynolds Metals preferred stocks. The Tenneco preferred stock has a protective provision that provides preferred stockholders with voting rights whenever six quarterly dividends are in arrears. At that point the preferred shareholders are given the power to elect a majority of the board of directors. The Reynolds Metals preferred stock includes a protective provision that precludes the payment of common stock dividends during any period in which the preferred stock sinking fund is in default. Both provisions, which yield protection beyond that provided by the cumulative provision and thereby reduce shareholder risk, are desirable. Given these protective provisions for the investor they reduce the cost of preferred stock to the issuing firm.

Convertibility. Much of the preferred stock that is issued today is convertible at the discretion of the holder into a predetermined number of shares of common stock. In fact, today about one-third of all preferred stock issued has a convertibility feature. The convertibility feature is, of course, desirable to the investor and thus reduces the cost of the preferred stock to the issuer.

Adjustable rate preferred stock. In the early 1980s, another new financing alternative was developed aimed at providing investors with some protection against wide swings in principal that occur when interest rates move up and down. This financing vehicle is called adjustable rate preferred stock. With adjustable rate preferred stock, quarterly dividends fluctuate with interest rates under a formula that ties the dividend payment at either a premium or discount to the highest of:

1. the three-month Treasury bill rate
2. the 10-year Treasury bond rate
3. the 20-year Treasury bond rate.

Although adjustable rate preferred stock allows dividend rates to be tied to the rates on Treasury securities, it also provides a maximum and a minimum level to which they can climb or fall, called the dividend rate band. The purpose of allowing the interest rate on this preferred stock to fluctuate is, of course, to minimize the fluctuation in the value of the preferred stock.

Participation. Although participating features are infrequent in preferred stock, their inclusion can greatly affect its desirability and cost. The participation feature allows the preferred stockholder to participate in earnings beyond the payment of the stated dividend. This is usually done in accordance with some set formula. For example, Borden Series A preferred stock currently provides for a dividend of no less than 60 cents per share, to be determined by the board of directors. Preferred stock of this sort actually resembles common stock as much as it does normal preferred stock. Although a participating feature is certainly desirable from the point of view of the investor, it is infrequently included in preferred stock.

PIK preferred. One by-product of the acquisition boom of the late 1980s was the creation of pay-in-kind (PIK) preferred stock. With PIK preferred, investors receive no dividends initially; they merely get more preferred stock, which in turn pays dividends in even more preferred stock. Eventually usually after five or six years if all goes well for the issuing company cash dividends should replace the preferred stock dividends. Needless to say, the issuing firm has to offer hefty dividends, generally ranging from 12% to 18%, to entice investors to purchase PIK preferred.

Retirement features. Although preferred stock does not have a set maturity associated with it, issuing firms generally provide for some method of retirement. If preferred stock could not be retired, issuing firms could not take advantage of falling interest rates.

Callable preferred. Most preferred stock has some type of call provision associated with it. In fact, the Securities and Exchange Commission discourages the issuance of preferred stock without some call provision. The SEC has taken this stance on the grounds that if a method of retirement is not provided, the issuing firm will not be able to replace its preferred stock if interest rates fall.

The call provision on preferred stock usually involves an initial premium above the value or issuing price of the preferred of approximately 10%. Then, over time, the call premium generally falls. For example, Quaker Oats in 1976 issued $9.56 preferred stock without par value for $100 per share. This issue was not callable until 1980 and then was callable at $109.56. After that the call price gradually drops to $100 in the year 2000, as shown in Exhibit 17-3.

By setting the initial call price above the initial issue price and allowing it to decline slowly over time, the firm protects the investor from an early call that carries no premium. A call provision also allows the issuing firm to plan the retirement of its preferred stock at predetermined prices.

Sinking-fund provisions. A sinking-fund provision requires the firm periodically to set aside an amount of money for the retirement of its preferred stock. This money is then used to purchase the preferred stock in the open market or through the use of the

Exhibit 17-3 Call Provision of Quaker Oats $9.56 Cumulative Preferred

	Date	Call Price
Date of issue	until 7/19/80	Not callable
7/20/80	until 7/19/85	$109.56
7/20/85	until 7/19/90	107.17
7/20/90	until 7/19/95	104.78
7/20/95	until 7/19/00	102.39
After 7/19/00		100.00

call provision, whichever method is cheaper. Although preferred stock does not have a maturity date associated with it, the use of a call provision in addition to a sinking fund can effectively create a maturity date. For example, the Quaker Oats issue we just examined has associated with it an annual sinking fund, operating between the years 1981 and 2005, which requires the annual elimination (retiring) of a minimum of 20,000 shares and a maximum of 40,000 shares. The minimum payments are designed so that the entire issue will be retired by the year 2005. If any sinking-fund payments are made above the minimum amount, the issue will be retired prior to 2005. Thus, the Quaker Oats issue of preferred stock has a maximum life of 30 years, and the size of the issue outstanding decreases each year after 1981.

Valuing Preferred Stock

As already explained, the owner of preferred stock generally receives a constant income from the investment in each period. However, the return from preferred stock comes in the form of dividends rather than interest. In addition, while bonds generally have a specific maturity date, most preferred stocks are perpetuities (non-maturing). In this instance, finding the value (present value) of preferred stock, Vps, a level cash flow stream continuing indefinitely, may best be explained by an example.

Consider a preferred stock that pays an annual dividend of $3.64. The shares do not have a maturity date, and the investor's required rate of return is 7.28%. What is the present value of the preferred stock expected dividends discounted at the investor's required rate of return? The valuation model is defined as follows:

$$V_{ps} = \frac{D}{K_{ps}}$$

where V_{ps} = Present value of a preferred stock

D = Annual dividend
K_{ps} = Investor's required rate of return

Because the dividends in each period are equal for preferred stock, we can calculate the value of a preferred stock as follows:

V_{ps} = Annual dividend / required rate of return
= $3.64 / (7.28%/100)
= $3.63 / 0.0728
= $50.00

This means that an investor with a required rate of return of 7.28% would not be willing to pay more than $50.00 for a preferred stock that paid a dividend of $3.64.

COMMON STOCK

Common stock involves ownership in the corporation. In effect, bondholders and preferred stockholders can be viewed as creditors, whereas the common stockholders are the true owners of the firm. Common stock does not have a maturity date, but exists as long as the firm does, nor does common stock have an upper limit on its dividend payments. Dividend payments must be declared by the firm's board of directors before they are issued. In the event of bankruptcy the common stockholders, as owners of the corporation, cannot exercise claims on assets until the firm's creditors, including the bondholders and preferred shareholders, have been satisfied.

In examining common stock, we will look first at several of its features or characteristics. Then we will focus on valuing common stock.

Features or Characteristics of Common Stock

We now examine common stock's claim on income and assets, stockholder voting rights, preemptive rights, and the meaning and importance of its limited-liability feature.

Claim on income. As the owners of the corporation, the common shareholders have the right to the residual income after bondholders and preferred stockholders have been paid. This income may be paid directly to the shareholders in the form of dividends or retained and reinvested by the firm. Although it is obvious the shareholder benefits immediately from the distribution of income in the form of dividends, the reinvestment of earnings also benefits the shareholder. Plowing back earnings into the firm results in an increase in the value of the firm, in its earning power, and in its future dividends. This action in turn results in an increase in the value of the stock. In effect, residual income is distributed directly to shareholders in the form of dividends or indirectly in the form of capital gains on their common stock. The right to residual income has both advantages and disadvantages for the common stockholder. The advantage is that the potential return is limitless. Once the claims of the most senior securities (bonds and preferred stock) have been satisfied, the remaining income flows to the common stockholders in the form of dividends or capital gains. The disadvantage: If the bond and preferred stock claims on income totally absorb earnings, common shareholders receive nothing. In years when earnings fall, it is the common shareholder who suffers first.

Claim on assets. Just as common stock has a residual claim on income, it also has a residual claim on assets in the case of liquidation. Only after the claims of debt holders and preferred stockholders have been satisfied do the claims of common shareholders receive attention. Unfortunately, when bankruptcy does occur, the claims of the common shareholders generally go unsatisfied. This residual claim on assets adds to the risk of common stock. Thus, while common stock has historically provided a large return, averaging 10% annually since the late 1920s, it also has large risks associated with it.

Voting rights. The common stock shareholders are entitled to elect the board of directors and are in general the only security holders given a vote. Early in this century it was not uncommon for a firm to issue two classes of common stock, which were identical except that only one carried voting rights. For example, both the Parker Pen Co. and the Great Atlantic and Pacific Tea Co. (A&P) had two such classes of common stock. This practice was virtually eliminated by

1. The Public Utility Holding Company Act of 1935, which gave the Securities and Exchange Commission the power to require that newly issued common stock carry voting rights

2. The New York Stock Exchange's refusal to list common stock without voting privileges, and

3. Investor demand for the inclusion of voting rights.

However, with the merger boom of the 1980s, dual classes of common stock with different voting rights again emerged, this time as a defensive tactic used to prevent takeovers.

Common shareholders not only have the right to elect the board of directors, they also must approve any change in the corporate charter. A typical charter change might involve the authorization to issue new stock or perhaps a merger proposal.

Voting for directors and charter changes occurs at the corporation's annual meeting. While shareholders may vote in person, the majority generally vote by proxy. A proxy gives a designated party the temporary power of attorney to vote for the signee at the corporation's annual meeting. The firm's management generally solicits proxy votes and, if the shareholders are satisfied with its performance, has little problem securing them. However, in times of financial distress or when management takeovers are threatened, **proxy fights**—battles between rival groups for proxy votes—occur.

While each share of stock carries the same number of votes, the voting procedure is not always the same from company to company. The two procedures commonly used are majority and cumulative voting. Under **majority voting,** each share of stock allows the shareholder one vote, and each position on the board of directors is voted on separately. Because each member of the board of directors is elected by a simple majority, a majority of shares has the power to elect the entire board of directors.

With **cumulative voting,** each share of stock allows the shareholder a number of votes equal to the number of directors being elected. The shareholder can then cast all of his or her votes for a single candidate or split them among the various candidates. The advantage of a cumulative voting procedure is that it gives minority shareholders the power to elect a director.

Preemptive rights. The **preemptive right** entitles the common shareholder to maintain a proportionate share of ownership in the firm. When new shares are issued, common shareholders have the first right of refusal. If a shareholder owns 25% of the corporation's stock, then he or she is entitled to purchase 25% of the new shares. Certificates issued to the shareholders giving them an option to purchase a stated number of new shares of stock at a specified price during a 2- to 10-week period are called rights. These rights can be exercised (generally at a price set by management below the common stock's current market price), can be allowed to expire, or can be sold in the open market.

Limited liability. Although the common shareholders are the actual owners of the corporation, their liability in the case of bankruptcy is limited to the amount of their investment. The advantage is that investors who might not otherwise invest their funds in the firm become willing to do so. This limited-liability feature aids the firm in raising funds.

Valuing Common Stock

Like both bonds and preferred stock, a common stock's value is equal to the present value of all future cash flow expected to be received by the stockholder. However, in contrast to bonds, common stock does not promise its owners interest income or a maturity payment at some specified time in the future. Nor does common stock entitle the holder to a predetermined constant dividend, as does preferred stock. For common stock, the dividend is based on the profitability of the firm and on management's decision to pay dividends or to retain the profits for reinvestment purposes. As a consequence, dividend streams tend to increase with the growth in corporate earnings. Thus, the growth of future dividends is a prime distinguishing feature of common stock.

The Growth Factor in Valuing Common Stock

What is meant by the term "growth" when used in the context of valuing common stock? A company can grow in a variety of ways. It can become larger by borrowing money to invest in new projects. Likewise, it can issue new stock for expansion. Management could also acquire another company to merge with the existing firm, which would increase the firm's assets. In all these cases, the firm is growing through the use of new financing, by issuing debt or common stock. Although management could accurately say that the firm has grown, the original stockholders may or may not participate in this growth. Growth is realized through the infusion of new capital. The firm size has clearly increased, but unless the original investors increase their investment in the firm, they will own a smaller portion of the expanded business.

Another means of growing is internal growth, which requires that management retain some or all of the firm's profits for reinvestment in the firm, resulting in the growth of future earnings and hopefully the value of the common stock.

To illustrate the nature of internal growth, assume that the return on equity for a company is 16%. If the company's management decides to pay all the profits out in dividends to its stockholders, the firm will experience no growth internally. It might become larger by borrowing more money or issuing new stock, but internal growth will come only through the retention of profits. If, on the other hand, the company retained all the profits, the stockholders' investment in the firm would grow by the amount of profits retained, or by 16%. If, however, management kept only 50% of the profits for reinvestment, the common shareholders' investment would increase only by half of the 16% return on equity, or by 8%. Generalizing this relationship, we have

$$G = ROE \times r$$

where

g = the growth rate of future earnings and the growth in the common stockholders investment in the firm.

ROE = the return on equity (net income/common book value).

r = the company's percentage of profits retained, called the profit-retention rate.

Therefore, if only 25% of the profits were retained by the company we would expect the common stockholders' investment in the firm and the value of the stock price to increase or grow by 4%, that is,

$$g = 16\% \times .25 = 4\%$$

The common stockholders frequently rely on an increase in the stock price as a source of return. If the company is retaining a portion of its earnings for reinvestment, future profits and dividends should grow. This growth should be reflected in an increased market price of the common stock in future periods, provided that the return on the funds reinvested exceeds the investor's required rate of return. Therefore, both types of return (dividends and price appreciation) are necessary in the development of a valuation model for common stock.

To explain this process, let us begin by examining how an investor might value a common stock that is to be held for only one year.

Common Stock Valuation—Single Holding Period

For an investor holding a common stock for only one year, the value of the stock should equal the present value of both the expected dividend to be received in one year, and the anticipated market price of the share at year end. The value of the stock can be found by using the following equation:

$$V_{cs} = \frac{D_1}{(1+k_{cs})} + \frac{P_1}{(1+k_{cs})}$$

where V_{cs} = common stock value
                 D_1 = of dividend in one year
                 P_1 = of market price in one year
                 K_{cs} = represents a common stockholder's required rate of return

Suppose an investor is contemplating the purchase of common stock at the beginning of this year. The dividend at year end is expected to be $1.64, and the market price by the end of the year is projected to be $22. If the investors required rate of return is 18%, the value of the stock would be

$$V_{cs} = \frac{\$1.64}{1+.18} + \frac{\$22}{1+.18}$$

$$= \frac{\$1.64}{(1.180)} + \frac{\$22.00}{(1.18\%)}$$

$$= \$1.39 + \$18.64$$

$$= \$20.03$$

Valuating a share of stock for a single holding period is a three-step process.

1. Estimate the expected future cash flows from common stock ownership (a $1.64 dividend and a $22 end-of-year expected share price).
2. Estimate the investor's required rate of return after assessing the riskiness of the expected cash flows (assumed to be 18%).
3. Discount the expected dividend and end-of-year share price back to the present at the investor's required rate of return.

Common Stock Valuation—Multiple Holding Periods

Since common stock has no maturity date and is frequently held for many years, a multiple-holding-period valuation model can be defined as follows:

$$V_{cs} = \frac{D_1}{(1+k_{cs})^1} + \frac{D_2}{(1+k_{cs})^2} + \frac{D_3}{(1+k_{cs})^n}$$

where V_{cs} = common stock value
                 D_1 = present value of dividend in one year
                 K_{cs} = a common stockholder's required rate of return
                 n = number of periods

The above equation indicates that we are discounting the dividend at the end of the first year, Dl, back one year; the dividend in the second year, D2, back two years; the dividend in the nth year back n years; and so on for an infinite number of years. The required rate of return is k_{cs}. In using equation (4), note that the value of the stock is established at the beginning of the year, say January 1, 1998. The most recent past dividend, D_0 would have been paid the previous day, December 31, 1997. Thus, if we purchased the stock on January 1, the first dividend would be received in 12 months, on December 31, 1998, which is represented by D1.

Fortunately, this equation can be reduced to a much more manageable form if dividends grow each year at a constant rate, g. The constant growth common stock valuation equation may be presented as follows:

$$\text{common stock value} = \frac{\text{dividend in year 1}}{\text{required rate of return} - \text{growth rate}}$$

$$V_{cs} = \frac{D_1}{k_{cs} - g}$$

Consider the valuation of a share of common stock that paid a $2 dividend at the end of the last year and is expected to pay a cash dividend every year from now to infinity. Each year the dividends are expected to grow at a rate of 10%. Based on an assessment of the riskiness of the common stock, the investor's required rate of return is 15%. Using this information, we would compute the value of the common stock as follows:

1. Since the $2 dividend was paid last year (D^0) we must compute the next dividend to be received, which is, (D_1). This can be done using the following model:

$$
\begin{aligned}
D1 &= D0(1 + g) \\
&= \$2.00\,(1 + 10\%) \\
&= \$2.00\,(1.10) \\
&= \$2.20
\end{aligned}
$$

2. Once the next dividend is determined we can now solve the equation,

$$
\begin{aligned}
V_{cs} &= \frac{D_1}{k_{cs} - g} \\
&= \frac{\$2.20}{.15 - .10} \\
&= \frac{\$2.20}{.05} \\
&= \$44.00
\end{aligned}
$$

As we can see, the value of a common stock is equal to the present value of all future dividends, which is a fundamental premise of finance. In practice, however, managers, along with many security analysts, often talk about the relationship between stock value and earnings, rather than dividends. We would encourage you to be very cautious in using earnings to value a stock. Even though it may be a popular practice, the evidence available suggests that investors look to the cash flows generated by the firm, not the earnings, for value. A firm's value truly is the present value of the cash flows it produces.

STOCKHOLDERS' EXPECTED RATE OF RETURN

The expected rate of return is the return the investor expects to receive on an investment when the existing market price is paid for the security. This rate of return is of interest to the financial manager because it tells the manager about the investor's expectations.

The Preferred Stockholder's Expected Rate of Return

In computing the preferred stockholder's expected rate of return, we use the valuation equation for preferred stock. Earlier, the equation specified the value of a preferred stock, V*ps* as

$$V_{ps} = \frac{\text{annual dividend}}{\text{required rate of return}} = \frac{D}{k_{ps}}$$

we can rewrite this equation and solve for K*ps*:

$$k_{ps} = \frac{\text{annual dividend}}{\text{value}} = \frac{D}{V_{ps}}$$

That is, preferred stockholder's required rate of return simply equals the stock's annual dividend divided by the intrinsic value. We may also restate equation to

$$\text{expected rate of return} = \frac{\text{annual dividend}}{\text{market price}} = \frac{D}{P_0}$$

Note that we have merely substituted the current market price P*o*, for the intrinsic value, V*ps*. The expected rate of return, therefore, equals the annual dividend relative to the price the stock is presently selling for, P*o*. Thus, the expected rate of return is the rate of return the investor can expect to earn from the investment if bought at the current market price. For example, if the present market price of a preferred stock is $50 and it pays a $3.64 annual dividend, the expected rate of return implicit in the present market price is

$$\text{expected rate of return} = \frac{D}{P_0} = \frac{\$3.64}{\$50} = 7.28\%$$

Therefore, investors who pay $50.00 per share for a preferred stock that is paying a dividend of $3.64 annually are expecting a 7.28% rate of return on this investment.

The Common Stockholder's Expected Rate of Return

The valuation equation for common stock was defined earlier. Owing to the difficulty of discounting to infinity, we made the key assumption that the dividends increase at a constant annual compound growth rate. Using this assumption we may express the stock's expected rate of return equation as follows:

$$\text{expected rate of return} = \frac{\text{dividend in year 1}}{\text{market price}} + \text{growth rate} = \frac{D_1}{P_0} + g$$

Example. As an example of computing the expected rate of return for a common stock where dividends are anticipated to grow at a constant rate to infinity, assume that a firm's common stock has a current market price of $44. If the expected dividend at the conclusion of this year is $2.20 and dividends and earnings are growing at a 10% annual rate (last year's dividend was $2), the expected rate of return implicit in the $44 stock price is as follows:

$$\text{expected rate of return} = \frac{\$2.20}{\$44} + 10\%$$
$$= .05 + .10$$
$$= 15\%$$

As a final note, we should understand that the expected rate of return implied by a given market price equals the required rate of return for investors at the margin. For these investors, the expected rate of return is just equal to their required rate of return, and, therefore, they are willing to pay the current market price for the security. These investors' required rate of return is of particular significance to the financial manager because it represents the cost of new financing to the firm.

SUMMARY

Valuation is an important issue if we are to manage the company effectively. An understanding of the concepts and how to compute the value of a security underlie much that we do in finance and in making correct decisions for the firm as a whole. Only if we know what matters to our investors can we maximize the firm's value.

For our purposes, value is the present value of future cash flows expected to be received from an investment discounted at the investor's required rate of return. In this context, the value of a security is a function of

(1) the expected cash inflows from the asset

(2) the riskiness of the investment

(3) the investor's required rate of return.

Valuing an asset with a finite stream of cash flows involves computing the present value of the individual cash receipts for each period. A bond that matures on a designated date is an example of such an asset. Here we find both the present value of the interest payments and the present value of the maturity or par value.

The expected rate of return on a bond is the required rate of return of the bondholders who are willing to pay the present market price for the bond, but no more. This rate is reached at the point where the present value of future cash flows to be received by the bondholder is just equal to the present market price of the bond. This rate of return is important to the financial manager because it equals the required rate of return of the firm's investors.

Certain key relationships exist in bond valuation, three of these being:

1. A decrease in interest rates (required rates of return) will cause the value of a bond to increase; an interest rate increase will cause a decrease in value. The change in value caused by changing interest rates is called interest-rate risk.

2. If the bondholder's required rate of return (current interest rate):

    a. Equals the coupon interest rate, the bond will sell at par, or maturity value.

    b. Exceeds the bond's coupon rate, the bond will sell below par value, or at a discount.

    c. Is less than the bond's coupon rate, the bond will sell above par value, or at a premium.

3. A bondholder owning a long-term bond is exposed to greater interest-rate risk than one owning a short-term bond.

Although the valuation of any security entails the same basic principles, the procedures used in each situation vary. For example, valuing a finite stream of cash flows involves computing the present value of the individual cash receipts for each period. An example of this type of valuation problem would be a bond that is scheduled to mature on a designated date. A second category of cash flow patterns involves an infinite cash flow stream, such as those from preferred stock and common stock. Although the underlying premise of valuation does not change—that is, value equals the present value of future cash flows—valuing such an asset requires a modification in the procedure. For securities with cash flows that are constant in each year, such as preferred stock, the present value equals the dollar amount of the annual dividend divided by the investor's required rate of return. Furthermore, for common stock where the future dividends are expected to increase at a constant growth rate, value may be given by the following equation:

$$\text{Value} = \frac{\text{dividend in year 1}}{\text{required rate of return} - \text{growth rate}}$$

The expected rate of return on a security is the required rate of return of investors who are willing to pay the present market price for the security, but no higher price. This rate of return is important to the financial manager because it equals the required rate of return of the firm's investors. This rate is reached at the point where the present value of future cash flows to be received by the investor is just equal to the present market price of the security.

SELF-CORRECTION PROBLEMS

1. Trico bonds have a coupon rate of 8%, a par value of $1,000, and will mature in 20 years. If you require a return of 7%, what price would you be willing to pay for the bond? What happens if you pay move for the bond? What happens if you pay less for the bond?

2. Sunn Co.'s bonds, maturing in seven years, pay 8% interest on a $1,000 face value. However, interest is paid semiannually. If your required rate of return is 10%, what is the value of the bond? How would your answer change if the interest were paid annually?

3. What is the value of a preferred stock where the dividend rate is 16% on a $100 par value? The appropriate discount rate for a stock of this risk level is 12%.

4. You own 250 shares of Dalton Resources' preferred stock, which currently sells for $38.50 per share and pays annual dividends of $3.25 per share.
   a. What is your expected return?
   b. If you require an 8% return, given the current price, should you sell or buy more stock?

5. Blackburn & Smith's common stock currently sells for $23 per share. The company's executives anticipate a constant growth rate of 10.5% and an end-of-year dividend of $2.50.
   a. What is your expected rate of return?
   b. If you require a 17% return, should you purchase the stock?

SOLUTIONS TO SELF-CORRECTION PROBLEMS

1. Present value of interest: $80 (10.594)   = $847.52
   Present value of par value: $1,000 (0258) =   258.00
   Value of bond   = $1,105.52

   If you pay more for the bond, your required rate of return will not be satisfied. In other words, by paying an amount for the bond that exceeds $1,105.52, the expected rate of return for the bond is less than the required rate of return. If you have the opportunity to pay less for the bond, the expected rate of return exceeds the 7% required rate of return.

2. If interest is paid semiannually:

   $40 (9.899)   = $395.96
   $1,000 (0.505) =   505.00
   Value of bond = $900.96

   if interest is paid annually.

   Value of bond = $80 (4.868) + $1,000 (0.513)
                   = $902.44

3. $$V_{ps} = \frac{.16 \times \$100}{.12} = \frac{\$16}{12} = \$133.33$$

4. a. Expected rate of return $= \dfrac{\text{Dividend}}{\text{Market Price}} = \dfrac{\$3.25}{\$38.50} = 0.0844 = 8.44\%$

   b. Given your 8% required rate of return, the stock is worth $40.62 to you:

   $$\text{Value} = \frac{\text{Dividend}}{\text{Required Rate of Return}} = \frac{\$3.25}{0.08} = \$40.62$$

   Because the expected rate of return (8.44%) is greater than your required rate of return of (8%) and the current market price ($38.50) is less than $40.62, the stock is undervalued; thus, you should buy it.

5. a. Expected rate of return $= \dfrac{\text{Dividend in Year 1}}{\text{Market Price}} + \text{growth rate } 8.44\%$

   $$= \frac{\$2.50}{\$23.00} + 10.5\%$$

   $$= .1087 + .1050$$

   $$= .2137 \text{ or } 21.37\%$$

   b. $\text{Value} = \dfrac{\text{dividend in year 1}}{\text{required rate of return} - \text{growth rate}}$

   $$= \frac{\$2.50}{.17 - .10\%} = \frac{\$2.50}{0.065} = \$38.46$$

   The expected rate of return exceeds your required rate of return. This means that the value of the stock to you is greater than the current market price. Thus, you should buy the stock.

QUESTIONS

1. What are the basic differences between book value, liquidation value, market value, and intrinsic value?
2. Explain the three factors that determine the intrinsic or economic value of an asset.
3. Explain the relationship between an investor's required rate of return and the value of a security.
4. a. How does a bond's par value differ from its market value?
   b. Explain the difference between a bond's coupon interest rate, the current yield, and a bondholder's required rate of return.
5. Describe the bondholder's claim on the firm's assets and income.
6. Distinguish between debentures and mortgage bonds.
7. Define (a) Eurobonds, (b) zero coupon bonds, and (c) junk bonds.
8. Define the bondholder's expected rate of return.
9. Why is preferred stock referred to as a hybrid security? It is often said to combine the worst features of common stock and bonds. What is meant by this statement?

10. Why would a preferred stockholder want the stock to have a cumulative dividend feature and protective provisions?

11. Distinguish between fixed rate preferred stock and adjustable rate preferred stock. What is the rationale for a firm issuing adjustable rate preferred stock?

12. Why is preferred stock frequently convertible? Why would it be callable?

13. Compare valuing preferred stock and common stock.

14. The common stockholders receive two types of return from their investment. What are they?

PROBLEMS

1. Bond Valuation. Calculate the value of a bond that expects to mature in 12 years and has a $1,000 face value. The coupon interest rate is 8% and the investors' required rate of return is 12%.

2. Bond Valuation. Enterprise, Inc. bonds have a 9%, coupon rate. The interest is paid semiannually and the bonds mature in eight years. Their par value is $1,000. If your required rate of return is 8%, what is the value of the bond? What is its value if the interest is paid annually?

3. Bond Valuation. National Steel 15-year, $1,000 par value bonds pay 8% interest annually. The market price of the bonds is $1,085 and your required rate of return is 10%.

   a. Compute the bond's expected rate of return.

   b. Determine the value of the bond to you, given your required rate of return.

   c. Should you purchase the bond?

4. Bond Valuation. You own a bond that pays $100 in annual interest, with a $1,000 par value. It matures in 15 years. Your required rate of return is 12%.

   a. Calculate the value of the bond.

   b. How does the value change if your required rate of return (i) increases to 15% or (ii) decreases to 8%?

   c. Explain the implications of your answers in part (b) as they relate to interest rate risk, premium bonds, and discount bonds.

   d. Assume that the bond matures in 5 years instead of 15 years. Recompute your answers in part (b).

   e. Explain the implications of your answers in part (d) as they relate to interest rate risk, premium bonds, and discount bonds.

5. Bond Valuation. Arizona Public Utilities issued a bond that pays $80 in annual interest, with a $1,000 par value. It matures in 20 years. Your required rate of return is 7%.

   a. Calculate the value of the bond.

   b. How does the value change if your required rate of return (i) increases to 10% or (ii) decreases to 6%?

   c. Explain the implications of your answers in part (b) as they relate to interest rate risk, premium bonds, and discount bonds.

   d. Assume that the bond matures in 10 years instead of 20 years. Recompute your answers in part (b).

   e. Explain the implications of your answers in part (d) as they relate to interest rate risk, premium bonds, and discount bonds.

6. Preferred Stockholder Expected Return. You own 200 shares of Somner Resources' preferred stock, which currently sells for $40 per share and pays annual dividends of $3.40 per share.

    a. What is your expected return?

    b. If you require an 8%, return, given the current price should you sell or buy more stock?

7. Common Stock Valuation. You intend to purchase Marigo common stock at $50 per share, hold it one year, and sell after a dividend of $6 is paid. How much will the stock price have to appreciate for you to satisfy your required rate of return of 15%?

8. Common Stockholder Expected Return. Made-It's common stock currently sells for $22.50 per share. The company's executives anticipate a constant growth rate of 10% and an end-of-year dividend of $2.

    a. What is your expected rate of return if you buy the stock for $22.50?

    b. If you require a 17%, return, should you purchase the stock?

9. Common Stock Valuation. Header Motor, Inc. paid a $3.50 dividend last year. At a constant growth rate of 5%, what is the value of the common stock if the investors require a 20% rate of return?

INTERNET EXERCISES

Fixed-Income Securities

1. Visit www.moneyadvisor.com web site and use their human life value calculator to find the monetary value of your life. Based on their calculations, what is your life worth? Do you agree ? Why?

Common Stock

2. Use the Motley Fool (www.foolnet.com) web site to analyze your stock portfolio situation. Based on your findings, what changes (sell, buy, hold) should you make in your investment portfolio?

SECTION X
INTERNATIONAL FINANCIAL MANAGEMENT

Chapter 18: International Finance Concepts and Applications

INTERNATIONAL FINANCE CONCEPTS AND APPLICATIONS

Today, international economic boundaries no longer exist. In financial manage-ment, when we ask, Where can funds be raised least expensively? Where can this new product be produced least expensively? Where will our major competition come from? The answer will quite likely involve a foreign country. If we are going to be successful in business, we must have an international perspective in our decision making.

The case of the biotechnology industry typifies how the internationalization of business coupled with recent technological breakthroughs have created both competition and opportunities for U.S. firms. Here, we as financial managers must be able to look at new projects and see both their potential and risks from an international perspective.

One business battle presently being fought in the international arena is for dominance in biotechnology products. Not only are the profits from success going to come from sales around the world, but the competition is also international in perspective. The United States has been at the forefront of biotechnology, but Japanese companies are quickly gaining ground. Drawing on a strategy that has served them well in other industries, the Japanese are heavily relying on "piggy-backing." The key to this strategy is to use their considerable financial assets to supply needed cash to biotechnology laboratories around the world, which then grant the Japanese access to technological breakthroughs. By riding "piggyback" on basic research conducted in other countries, the Japanese companies, in effect, augment their own research budgets, freeing resources for perfecting prod-ucts that have the best chance of dominating markets around the world. Takeda, for example, which has a joint venture with Abbott Labs and alliances in West Germany, France, and Italy, funds research at Harvard University.

Today, the United States is spending three times the Japanese investment per year on biotech R&D and still holds a considerable lead in most areas of research. However, only time will tell how this will all turn out. What is important to us is that we recognize that businesses are no longer bound by international boundaries, and that we must be able to apply our trade around the world.

GLOBALIZATION OF PRODUCT AND FINANCIAL MARKETS

World trade has grown much faster over the last few decades than world aggregate output (gross national product or GNP). The dollar value of world export has grown from five hundred billion in 1970 to more than several trillion dollars. This remarkable increase in international trade is reflected in the increased openness of almost all national economies to international influences. For example, the proportion of U.S. GNP accounted for by exports and imports (about one fifth) is now double what it was two decades ago, and is even higher for manufactured goods. The U.S. Department of Commerce estimates that the United States exports about one fifth of its industrial production and that about 70% of all U.S. goods compete directly with foreign goods.

Some industries and states are highly dependent on the international economy. For example, the electronic consumer products and automobile industries are widely considered to be global industries. Ohio ranks fourth in terms of manufactured exports, and more than half of all Ohio workers are employed by firms that depend to some extent on exports.

There has also been a rise in the global level of international portfolio and direct investment. Both direct and portfolio investment in the United States have been increasing faster than U.S. investment overseas. Direct investment occurs when the multinational corporation (MNC) has control over the investment, such as when it builds an offshore manufacturing facility. Portfolio investment involves financial assets with maturities greater than one year, such as the purchase of foreign stocks and bonds. Total foreign investment in the U.S. now exceeds such U.S. investment overseas.

A major reason for long-run overseas investments of United States companies is the high rates of return obtainable from these investments. The amount of United States direct foreign investments (DFI) abroad is large and growing. Significant amounts of the total assets, sales, and profits of American MNCs are attributable to foreign investments and foreign operations. Direct foreign investment is not limited to American firms. Many European and Japanese firms have operations abroad, too. During the last decade, these firms have been increasing their sales and setting up production facilities abroad, especially in the United States.

Capital flows between countries for international financial investment purposes have also been increasing. Many firms, investment companies, and individuals invest in the capital markets in foreign countries. The motivation is twofold: to obtain returns higher than those obtainable in the domestic capital markets, and to reduce portfolio risk through international diversification. The increase in world trade and investment activity is reflected in the recent globalization of financial markets. The Eurodollar market is larger than any domestic financial market. U.S. companies are increasingly turning to this market for funds. Even companies and public entities that have no overseas presence are beginning to rely on this market for financing.

In addition, most national financial markets are becoming more integrated with global markets because of the rapid increase in the volume of interest rate and currency swaps. Because of the widespread availability of these swaps, the currency denomination and the source country of financing for many globally integrated companies are dictated by accessibility and relative cost considerations regardless of the currency ultimately needed by the firm.

The foreign exchange markets have also grown rapidly, and the weekly trading volume in these globally integrated markets, between $3 and $5 trillion, exceeds the annual trading volume on the world's securities markets. Even a purely domestic firm that buys all its inputs and sells all its output in its home country is not immune to foreign competition, nor can it totally ignore the workings of the international financial markets.

EXCHANGE RATES

Recent History of Exchange Rates

Between 1949 and 1970, the exchange rates between the major currencies were fixed. All countries were required to set a specific parity rate for their currency vis-a-vis the United States dollar. For example, consider the German currency, the Deutsche mark (DM). In 1949, the parity rate was set at 4.0 DM to $1. The actual exchange rate prevailing on any day was allowed to lie within a narrow band around the parity rate. The DM was allowed to fluctuate between 4.04 and 3.96 per dollar. A country could effect a major adjustment in the exchange rate by changing its parity rate with respect to the dollar. When the currency was made cheaper with respect to the dollar, this adjustment was called a devaluation. A revaluation resulted when a currency became more expensive with respect to the dollar. In 1969, the DM parity rate was adjusted to 3.66 per dollar. This adjustment was a revaluation of the DM parity by 9.3%.

The new bands around the parity were 3.7010 and 3.6188 DM per dollar. The DM strengthened against the dollar since fewer DM were needed to buy a dollar. Since 1973, a floating-rate international currency system has been operating. For most currencies, there are no parity rates and no bands within which the currencies fluctuate.[1] Most major currencies, including the United States dollar, fluctuate freely, depending upon their values as perceived by the traders in foreign exchange markets. The country's relative economic strengths, its level of exports and imports, the level of monetary activity, and the deficits or surpluses in its balance of payments (BOP) are all important factors in the determination of exchange rates.[2] Short-term, day-to-day fluctuations in exchange rates are caused by changing supply and demand conditions in the foreign exchange market.

The Foreign Exchange Market

The foreign exchange market provides a mechanism for the transfer of purchasing power from one currency to another. This market is not a physical entity like the New York Stock Exchange; it is a network of telephone and computer connections among banks, foreign exchange dealers, and brokers. The market operates simultaneously at three levels. At the first level, customers buy and sell foreign exchange (that is, foreign currency) through their banks. At the second level, banks buy and sell foreign exchange from other banks in the same commercial center. At the last level, banks buy and sell foreign exchange from banks in commercial centers in other countries. Some important commercial centers for foreign exchange trading are New York, London, Zurich, Frarkfurt, Hong Kong, Singapore, and Tokyo.

An example will illustrate this multilevel trading. A trader in Texas may buy foreign exchange (pounds) from a bank in Houston for payment to a British supplier against some purchase made. The Houston bank, in turn, may purchase the foreign currency (pounds) from a New York bank. The New York bank may buy the pounds from another bank in New York or from a bank in London.

Because this market provides transactions in a continuous manner for a very large volume of sales and purchases, the currency markets are efficient. In other words, it is difficult to make a profit by shopping around from one bank to another. Minute differences in the quotes from different banks are quickly eliminated. Because of the arbitrage mechanism, simultaneous quotes to different buyers in London and New York are likely to be the same.

Two major types of transactions are carried out in the foreign exchange markets: spot and forward transactions.

Spot Exchange Rates

A typical spot transaction involves an American firm buying foreign currency from its bank and paying for it in dollars. The price of foreign currency in terms of the domestic currency is the exchange rate. Another type of spot transaction is when an American firm receives foreign currency from abroad. The firm typically would sell the foreign currency to its bank for dollars. These are both spot transactions because one currency is exchanged for another currency today. The actual exchange rate quotes are expressed in several different ways, as discussed later. To allow time for the transfer of funds, the value date when the currencies are actually exchanged is two days after the spot transaction occurs. Four banks could easily be involved in the transactions: the local banks of the buyer and seller of the foreign exchange, and the money-center banks that handle the purchase and sale in the interbank market. Perhaps the buyer or seller will have to move the funds from one of its local banks to another, bringing even more banks into the transaction.

On the spot exchange market the quoted exchange rate is typically called a direct quote. A direct quote indicates the number of units of the home currency required to buy one unit of the foreign currency. That is, in New York the typical exchange rate quote indicates the number of dollars needed to buy one unit of the home foreign currency: dollars per pound, dollars per mark, and so on. The spot rates in columns 2 and 3 of Exhibit 18-1 are the direct exchange quotes taken from *The Wall Street Journal* on July 19, 1994. To buy one pound on July 18, 1994, 1.5615 dollars were needed. To buy one franc and one mark, 18.848 cents and 64.66 cents were needed, respectively. The quotes in the spot exchange market in Paris are given in terms of francs and those in Frankfurt in terms of Deutsche marks.

An indirect quote indicates the number of units of foreign currency that can be bought for one unit of the home currency. This reads as pounds per dollar, francs per dollar, and so on. Indirect quotes are given in the last two columns of Exhibit 18-1.

In summary, a direct quote is the dollar/foreign currency rate (\$/FC), and an indirect quote is the foreign currency/dollar rate (FC/\$). Therefore, an indirect quote is the reciprocal of a direct quote and vice versa. The following example illustrates the computation of an indirect quote from a given direct quote.

Example

Suppose you want to compute the indirect quotes from the direct quotes of spot rates for pounds, francs, and marks given in column 2 of Exhibit 18-1. The direct quotes are: pound, 1.5615; French franc, .18848; and Deutsche mark, .6466. The related indirect quotes are calculated as the reciprocal of the direct quote as follows:

$$\text{Indirect quote} = \frac{1}{\text{direct quote}}$$

Thus

Pounds:
$$\frac{1}{\$1.5615/\pounds} = \pounds.6404/\$$$

Francs:
$$\frac{1}{\$.18848/FF} = FF5.3055/\$$$

Deutsche marks:
$$\frac{1}{\$.6466/DM} = DM1.5465/\$$$

Exhibit 18-1 Foreign Exchange Rates Reported on July 19, 1994

Country	U.S. $ equiv.		Currency[a] per U.S. $	
	Mon.	Fri.	Mon.	Fri.
Argentina (Peso)	1.01	1.01	.99	.99
Australia (Dollar)	.7303	.7335	1.3693	1.3633
Austria (Schilling)	.09187	.09146	10.88	10.93
Belgium (Franc)	.03137	.03122	31.88	32.03
Brazil (Real)	1.0989011	1.0729614	.91	.93
Britain (Pound)	1.5615	1.5607	.6404	.6407
30-Day Forward	1.5609	1.5601	.6407	.6410
90-Day Forward	1.5605	1.5597	.6408	.6411
180-Day Forward	1.5603	1.5595	.6409	.6412
Canada (Dollar)	.7265	.7260	1.3765	1.3775
30-Day Forward	.7256	.7251	1.3782	1.3792
90-Day Forward	.7236	.7231	1.3820	1.3830
180-Day Forward	.7196	.7191	1.3896	1.3906
China (Renminbi)	.115221	.115221	8.6790	8.6790
France (Franc)	.18848	.18758	5.3055	5.3310
30-Day Forward	.18829	.18739	5.3110	5.3365
90-Day Forward	.18809	.18719	5.3167	5.3422
180-Day Forward	.18795	.18706	5.3205	5.3460
Germany (Mark)	.6466	.6433	1.5465	1.5545
30-Day Forward	.6450	.6416	1.5505	1.5585
90-Day Forward	.6467	.6434	1.5462	1.5542
180-Day Forward	.6480	.6447	1.5431	1.5511
Hong Kong (Dollar)	.12945	.12945	7.7250	7.7250
India (Rupee)	.03212	.03212	31.13	31.13
Ireland (Punt)	1.5406	1.5372	.6491	.6505
Israel (Shekel)	.3298	.3298	3.0320	3.0320
Italy (Lira)	.0006447	.0006452	1551.14	1549.86
Japan (Yen)	.010168	.010220	98.35	97.85
Mexico (Peso)				
Floating rate	.2943341	.2942475	3.3975	3.3985
Netherland (Guilder)	.5765	.5737	1.7346	1.7431
Norway (Krone)	.1477	.1470	6.7721	6.8033
Philippines (Peso)	.03821	.03861	26.17	25.90
Portugal (Escudo)	.006277	.006249	159.30	160.04
Saudi Arabia (Riyal)	.26667	.26665	3.7500	3.7503
South Korea (Won)	.0012392	.0012408	807.00	805.90
Spain (Peseta)	.007824	.007783	127.82	128.48
Sweden (Krona)	.1300	.1292	7.6900	7.7414
Switzerland (Franc)	.7664	.7642	1.3048	1.3085
Taiwan (Dollar)	.037622	.037509	26.58	26.66
SDR[b]	1.46680	1.46321	.68176	.68343
ECU[c]	1.23320	1.22950	—	—

[a] Exchange Rates: Monday, July 18, 1994. The New York foreign exchange selling rates apply to trading among banks in amounts of $1 million and more, as quoted at 3 P.M. Eastern time by Bankers Trust Co., Dow Jones Telerate Systems, Inc, and other sources.

Retail transactions provide fewer units of foreign currency per dollar.

[b] Special Drawing Rights (SDR) are based on exchange rates for the U.S., German, British, French, and Japanese currencies. *Source:* International Monetary Fund.

[c] European Currency Unit (ECU) is based on a basket of community currencies. *Source:* European Community Commission.

Notice that the direct quotes and indirect quotes on page 411 are identical to those shown in columns 2 and 4 of Exhibit 18-1.

Direct and indirect quotes are useful in conducting international transactions, as the following examples show.

Example

An American business must pay 1,000 marks to a German firm on July 18, 1994. How many dollars will be required for this transaction?

$$\$.6466/DM \times DM1{,}000 = \$646.60$$

Example

An American business must pay $2,000 to a British resident on July 18, 1994. How many pounds will the British resident receive?

$$£.6406/\$ \times \$2000 = £1281.20$$

Exchange Rates and Arbitrage

The foreign exchange quotes in two different countries must be in line with each other. The direct quote for U.S. dollars in London is given in pounds/dollar. Because the foreign exchange markets are efficient, the direct quotes for the United States dollar in London, on July 18, 1994, must be very close to the indirect rate of .6406 pounds/dollar prevailing in New York on that date.

If the exchange rate quotations between the London and New York spot exchange markets were out of line, then an enterprising trader could make a profit by buying in the market where the currency was cheaper and selling it in the other. Such a buy-and-sell strategy would involve a zero net investment of funds and no risk bearing yet would provide a sure profit. Such a person is called an arbitrager, and the process of buying and selling in more than one market to make a riskless profit is called arbitrage. Spot exchange markets are efficient in the sense that arbitrage opportunities do not persist for any length of time. That is, the exchange rates between two different markets are quickly brought in line, aided by the arbitrage process. Simple arbitrage eliminates exchange rate differentials across the markets for a single currency, as in the following example for the New York and London quotes. Triangular arbitrage does the same across the markets for all currencies. Covered interest arbitrage eliminates differentials across currency and interest rate markets.

Suppose that London quotes £.6600/$ instead of £.6406/$. If you simultaneously bought a pound in New York for £.6406/$ and sold a pound in London for £.6600/$, you would have (1) taken a zero net investment position since you bought £1 and sold £1, (2) locked in a sure profit of £.0194/$ no matter which way the pound subsequently moves, and (3) set in motion the forces that will eliminate the different quotes in New York and London. As others in the marketplace learn of your transaction, they will attempt to make the same transaction. The increased demand to buy pounds in New York will lead to a higher quote there and the increased supply of pounds will lead to a lower quote in London. The workings of the market will produce a new spot rate that lies between £.6406/$ and £.6600/$ and is the same in New York and in London.

Asked and Bid Rates

Two types of rates are quoted in the spot exchange market: the asked and the bid rates. The asked rate is the rate the bank or the foreign exchange trader "asks" the customer to pay in home currency for foreign currency when the bank is selling and the customer is buying. The asked rate is also known as the selling rate or the offer rate. The bid rate is the rate at which the bank buys the foreign currency from the customer by paying in home currency. The bid rate is also known as the buying rate. Note that Exhibit 18-1 contains only the selling, offer, or asked rates, and not the buying rate.

The bank sells a unit of foreign currency for more than it pays for it. Therefore, the direct asked quote ($/FC) is greater than the direct bid quote. The difference is known as the bid-asked spread. When there is a large volume of transactions and the trading is continuous, the spread is small and can be less than .5% (.005) for the major currencies. The spread is much higher for infrequently traded currencies. The spread exists to compensate the banks for holding the risky foreign currency and for providing the service of converting currencies.

Forward Exchange Rates

A forward exchange contract requires delivery, at a specified future date, of one currency for a specified amount of another currency. The exchange rate for the forward transaction is agreed on today; the actual payment of one currency and the receipt of another currency take place at the future date. For example, a thirty-day contract on March 1 is for delivery on March 31. Note that the forward exchange rate is not the same as the spot rate that will prevail in the future. The actual spot rate that will prevail is not known today; only the forward rate is known. The actual spot rate will depend on the market conditions at that time; it may be more or less than today's forward rate. Exchange rate risk is the risk that tomorrow's exchange rate will differ from today's rate.

As indicated earlier, it is extremely unlikely that the future spot rate will be exactly the same as the forward rate quoted today. Assume that you are going to receive a payment denominated in pounds from a British customer in thirty days. If you wait for thirty days and exchange the pounds at the spot rate, you will receive a dollar amount reflecting the exchange rate thirty days hence (that is, the future spot rate). As of today, you have no way of knowing the exact dollar value of your future pound receipts. Consequently, you cannot make precise plans about the use of these dollars. If, conversely, you buy a future contract, then you know the exact dollar value of your future receipts, and you can make precise plans concerning their use. The forward contract, therefore, can reduce your uncertainty about the future, and the major advantage of the forward market is that of risk reduction.

Forward exchange contracts are usually quoted for periods of 30, 90, and 180 days. A contract for any intermediate date can be obtained, usually with the payment of a small premium. Forward contracts for periods longer than 180 days can be obtained by special negotiations with banks. Contracts for periods greater than one year can be costly.

Forward rates, like spot rates, are quoted in both direct and indirect form. The direct quotes for the thirty-day and ninety-day forward contracts on pounds, francs, and marks are given in column 2 of Exhibit 18-1. The indirect quotes for forward contracts, like spot rates, are reciprocals of the direct quotes. The indirect quotes are indicated in column 4 of Exhibit 18-1. The direct quotes are the dollar/foreign currency rate, and the indirect quotes are the foreign currency/dollar rate similar to the spot exchange quotes.

The thirty-day forward quote for pounds is $1.5609 per pound. This means that if one purchases the contract for forward pounds on July 18, 1994, the bank will deliver a pound against the payment of $1.5609 on August 17,1994. The bank is contractually bound to deliver the pound at this price, and the buyer of the contract is legally obligated to buy it at this price on August 17, 1994. Therefore, this is the price the customer must pay regardless of the actual spot rate prevailing on August 17, 1994. If the spot price of the pound is less than $1.5609, then the customer pays more than the spot price. If the spot price is greater than $1.5609, then the customer pays less than the spot price.

INTEREST RATE PARITY THEORY

Forward rates generally entail a premium or a discount relative to current spot rates. However, these forward premiums and discounts differ between currencies and maturities. These differences depend solely on the difference in the level of interest rates between two countries, called the interest rate differential. The value of the premium or discount can be theoretically computed from the interest rate parity (IRP) theory. This theory states that (except for the effects of small transactions costs) the forward premium or discount should be equal to the difference in the national interest rates for securities of the same maturity.

Stated very simply, what does all this mean? It means that because of arbitrage, the interest rate differential between two countries must be equal to the difference between the forward and spot exchange rates. If this were not true, arbitragers would buy in the forward market and sell in the spot market (or vice versa) until prices were back in line and there were no profits left to be made. For example, if prices in the forward market were too low, arbitragers would enter the market, increase the demand for the forward foreign currency, and drive up the prices in the forward market until those prices obeyed the interest rate parity theory.

PURCHASING POWER PARITY

Long-run changes in exchange rates are influenced by international differences in inflation rates and the purchasing power of each nation's currency. Exchange rates of countries with high rates of inflation will tend to decline. According to the purchasing power parity (PPP) theory, exchange rates will tend to adjust in such a way that each currency will have the same purchasing power (especially in terms of internationally traded goods). Thus, if the United Kingdom experiences a 10% rate of inflation in a year that Germany experiences only a 6% rate, the U.K. currency (the pound) will be expected to decline in value approximately by 3.77% (1.10/1.06) against the German currency (the Deutsche mark). More accurately, according to the PPP

Expected spot rate = Current spot rate × Expected difference in inflation rate

$$
\begin{matrix} \text{expected spot rate} \\ \text{(domestic currency} \\ \text{per unit of foreign} \\ \text{currency)} \end{matrix} = \begin{matrix} \text{current spot rate} \\ \text{(domestic currency} \\ \text{per unit of foreign} \\ \text{currency)} \end{matrix} \times \frac{(1 + \text{expected domestic inflation rate})}{(1 + \text{expected foreign inflation rate})}
$$

Thus, if the beginning value of the mark was £0.40, with a 6% inflation rate in Germany and a 10% inflation rate in the United Kingdom, according to the PPP, the expected value of the Deutsche mark at the end of that year will be £.40 × [1.10/1.06], or £.4151.

Stated very simply, what does this mean? It means that a dollar should have the same purchasing power anywhere in the world—well at least on average. Obviously, this is not quite true. However, the purchasing power parity theory tells us that we should expect, on average, that differences in inflation rates between two countries should be reflected in changes in the exchange rates. In effect, the best forecast of the difference in inflation rates between two countries should also be the best forecast of the change in the spot rate of exchange expected spot rate.

The Law of One Price

Underlying the PPP relationship is the Law of One Price. This law is actually a proposition that in competitive markets where there are 170 transportation costs or barriers to trade, the same good sold in different countries sells for the same price if all the different prices are expressed in terms of the same currency. The idea is that the worth, in terms of marginal utility, of a good does not depend on where it is bought or sold. Because inflation will erode the purchasing power of any currency, its exchange rate must adhere to the PPP relationship if the Law of One Price is to hold over time.

There are enough obvious exceptions to the concept of purchasing power parity that it may, at first glance, seem difficult to accept. For example, in the Spring of 1995 a Big Mac cost $1.80 in the United States and, given the then existing exchange rates, it cost an equivalent of $1.42 in Mexico, $2.91 in Japan and $3.09 in Germany. On the surface this might appear to violate the purchasing power parity theory and the Law of One Price; however, we must remember that this theory is based upon the concept of arbitrage. In the case of a Big Mac, it's pretty hard to imagine buying Big Macs in Mexico for $1.42, shipping them to Germany, and reselling them for $3.09. But for commodities like gold and other items that are relatively inexpensive to ship and do not have to be consumed immediately, the Law of One Price holds much better.

International Fisher Effect. According to the domestic Fisher Effect (FE), nominal interest rates reflect the expected inflation rate and a real rate of interest. In other words,

$$\frac{\text{nominal}}{\text{interest rate}} = \frac{\text{expected}}{\text{inflation rate}} + \frac{\text{real rate}}{\text{of interest}}$$

While there is mixed empirical support for the FE internationally, it is widely thought that, for the major industrial countries the real rate of interest is about 3% when a long-term period is considered. In such a case, with the previous assumption regarding inflation rates, interest rates in the United Kingdom and Germany would be (.10+ .03 + .003) or 13.3% and (.06+ .03 + .0018) or 9.18 %, respectively.

In effect, the International Fisher Effect (IFE) states that the real interest rate should be the same all over the world, with the difference in nominal or stated interest rates simply resulting from the difference in expected inflation rates. As we look at interest rates around the world, this tells us that we should not necessarily send our money to a bank account in the country with the highest interest rates. That course of action might only result in us sending our money to a bank in the country with the highest expected level of inflation.

EXPOSURE TO EXCHANGE RATE RISK

An asset denominated or valued in terms of foreign currency cash flows will lose value if that foreign currency declines in value. It can be said that such an asset is exposed to exchange rate risk. However, this possible decline in asset value may be offset by the decline in value of any liability that is also denominated or valued in terms of that foreign currency. Thus, a firm would normally be interested in its net exposed position (exposed assets – exposed liabilities) for each period in each currency.

While expected changes in exchange rates can often be included in the cost-benefit analysis relating to such transactions, in most cases there is an unexpected component in exchange rate changes and often the cost-benefit analysis for such transactions does not fully capture even the expected change in the exchange rate. For example, price increases for the foreign operations of many MNCs often have to be less than those necessary to fully offset exchange rate changes, owing to the competitive pressures generated by local businesses, as the Japanese car makers found in 1988 for their U.S. sales.

Three measures of foreign exchange exposure are translation exposure, transactions exposure, and economic exposure. Translation exposure arises because the foreign operations of MNCs have accounting statements denominated in the local currency of the country in which the operation is located. For U.S. MNCs, the reporting currency for its consolidated financial statements is the dollar, so the assets, liabilities, revenues, and expenses of the foreign operations must be translated into dollars. International transactions often require a payment to be made or received in a foreign currency in the future, so these transactions are exposed to exchange rate risk. Economic exposure exists over the long term because the value of future cash flows in the reporting currency (that is, the dollar) from foreign operations are exposed to exchange rate risk. Indeed, the whole stream of future cash flows is exposed. The Japanese automaker situation highlights the effect of economic exposure on an MNC's revenue stream. The three measures of exposure now are examined more closely.

Translation Exposure

Foreign currency assets and liabilities are considered exposed if their foreign currency value for accounting purposes is to be translated into the domestic currency using the current exchange rate—the exchange rate in effect on the balance sheet date. Other assets and liabilities and equity amounts that are translated at the historic exchange rate—the rate in effect when these items were first recognized in the company's accounts—are not considered to be exposed. The rate (current or historic) used to translate various accounts depends on the translation procedure used. While transaction exposure can result in exchange rate change-related losses and gains that are realized and have an impact on both reported and taxable income, translation exposure results in exchange rate losses and gains that are reflected in the company's accounting books, but are unrealized and have little or no impact on taxable income. Thus, if financial markets are efficient and managerial goals are consistent with owner wealth maximization, a firm should not have to waste real resources hedging against possible paper losses caused by translation exposure. However, if there are significant agency or information costs or if markets are not efficient, a firm may indeed find it economical to hedge against translation losses or gains.

Transactions Exposure

Receivables, payables, and fixed-price sales or purchase contracts are examples of foreign currency transactions whose monetary value was fixed at a time different from the time when these transactions are actually completed. Transactions exposure is a term that describes the net contracted foreign currency transactions for which the settlement amounts are subject to changing exchange rates. A company normally must set up an additional reporting system to track transactions exposure because several of these amounts are not recognized in the accounting books of the firm.

Exchange risk may be neutralized or hedged by a change in the asset and liability position in the foreign currency. An exposed asset position (such as an account receivable) can be hedged or covered by creating a liability of the same amount and maturity denominated in the foreign currency (such as a forward contract to sell the foreign currency). An exposed liability position (such as an account payable) can be covered by acquiring assets of the same amount and maturity in the foreign currency (such as a forward contract to buy the foreign currency). The objective is to have a zero net asset position in the foreign currency. This eliminates exchange risk, since the loss (gain) in the liability (asset) is exactly offset by the gain (loss) in the value of the asset (liability) when the foreign currency appreciates (depreciates). Two popular forms of hedge are the money market hedge and the exchange market or forward market hedge. In both types of hedge the amount and the duration of the asset (liability) positions are matched. Note as you read the next two subsections how IRP theory assures that each hedge provides the same cover.

Money-Market Hedge. In a money-market hedge, the exposed position in a foreign currency is offset by borrowing or lending in the money market. Consider the case of the

American firm with a net liability position (that is the, amount it owes) of 3,000 pounds. The firm knows the exact amount of its pound liability in thirty days, but it does not know the liability in dollars. Assume that the thirty-day money market rates in both the United States and United Kingdom are, respectively, 1% for lending and 1.5% for borrowing. The American business can take the following steps:

Step 1: Calculate the present value of the foreign currency liability (3000£) that is due in thirty days. Use the money market rate applicable for the foreign country (1 percent in the United Kingdom). The present value of 3,000 pounds is 2,970.30 pounds computed as follows: $3000/(1 + .01)$.

Step 2: Exchange dollars on today's spot market to obtain the 2,970.30 pounds. The dollar amount needed today is $4,638.12 ($2970.30 \times 1.5615$).

Step 3: Invest 2,970.30 pounds in a United Kingdom one-month money market instrument. This investment will compound to exactly 3,000 pounds in one month. The future liability of 3,000 pounds is covered by the 2,970.30 pound investment.*

*Observe that 2970.30 pounds $\times (1 + .01) = 3,000$ pounds.

Note: if the American business does not own this amount today, it can borrow $4638.12 from the United States money market at the going rate of 1.5 percent. In thirty days the American business will need to repay $4,707.69 [$4,638.12 \times (1 + .015)$]

Assuming that the American business borrows the money, its management may base its calculations on the knowledge that the British goods, on delivery in thirty days, will cost it $4,707.69. The British business will receive 3,000 pounds. The American business need not wait for the future spot exchange rate to be revealed. On today's date, the future dollar payment of the contract is known with certainty. This certainty helps the American business in making its pricing and financing decisions.

Many businesses hedge in the money market. The firm needs to borrow (creating a liability) in one market, lend or invest in the other money market, and use the spot exchange market on today's date. The mechanics of covering a net asset position in the foreign currency are the exact reverse of the mechanics of covering the liability position. With a net asset position in pounds: Borrow in the United Kingdom money market in pounds, convert to dollars on the spot exchange market, invest in the United States money market. When the net assets converted into pounds (i.e., when the firm receives what it is owed), pay off the loan and the interest. The cost of hedging in the money market is the cost of doing business in three different markets. Information about the three markets is needed, and analytical calculations of the type indicated here must be made.

Many small and infrequent traders find the cost of the money market hedge prohibitive, owing especially to the need for information about the market. These traders use the exchange or the forward market hedge, which has very similar hedging benefits.

The Forward Market Hedge. The forward market provides a second possible hedging mechanism. It works as follows: A net asset (liability) position is covered by a liability (asset) in the forward market. Consider again the case of the American firm with a liability of 3000 pounds that must be paid in thirty days. The firm may take the following steps to cover its liability position:

Step 1: Buy a forward contract today to purchase 3,000 pounds in thirty days. The thirty-day forward rate is, $1.5609 per pound.

Step 2: On the thirtieth day pay the banker $4,682.70 ($3000 \times \$1.5609$) and collect 3,000 pounds. Pay these pounds to the British supplier.

By the use of the forward contract, the American business knows the exact worth of the future payment in dollars ($4,682.70). The exchange risk in pounds is totally eliminated by the net asset position in the forward pounds. In the case of a net asset exposure, the steps open to the American firm are the exact opposite: Sell the pounds forward, and on the future day receive and deliver the pounds to collect the agreed-on dollar amount.

The use of the forward market as a hedge against exchange risk is simple and direct. That is, match the liability or asset position against an offsetting position in the forward market. The forward market hedge is relatively easy to implement. The firm directs its banker that it needs to buy or sell a foreign currency on a future date, and the banker gives a quote.

The forward hedge and the money market hedge give an identical future dollar payment (or receipt) if the forward contracts are priced according to the interest rate parity theory. The alert student may have noticed that the dollar payments in the money market hedge and the forward market hedge examples were, respectively, $4707.69 and $4682.70. Recall from our previous discussions that in efficient markets, the forward contracts do indeed conform to IRP theory. However, the numbers in our example are not identical because the forward rate used in the forward hedge is not exactly equal to the interest rates in the money market hedge.

Economic Exposure

The economic value of a company can vary in response to exchange rate changes. This change in value may be caused by a rate-change-induced decline in the level of expected cash flows and/or by an increase in the riskiness of these cash flows. Economic exposure refers to the overall impact of exchange rate changes on the value of the firm and includes not only the strategic impact of changes in competitive relationships that arise from exchange rate changes, but also the economic impact of transactions exposure and, if any, of translation exposure.

Economic exposure to exchange rate changes depends on the competitive structure of the markets for a firm's inputs and its outputs and how these markets are influenced by changes in exchange rates. This influence, in turn, depends on several economic factors, including price elasticities of the products, the degree of competition from foreign markets and direct (through prices) and indirect (through incomes) impact of exchange rate changes on these markets. Assessing the economic exposure faced by a particular firm thus depends on the ability to understand and model the structure of the markets for its major inputs (purchases) and outputs (sales).

A company need not engage in any cross-border business activity to be exposed to exchange rate changes because product and financial markets in most countries are related and influenced to a large extent by the same global forces. The output of a company engaged in business activity only within one country may be competing with imported products, or it may be competing for its inputs with other domestic and foreign purchasers. For example, a Canadian chemical company that did no cross-border business nevertheless found that its profit margins depended directly on the United States dollar–Japanese yen exchange rate. The company used coal as an input in its production process, and the Canadian price of coal was heavily influenced by the extent to which the Japanese bought United States coal, which in turn depended on the dollar-yen exchange rate. Although transaction exposure need not be managed, it might be useful for a firm to manage its transaction and economic exposures because they affect firm value directly. In most companies, transaction exposure is generally tracked and managed by the office of the corporate treasurer. Economic exposure is difficult to define in operating terms, and very few companies manage it actively. In most companies, economic exposure is generally considered part of the strategic planning process, rather than as a treasurer's or finance function.

INTERNATIONAL FINANCING AND CAPITAL STRUCTURE DECISIONS

An MNC has access to many more financing sources than a domestic firm. It can tap not only the financing sources in its home country that are available to its domestic counterparts, but also sources in the foreign countries in which it operates. Host countries often provide access to low-cost subsidized financing to attract foreign investment. In addition, the MNC may enjoy preferential credit standards because of its size and investor preference for its home currency. An MNC may be able to access third-country capital markets—countries in which it does not operate but which may have large, well-functioning capital markets. Finally, an MNC can also access external currency markets: Eurodollar, Euro-currency, or Asian-dollar markets. These external markets are unregulated, and because of their lower spread, can offer very attractive rates for financing and for investments. With the increasing availability of interest rate and currency swaps, a firm can raise funds in the lowest-cost maturities and currencies and swap them into funds with the maturity and currency denomination it requires. Because of its ability to tap a larger number of financial markets, the MNC may have a lower cost of capital; and because it may better be able to avoid the problems or limitations of any one financial market, it may have a more continuous access to external finance compared to a domestic company.

Access to national financial markets is regulated by governments. For example, in the United States, access to capital markets is governed by SEC regulations. Access to Japanese capital markets is governed by regulations issued by the Ministry of Finance. Some countries have extensive regulations; other countries have relatively open markets. These regulations may differ depending on the legal residency terms of the company raising funds. A company that cannot use its local subsidiary to raise funds in a given market will be treated as foreign. In order to increase their visibility in a foreign capital market, a number of MNCs are now listing their equities on the stock exchanges of many of these countries.

The external currency markets are predominantly centered in Europe, and about 80 percent of their value is denominated in terms of the U.S. dollar. Thus, most external currency markets can be characterized as Eurodollar markets. Such markets consist of an active short-term money market and an intermediate-term capital market with maturities ranging up to fifteen years and averaging about seven to nine years. The intermediate-term market consists of the Eurobond and the Syndicated Euro-credit markets. Eurobonds are usually issued as unregistered bearer bonds and generally tend to have higher flotation costs but lower coupon rates compared to similar bonds issued in the United States. A Syndicated Euro-credit loan is simply a large term loan that involves contributions by a number of lending banks.

In arriving at its capital structure decisions, an MNC has to consider a number of factors. First, the capital structure of its local affiliates is influenced by local norms regarding capital structure in that industry and in that country. Local norms for companies in the same industry can differ considerably from country to country. Second, the local affiliate capital structure must also reflect corporate attitudes toward exchange rate and political risk in that country, which would normally lead to higher levels of local debt and other local capital. Third, local affiliate capital structure must reflect home country requirements with regard to the company's consolidated capital structure. Finally, the optimal MNC capital structure should reflect its wider access to financial markets, its ability to diversify economic and political risks, and its other advantages over domestic companies.

DIRECT FOREIGN INVESTMENT

An MNC often makes direct foreign investments abroad in the form of plants and equipment. The decision process for this type of investment is very similar to the capital-budgeting decision in the domestic context—with some additional twists.

Most real-world capital budgeting decisions are made with uncertain future outcomes. Recall that a capital budgeting decision has three major components: the estimation of the future cash flows (including the initial cost of the proposed investment), the estimation of the risk in these cash flows, and the choice of the proper discount rate. We will assume that the net present value is appropriate as we examine (1) the risks associated with direct foreign investment, and (2) factors to be considered in making the investment decision that may be unique to the international scene.

Risks in Direct Foreign Investments

Risks in domestic capital budgeting arise from two sources: business risk and financial risk. The international capital-budgeting problem incorporates these risks as well as political risk and exchange risk.

Business Risk and Financial Risk. International business risk is due to the response of business to economic conditions in the foreign country. Thus, the U.S. MNC needs to be aware of the business climate in both the United States and the foreign country. Additional business risk is due to competition from other MNCs, local businesses, and imported goods. Financial risk refers to the risks introduced in the profit stream by the firm's financial structure. The financial risks of foreign operations are not very different from those of domestic operations.

Political Risk. Political risk arises because the foreign subsidiary conducts its business in a political system different from that of the home country. Many foreign governments, especially those in the Third World, are less stable than the U.S. government. A change in a country's political setup frequently brings a change in policies with respect to businesses—and especially with respect to foreign businesses. An extreme change in policy might involve nationalization or even outright expropriation of certain businesses. These are the political risks of conducting business abroad. A business with no investment in plants and equipment is less susceptible to these risks. Some examples of political risk are listed below:

1. Expropriation of plants and equipment without compensation.
2. Expropriation with minimal compensation that is below actual market value.
3. Non-convertibility of the subsidiary's foreign earnings into the parent's currency, the problem of blocked funds.
4. Substantial changes in the laws governing taxation.
5. Governmental controls in the foreign country regarding the sale price of the products, wages, and compensation to personnel, hiring of personnel, making of transfer payments to the parent, and local borrowing.
6. Some governments require certain amounts of local equity participation in the business. Some require that the majority of the equity participation belong to their country.

All these controls and governmental actions introduce risks in the cash flows of the investment to the parent company. These risks must be considered before making the foreign investment decision. The MNC may decide against investing in countries with risks of types 1 and 2. Other risks can be borne—provided that the returns from the foreign investments are high enough to compensate for them. Insurance against some types of political risks may be purchased from private insurance companies or from the U.S. government Overseas Private Investment Corporation. It should be noted that although an MNC cannot protect itself against all foreign political risks, political risks are also present in domestic business.

Exchange Risk. The exposure of the fixed assets is best measured by the effects of the exchange rate changes on the firm's future earnings stream: that being economic exposure rather than translation exposure. For instance, changes in the exchange rate may adversely affect sales by making competing imported goods cheaper. Changes in the cost of goods sold may result if some components are imported and their price in the foreign currency changes because of exchange rate fluctuations. The thrust of these examples is that the effect of exchange rate changes on income statement items should be properly measured to evaluate exchange risk. Finally, exchange risk affects the dollar-denominated profit stream of the parent company, whether or not it affects the foreign-currency profits.

SUMMARY

The growth of our global economy, the increasing number of multinational corporations, and the increase in foreign trade itself underscore the importance of the study of international finance. Exchange-rate mechanics are discussed in the context of the prevailing floating rates. Under this system, exchange rates between currencies vary in an apparently random fashion in accordance with the supply and demand conditions in the exchange market. Important economic factors affecting the level of exchange rates include the relative economic strengths of the countries involved, the balance-of-payments mechanism, and the countries' monetary policies. Several important exchange-rate terms are introduced. These include the asked and the bid rates, which represent the selling and buying rates of currencies. The direct quote is the units of home currency per unit of foreign currency, and the indirect quote is the reciprocal of the direct quote.

- The forward exchange market provides a valuable service by quoting rates for the delivery of foreign currencies in the future. The foreign currency is said to sell at a premium (discount) forward from the spot rate when the forward rate is greater (less) than the spot rate, in direct quotation. In addition, the influences of purchasing power parity (PPP) and the International Fisher Effect (IFE) in determining the exchange rate are discussed. In rational and efficient markets, forward rates are unbiased forecasts of future spot rates that are consistent with the PPP.

- Exchange risk exists because the exact spot rate that prevails on a future date is not known with certainty today. The concept of exchange risk is applicable to a wide variety of businesses including export-import firms and firms involved in making direct foreign investments or international investments in securities. Exchange exposure is a measure of exchange risk. There are different ways of measuring the foreign exposure including the net asset (net liability) measurement. Different strategies are open to businesses to counter the exposure to this risk including the money market hedge and the forward market hedge. Each involves different costs.

- Funds positioning is a useful tool for reducing exchange risk exposure. The MNC may have a lower cost of capital because it has access to a larger set of financial markets than a domestic company. In addition to the home, host, and third-country financial markets, the MNC can tap the rapidly growing external currency markets. In making capital structure decisions, the MNC must consider political and exchange risks and host and home country capital structure norms.

- The complexities encountered in the direct foreign investment decision include the usual sources of risk—business and financial—and additional risks associated with fluctuating exchange rates and political factors. Political risk is due to differences in political climates, institutions, and processes between the home country and abroad.

Under these conditions, the estimation of future cash flows and the choice of the proper discount rates are more complicated than for the domestic investment situation.

SELF-CORRECTION PROBLEM

Selling Quotes for the German Mark in New York

Country	Contract	$/Foreign Currency
Germany—mark	Spot	.3893
	30-day	.3910
	90-day	.3958

You own $10,000. The dollar rate on the German mark is $2.5823/DM. The German mark rate is given in the table above. Are arbitrage profits possible? Set up an arbitrage scheme with your capital. What is the gain (loss) in dollars?

SOLUTION TO SELF-CORRECTION PROBLEM

The German rate is 2.5823 marks/$1, while the (indirect) New York rate is 1/.3893 = 2.5687 marks/$.

Assuming no transaction costs, the rates between German and New York are out of line. Thus, arbitrage profits are possible.

Step 1:   Because the mark is cheaper in Germany, buy $10,000 worth of marks in Germany. The number of marks purchased would be $10,000 × 2.5823 = 25,823 marks

Step 2:   Simultaneously sell the marks in New York at the prevailing rate. The amount received upon the sale of the marks would be:
25,823 marks × $.3893/mark = $10,052.89
net gain is $10,052.89 − $10,000 = $52.89

QUESTIONS

1. What additional factors are encountered in international as compared with domestic financial management? Discuss each briefly.
2. What different types of businesses operate in the international environment? Why are the techniques and strategies available to these firms different?
3. What is meant by arbitrage profits?
4. How do the purchasing power parity, interest rate parity, and the Fisher effect explain the relationships between the current spot rate, the future spot rate, and the forward rate?
5. What is meant by (a) exchange risk, (b) political risk?
6. What are the differences between transaction, translation, and economic exposures? Should all of them be ideally reduced to zero?
7. What steps can a firm take to reduce exchange risk? Indicate at least two different techniques.

8. How are the forward market and the money market hedges affected? What are the major differences between these two types of hedges?

9. In the New York exchange market, the forward rate for the Indian currency, the rupee, is not quoted. If you were exposed to exchange risk in rupees, how could you cover your position?

10. Compare and contrast the use of forward contracts, futures contracts, and options to reduce foreign exchange exposure. When is each instrument most appropriate?

11. Indicate two working-capital management techniques that are useful for international businesses to reduce exchange risk and potentially increase profits.

12. How do the financing sources available to an MNC differ from those available to a domestic firm? What do these differences mean for the company's cost of capital?

13. What risks are associated with direct foreign investment? How do these risks differ from those encountered in domestic investment?

14. How is the direct foreign investment decision made? What are the inputs to this decision process? Are the inputs more complicated than those to the domestic investment problem? If so, why?

15. A corporation desires to enter a particular foreign market. The DFI analysis indicates that a direct investment in the plant in the foreign country is not profitable. What other course of action can the company take to enter the foreign market? What are the important considerations?

PROBLEMS

The data for Problems 1 through 6 are given in the following table:

Selling Quotes for Foreign Currencies in New York

Country	Contract	$/Foreign Currency
Canada—dollar	Spot	.8437
	30-day	.8417
	90-day	.8395
Japan—yen	Spot	.004684
	30-day	.004717
	90-day	.004781
Switzerland—franc	Spot	.5139
	30-day	.5169
	90-day	.5315

1. An American business needs to pay (a) 10,000 Canadian dollars, (b) 2 million yen, and (c) 50,000 Swiss francs to businesses abroad. What are the dollar payments to the respective countries?

2. An American business pays $10,000, $13,000, and $20,000 to suppliers in, respectively, Japan, Switzerland, and Canada. How much in local currencies do the suppliers receive?

3. Compute the indirect quote for the spot and forward Canadian dollar, yen, and Swiss franc contracts.

4. The spreads on the contracts as a percent of the asked rates are 2% for yen, 3% for Canadian dollars, and 5% for Swiss francs. Show, in a table similar to the one above, the bid rates for the different spot and forward rates.

5. You own $10,000. The dollar rate in Tokyo is 216.6743. The yen rate in New York is given in the previous table. Are arbitrage profits possible? Set up an arbitrage scheme with your capital. What is the gain (loss) in dollars?

6. Compute the Canadian dollar/yen and the yen/Swiss franc spot rate from the data in the table above.

INTERNET EXERCISE

Go to http://www.marketedge.com and click on "currencies." Using the current information on this page update the direct quotes used in the example on page 410.

Notes

[1] The system of floating rates is referred to as the "floating-rate regime."

[2] The balance of payments for the United States reflects the difference between the imports and exports of goods (the trade balance) and services. Capital inflows and outflows are tabulated in the capital account.

APPENDICES

Appendix A: Using a Calculator

Appendix B: Future Value of \$1 ($FVIF_{i,n}$)

Appendix C: Present Value of \$1 ($PVIF_{i,n}$)

Appendix D: Future Value of an Annuity of \$1 for n Periods ($FVIFA_{i,n}$)

Appendix E: Present Value of an Annuity of \$1 for n Periods ($PVIFA_{i,n}$)

Using a Calculator

As you prepare for a career in business, the ability to use a financial calculator is essential, whether you are in the finance division or the marketing department. For most positions, it will be assumed that you can use a calculator in making computations that at one time were simply not possible without extensive time and effort. The following examples let us see what is possible, but they represent only the beginning of using the calculator in finance.

In demonstrating how calculators may make our work easier, we must first decide which calculator to use. The options are numerous and largely depend on personal preference. We have chosen to demonstrate the Hewlett-Packard HP 17BII.

I. Introductory Comments

In the examples that follow, you are told (1) which keystrokes to use, (2) the resulting appearance of the calculator display, and (3) a supporting explanation. The keystrokes column tells you which keys to press. The keystrokes shown in an unshaded box tell you to use one of the calculator's dedicated or "hard" keys. For example if +/− is shown in the keystrokes instruction column, press that key on the keyboard of the calculator. To use a function printed in gold lettering above a dedicated key, always press the gold key ▭ first, then the function key. For example, keying in 2 and pressing ▭ +/− calculates the square root of 2.

When the calculator is on, a set of labels appears across the bottom of the display. This is called a *menu* because it presents you with the choices of what you can do next. Press the key directly beneath the menu label to access that function. Menu keys are represented with a shaded box in the keystrokes column. For example, TIME displays the current date and time and the other TIME menu options.

II. An Important Starting Point

Purpose: Before each new calculation, clear the variables, and if need be, change the number of digits displayed, the number of payments per period, and the beginning or end mode.

Example: You want to display four numbers to the right of the decimal.

Keystrokes	Display	Explanation
DSP	Select display format	Sets display to show four numbers to the right of the decimal
FIX 4		
INPUT	0.0000	
CLR	0.0000	Clears display

Example: You can display two payments per year to be paid at the end of each period

Keystrokes	Display	Explanation
FIN TVM		Sets number of payments per year at 2 and timing
OTHER		of payment at the end of each period
2 P/YR		
END EXIT	2 P/YR END MODE	

III. Calculating Table Values for:

A. The compound sum of $1 (Appendix B)

Purpose: Compute the table values for Appendix B, the future value of $1.

Method: Solve for the future value of $1: $FVIF_{i,n} = \$1(1 + i)^n$

Example: What is the table value for the compound sum of $1 for 5 years at 12% annual interest rate?

Keystrokes	Display	Explanation
FIN TVM		Displays TVM menu
OTHER 1 P/YR END EXIT		Sets 1 payment per year; END mode
▨ CLEAR DATA	1 P/YR	Clears TVM variables
1 +/− PV	PV = -1.0000	Stores initial $1 as a negative present value Otherwise the answer will appear as a negative
5 N	N = 5.0000	Stores number of periods
12 1% YR	1%YR = 12.0000	Stores interest rate
FV	FV = 1.7623	Table value

B. The present value of $1 (Appendix C)

Purpose: Compute the table values for Appendix C, the present value of $1.

Method: Solve for the present value of $1: $PVIF_{i,n} = \dfrac{\$1}{(1+i)^n}$

Example: What is the table value for the present value of $1 for 8 years at a 10% annual interest rate?

Keystrokes	Display	Explanation
FIN TVM ▨ CLEAR DATA		Clears TVM variable; verifies the correct number of payments per year and the BEG or END mode
1 +/− FV	FV = 1.0000	Stores future amount as negative value
8 N	N = 8.0000	Stores number of periods
12 1% YR	I%YR = 10.0000	Stores interest rate
FV	FV = 0.4665	Table value

C. The sum of an annuity of $1 for n periods (Appendix D)

Purpose: Compute the table values for Appendix D, the sum of an annuity of $1.

Method: Solve for the future value of an annuity of $1:

$$FVIFA_{i,n} = \$1 \sum_{t=0}^{n-1} (1+i)^t$$

which may also be solved as $FVIFA_{i,n} = \dfrac{(1+i)^n - 1}{i}$

Example: What is the table value for the compound sum of an annuity of $1 for 6 years at a 14% annual interest rate?

Keystrokes	Display	Explanation
FIN TVM CLEAR DATA		Clears TVM variable; verifies the correct number of payments per year and the BEG or END mode.
1 +/- FV	FV = –1.0000	Stores annual payment (annuity) as a negative number. Otherwise the answer will appear as a negative.
6 N	N = 6.0000	Stores number of periods
14 I% YR	I%YR = 14.0000	Stores interest rate
FV	FV = 8.5355	Table value

D. The present value of an annuity of $1 for n periods (Appendix E)

Purpose: Compute the table values for Appendix E, the present value of an annuity of $1.

Method: Solve for the present value of an annuity of $1:

$$PVIFA_{i,n} = \$1 \sum_{i=1}^{n} \frac{\$1}{(1+i)^n}$$

which may also be solved as $PVIFA_{i,n} = \dfrac{1-[1/(1+i)^n]}{i}$

Example: What is the table for the present value of an annuity of $1 for 12 years at a 9% annual interest rate?

Keystrokes	Display	Explanation
FIN TVM CLEAR DATA		Clears TVM variable, and verifies the correct number of payments per year and the BEG or END mode.
1 +/- PMT	PMT = 1.0000	Stores annual payment (annuity) as a negative number. Otherwise the answer will appear as a negative.
12 N	N = 12.0000	Stores number of periods
9 I% YR	I%YR = 9.0000	Stores interest rate
PV	PV = 7.1607	Table value

FUTURE VALUE OF $1 (FVIF$_{i,n}$)

n	1%	2%	3%	4%	5%	6%	7%	8%	9%	10%
1	1.010	1.020	1.030	1.040	1.050	1.060	1.070	1.080	1.090	1.100
2	1.020	1.040	1.061	1.082	1.102	1.124	1.145	1.166	1.188	1.210
3	1.030	1.061	1.093	1.125	1.158	1.191	1.225	1.260	1.295	1.331
4	1.041	1.082	1.126	1.170	1.216	1.262	1.311	1.360	1.412	1.464
5	1.051	1.104	1.159	1.217	1.276	1.338	1.403	1.469	1.539	1.611
6	1.062	1.126	1.194	1.265	1.340	1.419	1.501	1.587	1.677	1.772
7	1.072	1.149	1.230	1.316	1.407	1.504	1.606	1.714	1.828	1.949
8	1.083	1.172	1.267	1.369	1.477	1.594	1.718	1.851	1.993	2.144
9	1.094	1.195	1.305	1.423	1.551	1.689	1.838	1.999	2.172	2.358
10	1.105	1.219	1.344	1.480	1.629	1.791	1.967	2.159	2.367	2.594
11	1.116	1.243	1.384	1.539	1.710	1.898	2.105	2.332	2.580	2.853
12	1.127	1.268	1.426	1.601	1.796	2.012	2.252	2.518	2.813	3.138
13	1.138	1.294	1.469	1.665	1.886	2.133	2.410	2.720	3.066	3.452
14	1.149	1.319	1.513	1.732	1.980	2.261	2.579	2.937	3.342	3.797
15	1.161	1.346	1.558	1.801	2.079	2.397	2.759	3.172	3.642	4.177
16	1.173	1.373	1.605	1.873	2.183	2.540	2.952	3.426	3.970	4.595
17	1.184	1.400	1.653	1.948	2.292	2.693	3.159	3.700	4.328	5.054
18	1.196	1.428	1.702	2.026	2.407	2.854	3.380	3.996	4.717	5.560
19	1.208	1.457	1.753	2.107	2.527	3.026	3.616	4.316	5.142	6.116
20	1.220	1.486	1.806	2.191	2.653	3.207	3.870	4.661	5.604	6.727
21	1.232	1.516	1.860	2.279	2.786	3.399	4.140	5.034	6.109	7.400
22	1.245	1.546	1.916	2.370	2.925	3.603	4.430	5.436	6.658	8.140
23	1.257	1.577	1.974	2.465	3.071	3.820	4.740	5.871	7.258	8.954
24	1.270	1.608	2.033	2.563	3.225	4.049	5.072	6.341	7.911	9.850
25	1.282	1.641	2.094	2.666	3.386	4.292	5.427	6.848	8.623	10.834
30	1.348	1.811	2.427	3.243	4.322	5.743	7.612	10.062	13.267	17.449
40	1.489	2.208	3.262	4.801	7.040	10.285	14.974	21.724	31.408	45.258
50	1.645	2.691	4.384	7.106	11.467	18.419	29.456	46.900	74.354	117.386

n	11%	12%	13%	14%	15%	16%	17%	18%	19%	20%
1	1.110	1.120	1.130	1.140	1.150	1.160	1.170	1.180	1.190	1.200
2	1.232	1.254	1.277	1.300	1.322	1.346	1.369	1.392	1.416	1.440
3	1.368	1.405	1.443	1.482	1.521	1.561	1.602	1.643	1.685	1.728
4	1.518	1.574	1.630	1.689	1.749	1.811	1.874	1.939	2.005	2.074
5	1.685	1.762	1.842	1.925	2.011	2.100	2.192	2.288	2.386	2.488
6	1.870	1.974	2.082	2.195	2.313	2.436	2.565	2.700	2.840	2.986
7	2.076	2.211	2.353	2.502	2.660	2.826	3.001	3.185	3.379	3.583
8	2.305	2.476	2.658	2.853	3.059	3.278	3.511	3.759	4.021	4.300
9	2.558	2.773	3.004	3.252	3.518	3.803	4.108	4.435	4.785	5.160
10	2.839	3.106	3.395	3.707	4.046	4.411	4.807	5.234	5.695	6.192
11	3.152	3.479	3.836	4.226	4.652	5.117	5.624	6.176	6.777	7.430
12	3.498	3.896	4.334	4.818	5.350	5.936	6.580	7.288	8.064	8.916
13	3.883	4.363	4.898	5.492	6.153	6.886	7.699	8.599	9.596	10.699
14	4.310	4.887	5.535	6.261	7.076	7.987	9.007	10.147	11.420	12.839
15	4.785	5.474	6.254	7.138	8.137	9.265	10.539	11.974	13.589	15.407
16	5.311	6.130	7.067	8.137	9.358	10.748	12.330	14.129	16.171	18.488
17	5.895	6.866	7.986	9.276	10.761	12.468	14.426	16.672	19.244	22.186
18	6.543	7.690	9.024	10.575	12.375	14.462	16.879	19.673	22.900	26.623
19	7.263	8.613	10.197	12.055	14.232	16.776	19.748	23.214	27.251	31.948
20	8.062	9.646	11.523	13.743	16.366	19.461	23.105	27.393	32.429	38.337
21	8.949	10.804	13.021	15.667	18.821	22.574	27.033	32.323	38.591	46.005
22	9.933	12.100	14.713	17.861	21.644	26.186	31.629	38.141	45.923	55.205
23	11.026	13.552	16.626	20.361	24.891	30.376	37.005	45.007	54.648	66.247
24	12.239	15.178	18.788	23.212	28.625	35.236	43.296	53.108	65.031	79.496
25	13.585	17.000	21.230	26.461	32.918	40.874	50.656	62.667	77.387	95.395
30	22.892	29.960	39.115	50.949	66.210	85.849	111.061	143.367	184.672	237.373
40	64.999	93.049	132.776	188.876	267.856	378.715	533.846	750.353	1051.642	1469.740
50	184.559	288.996	450.711	700.197	1083.619	1670.669	2566.080	3927.189	5988.730	9100.191

Future Value of $1 (FVIF$_{i,n}$), (continued)

n	21%	22%	23%	24%	25%	26%	27%	28%	29%	30%
1	1.210	1.220	1.230	1.240	1.250	1.260	1.270	1.280	1.290	1.300
2	1.464	1.488	1.513	1.538	1.562	1.588	1.613	1.638	1.664	1.690
3	1.772	1.816	1.861	1.907	1.953	2.000	2.048	2.097	2.147	2.197
4	2.144	2.215	2.289	2.364	2.441	2.520	2.601	2.684	2.769	2.856
5	2.594	2.703	2.815	2.932	3.052	3.176	3.304	3.436	3.572	3.713
6	3.138	3.297	3.463	3.635	3.815	4.001	4.196	4.398	4.608	4.827
7	3.797	4.023	4.259	4.508	4.768	5.042	5.329	5.629	5.945	6.275
8	4.595	4.908	5.239	5.589	5.960	6.353	6.767	7.206	7.669	8.157
9	5.560	5.987	6.444	6.931	7.451	8.004	8.595	9.223	9.893	10.604
10	6.727	7.305	7.926	8.594	9.313	10.086	10.915	11.806	12.761	13.786
11	8.140	8.912	9.749	10.657	11.642	12.708	13.862	15.112	16.462	17.921
12	9.850	10.872	11.991	13.215	14.552	16.012	17.605	19.343	21.236	23.298
13	11.918	13.264	14.749	16.386	18.190	20.175	22.359	24.759	27.395	30.287
14	14.421	16.182	18.141	20.319	22.737	25.420	28.395	31.691	35.339	39.373
15	17.449	19.742	22.314	25.195	28.422	32.030	36.062	40.565	45.587	51.185
16	21.113	24.085	27.446	31.242	35.527	40.357	45.799	51.923	58.808	66.541
17	25.547	29.384	33.758	38.740	44.409	50.850	58.165	66.461	75.862	86.503
18	30.912	35.848	41.523	48.038	55.511	64.071	73.869	85.070	97.862	112.454
19	37.404	43.735	51.073	59.567	69.389	80.730	93.813	108.890	126.242	146.190
20	45.258	53.357	62.820	73.863	86.736	101.720	119.143	139.379	162.852	190.047
21	54.762	65.095	77.268	91.591	108.420	128.167	151.312	178.405	210.079	247.061
22	66.262	79.416	95.040	113.572	135.525	161.490	192.165	228.358	271.002	321.178
23	80.178	96.887	116.899	140.829	169.407	203.477	244.050	292.298	349.592	417.531
24	97.015	118.203	143.786	174.628	211.758	256.381	309.943	374.141	450.974	542.791
25	117.388	144.207	176.857	216.539	264.698	323.040	393.628	478.901	581.756	705.627
30	304.471	389.748	497.904	634.810	807.793	1025.904	1300.477	1645.488	2078.208	2619.936
40	2048.309	2846.941	3946.340	5455.797	7523.156	10346.879	14195.051	19426.418	26520.723	36117.754
50	13779.844	20795.680	31278.301	46889.207	70064.812	104354.562	154942.687	229345.875	338440.000	497910.125

n	31%	32%	33%	34%	35%	36%	37%	38%	39%	40%
1	1.310	1.320	1.330	1.340	1.350	1.360	1.370	1.380	1.390	1.400
2	1.716	1.742	1.769	1.796	1.822	1.850	1.877	1.904	1.932	1.960
3	2.248	2.300	2.353	2.406	2.460	2.515	2.571	2.628	2.686	2.744
4	2.945	3.036	3.129	3.224	3.321	3.421	3.523	3.627	3.733	3.842
5	3.858	4.007	4.162	4.320	4.484	4.653	4.826	5.005	5.189	5.378
6	5.054	5.290	5.535	5.789	6.053	6.328	6.612	6.907	7.213	7.530
7	6.621	6.983	7.361	7.758	8.172	8.605	9.058	9.531	10.025	10.541
8	8.673	9.217	9.791	10.395	11.032	11.703	12.410	13.153	13.935	14.758
9	11.362	12.166	13.022	13.930	14.894	15.917	17.001	18.151	19.370	20.661
10	14.884	16.060	17.319	18.666	20.106	21.646	23.292	25.049	26.924	28.925
11	19.498	21.199	23.034	25.012	27.144	29.439	31.910	34.567	37.425	40.495
12	25.542	27.982	30.635	33.516	36.644	40.037	43.716	47.703	52.020	56.694
13	33.460	36.937	40.745	44.912	49.469	54.451	59.892	65.830	72.308	79.371
14	43.832	49.756	54.190	60.181	66.784	74.053	82.051	90.845	100.509	111.120
15	57.420	64.358	72.073	80.643	90.158	100.712	112.410	125.366	139.707	155.567
16	75.220	84.953	95.857	108.061	121.713	136.968	154.002	173.005	194.192	217.793
17	98.539	112.138	127.490	144.802	164.312	186.277	210.983	238.747	269.927	304.911
18	129.086	148.022	169.561	194.035	221.822	253.337	289.046	329.471	375.198	426.875
19	169.102	195.389	225.517	260.006	299.459	344.537	395.993	454.669	521.525	597.625
20	221.523	257.913	299.937	348.408	404.270	468.571	542.511	627.443	724.919	836.674
21	290.196	340.446	398.916	466.867	545.764	637.256	743.240	865.871	1007.637	1171.343
22	380.156	449.388	530.558	625.601	736.781	865.668	1018.238	1194.900	1400.615	1639.878
23	498.004	593.192	705.642	838.305	994.653	1178.668	1394.986	1648.961	1946.854	2295.829
24	652.385	783.013	938.504	1123.328	1342.781	1602.988	1911.129	2275.564	2706.125	3214.158
25	854.623	1033.577	1248.210	1505.258	1812.754	2180.063	2618.245	3140.275	3761.511	4499.816
30	3297.081	4142.008	5194.516	6503.285	8128.426	10142.914	12636.086	15716.703	19517.969	24201.043
40	49072.621	66519.313	89962.188	121388.437	163433.875	219558.625	294317.937	393684.687	525508.312	700022.688

PRESENT VALUE OF $1 (PVIF$_{i,n}$) APPENDIX C

n	1%	2%	3%	4%	5%	6%	7%	8%	9%	10%
1	.990	.980	.971	.962	.952	.943	.935	.926	.917	.909
2	.980	.961	.943	.925	.907	.890	.873	.857	.842	.826
3	.971	.942	.915	.889	.864	.840	.816	.794	.772	.751
4	.961	.924	.888	.855	.823	.792	.763	.735	.708	.683
5	.951	.906	.863	.822	.784	.747	.713	.681	.650	.621
6	.942	.888	.837	.790	.746	.705	.666	.630	.596	.564
7	.933	.871	.813	.760	.711	.665	.623	.583	.547	.513
8	.923	.853	.789	.731	.677	.627	.582	.540	.502	.467
9	.914	.837	.766	.703	.645	.592	.544	.500	.460	.424
10	.905	.820	.744	.676	.614	.558	.508	.463	.422	.386
11	.896	.804	.722	.650	.585	.527	.475	.429	.388	.350
12	.887	.789	.701	.625	.557	.497	.444	.397	.356	.319
13	.879	.773	.681	.601	.530	.469	.415	.368	.326	.290
14	.870	.758	.661	.577	.505	.442	.388	.340	.299	.263
15	.861	.743	.642	.555	.481	.417	.362	.315	.275	.239
16	.853	.728	.623	.534	.458	.394	.339	.292	.252	.218
17	.844	.714	.605	.513	.436	.371	.317	.270	.231	.198
18	.836	.700	.587	.494	.416	.350	.296	.250	.212	.180
19	.828	.686	.570	.475	.396	.331	.277	.232	.194	.164
20	.820	.673	.554	.456	.377	.312	.258	.215	.178	.149
21	.811	.660	.538	.439	.359	.294	.242	.199	.164	.135
22	.803	.647	.522	.422	.342	.278	.226	.184	.150	.123
23	.795	.634	.507	.406	.326	.262	.211	.170	.138	.112
-14	.788	.622	.492	.390	.310	.247	.197	.158	.126	.102
25	.780	.610	.478	.375	.295	.233	.184	.146	.116	.092
30	.742	.552	.412	.308	.231	.174	.131	.099	.075	.057
40	.672	.453	.307	.208	.142	.097	.067	.046	.032	.022
50	.608	.372	.228	.141	.087	.054	.034	.021	.013	.009

n	11%	12%	13%	14%	15%	16%	17%	18%	19%	20%
1	.901	.893	.885	.877	.870	.862	.855	.847	.840	.833
2	.812	.797	.783	.769	.756	.743	.731	.718	.706	.694
3	.731	.712	.693	.675	.658	.641	.624	.609	.593	.579
4	.659	.636	.613	.592	.572	.552	.534	.516	.499	.482
5	.593	.567	.543	.519	.497	.476	.456	.437	.419	.402
6	.535	.507	.480	.456	.432	.410	.390	.370	.352	.335
7	.482	.452	.425	.400	.376	.354	.333	.314	.296	.279
8	.434	.404	.376	.351	.327	.305	.285	.266	.249	.233
9	.391	.361	.333	.308	.284	.263	.243	.225	.209	.194
10	.352	.322	.295	.270	.247	.227	.208	.191	.176	.162
11	.317	.287	.261	.237	.215	.195	.178	.162	.148	.135
12	.286	.257	.231	.208	.187	.168	.152	.137	.124	.112
13	.258	.229	.204	.182	.163	.145	.130	.116	.104	.093
14	.232	.205	.181	.160	.141	.125	.111	.099	.088	.078
15	.209	.183	.160	.140	.123	.108	.095	.084	.074	.065
16	.188	.163	.141	.123	.107	.093	.081	.071	.062	.054
17	.170	.146	.125	.108	.093	.080	.069	.060	.052	.045
18	.153	.130	.111	.095	.081	.069	.059	.051	.044	.038
19	.138	.116	.098	.083	.070	.060	.051	.043	.037	.031
20	.124	.104	.087	.073	.061	.051	.043	.037	.031	.026
21	.112	.093	.077	.064	.053	.044	.037	.031	.026	.022
22	.101	.083	.068	.056	.046	.038	.032	.026	.022	.018
23	.091	.074	.060	.049	.040	.033	.027	.022	.018	.015
24	.082	.066	.053	.043	.035	.028	.023	.019	.015	.013
25	.074	.059	.047	.038	.030	.024	.020	.016	.013	.010
30	.044	.033	.026	.020	.015	.012	.009	.007	.005	.004
40	.015	.011	.008	.005	.004	.003	.002	.001	.001	.001
50	.005	.003	.002	.001	.001	.001	.000	.000	.000	.000

Present Value of $1 (PVIF$_{i,n}$), (continued)

n	21%	22%	23%	24%	25%	26%	27%	28%	29%	30%
1	.826	.820	.813	.806	.800	.794	.787	.781	.775	.769
2	.683	.672	.661	.650	.640	.630	.620	.610	.601	.592
3	.564	.551	.537	.524	.512	.500	.488	.477	.466	.455
4	.467	.451	.437	.423	.410	.397	.384	.373	.361	.350
5	.386	.370	.355	.341	.328	.315	.303	.291	.280	.269
6	.319	.303	.289	.275	.262	.250	.238	.227	.217	.207
7	.263	.249	.235	.222	.210	.198	.188	.178	.168	.159
8	.218	.204	.191	.179	.168	.157	.148	.139	.130	.123
9	.180	.167	.155	.144	.134	.125	.116	.108	.101	.094
10	.149	.137	.126	.116	.107	.099	.092	.085	.078	.073
11	.123	.112	.103	.094	.086	.079	.072	.066	.061	.056
12	.102	.092	.083	.076	.069	.062	.057	.052	.047	.043
13	.084	.075	.068	.061	.055	.050	.045	.040	.037	.033
14	.069	.062	.055	.049	.044	.039	.035	.032	.028	.025
15	.057	.051	.045	.040	.035	.031	.028	.025	.022	.020
16	.047	.042	.036	.032	.028	.025	.022	.019	.017	.015
17	.039	.034	.030	.026	.023	.020	.017	.015	.013	.012
18	.032	.028	.024	.021	.018	.016	.014	.012	.010	.009
19	.027	.023	.020	.017	.014	.012	.011	.009	.008	.007
20	.022	.019	.016	.014	.012	.010	.008	.007	.006	.005
21	.018	.015	.013	.011	.009	.008	.007	.006	.005	.004
22	.015	.013	.011	.009	.007	.006	.005	.004	.004	.003
23	.012	.010	.009	.007	.006	.005	.004	.003	.003	.002
24	.010	.008	.007	.006	.005	.004	.003	.003	.002	.002
25	.009	.007	.006	.005	.004	.003	.003	.002	.002	.001
30	.003	.003	.002	.002	.001	.001	.001	.001	.000	.000
40	.000	.000	.000	.000	.000	.000	.000	.000	.000	.000
50	.000	.000	.000	.000	.000	.000	.000	.000	.000	.000

n	31%	32%	33%	34%	35%	36%	37%	38%	39%	40%
1	.763	.758	.752	.746	.741	.735	.730	.725	.719	.714
2	.583	.574	.565	.557	.549	.541	.533	.525	.518	.510
3	.445	.435	.425	.416	.406	.398	.389	.381	.372	.364
4	.340	.329	.320	.310	.301	.292	.284	.276	.268	.260
5	.259	.250	.240	.231	.223	.215	.207	.200	.193	.186
6	.198	.189	.181	.173	.165	.158	.151	.145	.139	.133
7	.151	.143	.136	.129	.122	.116	.110	.105	.100	.095
8	.115	.108	.102	.096	.091	.085	.081	.076	.072	.068
9	.088	.082	.077	.072	.067	.063	.059	.055	.052	.048
10	.067	.062	.058	.054	.050	.046	.043	.040	.037	.035
11	.051	.047	.043	.040	.037	.034	.031	.029	.027	.025
12	.039	.036	.033	.030	.027	.025	.023	.021	.019	.018
13	.030	.027	.025	.022	.020	.018	.017	.015	.014	.013
14	.023	.021	.018	.017	.015	.014	.012	.011	.010	.009
15	.017	.016	.014	.012	.011	.010	.009	.008	.007	.006
16	.013	.012	.010	.009	.008	.007	.006	.006	.005	.005
17	.010	.009	.008	.007	.006	.005	.005	.004	.004	.003
18	.008	.007	.006	.005	.005	.004	.003	.003	.003	.002
19	.006	.005	.004	.004	.003	.003	.003	.002	.002	.002
20	.005	.004	.003	.003	.002	.002	.002	.002	.001	.001
21	.003	.003	.003	.002	.002	.002	.001	.001	.001	.001
22	.003	.002	.002	.002	.001	.001	.001	.001	.001	.001
23	.002	.002	.001	.001	.001	.001	.001	.001	.001	.000
24	.002	.001	.001	.001	.001	.001	.001	.000	.000	.000
25	.001	.001	.001	.001	.001	.000	.000	.000	.000	.000
30	.000	.000	.000	.000	.000	.000	.000	.000	.000	.000
40	.000	.000	.000	.000	.000	.000	.000	.000	.000	.000

FUTURE VALUE OF AN ANNUITY OF $1 FOR N PERIODS (FVIFA$_{I,N}$)

n	1%	2%	3%	4%	5%	6%	7%	8%	9%	10%
1	1.000	1.000	1.000	1.000	1.000	1.000	1.000	1.000	1.000	1.000
2	2.010	2.020	2.030	2.040	2.050	2.060	2.070	2.080	2.090	2.100
3	3.030	3.060	3.091	3.122	3.152	3.184	3.215	3.246	3.278	3.310
4	4.060	4.122	4.184	4.246	4.310	4.375	4.440	4.506	4.573	4.641
5	5.101	5.204	5.309	5.416	5.526	5.637	5.751	5.867	5.985	6.105
6	6.152	6.308	6.468	6.633	6.802	6.975	7.153	7.336	7.523	7.716
7	7.214	7.434	7.662	7.898	8.142	8.394	8.654	8.923	9.200	9.487
8	8.286	8.583	8.892	9.214	9.549	9.897	10.260	10.637	11.028	11.436
9	9.368	9.755	10.159	10.583	11.027	11.491	11.978	12.488	13.021	13.579
10	10.462	10.950	11.464	12.006	12.578	13.181	13.816	14.487	15.193	15.937
11	11.567	12.169	12.808	13.486	14.207	14.972	15.784	16.645	17.560	18.531
12	12.682	13.412	14.192	15.026	15.917	16.870	17.888	18.977	20.141	21.384
13	13.809	14.680	15.618	16.627	17.713	18.882	20.141	21.495	22.953	24.523
14	14.947	15.974	17.086	18.292	19.598	21.015	22.550	24.215	26.019	27.975
15	16.097	17.293	18.599	20.023	21.578	23.276	25.129	27.152	29.361	31.772
16	17.258	18.639	20.157	21.824	23.657	25.672	27.888	30.324	33.003	35.949
17	18.430	20.012	21.761	23.697	25.840	28.213	30.840	33.750	36.973	40.544
18	19.614	21.412	23.414	25.645	28.132	30.905	33.999	37.450	41.301	45.599
19	20.811	22.840	25.117	27.671	30.539	33.760	37.379	41.446	46.018	51.158
20	22.019	24.297	26.870	29.778	33.066	36.785	40.995	45.762	51.159	57.274
21	23.239	25.783	28.676	31.969	35.719	39.992	44.865	50.422	56.764	64.002
22	24.471	27.299	30.536	34.248	38.505	43.392	49.005	55.456	62.872	71.402
23	25.716	28.845	32.452	36.618	41.430	46.995	53.435	60.893	69.531	79.542
24	26.973	30.421	34.426	39.082	44.501	50.815	58.176	66.764	76.789	88.496
25	28.243	32.030	36.459	41.645	47.726	54.864	63.248	73.105	84.699	98.346
30	34.784	40.567	47.575	56.084	66.438	79.057	94.459	113.282	136.305	164.491
40	48.885	60.401	75.400	95.024	120.797	154.758	199.630	295.052	337.872	442.580
50	64.461	84.577	112.794	152.664	209.341	290.325	406.516	573.756	815.051	1163.865

n	11%	12%	13%	14%	15%	16%	17%	18%	19%	20%
1	1.000	1.000	1.000	1.000	1.000	1.000	1.000	1.000	1.000	1.000
2	2.110	2.120	2.130	2.140	2.150	2.160	2.170	2.180	2.190	2.200
3	3.342	3.374	3.407	3.440	3.472	3.506	3.539	3.572	3.606	3.640
4	4.710	4.779	4.850	4.921	4.993	5.066	5.141	5.215	5.291	5.368
5	6.228	6.353	6.480	6.610	6.742	6.877	7.014	7.154	7.297	7.442
6	7.913	8.115	8.323	8.535	8.754	8.977	9.207	9.442	9.683	9.930
7	9.783	10.089	10.405	10.730	11.067	11.414	11.772	12.141	12.523	12.916
8	11.859	12.300	12.757	13.233	13.727	14.240	14.773	15.327	15.902	16.499
9	14.164	14.776	15.416	16.085	16.786	17.518	18.285	19.086	19.923	20.799
10	16.722	17.549	18.420	19.337	20.304	21.321	22.393	23.521	24.709	25.959
11	19.561	20.655	21.814	23.044	24.349	25.733	27.200	28.755	30.403	32.150
12	22.713	24.133	25.650	27.271	29.001	30.850	32.824	34.931	37.180	39.580
13	26.211	28.029	29.984	32.088	34.352	36.786	39.404	42.218	45.244	48.496
14	30.095	32.392	34.882	37.581	40.504	43.672	47.102	50.818	54.841	59.196
15	34.405	37.280	40.417	43.842	47.580	51.659	56.109	60.965	66.260	72.035
16	39.190	42.753	46.671	50.980	55.717	60.925	66.648	72.938	79.850	87.442
17	44.500	48.883	53.738	59.117	65.075	71.673	78.978	87.067	96.021	105.930
18	50.396	55.749	61.724	68.393	75.836	84.140	93.404	103.739	115.265	128.116
19	56.939	63.439	70.748	78.968	88.211	98.603	110.283	123.412	138.165	154.739
20	64.202	72.052	80.946	91.024	102.443	115.379	130.031	146.626	165.417	186.687
21	72.264	81.698	92.468	104.767	118.809	134.840	153.136	174.019	197.846	225.024
22	81.213	92.502	105.489	120.434	137.630	157.414	180.169	206.342	236.436	271.028
23	91.147	104.602	120.203	138.295	159.274	183.600	211.798	244.483	282.359	326.234
24	102.173	118.154	136.829	158.656	184.166	213.976	248.803	289.490	337.007	392.480
25	114.412	133.333	155.616	181.867	212.790	249.212	292.099	342.598	402.038	471.976
30	199.018	241.330	293.192	356.778	434.738	530.306	647.423	790.932	966.698	1181.865
40	581.812	767.080	1013.667	1341.979	1779.048	2360.724	3134.412	4163.094	5529.711	7343.715
50	1668.723	2399.975	3459.344	4994.301	7217.488	10435.449	15088.805	21812.273	31514.492	45496.094

Future Value of an Annuity of $1 for *n* Periods (FVIFA$_{i,n}$), (continued)

n	21%	22%	23%	24%	25%	26%	27%	28%	29%	30%
1	1.000	1.000	1.000	1.000	1.000	1.000	1.000	1.000	1.000	1.000
2	2.210	2.220	2.230	2.240	2.250	2.260	2.270	2.280	2.290	2.300
3	3.674	3.708	3.743	3.778	3.813	3.848	3.883	3.918	3.954	3.990
4	5.446	5.524	5.604	5.684	5.766	5.848	5.931	6.016	6.101	6.187
5	7.589	7.740	7.893	8.048	8.207	8.368	8.533	8.700	8.870	9.043
6	10.183	10.442	10.708	10.980	11.259	11.544	11.837	12.136	12.442	12.756
7	13.321	13.740	14.171	14.615	15.073	15.546	16.032	16.534	17.051	17.583
8	17.119	17.762	18.430	19.123	19.842	20.588	21.361	22.163	22.995	23.858
9	21.714	22.670	23.669	24.712	25.802	26.940	28.129	29.369	30.664	32.015
10	27.274	28.657	20.113	31.643	33.253	34.945	36.723	38.592	40.556	42.619
11	34.001	35.962	38.039	40.238	42.566	45.030	47.639	50.398	53.318	56.405
12	42.141	44.873	47.787	50.895	54.208	57.738	61.501	65.510	69.780	74.326
13	51.991	55.745	59.778	64.109	68.760	73.750	79.106	84.853	91.016	97.624
14	63.909	69.009	74.528	80.496	86.949	93.925	101.465	109.611	118.411	127.912
15	78.330	85.191	92.669	100.815	109.687	119.346	129.860	141.302	153.750	167.285
16	95.779	104.933	114.983	126.010	138.109	151.375	165.922	181.867	199.337	218.470
17	116.892	129.019	142.428	157.252	173.636	191.733	211.721	233.790	258.145	285.011
18	142.439	158.403	176.187	195.993	218.045	242.583	269.885	300.250	334.006	371.514
19	173.351	194.251	217.710	244.031	273.556	306.654	343.754	385.321	431.868	483.968
20	210.755	237.986	268.783	303.598	342.945	387.384	437.568	494.210	558.110	630.157
21	256.013	291.343	331.603	377.461	429.681	489.104	556.710	633.589	720.962	820.204
22	310.775	356.438	408.871	469.052	538.101	617.270	708.022	811.993	931.040	1067.265
23	377.038	435.854	503.911	582.624	673.626	778.760	900.187	1040.351	1202.042	1388.443
24	457.215	532.741	620.810	723.453	843.032	982.237	1144.237	1332.649	1551.634	1805.975
25	554.230	650.944	764.596	898.082	1054.791	1238.617	1454.180	1706.790	2002.608	2348.765
30	1445.111	1767.044	2160.459	2640.881	3227.172	3941.953	4812.891	5873.172	7162.785	8729.805
40	9749.141	12936.141	17153.691	22728.367	30088.621	39791.957	52570.707	69376.562	91447.375	120389.375

n	31%	32%	33%	34%	35%	36%	37%	38%	39%	40%
1	1.000	1.000	1.000	1.000	1.000	1.000	1.000	1.000	1.000	1.000
2	2.310	2.320	2.330	2.340	2.350	2.360	2.370	2.380	2.390	2.400
3	4.026	4.062	4.099	4.136	4.172	4.210	4.247	4.284	4.322	4.360
4	6.274	6.362	6.452	6.542	6.633	6.725	6.818	6.912	7.008	7.104
5	9.219	9.398	9.581	9.766	9.954	10.146	10.341	10.539	10.741	10.946
6	13.077	13.406	13.742	14.086	14.438	14.799	15.167	15.544	15.930	16.324
7	18.131	18.696	19.277	19.876	20.492	21.126	21.779	22.451	23.142	23.853
8	24.752	25.678	26.638	27.633	28.664	29.732	30.837	31.982	33.167	34.395
9	33.425	34.895	36.429	38.028	39.696	41.435	43.247	45.135	47.103	49.152
10	44.786	47.062	49.451	51.958	54.590	57.351	60.248	63.287	66.473	69.813
11	59.670	63.121	66.769	70.624	74.696	78.998	83.540	88.335	93.397	98.739
12	79.167	84.320	89.803	95.636	101.840	108.437	115.450	122.903	130.822	139.234
13	104.709	112.302	120.438	129.152	138.484	148.474	159.166	170.606	182.842	195.928
14	138.169	149.239	161.183	174.063	187.953	202.925	219.058	236.435	255.151	275.299
15	182.001	197.996	215.373	234.245	254.737	276.978	301.109	327.281	355.659	386.418
16	239.421	262.354	287.446	314.888	344.895	377.690	413.520	452.647	495.366	541.985
17	314.642	347.307	383.303	422.949	466.608	514.658	567.521	625.652	689.558	759.778
18	413.180	459.445	510.792	567.751	630.920	700.935	778.504	864.399	959.485	1064.689
19	542.266	607.467	680.354	761.786	852.741	954.271	1067.551	1193.870	1334.683	1491.563
20	711.368	802.856	905.870	1021.792	1152.200	1298.809	1463.544	1648.539	1856.208	2089.188
21	932.891	1060.769	1205.807	1370.201	1556.470	1767.380	2006.055	2275-982	2581.128	2925.862
22	1223.087	1401.215	1604.724	1837.068	2102.234	2404.636	2749.294	3141.852	3588.765	4097.203
23	1603.243	1850.603	2135.282	2462.669	2839.014	3271.304	3767.532	4336.750	4989.379	5737.078
24	2101.247	2443.795	2840.924	3300.974	3833.667	4449.969	5162.516	5985.711	6936.230	8032.906
25	2753.631	3226.808	3779.428	4424.301	5176.445	6052.957	7073.645	8261.273	9642.352	11247.062
30	10632.543	12940.672	15737.945	19124.434	23221.258	28172.016	34148.906	41357.227	50043.625	60500.207

PRESENT VALUE OF AN ANNUITY OF $1 FOR N PERIODS (PVIFA$_{I,N}$)

n	1%	2%	3%	4%	5%	6%	7%	8%	9%	10%
1	.990	.980	.971	.962	.952	.943	.935	.926	.917	.909
2	1.970	1.942	1.913	1.886	1.859	1.833	1.808	1.783	1.759	1.736
3	2.941	2.884	2.829	2.775	2.723	2.673	2.624	2.577	2.531	2.487
4	3.902	3.808	3.717	3.630	3.546	3.465	3.387	3.312	3.240	3.170
5	4.853	4.713	4.580	4.452	4.329	4.212	4.100	3.993	3.890	3.791
6	5.795	5.601	5.417	5.242	5.076	4.917	4.767	4.623	4.486	4.355
7	6.728	6.472	6.230	6.002	5.786	5.582	5.389	5.206	5.033	4.868
8	7.652	7.326	7.020	6.733	6.463	6.210	5.971	5.747	5.535	5.335
9	8.566	8.162	7.786	7.435	7.108	6.802	6.515	6.247	5.995	5.759
10	9.471	8.983	8.530	8.111	7.722	7.360	7.024	6.710	6.418	6.145
11	10.368	9.787	9.253	8.760	8.306	7.887	7.499	7.139	6.805	6.495
12	11.255	10.575	9.954	9.385	8.863	8.384	7.943	7.536	7.161	6.814
13	12.134	11.348	10.635	9.986	9.394	8.853	8.358	7.904	7.487	7.103
14	13.004	12.106	11.296	10.563	9.899	9.295	8.746	8.244	7.786	7.367
15	13.865	12.849	11.938	11.118	10.380	9.712	9.108	8.560	8.061	7.606
16	14.718	13.578	12.561	11.652	10.838	10.106	9.447	8.851	8.313	7.824
17	15.562	14.292	13.166	12.166	11.274	10.477	9.763	9.122	8.544	8.022
18	16.398	14.992	13.754	12.659	11.690	10.828	10.059	9.372	8.756	8.201
19	17.226	15.679	14.324	13.134	12.085	11.158	10.336	9.604	8.950	8.365
20	18.046	16.352	14.878	13.590	12.462	11.470	10.594	9.818	9.129	8.514
21	18.857	17.011	15.415	14.029	12.821	11.764	10.836	10.017	9.292	8.649
22	19.661	17.658	15.937	14.451	13.163	12.042	11.061	10.201	9.442	8.772
23	20.456	18.292	16.444	14.857	13.489	12.303	11.272	10.371	9.580	8.883
24	21.244	18.914	16.936	15.247	13.799	12.550	11.469	10.529	9.707	8.985
25	22.023	19.524	17.413	15.622	14.094	12.783	11.654	10.675	9.823	9.077
30	25.808	22.397	19.601	17.292	15.373	13.765	12.409	11.258	10.274	9.427
40	32.835	27.356	23.115	19.793	17.159	15.046	13.332	11.925	10.757	9.779
50	39.197	31.424	25.730	21.482	18.256	15.762	13.801	12.234	10.962	9.915

n	11%	12%	13%	14%	15%	16%	17%	18%	19%	20%
1	.901	.893	.885	.877	.870	.862	.855	.847	.840	.833
2	1.713	1.690	1.668	1.647	1.626	1.605	1.585	1.566	1.547	1.528
3	2.444	2.402	2.361	2.322	2.283	2.246	2.210	2.174	2.140	2.106
4	3.102	3.037	2.974	2.914	2.855	2.798	2.743	2.690	2.639	2.589
5	3.696	3.605	3.517	3.433	3.352	3.274	3.199	3.127	3.058	2.991
6	4.231	4.111	3.998	3.889	3.784	3.685	3.589	3.498	3.410	3.326
7	4.712	4.564	4.423	4.288	4.160	4.039	3.922	3.812	3.706	3.605
8	5.146	4.968	4.799	4.639	4.487	4.344	4.207	4.078	3.954	3.837
9	5.537	5.328	5.132	4.946	4.772	4.607	4.451	4.303	4.163	4.031
10	5.889	5.650	5.426	5.216	5.019	4.833	4.659	4.494	4.339	4.192
11	6.207	5.938	5.687	5.453	5.234	5.029	4.836	4.656	4.487	4.327
12	6.492	6.194	5.918	5.660	5.421	5.197	4.988	4.793	4.611	4.439
13	6.750	6.424	6.122	5.842	5.583	5.342	5.118	4.910	4.715	4.533
14	6.982	6.628	6.303	6.002	5.724	5.468	5.229	5.008	4.802	4.611
15	7.191	6.811	6.462	6.142	5.847	5.575	5.324	5.092	4.876	4.675
16	7.379	6.974	6.604	6.265	5.954	5.669	5.405	5.162	4.938	4.730
17	7.549	7.120	6.729	6.373	6.047	5.749	5.475	5.222	4.990	4.775
18	7.702	7.250	6.840	6.467	6.128	5.818	5.534	5.273	5.033	4.812
19	7.839	7.366	6.938	6.550	6.198	5.877	5.585	5.316	5.070	4.843
20	7.963	7,469	7.025	6.623	6.259	5.929	5.628	5.353	5.101	4.870
21	8.075	7.562	7.102	6.687	6.312	5.973	5.665	5.384	5.127	4.891
22	8.176	7.645	7.170	6.743	6.359	6.011	5.696	5.410	5.149	4.909
23	8.266	7.718	7.230	6.792	6.399	6.044	5.723	5.432	5.167	4.925
24	8.348	7.784	7.283	6.835	6.434	6.073	5.747	5.451	5.182	4.937
25	8.442	7.843	7.330	6.873	6.464	6.097	5.766	5.467	5.195	4.948
30	8.694	8.055	7.496	7.003	6.566	6.177	5.829	5.517	5.235	4.979
40	8.951	8.244	7.634	7.105	6.642	6.233	5.871	5.548	5.258	4.997
50	9.042	8.305	7.675	7.133	6.661	6.246	5.880	5.554	5.262	4.999

Present Value of an Annuity of $1 for n Periods (PVIFA$_{i,n}$), (continued)

n	21%	22%	23%	24%	25%	26%	27%	28%	29%	30%
1	.826	.820	.813	.806	.800	.794	.787	.781	.775	.769
2	1.509	1.492	1.474	1.457	1.440	1.424	1.407	1.392	1.376	1.361
3	2.074	2.042	2.011	1.981	1.952	1.923	1.896	1.868	1.842	1.816
4	2.540	2.494	2.448	2.404	2.362	2.320	2.280	2.241	2.203	2.166
5	2.926	2.864	2.803	2.745	2.689	2.635	2.583	2.532	2.483	2.436
6	3.245	3.167	3.092	3.020	2.951	2.885	2.821	2.759	2.700	2.643
7	3.508	3.416	3.327	3.242	3.161	3.083	3.009	2.937	2.868	2.802
8	3.726	3.619	3.518	3.421	3.329	3.241	3.156	3.076	2.999	2.925
9	3.905	3.786	3.673	3.566	3.463	3.366	3.273	3.184	3.100	3.019
10	4.054	3.923	3.799	3.682	3.570	3.465	3.364	3.269	3.178	3.092
11	4.177	4.035	3.902	3.776	3.656	3.544	3.437	3.335	3.239	3.147
12	4.278	4.127	3.985	3.851	3.725	3.606	3.493	3.387	3.286	3.190
13	4.362	4.203	4.053	3.912	3.780	3.656	3.538	3.427	3.322	3.223
14	4.432	4.265	4.108	3.962	3.824	3.695	3.573	3.459	3.351	3.249
15	4.489	4.315	4.153	4.001	3.859	3.726	3.601	3.483	3.373	3.268
16	4.536	4.357	4.189	4.033	3.887	3.751	3.623	3.503	3.390	3.283
17	4.576	4.391	4.219	4.059	3.910	3.771	3.640	3.518	3.403	3.295
18	4.608	4.419	4.243	4.080	3.928	3.786	3.654	3.529	3.413	3.304
19	4.635	4.442	4.263	4.097	3.942	3.799	3.664	3.539	3.421	3.311
20	4.657	4.460	4.279	4.110	3.954	3.808	3.673	3.546	3.427	3.316
21	4.675	4.476	4.292	4.121	3.963	3.816	3.679	3.551	3.432	3.320
22	4.690	4.488	4.302	4.130	3.970	3.822	3.684	3.556	3.436	3.323
23	4.703	4.499	4.311	4.137	3.976	3.827	3.689	3.559	3.438	3.325
24	4.713	4.507	4.318	4.143	3.981	3.831	3.692	3.562	3.441	3.327
25	4.721	4.514	4.323	4.147	3.985	3.834	3.694	3.564	3.442	3.329
30	4.746	4.534	4.339	4.160	3.995	3.842	3.701	3.569	3.447	3.332
40	4.760	4.544	4.347	4.166	3.999	3.846	3.703	3.571	3.448	3.333
50	4.762	4.545	4.348	4.167	4.000	3.846	3.704	3.571	3.448	3.333

n	31%	32%	33%	34%	35%	36%	37%	38%	39%	40%
1	.763	.758	.752	.746	.741	.735	.730	.725	.719	.714
2	1.346	1.331	1.317	1.303	1.289	1.276	1.263	1.250	1.237	1.224
3	1.791	1.766	1.742	1.719	1.696	1.673	1.652	1.630	1.609	1.589
4	2.130	2.096	2.062	2.029	1.997	1.966	1.935	1.906	1.877	1.849
5	2.390	2.345	2.302	2.260	2.220	2.181	2.143	2.106	2.070	2.035
6	2.588	2.534	2.483	2.433	2.385	2.339	2.294	2.251	2.209	2.168
7	2.739	2.677	2.619	2.562	2.508	2.455	2.404	2.355	2.308	2.263
8	2.854	2.786	2.721	2.658	2.598	2.540	2.485	2.432	2.380	2.331
9	2.942	2.868	2.798	2.730	2.665	2.603	2.544	2.487	2.432	2.379
10	3.009	2.930	2.855	2.784	2.715	2.649	2.587	2.527	2.469	2.414
11	3.060	2.978	2.899	2.824	2.752	2.683	2.618	2.555	2.496	2.438
12	3.100	3.013	2.931	2.853	2.779	2.708	2.641	2.576	2.515	2.456
13	3.129	3.040	2.956	2.876	2.799	2.727	2.658	2.592	2.529	2.469
14	3.152	3.061	2.974	2.892	2.814	2.740	2.670	2.603	2.539	2.477
15	3.170	3.076	2.988	2.905	2.825	2.750	2.679	2.611	2.546	2.484
16	3.183	3.088	2.999	2.914	2.834	2.757	2.685	2.616	2.551	2.489
17	3.193	3.097	3.007	2.921	2.840	2.763	2.690	2.621	2.555	2.492
18	3.201	3.104	3.012	2.926	2.844	2.767	2.693	2.624	2.557	2.494
19	3.207	3.109	3.017	2.930	2.848	2.770	2.696	2.626	2.559	2.496
20	3.211	3.113	3.020	2.933	2.850	2.772	2.698	2.627	2.561	2.497
21	3.215	3.116	3.023	2.935	2.852	2.773	2.699	2.629	2.562	2.498
22	3.217	3.118	3.025	2.936	2.853	2.775	2.700	2.629	2.562	2.498
23	3.219	3.120	3.026	2.938	2.854	2.775	2.701	2.630	2.563	2.499
24	3.221	3.121	3.027	2.939	2.855	2.776	2.701	2.630	2.563	2.499
25	3.222	3.122	3.028	2.939	2.856	2.776	2.702	2.631	2.563	2.499
30	3.225	2.124	3.030	2.941	2.857	2.777	2.702	2.631	2.564	2.500
40	3.226	3.125	3.030	2.941	2.857	2.778	2.703	2.632	2.564	2.500
50	3.226	3.125	3.030	2.941	2.857	2.778	2.703	2.632	2.564	2.500

ACCOUNTING GLOSSARY

absorption approach A costing approach that considers all factory overhead (both variable and fixed) to be product (inventoriable) costs that become an expense in the form of manufacturing cost of goods sold only as sales occur.

accelerated depreciation Any pattern of depreciation that writes off depreciable assets more quickly than does ordinary straight-line depreciation.

account Each item in a financial statement.

account analysis Selecting a volume-related cost driver and classifying each account as a variable cost or as a fixed cost.

accounting rate-of-return (ARR) model A non-DCF capital-budgeting model expressed as the increase in expected average annual operating income divided by the initial increase in required investment.

accounting system A formal mechanism for gathering, organizing, and communicating information about an organization's activities.

accounts payable Amounts owed on open accounts whereby the buyer pays cash some time after the date of sale.

accounts receivable Amounts owed to a company by customers who buy on open account.

accrual basis A process of accounting that recognizes the impact of transactions on the financial statements in the time periods when revenues and expenses occur instead of when cash is received or disbursed.

accrue To accumulate a receivable or payable during a given period even though no explicit transaction occurs.

activity analysis The process of identifying appropriate cost drivers and their effects on the costs of making a product or providing a service.

activity-based accounting (ABA) A system that first accumulates overhead costs for each of the activities of an organization, and then assigns the costs of activities to the products, services, or other cost objects that caused that activity.

activity-based costing (ABC) *See* activity-based accounting.

activity-level variances The differences between the master budget amounts and the amounts in the flexible budget.

adjustments Recording of implicit transactions, in contrast to the explicit transactions that trigger nearly all day-to-day routine entries.

agency theory A theory used to describe the formal choices of performance measures and rewards.

assets Economic resources that are expected to benefit future activities.

attention directing Reporting and interpreting information that helps managers to focus on operating problems, imperfections, inefficiencies, and opportunities.

audit An examination or in-depth inspection that is made in accordance with generally accepted auditing standards. It culminates with the accountant's testimony that management's financial statements are in conformity with generally accepted accounting principles.

avoidable costs Costs that will not continue if an ongoing operation is changed or deleted.

backflush costing An accounting system that applies costs to products only when the production is complete.

balance sheet A snapshot of financial status at an instant of time.

balanced scorecard A performance measurement system that strikes a balance between financial and operating measures, links performance to rewards, and gives explicit recognition to the diversity of stakeholder interests.

behavioral implications The accounting system's effect on the behavior (decisions) of managers.

bench marks General rules of thumb specifying appropriate levels for financial ratios.

book value The original cost of equipment less accumulated depreciation, which is the summation of depreciation charged to past periods.

breakeven point The level of sales at which revenue equals expenses and net income is zero.

budget A quantitative expression of a plan of action and an aid to coordinating and implementing the plan.

budgeted factory-overhead rate The budgeted total overhead divided by the budgeted cost-driver activity.

by-product A product that, like a joint product, is not individually identifiable until manufacturing reaches a split-off point, but has relatively insignificant total sales value.

capacity costs The fixed costs of being able to achieve a desired level of production or to provide a desired level of service while maintaining product or service attributes, such as quality.

capital budget A budget that details the planned expenditures for facilities, equipment, new products, and other long-term investments.

capital turnover Revenue divided by invested capital.

capital-budgeting decisions Decisions that have significant financial effects beyond the current year.

cash basis A process of accounting where revenue and expense recognition would occur when cash is received and disbursed.

cash budget A statement of planned cash receipts and disbursements.

cash equivalents Short-term investments that can easily be converted into cash with little delay.

cash flow Usually refers to the net cash flow from operating activities.

cash flows from operating activities The first major section in the statement of cash flows.

cellular manufacturing A production system where machines are organized in cells according to the specific requirements of a product family.

Certified Management Accountant (CMA) The management accountant's counterpart to the CPA.

Certified Public Accountant (CPA) In the United States, an accountant earns this designation by a combination of education, qualifying experience, and the passing of a two-day written national examination.

coefficient of determination (R^2) A measurement of how much of the fluctuation of a cost is explained by changes in the cost driver.

committed fixed costs Costs arising from the possession of facilities, equipment, and a basic organization: large, indivisible chunks of cost that the organization is obligated to incur or usually would not consider avoiding.

common costs Those costs of facilities and services that are shared by users.

common stock Stock that has no predetermined rate of dividends and is the last to obtain a share in the assets when the corporation is dissolved. It usually has voting power in the management of the corporation.

common-size statements Financial statements expressed in component percentages.

component percentages Analysis and presentation of financial statements in percentage form to aid comparability, frequently used when companies differ in size.

computer-integrated manufacturing (CIM) systems Systems that use computer-aided design and computer-aided manufacturing, together with robots and computer-controlled machines.

conservatism convention Selecting the method of measurement that yields the gloomiest immediate results.

consolidated financial statements Financial statements that combine the financial statements of the parent company with those of various subsidiaries, as if they were a single entity.

constant dollars Nominal dollars that are restated in terms of current purchasing power.

continuity convention The assumption that in all ordinary situations an entity persists indefinitely.

continuous budget A common form of master budget that adds a month in the future as the month just ended is dropped.

contribution approach A method of internal (management accounting) reporting that emphasizes the distinction between variable and fixed costs for the purpose of better decision making.

contribution margin The sales price minus the variable cost per unit.

controllable cost Any cost that is influenced by a manager's decisions and actions.

controller/comptroller The top accounting officer of an organization. The term comptroller is used primarily in government organizations.

conversion costs Direct labor costs plus factory overhead costs.

corporation A business organized as a separate legal entity and owned by its stockholders.

cost A sacrifice or giving up of resources for a particular purpose, frequently measured by the monetary units that must be paid for goods and services.

cost accounting That part of the accounting system that measures costs for the purposes of management decision making and financial reporting.

cost accounting systems The techniques used to determine the cost of a product, service, or other cost objective by collecting and classifying costs and assigning them to cost objects.

cost accumulation Collecting costs by some natural classification such as materials or labor.

cost allocation Tracing and reassigning costs to one or more cost objectives such as departments, customers, or products.

cost allocation base A cost driver when it is used for allocating costs.

cost application The allocation of total departmental costs to the revenue-producing products or services.

cost behavior How the activities of an organization affect its costs.

cost center A responsibility center for which costs are accumulated.

cost drivers Activities that affect costs.

cost function An algebraic equation used by managers to describe the relationship between a cost and its cost driver(s).

cost measurement The first step in estimating or predicting costs as a function of appropriate cost drivers.

cost method The method of accounting for investments whereby the initial investment is recorded at cost and dividends are recognized as income when they are received.

cost object *See* cost objective.

cost objective Any activity or resource for which a separate measurement of costs is desired. Examples include departments, products, and territories.

cost of capital What a firm must pay to acquire more capital, whether or not it actually has to acquire more capital to take on a project.

cost of goods sold The cost of the merchandise that is acquired or manufactured and resold.

cost of quality report A report that displays the financial impact of quality.

cost pool A group of individual costs that is allocated to cost objectives using a single cost driver.

cost prediction The application of cost measures to expected future activity levels to forecast future costs.

cost recovery A concept in which assets such as inventories, prepayments, and equipment are carried forward as assets because their costs are expected to be recovered in the form of cash inflows (or reduced cash outflows) in future periods.

cost-allocation base A cost driver when it is used for allocating costs.

cost-benefit balance Weighing estimated costs against probable benefits, the primary consideration in choosing among accounting systems and methods.

cost-benefit criterion An approach that implicitly underlies the decisions about the design of accounting systems. As a system is changed, its potential benefits should exceed its additional costs.

cost-management system Identifies how management's decisions affect costs, by first measuring the resources used in performing the organization's activities and then assessing the effects on costs of changes in those activities.

cost-volume-profit (CVP) analysis The study of the effects of output volume on revenue (sales), expenses (costs), and net income (net profit).

credit An entry on the right side of an account.

cross-sectional comparisons Comparisons of a company's financial ratios with ratios of other companies or with industry averages for the same period.

current assets Cash and all other assets that are reasonably expected to be converted to cash or sold or consumed during the normal operating cycle.

current cost The cost to replace an asset, as opposed to its historical cost.

current liabilities An organization's debts that fall due within the coming year or within the normal operating cycle if longer than a year.

current-cost method The measurement method that uses current costs and nominal dollars.

currently attainable standards Levels of performance that can be achieved by realistic levels of effort.

cycle time The time taken to complete a product or service, or any of the components of a product or service.

debentures Formal certificates of indebtedness that are accompanied by a promise to pay interest at a specified annual rate.

debit An entry on the left side of an account.

decentralization The delegation of freedom to make decisions. The lower in the organization that this freedom exists, the greater the decentralization.

decision making The purposeful choice from among a set of alternative courses of action designed to achieve some objective.

decision model Any method for making a choice, sometimes requiring elaborate quantitative procedures.

deferred revenue *See* unearned revenue.

depreciation The periodic cost of equipment which is spread over (or charged to) the future periods in which the equipment is expected to be used.

differential approach An approach that compares two alternatives by computing the differences in cash flows between alternatives and then converting these differences in cash flows to their present values.

differential cost The difference in total cost between two alternatives.

direct costs Costs that can be identified specifically and exclusively with a given cost objective in an economically feasible way.

direct method A method for allocating service department costs that ignores other service departments when any given service department's costs are allocated to the revenue-producing (operating) departments.

direct-labor costs The wages of all labor that can be traced specifically and exclusively to the manufactured goods in an economically feasible way.

direct-material costs The acquisition costs of all materials that are physically identified as a part of the manufactured goods and that may be traced to the manufactured goods in an economically feasible way.

discount rate *See* required rate of return.

discounted-cash-flow (DCF) models A type of capital-budgeting model that focuses on cash inflows and outflows and explicitly and systematically incorporates the time value of money.

discretionary fixed costs Costs determined by management as part of the periodic planning process in order to meet the organization's goals.

discriminatory pricing Charging different prices to different customers for the same product or service.

dividends Distributions of assets to stockholders that reduce retained income.

double-entry system A method of record keeping in which at least two accounts are affected by each transaction.

dysfunctional behavior Any action taken in conflict with organizational goals.

earnings *See* profits.

earnings per share Net income divided by the average number of common shares outstanding during the year.

effectiveness The degree to which a goal, objective, or target is met.

efficiency The degree to which inputs are used in relation to a given level of outputs.

efficiency variance *See* usage variance.

efficient capital market A market in which market prices fully reflect all information available to the public.

engineering analysis The systematic review of materials, supplies, labor, support services, and facilities needed for products and services: measuring cost behavior according to what costs should be, not by what costs have been.

equities The claims against, or interests in, an organization's assets.

equity method Accounts for the investment at the acquisition cost adjusted for the investor's share of dividends and earnings or losses of the investee after the date of investment.

equivalent units The number of completed units that could have been produced from the inputs applied.

expected cost The cost most likely to be attained.

expenses Gross decreases in assets from delivering goods or services.

factory burden *See* factory-overhead costs.

factory-overhead costs All costs other than direct material or direct labor that are associated with the manufacturing process.

favorable expense variable A variance that occurs when actual expenses are less than budgeted expenses.

Financial Accounting Standards Board (FASB) The primary regulatory body over accounting principles and practices. Consisting of seven full-time members, it is an independent creation of the private sector.

financial accounting The field of accounting that develops information for external decision makers such as stockholders, suppliers, banks, and government regulatory agencies.

financial budget The part of a master budget that focuses on the effects that the operating budget and other plans (such as capital budgets and repayments of debt) will have on cash.

financial capital maintenance The concept that income emerges after financial resources are recovered.

financial planning models Mathematical models of the master budget that can react to any set of assumptions about sales, costs, or product mix.

first-in, first-out (FIFO) An inventory method that assumes that the stock acquired earliest is sold (used up) first.

first-in, first-out (FIFO) process-costing method A process-costing method that sharply distinguishes the current work done from the previous work done on the beginning inventory of work in process.

fixed assets Physical items that can be seen and touched, such as property, plant, and equipment.

fixed cost A cost that is not immediately affected by changes in the cost driver.

fixed overhead rate The amount of fixed manufacturing overhead applied to each unit of production. It is determined by dividing the budgeted fixed overhead by the expected volume of production for the budget period.

flexible budget A budget that adjusts for changes in sales volume and other cost-driver activities.

flexible-budget variances The variances between the flexible budget and the actual results.

Foreign Corrupt Practices Act U.S. law forbidding bribery and other corrupt practices and requiring that accounting records be maintained in reasonable detail and accuracy, and that an appropriate system of internal accounting controls be maintained.

full cost The total of all manufacturing costs plus the total of all selling and administrative costs.

fully allocated cost *See* full cost.

general ledger A collection of the group of accounts that supports the items shown in the major financial statements.

general price index A comparison of the average price of a group of goods and services at one date with the average price of a similar group at another date.

generally accepted accounting principles (GAAP) Broad concepts or guidelines and detailed practices, including all conventions, rules, and procedures that together make up accepted accounting practice at a given time.

goal congruence A condition where employees, working in their own personal interests make decisions that help meet the overall goals of the organization.

going concern convention *See* continuity convention.

goodwill The excess of the cost of an acquired company over the sum of the fair market values of its identifiable individual assets less its liabilities.

gross book value The original cost of an asset before deducting accumulated depreciation.

gross margin The excess of sales over the total cost of goods sold.

gross profit *See* gross margin.

half-year convention A requirement of the modified accelerated cost recovery system that treats all assets as if they were placed in service at the midpoint of the tax year.

high-low method A simple method for measuring a linear cost function from past cost data, focusing on the highest-activity and lowest-activity points and fitting a line through these two points.

historical cost The amount originally paid to acquire an asset.

holding gains (or losses) Increases (or decreases) in the replacement costs of the assets held during the current period.

hurdle rate *See* required rate of return.

hybrid-costing system An accounting system that is a blend of ideas from both job costing and process costing.

ideal standards *See* perfection standards.

idle time An indirect labor cost consisting of wages paid for unproductive time caused by machine breakdowns, material shortages, and sloppy scheduling.

imperfect competition A market in which a firm's price will influence the quantity it sells.

incentives Those formal and informal performance-based rewards that enhance managerial effort toward organizational goals.

income *See* profits.

income percentage of revenue Income divided by revenue.

income statement A statement that measures the performance of an organization by matching its accomplishments (revenue from customers, which is usually called sales) and its efforts (cost of goods sold and other expenses).

incremental cost *See* differential cost.

incremental effect The change in total results (such as revenue, expenses, or income) under a new condition in comparison with some given or known condition.

indirect costs Costs that cannot be identified specifically and exclusively with a given cost objective in an economically feasible way.

indirect labor All factory labor wages, other than those for direct labor and manager salaries.

indirect method In a statement of cash flows, the method that reconciles net income to the net cash provided by operating activities.

inflation A general decline in the purchasing power of the monetary unit.

Institute of Management Accountants (IMA) The largest U.S. professional organization of accountants whose major interest is management accounting.

intangible assets Long-lived assets that are not physical in nature. Examples are goodwill, franchises, patents, trade-marks, and copyrights.

internal control system Methods and procedures to prevent errors and irregularities, detect errors and irregularities, and promote operating efficiency

internal rate of return (IRR) The discount rate that makes the net present value of the project equal to zero.

inventory turnover The number of times the average inventory is sold per year.

investment center A responsibility center whose success is measured not only by its income but also by relating that income to its invested capital, as in a ratio of income to the value of the capital employed.

investments in affiliates Investments in equity securities that represent 20% to 50% ownership. They are usually accounted for under the equity method.

investments in associates *See* investments in affiliates.

job costing *See* job-order costing.

job order *See* job-cost record.

job-cost record A document that shows all costs for a particular product, service, or batch of products.

job-cost sheet *See* job-cost record.

job-order costing The method of allocating costs to products that are readily identified by individual units or batches, each of which requires varying degrees of attention and skill.

joint costs The costs of manufacturing joint products prior to the split-off point.

joint products Two or more manufactured products that (1) have relatively significant sales values and (2) are not separately identifiable as individual products until their split-off point.

just-in-time (JIT) philosophy A philosophy to eliminate waste by reducing the time products spend in the production process and eliminating the time laborers spend on activities that do not add value.

just-in-time (JIT) production system A system in which an organization purchases materials and parts and produces components just when they are needed in the production process, the goal being to have zero inventory, because holding inventory is a non-value-added activity.

labor time tickets The record of the time a particular direct laborer spends on each job.

last-in, first-out (LIFO) An inventory method that assumes that the stock acquired most recently is sold (used up) first.

least-squares regression Measuring a cost function objectively by using statistics to fit a cost function to all the data.

ledger accounts A method of keeping track of how multitudes of transactions affect each particular asset, liability, revenue, and expense.

legal value *See* par value.

liabilities The entity's economic obligations to non-owners.

LIFO layers Separately identifiable additional layers of LIFO inventory.

LIFO increments *See* LIFO layers.

limited liability Creditors cannot seek payment from shareholders as individuals if the corporation itself cannot pay its debts.

limiting factor The item that restricts or constrains the production or sale of a product or service.

line authority Authority exerted downward over subordinates.

linear-cost behavior Activity that can be graphed with a straight line when a cost changes proportionately with changes in a cost driver.

liquidation Converting assets to cash and using the cash to pay off outside claims.

long-range planning Producing forecasted financial statements for five- or ten-year periods.

long term liabilities *See* noncurrent liabilities.

lower-of-cost-or-market (LCM) An inventory method in which the current market price of inventory is compared with its cost (derived by specific identification, FIFO, LIFO, or weighted average) and the lower of the two is selected as the basis for the valuation of goods at a specific inventory date.

management accounting The process of identifying, measuring, accumulating, analyzing, preparing, interpreting, and communicating information that helps managers fulfill organizational objectives.

management audit A review to determine whether the policies and procedures specified by top management have been implemented.

management by exception Concentrating on areas that deviate from the plan and ignoring areas that are presumed to be running smoothly.

management by objectives (MBO) The joint formulation by a manager and his or her superior of a set of goals and plans for achieving the goals for a forthcoming period.

management control system A logical integration of management accounting tools to gather and report data and to evaluate performance.

managerial effort Exertion toward a goal or objective including all conscious actions (such as supervising, planning, and thinking) that result in more efficiency and effectiveness.

manufacturing overhead *See* factory-overhead costs.

margin of safety Equal to the planned unit sales less the breakeven unit sales; it shows how far sales can fall below the planned level before losses occur.

marginal cost The additional cost resulting from producing and selling one additional unit.

marginal income *See* contribution margin.

marginal income tax rate The tax rate paid on additional amounts of pretax income.

marginal revenue The additional revenue resulting from the sale of an additional unit.

markup The amount by which price exceeds cost.

master budget A budget that summarizes the planned activities of all subunits of an organization.

master budget variance The variance of actual results from the master budget.

matching The relating of accomplishments or revenues (as measured by the selling prices of goods and services delivered) and efforts or expenses (as measured by the cost of goods and services used) to a particular period for which a measurement of income is desired.

materiality The accounting convention that justifies the omission of insignificant information when its omission or misstatement would not mislead a user of the financial statements.

materials requisitions Records of materials issued to particular jobs.

measurement of cost behavior Understanding and quantifying how activities of an organization affect levels of costs.

minority interests An account that shows the outside stockholders' interest, as opposed to the parent's interest, in a subsidiary corporation.

mixed costs Costs that contain elements of both fixed and variable-cost behavior.

motivation The drive for some selected goal that creates effort and action toward that goal.

net book value The original cost of an asset less any accumulated depreciation. *See* book value.

net income The popular "bottom line"—the residual after deducting from revenues all expenses, including income taxes.

net worth A synonym for owner's equity.

net-present-value (NPV) method A discounted-cash-flow approach to capital budgeting that discounts all expected future cash flows to the present using a minimum desired rate of return.

nominal dollars Dollar measurements that are not restated for fluctuations in the general purchasing power of the monetary unit.

nominal rate Quoted market interest rate that includes an inflation element.

non-value-added costs Costs that can be eliminated without affecting a product's value to the customer.

noncurrent liabilities An organization's debts that fall due beyond one year.

normal costing A cost system that applies actual direct materials and actual direct-labor costs to products or services but uses standards for applying overhead.

normal costing system The cost system in which overhead is applied on an average or normalized basis in order to get representative or normal inventory valuations.

objectivity Accuracy supported by a high extent of consensus among independent measures of an item.

operating budget A major part of a master budget that focuses on the income statement and its supporting schedules.

operating cycle The time span during which cash is spent to acquire goods and services that are used to produce the organization's output, which in turn is sold to customers, who in turn pay for their purchases with cash.

operating leverage A firm's ratio of fixed to variable costs.

operation A hybrid-costing system often used in the batch or group manufacturing of goods that have some common characteristics plus some individual characteristics.

opportunity cost The maximum available contribution to profit forgone (or passed up) by using limited resources for a particular purpose.

outlay cost A cost that requires a cash disbursement.

overapplied overhead The excess of overhead applied to products over actual overhead incurred.

overtime premium An indirect labor cost, consisting of wages paid to all factory workers in excess of their straight-time wage rates.

owners' equity The excess of the assets over the liabilities.

paid-in capital The ownership claim against, or interest in, the total assets arising from any paid-in investment.

par value The value that is printed on the face of the certificate.

parent company A company owning more than 50% of another business's stock.

participative budgeting Budgets formulated with the active participation of all affected employees.

partnership An organization that joins two or more individuals together as co-owners.

payback period *See* payback time.

payback time The measure of the time it will take to recoup, in the form of cash inflows from operations, the initial dollars of outlay.

payroll fringe costs Employer contributions to employee benefits such as social security, life insurance, health insurance, and pensions.

perfect competition A market in which a firm can sell as much of a product as it can produce, all at a single market price.

perfection standards Expressions of the most efficient performance possible under the best conceivable conditions, using existing specifications and equipment.

performance reports Feedback provided by comparing results with plans and by highlighting variances.

period costs Costs that are deducted as expenses during the current period without going through an inventory stage.

physical capital maintenance The concept that income emerges only after recovering an amount that allows physical operating capability to be maintained.

postaudit A follow-up evaluation of capital budgeting decisions.

practical capacity Maximum or full capacity.

predatory pricing Establishing prices so low that competitors are driven out of the market so that the predatory pricer then has no significant competition and can raise prices dramatically.

preferred stock Stock that typically has some priority over other shares regarding dividends or the distribution of assets upon liquidation.

price elasticity The effect of price changes on sales volumes.

price variance The difference between actual input prices and expected input prices multiplied by the actual quantity of inputs used.

prime costs Direct labor costs plus direct materials costs.

pro forma statement *See* master budget.

problem solving Aspect of accounting that quantifies the likely results of possible courses of action and often recommends the best course of action to follow.

process costing The method of allocating costs to products by averaging costs over large numbers of nearly identical products.

product costs Costs identified with goods produced or purchased for resale.

product life cycle The various stages through which a product passes, from conception and development through introduction into the market through maturation and, finally, withdrawal from the market.

production cycle time The time from initiating production to delivering the goods to the customer.

production-volume variance A variance that appears whenever actual production deviates from the expected volume of production used in computing the fixed overhead rate. It is calculated as (actual volume – expected volume) x fixed-overhead rate.

productivity A measure of outputs divided by inputs.

profit centers A responsibility center for controlling revenues as well as costs (or expenses)—that is, profitability.

profit plan *See* operating budget.

profits The excess of revenues over expenses.

prorate To assign underapplied overhead or overapplied overhead in proportion to the sizes of the ending account balances.

prorating the variance Assigning the variances to the inventories and cost of goods sold related to the production during the period the variances arose.

quality control The effort to ensure that products and services perform to customer requirements.

quality-control chart The statistical plot of measures of various product dimensions or attributes.

quantity variance *See* usage variance.

recovery period The number of years over which an asset is depreciated for tax purposes.

regression analysis *See* least-squares regression.

relevant information The predicted future costs and revenues that will differ among alternative courses of action.

relevant range The limit of cost-driver activity within which a specific relationship between costs and the cost driver is valid.

required rate of return The minimum desired rate of return, based on the firm's cost of capital.

residual income Net income less "imputed" interest.

residual value The predicted sales value of a long-lived asset at the end of its useful life.

responsibility accounting Identifying what parts of the organization have primary responsibility for each objective, developing measures of achievement of objectives, and creating reports of these measures by organization subunit or responsibility center.

responsibility center A set of activities assigned to a manager, a group of managers, or other employees.

retained earnings *See* retained income.

retained income The ownership claim arising as a result of profitable operations.

return on investment (ROT) A measure of income or profit divided by the investment required to obtain that income or profit.

return on sales *See* income percentage of revenue.

revaluation equity A portion of stockholders' equity that shows all accumulated holding gains.

revenue A gross increase in assets from delivering goods or services.

rolling budget *See* continuous budget.

sales budget The result of decisions to create conditions that will generate a desired level of sales.

sales forecast A prediction of sales under a given set of conditions.

sales mix The relative proportions or combinations of quantities of products that constitute total sales.

sales-activity variances Variances that measure how effective managers have been in meeting the planned sales objective, calculated as actual unit sales less master budget unit sales times the budgeted unit contribution margin.

scarce resource *See* limiting factor.

scorekeeping The accumulation and classification of data.

Securities and Exchange Commission (SEC) By federal law, the agency with the ultimate responsibility for specifying the generally accepted accounting principles for U.S. companies whose stock is held by the general investing public.

segment autonomy The delegation of decision-making power to managers of segments of an organization.

segments Responsibility centers for which a separate measure of revenues and costs is obtained.

sensitivity analysis The systematic varying of budget data input to determine the effects of each change on the budget.

separable costs Any cost beyond the split-off point.

service departments Units that exist only to support other departments.

sole proprietorship A business entity with a single owner.

source documents Explicit evidence of any transactions that occur in the entity's operation, for example, sales slips and purchase invoices.

specific identification An inventory method that recognizes the actual cost paid for the specific item sold.

specific price index An index used to approximate the current costs of particular assets or types of assets.

split-off point The juncture of manufacturing where the joint products become individually identifiable.

staff authority Authority to advise but not command. It may be exerted downward, laterally, or upward.

standard cost A carefully determined cost per unit that should be attained.

standard cost systems Accounting systems that value products according to standard costs only.

Standards of Ethical Conduct for Management Accountants Codes of conduct developed by the Institute of Management Accountants, which include competence, confidentiality, integrity, and objectivity.

stated value *See* par value.

statement of cash flows A statement that reports the cash receipts and cash payments of an organization during a particular period.

statement of financial condition *See* balance sheet.

statement of financial position *See* balance sheet.

statement of retained earnings A financial statement that analyzes changes in the retained earnings or retained income account for a given period.

statement of retained income *See* statement of retained earnings.

static budget variance *See* master budget variance.

step costs Costs that change abruptly at intervals of activity because the resources and their costs come in indivisible chunks.

step-down method A method for allocating service department costs that recognizes that some service departments support the activities in other service departments as well as those in production departments.

stockholders' equity The excess of assets over liabilities of a corporation.

strategic plan A plan that sets the overall goals and objectives of the organization.

subordinated A creditor claim that is junior to the other creditors in exercising claims against assets.

subsidiary A company owned by a parent company that owns more than 50% of its stock.

sunk cost A cost that has already been incurred and, therefore, is irrelevant to the decision-making process. Synonyms are historical cost or past cost.

tangible assets *See* fixed assets.

target costing A strategy in which companies first determine the price at which they can sell a new product or service and then design a product or service that can be produced at a low enough cost to provide an adequate profit margin.

tax shields Depreciation deductions and similar deductions that protect that amount of income from taxation. All allowable expenses, both cash and noncash items, could be called tax shields because they reduce income and thereby reduce income taxes.

time cards *See* labor time tickets.

time-series comparisons Comparison of a company's financial ratios with its own historical ratios.

total project approach An approach that compares two or more alternatives by computing the total impact on cash flows for each alternative and then converting these total cash flows to their present values.

total quality management (TQM) The application of quality principles to all of the organization's endeavors to satisfy customers.

transaction Any event that affects the financial position of an organization and requires recording.

transaction-based costing Activity-based costing.

transfer price The amount charged by one segment of an organization for a product or service that it supplies to another segment of the same organization.

transferred-in costs In process costing, costs incurred in a previous department for items that have been received by a subsequent department.

treasury stock A corporation's own stock that has been issued and subsequently repurchased by the company and is being held for a specific purpose.

unavoidable costs Costs that continue even if an operation is halted.

uncontrollable cost Any cost that cannot be affected by the management of a responsibility center within a given time span.

underapplied overhead The excess of actual overhead over the overhead applied to products.

unearned revenue Collections from customers received and recorded before they are earned.

unexpired cost Any asset that ordinarily becomes an expense in future periods, for example, inventory and prepaid rent.

unfavorable expense variance A variance that occurs when actual expenses are more than budgeted expenses.

usage variance The difference between the quantity of inputs actually used and the quantity of inputs that should have been used to achieve the actual quantity of output multiplied by the expected price of input.

value chain The sequence of functions that adds value to the company's products or services.

value-added cost The necessary cost of an activity that cannot be eliminated without affecting a product's value to the customer.

variable budget *See* flexible budget.

variable cost A cost that changes in direct proportion to changes in the cost driver.

variable-cost percentage *See* variable-cost ratio.

variable-cost ratio All variable costs divided by sales.

variable-overhead efficiency variance When actual cost-driver activity differs from the standard amount allowed for the actual output achieved.

variable-overhead spending variance The difference between the actual variable overhead and the amount of variable overhead budgeted for the actual level of cost-driver activity.

variances Deviations from plans.

verifiability *See* objectivity.

visual-fit method A method in which the cost analyst visually fits a straight line through a plot of all the available data, not just between the high point and the low point, making it more reliable than the high-low method.

FINANCE GLOSSARY

A-B-C system An *ad hoc* technique of monitoring inventory. A-items are high value, C-items are low value, and *B*-items fall between.

accounting profit Earnings amount derived *from* accrual accounting practices that correspond with generally accepted accounting principles.

accounting rate of return Nondiscounted profitability measure that divides accounting earnings by average investment.

accounts receivable turnover ratio Method of monitoring trends in customer payments; higher turnover is considered positive.

add-on interest Interest calculated on the amount of funds to be lent and added to the loaned amount to determine the loan's face value.

adjustable-rate preferred stock (ARFS) A capital market security that periodically adjusts the dividend amount in the direction of interest rate movements.

adjusted present value (APV) A value derived by evaluating financing cash flows separate from operating cash flows.

agent A person who performs activities for another person, called a *principal*. Managers are agents of the firm.

aging schedule Process of classifying accounts by the amount of time they have been outstanding. The schedule usually displays the percentage of receivables that are one month old, two months old, and so on.

American depository receipt (ADR) Receipt issued by a bank; represents ownership of foreign company's common stock. The shares of the foreign companies are held in trust.

amortizing term loan A loan with serial payments for principal and interest.

annual clean-up period Period of time the bank wants the borrower to be free of bank credit or to have the balance below some agreed amount. The purpose is to show the bank that the firm does not need the loan as a source of permanent financing.

annual operating cash flows The cash outflows incurred for material, labor, and overhead; excludes all financing costs.

annual percentage rate (APR) The rate per period times the number of periods per year.

annual report The formal financial statement issued yearly by a corporation. The annual report shows assets, liabilities, income, and how the company stood at the close of the business year. It usually also includes other information of interest to shareholders.

annualized cost of a missed discount (ACD) The cost of foregoing cash discounts and paying at some date beyond the discount period.

annuity due A series of equal cash payments occurring at the beginning of each period with equal amounts of time between each payment.

asked price The lowest price at which a dealer offers to sell securities the sell side of the bid-asked spread.

average collection period (ACP) The amount of time accounts receivable are outstanding; used to evaluate the quality of the investment in accounts receivable.

balance proportions An accounts receivable monitoring technique that relates the outstanding balance to the sale that generated the receivable.

balance sheet Statement of a firm's financial position on a given date. Shows what the firm owns (its assets), what it owes (its liabilities), and the residual or equity of the owners (the net worth).

bank discount rate method Interest calculated on the face amount of the loan. The lender deducts the interest in advance.

bankruptcy A legal proceeding to decide whether to liquidate or reorganize a company and the administration thereof.

bar chart A graph of a period's high, low, and closing price. The price range is a vertical bar. The close is a short horizontal bar.

bass point One hundredth of a percentage point. Used to express changes in interest rates.

Baumol EOQ model A mathematical model for calculating the optimal cash order size. The model minimizes the total ordering and holding costs.

bearer bond A bond issued without a record of the owner's name. Payment is made to whomever holds the bond.

beta A measure of a security's nondiversifiable risk; shows the relationship between an individual security's performance and the performance of a market index.

bid price The price at which a dealer offers to buy a security.

bill (T-bill) Short-term (one year or less) security issued by the U.S. Treasury. A T-bill is issued at a discount and pays no coupon.

bond Long-term (over ten years) security that pays a specified sum (called the principal) either at a future date or periodically over the length of a loan, during which time a fixed rate of interest may be paid on certain dates.

bond market Financial market for trading long-term debt instruments issued by firms and governments; bonds represent promises to repay specified amounts at a future time.

book value of assets Historical value of the assets adjusted for depreciation of fixed assets and other asset writedowns.

business organization An institution that buys material and labor and organizes them to produce and sell goods and services.

business risk The risk associated with the returns generated by a firm's assets as if the firm were financed entirely by equity. Risk associated with debt financing is ignored.

business sector Part of the economy that consists of units that produce and provide goods and services to households and other businesses.

buy-and-hold strategy Investment strategy of buying securities and holding them for a period of time. Opposite of trading in an attempt to sell at each market high and buy at each market low.

buyout specialists Organizations that use borrowed funds to buy public firms and privatize them.

call provision A feature of the trust indenture of a bond that allows the issuer to repurchase outstanding bonds at a given price from the holders after a given date.

callable preferred stock Preferential stock that can be retired by the issuer; unlike equity security, may not have infinite life.

capital budgeting Process of identifying, evaluating, and implementing approved capital expenditures.

capital gain Increase in value of a security over its original cost.

capital gains tax Tax on the excess of proceeds over cost from the sale of capital asset as defined by the Internal Revenue Code. The Tax Reform Act of 1986 made the capital gains tax rate the same as the tax on other income.

capital investments Expenditures of a firm for assets, such as plant and equipment.

capital loss Decrease in value of a security from its original cost.

capital market line (CML) The relationship between risk and return in well-diversified portfolios.

capital market A market for securities with maturities beyond one year.

capital rationing A situation in which new investments are limited to less than those economically justifiable.

capitalizing cash flow The process of dividing future cash flow amounts by an interest rate representing the minimum return the cash flows should earn; for example, if future cash flow is $10 per year in perpetuity and the interest rate is 4%, the cash flows have a capitalized (economic) value of $10 – 0.04 = $250.

cash budget A schedule of expected cash receipts and disbursements and the borrowing requirements for a given period of time.

cash conversion cycle The operating cycle less the accounts payable and accrued liabilities deferral period.

cash dividend Cash payment from the firm to its shareholders.

cash inadequacy Insufficient cash to meet current obligations.

causal model Assumes that the factor to be forecast exhibits a cause-and-effect relationship with a number of other factors.

certainty equivalent (CE) A technique used to adjust uncertain cash flows downward to a level that the decision maker is indifferent between the risky unadjusted cash flows and the certain adjusted cash flows.

collateral trust bond A *bond* secured by pledges of stocks and bonds.

common-size analysis Accounting statements expressed as a percentage of net sales or total assets to aid comparison.

compensating balance A bank's requirement that the borrower maintain a minimum noninterest-bearing average balance; used to compensate banks for services; borrower pays interest on these balances.

compound interest Interest computed on both the principal sum and the interest earned by the principal sum as of a given date.

compounding Process by which a given amount is adjusted to yield a future value. Compounding is the opposite of *discounting*.

concentration bank A bank to which a company transfers all excess cash balances daily.

contribution margin proportion The proportion of each sales dollar left after paying *variable costs;* ratio of (sales-variable costs) sales.

convertible bond A bond that pays fixed interest payments and has a specified maturity, just like an ordinary bond, but differs in that it can be exchanged for a specified number of shares of common stock.

correlation Measure of the degree to which two variables move together.

cost of capital Minimum market rate of return on new investments required to maintain the value of the firm.

cost of debt *Yield to maturity* of the instrument.

cost of equity Market rate of return required by investors to hold the company's common stock.

cost of preferred stock Preferred stock dividend divided by the market price of the stock.

covariance A statistical term used to reflect the extent to which two variables move together. A positive value means that on average, they move in the same direction. The covariance depends not only on the correlation between the two variables but also the *standard deviations* of each variable.

covenants Restrictions placed on the borrower requiring specific standards be met, as verified by the trustee.

credit Arrangement that allows a customer to take goods or services and delay paying for them.

credit standards Criteria used to determine which customers receive credit. Usually encompasses an examination of the customer's credit rating, credit references, outstanding debt, and financial statements.

credit terms The payment provisions that are part of a credit arrangement.

cumulative voting A voting system in which a shareholder may cast votes equal to the number of shares owned times the number of directors to be elected. The votes may be cast for only one director but in any combination.

currency risk The risk that fluctuating exchange rates will adversely affect the investment.

current assets Assets that will turn into cash within the normal business cycle.

current liabilities Liabilities that are payable within the firm's business cycle.

current ratio A measure of liquidity, defined as current assets divided by current liabilities.

debenture A debt obligation not secured by specific property but backed by the general credit of the issuing company

debt security Agreement to pay a specified sum (called the principal) either at a future date or over the course of a loan, during which time interest may be paid on certain dates.

declaration date The date the firm's directors issue a statement declaring a dividend. The dividend becomes a legally binding obligation of the corporation.

default (credit) risk The chance that interest or principal on a debt security will not be paid on a payment date and in the promised amount.

default risk premium The premium on a loan charged in case the borrower fails to make a contracted payment.

defensive interval ratio A measurement of the number of days of normal cash expenditures covered by quick assets.

deficit (borrowing) units Net borrowers, who spend more than they save. The business sector is considered a net deficit unit.

degree of financial leverage (DFL) The percentage change in net income for a given change in earnings before interest and taxes.

degree of operating leverage (DOL) The percentage change in earnings before interest and taxes for a given change in sales.

degree of total leverage (DTL) The percentage change in net income for a given change in sales.

dependency The degree of association, or *correlation*, between two variables. Dependency is low for small levels of correlation and high for high levels of correlation.

depository transfer check (DTC) An instrument used to transfer funds between bank accounts of the same firm. No signature is required. The DTC clears through the normal channels, similar to a check.

direct send The check clearing process bypasses at least part of the normal Federal Reserve collection system in an effort to accelerate collection of funds.

discount The amount by which a bond (or preferred stock) sells below its par value. The security trades at a discount when the coupon rate is lower than the market rate of interest.

discount factor Present value of $1 received at a stated future date.

discount rate Interest rate charged to member banks on their loans from the *Federal Reserve Banks.* It is so called because the interest on a loan is discounted when the loan is made, rather than collected when the loan is repaid.

discounted cash flow analysis The process of converting future cash flows to their present values. This process is the opposite of *future value analysis.*

discounted payback period A discounted cash flow technique that calculates the time it takes to recover the original investment.

discounting Process by which a given amount is adjusted at interest to yield a present value. Discounting is the opposite of *compounding.*

diversifiable risk The amount of risk that can be eliminated through proper *diversification.*

diversification Investing in more than one asset to reduce risk.

dividend payout ratio The proportion of earnings paid out in dividends.

Dow Jones Industrial Average A price index of 30 listed stocks. The price of the stocks is added and divided by a number that adjusts for *stock splits.* An example of a stock split is when a share selling for $90 is split into two shares selling for $45 each.

duration A number which summarizes the various factors that affect a bond's price sensitivity to changes in interest rates.

Dutch auction A process where investors submit bids for securities. The issuer ranks the bids from high to low and sequentially selects those bids that are most advantageous to the issuer.

earnings available to common shareholders Net income less dividends paid to preferred shareholders.

EBIT indifference level The level of earnings before interest and taxes to which management is indifferent between financing alternatives.

economic returns Payments to a firm in excess of the economic costs, including normal profit.

economic system Relationship between the components of an economy (such as its households, firms, and government) and the institutional framework of laws and customs within which these components operate.

economic value of assets The expected value of an asset derived by capitalizing future cash flows at an appropriate interest rate. See *capitalizing cash flows.*

economic value of cash The expected return that a firm gives up when it invests in cash rather than in a risk-free security.

effective annual rate (EAR) The true interest rate that is paid on a loan.

efficiency ratios Measures that portray how quickly assets or liabilities are used. The higher an efficiency ratio, the more efficient management is perceived in utilizing the resources committed to the measured activity.

efficient financial market Prices for traded securities embody all currently available relevant information. Characteristics of efficient markets include low transaction costs, freely accessible information, many investors, and quick price corrections.

efficient frontier The frontier is the boundary line marking off the best risk-and-return combinations available to the investor.

efficient investment An investment offering the best expected return for a given risk, or the lowest risk for a given expected return.

efficient market Market condition in which prices always fully reflect all available information. Adjustment to new information is virtually instantaneous.

efficient market hypothesis (EMH) The concept that competition in the financial markets alerts investors to information so that prices adjust almost instantaneously to new information.

electronic depository transfer check (EDTC) An electronic version of the DTC. Funds are transferred by wire.

electronic wire transfer A means of effecting the immediate transfer of funds from one bank account to an account at another bank.

EOQ model A mathematical model for calculating the optimal inventory order size; it minimizes the total ordering and holding costs.

equilibrium price Price of a commodity or service determined in the market by the intersection of supply and demand; the price at which the market clears.

equipment trust certificate (ETC) A bond issued to pay for new equipment; secured by a lien on the purchased equipment.

equity security Security which provides ownership in the firm issuing it. The security has no maturity date. equivalent annual annuity (EAA) An even cash flow that yields the same present value amount as the project's net present value.

Eurobond An international debt instrument denominated in a currency different from the currency of the country in which it is sold.

Eurocapital market An international market for debt and equity securities.

Eurocurrency loans Loans by commercial banks denominated in currencies other than the currency of the country in which the bank resides.

Eurodollar market A market for dollar-denominated deposits outside the United States.

Euroequity An ownership financial instrument denominated in a currency different from the currency of the country in which it is sold.

excess profits Returns in excess of profits required to satisfy the investor for the amount of risk involved.

excess reserves Quantity of a bank's legal reserves over and above its required reserves. Excess reserves are the key to a bank's lending power.

ex-dividend date Date when ownership of the Security is without the right to a dividend about to be paid by a *firm*.

expected inflation premium The premium investors require to compensate them for the expected eroding effect of inflation on the value of money.

expected portfolio return The weighted arithmetic average of all possible outcomes for the *portfolio,* where the weights are the probabilities that each outcome will occur.

expected return The weighted average of all possible outcomes, where the weights are the probabilities that each outcome will occur. It is the expected value, or mean, of a probability distribution.

expected return-risk principle Given the risk exposure, securities are priced to provide investors with a return that compensates for the risk.

external financing requirement (EFR) The amount of funds that must be supplied by creditors or investors to satisfy financing needs.

factor A company in the business of buying accounts receivable from other businesses at a discount to their face value.

factoring Selling accounts receivable at a discount to a financial institution. *The factor* usually bears the risk of collection.

favorable financial leverage Positive effects of debt financing on shareholders' claims on earnings.

federal funds rate Interest rate at which banks borrow excess reserves from other banks' accounts at the Fed, usually overnight, to keep required reserves from falling below the legal level. In general, the lower the volume of excess reserves, the higher the federal funds rate. Therefore, the federal funds rate is an important indicator that the Fed watches to decide whether to add to banks' reserves or take away from them.

Federal Reserve Bank (Fed) One of the 12 banks (and branches) which make up the Federal Reserve System. Each serves as a "banker's bank" for the member banks in its district by acting as a source of credit and a depository of resources.

finance The study and practice of making money-denominated decisions. As a discipline, finance can be classified into three areas: managerial, investments, and markets and institutions.

finance subsidiary A separate legal entity owned by the parent corporation that specializes in financing the company's sales.

financial assets Financial instruments with claims on real *assets.*

financial (capital) lease A long-term, noncancelable *lease* that has many characteristics of debt. The lease obligation is shown directly on the balance sheet.

financial intermediaries Financial institutions that serve as middlemen between lenders and borrowers. They create and issue financial claims against themselves in order to acquire financial claims against others. Examples: banks, savings and loans associations, and pension funds.

financial intermediation The process of wholesaling or retailing funds between lenders and borrowers *by financial intermediaries.*

financial leverage The effects of debt financing on shareholders' claims on earnings.

financial leverage ratios Measures that show how the use of debt affects the firm's ability to repay the obligations.

financial markets One of the three areas of finance. Markets of the economy in which both short-term and long-term securities are exchanged.

financial risk Variability in the earnings stream of a company that results from the use of debt.

financial system The channel through which the savings of surplus sectors flow to the deficit sectors that wish to borrow.

First-in, first-out (FIFO) A method of inventory accounting in which the oldest item in inventory is assumed to be sold first.

fiscal policy Deliberate exercise of government's power to tax and spend in order to achieve price stability, help dampen the swings of business cycles, and bring the nation's output and employment to desired levels.

five C's of credit An *ad hoc* approach for evaluating credit applicants that looks at the customer's character, capacity, capital, collateral, and conditions.

fixed-charge coverage ratio A risk ratio to measure the level of earnings available per dollar of interest, fixed charges, and principal payments. Does not reflect the true cash flows available to meet the obligations.

fixed cost A cost that remains relatively constant regardless of the volume of operations. Examples: rent, depreciation, and property taxes.

fixed income securities Debt and preferred stock securities which make fixed dollar payments to investors over their lives.

float Checks in the process of collection.

floating-rate preferred A preferential security whose dividend adjusts periodically to track changing interest rates.

forward exchange rate Foreign exchange bought (or sold) at a given time and at a stipulated current or "spot" price, but payable at a future date. By buying or selling forward exchange, importers and exporters can protect themselves against the risks of fluctuations in the current exchange market.

forward rates Future interest rates implied by currently available spot interest rates.

fourth market Direct trading of securities between institutions without the service of dealers or brokers.

fractional reserve banking system The practice of keeping only a fraction of the deposits of depository institutions as cash reserves.

free reserves Excess banking reserves minus reserves borrowed from the Federal Reserve by depository institutions.

funding constraint A fixed amount of money available for investments aggregating in excess of the amount of funds. Any means of payment.

future value analysis The determination of the future worth of a series of cash flows. This process is the opposite of discounted cash flow analysis.

future value formula The value of $(1 + r)^n$, where r is the interest rate and n is the number of time periods.

future value of an annuity due The value at a known future date of a series of constant cash flows for a known number of periods with the cash flows occurring at the beginning of each period.

future value annuity factor (FVIFA) The sum of the future value of $1 amounts, using the future value formula, which occurs in periods $1, 2...., n$.

general obligation bond (GO) A municipal bond for which the coupon and maturity payments are backed by the "full faith and credit" of the issuing municipality.

geometric average The nth root of the product of n observations.

goodwill The excess of the purchase price over the assessed value of the *tangible assets* acquired.

hedge To take an action to remove or reduce an exposure or a position.

hedging strategy The matching of asset and liability cash flows.

holder-of-record date The date as of which all shareholders listed in a company's records are noted to receive the declared cash or stock dividend when it is paid.

holding-period rate of return Rate of return earned from holding an asset during a given time period.

horizontal analysis Common-size analysis that compares the same accounts from year to year.

household sector Part of the economy that consists of units that consume and provide funds and labor to the business sector. Households purchase goods and services from the business sector.

imperfect competition A market type in which a large number of firms compete with one another by making similar but slightly different products; there is *asymmetrical information*—not all firms know what other firms are doing.

income Revenues for the period minus the costs for the period.

income statement Financial statement of a firm showing its revenues, costs, and profit during a given period. Also known as a profit-and-loss statement.

incremental expense cash flow Additional cash outflows for expenses that result from accepting a *capital budgeting* project.

incremental investment The additional investment the firm will encounter as a result of implementing a new credit policy.

incremental operating cash costs The additional cash operating costs that result from the acceptance of a *capital budgeting* project.

incremental sales The additional sales that result from the acceptance of a *capital budgeting* project.

indenture A contract specifying the legal requirements between the bond issuer and the bond holders.

independence No association, or *correlation,* exists between two variables.

inflation Rise in the general price level of all goods and services or equivalently, a decline in the purchasing power of a unit of money (such as the dollar).

informational signaling An increase in the dividend signals positive information; a decrease signals negative information.

insider trading Process of trading in a company's stock to profit from information that is not available to the public.

installed cash cost Cash expenditure to buy, install, and make operative the item proposed by the *capital budgeting* proposal.

interest coverage ratio Measures the amount of earnings before interest and taxes available to pay interest. Its shortcoming is that earnings are not cash flow.

interest rate The price paid for borrowing money It is the rate of exchange of present consumption for future consumption, or the price of current dollars in terms of future dollars.

interest rate parity An economic principle that holds that the differential in interest rates between countries is the only determinant of the difference between the spot and forward currency rates.

interim loan A bridge loan until permanent financing is arranged.

internal rate of return (IRR) A time value of money technique that finds the interest rate that equates the present value of cash inflows with the present value of cash outflows.

intraperiod interest rate The annual interest rate divided by the number of compounding periods within one year intrinsic value. The "real" value that a stock "should" have based on fundamental factors affecting value.

inventory turnover A ratio used to evaluate the number of times average inventory has been sold during the period

investment banker A financial organization that specializes in selling newly issued securities. Investment bankers also advise clients on financial matters, negotiate mergers and takeovers, and sell previously issued securities.

investment decisions Decisions pertaining to the selection and diversification of the purchase of assets.

investment goods Additions to the economy's real capital stock, that is, all final purchases of capital equipment (machinery, tools), all construction, both residential and nonresidential, and changes in inventory.

investment grade rating Bond ratings *BBB* (by S&P) or *Baa* (by Moody's) or above.

investment opportunity schedule A graph of the firm's investment projects ranked in order of their rates of return.

investment tax credit (ITC) A tax deduction approved by the federal income tax statutes allowed corporations investing in equipment. Politicians approve it and repeal it depending on what they think is good for the economy.

investment turnover The amount of sales that each $1 of investment generates.

investment-type cash flow An initial cash outflow followed by positive cash inflows in future periods.

investments One of the three areas of finance. It deals with the commitment of funds toward the purchase of securities or assets issued by firms, governments, or individuals.

irrelevant cash flow Cash flow that does not change as a result of some specific action.

judgmental forecast A nonstatistical technique that relies on the forecaster's experience or best estimate. Junk bonds, bonds rated below investment grade-rated *BB* (by S&P) or *Ba* (by Moody's) or below.

Just-in-time (JIT) inventory system A production and management system in which inventory is cut down to a minimum through adjustments to the time and physical distance between the various production operations.

last-in, first-out (LIFO) A method of inventory accounting in which the newest item in inventory is assumed to be sold first.

lease A contractual agreement between the owner of an asset (lessor) and the user of the asset (lessee), which calls for the lessee to pay the lessor an established lease payment.

line of credit Prearranged agreement with a lender for short-term borrowings on demand under prespecified terms. There is no legal commitment on the part of the lender to provide the stated credit.

liquidation The termination of the firm. Assets are sold and the proceeds are paid to creditors. Any monies remaining after paying creditors is distributed to shareholders liquidity A characteristic of a security that refers to its risk, both credit risk and *market risk,* and its marketability. High liquidity requires low risk and high marketability.

liquidity effect The fall (rise) in the rate of interest caused by an increase (decrease) in the supply of money balances.

loan-type cash flows An initial cash inflow followed by cash outflows in future periods.

lock box A post office box address to which credit customers mail payments.

long-term value index (LVI) The proportion of the stock price that is based on cash flows expected to be received after the first five years.

majority voting A voting system in which the number of votes a shareholder may cast for any director may not exceed the number of shares owned.

managerial finance One of the three areas of finance. It deals with management decisions relating to obtaining funds and assets for the firm, controlling costs, and managing the firm's cash flows.

margin of safety The amount long-term financing exceeds permanent asset investment in current and fixed assets.

market anomalies Situations in which the *efficient market hypothesis* is not supported.

market portfolio An imaginary *portfolio* that includes all risky assets in proportion to their market value.

market risk The risk inherent in the ownership of any security because the market fluctuates. This risk cannot be eliminated.

market structure indicators Factors that measure actions of the market in terms of highs and lows, breadth, volume, and strength.

market timing Strategy of varying the proportion of certain types of securities in a portfolio depending on where the investor views the market to be at a particular time.

market value of assets The value exchanged in an arm's-length transaction between a willing buyer and a willing seller.

materials requirement planning (MRP) A computerized system for determining inventory requirements and when to place orders.

maximize shareholders' wealth The theoretical objective management should follow to increase the long-term value of the company's common stock.

Miller-Orr model A cash management control limit model that allows irregular cash patterns in order to minimize costs of investing in cash.

mini-muni Municipal bond with a par value of less than $1000.

monetary indicators Factors that signal monetary changes in the economy which influence stock prices.

monetary policy Deliberate exercise of a country's monetary authority's (for example, Federal Reserve's) power to induce expansions or contractions in the money supply in order to help dampen the swings of business cycles and bring the nation's output and employment to desired levels.

money market A market for securities with less than one year to maturity. Typical securities are Treasury bills, repurchase agreements, negotiable certificates of deposit, and bankers' acceptances.

money market preferred stock (MMPS) *Preferred stock* with a short life that trades in the money market.

money supply Money is a medium of exchange. The money supply measures the amount of the exchange medium available.

mortgage bond A bond secured with a lien on real property.

multinational firm A business with investments and operating facilities in more than one country.

mutual fund An investment company that issues redeemable shares (sometimes called units) to the public and invests the proceeds in a portfolio of securities.

mutually exclusive Either-or decision; take one project or the other.

net advantage to leasing The difference between the cost to purchase the asset and the present value of lease payments.

net cash flow from financing (NCFFF) Shown in the Statement of Cash Flows as cash generated or reduced from the sales or repurchase of securities used to finance the business or the payment of dividends.

net cash flow from investing (NCFLI) Shown in the Statement of Cash Flows as cash generated or reduced from the sales or purchases of investment in long-term securities or plant and equipment.

net cash flow from operations (NCFFO) Shown in the Statement of Cash Flows as cash generated or consumed by the productive activities of a firm over a period of time; represents cash profits.

net present value (NPV) A time value of money technique that nets the present value of cash inflows against the present value of cash outflows.

net working capital The excess of current assets over current liabilities. Alternatively, the excess of equity and long-term debt over fixed and other noncurrent assets. As it applies to capital expenditures, it is defined as current assets less noninterest bearing current liabilities that change as a result of a capital budgeting decision.

net worth The ownership interests of common and, perhaps, preferred shareholders in a company; on a balance sheet, equity equals total assets less all liabilities.

neutral financial leverage The effect of debt financing has no effect on shareholders' claims on earnings.

New York Stock Exchange Composite Index Value-weighted price index based on all stocks traded on the New York Stock Exchange. *Value-weighted* means the market value of the firm's equity relative to the aggregate equity market value of all firms traded on the exchange.

no-growth firm Firm whose investment opportunities simply earn the required market rate.

nominal interest rate The observed rate of interest, uncorrected for inflation. *Nominal* means in name only and, thus, is likely not the effective rate of interest.

nonspontaneous financing Financing that has either an explicit or an implicit cost associated with it.

note Medium-term (one to ten years) security. Note holder receives coupon payments.

odd lot The quantity of securities that is less than the established unit for trading.

open market operations Purchases and sales of government securities by the Federal Reserve System. Purchases of securities are expansionary because they add to commercial banks' reserves; sales of securities are contractionary because they reduce commercial banks' reserves.

open market purchase Purchase of shares on the exchanges or in the over-the-counter market without any public announcement.

operating breakeven sales level The point at which the firm's operating revenues equal its operating costs. To compute the breakeven point, costs are divided into fixed and variable components.

operating costs Expenses incurred in operating a business, excluding all financing expenses.

operating cycle The period of time between the acquisition of material, labor, and overhead inputs for production and the collection of sales receipts.

operating lease A lease in which the present value of the lease payments is less than 90% of the initial cost of the asset; the life of the lease is less than 75% of the economic life of the asset; no bargain purchase option exists in the lease; and no transfer of ownership of the lease asset to the user exists.

operating leverage The effect of fixed operating costs on earnings when sales revenue changes.

operating loan Bank credit used to finance a temporary need for working capital funds.

operating return on assets A measure of the productivity of assets on a before tax basis; defined as EBIT + assets.

ordinary annuity A stream of cash flows of equal amount occurring at the end of each period for a specified number of periods.

over-the-counter-market (OTC) Secondary markets conducted by dealers who supply buy-sell quotes on the securities in which they deal. If the securities are listed on an organized exchange, the market is called the *third market.*

payback period A nondiscounted cash flow technique that determines the estimated time it takes to recover the original investment.

payment date Date company actually mails out dividend checks to stockholders.

perfect competition A theoretical state that occurs in markets in which a large number of firms sell an identical product; there are many buyers; there are no restrictions on entry; firms have no advantage over potential new entrants; and all firms and buyers are fully informed about the prices of each and every firm.

perpetuity An investment offering a level stream of cash flows with no maturity date.

point and figure chart A charting device that records every price change of a certain minimum amount, rather than every price change.

points An up-front fee where one point is 1% of the value of the loan.

portfolio A combination of multiple securities that attempt to obtain the best balance between risk and return.

portfolio beta An index representing the undiversifiable risk of a group of stocks formed into a *portfolio.*

portfolio risk The variability associated with a collection of securities grouped into a *portfolio.*

preemptive right A provision in the corporate charter or in state law that allows the existing stockholders to purchase additional shares of stock before they are offered for sale to the public. This allows existing stockholders to maintain their proportionate ownership in the firm.

preferred stock Shares of stock that receive priority over common stock at a fixed rate in the distribution of dividends, or in the distribution of assets if the company is liquidated.

premium The amount by which a bond (or preferred stock) sells above its par value. The security trades at a premium when the coupon rate is above the market rate of interest.

present value annuity factor (PVIFA) The sum of the present value of $1 amounts, using the *present value formula,* which occurs in periods 1,2,. . ., *n.*

present value formula A formula showing how the current price of an asset is related to its expected future cash flows through the use of a rate of interest. The formula is 11 $(1 + r)$" where *r is* an interest rate and *n* is time periods.

present value of an annuity due The value today of a series of constant cash flows for a known number of periods, with the cash flows occurring at the beginning of each period.

present value of growth opportunities (PVGO) Projects available to a firm that have an expected return in excess of the firm's required market return.

primary market The market in which the initial sale of securities occur.

principal An individual who establishes a compensation scheme to motivate an agent to choose activities advantageous to the principal. Shareholders are *principals* of the firm.

principal The face (or par) value of a bond that must be repaid at maturity.

Principal-agent problem The possibility that an agent will act in her or his own self-interest to the detriment of the principal for whom she or he is acting.

private placement A securities issue offering made to institutional investors. The securities are not registered with the Securities and Exchange Commission.

production opportunities The diversion of some present wealth into activities which result in increased future wealth.

profitability index A discounted cash flow technique that compares the present value of future cash flows to the initial cash outflow.

prospectus A legal document provided to potential investors in a new securities issue detailing all pertinent facts concerning the securities to be offered.

proxy A document that a stockholder gives to another party for the purpose of voting the shares.

purchasing power parity A principle stating that comparable goods should sell for equivalent prices regardless of the currency used to price the goods.

purchasing power risk The risk that an investment's principal and income will lose their purchasing power because of *inflation*.

pure time value of money. Theoretical interest rate on a long-term, riskless loan, where the interest payments are made solely for the use of someone else's money. In practice, this rate is often approximated by the interest rate on long-term negotiable government bonds.

quick ratio (acid test ratio) A measure of liquidity, defined as cash, marketable securities, and accounts receivable divided by current liabilities.

range A crude measure of dispersion defined as the difference between the highest value and the lowest value in a data set.

rate of return In a financial framework, it is the interest rate that equates the present value of cash returns on an investment with the present value of the cash expenditures relating to the investment.

ratio projection method The historical proportion of cash to sales to estimate the amount of cash that should be held.

real assets Land, buildings, plant and equipment, inventories, and consumer durable goods.

real interest rate The observable *(nominal)* rate of interest minus the rate of *inflation*.

recaptured depreciation The difference between the selling price of a depreciable asset and its net book value, up to the original cost of the asset.

registered bond A bond issued with a record name of the owner. Payment is made directly to the registered owner of the bond.

reinvestment (interest rate) risk Uncertainty about the rate of return that will be earned by future cash flows from an investment.

relevant cash flow Cash flow that changes as a result of some specific action.

reorganization A legal process in which all financial claims against the company are settled to reflect the firm's intrinsic value. The firm continues its operations.

reserve requirements Minimum amount of legal reserves that a bank is required by law to keep behind its deposit liabilities.

return on assets An accounting based ratio showing the profitability of the book value of assets.

return on beginning equity An accounting profitability measure, which divides profits by beginning equity shown on the balance sheet.

return on equity An accounting based ratio showing the return on the book value of equity.

return on sales A measure of the proportion of each sales dollar that is left after meeting all expenses.

revenue bond A municipal bond for which the coupon and maturity payments are paid from revenues from a specific revenue-generating project, such as a toll road.

revolving loan Legally assured *line of credit* with a bank. Interest charged at one rate for the amount used and at a lower rate for the amount not used.

risk Quantitative measurement of an outcome, such as a gain or loss; the chance of an outcome.

risk aversion It is a dislike for risk. Higher risk requires higher expected return.

risk-free rate The interest rate for an asset that is virtually riskless. For example, debt issued by the government maturing in one year has a precisely predictable rate of return for one year.

risk premium The actual return on a security minus the risk-free rate of return.

round lot A unit of trading of a security.

S&P 500 Index A value-weighted price index made up of 500 large companies traded on the New York Stock Exchange. *Value-weigh fed* means the market value of the firm's equity relative to the aggregate equity market value of all firms traded on the exchange.

salvage value The resale value of an asset.

salvage value tax adjustment The calculation of income taxes on an asset that is sold for either more or less than its depreciated book value.

secondary market Securities markets that handle transactions in existing securities. Often contrasted with *primary market.*

secured loan Financing that is backed by the pledge of some asset. In liquidation, the secured creditor receives the cash from the sale of the pledged asset to the extent of the loan value.

securitization of accounts receivable Substitution of tradable financial securities for privately negotiated accounts receivable.

security interest A legal term meaning a lender has a secured interest in an asset. Unsecured lenders cannot look to the secured asset for repayment.

Semistrong-form efficiency Market condition in which current prices not only reflect all informational content of historical prices but also reflect all publicly available knowledge about the firm under study.

sentiment indicators Factors that attempt to measure the buying and selling psychology of investors.

shelf registration Securities and Exchange Commission Rule 415, which allows companies to register all securities they plan to issue over the following two years. The companies then file short statements when they wish to sell any part of these securities during the period.

sample discount The difference between the future value and present value when simple interest is used.

simple interest Interest computed by multiplying the original principal by the percent of interest by the time period involved. It is paid when the loan matures.

specialist Broker to the brokers.

sponsored ADR ADR issued by a single depository institution.

spontaneous asset An asset that increases or decreases as sales increase or decrease.

spontaneous financing Those liabilities such as accounts payable and accrued wages that arise automatically, without negotiation, in the course of doing business.

spontaneous liability A liability that increases or decreases as sales increase or decrease.

spot exchange rate The rate at which one currency can be converted into another, or the price of one currency in terms of another. For example, if the price of the German mark were $0.25 per mark, it would require $0.25 to purchase one mark or four marks to purchase $1.

spread In *underwriting,* the difference between the price that the underwriter pays the company for the new securities and the price at which the securities are sold to the public or are privately placed.

stakeholders Claimants on cash flows of the firm.

standard deviation A statistic used to measure dispersion about an expected value. A high (low) standard deviation is associated with high (low) risk. It is the square root of the variance.

standby credit A *term loan* that matures at the expiration date of the loan. It cannot be paid down and reused again without being renegotiated.

statement of cash flows An accounting statement that traces the sources and uses of cash as a result of organizational activity.

stock dividend A dividend paid in securities rather than cash.

stock exchange A physical location where securities trade like at an auction. Securities are always bought by the highest bidders and sold by the lowest offerers.

stock market The financial market for trading claims (shares) of a firm.

stock split The division of a corporation's outstanding shares into a larger number of shares.

straight bond value That component of a callable bond that acts like an ordinary bond.

strategic decisions The set of decisions resulting in the formulation and implementation of strategies, or plans, designed to achieve the objectives of the organization.

stretching accounts payable Failing to pay within the prescribed trade credit period.

strong-form efficiency Market condition in which no information that is available, be it public or private, can be used to earn superior investment returns consistently.

sunk costs Cash flow expended in the past.

surplus (saving) units Net savers, who save more than they spend. The *household sector* is considered a net surplus sector.

sustainable growth Growth the firm can maintain over time given its dividend policy, financing policy, asset management performance, and profitability of sales.

tactical decisions The set of decisions designed to carry out daily activities so as to meet strategic objectives.

tangible assets Physical assets such as plant and equipment.

tax-loss carryovers Taxable losses carried forward into future years to offset tax liability of those years.

tender offer A publicly announced offer to buy the stock of a firm directly from its shareholders.

term loan A loan with a maturity greater than one year, term structure of interest rates. The relationship between yield and time to maturity of a debt security.

terminal nonoperating cash flows Cash flow occurring at the end of the investment's life; included are *salvage value,* taxes on sale of asset, and liquidation of all net working capital associated with the investment.

terminal value The value of cash flows compounded forward to some later time at an appropriate interest rate.

third market Over-the-counter trading of securities that are listed on organized exchanges.

time deposit Bank accounts and other deposits that earn a higher interest than savings accounts but which must be left on deposit for a specified period of time (their maturity).

time preference rate Human desire for a good in the present as opposed to the future. The rate is reflected by the price people are willing to pay for immediate possession of the good, as opposed to the price they are willing to pay for future possession.

time value of money A principle stating that dollars at different points in time can only be directly compared when they are first adjusted by the interest rate representing the opportunity cost of money.

timeliness Indicator used by Value Lines Investment Services to signify the potential price changes in stocks.

total debt-to-equity ratio A measure of financial leverage risk, defined as total debt divided by shareholders' equity.

total risk Diversifiable risk + nondiversifiable risk.

trades on the equity The use of debt to increase the expected return on equity.

trading The buying and selling of securities to take advantage of price swings.

trading post Place on the exchange floor where a company's stock trades.

treasury stock Common stock that has been repurchased by the company that originally issued it.

trend analysis A variable of interest is analyzed against time.

Treynor index A measure of reward per unit of risk. It indicates the rate of return on the market index required to make the expected rate of return on a portfolio equal to the risk-free rate.

underwriting A guarantee by investment banking firms to an issuing corporation that a definable sum of money will be paid on a specified date for the issue of stocks or bonds.

unfavorable financial leverage Negative effects of debt financing on shareholders' claims on earnings.

unlevered firm A firm financed entirely with equity financing.

unsecured loan Financing that requires no assets as collateral but allows the lender a general claim against the borrower, rather than a lien against specific assets.

unsponsored ADR *ADR* issued by more than one depository institution

valuation The worth of an economic asset.

value of unlevered firm Value of a firm that is financed entirely with equity.

variable cost A cost that moves directly with a firm's output, rising as output increases over a full range of production. Examples: raw materials and sales commissions.

variance A statistic that measures dispersion about the expected value. A high (low) variance is associated with high (low) risk. It is the *standard deviation* squared.

vertical analysis Common-size analysis that compares accounts in the income statement to net sales and amounts in the balance sheet to total assets.

weak-form efficiency Market condition in which current prices reflect all information that is contained in the historical sequence of prices.

weighted average cost of capital The minimum rate of return that is acceptable on new non-risk changing investments in order to maintain the value of the firm.

window dressing Making financial statements appear more favorable than they really are.

Yankee bond A foreign bond denominated in U.S. dollars.

yield curve A pictorial representation of the *term structure of interest rates.*

yield to maturity (YTM) Percentage figure reflecting the effective yield on a bond, based on the difference between its purchase and redemption prices, and any returns received by the bondholder in the interim.

zero balance account (ZBA) A demand deposit account that has a zero balance at the end of the day. Checks presented against the account are covered by funds transferred from another account.

zero coupon security A note or bond that earns no annual interest payments. The difference between the purchase price and the par value at maturity represents interest to the holder.

INDEX

income tax, 37, 46, 48, 49, 53, 54, 56, 144, 161, 230, 285, 335
income tax expense, 37, 48
income tax rate, 294
income taxes payable, 40
incremental approach, 131, 132, 133
incremental cash flows, 284, 296
incremental costs, 284, 309
indenture, 384
indirect costs, 93
indirect labor, 117, 118
indirect quotes, 410, 412, 413, 421
indirect securities, 240, 241
inflation, 10, 45, 48, 252, 415
inflation-risk premium, 251
initial public offering of stock (IPO), 233
input controls, 207
insider trading, 250
interest, 62, 79, 262, 266, 275, 316, 333, 337, 345, 347, 351, 388
interest rate, 226, 228, 263, 274, 338, 339, 340, 341, 342, 373, 375, 408, 419, 428, 430
interest rate differential, 414
interest rate parity (IRP) theory, 414, 416, 418
interest rate risk, 314, 315
interest rates, 79, 221, 237, 238, 251, 252, 254, 277, 314, 389, 391, 418
interest-coverage ratio, 79
intermediate-term market, 419
internal control, 201, 202, 206, 207, 211
internal rate of return (IRR), 288, 290, 291, 296, 368, 372
Internal Revenue Service (IRS), 54, 348
international business risk, 420
International Fisher Effect (IFE), 415, 421
international transactions, 416
interpolation method, 288
intrinsic value, 382
inventory, 17, 40, 45, 46, 49, 56, 73, 75, 76, 78, 97, 98, 130, 138, 154, 156, 157, 159, 171, 210, 223, 238, 305, 322, 323, 325
inventory liquidation, 49
inventory loans, 340
inventory management, 322, 323, 327
inventory profit, 49
inventory shrinkage, 209, 210
inventory turnover, 76, 77, 85
inventory turnover ratio, 76
investment, 7, 73, 224, 226, 238, 250, 294, 295, 317, 318, 320, 327, 368, 371, 373, 397, 407
investment banker, 246, 247, 248, 255
investment banking, 233, 242, 246, 247, 254, 255
investment decision rules, 228

investment proposals, 261, 286, 289, 290, 291, 294, 295, 296
investments, 76, 222, 223, 225, 226, 228, 230, 233, 277, 283, 408

J

journal, 30
journal entries, 18
junk bonds, 387, 388
just-in-time (JIT) production system, 110, 111
just-in-time inventory control, 325, 326
just-in-time inventory system, 326

L

labor, 94
labor costs, 117
last-in, first-out (LIFO), 45, 46, 48, 49, 50, 56
Law of One Price, 414, 415
lease, 346
lease agreement, 362
lease-back arrangement, 354
ledger, 19, 27, 30
lessee, 346, 347, 348, 361
lessor, 346, 347, 349
leverage, 81, 222, 225, 227, 234
leverage leasing, 347
liabilities, 7, 15, 16, 20, 21, 22, 25, 27, 28, 30, 40, 43, 56, 326
lien, 345
LIFO liquidation, 49
limited liability, 394
line authority, 6
line of credit, 336
liquidation value, 381
liquidity, 75, 304, 306, 314, 315, 318, 326, 327, 344
Liquidity Preference Theory, 254
loan agreement, 342, 343, 344
loan amortization schedule, 275
lock-box arrangement, 308, 309, 310
long-range planning, 150
long-term assets, 38, 40, 42
long-term capital, 237, 243, 245, 249
long-term debt, 40, 41, 62, 66, 71, 73, 79, 85, 305, 343, 344, 384, 386, 390
long-term financial instruments, 241, 242
long-term liabilities, 40, 41
long-term solvency, 62
losses, 37

Q

R

S

safety stock, 324, 325, 327
sale and leaseback arrangement, 346
sales budget, 156, 160, 161
sales forecasting, 161
sales forecasts, 160, 162, 172
sales mix, 129, 142, 143
sales-activity variances, 181, 183
salvage value, 285, 286, 349
secondary market, 239, 242, 244, 250, 255, 256, 317
secured credit, 353
securities, 222, 223, 226, 228, 233, 238, 239, 242, 243, 244, 246, 247, 248, 250, 254, 255, 256, 303, 305, 306, 309, 310, 314, 315, 316, 317, 318, 326, 327, 367, 369, 370, 371, 372, 376, 384, 387, 399, 409, 421
Securities Act of 1933, 249, 256
Securities and Exchange Commission (SEC), 3, 61, 232, 233, 243, 248, 249, 250, 256, 317, 387, 391, 419
Securities Exchange Act of 1934, 250, 256
securities markets, 233, 247, 249, 382
security prices, 243
selling rate, 413
sensitivity analysis, 172, 173
separation of duties, 203, 204, 211
shareholders, 7, 8, 80, 228, 229, 233, 234, 367, 368, 393, 394
shareholders' equity, 28
shareholders' investment (owners' equity), 41
shares of stock, 8
short-term credit, 333, 334, 335, 336, 338, 339, 340, 353
short-term debt, 242, 255, 337
short-term lease, 354
short-term liabilities, 223, 333
short-term liquidity, 62
short-term loans, 304, 333
short-term notes, 40
short-term notes payable, 305
sinking-fund provision, 391
specific unit cost, 45, 46, 56
specific-unit-cost method, 46
spot exchange market, 410, 412, 417
spot exchange rate, 417
spot transaction, 410
stable-monetary-unit concept, 10, 12
staff authority, 6
stakeholders, 229
standard costs, 182, 191
statement of cash flows, 28, 35, 38, 41, 43, 56, 61, 70, 71, 85
statement of financial position, 38
statement of operations, 35
statement of retained earnings, 28, 35, 37, 38, 41, 43, 56
static budget, 176
stock, 7, 8, 43, 62, 69, 82, 228, 229, 233, 245, 289, 290, 295, 296
stockholders, 5, 7, 8, 16, 38, 41, 43, 53, 74, 81, 84, 85, 250, 284, 368, 394, 395
stockholders' equity, 16, 21, 22, 25, 26, 27, 28, 30, 43, 63, 83
stocks, 222, 224, 225, 233, 238, 241, 243, 244
straight-line depreciation, 50, 51, 52, 53, 54, 286, 291, 293
straight-line method, 53, 55, 56
strategic plan, 150
sunk costs, 284
systematic risk, 289

T

T-account, 17, 18, 217
Tax Reform Act of 1986, 54, 230
tax shield, 293
taxability, 314, 327
temporary asset investments, 304
term financing, 333, 341
term loans, 341, 342, 354
term structure of interest rates, 252, 254
term value, 381
terminal warehouse agreement, 341
terms of sale, 320
time value of money, 222, 226, 234, 261, 277
time-period concept, 11
times-interest-earned ratio, 79, 85
total assets, 43
total liabilities, 40, 41, 43
trade, 224, 243
trade credit, 305, 335
trading, 224
transaction exposure, 418
transaction loans, 336, 337
transactions, 10, 30, 238
transactions balances, 305
transactions exposure, 415
transit float, 307
translation exposure, 415, 418
treasurer, 6, 12
treasury stock, 38
trend percentages, 65, 85
trial balance, 27